BRITISH RAILWAYS
LOCOMOTIVES & COACHING STOCK
2001

The Complete Guide to all Locomotives & Coaching Stock which operate on Britain's Mainline Railways

Neil Webster, Peter Hall & Peter Fox

ISBN 1 902336 19 4

© 2001. Platform 5 Publishing Ltd., 3 Wyvern House, Sark Road, Sheffield, S2 4HG, England.

CONTENTS

SECTION 5 – LOCO-HAULED NON-PASSENGER COACHING STOCK

SECTION 6 – CODES

SECTION 7 – LIGHT RAIL SYSTEMS & METROS

UPDATES

A comprehensive update to this book is published every month in the Platform 5 magazine, *Today's Railways*, which also contains news and rolling stock information on railways throughout Europe. For further details of *Today's Railways,* please see the advertisements elsewhere within this book.

Information in this edition is intended to illustrate the actual situation on Britain's railways, rather than necessarily agree with TOPS, RSL and other computer records. Information is updated to 1 January 2001.

COVER PHOTOGRAPHS

Front Cover: A GNER Newcastle–London King's Cross HST service seen at Bolton Grange near York on 28 August 1999. Power cars are 43169 and 43117.
Paul Senior

Rear Cover: Connex Class 508/2 EMU 508203 approaches Coulsdon South with the 16.57 London Bridge–Reigate service on 21 July 2000. **David Brown**

READERS' COMMENTS

With such a wealth of information as contained in this book, it is inevitable a few inaccuracies may be found. The authors will be pleased to receive notification from readers of any such inaccuracies, and also of any additional information to supplement our records and thus enhance future editions. Please send comments to:

Locomotives, DMUs & EMUs: Neil Webster, Metro Enterprises Ltd., 312 Leeds Road, Birstall, Batley, West Yorkshire, WF17 0HS.
(Tel: 01924 470235; Fax: 01924 473675; e-mail: neil.webster2@ntlworld.com)

Coaching Stock: Peter Hall, 4 Ladies Spring Court, Ladies Spring Grove, Dore, Sheffield, S17 3LR. (Tel: 0114 2620693; e-mail: peter@hall59.freeserve.co.uk)

Light Rail & Metros: Peter Fox, Platform 5 Publishing Ltd., Wyvern House, Sark Road, Sheffield, South Yorkshire, S2 4HG. (Tel: 0114 255 2625; Fax: 0114 255 2471; e-mail:peter@platfive.freeserve.co.uk)

Readers are advised that both the authors and publisher regret they are unable to answer ANY specific locomotive and rolling stock queries (concerning the UK or elsewhere) other than through the 'Q & A' section in the Platform 5 magazine *Today's Railways*.

ACKNOWLEDGEMENTS

The author would like to thank the following companies and individuals for their help and co-operation with the compilation of this book:

Alstom Ltd.
English Welsh & Scottish Railway Ltd.
Enron Teesside Operations Ltd.
The Felixstowe Dock & Railway Company Ltd.
Freightliner Ltd.
Harry Needle Railroad Company Ltd.
HSBC Rail (UK) Ltd.
Porterbrook Leasing Company Ltd.
Virgin Trains

Thanks are also due to the following individuals for their reports of changes observed during 2000:

Kevin Adlam, Mark Beal, Donald J. Bishop, Tony Booth, Carl Bowman, Don Brayford, Andrew Burchell, Graham Campbell, Phil Vhilton, L. Clearie, Alan Costello, Roger Elliott, Les Forshaw, Keith Foster, Ian Furness, Brian Garvin, John Hall, David Haydock, M.J. Haywood, John Henley, Graham Holden, Bob Jamie, Paul Jeffries, Kevin Lee, David Lewis, D. John Lewis, Colin J. Marsden, Paul Moore, Brian Morrison, Gordon Parrish, Kenneth Pitt, R.D. Richardson, Simon Rudge, Tony Russell, John E. Salmon, David F. Smith, Alan Spencer, Alan Sugden, Edward Tucker, Stephen Turk, Robert Volland, Robert K. Walker, Bill Wise and Steven Woodhouse, plus those who wish to remain anonymous.

ORGANISATION & OPERATION OF BRITAIN'S RAILWAY SYSTEM

INFRASTRUCTURE & OPERATION

Britain's national railway infrastructure (i.e. the track, signalling, stations and associated power supply equipment) is owned by a public company – Railtrack PLC. Many stations and maintenance depots are leased to and operated by Train Operating Companies (TOCs), but some larger stations remain under Railtrack control. The only exception is the infrastructure on the Isle of Wight, which is nationally owned and is leased to the Island Line franchisee.

Trains are operated by TOCs over the Railtrack network, regulated by access agreements between the parties involved. In general, TOCs are responsible for the provision and maintenance of the locomotives, rolling stock and staff necessary for the direct operation of services, whilst Railtrack is responsible for the provision and maintenance of the infrastructure and also for staff needed to regulate the operation of services.

DOMESTIC PASSENGER TRAIN OPERATORS

The large majority of passenger trains are operated by the TOCs on fixed term franchises. Franchise expiry dates are shown in parentheses in the list of franchisees below:

Franchise	Franchisee	Trading Name
Anglia Railways	GB Railways Ltd. (until 4 April 2004)	Anglia Railways
Cardiff Railway	National Express Group PLC (until 30 April 2004)	Cardiff Railways
Central Trains	National Express Group PLC (until 1 April 2004)	Central Trains
Chiltern Railways	M40 Trains Ltd. (until 20 July 2003)	Chiltern Railways
Cross Country	Virgin Rail Group Ltd. (until 4 January 2012)	Virgin Trains
Gatwick Express	National Express Group PLC (until 27 April 2011)	Gatwick Express
Great Eastern Railway	First Group PLC (until 4 April 2004)	First Great Eastern
Great Western Trains	First Group PLC (until 3 February 2006)	First Great Western
InterCity East Coast	GNER Holdings Ltd. (until 4 April 2004)	Great North Eastern Railway

InterCity West Coast	Virgin Rail Group Ltd. (until 8 March 2012)	Virgin Trains
Island Line	Stagecoach Holdings PLC (until 12 October 2001)	Island Line
LTS Rail	National Express Group PLC (until 25 May 2011)	c2c
Merseyrail Electrics	Arriva PLC (by 18 February 2003)	Merseyrail Electrics
Midland Main Line	National Express Group PLC (until 27 April 2008)	Midland Mainline
North London Railways	National Express Group PLC (until 1 September 2004)	Silverlink Train Services
North West Regional Railways	First Group PLC (until 1 April 2004)	First North Western
Regional Railways North East	Arriva PLC (by 18 February 2003)	Northern Spirit
Scotrail	National Express Group PLC (until 30 March 2004)	ScotRail
South Central	Connex Transport UK Ltd. (until 25 May 2003)	Connex
South Eastern	Connex Transport UK Ltd. (until 12 October 2011)	Connex
South Wales & West	National Express Group PLC (until 30 April 2004)	Wales & West Passenger Trains
South West	Stagecoach Holdings PLC (until 3 February 2003)	South West Trains
Thames	Victory Railways Holdings Ltd. (until 12 April 2004)	Thames Trains
Thameslink	GOVIA Ltd. (until 1 April 2004)	Thameslink Rail
Great Northern	National Express Group PLC (until 30 April 2004)	WAGN
West Anglia	National Express Group PLC (until 4 April 2004)	WAGN

Many of the shorter-term franchises are currently subject to re-negotiation. The Shadow Strategic Rail Authority has already announced M40 Trains Ltd. as preferred bidder for an extended Chiltern franchise, and GOVIA Ltd. as preferred bidder for replacement of the South Central franchise. Announcements regarding the future of other franchises were regarded as imminent as this edition closed for press.

The above companies may also operate other services under 'Open Access' arrangements.

The following operate non-franchised services only:

Operator	Trading Name	Route
British Airports Authority	Heathrow Express	London Paddington–Heathrow Airport
Hull Trains	Hull Trains	London King's Cross–Hull
West Coast Railway	West Coast Railway	Fort William–Mallaig

INTERNATIONAL PASSENGER OPERATIONS

Eurostar (UK) Ltd. operates international passenger-only services between the United Kingdom and continental Europe, jointly with French National Railways (SNCF) and Belgian National Railways (SNCB/NMBS). Eurostar (UK) is a subsidiary of London & Continental Railways Ltd., which is jointly owned by National Express Group plc and British Airways plc.

In addition, the tunnel operating company, Eurotunnel, provides a service for the conveyance of accompanied road vehicles through the Channel Tunnel.

FREIGHT TRAIN OPERATIONS

The following operators operate freight train services under 'Open Access' arrangements:

English Welsh & Scottish Railway Ltd. (EWS)
Freightliner Ltd.
GB Railfreight Ltd.
Direct Rail Services Ltd.
Mendip Rail Ltd.

1. LOCOMOTIVES

USING THIS SECTION – LAYOUT OF INFORMATION

Railtrack registered locomotives are listed in numerical order of class number, and then in numerical order of individual locomotives – using current numbers as allocated by the Rolling Stock Library (RSL) – the national registry of rail vehicles. The only exceptions are locomotives numbered in the 89xxx series (see page 9), which are listed under their previous class numbers. Where numbers actually carried are different to those officially allocated, these are noted in class headings where appropriate. Where locomotives have been renumbered since the previous edition of this book, the most immediate previous number is shown in parentheses. Each locomotive entry is laid out as in one of the following examples:

Class 08 & 09 Shunting Locomotives

RSL No.	Detail	Livery	Owner	Pool		Allocn.	Location
08308	a	**SS**	RT	HASS		IS	*Inverness CARMD*

Official names carried are appended in a table following each class as appropriate.

Other Locomotives

RSL No.	Detail	Livery	Owner	Pool		Allocn.	Name
37682	r§	**E**	E	WKSN		TO	Hartlepool Pipe Mill

Eurotunnel locomotives are listed in numerical order of painted number. Each locomotive entry is laid out as in the following example:

No.	Detail	Livery	Owner	Allocn.	Name
9001		**ET**	ET	CO	LESLEY GARRETT

CLASS HEADINGS

Principal details and dimensions are quoted for each class in metric and/or imperial units as considered appropriate bearing in mind common UK usage. Abbreviations used are shown in Section 6.9.

All dimensions and weights are quoted for locomotives in an 'as new' condition with all necessary supplies (e.g. oil, water and sand) on board. Dimensions are quoted in the order Length – Width – Height. Lengths quoted are over buffers or couplings as appropriate. All width and height dimensions quoted are maxima. For overhead supply system electric locomotives, the height quoted is with pantograph lowered. Where two different wheel diameter dimensions are shown, the first refers to powered wheels and the second refers to non-powered wheels.

DETAIL DIFFERENCES

Only detail differences which currently affect the areas and types of train which locomotives may work are shown. All other detail differences are specifically excluded. Where such differences occur within a class or part class, they are shown in the 'Detail' column alongside the individual locomotive number. Standard abbreviations used are:

a	Train air brake equipment only.
b	Drophead buckeye couplers.
c	Scharfenberg couplers.
j	RCH jumper cables for operating with Propelling Control Vehicles.
k	Swinghead automatic combination couplers.
p	Train air, vacuum and electro-pneumatic brakes.
r	Radio Electronic Token Block (RETB) equipment.
s	Slow Speed Control equipment.
v	Train vacuum brake only.
x	Train air and vacuum brakes ('Dual brakes').
+	Additional fuel tank capacity.
§	Sandite laying equipment.

In all cases use of the above abbreviations indicates the equipment indicated is normally operable. Meaning of non-standard abbreviations and symbols is detailed in individual class headings.

LIVERY CODES

Livery codes are used to denote the various liveries carried. It is impossible in a publication of this size to list every livery variation which currently exists. In particular items ignored for the purposes of this publication include:

* Minor colour variations.
* Omission of logos.
* All numbering, lettering and branding.

Descriptions quoted are thus a general guide only. Logos as appropriate for each livery are normally deemed to be carried. A complete list of livery codes used appears in Section 6.1.

OWNER CODES

Owner codes are used to denote the owners of locomotives listed. A complete list of owner codes used appears in Section 6.2.

POOL CODES

Locomotives are split into operational groups ('pools') for diagramming and maintenance purposes. The official codes used to denote these pools are shown in this publication. A complete list of the pool codes used appears in Section 6.3.

ALLOCATION & LOCATION CODES

Allocation codes are used in this publication to denote the normal maintenance base of each operational locomotive (except Freightliner operated locomotives). However, maintenance may be carried out at other locations and may also be carried out by mobile maintenance teams.

The codes FD and FE are used for locomotives operated by Freightliner. This company does not operate a depot based maintenance system for its locomotives, instead using mobile maintenance teams to carry out day-to-day maintenance, with heavier repairs being performed by contractors.

Location codes are used to denote the current actual location of stored vehicles. A location code will always be followed by (S) to denote stored.

A complete list of allocation and location codes used appears in Section 6.6.

A complete list of the abbreviations used to denote different types of depots appears in Section 6.7.

SHUNTING LOCOMOTIVE LOCATIONS

The actual location of operational shunting locomotives of classes 08 & 09, updated to reports received as at 4 January 2001, is included as a guide to readers as to where these locomotives may be found. Whilst some locomotives remain at certain locations for considerable lengths of time, others may move around far more frequently. Readers must appreciate the listing of a locomotive at a location is no absolute guarantee the locomotive concerned (or any other locomotive) will remain present on a subsequent date.

NAMES

Only names carried with official sanction are listed in this publication. As far as possible names are shown in UPPER/lower case characters as actually shown on the name carried on the locomotive. Names known to be carried on one side only are suffixed [1] (e.g. Back Tor[1]).

GENERAL INFORMATION

CLASSIFICATION AND NUMBERING

All locomotives are classified and allocated numbers by the Rolling Stock Library under the TOPS numbering system, introduced in 1972. This comprises a two-digit class number followed by a three-digit serial number. Where the actual number carried by a locomotive differs from the allocated number, or where an additional number is carried to the allocated number, this is shown by a note in the class heading.

For diesel locomotives, class numbers offer an indication of engine horsepower as shown in the table below.

Class No. Range	Engine h.p.
01–14	0–799
15–20	800–1000
21–31	1001–1499
32–39	1500–1999
40–54, 57	2000–2999
55–56, 58–69	3000+

For electric locomotives class numbers are allocated in ascending numerical order under the following scheme:

Class 70–80   direct current and d.c./diesel dual system locomotives.
Class 81 onwards   alternating current and a.c./d.c. dual system locos.

Numbers in the 89xxx series (except 89001) are allocated by the Rolling Stock Library to locomotives which have been de-registered but subsequently re-registered for use on the Railtrack network and whose original number has already been re-used. 89xxx numbers are normally only carried inside locomotive cabs and are not carried externally in normal circumstances.

WHEEL ARRANGEMENT

For main line locomotives the system whereby the number of driven axles on a bogie or frame is denoted by a letter (A = 1, B = 2, C = 3 etc.) and the number of non-powered axles is denoted by a number is used. The use of the letter 'o' after a letter indicates each axle is individually powered, whilst the '+' symbol indicates bogies are inter-coupled.

For shunting locomotives, the Whyte notation is used. In this notation the number of leading wheels are given, followed by the number of driving wheels and then the trailing wheels.

HAULAGE CAPABILITY OF DIESEL LOCOMOTIVES

The haulage capability of a diesel locomotive depends upon three basic factors:

1. Adhesive weight. The greater the weight on the driving wheels, the greater the adhesion and more tractive power can be applied before wheelslip occurs.

2. The characteristics of its transmission. To start a train the locomotive has to exert a pull at standstill. A direct drive diesel engine cannot do this, hence the need for transmission. This may be mechanical, hydraulic or electric. The present British Standard for locomotives is electric transmission. Here the diesel engine drives a generator or alternator and the current produced is fed to the traction motors. The force produced by each driven wheel depends on the current in its traction motor. In other words, the larger the current, the harder it pulls. As the locomotive speed increases, the current in the traction motor falls, hence the *Maximum Tractive Effort* is the maximum force at its wheels the locomotive can exert at a standstill. The electrical equipment cannot take such high currents for long without overheating. Hence the *Continuous Tractive Effort* is quoted which represents the current which the equipment can take continuously.

3. The power of its engine. Not all power reaches the rail, as electrical machines are approximately 90% efficient. As the electrical energy passes through two such machines (the generator or alternator and the traction motors), the *Power at Rail* is approximately 81% (90% of 90%) of the engine power, less a further amount used for auxiliary equipment such as radiator fans, traction motor blowers, air compressors, battery charging, cab heating, Electric Train Supply (ETS) etc. The power of the locomotive is proportional to the tractive effort times the speed. Hence when on full power there is a speed corresponding to the continuous tractive effort.

HAULAGE CAPABILITY OF ELECTRIC LOCOMOTIVES

Unlike a diesel locomotive, an electric locomotive does not develop it power on board and its performance is determined only by two factors, namely its weight and the characteristics of its electrical equipment. Whereas a diesel locomotive tends to be a constant power machine, the power of an electric locomotive varies considerably. Up to a certain speed it can produce virtually a constant tractive effort. Hence power rises with speed according to the formula given in section three above, until a maximum speed is reached at which tractive effort falls, such that the power also falls. Hence the power at the speed corresponding to the maximum tractive effort is lower than the maximum speed.

BRAKE FORCE

The brake force is a measure of the braking power of a locomotive. This is shown on the locomotive data panels so operating staff can ensure sufficient brake power is available on freight trains.

ELECTRIC TRAIN SUPPLY (ETS)

A number of locomotives are equipped to provide a supply of electricity to the train being hauled to power auxiliaries such as heating, cooling fans, air conditioning and kitchen equipment. ETS is provided from the locomotive by means of a separate alternator (except Class 33 locos, which have a d.c. generator). The ETS index of a locomotive is a measure of the electrical power available for train supply.

Similarly, most loco-hauled coaches also have an ETS index, which in this case is a measure of the power required to operate equipment mounted in the coach. The sum of the ETS indices of all the hauled vehicles in a train must not exceed the ETS index of the locomotive.

ETS is commonly (but incorrectly) known as ETH (Electric Train Heating), which term is a throwback to the days before loco-hauled coaches were equipped with electrically powered auxiliary equipment other than for train heating.

ROUTE AVAILABILITY (RA)

This is a measure of a railway vehicle's axle load. The higher the axle load of a vehicle, the higher the RA number on a scale from 1 to 10. Each Railtrack route has a RA number and in general no vehicle with a higher RA number may travel on that route without special clearance. A map showing route availability on all routes is published on the Railtrack internet web site.

MULTIPLE & PUSH-PULL WORKING

Multiple working between vehicles (i.e. two or more powered vehicles being driven from one cab) is facilitated by jumper cables connecting the vehicles. However, not all types are compatible with each other, and a number of different systems are in use, each system being incompatible with any other.

Association of American Railroads (AAR) System: Classes 59, 66, and 67.
Blue Star Coupling Code: Classes 20, 25, 31, 33, & 37.
Green Circle Coupling Code: Class 47 (not all equipped).
Orange Square Coupling Code: Class 50.
Red Diamond Coupling Code: Classes 56 and 58.
SR System: Classes 33/1, 73 and various electric multiple units.
Within Own Class only: Classes 43 and 60.

Class 47 locos 47701–47717 use a TDM system for push-pull working which utilises the existing RCH jumper cables fitted to coaching stock vehicles. Previously these cables had only been used to control train lighting and public address systems.

A number of other locomotives are equipped with a more modern TDM system for push-pull working which also facilitates multiple working.

1.1 DIESEL LOCOMOTIVES

Note: All diesel locomotives authorised to operate under their own power on the Railtrack network are listed in this section. Diesel locomotives authorised to operate solely on the Eurotunnel network are listed in section 1.6.

SERIES 01/5   BARCLAY/RR   0-6-0

Built: 1985–86 by Andrew Barclay at Kilmarnock (Works Nos. 663 & 668 respectively), for the Ministry of Defence Army Department (Nos. 626 and 631 respectively). Registered for use on the Railtrack network in 1999. Loading gauge restrictions preclude use of these locomotives other than between Kineton and Fenny Compton.
Engine: Rolls Royce CV12TCE of 445 kW (600 h.p.) at ? r.p.m.
Transmission: Hydraulic.
Maximum Tractive Effort:
Continuous Tractive Effort: **Train Brakes:** Air.
Brake Force: 46 t.   **Dimensions:** 9.45 x ? x ? m.
Weight: 61.0 t.   **Wheel Diameter:**
Design Speed: 60 km/h.   **Maximum Speed:** 10 m.p.h.
Fuel Capacity: 3000 litres.   **RA:** 7.
Train Supply: Not equipped.   **Multiple Working:** Not equipped.

01505	**MD**	MD	MBDL	KN
01506	**MD**	MD	MBDL	KN

SERIES 01/5   H-B/CATERPILLAR   0-6-0

Built: 1971 by The Hunslet Engine Company at Leeds (Works No. 7018), for the National Coal Board, Western Area (No. 8D). Subsequently sold to Hunslet-Barclay, Kilmarnock and rebuilt prior to sale to The Felixstowe Dock and Railway Company in 1999. Registered for use on the Railtrack network in 1999. Normally used at Felixstowe South Container Terminal.
Engine: Caterpillar 3412C DITA of 475 kW (640 h.p.) at ? r.p.m.
Transmission: Hydraulic. Twin Disc 13800 series torque converter coupled to a Hunslet final drive.
Maximum Tractive Effort: 180 kN (40365 lbf).
Continuous Tractive Effort: 235 kN (52700 lbf) at ?? m.p.h.
Train Brakes: Air.
Brake Force: 48 t.   **Dimensions:** 3.95 x 2.51 x 3.80 m.
Weight: 64.3 t.   **Wheel Diameter:** 1143 mm.
Design Speed: 15 m.p.h.   **Maximum Speed:** 15 m.p.h.
Fuel Capacity: 930 litres.   **RA:** 7.
Train Supply: Not equipped.   **Multiple Working:** Not equipped.

Non standard numbering:
• 01531 also carries number H4323.

01531	**FX**	FX	MBDL	FX	COLONEL TOMLINE

SERIES 01/5   ENGLISH ELECTRIC/RR   0–4–0

Built: 1966 by English Electric at Vulcan Foundry, Newton le Willows (Works No. D1122), for the Central Electricity Generating Board at Croydon 'B' Power Station (No. 2). Subsequently acquired by RFS(E), Doncaster (now Wabtec). Registered for use on the Railtrack network in 2000, and hired to Aggregate Industries UK for use at Croft Quarry, Leicestershire.
Engine: ? of 235 kW (315 h.p.) at ? r.p.m.
Transmission: Hydraulic.
Maximum Tractive Effort:
Continuous Tractive Effort:
Train Brakes: Air.

Brake Force: 10 t.	**Dimensions:** 7.32 x ? x ? m.
Weight: 24.0 t.	**Wheel Diameter:**
Design Speed: 10 m.p.h.	**Maximum Speed:** 10 m.p.h.
Fuel Capacity: 1365 litres.	**RA:** 0.
Train Supply: Not equipped.	**Multiple Working:** Not equipped.

Non standard livery:
• 01551 is in RFS(E) livery of blue, lined out in silver.

01551   **0**   WₐA   MBDL   ZB

SERIES 01/5   HNRC/ROLLS-ROYCE   0–6–0

Built: 1966 by Thomas Hill at Vanguard Works, Kilnhurst (Works No. 167V), for ICI Billingham (No. D3). Subsequently sold to Harry Needle Railroad Company in 1995 and rebuilt 2000. Registered for use on the Railtrack network in 2000, and hired to Creative Logistics, for use at Salford International Railfreight Terminal.
Engine: Rolls Royce 8-cylinder of 275 kW (370 h.p.) at ? r.p.m.
Transmission: Hydraulic. Twin Disc 11800 torque converter coupled to a RF final drive unit.
Maximum Tractive Effort:
Continuous Tractive Effort:
Train Brakes: Air.

Brake Force: 19 t.	**Dimensions:** 9.14 x ? x ? m.
Weight: 49.0 t.	**Wheel Diameter:**
Design Speed: 10 m.p.h.	**Maximum Speed:** 10 m.p.h.
Fuel Capacity: 1360 litres.	**RA:** 5.
Train Supply: Not equipped.	**Multiple Working:** Not equipped.

Non standard livery:
• 01552 is in Creative Logistics livery of blue and green.

01552   **0**   HN   HNRL   BH

SERIES 01/5   BR/ENGLISH ELECTRIC   0-6-0

Built: 1950 by BR at Derby Locomotive Works as BR 12082. Withdrawn from service in 1971 and sold to Shellstar (UK), Ince (later UK Fertilisers) in 1972. Purchased by Harry Needle in 19??, and registered for use on the Railtrack network in 2000. Part of the Harry Needle Railroad Company hire fleet.
Engine: English Electric 6KT of 260 kW (350 h.p.) at 600 r.p.m.
Main Generator: English Electric 801.
Traction Motors: Two English Electric 506.
Maximum Tractive Effort: 156 kN (35000 lbf).
Continuous Tractive Effort: ? at 8.5 m.p.h.

Power at Rail:	**Train Brakes:** Air.
Brake Force: 19 t.	**Dimensions:** 8.88 x 2.59 x 3.78 m.
Weight: 48.60 t.	**Wheel Diameter:** 1232 mm.
Design Speed: 20 m.p.h.	**Maximum Speed:** 20 m.p.h.
Fuel Capacity: 3000 litres.	**RA:** 5.
Train Supply: Not equipped.	**Multiple Working:** Not equipped.

Non-standard numbering:
• 01553 also carries number 12082.

01553	**HN**	HN	HNRL	BH	

CLASS 03   BR/GARDNER   0-6-0

Built: 1962 by BR at Swindon Works. Normally used at Hornsey T&RSMD.
Engine: Gardner 8L3 of 152 kW (204 h.p.) at 1200 r.p.m.
Transmission: Mechanical. Fluidrive type 23 hydraulic coupling to Wilson-Drewry CA5R7 gearbox with SCG type RF11 final drive.
Maximum Tractive Effort: 68 kN (15300 lbf).
Continuous Tractive Effort: 68 kN (15300 lbf) at 3.75 m.p.h.

Train Brakes: Air & vacuum.	
Brake Force: 13 t.	**Dimensions:** 7.93 x 2.59 x 3.73 m.
Weight: 31.3 t.	**Wheel Diameter:** 1092 mm.
Design Speed: 28.5 m.p.h.	**Maximum Speed:** 28.5 m.p.h.
Fuel Capacity: 1364 litres.	**RA:** 1.
Train Supply: Not equipped.	**Multiple Working:** Not equipped.

03179	**WN**	WN	HQXX	HE	CLIVE

CLASS 07 RUSTON & HORNSBY/PAXMAN 0-6-0

Built: 1962 by Ruston & Hornsby, Lincoln, as BR D2985 for shunting duties in Southampton Docks. Withdrawn from service in 1977 and sold to Tilsley & Lovatt, Stoke-on-Trent in 1978. Resold to Staveley Lime Company (later Peakstone Ltd.), Peak Dale, in 1978. Purchased by Harry Needle in 1989 and registered for use on the Railtrack network in 2000. Part of the Harry Needle Railroad Company hire fleet.
Engine: Paxman 6RPHL Mk. 3 of 204 kW (275 h.p.) at 1360 r.p.m.
Main Generator: AEI RTB 6652.
Traction Motors: AEI RTA 6652.

Maximum Tractive Effort: 126 kN (28240 lbf).
Continuous Tractive Effort: ? at 4.4 m.p.h.
Power at Rail:
Brake Force: 21 t.
Weight: 42.25 t.
Design Speed: 20 m.p.h.
Fuel Capacity:
Train Supply: Not equipped.

Train Brakes: Air.
Dimensions: 8.13 x 2.57 x 3.86 m.
Wheel Diameter: 1067 mm.
Maximum Speed: 20 m.p.h.
RA: 6.
Multiple Working: Not equipped.

07001	**HN**	HN	HNRL	BH

CLASS 08   BR/ENGLISH ELECTRIC   0-6-0

Built: 1955–62 by BR at Crewe, Darlington, Derby Locomotive, Doncaster or Horwich Works.
Engine: English Electric 6KT of 298 kW (400 h.p.) at 680 r.p.m.
Main Generator: English Electric 801.
Traction Motors: Two English Electric 506.
Maximum Tractive Effort: 156 kN (35000 lbf).
Continuous Tractive Effort: 49 kN (11100 lbf) at 8.8 m.p.h.
Power At Rail: 194 kW (260 h.p.).
Brake Force: 19 t.
Weight: 49.6–50.4 t.
Design Speed: 20 m.p.h.
Fuel Capacity: 3037 litres.
Train Supply: Not equipped.

Train Brakes: Air & vacuum.
Dimensions: 8.92 x 2.59 x 3.89 m.
Wheel Diameter: 1372 mm.
Maximum Speed: 15 m.p.h.
RA: 5.
Multiple Working: Not equipped.

Notes: † – Equipped with remote control (Hima Sella system) for working at Allied Steel & Wire, Cardiff.
‡ – Equipped with remote control (Cattron system) for evaluation purposes.

Non-standard liveries/numbering:
* 08397 is as **F**, but with BR Railfreight General yellow & red logos.
* 08414 is as **DG**, but with BR & Railfreight Distribution logos and large bodyside numbers. Also carries number D3529.
* 08460 is light grey with black underframe, cab doors, window surrounds and roof. Also carries number D3575.
* 08500 is red, lined out in black & white. Also carries bodyside number 1.
* 08527 is light grey with a black roof, blue bodyside stripe and 'Ilford Level 5' branding.
* 08573 is light grey and unnumbered.
* 08593 is Great Eastern Railway style blue. Also carries number D3760.
* 08601 is London Midland & Scottish Railway style black.
* 08616 carries number 3783.
* 08617 is in Virgin Trains 'Pitstop' livery of black with a large red and black bodyside flag.
* 08642 is London & South Western Railway style black. Also carries number D3809.
* 08649 is grey with blue, white and red stripes and WTL logo. Also carries number D3816.
* 08682 is dark blue with a grey roof.
* 08715 is 'Dayglo' orange.

- 08721 is as **B**, but with a red and yellow stripe.
- 08834 is in RFS(E) livery of blue with silver lining.
- 08730/867 are in plain black livery.
- 08785 is silver grey.
- 08801 carries number 801.
- 08805 is London Midland & Scottish Railway style maroon. Also carries number 3973.
- 08809 is light grey with orange lettering.
- 08879 is green and black with Railfreight Distribution logos.
- 08883 is Caledonian Railway style blue.
- 08928 is as **F0**, with large bodyside numbers and light blue solebar.

Class 08/0. Standard Design.

08077	**RF**	P	DFLS	FD	*Southampton Maritime Freightliner Terminal*
08308	a	**SS**	RT	HASS	IS	*Inverness CARMD*
08331		**GN**	WA	RFSH	EC	*Craigentinny T&RSMD*
08375	a	**RT**	RT	DFLS	FD	*Ipswich Yard*
08389	a	**B**	EF	WSXX	OC(S)	
08393	a	**FE**	EF	WSSE	OC	*Dagenham Dock Up Sidings*
08397	a	**0**	E	WSWM	BS	*Padeswood Hall Cement Works*
08401	a	**DG**	E	WSYH	IM	*Scunthorpe Trent Yard*
08402	a	**DG**	E	WSXX	BK(S)	
08405	a	**DG**	E	WSYH	IM	*Immingham Reception Sidings*
08410	a	**GL**	FW	HJSL	LA	*Laira T&RSMD*
08411	a	**B**	E	WSSC	ML	*Ayr SD*
08414	a	**0**	E	WSWX	OC(S)	
08417	a	**B**	SO	XYPS	MD	*Merehead*
08418	a	**F**	E	WSWM	BS	*Blue Circle Cement, Washwood Heath*
08428	a	**E**	E	WSYH	IM	*Rotherham Steel Terminal*
08441	a	**B**	E	WSSC	ML	*Ferrybridge T&RSMD*
08442	a	**F**	E	WSYH	IM	*Immingham TMD*
08451		**B**	VW	HFSN	WN	*Willesden TMD*
08454		**VP**	VW	HFSN	WN	*Willesden TMD*
08460	a	**0**	E	WSNW	AN	*Allerton T&RSMD*
08466	at†	**E**	E	WSAW	CF	*Allied Steel & Wire, Cardiff*
08472	a	**BR**	WA	RFSH	EC	*Craigentinny T&RSMD*
08480	a	**G**	E	WSSW	CF	*Didcot Yard*
08481		**B**	E	WSAW	CF	*Allied Steel & Wire, Cardiff*
08482	a	**FD**	E	WSSE	OC	*Willesden Euroterminal*
08483	a	**GL**	FW	HJXX	PM	*St. Phillips Marsh T&RSMD*
08484	a	**DG**	RC	KWSW	ZN	*Railcare, Wolverton*
08485	a	**B**	EF	WSNW	AN	*Guide Bridge Brookside Sidings*
08489	a	**F**	E	WSWX	WA(S)	
08492	a	**B**	E	WSXX	ML(S)	
08493	a	**B**	E	WSXX	CF(S)	
08495		**E**	E	WSYH	IM	*Worksop Yards*
08499	a	**F**	E	WSXX	KY(S)	
08500		**0**	E	WSWS	EH	*Bristol Barton Hill T&RSMD*
08506	a	**B**	E	WSSE	OC	*Old Oak Common T&RSMD*
08509	a	**F**	E	WSWX	IM(S)	

08510	a	B	E	WSYH	IM	*Tinsley Yard*
08511	a	E	E	WSEM	TO	*Toton Up Yard*
08512	a	F	E	WSYH	IM	*Doncaster Railfreight Terminal*
08514	a	B	E	WSYH	IM	*Worksop Yards*
08516	a	DG	E	WSEM	TO	*Peterborough SD*
08523		ML	E	WSXX	CD(S)	
08525		F	MA	HISL	NL	*Neville Hill (InterCity)T&RSMD*
08526		E	E	WSSE	OC	*Stratford SD*
08527		0	AD	KCSI	ZI	*Adtranz, Ilford*
08528		DG	E	WSEM	TO	*Castle Cement, Ketton*
08529		B	E	WSXX	DR(S)	
08530		DG	P	DFLS	FD	*Barrow Hill T&RSMD*
08531	a	DG	P	DFLS	FD	*Tilbury Container Terminal*
08534		DG	E	WSSC	ML	*Mossend Yard*
08535		DG	EF	WSXX	CD(S)	
08536		B	MA	HISE	DY(S)	
08538		DG	E	WSEM	TO	*Peterborough Yards*
08540		DG	E	WSWM	BS	*Crewe Diesel TMD*
08541		DG	E	WSWX	OC(S)	
08542		F	E	WSXX	BS(S)	
08543		DG	E	WSWM	BS	*Washwood Heath Up Sidings*
08561		B	E	WSNW	AN	*Allerton T&RSMD*
08567		B	E	WSWM	BS	*BescotTMD*
08568	a	B	RC	KGSS	ZH(S)	
08569		E	EF	WSEM	TO	*Toton WRD*
08571	a	B	WA	RFSH	WH	*Whatley Quarry*
08573		0	AD	KCSI	ZI	*Adtranz, Ilford*
08575		B	P	DFLS	FD	*Southampton Maritime SD*
08576		B	E	WSXX	CF(S)	
08577		B	E	WSNE	TE	*Tyne Yard*
08578		RG	E	WSNW	AN	*Trafford Park Freight Terminal*
08580		B	E	WSWM	BS	*Northampton Castle Yard*
08582	a	DG	E	WSNE	TE	*Tees Yard*
08585		B	P	DFLS	FD	*Trafford Park Container Terminal*
08587		B	E	WSYH	IM	*Doncaster Decoy Up Yard*
08588		BR	MA	HISL	NL(S)	
08593		0	E	WSSE	OC	*Wembley Yards*
08596	a†	WA	WA	RFSH	ZB	*Leeds Station*
08597		B	E	WSYH	IM	*Healey Mills Yard*
08599		B	E	WSNW	AN	*Peak Forest Sorting Sidings*
08601		0	E	WSXX	AN(S)	
08605		B	E	WSYH	IM	*Knottingley T&RSMD*
08611		V	VW	HFSL	LO	*Longsight T&RSMD*
08616		GW	MA	HGSS	TS	*Soho T&RSMD*
08617		0	VW	HFSN	WN	*Willesden TMD*
08623		B	E	WSWM	BS	*Wolverhampton Steel Terminal*
08624		B	P	DFLS	FD	*Felixstowe North Container Terminal*
08628		B	E	WSXX	SY(S)	
08629		RP	RC	KWSW	ZN	*Railcare, Wolverton*
08630		E	E	WSSC	ML	*Mossend Yard*
08631		N	PO	HSSN	NC	*Norwich Crown Point T&RSMD*

08632		B	E	WSXX	CD(S)	
08633		RX	E	WSNE	TE	Thornaby T&RSMD
08635		B	E	WSSE	OC	Tilbury Grain Terminal
08641		DG	FW	HJSL	LA	Plymouth Station
08642		O	P	DFLS	ST	Southampton Maritime SD
08643		GL	FW	HJXX	PM	St. Phillips Marsh T&RSMD
08644		IM	FW	HJSL	LA	Penzance
08645		DG	FW	HJSL	LA	Laira T&RSMD
08646		F	E	WSWS	EH	Eastleigh Yards
08648		DG	FW	HJSL	LA(S)	
08649		O	AM	KESE	ZG	Alstom, Eastleigh
08651	a	DG	E	WSAW	CF	Allied Steel & Wire, Cardiff
08653		FE	EF	WSWS	EH	Bristol Barton Hill T&RSMD
08655		F	EF	WSYH	IM	Knottingley Yard
08661	a	F	EF	WSYX	AN(S)	
08662		B	E	WSYH	IM	Doncaster TMD
08663	a	GL	FW	HJSL	LA	Plymouth Station
08664		E	E	WSWS	EH	Westbury Yard
08665		B	E	WSYH	IM	Immingham TMD
08666		B	E	WSYX	AN(S)	
08670	a	B	E	WSSC	ML	Wabtec, Doncaster
08673		IM	E	WSYX	AN(S)	
08675		F	E	WSXX	ML(S)	
08676		B	E	WSYH	IM	Tinsley Yard
08682		O	AD	KDSD	ZF	Adtranz, Doncaster
08683		B	E	WSWM	BS	Bescot TMD
08685		B	E	WSSC	ML	Mossend Yard
08689	a	E	E	WSYH	IM	Immingham Reception Sidings
08690		MA	MA	HISE	DY	Etches Park T&RSMD
08691		G	WA	DFLS	FD	Crewe Carriage T&RSMD
08694	a	E	EF	WSSE	OC	Old Oak Common T&RSMD
08695	a	E	E	WSWM	BS	Wolverhampton Steel Terminal
08696	a	V	VW	HFSL	LO	Liverpool Downhill CSD
08697		B	MA	HISE	DY(S)	
08698	a	E	E	WSWM	BS	Bescot TMD
08701	a	RX	E	WSNW	AN	Warrington Yards
08702		B	E	WSXX	ZB(S)	
08703	a	B	EF	WSNW	AN	Warrington Yards
08706		B	E	WSEM	TO	Toton TMD
08709		B	E	WSNW	AN	Carlisle Currock WRD
08711		RX	E	WSSE	OC	London International Freight Terminal
08714		RX	E	WSEM	TO	Toton TMD
08715	v	O	E	WSXX	SF(S)	
08720	a	E	E	WSSC	ML	Deanside Transit, Hillingdon
08721		O	VW	HFSL	LO	Longsight T&RSMD
08724		WA	WA	RFSH	ZB	Leeds Neville Hill
08730		O	RC	KGSS	ZH	Railcare, Glasgow
08735		DG	E	WSWX	DR(S)	
08737	a	FE	EF	WSNW	AN	Trafford Park Freight Terminal
08738		E	E	WSWM	BS	Crewe Diesel TMD
08739		B	EF	WSXX	AN(S)	

08740		**F**	E	WSXX	SF(S)	
08742		**RX**	E	WSWM	BS	*Longport Sidings*
08743		**EN**	EN	MBDL	BG	*ICI, Billingham*
08745		**FE**	P	DFLS	CD(S)	
08746		**DG**	E	WSXX	DR(S)	
08750	a	**B**	RT	KESE	ZG	*Alstom, Eastleigh*
08751		**F**	EF	WSXX	ZB(S)	
08752	†	**CE**	E	WSAW	CF	*Cardiff Docks*
08754		**FL**	RT	DFLS	FD	*Allerton T&RSMD*
08756		**DG**	E	WSXX	CF(S)	
08757		**E**	E	WSEM	TO	*Toton Up Yard*
08758		**B**	E	WSXX	SF(S)	
08762		**B**	RT	DFLS	FD	*Dagenham Dock Up Sidings*
08765		**DG**	E	WSWM	BS	*Hams Hall Freight Terminal*
08768		**B**	E	WSYX	ML(S)	
08770	a	**DG**	E	WSAW	CF	*Cardiff Canton TMD*
08775		**E**	E	WSSE	OC	*Willesden Brent Yard*
08776	a	**DG**	E	WSSE	OC	*Sherness Dockyard*
08780		**B**	FW	HJSE	LE	*Landore T&RSMD*
08782	a	**B**	E	WSXX	CD(S)	
08783		**B**	E	WSYH	IM	*Daventry International Railfreight Terminal*
08784		**B**	EF	WSNW	AN	*Warrington Yards*
08785	a	**O**	P	DFLS	FD	*Crewe Basford Hall Yard*
08786	a	**DG**	E	WSWS	EH	*Eastleigh Yards*
08788		**RT**	RT	HASS	IS	*Inverness T&RSMD*
08790		**B**	VW	HFSL	LO	*Longsight T&RSMD*
08792		**T**	E	WSSW	CF	*Onllwyn*
08795		**IM**	FW	HJSE	LE	*Landore T&RSMD*
08798		**B**	E	WSWS	EH	*Tavistock Junction*
08799	a	**E**	EF	WSSE	OC	*Ripple Lane Yard*
08801		**B**	E	WSXX	CF(S)	
08802		**RX**	E	WSWM	BS	*Crewe Diesel TMD*
08804		**B**	E	WSWS	EH	*Eastleigh T&RSMD*
08805		**O**	MA	HGSS	TS	*Tyseley T&RSMD*
08806	a	**F**	E	WSNE	TE	*Thornaby T&RSMD*
08807		**BR**	E	WSSC	ML	*Ayr SD*
08809		**O**	HN	DFLS	FD	*Coatbridge Freightliner Terminal*
08810	a	**AR**	AR	HSSN	NC	*Norwich Crown Point T&RSMD*
08813		**DG**	E	WSYX	TE(S)	
08815		**B**	E	WSYX	AN(S)	
08817		**BR**	E	WSXX	AN(S)	
08818		**B**	HN	DFLS	FD	*Crewe Basford Hall Yard*
08819		**DG**	E	WSXX	CF(S)	
08822		**GL**	FW	HJXX	OO	*Old Oak Common HST Depot*
08824		**F**	E	WSYH	IM	*Ferrybridge T&RSMD*
08825	a	**B**	EF	WSXX	OC(S)	
08827	a	**B**	E	WSYX	ML(S)	
08828	a	**E**	E	WSSW	CF	*Onllwyn*
08830		**LW**	CA	HLSV	CP	*Crewe Carriage Depot*
08834		**O**	WA	RFSH	BN	*Bounds Green T&RSMD*
08836		**IM**	FW	HJXX	OO	*Old Oak Common HST Depot*

08837		**DG**	EF	WSXX	AN(S)	
08842		**B**	EF	WSNW	AN	*Immingham TMD*
08844		**B**	EF	WSYH	IM	*Doncaster TMD*
08847		**B**	AM	KESE	ZG(S)	
08853	a	**B**	WA	RFSH	ZB	*Wabtec, Doncaster*
08854	†	**E**	E	WSAW	CF	*Allied Steel & Wire, Cardiff*
08856		**B**	EF	WSWS	EH	*Cardiff Canton TMD*
08865		**B**	E	WSSE	OC	*Old Oak Common TMD*
08866		**B**	E	WSWM	BS	*Dee Marsh Sidings*
08867		**O**	E	WSXX	DE(S)	
08868		**B**	HN	DFLS	FD	*Crewe Basford Hall Yard*
08869		**G**	AR	HSSN	NC(S)	
08870		**RL**	RL	MBDL	DE	*Brunner-Mond, Northwich*
08872		**DG**	EF	WSSE	OC	*Wembley Yards*
08873		**RX**	RT	HDXX	CP	*Crewe Carriage Depot*
08874		**SL**	RT	HPXX	BY	*Bletchley T&RSMD*
08877		**DG**	E	WSWX	SP(S)	
08879		**O**	EF	WSYH	IM	*Doncaster Up Yard*
08880		**B**	E	WSXX	AN(S)	
08881		**DG**	E	WSSC	ML	*Ayr SD*
08882		**B**	E	WSSC	ML	*Falkland Yard*
08883		**O**	E	WSSC	ML	*Perth Yard*
08884		**B**	E	WSWM	BS	*Bordesley Yard*
08886	‡	**E**	E	WSYH	IM	*Immingham Reception Sidings*
08887	a	**VP**	VW	HFSL	LO	*Longsight T&RSMD*
08888		**E**	E	WSWM	BS	*Daventry International Railfreight Terminal*
08890		**DG**	E	WSSE	OC	*Willesden South West Sidings*
08891		**B**	P	DFLS	FD	*Garston Freightliner Terminal*
08892		**GN**	WA	RFSH	BN	*Bounds Green T&RSMD*
08893		**DG**	E	WSYX	ZB(S)	
08894		**B**	E	WSXX	AN(S)	
08896		**E**	E	WSWS	EH	*Avonmouth Bulk Terminal*
08897		**E**	E	WSWM	BS	*Crewe Diesel TMD*
08899		**MM**	MA	HISE	DY	*Etches Park T&RSMD*
08900		**DG**	E	WSWS	EH	*Eastleigh T&RSMD*
08901		**B**	E	WSYX	FB(S)	
08902		**B**	EF	WSXX	AN(S)	
08903		**EN**	EN	MBDL	BG	*ICI, Billingham*
08904		**B**	E	WSWS	EH	*Didcot Yard*
08905		**B**	EF	WSWM	BS	*Saltley SD*
08906		**B**	E	WSXX	ML(S)	
08907		**LW**	EF	WSWM	BS	*Crewe Diesel TMD*
08908		**MM**	MA	HISL	NL	*Leeds Neville Hill (InterCity) T&RSMD*
08909		**ML**	E	WSNW	AN	*Allerton T&RSMD*
08910		**B**	E	WSSC	ML	*Millerhill Yard*
08911		**DG**	E	WSNE	TE	*Tees WRD*
08912		**B**	E	WSNW	AN	*Carlisle Kingmoor Yard*
08913		**DG**	EF	WSSE	OC	*Stratford SD*
08914		**B**	E	WSXX	ZB(S)	
08915		**F**	E	WSNW	AN	*Warrington Yards*

08918		**DG**	E	WSSE	OC	*Wembley Yards*
08919		**RX**	E	WSSE	OC	*Temple Mills Yard*
08920		**F**	E	WSWM	BS	*Bescot TMD*
08921	†	**E**	E	WSAW	CF	*Cardiff Canton TMD*
08922		**DG**	E	WSNW	AN	*Carlisle Kingmoor Yard*
08924		**DG**	E	WSXX	ZB(S)	
08925		**B**	E	WSWX	AN(S)	
08926		**DG**	EF	WSXX	AN(S)	
08927		**B**	E	WSYH	IM	*Doncaster TMD*
08928		**O**	AR	HSSN	NC(S)	
08931		**B**	E	WSYX	FB(S)	
08932		**B**	E	WSXX	CD(S)	
08933		**E**	E	WSSC	ML	*Polmadie T&RSMD*
08934	a	**VP**	VW	HFSN	WN	*Willesden TMD*
08939		**B**	EF	WSWM	BS	*Ferrybridge T&RSMD*
08940		**B**	E	WSYX	AN(S)	
08941		**B**	E	WSWS	EH	*St. Blazey SD*
08942		**B**	E	WSXX	ZB(S)	
08946		**FE**	EF	WSWM	BS	*Dee Marsh Sidings*
08947		**B**	E	WSWS	EH	*Eastleigh Yards*
08948	c	**EP**	EU	GPSS	OC	*North Pole International T&RSMD*
08950		**IM**	MA	HISL	NL(S)	
08951	†	**DG**	EF	WSAW	CF	*Allied Steel & Wire Cardiff*
08953	a	**DG**	E	WSWS	EH	*St. Blazey Yard*
08954		**T**	E	WSYH	IM	*York Up Yard*
08955		**T**	E	WSXX	CF(S)	
08956		**B**	SO	CDJD	DY	*Serco Railtest, Derby*
08957		**E**	E	WSSW	CF	*Cardiff Canton TMD*
08958		**B**	E	WSXX	SF(S)	

Class 08/9. Reduced height cab. Details as Class 08/0 except:

Converted: 1985–87 by BR at Landore T&RSMD.
Dimensions: 8.92 x 2.59 x 3.60 m.

08993		**E**	E	WSSW	CF	*Swansea Burrows Sidings*
08994	a	**E**	E	WSSW	CF	*Margam SD*
08995	a	**E**	E	WSSW	CF	*Margam*

Names:

08578	Lybert Dickinson	08874	Catherine
08629	BRML WOLVERTON LEVEL 5	08879	Sheffield Childrens Hospital
08649	G.H. Stratton	08896	STEPHEN DENT
08682	Lionheart	08903	John W Antill
08694	PAT BARR	08919	Steep Holm
08701	The Sorter	08950	Neville Hill 1st
08714	Cambridge	08993	ASHBURNHAM
08743	Bryan Turner	08994	GWENDRAETH
08790	M.A. SMITH	08995	KIDWELLY
08869	THE CANARY		

R. T. RAILTOURS LTD

Class 08 Shunting Locomotive for
HIRE, Duel braked newly overhauled at
Wabtec Doncaster Works. Railtrack
certified for mainline / siding use.
Link-up approved supplier. With or
without maintenance.

Please apply in writing by Fax or E-mail to:-
rt.rail@lineone.net
Tel: 01270 - 611799   Fax: 01270 - 611855

CLASS 09   BR/ENGLISH ELECTRIC   0–6–0

Built: 1959–62 by BR at Darlington or Horwich Works.
Engine: English Electric 6KT of 298 kW (400 h.p.) at 680 r.p.m.
Main Generator: English Electric 801.
Traction Motors: English Electric 506.
Maximum Tractive Effort: 111 kN (25000 lbf).
Continuous Tractive Effort: 39 kN (8800 lbf) at 11.6 m.p.h.
Power At Rail: 201 kW (269 h.p.).   **Train Brakes:** Air & vacuum.
Brake Force: 19 t.   **Dimensions:** 8.92 x 2.59 x 3.89 m.
Weight: 50 t.   **Wheel Diameter:** 1372 mm.
Design Speed: 27 m.p.h.   **Maximum Speed:** 27 m.p.h.
Fuel Capacity: 3037 litres.   **RA:** 5.
Train Supply: Not equipped.   **Multiple Working:** Not equipped.

Class 09/0. Standard Design.

09001		**E**	E	WSWS	EH	*Fowey Docks*
09003		**E**	E	WSSW	CF	*Port Talbot Steelworks*
09005		**DG**	E	WSYH	IM	*Bombardier Prorail, Horbury Jn.*
09006		**ML**	E	WSSE	OC	*Hoo Junction*
09007		**ML**	E	WSYH	IM	*Hull King George Dock*
09008		**E**	E	WSWS	EH	*Tavistock Junction*
09009		**E**	E	WSSE	OC	*Parkeston Yard*
09010		**DG**	E	WSSE	OC	*Old Oak Common T&RSMD*
09011		**DG**	EF	WSWM	BS	*Bescot Down Sidings*
09012		**DG**	E	WSSE	OC	*Hoo Junction*
09013		**DG**	E	WSSW	CF	*Margam SD*
09014		**DG**	E	WSYH	IM	*Goole Docks*
09015		**DG**	E	WSSW	CF	*Sudbrook Pumping Station*
09016		**DG**	E	WSWS	EH	*Tavistock Junction*
09017		**E**	E	WSSW	CF	*Newport Alexandra Dock Junction*
09018		**E**	E	WSSE	OC	*Adtranz, Ilford*
09019		**ML**	E	WSSE	OC	*Hither Green TMD*
09020		**B**	E	WSXX	ZB(S)	
09021		**E**	EF	WSWM	BS	*Oxley CARMD*
09022	a	**E**	EF	WSNW	AN	*Ditton Junction*
09023	a	**E**	E	WSNE	TE	*Tyne Yard SD*
09024		**ML**	E	WSSE	OC	*Hither Green TMD*
09025		**CX**	SC	HWSU	BI	*Brighton T&RSMD*
09026		**G**	SC	HWSU	BI	*Brighton T&RSMD*

Names:

09009	Three Bridges C.E.D	09026 William Pearson
09012	Dick Hardy	

Class 09/1. Converted from Class 08/0. 110 V electrical equipment. Details as Class 09/0 except:

Built: 1960–61 by BR at Crewe, Derby Locomotive or Horwich Works as Class 08. Converted 1992–93 by RFS Industries, Kilnhurst.

09101	**DG**	E	WSWS	EH	*Swindon Cocklebury Yard*

09102	**DG**	E	WSSW	CF	*Barry Docks*
09103	**DG**	E	WSWM	BS	*Rugby Up Sidings*
09104	**DG**	E	WSSC	ML	*PolmadieT&RSMD*
09105	**DG**	E	WSSW	CF	*East Usk Yard*
09106	**DG**	E	WSNE	TE	*Thornaby T&RSMD*
09107	**DG**	E	WSSW	CF	*Newport Godfrey Road*

Class 09/2. Converted from Class 08/0. 90 V electrical equipment.
Details as Class 09/0 except:

Built: 1958–60 by BR at Crewe or Derby Locomotive Works as Class 08.
Converted 1992 by RFS Industries, Kilnhurst.

09201	a	**DG**	E	WSYH	IM	*FerrybridgeT&RSMD*
09202		**DG**	E	WSYH	IM	*Doncaster Wood Yard*
09203		**DG**	E	WSSW	CF	*Cardiff Canton TMD*
09204		**DG**	E	WSNE	TE	*Thornaby T&RSMD*
09205		**DG**	E	WSSC	ML	*Millerhill Yard*

CLASS 20   ENGLISH ELECTRIC   Bo–Bo

Built: 1957–68 by English Electric Company at Vulcan Foundry, Newton le
Willows or by Robert Stephenson & Hawthorn at Darlington.
Engine: English Electric 8SVT Mk. II of 746 kW (1000 h.p.) at 850 r.p.m.
Main Generator: English Electric 819/3C.
Traction Motors: English Electric 526/5D or 526/8D.
Maximum Tractive Effort: 187 kN (42000 lbf).
Continuous Tractive Effort: 111 kN (25000 lbf) at 11 m.p.h.

Power At Rail: 574 kW (770 h.p.).	**Train Brakes:** Air & vacuum.
Brake Force: 35 t.	**Dimensions:** 14.25 x 2.67 x 3.86 m.
Weight: 73.4–73.5 t.	**Wheel Diameter:** 1092 mm.
Design Speed: 75m.p.h.	**Maximum Speed:** 60 m.p.h.
Fuel Capacity: 1727 litres.	**RA:** 5.
Train Supply: Not equipped.	**Multiple Working:** Blue Star.

Class 20/0. Standard Design.

| 20189 | **G** | RT | MOLO | ES | |

Class 20/3. Direct Rail Services refurbished locos. Details as Class 20/0 except:

Refurbished: 1995–96 by Brush Traction at Loughborough (20301–305) or
1997–98 by RFS(E) at Doncaster (20306–315).

Train Brakes: Air.	**Maximum Speed:** 75 m.p.h.
Brake Force: 31 t.	**Fuel Capacity:** 2900 (+ 4909) litres.
Multiple Working: Blue Star (20301–305 at nose end only).	

20301	+	**DR**	DR	XHSD	KD	Max Joule 1958–1999
20302		**DR**	DR	XHSD	KD	
20303	+	**DR**	DR	XHSD	KD	
20304		**DR**	DR	XHSD	KD	
20305		**DR**	DR	XHSD	KD	
20306	+	**DR**	DR	XHSD	KD	
20307	+	**DR**	DR	XHSD	KD	
20308	+	**DR**	DR	XHSD	KD	

```
20309  +  DR   DR   XHSD   KD
20310  +  DR   DR   XHSD   KD
20311  +  DR   DR   XHSD   KD
20312  +  DR   DR   XHSD   KD
20313  +  DR   DR   XHSD   KD
20314  +  DR   DR   XHSD   KD
20315  +  DR   DR   XHSD   KD
```

Class 20/9. Direct Rail Services (former Hunslet-Barclay) refurbished locos.
Details as Class 20/0 except:

Refurbished: 1989 by Hunslet-Barclay at Kilmarnock.
Train Brakes: Air.   **Fuel Capacity:** 1727 (+ 4727) litres.

```
20901     DR   DR   XHSD   KD
20902  +  DR   DR   XHSD   KD
20903  +  DR   DR   XHSD   KD
20904     DR   DR   XHSD   KD
20905  +  HB   DR   XHSS   KD(S)
20906     DR   DR   XHSD   KD
```

CLASS 25   BEYER PEACOCK/SULZER   Bo–Bo

Built: 1965 by Beyer Peacock at Gorton. Authorised for use on Railtrack between Grosmont & Whitby only.
Engine: Sulzer 6LDA28-B of 930 kW (1250 h.p.) at 750 r.p.m.
Main Generator: AEI RTB15656.   **Traction Motors:** AEI 253AY.
Maximum Tractive Effort: 200 kN (45000 lbf).
Continuous Tractive Effort: 93 kN (20800 lbf) at 17.1 m.p.h.
Power At Rail: 708 kW (949 h.p.).   **Train Brakes:** Air & vacuum.
Brake Force: 38 t.   **Dimensions:** 15.39 x 2.73 x 3.86 m.
Weight: 71.45 t.   **Wheel Diameter:** 1143 mm.
Design Speed: 90 m.p.h.   **Maximum Speed:** 60 m.p.h.
Fuel Capacity: 2270 litres.   **RA:** 5.
Train Supply: Not equipped.   **Multiple Working:** Blue Star.

Non-standard numbering:
• 25278 carries number D7628.

```
25278    GG   NY   MBDL   NY    SYBILIA
```

CLASS 31   BRUSH/ENGLISH ELECTRIC   A1A–A1A

Built: 1958–62 by Brush Traction at Loughborough.
Engine: English Electric 12SVT of 1100 kW (1470 h.p.) at 850 r.p.m.
Main Generator: Brush TG160-48.   **Traction Motors:** Brush TM73-68.
Maximum Tractive Effort: 160 kN (35900 lbf).
Continuous Tractive Effort: 83 kN (18700 lbf) at 23.5 m.p.h.
Power At Rail: 872 kW (1170 h.p.). **Train Brakes:** Air & vacuum.
Brake Force: 49 t.   **Dimensions:** 17.30 x 2.67 x 3.87 m.
Weight: 106.7–111 t.   **Wheel Diameter:** 1092/1003 mm.
Design Speed: 90 m.p.h.   **Maximum Speed:** 60 m.p.h.

Fuel Capacity: 2409 litres.   **RA:** 5 or 6.
Train Supply: Not equipped.   **Multiple Working:** Blue Star.

Non-standard numbering:
• 31110 carries number D5528.

Class 31/1. Standard Design. RA: 5.

31110	**G**	E	WMAC	OC	TRACTION magazine
31113	**CE**	E	WNXX	OM(S)	
31119	**CE**	E	WNYX	CL(S)	
31144	**CE**	E	WNYX	CL(S)	
31154	**CE**	E	WNYX	OM(S)	
31190	**FR**	PO	SDFR	TM	GRYPHON
31203	**CE**	E	WNXX	OM(S)	
31207	**CE**	E	WMAC	OC	
31233	**CE**	E	WNYX	OM(S)	Severn Valley Railway
31285	**CE**	E	WNYX	CL(S)	
31306	**CE**	E	WNXX	OM(S)	
31308	**CE**	E	WNXX	OM(S)	
31327	**FQ**	E	WNYX	CL(S)	

Class 31/4. Electric Train Supply equipment. Details as Class 31/1 except:

Maximum Speed: 90 m.p.h.   **RA:** 6.
Train Supply: Electric, but not operational (e – Electric, index 66).

31420	e	**IM**	E	WMAC	OC	
31427		**B**	E	WNXX	SF(S)	
31434		**B**	E	WNXX	HM(S)	
31452	e	**FR**	FR	SDFR	TM	MINOTAUR
31459	e	**FR**	FR	SDFR	TM	CERBERUS
31460		**B**	E	WNYX	BC(S)	
31465		**RR**	E	WNXX	OM(S)	
31466	ae	**E**	E	WMAC	OC	
31468	e	**FR**	FR	SDFR	TM	HYDRA

Class 31/1 ('31/5'). ETS equipment isolated. Details as Class 31/1 except:

Maximum Speed: 60 m.p.h.   **RA:** 6.
Train Supply: Electric, isolated.

31512	**CE**	E	WNYX	BS(S)	
31514	**CE**	E	WNXX	OM(S)	
31530	**CE**	E	WNXX	SP(S)	
31533	**CE**	E	WNYX	BC(S)	
31538	**B**	E	WNYX	CL(S)	
31554	**CE**	E	WNXX	WA(S)	
31556	**CE**	E	WNYX	CL(S)	

Class 31/6. ETS through wiring and controls. Details as Class 31/1 except:

Maximum Speed: 90 m.p.h.   **Train Supply:** Electric through wired.

31601	**FR**	FR	SDFR	TM	BLETCHLEY PARK 'STATION X'
31602	**FR**	FR	SDFR	TM	CHIMAERA

CLASS 33   BRCW/SULZER   Bo–Bo

Built: 1960–62 by the Birmingham Railway Carriage & Wagon Company at Smethwick.
Engine: Sulzer 8LDA28 of 1160 kW (1550 h.p.) at 750 r.p.m.
Main Generator: Crompton Parkinson CG391B1.
Traction Motors: Crompton Parkinson C171C2.
Maximum Tractive Effort: 200 kN (45000 lbf).
Continuous Tractive Effort: 116 kN (26000 lbf) at 17.5 m.p.h.

Power At Rail: 906 kW (1215 h.p.).	**Train Brakes:** Air & vacuum.
Brake Force: 35 t.	**Dimensions:** 15.47 x 2.82 x 3.86 m.
Weight: 77.7 t.	**Wheel Diameter:** 1092 mm.
Design Speed: 85 m.p.h.	**Maximum Speed:** 60 (* 75, † 85) m.p.h.
Fuel Capacity: 3410 litres.	**RA:** 6.

Train Supply: Electric, not operational (e – index 48 (750 V d.c. only).
Multiple Working: Blue Star.

Non-standard numbering:
- 33051 also carries number 6569.
- 33109 also carries number D6525.
- 33116 also carries number D6535.
- 33208 carries number D6593.

Class 33/0. Standard Design.

33019		**CE**	E	WNYX	ML(S)
33021	e†	**R**	WF	SDFR	TM	Eastleigh
33025	*	**CE**	E	WSAC	ML
33026		**CE**	E	WNYX	EH(S)
33030	*	**E**	E	WSAC	ML
33046		**CE**	E	WNYX	EH(S)
33051		**B**	E	WNYX	EH(S)	Shakespeare Cliff

Class 33/1. Blue Star & SR Multiple Working Equipment. Details as Class 33/0 except:

Train Brakes: Air, vacuum & electro-pneumatic.
Weight: 78.5 t.   **Multiple Working:** Blue Star & SR System.

33103	be†	**G**	CM	CTLO	TM
33108	be†	**B**	PO	SDFR	TM
33109	be†	**B**	HL	HYSB	RL	Captain Bill Smith RNR
33116	b	**B**	E	WNXX	OC(S)

Class 33/2. Narrow body profile. Details as Class 33/0 except:

Weight: 77.5 t.   **Dimensions:** 15.47 x 2.64 x 3.86 m.

33202		**CE**	E	WNXX	EH(S)
33208	e*	**G**	HL	MBDL	RL

CLASS 37   ENGLISH ELECTRIC   Co–Co

Built: 1960–65 by English Electric Company at Vulcan Foundry, Newton le Willows or by Robert Stephenson & Hawthorn at Darlington.
Engine: English Electric 12CSVT of 1300 kW (1750 h.p.) at 850 r.p.m.
Main Generator: English Electric 822/10G.
Traction Motors: English Electric 538/A.
Maximum Tractive Effort: 245 kN (55500 lbf).
Continuous Tractive Effort: 156 kN (35000 lbf) at 13.6 m.p.h.
Power At Rail: 932 kW (1250 h.p.). **Train Brakes:** Air & vacuum.
Brake Force: 50 t.   **Dimensions:** 18.75 x 2.74 x 3.94 or 3.99 m.
Weight: 102.8–108.4 t.   **Wheel Diameter:** 1092 mm.
Design Speed: 90 m.p.h.   **Maximum Speed:** 80 m.p.h.
Fuel Capacity: 4046 (+ 7678) litres. **RA:** 5 (§ 6).
Train Supply: Not equipped.   **Multiple Working:** Blue Star.

Notes: 37073/074/131–308/358/370–383 have roof mounted horns and are 3.99 m. high. The remainder have nose mounted horns and are 3.94 m. high.

Non-standard liveries/numbering:
* 37116 is as **B**, but with Transrail markings.
* 37131 also carries number 6831.
* 37351 carries number 37002 on one side only.
* 37403 carries number D6607.

Class 37/0. Standard Design. Details as above.

37010	a	**CE**	E	WNYX	SP(S)
37013	+	**ML**	E	WNYX	SF(S)
37023		**ML**	E	WNXX	OC(S)	Stratford TMD Quality Approved
37029		**B**	RV	RTLO	CP
37037	a	**F**	E	WNYX	SP(S)
37038		**CE**	IR	MBDL	BQ
37040		**E**	E	WNXX	SP(S)
37042	+	**E**	E	WKAC	OC
37046	a	**CE**	E	WNXX	TY(S)
37047	+	**ML**	E	WKAC	OC
37051		**E**	E	WNXX	DR(S)	Merehead
37054		**CE**	E	WNYX	ML(S)
37055	+	**ML**	E	WNXX	EH(S)
37057	+	**E**	E	WKAC	OC	Viking
37058	a+	**CE**	E	WNXX	TY(S)
37059	a+	**FD**	E	WNYX	IM(S)
37065	+	**ML**	E	WKAC	OC
37069	a+	**CE**	E	WNYX	SP(S)
37071	a+	**CE**	E	WNYX	SP(S)
37073	a+	**T**	E	WNYX	SP(S)
37074	a+	**ML**	E	WNYX	SP(S)
37077	a	**ML**	E	WNXX	TY(S)
37087		**CE**	E	WNYX	CW(S)
37097		**CE**	E	WNYX	MH(S)
37100	a	**T**	E	WNXX	TY(S)

37109		E	E	WKAD	CD	
37114	r+	E	E	WKAD	CD	City of Worcester
37116	+	O	E	WKAD	CD	Sister Dora
37131	+	F	E	WNYX	SP(S)	
37133	a	CE	E	WNYX	SP(S)	
37146	a	CE	E	WNXX	TY(S)	
37152		IS	E	WNYX	ML(S)	
37162	+	DG	E	WNYX	SP(S)	
37165	a+	TC	E	WNYX	TT(S)	
37170	a	TC	E	WNYX	SP(S)	
37174	a	E	E	WKAC	OC	
37175	a	CE	E	WNYX	OM(S)	
37178	+	F	E	WNYX	EH(S)	
37185	+	CE	E	WNYX	CF(S)	
37196	a	CE	E	WNXX	TY(S)	
37198	+	ML	E	WNXX	TO(S)	
37203		ML	E	WKAC	OC	
37211		CE	E	WNYX	TE(S)	
37212	+	T	E	WNYX	EH(S)	
37216	+	ML	E	WKAD	CD	
37217	+	B	E	WNYX	AY(S)	
37219		ML	E	WKAC	OC	
37220	+	E	E	WNXX	TO(S)	
37221	a	T	E	WNXX	TY(S)	
37225	+	F	E	WNYX	CF(S)	
37230	+	TC	E	WNYX	TO(S)	
37238	a+	F	E	WNXX	TY(S)	
37248	+	ML	E	WKAC	OC	Midland Railway Centre
37250	a+	T	E	WNXX	TY(S)	
37252		FD	E	WNYX	DD(S)	
37261	a+	FD	E	WNYX	OM(S)	
37262	+	DG	E	WNYX	SP(S)	Dounreay[1]
37263		CE	E	WNYX	EH(S)	
37264		CE	E	WNYX	CF(S)	
37275	+	B	E	WNYX	TO(S)	
37293	a+	ML	E	WNXX	TY(S)	
37294	a+	CE	E	WNXX	TY(S)	
37298	a+	E	E	WNYX	SP(S)	
37308	(37274)	+	B	E	WNXX	EH(S)

Class 37/3. Re-geared (CP7) bogies. Details as Class 37/0 except:

Maximum Tractive Effort: 250 kN (56180 lbf).
Continuous Tractive Effort: 184 kN (41250 lbf) at 11.4 m.p.h.
Design Speed: 80 m.p.h.

37331		FM	E	WNYX	DD(S)
37351	+	TC	E	WNXX	TE(S)
37358	+	F	E	WNYX	IM(S)
37370	a	E	E	WNYX	SP(S)
37372		ML	E	WKAD	CD
37375	a+	ML	E	WNXX	DR(S)

37376	a+	**F**	E	WNYX	SP(S)	
37377	+	**CE**	E	WNXX	EH(S)	
37379	a	**ML**	E	WKBM	ML	Ipswich WRD Quality Approved
37383	+	**ML**	E	WNYX	IM(S)	

Class 37/4. Refurbished with train supply equipment. Main generator replaced by alternator. Re-geared (CP7) bogies. Details as class 37/0 except:

Main Alternator: Brush BA1005A.   **Power At Rail:** 935 kW (1254 h.p.).
Maximum Tractive Effort: 256 kN (57440 lbf).
Continuous Tractive Effort: 184 kN (41250 lbf) at 11.4 m.p.h.
Dimensions: 18.75 x 2.74 x 3.99 m.   **Weight:** 107 t.
Design Speed: 80 m.p.h.
Fuel Capacity: 7678 (z 4046) litres.   **Train Supply:** Electric, index 38.

37401		**E**	E	WKCD	CD	Mary Queen of Scots
37402		**F**	E	WNXX	CD(S)	Bont Y Bermo
37403	ar	**G**	E	WNXX	CF(S)	Ben Cruachan
37405	r	**E**	E	WKBM	ML	
37406		**T**	E	WNXX	CF(S)	The Saltire Society
37407		**T**	E	WNXX	CD(S)	
37408	r	**E**	E	WKBM	ML	Loch Rannoch
37409	r	**T**	E	WNXX	ML(S)	Loch Awe
37410		**T**	E	WNXX	ML(S)	Aluminium 100
37411	r	**E**	E	WKBM	ML	Ty Hafan
37412		**T**	E	WKCD	CD	Driver John Elliott
37413	r	**E**	E	WNXX	DR(S)	
37414		**RR**	E	WNYX	CF(S)	Cathays C & W Works 1846–1993
37415	r	**E**	E	WKBM	ML	
37416	r	**E**	E	WKBM	ML	
37417	a	**E**	E	WNXX	BW(S)	
37418	r	**E**	E	WKBM	ML	East Lancashire Railway
37419	r	**E**	E	WKBM	ML	
37420		**RR**	E	WNXX	CD(S)	The Scottish Hosteller
37421		**E**	E	WKCD	CD	
37422		**RR**	E	WNXX	BW(S)	
37423		**T**	E	WNXX	ML(S)	Sir Murray Morrison 1873-1948
						Pioneer of the British Aluminium Industry
37424		**T**	E	WNXX	ML(S)	
37425		**RR**	E	WNXX	CF(S)	Sir Robert McAlpine/Concrete Bob
37426		**E**	E	WKCD	CD	
37427	r	**E**	E	WKBM	ML	
37428	r	**GS**	E	WKBM	ML	
37429		**RR**	E	WKCD	CD	Eisteddfod Genedlaethol
37430	ar	**T**	E	WNXX	ML(S)	Cwmbrân

Class 37/5. Refurbished without train supply equipment. Main generator replaced by alternator. Re-geared (CP7) bogies. Details as Class 37/4 except:

Maximum Tractive Effort: 248 kN (55590 lbf).
Dimensions: 18.75 x 2.74 x 3.94 or 3.99 m.
Weight: 106.1–107.3 (§ 110.0) t.   **Train Supply:** Not equipped.

Notes: 37610–679/682–698/800–899 have roof mounted horns and are 3.99 m. high. The remainder have nose mounted horns and are 3.94 m. high.

37503	r§	**E**	E	WKAD	CD	
37505	a§	**T**	E	WNXX	AY(S)	British Steel Workington
37509	a§	**F**	E	WNXX	EH(S)	
37510	a	**IS**	E	WNXX	TE(S)	
37513	as§	**LH**	E	WNXX	OC(S)	
37515	as	**FM**	E	WNXX	TE(S)	
37516	s§	**LH**	E	WNXX	TE(S)	
37517	as§	**LH**	E	WNXX	TE(S)	
37518	a§	**FM**	E	WNXX	AY(S)	
37519		**FM**	E	WNYX	EH(S)	
37520	r§	**E**	E	WKAD	CD	
37521	r§	**E**	E	WKAD	CD	English China Clays

Class 37/6. Refurbished for Nightstar services. Main generator replaced by alternator, re-geared bogies and UIC jumpers. Details as class 37/5 except:

Maximum Speed: 80 († 90) m.p.h. **Train Brake:** Air.
Train Supply: Not equipped, but electric through wired.
Multiple Working: TDM († plus Blue Star).

Note: One (unspecified) locomotive is hired from Eurostar (UK) to Freightliner for use on the West Highland Line (Craigendoran Junction–Fort William). This locomotive is outbased at Motherwell T&RSMD.

37601		**EP**	EU	GPSV	OC
37602		**EP**	EU	GPSV	OC
37603		**EP**	EU	GPSV	OC
37604		**EP**	EU	GPSV	OC
37605		**EP**	EU	GPSV	OC
37606		**EP**	EU	GPSV	OC
37607	†	**DR**	DR	XHSD	KD
37608	†	**DR**	DR	XHSD	KD
37609	†	**DR**	DR	XHSD	KD
37610	†	**DR**	DR	XHSD	KD
37611	†	**DR**	DR	XHSD	KD
37612	†	**DR**	DR	XHSD	KD

Class 37/5 (Continued).

37667	rs§	**E**	E	WKAD	CD	Meldon Quarry Centenary
37668	s§	**E**	E	WKAD	CD	
37669	r§	**E**	E	WKBM	ML	
37670	r§	**E**	E	WKBM	ML	
37671	a	**T**	E	WNXX	TY(S)	
37672	as	**T**	E	WNXX	TE(S)	
37673	§	**T**	E	WNXX	TE(S)	
37674	§	**T**	E	WKAD	CD	St. Blaise Church 1445–1995
37675	as§	**T**	E	WNXX	EH(S)	
37676	a§	**F**	E	WKSN	TO	
37677	a§	**F**	E	WNXX	TE(S)	
37678	a§	**F**	E	WNXX	BS(S)	
37679	a§	**F**	E	WNXX	AY(S)	

37680	a§	**FA**	E	WKSN	TO	
37682	r§	**E**	E	WKAD	CD	Hartlepool Pipe Mill
37683	a	**T**	E	WNXX	TE(S)	
37684	ar§	**E**	E	WKAD	CD	Peak National Park
37685	a§	**IS**	E	WNXX	TE(S)	
37686	a	**FA**	E	WNYX	SP(S)	
37688	§	**E**	E	WKAD	CD	
37689	a§	**F**	E	WNXX	TE(S)	
37692	s§	**FC**	E	WNXX	TE(S)	
37693	as	**T**	E	WNXX	TY(S)	
37694	§	**E**	E	WKAD	CD	
37695	s§	**E**	E	WKAD	CD	
37696	as	**T**	E	WNXX	TY(S)	
37697	§	**E**	E	WNXX	TT(S)	
37698	s§	**LH**	E	WKAD	CD	

Class 37/7. Refurbished locos. Main generator replaced by alternator. Re-geared (CP7) bogies. Ballast weights added. Details as class 37/5 except:
Main Alternator: GEC G564AZ (37796–803) Brush BA1005A (others).
Maximum Tractive Effort: 276 kN (62000 lbf).
Weight: 120 t.   **RA:** 7.

37701	as	**T**	E	WNXX	OM(S)	
37702	s	**T**	E	WKAD	CD	Taff Merthyr
37703		**E**	E	WKGS	TE(S)	
37704	s	**E**	E	WKAD	CD	
37705		**MG**	E	WNXX	ML(S)	
37706		**E**	E	WKAD	CD	
37707		**E**	E	WKAD	CD	
37708	a	**FP**	E	WNXX	TY(S)	
37709		**MG**	E	WNXX	IM(S)	
37710		**LH**	E	WKAD	CD	
37711		**FM**	E	WNYX	TO(S)	
37712	a	**E**	E	WKAC	OC	
37713		**LH**	E	WNXX	CD(S)	
37714	a	**E**	E	WKGS	TO(S)	
37715		**MG**	E	WNYX	SP(S)	
37716		**E**	E	WKGS	EH(S)	
37717		**E**	E	WKAD	CD	Berwick Middle School, Railsafe Trophy Winners 1998
37718		**E**	E	WKGS	TO(S)	
37719	a	**FP**	E	WNXX	OM(S)	
37796	as	**FC**	E	WNXX	TY(S)	
37797	s	**E**	E	WKAD	CD	
37798		**ML**	E	WKAD	CD	
37799	as	**T**	E	WKAD	CD	Sir Dyfed/County of Dyfed
37800	a	**MG**	E	WNXX	TY(S)	
37801	s	**E**	E	WKAD	CD	
37802	s	**T**	E	WNXX	OM(S)	
37803	a	**ML**	E	WNXX	TY(S)	
37883		**E**	E	WKGS	CD(S)	
37884		**LH**	E	WKAD	CD	Gartcosh

37885		E	E	WKGS	EH(S)	
37886		E	E	WKAD	CD	
37887	s	T	E	WNXX	IM(S)	
37888	z	F	E	WNXX	TE(S)	
37889		T	E	WNYX	CD(S)	
37890	a	MG	E	WNXX	TY(S)	
37891	a	MG	E	WNXX	TY(S)	
37892		MG	E	WNXX	OM(S)	Ripple Lane[1]
37893		E	E	WKAD	CD	
37894	as	FC	E	WNXX	TY(S)	
37895	s	E	E	WKAD	CD	
37896	s	T	E	WNXX	TY(S)	
37897	s	T	E	WNXX	BS(S)	
37898	s	T	E	WNXX	CF(S)	Cwmbargoed DP
37899	s	E	E	WKGS	TE(S)	

Class 37/9. Refurbished locos. New power unit. Main generator replaced by alternator. Ballast weights added. Details as Class 37/4 except:

Engine: Mirrlees MB275T of 1340 kW (1800 h.p.) at 1000 r.p.m. (‡ Ruston RK270T of 1340 kW (1800 h.p.) at 900 r.p.m.).
Train supply: Not equipped.
Main Alternator: Brush BA1005A (‡ GEC G564AZ).
Maximum Tractive Effort: 279 kN (62680 lbf).
Continuous Tractive Effort: 184 kN (41250 lbf) at 11.4 m.p.h.
Weight: 120 t.   **RA:** 7.

37901	‡s	T	E	WNYX	CF(S)	Mirrlees Pioneer
37902		FM	E	WNYX	IM(S)	
37903		FM	E	WNYX	CD(S)	
37905	‡s	FM	E	WNYX	IM(S)	
37906	‡s	F0	E	WNYX	KR(S)	

CLASS 43   BREL/PAXMAN   Bo–Bo

Built: 1976–82 by BREL at Crewe Works.
Engine: Paxman Valenta 12RP200L of 1680 kW (2250 h.p.) at 1500 r.p.m. († Paxman 12VP185 of 2010 kW (2700 h.p.) at 1800 r.p.m.).
Main Alternator: Brush BA1001B.
Traction Motors: Brush TMH68–46 or GEC G417AZ, frame mounted.
Maximum Tractive Effort: 80 kN (17980 lbf).
Continuous Tractive Effort: 46 kN (10340 lbf) at 64.5 m.p.h.
Power At Rail: 1320 kW (1770 h.p.).   **Train Brakes:** Air.
Brake Force: 35 t.   **Dimensions:** 17.79 x 2.71 x 3.88 m.
Weight: 70 t.   **Wheel Diameter:** 1020 mm.
Design Speed: 125 m.p.h.   **Maximum Speed:** 125 m.p.h.
Fuel Capacity: 4500 litres.   **RA:** 5.
Train Supply: Three-phase electric.
Multiple Working: Within class, jumpers at non-driving end only.

43002	FG	A	IWRP	PM	TECHNI?UEST
43003	FG	A	IWRP	PM	
43004	FG	A	IWRP	PM	Borough of Swindon

43005	**FG**	A	IWRP	PM	
43006	**IS**	A	IWCP	LA	
43007	**IS**	A	IWCP	LA	
43008	**V**	A	IWCP	LA	
43009	**FG**	A	IWRP	PM	
43010	**FG**	A	IWRP	PM	
43011	**FG**	A	SCXL	ZC(S)	Reader 125
43012	**FG**	A	IWRP	PM	
43013	**V**	P	ICCP	LA	
43014	**V**	P	ICCP	LA	
43015	**FG**	A	IWRP	PM	
43016	**FG**	A	IWRP	PM	
43017	**FG**	A	IWRP	LA	
43018	**FG**	A	IWRP	LA	The Red Cross
43019	**FG**	A	IWRP	LA	Dinas Abertawe/City of Swansea
43020	**FG**	A	IWRP	LA	John Grooms
43021	**FG**	A	IWRP	LA	
43022	**FG**	A	IWRP	LA	
43023	**FG**	A	IWRP	LA	County of Cornwall
43024	**FG**	A	IWRP	LA	
43025	**FG**	A	IWRP	LA	Exeter
43026	**FG**	A	IWRP	LA	City of Westminster
43027	**FG**	A	IWRP	LA	Glorious Devon
43028	**FG**	A	IWRP	LA	
43029	**IS**	A	ICCP	LA	
43030	**FG**	A	IWRP	PM	Christian Lewis Trust
43031	**FG**	A	IWRP	PM	
43032	**FG**	A	IWRP	PM	The Royal Regiment of Wales
43033	**FG**	A	IWRP	PM	
43034	**FG**	A	IWRP	PM	The Black Horse
43035	**FG**	A	IWRP	PM	
43036	**FG**	A	IWRP	PM	
43037	**FG**	A	IWRP	PM	
43038	**GN**	A	IECP	EC	
43039	**GN**	A	IECP	EC	
43040	**FG**	A	IWRP	PM	
43041	**FG**	A	IWRP	LA	City of Discovery
43042	**FG**	A	IWRP	LA	
43043	**MM**	P	IMLP	NL	LEICESTERSHIRE COUNTY CRICKET CLUB
43044	**MM**	P	IMLP	NL	Borough of Kettering
43045	**MM**	P	IMLP	NL	
43046	**MM**	P	IMLP	NL	Royal Philharmonic
43047 †	**MM**	P	IMLP	NL	
43048	**MM**	P	IMLP	NL	
43049	**MM**	P	IMLP	NL	Neville Hill
43050	**MM**	P	IMLP	NL	
43051	**MM**	P	IMLP	NL	
43052	**MM**	P	IMLP	NL	
43053	**MM**	P	IMLP	NL	Leeds United
43054	**MM**	P	IMLP	NL	

43055	**MM**	P	IMLP	NL	Sheffield Star
43056	**MM**	P	IMLP	NL	
43057	**MM**	P	IMLP	NL	
43058	**MM**	P	IMLP	NL	MIDLAND PRIDE
43059 †	**MM**	P	IMLP	NL	
43060	**MM**	P	IMLP	NL	County of Leicestershire
43061	**MM**	P	IMLP	NL	
43062	**V**	P	ICCP	LA	
43063	**V**	P	ICCP	LA	Maiden Voyager
43064	**MM**	P	IMLP	NL	
43065	**V**	P	ICCP	LA	
43066	**MM**	P	IMLP	NL	Nottingham Playhouse
43067	**V**	P	ICCP	LA	
43068	**V**	P	ICCP	LA	The Red Arrows
43069	**V**	P	ICCP	LA	
43070	**V**	P	ICCP	LA	
43071	**V**	P	ICCP	LA	Forward Birmingham
43072	**MM**	P	IMLP	NL	Derby Etches Park
43073	**MM**	P	IMLP	NL	
43074 †	**MM**	P	IMLP	NL	BBC EAST MIDLANDS TODAY
43075 †	**MM**	P	IMLP	NL	
43076	**MM**	P	IMLP	NL	THE MASTER CUTLER 1947-1997
43077	**MM**	P	IMLP	NL	
43078	**V**	P	ICCP	LA	Golowan Festival Penzance
43079	**V**	P	ICCP	LA	
43080	**V**	P	ICCP	LA	
43081	**MM**	P	IMLP	NL	
43082	**MM**	P	IMLP	NL	DERBYSHIRE FIRST
43083	**MM**	P	IMLP	NL	
43084	**V**	P	ICCP	LA	County of Derbyshire
43085	**MM**	P	IMLP	NL	
43086	**V**	P	ICCP	LA	
43087	**V**	P	ICCP	LA	
43088	**V**	P	ICCP	LA	
43089	**V**	P	ICCP	LA	
43090	**V**	P	ICCP	LA	
43091	**V**	P	ICCP	LA	
43092	**V**	P	ICCP	LA	Institution of Mechanical
					Engineers 150th Anniversary
43093	**V**	P	ICCP	LA	Lady in Red
43094	**V**	P	ICCP	LA	
43095	**GN**	A	IECP	EC	
43096	**GN**	A	IECP	EC	The Great Racer
43097	**V**	P	ICCP	LA	
43098	**V**	P	ICCP	LA	railwaychildren
43099	**V**	P	ICCP	LA	
43100	**V**	P	ICCP	LA	
43101	**V**	P	ICCP	LA	
43102	**V**	P	ICCP	LA	
43103	**V**	P	ICCP	LA	
43104	**IS**	A	SCXL	ZC(S)	County of Cleveland

43105	GN	A	IECP	EC	
43106	GN	A	IECP	EC	
43107	GN	A	IECP	EC	
43108	GN	A	IECP	EC	Old Course St Andrews
43109	GN	A	IECP	EC	
43110	GN	A	IECP	EC	
43111	GN	A	IECP	EC	
43112	GN	A	IECP	EC	
43113	GN	A	IECP	EC	
43114	GN	A	IECP	EC	
43115	GN	A	IECP	EC	
43116	GN	A	IECP	EC	
43117	GN	A	IECP	EC	
43118	GN	A	IECP	EC	
43119	GN	A	IECP	EC	
43120	GN	A	IECP	EC	
43121	V	P	ICCP	LA	
43122	V	P	ICCP	LA	South Yorkshire Metropolitan County
43123	V	P	ICCP	LA	
43124	FG	A	IWRP	PM	
43125	FG	A	IWRP	PM	Merchant Venturer
43126	FG	A	IWRP	PM	City of Bristol
43127	FG	A	IWRP	PM	
43128	FG	A	IWRP	PM	
43129	FG	A	IWRP	PM	
43130	FG	A	IWRP	PM	Sulis Minerva
43131	FG	A	IWRP	PM	Sir Felix Pole
43132	FG	A	IWRP	PM	
43133	FG	A	IWRP	PM	
43134	FG	A	IWRP	PM	County of Somerset
43135	FG	A	IWRP	PM	
43136	FG	A	IWRP	PM	
43137	FG	A	IWRP	PM	Newton Abbot 150
43138	FG	A	IWRP	PM	
43139	FG	A	IWRP	PM	
43140	FG	A	IWRP	PM	
43141	FG	A	IWRP	PM	
43142	FG	A	IWRP	PM	
43143	FG	A	IWRP	PM	
43144	FG	A	IWRP	PM	
43145	FG	A	IWRP	PM	
43146	FG	A	IWRP	PM	
43147	FG	A	IWRP	PM	
43148	FG	A	IWRP	PM	
43149	FG	A	IWRP	PM	B.B.C. Wales Today
43150	FG	A	IWRP	PM	Bristol Evening Post
43151	FG	A	IWRP	PM	
43152	FG	A	IWRP	PM	
43153	V	P	ICCP	LA	THE ENGLISH RIVIERA TORQUAY PAIGNTON BRIXHAM
43154	V	P	ICCP	LA	INTERCITY

43155		V	P	ICCP	LA	City of Aberdeen
43156		V	P	ICCP	LA	
43157		V	P	ICCP	LA	
43158		V	P	ICCP	LA	Dartmoor Pony
43159		V	P	ICCP	LA	
43160		V	P	ICCP	LA	
43161		V	P	ICCP	LA	
43162		V	P	ICCP	LA	
43163		FG	A	IWRP	LA	
43164		FG	A	IWRP	LA	
43165		FG	A	IWRP	LA	
43166		IS	A	ICCP	LA	
43167	†	GN	A	IECP	EC	
43168	†	FG	A	IWRP	LA	
43169	†	FG	A	IWRP	LA	The National Trust
43170	†	FG	A	IWRP	LA	Edward Paxman
43171		FG	A	IWRP	LA	
43172		FG	A	IWRP	LA	
43174		FG	A	IWRP	LA	Bristol-Bordeaux
43175	†	FG	A	IWRP	LA	
43176		FG	A	IWRP	LA	
43177	†	FG	A	IWRP	LA	University of Exeter
43178		V	A	IWCP	LA	
43179	†	FG	A	IWRP	LA	Pride of Laira
43180		V	P	ICCP	LA	City of Newcastle upon Tyne
43181		FG	A	IWRP	LA	Devonport Royal Dockyard 1693–1993
43182		FG	A	IWRP	LA	
43183		FG	A	IWRP	LA	
43184		V	A	IWCP	LA	
43185		FG	A	IWRP	LA	Great Western
43186		FG	A	IWRP	LA	Sir Francis Drake
43187		FG	A	IWRP	LA	
43188		FG	A	IWRP	LA	City of Plymouth
43189		FG	A	IWRP	LA	RAILWAY HERITAGE TRUST
43190		FG	A	IWRP	LA	
43191	†	FG	A	IWRP	LA	Seahawk
43192		FG	A	IWRP	LA	City of Truro
43193		V	P	ICCP	LA	Plymouth SPIRIT OF DISCOVERY
43194		V	P	ICCP	LA	
43195		V	P	ICCP	LA	British Red Cross 125th Birthday 1995[1]
43196		V	P	ICCP	LA	The Newspaper Society Founded 1836
43197		V	P	ICCP	LA	
43198		V	P	ICCP	LA	HMS Penzance

CLASS 46   BR/SULZER   1Co–Co1

Built: 1963 by BR at Derby Locomotive Works.
Engine: Sulzer 12LDA28B of 1860 kW (2500 h.p.) at 750 r.p.m.
Main Generator: Brush TG160-60.   **Traction Motors:** Brush TM73-68 Mk3.
Maximum Tractive Effort: 245 kN (55000 lbf).
Continuous Tractive Effort: 141 kN (31600 lbf) at 22.3 m.p.h.
Power At Rail: 1460 kW (1960 h.p.).   **Train Brakes:** Air & vacuum.
Brake Force: 63 t.   **Dimensions:** 20.70 x 2.78 x 3.92 m.
Weight: 140 t.   **Wheel Diameter:** 914/1143 mm.
Design Speed: 90 m.p.h.   **Maximum Speed:** 75 m.p.h.
Fuel Capacity: 3591 litres.   **RA:** 7.
Train Supply: Not equipped.   **Multiple Working:** Not equipped.

Non-standard livery/numbering:
• 46035 carries number D172. Official RSL number is 89472.

46035	**G**	CN	MBDL	CQ	Ixion

CLASS 47   BR/BRUSH/SULZER   Co–Co

Built: 1963–67 by Brush Traction, at Loughborough or by BR at Crewe Works.
Engine: Sulzer 12LDA28C of 1920 kW(*‡ 1785 kW) (2580 (*‡2400) h.p.) at 750 r.p.m.
Main Generator: Brush TG160-60 Mk4 or TM172-50 Mk1.
Traction Motors: Brush TM64-68 Mk1 or Mk1A.
Maximum Tractive Effort: 267 kN (60000 lbf).
Continuous Tractive Effort: 133 kN (30000 lbf) at 26 m.p.h.
Power At Rail: 1550 kW (2080 h.p.).   **Train Brakes:** Air.
Brake Force: 61 t.   **Dimensions:** 19.38 x 2.79 x 3.9 m.
Weight: 111.5–120.6 t.   **Wheel Diameter:** 1143 mm.
Design Speed: 95 m.p.h.   **Maximum Speed:** 75 m.p.h.
Fuel Capacity: 3273 (+ 5550; † 4410 litres).
Train Supply: Not equipped.
Multiple Working: Green Circle (n – not equipped).

Notes:
d Dock Mode' slow speed traction control system for working trains from Felixstowe North Container Terminal.

Non-standard liveries/numbering:
• 47004 carries number D1524.
• 47114 is as **GG**, but with Freightliner logos.
• 47145 is dark blue with Railfreight Distribution logos.
• 47515 is livery **IM** on one side and all-over white on the other side).
• 47519 also carries number D1102.

Class 47/0 (Dual braked locos) or Class 47/2 (Air braked locos). Standard Design. Details as above.

47004	xn	**GG**	E	WNXX	KR(S)
47052	*	**FF**	P	DHLT	EH(S)
47053	+	**FE**	EF	WNYX	HM(S)

47095	+	**FE**	EF	WNYX	AN(S)	
47114	*+	**0**	FL	DFLM	FD	Freightlinerbulk
47145	+	**0**	EF	WNYX	CD(S)	MERDDIN EMRYS
47146	+	**FE**	EF	WNYX	CD(S)	
47150	*+	**FL**	FL	DFLM	FD	
47152	*+	**FF**	FL	DFLM	FD	
47157	*+	**FF**	P	DFLM	FD	Johnson Stevens Agencies
47186	+	**FE**	EF	WNYX	HM(S)	
47188	+	**FE**	EF	WNYX	CD(S)	
47193	n*	**FL**	P	DHLT	CG(S)	
47197	dn*	**FF**	P	DFFT	FD	
47200	*+	**FE**	EF	WNYX	HM(S)	
47201	*+	**FE**	EF	WNYX	HM(S)	
47205	*+	**FF**	FL	DFLM	FD	
47206	n*	**FF**	P	DFLT	FD	The Morris Dancer
47207	*+	**FF**	P	DFLM	FD	The Felixstowe Partnership
47209	*+	**FF**	P	DHLT	CG(S)	
47211	+	**FD**	EF	WNYX	EH(S)	
47212	xn‡	**FF**	P	DFLT	FD	
47213	+	**FD**	EF	WNYX	SP(S)	
47217	+	**FE**	EF	WNYX	SP(S)	
47218	+	**FE**	EF	WNYX	SP(S)	
47219	+	**FE**	EF	WNYX	HM(S)	
47221	xn†	**FP**	E	WNYX	LB(S)	
47224	xn‡	**F**	P	DFLT	FD	
47225	n*	**FF**	P	DHLT	CG(S)	
47226	+	**FD**	EF	WNYX	HM(S)	
47228	+	**FE**	EF	WNYX	HM(S)	
47229	+	**FD**	EF	WNYX	HM(S)	
47234	*+	**FF**	P	DFLM	FD	
47236	+	**FE**	EF	WNYX	SF(S)	
47237	+	**FE**	EF	WNYX	HM(S)	
47241	+	**FE**	EF	WNYX	CD(S)	
47245	+	**FE**	EF	WNYX	DD(S)	
47256	xn	**FD**	E	WNYX	DD(S)	
47258	*+	**FL**	FL	DFLM	FD	Forth Ports Tilbury
47270	dn*	**FF**	P	DFFT	FD	Cory Brothers 1842–1992
47279	*+	**FF**	P	DFLM	FD	
47280	+	**FD**	EF	WNYX	HM(S)	
47283	n*	**FF**	FL	DHLT	ST(S)	
47285	+	**FE**	EF	WNYX	TT(S)	
47287	*+	**F**	FL	DFLM	FD	
47289	*+	**FF**	P	DFLM	FD	
47290	*+	**FF**	FL	DHLT	CG(S)	
47292	*+	**F**	P	DFLM	FD	
47293	+	**FE**	EF	WNYX	HM(S)	
47295	dn‡	**F**	FL	DFFT	FD	
47296	xn*	**FF**	P	DFLT	FD	
47298	+	**FD**	EF	WNYX	HM(S)	

Class 47/3 (Dual braked locos) or Class 47/2 (Air braked locos). Details as Class 47/0 except:

Weight: 113.7 t.

47301	*+ **FF**	P	DFLM	FD	Freightliner Birmingham
47302	*+ **FF**	FL	DFLM	FD	
47303	*+ **FF**	P	DFLM	FD	Freightliner Cleveland
47305	n* **FF**	P	DHLT	CG(S)	
47306	+ **FE**	EF	WNXX	EH(S)	The Sapper
47307	+ **FE**	EF	WNYX	HM(S)	
47308	* **FE**	FL	DHLT	CG(S)	
47309	d*+**FF**	FL	DHLT	CB(S)	European Rail Operator of The Year
47310	+ **FE**	EF	WNYX	HM(S)	
47312	+ **FE**	EF	WNYX	CD(S)	
47313	+ **FD**	EF	WNYX	HM(S)	
47314	+ **FD**	EF	WNYX	HM(S)	
47316	+ **FE**	EF	WNYX	TT(S)	
47323	d*+**FF**	P	DFFT	FD	
47326	+ **FE**	EF	WNYX	CD(S)	Saltley Depot Quality Approved
47328	+ **FD**	EF	WNYX	CD(S)	
47330	*+ **FF**	FL	DHLT	CG(S)	
47331	xns **CE**	E	WNYX	SP(S)	
47334	n* **FF**	P	DFLT	FD	P & O Nedlloyd
47335	+ **FD**	EF	WNYX	HM(S)	
47337	*+ **FF**	FL	DHLT	CG(S)	
47338	+ **FE**	EF	WNYX	CD(S)	
47339	n* **FF**	P	DHLT	CG(S)	
47345	n* **FF**	P	DFLT	FD	
47348	+ **FE**	EF	WNYX	SF(S)	St. Christopher's Railway Home
47349	xn* **FF**	P	DFLT	FD	
47353	n* **FF**	FL	DHLT	CG(S)	
47354	* **FF**	FL	DHLT	CG(S)	
47357	xn **CE**	E	WNYX	BS(S)	
47358	*+ **FF**	P	DFLM	FD	
47360	+ **FE**	EF	WNYX	HM(S)	
47361	*+ **FF**	P	DFLM	FD	
47365	+ **FE**	EF	WNYX	CF(S)	Diamond Jubilee
47367	*+ **FF**	P	DFLM	FD	
47368	xn **F**	E	WNYX	SF(S)	
47370	*+ **FF**	P	DFLM	FD	Andrew A Hodgkinson
47371	n* **FF**	P	DHLT	CB(S)	
47372	n* **FF**	P	DHLT	CP(S)	
47375	+ **FE**	EF	WNYX	HM(S)	
47376	xn* **FF**	P	DFLT	FD	Freightliner 1995
47377	n* **FF**	P	DHLT	CD(S)	

Class 47/4. Electric Train Supply equipment. Details as Class 47/0 except:

Weight: 120.4–125.1 t.   **Maximum Speed:** 95 (* 75) m.p.h.
Fuel Capacity: 3273 (+ 5887) litres.   **RA:** 7.
Train Supply: Electric, index 66.
Multiple Working: Not equipped (m – Green Circle).

47462	x	RG	E	WNYX	TT(S)	
47471	x	I	E	WNYX	CW(S)	
47474	x	RG	E	WNYX	CD(S)	Sir Rowland Hill
47475	x	RX	E	WNYX	HM(S)	
47476	x	RG	E	WNYX	TT(S)	
47478	x	B	E	WNYX	SP(S)	
47481	x	BL	E	WNYX	CW(S)	
47488	x	GG	FR	IANA	TM	
47489		RG	E	WNYX	SP(S)	
47492	x	RX	E	WNYX	OM(S)	
47501	x	RG	E	WNYX	CD(S)	Craftsman[1]
47513	x	BL	E	WNYX	CD(S)	
47515	x	O	E	WNYX	CW(S)	
47519	x+	GG	E	WNYX	CD(S)	
47524	x	RX	E	WNYX	CW(S)	
47525	x	FE	E	WNYX	CD(S)	
47526	x	BL	E	WNYX	CW(S)	
47528	x	IM	E	WNYX	DD(S)	
47530	x	RX	E	WNYX	SP(S)	
47532	x	RX	E	WNYX	SP(S)	
47535	x	RX	E	WNYX	OM(S)	
47536	x	RX	E	WNYX	CD(S)	
47539		RX	E	WNYX	ZC(S)	
47540	xm	CE	E	WNYX	CW(S)	The Institution of Civil Engineers
47547		N	E	WNYX	CD(S)	
47550	x	IM	E	WNYX	IM(S)	
47566	x	RX	E	WNYX	SP(S)	
47574	x	RG	E	WNYX	CD(S)	
47575	x	RG	E	WHCD	CD	City of Hereford
47576	x	RX	E	WNYX	CD(S)	
47596	x	RX	E	WNYX	CD(S)	
47624	xj	RX	E	WNYX	AN(S)	
47634		RG	E	WHCD	CD	Holbeck
47635	xj	RG	E	WHCD	CD	
47640	j	RG	E	WNYX	CD(S)	University of Strathclyde

Class 47/7. Electric Train Supply and Push & Pull equipment (RCH System).
Details as Class 47/4 except:

Weight: 118.7 t.   **Fuel Capacity:** 5887 litres.

47701	x	FR	WF	SDFR	TM	Waverley
47702	x	V	E	WNYX	TO(S)	County of Suffolk
47703	x	FR	FR	SDFR	TM	HERMES
47705	x	LW	RV	RTLO	CP	GUY FAWKES
47707	x	RX	E	WNYX	CW(S)	Holyrood
47709	x	FR	FR	SDFR	TM	
47710	x	FR	FR	SDFR	TM	
47711	x	V	E	WNYX	TO(S)	County of Hertfordshire
47712	x	FR	FR	SDFR	TM	ARTEMIS
47714	x	RX	E	WNYX	CW(S)	
47715		N	E	WNYX	CW(S)	

| 47716 | x | **RX** | E | WNYX | CW(S) | |
| 47717 | x | **RG** | E | WNYX | CW(S) | |

Class 47/7. Electric Train Supply equipment and RCH Jumper Cables. Details as Class 47/4 except:

Weight: 118.7 t.   **Fuel Capacity:** 5887 litres.

47721		**RX**	E	WHCD	CD	Saint Bede
47722		**V**	E	ILRA	TO	The Queen Mother
47725		**RX**	E	WHCD	CD	The Railway Mission
47726		**RX**	E	WHTD	CD	Manchester Airport Progress
47727		**RX**	E	WHCD	CD	Duke of Edinburgh's Award
47732	x	**RX**	E	WHCD	CD	Restormel
47733		**RX**	E	WHTD	CD	Eastern Star
47734		**RX**	E	WHTD	CD	Crewe Diesel Depot Quality Approved
47736		**RX**	E	WHCD	CD	Cambridge Traction & Rolling Stock Depot
47737		**RX**	E	WHCD	CD	Resurgent
47738		**RX**	E	WNXX	CD(S)	Bristol Barton Hill
47739		**RX**	E	WHCD	CD	Resourceful
47741		**V**	E	ILRA	TO	Resilient
47742		**RX**	E	ILRA	TO	The Enterprising Scot
47744		**E**	E	WHCD	CD	
47745	x	**RX**	E	WNYX	TO(S)	Royal London Society for the Blind
47746		**RX**	E	WHCD	CD	The Bobby
47747		**V**	E	ILRA	TO	Graham Farish
47749		**RX**	E	WHCD	CD	Atlantic College
47750		**V**	E	ILRA	TO	ATLAS
47756		**RX**	E	WHCM	ML	Royal Mail Tyneside
47757		**RX**	E	WHCD	CD	Restitution
47758		**E**	E	WHCD	CD	Regency Rail Cruises
47759		**RX**	E	WHCD	CD	
47760		**E**	E	WHTD	CD	Ribblehead Viaduct
47761		**RX**	E	WHCD	CD	
47762		**RX**	E	WHCD	CD	
47763		**RX**	E	WNXX	ML(S)	
47764		**RX**	E	WHCD	CD	Resounding
47765	x	**RX**	E	WNXX	BK(S)	Ressaldar
47766	x	**RX**	E	WNXX	TT(S)	Resolute
47767		**RX**	E	WHCD	CD	Saint Columba
47768	x	**RX**	E	WNXX	CD(S)	
47769		**V**	E	ILRA	TO	Resolve
47770		**RX**	E	WNXX	CF(S)	Reserved
47771		**RX**	E	WNXX	CD(S)	Heaton Traincare Depot
47772	x	**RX**	E	WHCD	CD	
47773		**RX**	E	WHCM	ML	Reservist
47774	x	**RX**	E	WHCD	CD	Poste Restante
47775	x	**RX**	E	WHTD	CD	Respite
47776	x	**RX**	E	WHCD	CD	Respected
47777	x	**RX**	E	WNXX	TO(S)	Restored

47778	RX	E	WHCD	CD	Irresistible
47779	RX	E	WNXX	CD(S)	
47780	RX	E	WHCD	CD	
47781	RX	E	WHCD	CD	Isle of Iona
47782	RX	E	WNXX	CF(S)	
47783	RX	E	WHCD	CD	Saint Peter
47784	RX	E	WHCD	CD	Condover Hall
47785	E	E	WHCD	CD	Fiona Castle
47786	E	E	WHCD	CD	Roy Castle OBE
47787	RX	E	WHCD	CD	Victim Support
47789	RX	E	WHCD	CD	Lindisfarne
47790	RX	E	WHCM	ML	Dewi Sant/Saint David
47791	RX	E	WHCM	ML	
47792	RX	E	WHCD	CD	Saint Cuthbert
47793	RX	E	WHCD	CD	Saint Augustine

Class 47/7. Electric Train Supply equipment. Locos dedicated for Royal Train & (occasional) Charter Train use. Details as Class 47/4 except:

Weight: 118.7 t.   **Fuel Capacity:** 5887 litres.

47798	RP	E	WHRD	CD	Prince William
47799	RP	E	WHRD	CD	Prince Henry

Class 47/4 ("47/8") Continued.

47802	+	IS	E	WNYX	CD(S)	
47805	+	IS	P	ILRA	TO	
47806	+	V	P	ILRA	TO	
47807	+	V	P	ILRA	TO	The Lion of Vienna
47810	+	IS	P	ILRA	TO	PORTERBROOK
47811	+	GL	P	IWLA	LE	
47812	+	IS	P	ILRA	TO	
47813	+	GL	P	IWLA	LE	S.S. Great Britain
47814	+	V	P	ILRA	TO	Totnes Castle
47815	+	GL	P	IWLA	LE	Abertawe Landore
47816	+	GL	P	IWLA	LE	Bristol Bath Road Quality Approved
47817	+	V	P	ILRA	TO	The Institution of Mechanical Engineers
47818	+	V	P	ILRA	TO	Strathclyde
47822	+	V	P	ILRA	TO	Pride of Shrewsbury
47826	+	IS	P	ILRA	TO	
47827	+	V	P	ILRA	TO	
47828	+	IS	P	ILRA	TO	
47829	+	V	P	ILRA	TO	
47830	+	GL	P	IWLA	LE	
47831	+	V	P	ILRA	TO	Bolton Wanderer
47832	+	GL	P	IWLA	LE	
47839	+	V	P	ILRA	TO	
47840	+	V	P	ILRA	TO	NORTH STAR
47841	+	V	P	ILRA	TO	Spirit of Chester
47843	+	V	P	ILRA	TO	VULCAN
47844	+	V	P	ILRA	TO	

47845	+	V	P	ILRA	TO	County of Kent
47846	+	GL	P	IWLA	LE	THOR
47847	+	IS	P	ILRA	TO	
47848	+	V	P	ILRA	TO	Newton Abbot Festival of Transport
47849	+	V	P	ILRA	TO	Cadeirlan Bangor Cathedral
47851	+	V	P	ILRA	TO	
47853	+	V	P	ILRA	TO	
47854	+	IS	P	ILRA	TO	Women's Royal Voluntary Service

CLASS 50   ENGLISH ELECTRIC   Co–Co

Built: 1967–68 by English Electric at Vulcan Foundry, Newton-le-Willows.
Engine: English Electric 16CVST of 2010 kW (2700 h.p.) at 850 r.p.m.
Main Generator: English Electric 840/4B.
Traction Motors: English Electric 538/5A.
Maximum Tractive Effort: 216 kN (48500 lbf).
Continuous Tractive Effort: 147 kN (33000 lbf) at 23.5 m.p.h.
Power At Rail: 1540 kW (2070 h.p.).   **Train Brakes:** Air & vacuum.
Brake Force: 59 t.   **Dimensions:** 20.88 x 2.78 x 3.96 m.
Weight: 116.9 t.   **Wheel Diameter:** 1092 mm.
Design Speed: 105 m.p.h.   **Maximum Speed:** 90 (* 100) m.p.h.
Fuel Capacity: 4796 litres.   **RA:** 6.
Train Supply: Electric, index 66.   **Multiple Working:** Orange Square.

Non-standard livery/numbering:
• 50017 is 'LMS Coronation Scot' style maroon with four gold bands.
• 50031 carries number D431.
• 50044 carries number D444.
• 50049 carries number D449.

50017	*	0	JK	MBDL	CQ	
50031		B	50	MBDL	KR	
50044		B	50	MBDL	KR	
50049		B	PD	MBDL	KR	
50050		BL	HS	SDFR	BH(S)	Fearless

CLASS 55   ENGLISH ELECTRIC   Co–Co

Built: 1961 by English Electric at Vulcan Foundry, Newton-le-Willows.
Engine: Two Napier-Deltic D18-25 of 1230 kW (1650 h.p.) each at 1500 r.p.m.
Main Generators: Two English Electric 829.
Traction Motors: English Electric 538/A.
Maximum Tractive Effort: 222 kN (50000 lbf).
Continuous Tractive Effort: 136 kN (30500 lbf) at 32.5 m.p.h.
Power At Rail: 1969 kW (2640 h.p.).   **Train Brakes:** Air & vacuum.
Brake Force: 51 t.   **Dimensions:** 21.18 x 2.68 x 3.94 m.
Weight: 104.7 t.   **Wheel Diameter:** 1092 mm.
Design Speed: 105 m.p.h.   **Maximum Speed:** 100 m.p.h.
Fuel Capacity: 3755 litres.   **RA:** 5.
Train Supply: Electric, index 66.   **Multiple Working:** Not equipped.

Non-standard numbering:
- 55009 carries number D9009. Official RSL number is 89509.
- Official RSL number of 55019 is 89519.
- 55022 carries number D9000. Official RSL number is 89500.

55009	**GG**	DP	MBDL	CP	ALYCIDON
55019	**B**	DP	MBDL	CP	ROYAL HIGHLAND FUSILIER
55022	**GG**	90	SDFR	TM	ROYAL SCOTS GREY

CLASS 56   BRUSH/BR/PAXMAN   Co-Co

Built: 1976–84 by Electroputere at Craiova, Romania (as sub contractors for Brush) or BREL at Doncaster or Crewe Works.
Engine: Ruston Paxman 16RK3CT of 2460 kW (3250 h.p.) at 900 r.p.m.
Main Alternator: Brush BA1101A.
Traction Motors: Brush TM73-62.
Maximum Tractive Effort: 275 kN (61800 lbf).
Continuous Tractive Effort: 240 kN (53950 lbf) at 16.8 m.p.h.
Power At Rail: 1790 kW (2400 h.p.).   **Train Brakes:** Air.
Brake Force: 60 t.   **Dimensions:** 19.36 x 2.79 x 3.9 m.
Weight: 125.2 t.   **Wheel Diameter:** 1143 mm.
Design Speed: 80 m.p.h.   **Maximum Speed:** 80 m.p.h.
Fuel Capacity: 5228 litres.   **RA:** 7.
Train Supply: Not equipped.   **Multiple Working:** Red Diamond.

Note: All equipped with Slow Speed Control.

Non-standard livery:
- 56063 is as **F**, but with the light grey replaced by a darker grey.

56003	**LH**	E	WNXX	DD(S)	
56004	**B**	E	WNXX	OC(S)	
56006	**B**	E	WNXX	KR(S)	
56007	**T**	E	WGAI	IM	
56010	**T**	E	WNYX	DD(S)	
56011	**E**	E	WGAI	IM	
56018	**E**	E	WGAI	IM	
56019	**FQ**	E	WNYX	IM(S)	
56021	**LH**	E	WNXX	IM(S)	
56022	**T**	E	WNXX	IM(S)	
56025	**T**	E	WGAT	TE	
56027	**LH**	E	WGAT	TE	
56029	**T**	E	WNYX	DD(S)	
56031	**CE**	E	WGAI	IM	
56032	**E**	E	WNXX	IM(S)	
56033	**T**	E	WGAI	IM	Shotton Paper Mill
56034	**LH**	E	WNYX	TT(S)	Castell Ogwr/Ogmore Castle
56036	**TC**	E	WNXX	CT(S)	
56037	**E**	E	WGAT	TE	
56038	**E**	E	WGAT	TE	
56039	**LH**	E	WNYX	TE(S)	
56040	**T**	E	WNXX	IM(S)	
56041	**E**	E	WGAI	IM	

56043	FM	E	WNXX	CT(S)	
56044	T	E	WNXX	IM(S)	Cardiff Canton Quality Approved
56045	LH	E	WNXX	IM(S)	British Steel Shelton
56046	CE	E	WGAT	TE	
56047	TC	E	WNYX	IM(S)	
56048	CE	E	WGAT	TE	
56049	TC	E	WNXX	BW(S)	
56050	LH	E	WNYX	TT(S)	British Steel Teesside
56051	E	E	WGAT	TE	
56052	T	E	WNXX	DD(S)	
56053	T	E	WNXX	DD(S)	
56054	T	E	WGAT	TE	British Steel Llanwern
56055	LH	E	WGAT	TE	
56056	T	E	WGAT	TE	
56057	E	E	WNYX	IM(S)	British Fuels
56058	E	E	WGAT	TE	
56059	E	E	WGAI	IM	
56060	E	E	WGAT	TE	
56061	FM	E	WNYX	TT(S)	
56062	E	E	WGAI	IM	
56063	0	E	WGAT	TE	
56064	T	E	WNXX	CT(S)	
56065	E	E	WGAT	TE	
56066	T	E	WNYX	CF(S)	
56067	E	E	WGAT	TE	
56068	E	E	WGAT	TE	
56069	E	E	WGAI	IM	Wolverhampton Steel Terminal
56070	T	E	WNXX	BW(S)	
56071	E	E	WGAT	TE	
56072	T	E	WNXX	TO(S)	
56073	T	E	WGAT	TE	Tremorfa Steelworks
56074	LH	E	WGAI	IM	Kellingley Colliery
56075	F	E	WNYX	TT(S)	
56076	T	E	WNXX	IM(S)	
56077	LH	E	WNXX	CT(S)	
56078	F	E	WGAI	IM	
56079	T	E	WNXX	IM(S)	
56080	F	E	WNYX	SP(S)	Selby Coalfield
56081	E	E	WGAI	IM	
56082	F	E	WNXX	IM(S)	
56083	LH	E	WNXX	BW(S)	
56084	LH	E	WNXX	IM(S)	
56085	LH	E	WGAT	TE	
56086	T	E	WNXX	IM(S)	The Magistrates' Association
56087	E	E	WGAI	IM	ABP Port of Hull
56088	E	E	WGAI	IM	
56089	E	E	WGAT	TE	
56090	LH	E	WGAI	IM	
56091	E	E	WGAI	IM	Stanton
56093	T	E	WNXX	DD(S)	
56094	E	E	WGAT	TE	Eggborough Power Station

56095	E	E	WGAT	TE	
56096	E	E	WGAI	IM	
56098	F	E	WGAT	TE	
56099	T	E	WNXX	DD(S)	
56100	LH	E	WGAT	TE	
56101	T	E	WNXX	IM(S)	Mutual Improvement
56102	LH	E	WGAI	IM	
56103	E	E	WGAI	IM	STORA
56104	FC	E	WNXX	IM(S)	
56105	E	E	WGAT	TE	
56106	LH	E	WNXX	BW(S)	
56107	LH	E	WNXX	CT(S)	
56108	F	E	WNXX	TE(S)	
56109	LH	E	WNXX	CT(S)	
56110	LH	E	WGAI	IM	Croft[1]
56111	LH	E	WGAI	IM	
56112	LH	E	WGAI	IM	Stainless Pioneer
56113	E	E	WGAI	IM	
56114	E	E	WGAT	TE	
56115	E	E	WGAI	IM	
56116	LH	E	WGAI	IM	
56117	E	E	WGAT	TE	
56118	LH	E	WGAI	IM	
56119	E	E	WGAT	TE	
56120	E	E	WGAI	IM	
56121	T	E	WNYX	CU(S)	
56123	T	E	WNYX	IM(S)	Drax Power Station
56124	T	E	WNYX	KY(S)	
56125	F	E	WNXX	IM(S)	
56127	T	E	WGAT	TE	
56128	T	E	WNXX	IM(S)	
56129	T	E	WNXX	IM(S)	
56130	LH	E	WNXX	TT(S)	Wardley Opencast
56131	F	E	WGAI	IM	Ellington Colliery
56132	T	E	WNYX	TT(S)	
56133	F	E	WNXX	TT(S)	
56134	FC	E	WGAT	TE	Blyth Power
56135	F	E	WNYX	IM(S)	Port of Tyne Authority

CLASS 57   BRUSH/GM   Co–Co

Built: 1964–65 by Brush Traction at Loughborough or BR at Crewe Works as Class 47. Rebuilt 1997–2000 by Brush Traction at Loughborough.
Engine: General Motors 645-12E3 of 1860 kW (2500 h.p.) at 900 r.p.m.
Main Alternator: Brush BA1101A.
Traction Motors: Brush TM68-46.
Maximum Tractive Effort: 244.5 kN (55000 lbf).
Continuous Tractive Effort: 140 kN (31500 lbf) at ?? m.p.h.
Power at Rail: 1507 kW (2025 h.p.).   **Train Brakes:** Air.
Brake Force: 80 t.   **Dimensions:** 19.38 x 2.79 x 3.9 m.

Weight: 120.6 t.
Design Speed: 75 m.p.h.
Fuel Capacity: 3273 (+ 5550 litres).
Train Supply: Not equipped.
Wheel Diameter: 1143 mm.
Maximum Speed: 75 m.p.h.
RA: 6
Multiple Working: Not equipped.

57001	**FL**	P	DFHZ	FD	Freightliner Pioneer
57002	**FL**	P	DFHZ	FD	Freightliner Phoenix
57003	**FL**	P	DFHZ	FD	Freightliner Evolution
57004	**FL**	P	DFHZ	FD	Freightliner Quality
57005	**FL**	P	DFHZ	FD	Freightliner Excellence
57006	**FL**	P	DFHZ	FD	Freightliner Reliance
57007	**FL**	P	DFHZ	FD	Freightliner Bond
57008	**FL**	P	DFHZ	FD	Freightliner Explorer
57009	**FL**	P	DFHZ	FD	Freightliner Venturer
57010	**FL**	P	DFHZ	FD	Freightliner Crusader
57011	**FL**	P	DFHZ	FD	Freightliner Challenger
57012 +	**FL**	P	DFTZ	FD	Freightliner Envoy

Class 57/6. Electric Train Supply Equipment. Details as Class 57/0 except:

Fuel Capacity: 5887 litres.   **Train Supply:** Electric, index 95.

57601	(47825)	**P**	P	SBXL	LB(S)	Thomas Telford

CLASS 58   BREL/PAXMAN   Co–Co

Built: 1983–87 by BREL at Doncaster Works.
Engine: Ruston Paxman 12RK3ACT of 2460 kW (3300 h.p.) at 1000 r.p.m.
Main Alternator: Brush BA1101B. **Traction Motors:** Brush TM73-62.
Maximum Tractive Effort: 275 kN (61800 lbf).
Continuous Tractive Effort: 240 kN (53950 lbf) at 17.4 m.p.h.
Power At Rail: 1780 kW (2387 h.p.). **Train Brakes:** Air.
Brake Force: 62 t. **Dimensions:** 19.13 x 2.72 x 3.93 m.
Weight: 130 t. **Wheel Diameter:** 1120 mm.
Design Speed: 80 m.p.h. **Maximum Speed:** 80 m.p.h.
Fuel Capacity: 4214 litres. **RA:** 7.
Train Supply: Not equipped. **Multiple Working:** Red Diamond.

Note: All equipped with Slow Speed Control.

58001	**MG**	E	WNXX	KY(S)	
58002	**ML**	E	WNXX	EH(S)	Daw Mill Colliery
58003	**MG**	E	WNXX	TO(S)	Markham Colliery
58004	**MG**	E	WNXX	DD(S)	
58005	**ML**	E	WNXX	LR(S)	Ironbridge Power Station
58006	**MG**	E	WNXX	IW(S)	
58007	**MG**	E	WNXX	IW(S)	
58008	**ML**	E	WNXX	TO(S)	
58009	**MG**	E	WFAN	TO	
58010	**MG**	E	WNXX	SF(S)	
58011	**MG**	E	WNXX	SF(S)	
58012	**MG**	E	WNXX	DD(S)	
58013	**ML**	E	WFAN	TO	
58014	**ML**	E	WNXX	TO(S)	Didcot Power Station

58015	**MG**	E	WNXX	DD(S)	
58016	**E**	E	WFAN	TO	
58017	**MG**	E	WNXX	DD(S)	
58018	**MG**	E	WNXX	SF(S)	High Marnham Power Station
58019	**MG**	E	WFAN	TO	Shirebrook Colliery
58020	**MG**	E	WFAN	TO	Doncaster Works
58021	**ML**	E	WFAN	TO	Hither Green Depot
58022	**MG**	E	WNXX	DD(S)	
58023	**ML**	E	WNXX	DD(S)	
58024	**E**	E	WFAN	TO	
58025	**MG**	E	WFAN	TO	
58026	**MG**	E	WFAN	TO	
58027	**MG**	E	WNXX	DD(S)	
58028	**MG**	E	WNXX	TO(S)	
58029	**MG**	E	WFAN	TO	
58030	**E**	E	WFAN	TO	
58031	**MG**	E	WFAN	TO	
58032	**ML**	E	WNXX	SF(S)	Thoresby Colliery
58033	**E**	E	WFAN	TO	
58034	**MG**	E	WNXX	DD(S)	
58035	**MG**	E	WNXX	DD(S)	
58036	**ML**	E	WNXX	CD(S)	
58037	**E**	E	WFAN	TO	Worksop Depot
58038	**ML**	E	WNXX	TO(S)	
58039	**E**	E	WNXX	TO(S)	
58040	**MG**	E	WNXX	SF(S)	Cottam Power Station
58041	**MG**	E	WFAN	TO	Ratcliffe Power Station
58042	**ML**	E	WFAN	TO	
58043	**MG**	E	WFAN	TO	
58044	**MG**	E	WNXX	DD(S)	
58045	**MG**	E	WFAN	TO	
58046	**ML**	E	WNXX	LR(S)	Asfordby Mine
58047	**E**	E	WFAN	TO	
58048	**E**	E	WNXX	TO(S)	
58049	**E**	E	WFAN	TO	Littleton Colliery
58050	**E**	E	WFAN	TO	Toton Traction Depot

CLASS 59   GENERAL MOTORS   Co–Co

Built: 1985 (59001/002/004) or 1989 (59005) by General Motors, La Grange, Illinois, USA or 1990 (59101–4), 1994 (59201) and 1995 (59202–6) by General Motors, London, Ontario, Canada.
Engine: General Motors 645E3C two stroke of 2460 kW (3300 h.p.) at 900 r.p.m.
Main Alternator: General Motors AR11 MLD-D14A.
Traction Motors: General Motors D77B.
Maximum Tractive Effort: 506 kN (113 550 lbf).

Continuous Tractive Effort: 291 kN (65 300 lbf) at 14.3 m.p.h.
Power At Rail: 1889 kW (2533 h.p.).   **Train Brakes:** Air.
Brake Force: 69 t.   **Dimensions:** 21.35 x 2.65 x 3.9 m.
Weight: 121 t.   **Wheel Diameter:** 1067 mm.
Design Speed: 60 (* 75) m.p.h.   **Maximum Speed:** 60 (* 75) m.p.h.
Fuel Capacity: 4546 litres.   **RA:** 7.
Train Supply: Not equipped.   **Multiple Working:** AAR System.

Class 59/0. Owned by Foster-Yeoman.

59001	**FY**	FY	XYPO	MD	YEOMAN ENDEAVOUR
59002	**MR**	FY	XYPO	MD	ALAN J DAY
59004	**YO**	FY	XYPO	MD	PAUL A HAMMOND
59005	**FY**	FY	XYPO	MD	KENNETH J PAINTER

Class 59/1. Owned by Hanson Quarry Products.

59101	**HA**	HA	XYPA	MD	Village of Whatley
59102	**HA**	HA	XYPA	MD	Village of Chantry
59103	**HA**	HA	XYPA	MD	Village of Mells
59104	**HA**	HA	XYPA	MD	Village of Great Elm

Class 59/2. Owned by English Welsh & Scottish Railway.

59201	*	**E**	E	WDAG	HG	Vale of York
59202	*	**E**	E	WDAG	HG	Vale of White Horse
59203	*	**E**	E	WDAG	HG	Vale of Pickering
59204	*	**E**	E	WDAG	HG	Vale of Glamorgan
59205	b*	**E**	E	WDAG	HG	L. Keith McNair
59206	b*	**E**	E	WDAG	HG	Pride of Ferrybridge

CLASS 60   BRUSH/MIRRLEES   Co–Co

Built: 1989–1993 by Brush Traction at Loughborough.
Engine: Mirrlees 8MB275T of 2310 kW (3100 h.p.) at 1000 r.p.m.
Main Alternator: Brush BA1000.   **Traction Motors:** Brush TM216.
Maximum Tractive Effort: 500 kN (106500 lbf).
Continuous Tractive Effort: 336 kN (71570 lbf) at 17.4 m.p.h.
Power At Rail: 1800 kW (2415 h.p.).   **Train Brakes:** Air.
Brake Force: 74 (+ 62) t.   **Dimensions:** 21.34 x 2.64 x 3.95 m.
Weight: 129 (+ 131) t.   **Wheel Diameter:** 1118 mm.
Design Speed: 62 m.p.h.   **Maximum Speed:** 60 m.p.h.
Fuel Capacity: 4546 (+ 5225) litres.   **RA:** 7.
Train Supply: Not equipped.   **Multiple Working:** Within class.

Note: All equipped with Slow Speed Control.

Non-standard liveries:
• 60006/033 are in 'Corus' livery of silver with red logos.
• 60064/070 are as **F**, with Loadhaul logos.

60001		E	E	WCAT	TE	
60002	+	E	E	WCAT	TE	High Peak
60003	+	E	E	WCAK	CF	FREIGHT TRANSPORT ASSOCIATION
60004	+	E	E	WCAK	CF	
60005	+	E	E	WCAK	CF	BP Gas Avonmouth
60006		O	E	WCAT	TE	Scunthorpe Ironmaster
60007	+	LH	E	WCAI	IM	
60008		LH	E	WCAT	TE	GYPSUM QUEEN II
60009	+	MG	E	WCAI	IM	Carnedd Dafydd
60010	+	E	E	WCAK	CF	
60011		ML	E	WCAT	TE	
60012	+	E	E	WCAI	IM	
60013		F	E	WCAT	TE	Robert Boyle
60014		FP	E	WCAT	TE	Alexander Fleming
60015	+	T	E	WCAK	CF	Bow Fell
60016		E	E	WCAN	TO	RAIL Magazine
60017	+	E	E	WCAT	TE	Shotton Works Centenary Year 1996
60018		E	E	WCAT	TE	
60019		E	E	WCAN	TO	
60020	+	E	E	WCAI	IM	
60021	+	F	E	WCAI	IM	Pen-y-Ghent[1]
60022	+	E	E	WCAI	IM	
60023	+	E	E	WCAI	IM	
60024	+	E	E	WCAN	TO	
60025	+	E	E	WCAI	IM	Caledonian Paper
60026	+	E	E	WCAK	CF	
60027	+	E	E	WCAI	IM	
60028	+	F	E	WCAI	IM	John Flamsteed
60029		E	E	WCAN	TO	Clitheroe Castle
60030	+	E	E	WCAK	CF	
60031		FM	E	WCAN	TO	
60032		T	E	WCAN	TO	William Booth
60033	+	O	E	WCAT	TE	Tees Steel Express
60034		T	E	WCAN	TO	Carnedd Llewelyn[1]
60035		T	E	WCAT	TE	Florence Nightingale
60036		E	E	WCAN	TO	GEFCO
60037	+	E	E	WCAK	CF	Aberthaw/Aberddawan
60038	+	LH	E	WCAI	IM	
60039		E	E	WCAT	TE	
60040		E	E	WCAT	TE	
60041	+	E	E	WCAK	CF	
60042	+	E	E	WCAT	TE	The Hundred of Hoo
60043		E	E	WCAT	TE	
60044		ML	E	WCAT	TE	
60045		E	E	WCAT	TE	The Permanent Way Institution
60046	+	F	E	WCAN	TO	William Wilberforce[1]
60047	+	E	E	WCAN	TO	
60048		E	E	WCAT	TE	EASTERN
60049	+	E	E	WCAT	TE	
60050	+	E	E	WCAT	TE	
60051	+	E	E	WCAK	CF	

60052	+	**E**	E	WCAK	CF	Glofa Twr - The last deep mine in Wales - Tower Colliery
60053	+	**E**	E	WCAT	TE	NORDIC TERMINAL
60054	+	**FP**	E	WCAN	TO	Charles Babbage
60055	+	**T**	E	WCAI	IM	Thomas Barnardo
60056	+	**T**	E	WCAK	CF	William Beveridge
60057		**FC**	E	WCAN	TO	Adam Smith
60058	+	**T**	E	WCAI	IM	John Howard
60059	+	**LH**	E	WCAK	CF	Swinden Dalesman
60060		**FC**	E	WCAT	TE	James Watt
60061		**T**	E	WCAT	TE	Alexander Graham Bell
60062		**T**	E	WCAT	TE	Samuel Johnson
60063		**T**	E	WCAT	TE	James Murray
60064	+	**O**	E	WCAK	CF	Back Tor[1]
60065		**T**	E	WCAT	TE	Kinder Low[1]
60066		**FC**	E	WCAN	TO	John Logie Baird
60067	+	**F**	E	WCAN	TO	James Clerk-Maxwell
60068		**F**	E	WCAN	TO	Charles Darwin
60069		**F**	E	WCAN	TO	Humphry Davy
60070	+	**O**	E	WCAK	CF	John Loudon McAdam
60071	+	**MG**	E	WCAN	TO	Dorothy Garrod
60072		**MG**	E	WCAN	TO	Cairn Toul[1]
60073		**MG**	E	WCAT	TE	Cairn Gorm[1]
60074		**MG**	E	WCAT	TE	
60075		**MG**	E	WCAN	TO	
60076		**MG**	E	WCAN	TO	
60077	+	**MG**	E	WCAK	CF	Canisp[1]
60078		**ML**	E	WCAT	TE	
60079		**MG**	E	WCAT	TE	Foinaven
60080	+	**T**	E	WCAI	IM	Kinder Scout
60081	+	**GW**	E	WCAK	CF	ISAMBARD KINGDOM BRUNEL
60082		**T**	E	WCAT	TE	Mam Tor
60083		**E**	E	WCAT	TE	Mountsorrel
60084		**T**	E	WCAN	TO	Cross Fell
60085		**T**	E	WNWX	CF(S)	
60086		**MG**	E	WCAT	TE	Schiehallion
60087		**MG**	E	WCAN	TO	Slioch
60088		**MG**	E	WCAT	TE	Buachaille Etive Mor[1]
60089	+	**T**	E	WCAK	CF	Arcuil
60090	+	**FC**	E	WCAI	IM	Quinag
60091	+	**FC**	E	WCAK	CF	An Teallach
60092		**F**	E	WCAT	TE	Reginald Munns
60093		**T**	E	WCAT	TE	Jack Stirk
60094		**MG**	E	WCAN	TO	Tryfan
60095		**F**	E	WCAN	TO	
60096	+	**T**	E	WCAK	CF	Ben Macdui
60097	+	**T**	E	WCAI	IM	
60098	+	**E**	E	WCAK	CF	Charles Francis Brush
60099		**MG**	E	WCAT	TE	Ben More Assynt
60100		**MG**	E	WCAN	TO	Boar of Badenoch

CLASS 66   GENERAL MOTORS   Co–Co

Built: 1998–2001 by General Motors, London, Ontario, Canada (Model JT42CWR).
Engine: General Motors 12N-710G3B-EC two stroke of 2385 kW (3200 h.p.) at 900 r.p.m.
Main Alternator: General Motors AR8/C86.
Traction Motors: General Motors D43TR.
Maximum Tractive Effort: 409 kN (92000 lbf).
Continuous Tractive Effort: 260 kN (58390 lbf) at 15.9 m.p.h.
Power At Rail: 1850 kW (2480 h.p.).   **Train Brakes:** Air.
Brake Force: 68 t.   **Dimensions:** 21.35 x 2.64 x 3.90 m.
Weight: 126 t.   **Wheel Diameter:** 1120 mm.
Design Speed: 87.5 m.p.h.   **Maximum Speed:** 75 m.p.h.
Fuel Capacity: 6550 litres.   **RA:** 7.
Train Supply: Not equipped.   **Multiple Working:** AAR System.

Note: All equipped with Slow Speed Control.

Class 66/0. EWS operated locomotives.

66001		E	A	WBAT	TE	66032	k	E	A	WBAK	CF
66002		E	A	WBAN	TO	66033		E	A	WBAH	EH
66003		E	A	WBAT	TE	66034		E	A	WBAH	EH
66004		E	A	WBAN	TO	66035		E	A	WBAM	ML
66005	k	E	A	WBAI	IM	66036	k	E	A	WBAI	IM
66006		E	A	WBAT	TE	66037	k	E	A	WBAN	TO
66007		E	A	WBAI	IM	66038		E	A	WBAN	TO
66008		E	A	WBAK	CF	66039	k	E	A	WBAI	IM
66009	k	E	A	WBAH	EH	66040		E	A	WBAN	TO
66010		E	A	WBAI	IM	66041		E	A	WBAT	TE
66011	k	E	A	WBAI	IM	66042		E	A	WBAN	TO
66012		E	A	WBAI	IM	66043	k	E	A	WBAK	CF
66013		E	A	WBAH	EH	66044		E	A	WBAT	TE
66014		E	A	WBAI	IM	66045	k	E	A	WBAI	IM
66015		E	A	WBAH	EH	66046		E	A	WBAI	IM
66016	k	E	A	WBAH	EH	66047	k	E	A	WBAT	TE
66017		E	A	WBAN	TO	66048		E	A	WBAI	IM
66018		E	A	WBAI	IM	66049		E	A	WBAM	ML
66019	k	E	A	WBAK	CF	66050		E	A	WBAI	IM
66020	k	E	A	WBAT	TE	66051		E	A	WBAT	TE
66021		E	A	WBAK	CF	66052		E	A	WBAI	IM
66022		E	A	WBAN	TO	66053		E	A	WBAI	IM
66023		E	A	WBAI	IM	66054		E	A	WBAK	CF
66024		E	A	WBAN	TO	66055		E	A	WBAK	CF
66025		E	A	WBAN	TO	66056		E	A	WBAK	CF
66026	k	E	A	WBAI	IM	66057		E	A	WBAK	CF
66027	k	E	A	WBAI	IM	66058		E	A	WBAK	CF
66028		E	A	WBAM	ML	66059		E	A	WBAN	TO
66029	k	E	A	WBAK	CF	66060		E	A	WBAI	IM
66030		E	A	WBAT	TE	66061		E	A	WBAH	EH
66031	k	E	A	WBAK	CF	66062		E	A	WBAN	TO

66063	E	A	WBAI	IM		66114 kr	E	A	WBBM	ML
66064	E	A	WBAH	EH		66115	E	A	WBAK	CF
66065	E	A	WBAM	ML		66116	E	A	WBAM	ML
66066	E	A	WBAM	ML		66117	E	A	WBAN	TO
66067	E	A	WBAN	TO		66118	E	A	WBAT	TE
66068	E	A	WBAI	IM		66119	E	A	WBAN	TO
66069	E	A	WBAI	IM		66120 k	E	A	WBAI	IM
66070	E	A	WBAT	TE		66121	E	A	WBAI	IM
66071	E	A	WBAI	IM		66122	E	A	WBAH	EH
66072	E	A	WBAI	IM		66123	E	A	WBAI	IM
66073	E	A	WBAI	IM		66124	E	A	WBAI	IM
66074	E	A	WBAN	TO		66125 k	E	A	WBAT	TE
66075	E	A	WBAN	TO		66126	E	A	WBAN	TO
66076	E	A	WBAK	CF		66127	E	A	WBAK	CF
66077	E	A	WBAI	IM		66128	E	A	WBAI	IM
66078	E	A	WBAT	TE		66129	E	A	WBAN	TO
66079	E	A	WBAK	CF		66130	E	A	WBAI	IM
66080 k	E	A	WBAK	CF		66131	E	A	WBAI	IM
66081	E	A	WBAI	IM		66132	E	A	WBAH	EH
66082	E	A	WBAH	EH		66133	E	A	WBAM	ML
66083	E	A	WBAT	TE		66134	E	A	WBAI	IM
66084 k	E	A	WBAI	IM		66135	E	A	WBAK	CF
66085	E	A	WBAI	IM		66136	E	A	WBAM	ML
66086	E	A	WBAN	TO		66137	E	A	WBAI	IM
66087	E	A	WBAN	TO		66138	E	A	WBAT	TE
66088	E	A	WBAK	CF		66139	E	A	WBAI	IM
66089	E	A	WBAT	TE		66140	E	A	WBAT	TE
66090	E	A	WBAK	CF		66141	E	A	WBAI	IM
66091	E	A	WBAI	IM		66142	E	A	WBAN	TO
66092	E	A	WBAK	CF		66143	E	A	WBAK	CF
66093	E	A	WBAT	TE		66144	E	A	WBAK	CF
66094 k	E	A	WBAI	IM		66145	E	A	WBAK	CF
66095 kr	E	A	WBBM	ML		66146	E	A	WBAH	EH
66096 r	E	A	WBBM	ML		66147	E	A	WBAI	IM
66097 r	E	A	WBBM	ML		66148	E	A	WBAN	TO
66098 r	E	A	WBBM	ML		66149	E	A	WBAT	TE
66099 r	E	A	WBBM	ML		66150	E	A	WBAN	TO
66100 r	E	A	WBBM	ML		66151	E	A	WBAK	CF
66101 r	E	A	WBBM	ML		66152	E	A	WBAM	ML
66102 kr	E	A	WBBM	ML		66153	E	A	WBAI	IM
66103 r	E	A	WBBM	ML		66154	E	A	WBAI	IM
66104 r	E	A	WBBM	ML		66155	E	A	WBAI	IM
66105 r	E	A	WBBM	ML		66156	E	A	WBAT	TE
66106 r	E	A	WBBM	ML		66157	E	A	WBAK	CF
66107	E	A	WBBM	ML		66158 k	E	A	WBAI	IM
66108 r	E	A	WBBM	ML		66159	E	A	WBAN	TO
66109 kr	E	A	WBBM	ML		66160	E	A	WBAI	IM
66110 r	E	A	WBBM	ML		66161	E	A	WBAT	TE
66111 r	E	A	WBBM	ML		66162	E	A	WBAH	EH
66112 r	E	A	WBBM	ML		66163	E	A	WBAN	TO
66113 r	E	A	WBBM	ML		66164	E	A	WBAK	CF

▲ One of a number of shunters recently registered for use on Railtrack metals in the 01xxx series, No. 01531 is pictured at the Port of Felixstowe on 19th February 2000. **John Day**

▼ West Anglia Great Northern (WAGN) Railway liveried Class 03 No. 03179 'CLIVE' is pictured at the WAGN depot at Hornsey on 15th June 1999.

Ross Aitken

▲ Class 08 No. 08393, carrying Railfreight Distribution livery, is pictured passing through Stratford on 4th December 1999. **K. Conkey**

▼ English Welsh & Scottish Railway liveried Class 08 No. 08995 stands at Margam Yard on 28th June 2000. **Rodney Lissenden**

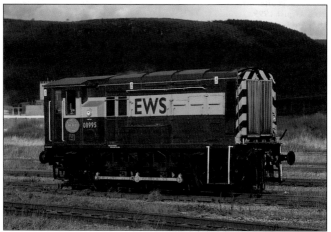

▲ Carrying EWS livery but without the branding, Class 09 No. 09009 'Three Bridges CED' stands at Harwich Parkeston Yard on 1st October 2000. **Alan Sargeant**

▼ Direct Rail Services liveried Class 20 No. 20309 is pictured nose first at Leiston, East Suffolk after arriving with a nuclear flask wagon from Sellafield. The date is 26th August 1999. **Michael J. Collins**

▲ A pair of Fragonset Railways livered Class 31s, Nos. 31601 'BLETCHLEY PARK 'STATION X'' and 31602 'CHIMAERA', pass Dore with a return Skegness–Derby charter on 15th July 2000. **Peter Fox**

▼ One of only two Class 33s in service with EWS, Civil-link liveried No. 33025 stands at Aberdeen Guild Street Yard on 31st May 2000. **G.W. Morrison**

▲ Loadhaul liveried Class 37 No. 37713 passes Bell Veu with a Ditton to Immingham Maritime Intermodal train on 26th March 1999.　**Ian A. Lyall**

▼ The 06.45 Newcastle–Plymouth, led by Virgin Trains liveried Class 43 Power Car No. 43084 'County of Derbyshire', runs along the sea wall at Horse Cove, Dawlish on 4th March 2000.　**John Chalcraft**

▲ BR Green Class 46 No. D 172 'Ixion' hauls three preserved locos and support coach through Oxford station on 4th August 2000. All four locos were en-route to Old Oak Common, where they exhibited at the open weekend held there on the 5th/6th August 2000. **Darren Ford**

▼ Still carrying the obsolescent Intercity livery, Class 47 No. 47805 enters Kensington Olympia with the 07.17 Manchester Piccadilly–Brighton service on 26th February 2000. **David Brown**

▲ First Great Western liveried Class 47 No. 47813 'SS Great Britain' hurries past Marazion on 13th July 2000 with the 12.52 Penzance–London Paddington.
John Chalcraft

▼ Class 50 No. 50017 carries a livery similar to one used by the LMS for the locomotives which worked the 'Coronation Scot' service. It is pictured here at Yate with the 17.06 Bath Spa–Manchester Piccadilly return charter on 22nd July 2000.
John Chalcraft

▲ BR blue Class 55 No. 55019 'ROYAL HIGHLAND FUSILIER' passes Normanton with a charter special on 8th September 1999. **G.W. Morrison**

▼ Transrail Freight liveried Class 56 No. 56079 hauls a Falkland Yard to Carlisle coal train past Troon Golf Course, Ayrshire on 28th April 1999. **Paul Senior**

▲ Freightliner liveried Class 57 No. 57012 'Freightliner Envoy' enters Ipswich with the 16.35 Felixstowe South FLT–Ipswich on 5th May 2000. **John Day**

▼ Class 58 No. 58041 'Ratcliffe Power Station', carrying two-tone grey livery with Mainline Freight branding, stands in Eastleigh East Yard with an engineers train on 19th December 1999. **Brian Denton**

▲ Carrying the new Mendip Rail livery, Class 59 No. 59002 'Alan J. Day' approaches Fairwood Junction as it leaves Westbury with the 11.46 Fareham–Whatley Quarry stone empties. The date is 31st May 2000.　　**John Chalcraft**

▼ Mainline Freight liveried Class 60 No. 60078 forks left at Brocklesby Junction with the 11.24 Santon–Immingham on 28th May 1999.　　**Anthony Underwood**

▲ English Welsh & Scottish Railway liveried Class 66 No. 66014 stands with a train of box wagons at Liverpool's Gladstone Dock on 1st June 1999.

Paul Shannon

▼ The 14.30 London Victoria–Gatwick Airport Gatwick Express service passes through Selhurst on 29th April 2000 with Class 73 No. 73204 providing the power. These locomotives are in the process of being withdrawn from these services in favour of Class 460 EMUs.

K. Conkey

Class 67s Nos. 67014 and 67016, both in English Welsh & Scottish Railway livery, pass Colton Junction on 23rd August 2000 with a Low Fell to London Royal Mail service.

Ian A. Lyall

▲ Anglia Railways liveried Class 86 No. 86217 'City University' at Barham, near Ipswich with the 14.30 Norwich–London Liverpool Street on 25th February 2000.

Michael J. Collins

▼ Rail express systems liveried Class 86 No. 86243 takes a Low Fell to Bristol Temple Meads Royal Mail service through Durham on 26th July 1999.

Ian A. Lyall

Class 87 No. 87008, in Virgin Trains livery, approaches Winwick Junction on 6th May 2000 with the 13.30 London Euston–Preston. **Paul Senior**

▲ Great North Eastern Railway liveried Class 89 No. 89001 waits to depart from Leeds with the 10.05 to London Kings Cross on 25th May 1999.   **G.W. Morrison**

▼ Class 90 No. 90145 hauls a southbound Freightliner at Greenholme during July 1998. The loco carries the old two-tone grey Freightliner colours now superceded by the green and yellow livery.   **Dave McAlone**

▲ The 07.00 London King Cross–Edinburgh races past Eaton Lane, Retford behind Great North Eastern Railway liveried Class 91 No. 91031 on 26th July 1999.
Ian A. Lyall

▼ European Passenger Services liveried Class 92 No. 92024 'J S Bach' coasts downgrade from Shap summit at Orton Moor on 27th August 1999 with the 14.48 Mossend Yard–Eastleigh Enterprise service. **Dave McAlone**

66165	k	E	A	WBAK	CF		66208	k	E	A	WBAN	TO

66165	k	E	A	WBAK	CF		66208	k	E	A	WBAN	TO
66166		E	A	WBAI	IM		66209	k	E	A	WBAI	IM
66167		E	A	WBAI	IM		66210	k	E	A	WBAN	TO
66168		E	A	WBAK	CF		66211	k	E	A	WBAT	TE
66169		E	A	WBAH	EH		66212	k	E	A	WBAK	CF
66170		E	A	WBAT	TE		66213	k	E	A	WBAI	IM
66171	k	E	A	WBAN	TO		66214	k	E	A	WBAK	CF
66172		E	A	WBAI	IM		66215	k	E	A	WBAK	CF
66173		E	A	WBAH	EH		66216	k	E	A	WBAH	EH
66174		E	A	WBAN	TO		66217	k	E	A	WBAH	EH
66175		E	A	WBAN	TO		66218	k	E	A	WBAN	TO
66176		E	A	WBAK	CF		66219	k	E	A	WBAN	TO
66177	k	E	A	WBAI	IM		66220	k	E	A	WBAI	IM
66178		E	A	WBAN	TO		66221	k	E	A	WBAI	IM
66179		E	A	WBAK	CF		66222	k	E	A	WBAK	CF
66180		E	A	WBAM	ML		66223	k	E	A	WBAT	TE
66181		E	A	WBAK	CF		66224	k	E	A	WBAT	TE
66182	k	E	A	WBAN	TO		66225	k	E	A	WBAN	TO
66183		E	A	WBAI	IM		66226	k	E	A	WBAI	IM
66184		E	A	WBAT	TE		66227	k	E	A	WBAT	TE
66185		E	A	WBAI	IM		66228	k	E	A	WBAI	IM
66186		E	A	WBAM	ML		66229	k	E	A	WBAK	CF
66187		E	A	WBAK	CF		66230	k	E	A	WBAI	IM
66188		E	A	WBAN	TO		66231	k	E	A	WBAN	TO
66189		E	A	WBAH	EH		66232	k	E	A	WBAN	TO
66190		E	A	WBAT	TE		66233	k	E	A	WBAT	TE
66191		E	A	WBAK	CF		66234	k	E	A	WBAI	IM
66192		E	A	WBAT	TE		66235	k	E	A	WBAK	CF
66193		E	A	WBAM	ML		66236	k	E	A	WBAK	CF
66194		E	A	WBAN	TO		66237	k	E	A	WBAI	IM
66195	k	E	A	WBAN	TO		66238	k	E	A	WBAH	EH
66196		E	A	WBAN	TO		66239	k	E	A	WBAK	CF
66197		E	A	WBAI	IM		66240	k	E	A	WBAI	IM
66198		E	A	WBAT	TE		66241	k	E	A	WBAK	CF
66199		E	A	WBAK	CF		66242	k	E	A	WBAI	IM
66200		E	A	WBAM	ML		66243	k	E	A	WBAN	TO
66201	k	E	A	WBAI	IM		66244	k	E	A	WBAT	TE
66202	k	E	A	WBAK	CF		66245	k	E	A	WBAI	IM
66203	k	E	A	WBAT	TE		66246	k	E	A	WBAN	TO
66204	k	E	A	WBAI	IM		66247	k	E	A	WBAN	TO
66205	k	E	A	WBAI	IM		66248	k	E	A	WBAM	ML
66206	k	E	A	WBAK	CF		66249	k	E	A	WBAH	EH
66207	k	E	A	WBAI	IM		66250	k	E	A	WBAK	CF

Class 66/5. Freightliner operated locomotives. Details as Class 66/0.

66501	FL	P	DFGM	FD	
66502	FL	P	DFGM	FD	
66503	FL	P	DFGM	FD	
66504	FL	P	DFGM	FD	
66505	FL	P	DFGM	FD	
66506	FL	H	DFRT	FD	Crewe Regeneration

66507	**FL**	H	DFRT	FD	
66508	**FL**	H	DFRT	FD	
66509	**FL**	H	DFRT	FD	
66510	**FL**	H	DFRT	FD	
66511	**FL**	H	DFRT	FD	
66512	**FL**	H	DFRT	FD	
66513	**FL**	H	DFRT	FD	
66514	**FL**	H	DFRT	FD	
66515	**FL**	H	DFRT	FD	
66516	**FL**	H	DFRT	FD	
66517	**FL**	H	DFRT	FD	
66518	**FL**	H	DFRT	FD	
66519	**FL**	H	DFRT	FD	
66520	**FL**	H	DFRT	FD	
66521	**FL**	H	DFHH	FD	
66522	**FL**	H	DFHH	FD	
66523	**FL**	H	DFGM	FD	
66524	**FL**	H	DFGM	FD	
66525	**FL**	H	DFGM	FD	
66526					
66527					
66528					
66529					
66530					
66531					

Class 66/6. Freightliner operated locomotives with modified gear ratios.
Details as Class 66/0 except:

Maximum Tractive Effort: 467 kN (105080 lbf).
Continuous Tractive Effort: 296 kN (66630 lbf) at 14.0 m.p.h.
Design Speed: 87.5 m.p.h.   **Maximum Speed:** 65 m.p.h.

66601	**FL**	P	DFHH	FD	The Hope Valley
66602	**FL**	P	DFRT	FD	
66603	**FL**	P	DFRT	FD	
66604	**FL**	P	DFRT	FD	
66605	**FL**	P	DFRT	FD	
66606	**FL**	P	DFRT	FD	

Class 66/7. GB Railfreight operated locomotives. Details as Class 66/0.

66701	**GB**	H			
66702	**GB**	H			
66703	**GB**	H			
66704	**GB**	H			
66705	**GB**	H			
66706	**GB**	H			
66707	**GB**	H			

CLASS 67   GENERAL MOTORS   Bo–Bo

Built: 1999–2000 by Alstom at Valencia, Spain, as sub-contractors for General Motors (General Motors model JT42 HW-HS).
Engine: General Motors 12N-710G3B-EC two stroke of 2385 kW (3200 h.p.) at 900 r.p.m.
Main Alternator: General Motors AR9/HE3/CA6B.
Traction Motors: General Motors D43FM.
Maximum Tractive Effort: 141 kN (31750 lbf).
Continuous Tractive Effort: 90 kN (20200 lbf) at ?? m.p.h.
Power At Rail: 1860 kW.   **Train Brakes:** Air.
Brake Force: 78 t.   **Dimensions:** 19.74 x 2.72 x 3.95 m.
Weight: 90 t.   **Wheel Diameter:** 965 mm.
Design Speed: 125 m.p.h.   **Maximum Speed:** 110 (*125) m.p.h.
Fuel Capacity: 4927 litres.   **RA:** 8.
Train Supply: Electric, index 66.   **Multiple Working:** AAR System.

Note: All equipped with Slow Speed Control and Swinghead Automatic Combination Couplers.

67001	E	A	WAAK	CF	Night Mail
67002	E	A	WNWX	TT(S)	Special Delivery
67003	E	A	WAAK	CF	
67004	E	A	WAAK	CF	Post Haste
67005	E	A	WAAK	CF	Queen's Messenger
67006	E	A	WAAK	CF	
67007	E	A	WAAK	CF	
67008	E	A	WAAK	CF	
67009	E	A	WAAK	CF	
67010	E	A	WAAK	CF	
67011	E	A	WAAK	CF	
67012	E	A	WAAK	CF	
67013	E	A	WAAK	CF	
67014	E	A	WAAK	CF	
67015	E	A	WAAK	CF	
67016	E	A	WAAK	CF	
67017	E	A	WAAK	CF	
67018	E	A	WAAK	CF	
67019	E	A	WAAK	CF	
67020	E	A	WAAK	CF	
67021	E	A	WAAK	CF	
67022	E	A	WAAK	CF	
67023	* E	A	WHPT	CF	
67024	E	A	WAAK	CF	
67025	E	A	WAAK	CF	
67026	E	A	WAAK	CF	
67027	E	A	WAAK	CF	
67028	E	A	WAAK	CF	
67029	E	A	WAAK	CF	
67030	E	A	WAAK	CF	

1.2. ELECTRIC & ELECTRO-DIESEL LOCOMOTIVES

CLASS 71   BR/ENGLISH ELECTRIC   Bo–Bo

Built: 1959 by BR at Doncaster Works.
Electric Supply System: 750 V d.c. from third rail.
Traction Motors: English Electric 532.
Maximum Tractive Effort: 195 kN (43800 lbf).
Continuous Rating: 1716 kW (2300 h.p.) giving a tractive effort of 55 kN (12400 lbf) at 69.6 m.p.h.   **RA:** 6.
Maximum Rail Power: 2239 kW (3000 h.p.).
Train Brakes: Air, vacuum & electro-pneumatic.
Brake Force: 41 t.   **Dimensions:** 15.42 x 2.82 x 3.99 m.
Weight: 76.2 t.   **Wheel Diameter:** 1219 mm.
Design Speed: 90 m.p.h.   **Maximum Speed:** 90 m.p.h.
Train Supply: Electric (300 kW maximum).
Multiple Working: SR System.

Non-standard numbering:
• 71001 carries number E5001. Official RSL number is 89403.

71001   **G**   NR   MBEL   SE

CLASS 73   BR/ENGLISH ELECTRIC   Bo–Bo

Built: 1962 by BR at Eastleigh Works.
Engine: English Electric 4SRKT of 447 kW (600 h.p.) at 850 r.p.m.
Main Generator: English Electric 824/3D.
Electric Supply System: 750 V d.c. from third rail.
Traction Motors: English Electric 542A.
Maximum Tractive Effort (Electric): 187 kN (42000 lbf).
Maximum Tractive Effort (Diesel): 152 kN (34100lbf).
Continuous Rating (Electric): 1060 kW (1420 h.p.) giving a tractive effort of 43 kN (9600 lbf) at 55.5 m.p.h.
Continuous Tractive Effort (Diesel): 72 kN (16100 lbf) at 10 m.p.h.
Maximum Rail Power (Electric): 1830 kW (2450 h.p.) at 37 m.p.h.
Train Brakes: Air, vacuum & electro-pneumatic († Air & electro-pneumatic).
Brake Force: 31 t.   **Dimensions:** 16.36 x 2.64 x 3.8 m.
Weight: 76.3 t.   **Wheel Diameter:** 1016 mm.
Design Speed: 80 m.p.h.   **Maximum Speed:** 60 m.p.h.
Fuel Capacity: 1545 litres.   **RA:** 6.
Train Supply: Electric, index 66 (on electric power only). May also deliver a reduced electric train supply when on diesel power whilst stationary.
Multiple Working: SR System.

Non-standard livery:
• 73005 is in non-standard blue livery with white roof.

Class 73/0. First build. Details as above.

73002	**BL**	ME	HEXX	KK(S)
73005	**0**	ME	HEBD	BD

Class 73/1. Later build. Details as Class 73/0 except:

Built: 1965–67 by English Electric Co. at Vulcan Foundry, Newton le Willows.
Main Generator: English Electric 824/5D.
Traction Motors: English Electric 546/1B.
Maximum Tractive Effort (Electric): 179 kN (40000 lbf).
Maximum Tractive Effort (Diesel): 160 kN (36000 lbf).
Continuous Rating (Electric): 1060 kW (1420 h.p.) giving a tractive effort of 35 kN (7800 lbf) at 68 m.p.h.
Continuous Tractive Effort (Diesel): 60 kN (13600 lbf) at 11.5 m.p.h.
Maximum Rail Power (Electric): 2350 kW (3150 h.p.) at 42 m.p.h.
Weight: 77 t.   **Dimensions:** 16.36 x 2.64 x 3.81m.
Design Speed: 90 m.p.h.   **Maximum Speed:** 60 (90*†) m.p.h.
Fuel Capacity: 1409 litres.
Train Supply: Electric, index 66 (on electric power only).

Note: ‡ Modified cabs for use on route learning duties.

73101	*	**PC**	E	WPAG	HG	The Royal Alex'
73103		**I**	E	WNXX	EH(S)	
73104	*	**I**	E	WNXX	EH(S)	
73105	*	**CE**	E	WNYX	OM(S)	
73106		**DG**	E	WNXX	HG(S)	
73107	*	**CE**	E	WNXX	OM(S)	Redhill 1844-1994
73108	*	**CE**	E	WPAG	HG	
73109	*	**ST**	SW	HYSB	BM	Battle of Britain 50th Anniversary
73110		**CE**	E	WPAG	HG	
73114	*	**ML**	E	WNYX	OM(S)	
73117		**I**	E	WNXX	EH(S)	University of Surrey
73118	†c	**EP**	EU	GPSN	OC	
73119	*	**CE**	E	WNXX	OM(S)	Kentish Mercury
73128	*	**E**	E	WPAG	HG	
73129	*	**N**	E	WPAG	HG	City of Winchester
73130	†c	**EP**	EU	GPSN	OC	
73131	*	**E**	E	WPAG	HG	
73132		**I**	E	WNXX	OM(S)	
73133	‡	**ML**	E	WPAG	HG	The Bluebell Railway
73134		**I**	E	WNXX	EH(S)	Woking Homes 1885-1985
73136	*	**ML**	E	WPAG	HG	Kent Youth Music
73138		**CE**	E	WNXX	OM(S)	
73139		**I**	E	WNXX	EH(S)	
73140		**I**	E	WNXX	OM(S)	
73141		**I**	E	WNXX	OM(S)	

Class 73/2. Locomotives originally dedicated to Gatwick Express-services. Details as Class 73/1 except:

Maximum Speed: 90 m.p.h.   **Train Brakes:** Air & electro-pneumatic.

73201	**GX**	P	IVGA	SL

73202	**GX**	P	IVGA	SL
73203	**GX**	P	IVGA	SL
73204	**GX**	P	SBXL	SU(S)
73205	**GX**	P	IVGA	SL
73206	**GX**	P	IVGA	SL
73207	**GX**	P	IVGA	SL
73208	**GX**	P	IVGA	SL
73209	**GX**	P	IVGA	SL
73210	**GX**	P	IVGA	SL
73211	**GX**	P	IVGA	SL
73212	**GX**	RK	QXXX	ZA(S)
73213	**GX**	P	IVGA	SL
73235	**GX**	P	IVGA	SL

Class 73/9. Merseyrail Electrics operated locomotives. Details as Class 73/0.

73901	**MS**	ME	HEXX	BD(S)
73906	**MS**	ME	HEBD	BD

CLASS 86   BR/ENGLISH ELECTRIC   Bo–Bo

Built: 1965–66 by English Electric Co. at Vulcan Foundry, Newton le Willows or by BR at Doncaster Works.
Electric Supply System: 25 kV a.c. 50 Hz overhead.
Traction Motors: AEI 282BZ axle hung.
Maximum Tractive Effort: 207 kN (46500 lbf).
Continuous Rating: 3010 kW (4040 h.p.) giving a tractive effort of 85 kN (19200 lbf) at 77.5 m.p.h.
Maximum Rail Power: 4550 kW (6100 h.p.) at 49.5 m.p.h.

Train Brakes: Air.	**Brake Force:** 40 t.
Dimensions: 17.83 x 2.65 x 3.98 m.	**Weight:** 83–86.8 t.
Wheel Diameter: 1156 mm.	**Design Speed:** 100 m.p.h.
Maximum Speed: 100 m.p.h.	**Train Supply:** Electric, index 74.
RA: 6.	**Multiple Working:** TDM system.

Class 86/1. Class 87-type bogies & motors. Details as above except:

Maximum Tractive Effort: 258 kN (58000 lbf).
Traction Motors: GEC 412AZ frame mounted.
Continuous Rating: 3730 kW (5000 h.p.) giving a tractive effort of 95 kN (21300 lbf) at 87 m.p.h.
Maximum Rail Power: 5860 kW (7860 h.p.) at 50.8 m.p.h.

Weight: 86.8 t.	**Wheel Diameter:** 1150 mm.
Design Speed: 110 m.p.h.	**Maximum Speed:** 110 m.p.h.

86101		**IS**	H	SAXL	CE(S)	Sir William A Stanier FRS
86102		**IS**	H	SAXL	CE(S)	Robert A Riddles
86103	x	**IS**	H	SAXL	ZH(S)	André Chapelon

Class 86/2. Standard Design. Details as in main class heading except:
Weight: 85–86.2 t.

Note: Locomotives from pool WEOE may be loaned on a day-to-day basis to West Coast Traincare for operation by Virgin West Cost in pool IWPA.

86204		IS	H	SAXL	ZH(S)	City of Carlisle
86205		V	H	IWPA	WN	City of Lancaster
86206		V	H	ICCA	LG	City of Stoke on Trent
86207		IS	H	ICCA	LG	City of Lichfield
86208		IS	E	WNXX	CE(S)	City of Chester
86209		V	H	SAXL	ZH(S)	City of Coventry
86210	x	RX	E	WNXX	CE(S)	C.I.T. 75th Anniversary
86212		V	H	ICCA	LG	Preston Guild 1328-1992
86213		V	H	SAXL	CE(S)	Lancashire Witch
86214		IS	H	ICCA	LG	Sans Pareil
86215		AR	H	IANA	NC	
86216		IS	H	SAXL	ZH(S)	Meteor
86217		AR	H	IANA	NC	City University
86218		AR	H	IANA	NC	NHS 50
86219		IS	H	SAXL	ZH(S)	Phoenix
86220		AR	H	IANA	NC	The Round Tabler
86221		AR	H	IANA	NC	B.B.C. Look East
86222		V	H	ICCA	LG	Clothes Show Live
86223		AR	H	IANA	NC	Norwich Union
86224		IS	H	ICCA	LG	
86225		V	H	ICCA	LG	Hardwicke
86226		V	H	ICCA	LG	CHARLES RENNIE MACKINTOSH
86227		IS	H	SAXL	ZH(S)	Sir Henry Johnson
86228		V	H	SAXL	CE(S)	Vulcan Heritage
86229		V	H	IWPA	WN	Lions Clubs International
86230		AR	H	IANA	NC	
86231		V	H	ICCA	LG	Starlight Express
86232		AR	H	IANA	NC	
86233		V	H	IWPA	WN	Laurence Olivier
86234		IS	H	ICCA	LG	J B Priestley OM
86235		AR	H	IANA	NC	Crown Point
86236		V	H	ICCA	LG	Josiah Wedgwood
86237		AR	H	IANA	NC	University of East Anglia
86238		AR	H	IANA	NC	European Community
86240		V	H	ICCA	LG	Bishop Eric Treacy
86241		RX	E	WNXX	CE(S)	Glenfiddich
86242		V	H	ICCA	LG	James Kennedy GC
86243	x	RX	E	WEOE	CE	
86244		V	H	ICCA	LG	The Royal British Legion
86245		V	H	IWPA	WN	Caledonian
86246		AR	H	IANA	NC	
86247		V	H	IWPA	WN	Abraham Darby
86248		V	H	ICCA	LG	Sir Clwyd/County of Clwyd
86249		IS	H	SAXL	NC(S)	County of Merseyside
86250		AR	H	IANA	NC	
86251		V	H	ICCA	LG	The Birmingham Post
86252		AR	H	IANA	NC	Sheppard 100
86253		IS	H	ICCA	LG	The Manchester Guardian
86254	x	RX	E	WEOE	CE	
86255		IS	H	WEOE	CE	Penrith Beacon
86256		V	H	ICCA	LG	Pebble Mill

86257		**AR**	H	IANA	NC
86258		**V**	H	ICCA	LG
86259		**V**	H	IWPA	WN	Greater MANCHESTER THE LIFE & SOUL OF BRITAIN
86260		**V**	H	IWPA	WN	Driver Wallace Oakes G.C.
86261	x	**E**	E	WEOE	CE	THE RAIL CHARTER PARTNERSHIP

Class 86/4. EWS owned locomotives. Details as Class 86/2 except:

Traction Motors: AEI 282AZ axle hung.
Maximum Tractive Effort: 258 kN (58000 lbf).
Weight: 83–83.9 t.
Continuous Rating: 2680 kW (3600 h.p.) giving a tractive effort of 89 kN (20000 lbf) at 67 m.p.h.
Maximum Rail Power: 4400 kW (5900 h.p.) at 38 m.p.h.

Note: Note: Locomotives from pool WEOE may be loaned on a day-to-day basis to West Coast Traincare for operation by Virgin West Cost in pool IWPA.

86401		**E**	E	WEOE	CE	Hertfordshire Rail Tours
86416	x	**RX**	E	WEOE	CE	
86417	x	**RX**	E	WEOE	CE	
86419	x	**RX**	E	WNXX	CE(S)	
86424		**RX**	E	WEOE	CE	
86425		**RX**	E	WEOE	CE	Saint Mungo
86426	x	**E**	E	WEOE	CE	Pride of the Nation
86430	x	**RX**	E	WEOE	CE	Saint Edmund

Class 86/5. Regeared locomotive operated by Freightliner. Details as Class 86/4 except:

Continuous Rating: 2680 kW (3600 h.p.) giving a tractive effort of 117 kN (26300 lbf) at 67 m.p.h.
Maximum Speed: 75 m.p.h.   **Train Supply:** Electric, isolated.

86501	(86608)	**FL**	FL	DFGC	FE

Class 86/6. Freightliner operated locomotives. Details as Class 86/4 except:

Maximum Speed: 75 m.p.h.   **Train Supply:** Electric, isolated.

86602		**FL**	FL	DFNC	FE	
86603		**FE**	FL	DHLT	CE(S)	
86604		**FF**	FL	DFNC	FE	
86605		**FF**	FL	DFNC	FE	
86606		**FF**	FL	DFNC	FE	
86607		**FL**	FL	DFNC	FE	
86609		**FL**	FL	DFNC	FE	
86610		**F**	FL	DFNC	FE	
86611		**FF**	FL	DFNC	FE	Airey Neave
86612		**FF**	P	DFNC	FE	Elizabeth Garrett Anderson
86613		**FL**	P	DFNC	FE	
86614		**FF**	P	DFNC	FE	Frank Hornby
86615		**F**	P	DFNC	FE	Rotary International
86618		**FF**	P	DFNC	FE	
86620		**FL**	P	DFNC	FE	Philip G Walton

86621	FF	P	DFNC	FE	London School of Economics
86622	FF	P	DFNC	FE	
86623	FF	P	DFNC	FE	
86627	FL	P	DFNC	FE	
86628	FF	P	DFNC	FE	Aldaniti
86631	FL	P	DFNC	FE	
86632	FL	P	DFNC	FE	
86633	FF	P	DFNC	FE	Wulfruna
86634	FL	P	DFNC	FE	
86635	FL	P	DFNC	FE	
86636	FL	P	DHLT	CE(S)	
86637	FF	P	DFNC	FE	
86638	FF	P	DFNC	FE	
86639	FF	P	DFNC	FE	

CLASS 87   BREL/GEC   Bo–Bo

Built: 1973–75 by BREL at Crewe Works.
Electric Supply System: 25 kV a.c. 50 Hz overhead.
Traction Motors: GEC G412AZ frame mounted.
Maximum Tractive Effort: 258 kN (58000 lbf).
Continuous Rating: 3730 kW (5000 h.p.) giving a tractive effort of 95 kN (21300 lbf) at 87 m.p.h.
Maximum Rail Power: 5860 kW (7860 h.p.) at 50.8 m.p.h.

Train Brakes: Air.	**Brake Force:** 40 t.
Dimensions: 17.83 x 2.65 x 3.96 m.	**Weight:** 83.3 t.
Wheel Diameter: 1150 mm.	**Design Speed:** 110 m.p.h.
Maximum Speed: 110 m.p.h.	**Train Supply:** Electric, index 95.
RA: 6.	**Multiple Working:** TDM system.

Class 87/0. Standard Design.

87001	V	P	IWCA	WN	Royal Scot
87002	V	P	IWCA	WN	Royal Sovereign
87003	V	P	IWCA	WN	Patriot
87004	V	P	IWCA	WN	Britannia
87005	V	P	IWCA	WN	City of London
87006	V·	P	IWCA	WN	George Reynolds
87007	V	P	IWCA	WN	City of Manchester
87008	V	P·	IWCA	WN	City of Liverpool
87009	V	P	IWCA	WN	City of Birmingham
87010	V	P	IWCA	WN	King Arthur
87011	V	P	IWCA	WN	
87012	V	P	IWCA	WN	
87013	V	P	IWCA	WN	John O'Gaunt
87014	V	P	IWCA	WN	Knight of the Thistle
87015	V	P	IWCA	WN	Howard of Effingham
87016	V	P	IWCA	WN	Willesden Intercity Depot
87017	V	P	IWCA	WN	Iron Duke
87018	V	P	IWCA	WN	Lord Nelson
87019	V	P	IWCA	WN	Sir Winston Churchill
87020	V	P	IWCA	WN	North Briton

87021	**V**	P	IWCA	WN	Robert The Bruce
87022	**V**	P	IWCA	WN	Lew Adams The Black Prince
87023	**V**	P	IWCA	WN	Polmadie
87024	**V**	P	IWCA	WN	Lord of the Isles
87025	**V**	P	IWCA	WN	County of Cheshire
87026	**V**	P	IWCA	WN	Sir Richard Arkwright
87027	**V**	P	IWCA	WN	Wolf of Badenoch
87028	**V**	P	IWCA	WN	Lord President
87029	**V**	P	IWCA	WN	Earl Marischal
87030	**V**	P	IWCA	WN	Black Douglas
87031	**V**	P	IWCA	WN	Hal o' the Wynd
87032	**V**	P	IWCA	WN	Kenilworth
87033	**V**	P	IWCA	WN	Thane of Fife
87034	**V**	P	IWCA	WN	William Shakespeare
87035	**V**	P	IWCA	WN	Robert Burns

Class 87/1. Thyristor Control. Details as Class 87/0 except:

Traction Motors: GEC G412BZ frame mounted.
Continuous Rating: 3620 kW (4850 hp) giving a tractive effort of 96 kN (21600 lbf) at 84 m.p.h.
Maximum Speed: 75 m.p.h.   **Weight:** 79.1 t.

| 87101 | **B** | EF | WNXX | CE(S) | STEPHENSON |

CLASS 89   BRUSH   Co–Co

Built: 1986 by BREL at Crewe Works (as sub-contractors for Brush).
Electric Supply System: 25 kV a.c. 50 Hz overhead.
Traction Motors: Brush. Frame mounted.
Maximum Tractive Effort: 205 kN (46000 lbf).
Continuous Rating: 4350 kW (5850 h.p.) giving a tractive effort of 105 kN (23600 lbf) at 92 m.p.h.

Maximum Rail Power:	**Train Brakes:** Air.
Brake Force: 50 t.	**Dimensions:** 19.80 x 2.74 x 3.98 m.
Weight: 104 t.	**Wheel Diameter:** 1150 mm.
Design Speed: 125 m.p.h.	**Maximum Speed:** 125 m.p.h.
Train Supply: Electric, index 95.	**RA:** 6.
Multiple Working: TDM system.	

| 89001 | **GN** | SI | IECB | BN |

CLASS 90   GEC   Bo–Bo

Built: 1987–90 by BREL at Crewe Works (as sub contractors for GEC).
Electric Supply System: 25 kV a.c. 50 Hz overhead.
Traction Motors: GEC G412CY frame mounted.
Maximum Tractive Effort: 258 kN (58000 lbf).
Continuous Rating: 3730 kW (5000 h.p.) giving a tractive effort of 95 kN (21300 lbf) at 87 m.p.h.
Maximum Rail Power: 5860 kW (7860 h.p.) at 68.3 m.p.h.
Train Brakes: Air.

Brake Force: 40 (* 50) t.
Weight: 84.5 t.
Design Speed: 110 m.p.h.
Train Supply: Electric, index 95.
Multiple Working: TDM system.

Dimensions: 18.80 x 2.74 x 3.97 m.
Wheel Diameter: 1156 mm.
Maximum Speed: 110 († 100) m.p.h.
RA: 7.

Non-standard liveries:
- 90029 is in German Federal Railways style red and white.
- 90036 is as FE, but has a yellow roof.

Class 90/0. Standard Design. Details as above.

Note: One (unspecified) locomotive is hired from EWS (Pool WEPE) to Great North Eastern Railway (Pool IECA) on a regular basis. This locomotive is used between London King's Cross and Leeds/Bradford Forster Square only.

90001	b	V	P	IWCA	WN	BBC Midlands Today
90002	b	V	P	IWCA	WN	Mission: Impossible
90003	b	V	P	IWCA	WN	THE HERALD
90004	b	V	P	IWCA	WN	City of Glasgow
90005	b	IS	P	IWCA	WN	Financial Times
90006	b	IS	P	IWCA	WN	High Sheriff
90007	b	IS	P	IWCA	WN	Lord Stamp
90008	b	IS	P	IWCA	WN	The Birmingham Royal Ballet
90009	b	V	P	IWCA	WN	The Economist
90010	b	V	P	IWCA	WN	275 Railway Squadron (Volunteers)
90011	b	V	P	IWCA	WN	West Coast Rail 250
90012	b	V	P	IWCA	WN	British Transport Police
90013	b	V	P	IWCA	WN	The Law Society
90014	b	V	P	IWCA	WN	
90015	b	V	P	IWCA	WN	The International Brigades SPAIN 1936-1939
90016	†b	RX	E	WEFE	CE	
90017	†b	RX	E	WEFE	CE	Rail express systems Quality Assured
90018	†b	RX	E	WEFE	CE	
90019	†b	RX	E	WEFE	CE	Penny Black
90020	†b	E	E	WEFE	CE	Sir Michael Heron
90021	*	FE	EF	WEPE	CE	
90022	*	FE	EF	WEPE	CE	Freightconnection
90023	*	FE	EF	WEPE	CE	
90024	*	GN	EF	WEPE	CE	
90025	*	FD	EF	WEPE	CE	
90026	†	FE	EF	WEFE	CE	Crewe International Electric Maintenance Depot
90027	*	FD	EF	WEPE	CE	Allerton T & RS Depot Quality Approved
90028	*	SB	EF	WEPE	CE	Vrachtverbinding
90029	†	O	EF	WEFE	CE	Frachtverbindungen
90030	†	E	EF	WEFE	CE	Crewe Locomotive Works
90031	†	E	EF	WEFE	CE	The Railway Children Partnership Working For Street Children Worldwide
90032	†	FE	EF	WEFE	CE	Cerestar
90033	*	FE	EF	WEPE	CE	
90034	†	FE	EF	WEFE	CE	

90035	†	**FE**	EF	WEFE	CE
90036	†	**0**	EF	WEFE	CE
90037	†	**FD**	EF	WEFE	CE
90038	*	**FE**	EF	WEPE	CE
90039	*	**FD**	EF	WEPE	CE
90040	†	**FD**	EF	WEFE	CE

Class 90/1. Freightliner leased locomotives. Details as Class 90/0 except:

Maximum Speed: 75 m.p.h.   **Train Supply:** Electric, isolated.

90141	**FF**	P	DFLC	FE	
90142	**FF**	P	DFLC	FE	
90143	**FF**	P	DFLC	FE	Freightliner Coatbridge
90144	**FF**	P	DFLC	FE	
90145	**FF**	P	DFLC	FE	
90146	**FF**	P	DFLC	FE	
90147	**FF**	P	DFLC	FE	
90148	**FF**	P	DFLC	FE	
90149	**FF**	P	DFLC	FE	
90150	**FF**	P	DFLC	FE	

CLASS 91   GEC   Bo–Bo

Built: 1988–91 by BREL at Crewe Works (as sub contractors for GEC).
Electric Supply System: 25 kV a.c. 50 Hz overhead.
Traction Motors: GEC G426AZ.   **Maximum Tractive Effort:**
Continuous Rating: 4540 kW (6090 h.p.) giving a tractive effort of ?? kN at ?? m.p.h.
Maximum Rail Power: 4700 kW (6300 h.p.) at ?? m.p.h.
Train Brakes: Air.
Brake Force: 45 t.   **Dimensions:** 19.41 x 2.74 x 3.76 m.
Weight: 84 t.   **Wheel Diameter:** 1000 mm.
Design Speed: 140 m.p.h.   **Maximum Speed:** 125 m.p.h.
Train Supply: Electric, index 95.   **RA:** 7.
Multiple Working: TDM system.

Note: r – This class is in the process of refurbishment at Adtranz, Doncaster. Refurbished locomotives will be reclassified 91/1 and will be renumbered by the addition of 100 to their existing number.

91001	**GN**	H	IECA	BN	
91002	**GN**	H	IECA	BN	Durham Cathedral
91003	**GN**	H	IECA	BN	
91004	**GN**	H	IECA	BN	Grantham
91005	**GN**	H	IECA	BN	
91006	**GN**	H	IECA	BN	
91007	**GN**	H	IECA	BN	
91008	**GN**	H	IECA	BN	
91009	**GN**	H	IECA	BN	The Samaritans
91010	**GN**	H	IECA	BN	
91011	**GN**	H	IECA	BN	Terence Cuneo
91012	**GN**	H	IECA	BN	County of Cambridgeshire

91013	**GN**	H	IECA	BN	County of North Yorkshire
91014	**GN**	H	IECA	BN	St. Mungo Cathedral
91015	**GN**	H	IECA	BN	Holyrood
91016	**GN**	H	IECA	BN	
91017	**GN**	H	IECA	BN	City of Leeds
91018	**GN**	H	IECA	BN	Bradford Film Festival
91019	**GN**	H	IECA	BN	County of Tyne & Wear
91020	**GN**	H	IECA	BN	
91021	**GN**	H	IECA	BN	Archbishop Thomas Cranmer
91022	**GN**	H	IECA	BN	Double Trigger
91023	**GN**	H	IECA	BN	
91024	**GN**	H	IECA	BN	Reverend W Awdry
91025	**GN**	H	IECA	BN	Berwick-upon-Tweed
91026	**GN**	H	IECA	BN	York Minster
91127 r	**GN**	H	IECA	BN	Edinburgh Castle
91028	**GN**	H	IECA	BN	Peterborough Cathedral
91029	**GN**	H	IECA	BN	Queen Elizabeth II
91030	**GN**	H	IECA	BN	
91031	**GN**	H	IECA	BN	County of Northumberland

CLASS 92   BRUSH   Co–Co

Built: 1993–96 by Brush Traction at Loughborough.
Electric Supply System: 25 kV a.c. 50 HZ overhead or 750 V d.c. third rail.
Traction Motors: Brush.
Maximum Tractive Effort: 400 kN (90 000 lbf).
Continuous Rating: 5040 kW (6760 h.p.) on a.c., 4000 kW (5360 h.p.) on d.c.
Maximum Rail Power: **Train Brakes:** Air.
Brake Force: 63 t.   **Dimensions:** 21.34 x 2.67 x 3.96 m.
Weight: 126 t.   **Wheel Diameter:** 1160 mm.
Design Speed: 140 km/h (87½ m.p.h.).
Maximum Speed: 140 km/h (87½ m.p.h.).
Train Supply: Electric, index 108 (a.c.), 70 (d.c.).   **RA:** 7.

Note: Locomotives in pool WTWE are also authorised to operate on the Eurotunnel network. These locomotives have temporarily had their d.c. shoegear removed and may only operate under power between Dollands Moor and Fréthun.

92001	**E**	E	WTWE	CE	Victor Hugo
92002	**EP**	E	WTWE	CE	H.G. Wells
92003	**EP**	E	WTWE	CE	Beethoven
92004	**EP**	E	WTAE	CE	Jane Austen
92005	**EP**	E	WTAE	CE	Mozart
92006	**EP**	SF	WTAE	CE	Louis Armand
92007	**EP**	E	WTAE	CE	Schubert
92008	**EP**	E	WTAE	CE	Jules Verne
92009	**EP**	E	WTAE	CE	Elgar
92010	**EP**	SF	WTWE	CE	Molière
92011	**EP**	E	WTAE	CE	Handel
92012	**EP**	E	WTWE	CE	Thomas Hardy
92013	**EP**	E	WTAE	CE	Puccini
92014	**EP**	SF	WTAE	CE	Emile Zola

92015	**EP**	E	WTAE	CE	D.H. Lawrence
92016	**EP**	E	WTAE	CE	Brahms
92017	**EP**	E	WTAE	CE	Shakespeare
92018	**EP**	SF	WTAE	CE	Stendhal
92019	**EP**	E	WTAE	CE	Wagner
92020	**EP**	EU	WTAE	CE	Milton
92021	**EP**	EU	WTAE	CE	Purcell
92022	**EP**	E	WTAE	CE	Charles Dickens
92023	**EP**	SF	WTAE	CE	Ravel
92024	**EP**	E	WTAE	CE	J.S. Bach
92025	**EP**	E	WTAE	CE	Oscar Wilde
92026	**EP**	E	WTAE	CE	Britten
92027	**EP**	E	WTWE	CE	George Eliot
92028	**EP**	SF	WTWE	CE	Saint Saëns
92029	**EP**	E	WTWE	CE	Dante
92030	**EP**	E	WTAE	CE	Ashford
92031	**EP**	E	WTWE	CE	
92032	**EP**	EU	WTAE	CE	César Franck
92033	**EP**	SF	WTAE	CE	Berlioz
92034	**EP**	E	WTAE	CE	Kipling
92035	**EP**	E	WTAE	CE	Mendelssohn
92036	**EP**	E	WTAE	CE	Bertolt Brecht
92037	**EP**	E	WTWE	CE	Sullivan
92038	**EP**	SF	WTWE	CE	Voltaire
92039	**EP**	E	WTWE	CE	Johann Strauss
92040	**EP**	EU	WTAE	CE	Goethe
92041	**EP**	E	WTAE	CE	Vaughan Williams
92042	**EP**	E	WTAE	CE	Honegger
92043	**EP**	SF	WTWE	CE	Debussy
92044	**EP**	EU	WTAE	CE	Couperin
92045	**EP**	EU	WTWE	CE	Chaucer
92046	**EP**	EU	WTAE	CE	Sweelinck

UNCLASSIFIED   METROPOLITAN VICKERS   Bo–Bo

Built: 1922 by Metropolitan Vickers at Gorton.
Electric Supply System: 750 V d.c. from third rail or four rail system.
Traction Motors:
Maximum Tractive Effort: 100 kN (22600 lbf).
Continuous Rating: 895 kW (1200 h.p.) giving a tractive effort of 65 kN (14700 lbf) at ? m.p.h.

Maximum Rail Power:	**RA:**
Brake Force:	**Train Brakes:** Air.
Weight: 76.2 t.	**Dimensions:**
Design Speed: 65 m.p.h.	**Wheel Diameter:** 1105 mm.
Train Supply: Not equipped.	**Maximum Speed:** 65 m.p.h.
	Multiple Working: Not equipped.

Non-standard livery/numbering:
• 12 is London Transport livery of maroon, lined out in straw with red window surrounds and solebar. Official RSL number is 89212.

| 12 | **0** | LU | MBEL | WR | SARAH SIDDONS |

1.3. LOCOMOTIVES AWAITING DISPOSAL

The list below comprises locomotives awaiting disposal which are stored on the Railtrack network, together with locomotives stored at other locations (e.g. repair facilites) which, although awaiting disposal, remain Railtrack registered. This includes locomotives for which sales have been agreed, but collection by the new owner had not been made at the time of going to press.

Non-standard liveries:
- 20169 and 47972 are in British Railways Board Central Services livery of red and grey.
- 37137 is being used for painting trials, hence livery carried may vary from time to time.
- 43173 is in Great Western Trains livery of Green and ivory.
- 47803 is yellow and white with a red stripe.

08515	**B**	X	WNZX	GD(S)	31320	**B**	X	WNZX	SF(S)
08517	**B**	X	WNZX	SF(S)	31407	**ML**	E	WNZX	BS(S)
08618	**B**	X	WNZX	GD(S)	31408	**B**	E	WNZX	SP(S)
08622	**B**	RL	MBDL	ML(S)	31411	**DG**	E	WNZX	BC(S)
08634	**B**	X	WNZX	SF(S)	31417	**DG**	E	WNZX	BC(S)
08700	**B**	X	WNZX	SF(S)	31421	**RR**	PO	WNZX	CW(S)
08731	**B**	X	WNZX	ML(S)	31428	**B**	HN	HNRS	BC(S)
08826	**B**	X	WNZX	ML(S)	31432	**B**	E	WNZX	SP(S)
08855	**B**	E	WNZX	ZB(S)	31442	**B**	E	WNZX	CQ(S)
20007	**B**	DR	XHSS	ZB(S)	31444	**CE**	E	WNZX	SP(S)
20032	**B**	DR	XHSS	ZB(S)	31516	**CE**	HN	HNRS	BC(S)
20059	**FQ**	E	WNZX	MG(S)	31519	**CE**	E	WNZX	SP(S)
20072	**B**	DR	XHSS	ZB(S)	31541	**CE**	E	WNZX	OM(S)
20119	**B**	E	WNZX	TT(S)	31545	**B**	E	WNZX	BC(S)
20121	**B**	DR	XHSS	ZB(S)	31548	**CE**	HN	HNRS	BS(S)
20168	**B**	E	WNZX	MG(S)	33038	**B**	HN	HNRS	SF(S)
20169	**O**	PO	WNZX	BC(S)	37012	**CE**	E	WNZX	SP(S)
20177	**B**	E	WNZX	TT(S)	37019	**FD**	E	WNZX	HM(S)
31102	**CE**	PO	WNZX	CD(S)	37043	**TC**	E	WNZX	SP(S)
31125	**CE**	HN	HNRS	BS(S)	37045	**F**	E	WNZX	TT(S)
31168	**B**	HN	HNRS	BC(S)	37048	**MG**	E	WNZX	TT(S)
31174	**CE**	HN	HNRS	BS(S)	37063	**FD**	HN	HNRS	ZB(S)
31196	**CE**	X	WNZX	SF(S)	37068	**FD**	E	WNZX	IM(S)
31200	**CE**	PO	WNZX	CW(S)	37072	**DG**	HN	HNRS	ZB(S)
31229	**CE**	HN	HNRS	BC(S)	37078	**FM**	E	WNZX	SP(S)
31263	**CE**	HN	HNRS	BC(S)	37079	**FD**	HN	HNRS	ZH(S)
31273	**CE**	X	WNZX	HM(S)	37088	**TC**	E	WNZX	SP(S)
31275	**F**	E	WNZX	CS(S)	37095	**CE**	HN	HNRS	ZB(S)
31282	**FQ**	HN	HNRS	BC(S)	37098	**CE**	X	WNZX	OM(S)
31283	**B**	X	WNZX	SF(S)	37137	**O**	E	WNZX	TT(S)
31286	**B**	HN	HNRS	BC(S)	37139	**FC**	E	WNZX	TE(S)
31296	**FA**	E	WHZX	CP(S)	37140	**CE**	E	WNZX	SP(S)
31299	**FO**	X	WNZX	SF(S)	37141	**CE**	E	WNZX	CD(S)
31319	**FC**	PO	WNZX	CW(S)	37142	**CE**	E	WNZX	CW(S)

37144	**FA**	E	WNZX	IM(S)	37904	**FM**	E	WNZX	CF(S)
37153	**TC**	E	WNZX	SP(S)	43173	**O**	A	SCXL	PY(S)
37188	**TC**	E	WNZX	TT(S)	45015	**B**	E	WNZX	TT(S)
37191	**CE**	E	WNZX	SP(S)	47033	**FE**	EF	WNZX	SP(S)
37201	**TC**	E	WNZX	BC(S)	47125	**FE**	PO	WNZX	CW(S)
37209	**BL**	E	WNZX	DD(S)	47156	**FD**	EF	WNZX	CW(S)
37213	**FC**	E	WNZX	TT(S)	47194	**FD**	EF	WNZX	SP(S)
37214	**T**	E	WNZX	SP(S)	47223	**F**	E	WNZX	CW(S)
37218	**F**	E	WNZX	IM(S)	47238	**FD**	PO	WNZX	BS(S)
37222	**MG**	E	WNZX	CF(S)	47276	**F**	EF	WNZX	SP(S)
37223	**FC**	E	WNZX	IM(S)	47294	**FD**	E	WNZX	TT(S)
37227	**MG**	X	WNZX	OM(S)	47297	**FE**	EF	WNZX	SP(S)
37229	**FC**	E	WNZX	CF(S)	47300	**CE**	E	WNZX	SP(S)
37235	**F**	E	WNZX	DD(S)	47341	**CE**	E	WNZX	TT(S)
37240	**CE**	E	WNZX	SP(S)	47344	**FE**	EF	WNZX	SP(S)
37242	**ML**	E	WNZX	SP(S)	47351	**FE**	EF	WNZX	SP(S)
37251	**IS**	PO	WNZX	SP(S)	47355	**FD**	EF	WNZX	HM(S)
37254	**CE**	HN	HNRS	ZH(S)	47363	**F**	EF	WNZX	SP(S)
37255	**CE**	E	WNZX	SP(S)	47484	**GW**	E	WNZX	CD(S)
37278	**FC**	E	WNZX	TT(S)	47565	**RX**	E	WNZX	SP(S)
37334	**F**	E	WNZX	IM(S)	47628	**RX**	E	WNZX	CW(S)
37340	**FD**	E	WNZX	IM(S)	47704	**RX**	E	WNZX	CD(S)
37341	**F**	E	WNZX	TE(S)	47803	**O**	E	WNZX	SF(S)
37343	**CE**	E	WNZX	TT(S)	47971	**BL**	E	WNZX	ZC(S)
37344	**FD**	E	WNZX	IM(S)	47972	**O**	E	WNZX	CD(S)
37345	**FD**	E	WHZX	IM(S)	56023	**FC**	E	WNZX	TT(S)
37359	**FP**	E	WNZX	TE(S)	56092	**T**	E	WNZX	SP(S)
37380	**MG**	E	WNZX	CD(S)	56097	**FM**	E	WNZX	SP(S)
37384	**CE**	E	WNZX	SP(S)	025031	**DG**	E		TO(S)
37404	**T**	E	WNZX	SP(S)	025032	**DG**	E		TO(S)

1.4. LOCOMOTIVES UNDERGOING RAILTRACK CERTIFICATION

The following locomotives are currently undergoing or have recently undergone restoration with a view to receiving Railtrack certification.

Non-standard liveries/numbering:

• 08168 is in black livery.
• 20092 is in British Railways Board Central Services livery of red and grey.

03170	B	HN	BH		31106	CE	HJ	ZA(S)
07013	B	HN	BH		31107	CE	HJ	BH(S)
08168	O	PO	ZA(S)		31128	FO	PO	TM(S)
08359	G	PO	TS(S)		31439	RR	FR	ZA(S)
08507	B	HN	BH(S)		31461	DG	FR	TM(S)
08936	B	HN	BH(S)		31537	CE	FR	ZA(S)
20016	B	DR	BS(S)		33002	CE	DR	BH(S)
20057	B	DR	BS(S)		33008	G	DR	BH(S)
20066	B	DR	BS(S)		33023	B	DR	KD(S)
20073	B	DR	BS(S)		33029	B	DR	KD(S)
20081	B	DR	BS(S)		33053	FA	DR	BH(S)
20092	O	DR	BS(S)		33057	CE	DR	BH(S)
20132	B	DR	BS(S)		33203	FD	DR	SR(S)
20138	FQ	DR	LT(S)		33205	FD	DR	OM(S)
20165	FQ	DR	KD(S)		33207	DR	DR	ZA(S)
20206	B	MO	ZB(S)		45112	B	PO	TM(S)
31105	T	FR	BH(S)					

1.5. EUROTUNNEL LOCOMOTIVES

DIESEL LOCOMOTIVES

0001–0005   MaK   Bo-Bo

Built: 1992–93 by MaK at Kiel, Germany (Model DE1004).
Engine: MTU 12V 396 Tc of 1180 kW (1580 h.p.) at 1800 rpm.
Main Alternator: BBC.   **Traction Motors:** BBC.
Maximum Tractive Effort: 305 kN (68600 lbf).
Continuous Tractive Effort: 140 kN (31500 lbf) at 20 mph.
Power At Rail: 750 kW (1012 h.p.).
Brake Force: 120 kN.   **Dimensions:** 16.50 x ?? x ?? m.
Weight: 84 t.   **Wheel Diameter:** 1000 mm.
Design Speed: 120 km/h.   **Maximum Speed:** 120 km/h.
Fuel Capacity: **Train Brakes:** Air.
Train Supply: Not equipped.   **Multiple Working:** Within class.

0001	**GY**	ET	CO
0002	**GY**	ET	CO
0003	**GY**	ET	CO
0004	**GY**	ET	CO
0005	**GY**	ET	CO

0032–0042   HUNSLET/SCHÖMA   0-4-0

Built: 1989–90 by Hunslet Engine Company at Leeds as 900 mm. gauge.
Rebuilt: 1993-94 by Schöma in Germany to 1435 mm. gauge.
Engine: Deutz of 270 kW (200 h.p.) at ???? rpm.
Transmission: Mechanical.   **Maximum Tractive Effort:**
Cont. Tractive Effort: **Power At Rail:**
Brake Force: **Dimensions:**
Weight: **Wheel Diameter:**
Design Speed: 50 km/h.   **Maximum Speed:** 50 km/h.
Fuel Capacity: **Train Brakes:** Air.
Train Supply: Not equipped.   **Multiple Working:** Not equipped.

0031	**Y**	ET	CO	FRANCES
0032	**Y**	ET	CO	ELISABETH
0033	**Y**	ET	CO	SILKE
0034	**Y**	ET	CO	AMANDA
0035	**Y**	ET	CO	MARY
0036	**Y**	ET	CO	LAWRENCE
0037	**Y**	ET	CO	LYDIE
0038	**Y**	ET	CO	JENNY
0039	**Y**	ET	CO	PACITA
0040	**Y**	ET	CO	JILL
0041	**Y**	ET	CO	KIM
0042	**Y**	ET	CO	NICOLE

ELECTRIC LOCOMOTIVES

9001–9113   BRUSH/ABB   Bo-Bo-Bo

Built: 1993–2001 by Brush Traction at Loughborough.
Supply System: 25 kV a.c. 50 Hz overhead.
Traction Motors: ABB 6PH.   **Maximum Tractive Effort:** 400 kN (90 000 lbf).
Continuous Rating: 5760 kW (7725 h.p.) giving a TE of 310 kN at 65 km/h.
Maximum Rail Power: **Multiple Working:** TDM system.
Brake Force: 50 t.   **Dimensions:** 22.01 x 2.97 x 4.20 m.
Weight: 132 t.   **Wheel Diameter:** 1090 mm.
Design Speed: 175 km/h.   **Maximum Speed:** 160 km/h.
Train Supply: Electric.   **Train Brakes:** Air.

CLASS 9/0. Mixed traffic locomotives.

9001	**ET**	ET	CO	LESLEY GARRETT
9002	**ET**	ET	CO	STUART BURROWS
9003	**ET**	ET	CO	BENJAMIN LUXON
9004	**ET**	ET	CO	VICTORIA DE LOS ANGELES
9005	**ET**	ET	CO	JESSYE NORMAN
9006	**ET**	ET	CO	REGINE CRESPIN
9007	**ET**	ET	CO	DAME JOAN SUTHERLAND
9008	**ET**	ET	CO	ELISABETH SODERSTROM
9009	**ET**	ET	CO	FRANÇOIS POLLET
9010	**ET**	ET	CO	JEAN-PHILLIPE COURTIS
9011	**ET**	ET	CO	JOSÉ VAN DAM
9012	**ET**	ET	CO	LUCIANO PAVAROTTI
9013	**ET**	ET	CO	MARIA CALLAS
9014	**ET**	ET	CO	LUCIA POPP
9015	**ET**	ET	CO	LÖTSCHBERG 1913
9016	**ET**	ET	CO	WILLARD WHITE
9017	**EG**	ET	CO	JOSÉ CARRERAS
9018	**ET**	ET	CO	WILHELMENA FERNANDEZ
9019	**ET**	ET	CO	MARIA EWING
9020	**ET**	ET	CO	Nicolai Ghiaurov
9021	**ET**	ET	CO	TERESA BERGANZA
9022	**ET**	ET	CO	DAME JANET BAKER
9023	**ET**	ET	CO	DAME ELISABETH LEGGE-SCHWARZKOPF
9024	**ET**	ET	CO	GOTTHARD 1882
9025	**ET**	ET	CO	JUNGFRAUJOCH 1912
9026	**ET**	ET	CO	FURKATUNNEL 1982
9027	**ET**	ET	CO	BARBARA HENDRICKS
9028	**ET**	ET	CO	DAME KIRI TE KANAWA
9029	**ET**	ET	CO	THOMAS ALLEN
9031	**ET**	ET	CO	
9032	**ET**	ET	CO	RENATA TEBALDI
9033	**ET**	ET	CO	MONTSERRAT CABALLE
9034	**ET**	ET	CO	MIRELLA FRENI
9035	**ET**	ET	CO	Nicolai Gedda

9036	**ET**	ET	CO	ALAIN FONDARY
9037	**ET**	ET	CO	GABRIEL BACQUIER
9038	**ET**	ET	CO	HILDEGARD BEHRENS
9040	**EG**	ET	CO	

CLASS 9/1. Freight Shuttle dedicated locomotives.

9101	**EG**	ET	CO
9102	**EG**	ET	CO
9103	**EG**	ET	CO
9104	**EG**	ET	CO
9105	**EG**	ET	CO
9106	**EG**	ET	CO
9107	**EG**	ET	CO
9108	**EG**	ET	CO
9109			
9110			
9111			
9112			
9113			

9201–9207   BRUSH/ADTRANZ   Bo-Bo-Bo

Built: 2001 by Brush Traction at Loughborough.
Supply System: 25 kV a.c. 50 Hz overhead.

Traction Motors:	**Maximum Tractive Effort:**
Continuous Rating: 7000 kW.	
Maximum Rail Power:	**Multiple Working:**
Brake Force:	**Dimensions:**
Weight:	**Wheel Diameter:**
Design Speed:	**Maximum Speed:**
Train Supply:	**Train Brakes:**

9201
9202
9203
9204
9205
9206
9207

2. LOCO-HAULED PASSENGER COACHING STOCK

INTRODUCTION

LAYOUT OF INFORMATION

Coaches are listed in numerical order of painted number in batches according to type.

Each coach entry is laid out as in the following example (former number column may be omitted where not applicable):

No.	Prev. No.	Notes	Livery	Owner	Operation	Depot/Location
2918	(40518)	*	**RP**	RT	*OR*	ZN

DETAILED INFORMATION & CODES

Under each type heading, the following details are shown:

- Diagram Code. This consists of the first three characters of the TOPS type code followed by two numbers which relate to the particular design of vehicle.
- 'Mark' of coach (see below).
- Descriptive text.
- Number of first class seats , standard class seats, lavatory compartments and wheelchair spaces shown as F/S nT nW respectively.
- Bogie type (see below).
- Additional features.
- ETH Index.

TOPS TYPE CODES

TOPS type codes are allocated to all coaching stock. For vehicles numbered in the passenger stock number series the code consists of:

(1) Two letters denoting the layout of the vehicle as follows:

AA	Gangwayed Corridor
AB	Gangwayed Corridor Brake
AC	Gangwayed Open (2+2 seating)
AD	Gangwayed Open (2+1 seating)
AE	Gangwayed Open Brake
AF	Gangwayed Driving Open Brake
AG	Micro-Buffet
AH	Brake Micro-Buffet
AI	As 'AC' but with drop-head buckeye and gangway at one end only

AJ Restaurant Buffet with Kitchen
AK Kitchen Car
AL As 'AC' but with disabled person's toilet (Mark 4 only)
AN Miniature Buffet
AP Pullman First with Kitchen
AQ Pullman Parlour First
AR Pullman Brake First
AS Sleeping Car
AT Royal Train Coach
AU Sleeping Car with Pantry
AX Generator Van (1000 V d.c.)
AZ Special Saloon
GF DMU/EMU/Mark 4 Barrier Vehicle
AX Generator Van (415 V a.c three-phase)
NM Sandite Coach

(2) A digit denoting the class of passenger accommodation:

1	First	4	Unclassified
2	Standard (formerly second)	5	None
3	Composite (first & standard)		

(3) A suffix relating to the build of coach.

1	Mark 1	C	Mark 2C	G	Mark 3 or 3A
Z	Mark 2	D	Mark 2D	H	Mark 3B
A	Mark 2A	E	Mark 2E	J	Mark 4
B	Mark 2B	F	Mark 2F		

OPERATING CODES

Operating codes used by train company operating staff (and others) to denote vehicle types in general. These are shown in parentheses adjacent to TOPS type codes. Letters useD are:

B	Brake	K	Side corridor with lavatory
C	Composite	O	Open
F	First Class	S	Standard Class (formerly second)

Various other letters are in use and the meaning of these can be ascertained by referring to the titles at the head of each type.

Readers should note the distinction between an SO (Open Standard) and a TSO (Tourist Open Standard) The former has 2+1 seating layout, whilst the latter has 2+2.

BOGIE TYPES

BR Mark 1 (BR1). Double bolster leaf spring bogie. Generally 90 m.p.h., but BR1 bogies may be permitted to run at 100 m.p.h. with special maintenance. Weight: 6.1 t.

BR Mark 2 (BR2). Single bolster leaf-spring bogie used on certain types of non-passenger stock and suburban stock (all now withdrawn). Weight: 5.3 t.

COMMONWEALTH (C). Heavy, cast steel coil spring bogie. 100 m.p.h. Weight: 6.75 t.

B4. Coil spring fabricated bogie. Generally 100 m.p.h., but B4 bogies may be permitted to run at 110 m.p.h. with special maintenance. Weight: 5.2 t.

B5. Heavy duty version of B4. 100 m.p.h. Weight: 5.3 t.

B5 (SR). A bogie originally used on Southern Region EMUs, similar in design to B5. Now also used on locomotive hauled coaches. 100 m.p.h.

BT10. A fabricated bogie designed for 125 m.p.h. Air suspension.

T4. A 125 m.p.h. bogie designed by BREL (now Adtranz).

BT41. Fitted to Mark 4 vehicles, designed by SIG in Switzerland. At present limited to 125 m.p.h., but designed for 140 m.p.h.

BRAKES

Air braking is now standard on British main line trains. Vehicles with other equipment are denoted:

v	Vacuum braked.
x	Dual braked (air and vacuum).

HEATING

Electric heating is now standard on British main-line trains. Certain coaches for use on charter services may in addition also have steam heating facilities, or be steam heated only.

PUBLIC ADDRESS

It is assumed all coaches are now fitted with public address equipment, although certain stored vehicles may not have this feature. In addition, it is assumed all vehicles with a conductor's compartment have public address transmission facilities, as have catering vehicles.

COOKING EQUIPMENT

It is assumed that Mark 1 catering vehicles have gas powered cooking equipment, whilst Mark 2, 3 and 4 catering vehicles have electric powered cooking equipment unless stated otherwise.

ADDITIONAL FEATURE CODES

d	Secondary door locking.
dg	Driver–Guard communication equipment.
f	Facelifted or fluorescent lighting.
k	Composition brake blocks (instead of cast iron).
n	Day/night lighting.
p	Public telephone.
pg	Public address transmission and driver-guard communication.

pt   Public address transmission facility.
q   Catering staff to shore telephone.
w   Wheelchair space.
z   Disabled persons' toilet.

Standard class coaches with wheelchair space also have one tip-up seat per space.

NOTES ON ETH INDICES

The sum of ETH indices in a train must not be more than the ETS index of the locomotive. The normal voltage on British trains is 1000 V. Suffix 'X' denotes 600 amp wiring instead of 400 amp. Trains whose ETH index is higher than 66 must be formed completely of 600 amp wired stock. Class 55 locomotives cannot provide a consistent electric train supply for Mark 2E or 2D FO 3192/3202, FK 13585–13607 & BFK 17163–17172. Class 33 locomotives cannot provide a suitable electric train supply for Mark 2D, Mark 2E, Mark 2F, Mark 3, Mark 3A, Mark 3B or Mark 4 coaches.

BUILD DETAILS

Lot Numbers
Vehicles ordered under the auspices of BR were allocated a lot (batch) number when ordered and these are quoted in class headings and sub-headings.

Builders
These are shown in class headings. Abbreviations used are found in section 6.8.

Information on sub-contracting works which built parts of vehicles e.g.the underframes etc. is not shown.

In addition to the above, certain vintage Pullman cars were built or rebuilt at the following works:

Metropolitan Carriage & Wagon Company, Birmingham (Now Alstom)
Midland Carriage & Wagon Company, Birmingham
Pullman Car Company, Preston Park, Brighton

Conversions have also been carried out at the Railway Technical centre, Derby, BR Salisbury Depot and Blakes Fabrications, Edinburgh.

Vehicle Numbers
Where a coach has been renumbered, the former number is shown in parentheses. If a coach has been renumbered more than once, the original number is shown first in parentheses, followed by the most recent previous number. Where the former number of a coach due to be converted or renumbered is known and the conversion and/or renumbering has not yet taken place, the coach is listed under both current number (with depot allocation) and under new number (without allocation).

Numbering Systems
Seven different numbering systems were in use on BR. These were the BR series, the four pre-nationalisation companies' series', the Pullman Car Company's series and the UIC (International Union of Railways) series. BR number

series coaches, former Pullman Car Company series and UIC series coaches are listed separately. There is also a separate listing of 'Saloon' type vehicles which are registered to run on the Railtrack network. Please note the Mark 2 Pullman vehicles were ordered after the Pullman Car Company had been nationalised and are therefore numbered in the BR series.

THE DEVELOPMENT OF BR STANDARD COACHES

The standard BR coach built from 1951 to 1963 was the Mark 1. This type features a separate underframe and body. The underframe is normally 64 ft. 6 in. long, but certain vehicles were built on shorter (57 ft.) frames. Tungsten lighting was standard and until 1961, BR Mark 1 bogies were generally provided. In 1959 Lot No. 30525 (TSO) appeared with fluorescent lighting and melamine interior panels, and from 1961 onwards Commonwealth bogies were fitted in an attempt to improve the quality of ride which became very poor when the tyre profiles on the wheels of the BR1 bogies became worn. Later batches of TSO and BSO retained the features of Lot No. 30525, but compartment vehicles – whilst utilising melamine panelling in standard class – still retained tungsten lighting. Wooden interior finish was retained in first class vehicles where the only change was to fluorescent lighting in open vehicles (except Lot No. 30648, which had tungsten lighting). In later years many Mark 1 coaches had BR 1 bogies replaced by B4.

In 1964, a new prototype train was introduced. Known as 'XP64', it featured new seat designs, pressure heating & ventilation, aluminium compartment doors and corridor partitions, foot pedal operated toilets and B4 bogies. The vehicles were built on standard Mark 1 underframes. Folding exterior doors were fitted, but these proved troublesome and were later replaced with hinged doors. All XP64 coaches have been withdrawn, but some have been preserved.

The prototype Mark 2 vehicle (W 13252) was produced in 1963. This was an FK of semi-integral construction and had pressure heating & ventilation, tungsten lighting, and was mounted on B4 bogies. This vehicle has been preserved by the National Railway Museum and is currently on display at Swindon. The production build was similar, but wider windows were used. The TSO and SO vehicles used a new seat design similar to that in the XP64 and fluorescent lighting was provided. Interior finish reverted to wood. Mark 2 vehicles were built from 1964–66.

The Mark 2A design, built 1967–68, incorporated the remainder of the features first used in the XP64 coaches, i.e. foot pedal operated toilets (except BSO), new first class seat design, aluminium compartment doors and partitions together with fluorescent lighting in first class compartments. Folding gangway doors (lime green coloured) were used instead of the traditional one-piece variety.

The following list summarises the changes made in the later Mark 2 variants:

Mark 2B: Wide wrap around doors at vehicle ends, no centre doors, slightly longer body. In standard class, one toilet at each end instead of two at one end as previously. Red folding gangway doors.

Mark 2C: Lowered ceiling with twin strips of fluorescent lighting and ducting for air conditioning, but air conditioning not fitted.

Mark 2D: Air conditioning. No opening top-lights in windows.

Mark 2E: Smaller toilets with luggage racks opposite. Fawn folding gangway doors.

Mark 2F: Plastic interior panels. Inter-City 70 type seats. Modified air conditioning system.

The Mark 3 design has BT10 bogies, is 75 ft. (23 m.) long and is of fully integral construction with Inter-City 70 type seats. Gangway doors were yellow (red in RFB) when new, although these are being changed on refurbishment. Loco-hauled coaches are classified Mark 3A, Mark 3 being reserved for HST trailers. A new batch of FO and BFO, classified Mark 3B, was built in 1985 with Advanced Passenger Train-style seating and revised lighting. The last vehicles in the Mark 3 series were the driving brake vans built for West Coast Main Line services.

The Mark 4 design was built by Metro-Cammell for use on the East Coast Main Line after electrification and features a body profile suitable for tilting trains, although tilt is not fitted, and is not intended to be. This design is suitable for 140 m.p.h. running, although is restricted to 125 m.p.h. pending installation of a more advanced signalling system on the route. The bogies for these coaches were built by SIG in Switzerland and are designated BT41. Power operated sliding plug exterior doors are standard.

2.1. BR NUMBER SERIES STOCK

AJ11 (RF)   RESTAURANT FIRST

Dia. AJ106. Mark 1. 325 spent most of its life as a Royal Train vehicle and was numbered 2907 for a time. Built with Commonwealth bogies, but B5 bogies substituted on 325. 24/–. ETH 2.

Lot No. 30633 Swindon 1961. 42.5 t C, 41t B5.

324	x	**CH**	NY	*ON*	NY
325		**PC**	VS	*ON*	SL

AP1Z (PFK)   PULLMAN FIRST WITH KITCHEN

Dia. AP101. Mark 2. Pressure Ventilated. 18/– 2T. B5 bogies. ETH 6.

Lot No. 30755 Derby 1966. 40t.

504	**PC**	WC	*ON*	CS	ULLSWATER
506	**PC**	WC	*ON*	CS	WINDERMERE

AQ1Z (PFP)   PULLMAN PARLOUR FIRST

Dia. AQ101. Mark 2. Pressure Ventilated. 36/– 2T. B4 bogies. ETH 5.

Lot No. 30754 Derby 1966. 35 t.

546	**PC**	WC	*ON*	CS	CONISTON WATER
548	**PC**	WC	*ON*	CS	GRASMERE
549	**PC**	WC	*ON*	CS	BASSENTHWAITE LAKE
550	**PC**	WC	*ON*	CS	RYDAL WATER
551	**PC**	WC	*ON*	CS	BUTTERMERE
552	**PC**	WC	*ON*	CS	ENNERDALE WATER
553	**PC**	WC	*ON*	CS	CRUMMOCK WATER

AR1Z (PFB)   PULLMAN BRAKE FIRST

Dia. AR101. Mark 2. Pressure Ventilated. 30/– 2T. B4 bogies. ETH 4.

Lot No. 30753 Derby 1966. 35 t.

586	**PC**	WC	*ON*		CS	DERWENTWATER

AJ21 (RG)   GRIDDLE CAR

Dia. AJ210. Mark 1. Rebuilt from RF. –/30. B5 bogies. ETH 2.

This vehicle was numbered DB975878 for a time when in departmental service for BR.

Lot No. 30013 Doncaster 1952. Rebuilt Wolverton 1965. 40 t.

1105	(302)	v	**G**	MH	*ON*	RL

AJ1F (RFB)   BUFFET OPEN FIRST

Dia. AJ104. Mark 2F. Air conditioned. Converted 1988–9/91 at BREL, Derby from Mark 2F FOs. 1200/1/3/6/11/14–17/20/21/50/2/5/6/9 have Stones equipment, others have Temperature Ltd. 25/– 1T 1W (except 1217 and 1253 which are 26/– 1T). B4 bogies. p. q. d. ETH 6X.

1200/3/6/11/14/16/20/52/5/6. Lot No. 30845 Derby 1973. 33 t.
1201/4/5/7/8/10/12/13/15/17–9/21/50/1/4/7/9. Lot No. 30859 Derby 1973–74. 33 t.
1202/9/53/8. Lot No. 30873 Derby 1974–75. 33 t.

† Fitted with new m.a. sets.

1200	(3287, 6459)	†	V	H	VX	MA
1201	(3361, 6445)	†	V	H	VX	MA
1202	(3436, 6456)	†	V	H	VX	MA
1203	(3291)	†		H	VX	MA
1204	(3401)	†	V	H	VX	MA
1205	(3329, 6438)	†	V	H	VX	MA
1206	(3319)	†	V	H	VX	MA
1207	(3328, 6422)	†	V	H	VX	MA
1208	(3393)		V	H	VX	MA
1209	(3437, 6457)	†	V	H	VX	MA
1210	(3405, 6462)	†.	V	H	VX	MA
1211	(3305)			H	VX	MA
1212	(3427, 6453)	†	V	H	VX	MA
1213	(3419)	†	V	H	VX	MA
1214	(3317, 6433)			H	VX	MA
1215	(3377)			H	VX	MA
1216	(3302)	†	V	H	VX	MA
1217	(3357, 6444)		SS	H	SR	IS
1218	(3332)		AR	H	AR	NC
1219	(3418)		AR	H	AR	NC
1220	(3315, 6432)	†	V	H	VX	MA
1221	(3371)			H	VX	MA
1250	(3372)	†	V	H	VX	MA
1251	(3383)	†	V	H	VX	MA
1252	(3280)	†	V	H	VX	MA
1253	(3432)	†	V	H	VX	MA
1254	(3391)	†	V	H	VX	MA
1255	(3284)	†	V	H	VX	MA
1256	(3296)	†		H	VX	MA
1258	(3322)	†	V	H	VX	MA
1259	(3439)	†	V	H	VX	MA
1260	(3378)	†	V	H	VX	MA

AK51 (RKB)   KITCHEN BUFFET

Dia. AK502. Mark 1. No seats. B5 bogies. ETH 1.

Lot No. 30624 Cravens 1960–61. 41 t.

1566	**M**	VS	ON	CP

AJ41 (RBR)   RESTAURANT BUFFET

Dia. AJ403. Mark 1. Built with 23 loose chairs (Dia. AJ402). All remaining vehicles refurbished with 23 fixed polypropylene chairs and fluorescent lighting. ETH 2 (2X*).

r Further refurbished with 21 chairs, payphone, wheelchair space and carpets (Dia. AJ416).
s Modified for use as servery vehicle with 14 chairs (1680) or 8 chairs (1698).

1653–1699. Lot No. 30628 Pressed Steel 1960–61. Commonwealth bogies. 39 t.
1730. Lot No. 30512 BRCW 1960–61. B5 bogies. 37t.

1653			RS		FK	1691	r	**G**	H		CP
1658		**BG**	RS	*ON*	BN	1692	xr	**CH**	RV	*ON*	CP
1659	x	**PC**	WT	*ON*	RL	1696		**G**	RS	*ON*	BN
1671	x*	**CC**	RS	*ON*	BN	1697	r		H		CP
1674			RS	*SO*	ZA	1698	s	**WV**	RS	*ON*	BN
1679		**G**	RS	*ON*	BN	1699	r		H		CP
1680	x*s	**SS**	WV	*ON*	BN	1730	x	**M**	BK	*ON*	BT
1683	r	**FT**	RV	*ON*	CP						

AN21 (RMB)   MINIATURE BUFFET CAR

Dia. AN203. Mark 1. –/44 2T. These vehicles are basically an open standard with two full window spaces removed to accommodate a buffet counter, and four seats removed to allow for a stock cupboard. All remaining vehicles now have fluorescent lighting. All vehicles have Commonwealth bogies except 1850 (B5). ETH 3.

1813–1832. Lot No. 30520 Wolverton 1960. 38t.
1840–1850. Lot No. 30507 Wolverton 1960. 37 t (1850 is 36 t).
1859–1863. Lot No. 30670 Wolverton 1961–62. 38t.
1871–1882. Lot No. 30702 Wolverton 1962. 38t.

1842/50/71 have been been refurbished and are fitted with a microwave oven and payphone. Dia. AN208.

1813	x	**CC**	RS	*ON*	BN	1860	x	**M**	WC	*ON*	CS
1832	x	**BG**	RS	*ON*	BN	1861	x	**M**	WC	*ON*	TM
1840	v	**G**	MH	*ON*	RL	1863	x	**CH**	RV	*ON*	CP
1842			H		ZN	1871	x		H		CP
1850			H		CP	1882	x	**M**	WC	*ON*	CS
1859	x	**M**	BK	*ON*	BT						

AJ41 (RBR)   RESTAURANT BUFFET

Dia. AJ414. Mark 1. This vehicle was built as an unclassified restaurant (RU). It was rebuilt with buffet counter and 23 fixed polypropylene chairs (RBS), then further refurbished by fitting fluorescent lighting and reclassified RBR. B4/B5 bogies. ETH 2X.

Lot No. 30575 Swindon 1960. 36.5 t.

1953   **M** VS   *ON*   CP

AS41   FIRST CLASS SLEEPING CAR

Dia. AS101. Mark 1. Pressure Ventilated. 11 single-berth compartments plus an attendant's compartment. ETH 3 (3X*).

2013. Lot No. 30159 Wolverton 1958. B5 bogies. 39t.
2127. Lot No. 30687 Wolverton 1961. Commonwealth bogies. 41t.

2013 was numbered 2908 for a time when in use with the Royal Train.

2013   **M** FS   SZ | 2127 *** M** GS   CS

AU51   CHARTER TRAIN STAFF COACHES

Dia. AU501. Mark 1. Converted from BCKs in 1988. Commonwealth bogies. ETH 2.

Lot No. 30732 Derby 1964. 37 t.

2833 (21270) **BG** RS *ON*   BN | 2834 (21267)   **WV** RS *SO*   ZA

AT5G   HM THE QUEEN'S SALOON

Dia. AT525. Mark 3. Converted from a FO built 1972. Consists of a lounge, bedroom and bathroom for HM The Queen, and a combined bedroom and bathroom for the Queen's dresser. One entrance vestibule has double doors. Air conditioned. BT10 bogies. ETH 9X.

Lot No. 30886 Wolverton 1977. 36 t.

2903 (11001)   **RP** RK *RP*   ZN

AT5G   HRH THE DUKE OF EDINBURGH'S SALOON

Dia. AT526. Mark 3. Converted from a TSO built 1972. Consists of a combined lounge/dining room, a bedroom and a shower room for the Duke, a kitchen and a valet's bedroom and bathroom. Air conditioned. BT10 bogies. ETH 15X.

Lot No. 30887 Wolverton 1977. 36 t.

2904 (12001)   **RP** RK *RP*   ZN

AT5B   ROYAL HOUSEHOLD COUCHETTES

Dia. AT527. Mark 2B. Converted from a BFK built 1969. Consists of luggage accommodation, guard's compartment, 350 kW diesel generator and staff sleeping accommodation. Pressure ventilated. B5 bogies. ETH 5X.

Lot No. 30888 Wolverton 1977. 46 t.

2905 (14105)   **RP** RK   ZN

Dia. AT528. Mark 2B. Converted from a BFK built 1969. Consists of luggage accommodation, guards compartment and staff accommodation. Pressure ventilated. B5 bogies. ETH 4X.

Lot No. 30889 Wolverton 1977. 35.5t.

2906 (14112)   **RP** RK   ZN

AT5G   ROYAL HOUSEHOLD SLEEPING CARS

Dia. AT531. Mark 3A. Built to similar specification as SLE 10646–732. 12 sleeping compartments for use of Royal Household with a fixed lower berth and a hinged upper berth. 2T plus shower room. Air conditioned. BT10 bogies. ETH 11X.

Lot No. 31002 Derby/Wolverton 1985. 42.5 t (44 t*).

2914		**RP**	RK		ZN
2915	*	**RP**	RK	*RP*	ZN

AT5G   ROYAL KITCHEN/DINING CAR

Dia AT537. Mark 3. Converted from HST TRUK built 1976. Large kitchen retained, but dining area modified for Royal use seating up to 14 at central table(s). Air conditioned. BT10 bogies. ETH 13X.

Lot No. 31059 Wolverton 1988. 43t.

2916 (40512)   **RP** RK *RP*   ZN

AT5G   ROYAL HOUSEHOLD KITCHEN/DINING CAR

Dia. AT539. Mark 3. Converted from HST TRUK built 1977. Large kitchen retained and dining area slightly modified with seating for 22 Royal Household members. Air conditioned. BT10 bogies. ETH 13X.

Lot No. 31084 Wolverton 1990. 43t.

2917 (40514)   **RP** RK *RP*   ZN

AT5G   ROYAL HOUSEHOLD CARS

Dia. AT538 (AT540*). Mark 3. Converted from HST TRUKs built 1976/7. Air conditioned. BT10 bogies. ETH 10X.

Lot Nos. 31083 (31085*) Wolverton 1989. 41.05t.

2918	(40515)		**RP**	RK	*RP*	ZN
2919	(40518)	*	**RP**	RK	*RP*	ZN

AT5B   ROYAL HOUSEHOLD COUCHETTES

Dia. AT536. Mark 2B. Converted from BFK built 1969. Consists of luggage accommodation, guard's compartment, workshop area, 350 kW diesel generator and staff sleeping accommodation. B5 bogies. ETH2X.

Lot No. 31044 Wolverton 1986. 48t.

2920   (14109, 17109)   **RP** RK *RP*   ZN

Dia. AT541. Mark 2B. Converted from BFK built 1969. Consists of luggage accommodation, kitchen, brake control equipment and staff accommodation. B5 bogies. ETH7X.

Lot No. 31086 Wolverton 1990. 41.5t.

2921   (14107, 17107)   **RP** RK *RP*   ZN

AT5G HRH THE PRINCE OF WALES'S SLEEPING CAR

Dia. AT534. Mark 3B. BT10 bogies. Air conditioned.ETH 7X.

Lot No. 31035 Derby/Wolverton 1987.

2922   **RP** RK *RP*   ZN

AT5G   HRH THE PRINCE OF WALES'S SALOON

Dia. AT535. Mark 3B. BT10 bogies. Air conditioned. ETH 6X.

Lot No. 31036 Derby/Wolverton 1987.

2923   **RP** RK *RP*   ZN

AD11 (FO)   OPEN FIRST

Dia. AD103. Mark 1. 42/– 2T. ETH 3. Many now fitted with table lamps.

3063–3069. Lot No. 30169 Doncaster 1955. B4 bogies. 33t.
3096–3100. Lot No. 30576 BRCW 1959. B4 bogies. 33t.

3064 and 3068 were numbered DB 975607 and DB 975606 for a time when in departmental service for British Rail.

3063	**BG**	VS		SL	3096	x **M**	BK *ON*	BT
3064	**BG**	VS		SL	3097	**WV**	RS *ON*	BN
3066	**RB**	VS	*ON*	CP	3098	x **CH**	RV *ON*	CP
3068	**RB**	VS	*ON*	CP	3100	x **CC**	RS *ON*	BN
3069	**RB**	VS	*ON*	CP				

Later design with fluorescent lighting, aluminium window frames and Commonwealth bogies.

3105–3128. Lot No. 30697 Swindon 1962–63. 36t.
3130–3150. Lot No. 30717 Swindon 1963. 36t.

3128/36/41/3/4/6/7/8 were renumbered 1058/60/3/5/6/8/9/70 when reclassified RUO, then 3600/5/8/9/2/6/4/10 when declassified, but have since regained their original numbers.

3105	x	**M**	WC *ON*	CS	3114		**G**	RS *ON*	BN
3107	x	**BG**	RS *ON*	BN	3115	x	**BG**	RS *ON*	BN
3110	x	**CC**	RS *ON*	BN	3117	x	**M**	WC *ON*	CS
3112	x	**CH**	RV *ON*	CP	3119	x	**CC**	RS *ON*	BN
3113	x	**M**	WC *ON*	CS	3120		**WV**	RS *ON*	BN

3121		**WV**	RS	*ON*	BN			
3122	x	**CH**	RV	*ON*	CP			
3123		**G**	RS	*ON*	BN			
3124		**G**	RS	*ON*	BN			
3125		**RB**	VS	*ON*	CP			
3127		**G**	RS	*ON*	BN			
3128	x	**M**	WC	*ON*	CS			
3130	v	**M**	WC	*ON*	CS			
3131	x	**CC**	RS	*ON*	BN			
3132	x	**CC**	RS	*ON*	BN			
3133	x	**CC**	RS	*ON*	BN			

3136			RS	*SO*	ZA
3140	x	**CH**	RV	*ON*	CP
3141		**WV**	RS	*ON*	BN
3143			FS		CS
3144	x	**CC**	RS	*ON*	BN
3146		**WV**	RS	*ON*	BN
3147		**WV**	RS	*ON*	BN
3148		**BG**	RS	*ON*	BN
3149			RS	*ON*	BN
3150		**G**	RS	*ON*	BN

AD1D (FO)   OPEN FIRST

Dia. AD105. Mark 2D. Air conditioned. 3172–88 have Stones equipment. 3192/3202 have Temperature Ltd. 42/– 2T. B4 bogies. ETH 5.

Lot No. 30821 Derby 1971–72. 32.5t.

3172		RK	*SO*	DY
3174	**VN**	VS	*ON*	CP
3178		VS		CP
3181	**RB**	RV	*ON*	CP
3182	**VN**	VS	*ON*	CP

3186		RS		DY
3187		E		CL
3188	**RB**	RV	*ON*	CP
3192		RK	*SO*	DY
3202		E		CL

AD1E (FO)   OPEN FIRST

Dia. AD106. Mark 2E. Air conditioned. Stones equipment. 42/– 2T (41/– 2T 1W w). B4 bogies. ETH 5.

* Seats removed to accommodate catering module. 40F 1T.
r Refurbished with new seats.
u Fitted with power supply for Mk. 1 RBR.

3255 was numbered 3525 for a time when fitted with a pantry.

Lot No. 30843 Derby 1972–73. 32.5t.

3223			RV		CP
3225			E		KN
3226			E		KN
3228	du		H		ZN
3229	d		H		ZN
3230			RK	*SO*	DY
3231			RA		CP
3232	dr	**FG**	H	*GW*	OO
3234	w		VS		CP
3235	u		H		PY
3237			RS		FK
3239			VS		CP
3240		**CH**	RV	*ON*	CP
3241	dr	**FG**	H	*GW*	OO
3242	wu		H		PY
3244	d		H		ZN

3246	w		RA		CP
3247		**VN**	VS	*ON*	CP
3248			RK	*SO*	DY
3251	*		RS		FK
3252	w		H		PY
3255	dr	**FG**	H	*GW*	OO
3256	w		H		PY
3257	w		VS		CP
3258	n		E		KN
3261	dw		H		ZN
3267		**VN**	VS	*ON*	CP
3268			RV		CP
3269	dr	**FG**	H	*GW*	OO
3270			VS		CP
3272			VS		CP
3273		**VN**	VS	*ON*	CP

3275   **VN** VS *ON*   CP |

AD1F (FO)   OPEN FIRST

Dia. AD107. Mark 2F. Air conditioned. 3277–3318/58–81 have Stones equipment, others have Temperature Ltd. 42/– 2T. All now refurbished with power-operated vestibule doors, new panels and new seat trim. B4 bogies. d. ETH 5X.

3277–3318. Lot No. 30845 Derby 1973. 33t.
3325–3428. Lot No. 30859 Derby 1973–74. 33t.
3429–3438. Lot No. 30873 Derby 1974–75. 33t.

r Further refurbished with table lamps, modified seats with burgundy seat trim and new m.a. sets.
s Further refurbished with table lamps and modified seats with burgundy seat trim.
u Fitted with power supply for Mk. 1 RBR.

3403 was numbered 6450 for a time when declassified.

No.						No.					
3277		**AR**	H	*AR*	NC	3352	r	**V**	H	*VW*	OY
3278	r	**V**	H	*VW*	OY	3353	s	**V**	H	*VW*	OY
3279	u	**AR**	H	*AR*	NC	3354	s	**V**	H	*VW*	OY
3285	s	**V**	H	*VW*	OY	3356	r	**V**	H	*VW*	OY
3290		**AR**	H	*AR*	NC	3358		**AR**	H	*AR*	NC
3292			H	*AR*	NC	3359	s	**V**	H	*VW*	OY
3293			H		NC	3360	s	**V**	H	*VW*	OY
3295		**AR**	H	*AR*	NC	3362	s	**V**	H	*VW*	OY
3299	r	**V**	H	*VW*	OY	3363	s	**V**	H	*VW*	OY
3300	s	**V**	H	*VW*	OY	3364	r	**V**	H	*VW*	OY
3303		**AR**	H	*AR*	NC	3366	s	**V**	H	*VW*	OY
3304	r	**V**	H	*VW*	OY	3368		**AR**	H	*AR*	NC
3309			H	*AR*	NC	3369	s	**V**	H	*VW*	OY
3312			H		NC	3373			H	*AR*	NC
3313	r	**V**	H	*VW*	OY	3374			H		NC
3314	r	**V**	H	*VW*	OY	3375		**AR**	H	*AR*	NC
3318			H	*AR*	NC	3379	u	**AR**	H	*AR*	NC
3325	r	**V**	H	*VW*	OY	3381			H	*AR*	NC
3326	r	**V**	H	*VW*	OY	3384	r	**V**	H	*VW*	OY
3330	r	**V**	H	*VW*	OY	3385	r	**V**	H	*VW*	OY
3331		**AR**	H	*AR*	NC	3386	r	**V**	H	*VW*	OY
3333	r	**V**	H	*VW*	OY	3387	s	**V**	H	*VW*	OY
3334		**AR**	H	*AR*	NC	3388		**AR**	H	*AR*	NC
3336	u	**AR**	H	*AR*	NC	3389	s	**V**	H	*VW*	OY
3337	r	**V**	H	*VW*	OY	3390	r	**V**	H	*VW*	OY
3338	u	**AR**	H	*AR*	NC	3392	r	**V**	H	*VW*	OY
3340	r	**V**	H	*VW*	OY	3395	r	**V**	H	*VW*	OY
3344	r	**V**	H	*VW*	OY	3397	r	**V**	H	*VW*	OY
3345	r	**V**	H	*VW*	OY	3399	u	**AR**	H	*AR*	NC
3348	r	**V**	H	*VW*	OY	3400		**AR**	H	*AR*	NC
3350	r	**V**	H	*VW*	OY	3402	s	**V**	H	*VW*	OY
3351		**AR**	H	*AR*	NC	3403	s	**V**	H	*VW*	OY

3408	s	**V**	H	*VW*	OY	3426	r	**V**	H	*VW*	OY
3411	s	**V**	H	*VW*	OY	3428	s	**V**	H	*VW*	OY
3414		**AR**	H	*AR*	NC	3429	r	**V**	H	*VW*	OY
3416			H	*AR*	NC	3431	r	**V**	H	*VW*	OY
3417		**AR**	H	*AR*	NC	3433	r	**V**	H	*VW*	OY
3424		**AR**	H	*AR*	NC	3434	s	**V**	H	*VW*	OY
3425	s	**V**	H	*VW*	OY	3438	s	**V**	H	*VW*	OY

AG1E (FO (T))   OPEN FIRST (PANTRY)

Dia. AG101. Mark 2E. Air conditioned. Converted from FO. Fitted with pantry containing microwave oven and space for a trolley. 36/– 1T. B4 bogies. p. d. ETH 5X.

Lot No. 30843 Derby 1972–73. 32.5t.

3520	(3253)		H		ZN	3523	(3238)	H	ZN
3521	(3271)	**AR**	H	*AR*	NC	3524	(3254)	H	IS
3522	(3236)		H		ZN				

AC21 (TSO)   OPEN STANDARD

Dia. AC204. Mark 1. These vehicles have 2+2 seating and are classified TSO ('Tourist second open'–a former LNER designation). –/64 2T. ETH 4.

3766. Lot No. 30079 York 1953. Commonwealth bogies (originally built with BR Mark 1 bogies). This coach has narrower seats than later vehicles. 36 t.
4198. Lot No. 30172 York 1956. BR Mark 1 bogies. 33t.

3766	x	**M**	WC	*ON*	CS	4198	v	**CH**	NY	*ON*	NY

AD21 (SO)   OPEN STANDARD

Dia. AD201. Mark 1. These vehicles have 2+1 seating and were often used as second class dining cars when new. –/48 2T. BR Mark 1 bogies. ETH 4.

4786. Lot No. 30376 York 1957. 33t.
4817. Lot No. 30473 BRCW 1957–59. 33t.

4786	v	**CH**	NY	*ON*	NY	4817	v	**CH**	NY	*ON*	NY

AC21 (TSO)   OPEN STANDARD

Dia. AC201. Mark 1. These vehicles are a development of Dia. AC204 with fluorescent lighting and modified design of seat headrest. Built with BR Mark 1 bogies. –/64 2T. ETH 4.

4831–4836. Lot No. 30506 Wolverton 1959. Commonwealth bogies. 33t.
4849–4880. Lot No. 30525 Wolverton 1959–60. B4 bogies. 33t.

4831	x	**M**	BK	*ON*	BT	4856	x	**M**	BK	*ON*	BT
4832	x	**M**	BK	*ON*	BT	4866		**RR**	H	*CA*	CF
4836	x	**M**	BK	*ON*	BT	4873		**RR**	H		CP
4849		**RR**	H	*CA*	CF	4875		**RR**	H	*CA*	CF
4854		**RR**	H	*CA*	CF	4876		**RR**	H	*CA*	CF

4880   **RR** H *CA* CF |

Lot No. 30646 Wolverton 1961. Built with Commonwealth bogies, but BR
Mark 1 bogies substituted by the SR on 4902/5/12/15/16. All now rebogied.
34 t B4, 36 t C.

4902	x B4	**CH**	RV	*ON*	CP	4915	x B4	**CC**	RS	*ON*	BN
4905	x C	**M**	WC	*ON*	TM	4916	x B4	**CC**	RS	*ON*	BN
4912	x C	**M**	WC	*ON*	CS	4917	x C	**RR**	H		CP

Lot No. 30690 Wolverton 1961–62. Commonwealth bogies and aluminium
window frames. 37 t.

4925		**G**	RS	*ON*	BN	4996	x	**CC**	RS	*ON*	BN
4927	x	**CH**	RV	*ON*	CP	4998		**BG**	RS	*ON*	BN
4931	v	**M**	WC	*ON*	CS	4999		**BG**	RS	*ON*	BN
4938		**BG**	RS	*ON*	BN	5002		**WR**	RS	*ON*	BN
4939			RS	*SO*	ZA	5005		**BG**	RS	*ON*	BN
4940	x	**M**	WC	*ON*	CS	5007		**G**	RS	*ON*	BN
4946	x	**CC**	RS	*ON*	BN	5008	x	**CC**	RS	*ON*	BN
4949		**BG**	RS	*ON*	BN	5009	x	**CH**	RV	*ON*	CP
4951	x	**M**	WC	*ON*	CS	5023		**G**	RS	*ON*	BN
4954	v	**M**	WC	*ON*	CS	5025	x	**CH**	RV	*ON*	CP
4956		**BG**	RS	*ON*	BN	5027		**G**	RS	*ON*	BN
4958	v	**M**	WC	*ON*	CS	5028	x	**M**	BK	*ON*	BT
4959		**BG**	RS	*ON*	BN	5029	x	**CH**	RV	*ON*	CP
4960	x	**M**	WC	*ON*	TM	5030	x	**CH**	RV	*ON*	CP
4963	x	**CH**	RV	*ON*	CP	5032	x	**M**	WC	*ON*	CS
4973	x	**M**	WC	*ON*	TM	5033	x	**M**	WC	*ON*	CS
4977		**G**	RS	*ON*	BN	5035	x	**M**	WC	*ON*	CS
4984	v	**M**	WC	*ON*	CS	5037		**G**	RS	*ON*	BN
4986		**G**	RS	*ON*	BN	5040	x	**CH**	RV	*ON*	CP
4991		**BG**	RS	*ON*	BN	5042	x		RS		FK
4994	x	**M**	WC	*ON*	CS	5044	x	**M**	WC	*ON*	CS

AC2Z (TSO)   OPEN STANDARD

Dia. AC205. Mark 2. Pressure ventilated. –/64 2T. B4 bogies. ETH 4.

Lot No. 30751 Derby 1965–67. 32 t.

5125	v	**G**	MH	*ON*	RL	5177	v	**RR**	H		TM
5132	v	**LN**	H		LT	5179	v	**RR**	H		TM
5135	v	**RR**	H		LT	5180	v	**RR**	H		LT
5148	v	**RR**	H		TM	5183	v	**RR**	H		TM
5154	v	**LN**	H		LT	5186	v	**RR**	H		TM
5156	v	**RR**	H		LT	5191	v	**CH**	H	*ON*	TM
5157	v	**RR**	H		TM	5193	v	**LN**	H		TM
5158	v	**RR**	H		LT	5194	v	**RR**	H		TM
5161	v	**RR**	H		LT	5198	v	**CH**	H	*ON*	TM
5163	v	**RR**	H		LT	5200	v	**G**	MH	*ON*	RL
5167	v	**RR**	H		LT	5207	v	**RR**	H		LT
5171	v	**G**	MH	*ON*	RL	5209	v	**RR**	H		LT
5174	v	**RR**	H		LT	5212	v	**LN**	H		TM

5213	v	**RR**	H		LT	5222	v **G**	MH	*ON*	RL
5216	v	**G**	MH	*ON*	RL	5225	v **RR**	H		LT
5221	v	**RR**	H		TM	5226	v **RR**	H		LT

AD2Z (SO)   OPEN STANDARD

Dia. AD203. Mark 2. Pressure ventilated. –/48 2T. B4 bogies. ETH 4.

Lot No. 30752 Derby 1966. 32 t.

5236	v	**G**	MH	*ON*	RL	5249	v **G**	MH	*ON*	RL
5237	v	**G**	MH	*ON*	RL	5254	**BG**	H		DY

AC2A (TSO)   OPEN STANDARD

Dia. AC206. Mark 2A. Pressure ventilated. –/64 2T (–/62 2T w). B4 bogies. ETH 4.

5265–5345. Lot No. 30776 Derby 1967–68. 32 t.
5350–5433. Lot No. 30787 Derby 1968. 32 t.

5265	**RR**	H		KN	5350	**FT**	RV	*ON*	CP
5266	**RR**	RV		CW	5353	**RR**	H		KN
5267	**RR**	H		KN	5354	**RR**	H		PY
5271	**RR**	H		KN	5364	**FT**	RV	*ON*	CP
5275	**FT**	RV	*ON*	CP	5365	**FT**	RV	*ON*	CP
5276	**RR**	H		CP	5366	**RB**	RV	*ON*	CP
5278	**RR**	H	*CA*	CF	5373	**FT**	RV	*ON*	CP
5282	**RR**	H		KN	5376	**FT**	RV	*ON*	CP
5290	**NB**	H		KN	5378	**FT**	RV	*ON*	CP
5292	**RB**	RV	*ON*	CP	5379	**RR**	H		KN
5293	**NB**	H		KN	5381 w	**RR**	H		CP
5299	**M**	WC	*ON*	CS	5384	**N**	RV		CW
5304	**RR**	RV		CW	5386 w	**RR**	H		CP
5307	**FT**	RV	*ON*	CP	5389 w	**RR**	H		CP
5309	**RR**	H		CP	5410	**N**	H		KN
5322	**RR**	H		CP	5412 w	**RR**	H	*CA*	CF
5331	**RR**	H		CP	5419 w	**RR**	H		CP
5335	**RR**	H		CP	5420 w	**RR**	H		CP
5341	**RB**	RV	*ON*	CP	5433 w	**RR**	H		CP
5345	**RR**	H		CP					

AC2B (TSO)   OPEN STANDARD

Dia. AC207. Mark 2B. Pressure ventilated. –/62 2T. B4 bogies. ETH 4.

Lot No. 30791 Derby 1969. 32 t.

Non-Standard Livery: 5453, 5478 and 5491 are royal blue with white lining.

5443	**N**	H		KN	5453 d	**O**	WC	*ON*	CS
5446	**N**	H		KN	5454	**N**	H		KN
5447	**N**	RV		CP	5462	**N**	RV		CP
5449	**N**	RV		CP	5463 d	**M**	WC	*ON*	CS
5450	**N**	RV		CP	5464	**N**	RV		CP

5471	**N**	H		KN		5480		**N**	H		KN
5472	**N**	H		KN		5487	d	**M**	WC	*ON*	CS
5475	**N**	H		KN		5491	d	**0**	WC	*ON*	CS
5478	d **0**	WC	*ON*	CS		5494		**N**	RV		CP

AC2C (TSO)   OPEN STANDARD

Dia. AC208. Mark 2C. Pressure ventilated. –/62 2T. B4 bogies. ETH 4.

Lot No. 30795 Derby 1969–70. 32t.

5554	**RR**	H		CW		5600	**M**	WC	*ON*	CS
5569	d **M**	WC	*ON*	CS		5614	**RR**	H		CW

AC2D (TSO)   OPEN STANDARD

Dia. AC209. Mark 2D. Air conditioned. Stones equipment. –/62 2T. B4 bogies. ETH 5.

Non-Standard Livery: 5630, 5732 & 5739 are **WV** without lining.

r Refurbished with new seats and end luggage stacks. –/58 2T.

Lot No. 30822 Derby 1971. 33t.

5616			RS		FK		5699			H		KN
5618			H		PY		5700	dr	**FG**	H	*GW*	OO
5620			H		PY		5701			H		KN
5623			H		PY		5704		**M**	WC	*ON*	CS
5629			H		PY		5710	dr	**FG**	H	*GW*	OO
5630		**0**	RV	*ON*	CP		5711			H		PY
5631	dr	**FG**	H	*GW*	OO		5714		**M**	WC	*ON*	CS
5632	dr	**FG**	H	*GW*	OO		5715			H		PY
5636	dr	**FG**	H	*GW*	OO		5716			H		KN
5640			H		PY		5718			H		KN
5647		**RB**	RV	*ON*	CP		5722			E		CL
5650			H		PY		5724			H		PY
5657	dr	**FG**	H	*GW*	OO		5726			H		PY
5661			H		KN		5727		**M**	WC	*ON*	CS
5662			H		ZN		5728			H		PY
5663			H		KN		5731			H		KN
5669	dr	**FG**	H	*GW*	OO		5732		**0**	RV	*ON*	CP
5674			H		KN		5737	dr	**FG**	H	*GW*	OO
5679	dr	**FG**	H	*GW*	OO		5738			H		KN
5687			H		KN		5739		**0**	RV		CP
5690			H		PY		5740	dr	**FG**	H	*GW*	OO
5694			H		KN							

AC2E (TSO)   OPEN STANDARD

Dia. AC210. Mark 2E. Air conditioned. Stones equipment. –/64 2T (w –/62 2T 1W). B4 bogies. d (except 5756 and 5879). ETH 5.

5744–5801. Lot No. 30837 Derby 1972. 33.5t.

5810–5906. Lot No. 30844 Derby 1972–73. 33.5t.

r Refurbished with new interior panelling.
s Refurbished with new interior panelling, modified design of seat headrest and centre luggage stack. –/60 2T (w –/58 2T 1W).
t Refurbished with new interior panelling and new seats.

No.						No.					
5744			H		ZN	5822	wspt	V	H	VX	MA
5745	s	V	H	VX	MA	5824	rw		H	VX	MA
5746	r	V	H	VX	MA	5827	r		H	VX	MA
5748	r pt		H	VX	MA	5828	ws	V	H	VX	MA
5750	s	V	H	VX	MA	5831		AR	H	AR	NC
5752	wrpt		H	VX	MA	5836		AR	H	AR	NC
5754	ws	V	H	VX	MA	5843	rw		H	VX	MA
5756		M	WC	ON	CS	5845	s	V	H	VX	MA
5769	r		H	VX	MA	5847	rw	V	H	VX	MA
5773	s pt	V	H	VX	MA	5852		AR	H	AR	NC
5775	s	V	H	VX	MA	5853	t		H	AR	NC
5776	r		H	VX	MA	5854	r		H	VX	MA
5778		AR	H	AR	NC	5859	s	V	H	VX	MA
5779	r		H	VX	MA	5863		AR	H	AR	NC
5780		AR	H	AR	NC	5866	r pt		H	VX	MA
5781		AR	H	AR	NC	5868	s pt	V	H	VX	MA
5784	r	V	H	VX	MA	5869	t		H	AR	NC
5787	s	V	H	VX	MA	5874	t		H	AR	NC
5788	r		H	VX	MA	5876	s pt	V	H	VX	MA
5789	r pt		H	VX	MA	5879				RV	CP
5791	wr		H	VX	MA	5881	ws	V	H	VX	MA
5792	r		H	VX	MA	5886	s	V	H	VX	MA
5793	wspt	V	H	VX	MA	5887	wr		H	VX	MA
5794	wr		H	VX	MA	5888	wr		H	VX	MA
5796	wr		H	VX	MA	5889	s	V	H	VX	MA
5797	r		H	VX	MA	5893	s	V	H	VX	MA
5800		AR	H	AR	NC	5897	r		H	VX	MA
5801	r	V	H	VX	MA	5899	s	V	H	VX	MA
5810	s	V	H	VX	MA	5900	wspt	V	H	VX	MA
5812	wr		H	VX	MA	5901	s	V	H	VX	MA
5814	r		H	VX	MA	5902	s	V	H	VX	MA
5815	ws	V	H	VX	MA	5903	s	V	H	VX	MA
5816	r pt		H	VX	MA	5905	s	V	H	VX	MA
5821	r pt	V	H	VX	MA	5906	wspt		H	VX	MA

AC2F (TSO)   OPEN STANDARD

Dia. AC211. Mark 2F. Air conditioned. Temperature Ltd. equipment. Inter-City 70 seats. All were refurbished in the 1980s with power-operated vestibule doors, new panels and new seat trim. –/64 2T. (w –/62 2T 1W) B4 bogies. d. ETH 5X.

5908–5958. Lot No. 30846 Derby 1973. 33t.
5959–6170. Lot No. 30860 Derby 1973–74. 33t.
6171–6184. Lot No. 30874 Derby 1974–75. 33t.

* Early Mark 2 style seats.

These vehicles have now undergone a second refurbishment with carpets and new seat trim .

Cross-Country vehicles:

r Standard refurbished vehicles with new m.a. sets.
s Also fitted with centre luggage stack. –/60 2T.
t Also fitted with centre luggage stack and wheelchair space. –/58 2T 1W.

West Coast vehicles:

r Standard refurbished vehicles with new seat trim and new m.a. sets.
u As 'r' but with two wheelchair spaces. –/60 2T 2W.
† Standard refurbished vehicles with new seat trim.

5908	r	**V**	H	*VW*	OY	5948	u	**V**	H	*VW*	OY
5910	u	**V**	H	*VW*	OY	5949	u	**V**	H	*VW*	OY
5911	s	**V**	H	*VX*	MA	5950		**AR**	H	*AR*	NC
5912	s	**V**	H	*VX*	MA	5951	r	**V**	H	*VX*	MA
5913	s		H	*VX*	MA	5952	r	**V**	H	*VW*	OY
5914	u	**V**	H	*VW*	OY	5953	†	**V**	H	*VW*	OY
5915	r	**V**	H	*VW*	OY	5954		**AR**	H	*AR*	NC
5916	t		H	*VX*	MA	5955	r	**V**	H	*VW*	OY
5917	s	**V**	H	*VX*	MA	5956			H	*AR*	NC
5918	t	**V**	H	*VX*	MA	5957	r	**V**	H	*VW*	OY
5919	s pt	**V**	H	*VX*	MA	5958	s		H	*VX*	MA
5920	†	**V**	H	*VW*	OY	5959	n	**AR**	H	*AR*	NC
5921		**AR**	H	*AR*	NC	5960	s	**V**	H	*VX*	MA
5922		**AR**	H	*AR*	NC	5961	s pt	**V**	H	*VX*	MA
5924		**AR**	H	*AR*	NC	5962	s pt	**V**	H	*VX*	MA
5925	s pt		H	*VX*	MA	5963	r	**V**	H	*VW*	OY
5926			H	*AR*	NC	5964		**AR**	H	*AR*	NC
5927		**AR**	H	*AR*	NC	5965	t		H	*VX*	MA
5928		**AR**	H	*AR*	NC	5966		**AR**	H	*AR*	NC
5929		**AR**	H	*AR*	NC	5967	t	**V**	H	*VX*	MA
5930	t	**V**	H	*VX*	MA	5968		**AR**	H	*AR*	NC
5931	†w	**V**	H	*VW*	OY	5969	u	**V**	H	*VW*	OY
5932	r	**V**	H	*VW*	OY	5971	s		H	*VX*	MA
5933	r	**V**	H	*VW*	OY	5973		**AR**	H	*AR*	NC
5934	r	**V**	H	*VW*	OY	5975	s	**V**	H	*VX*	MA
5935		**AR**	H	*AR*	NC	5976	t	**V**	H	*VX*	MA
5936		**AR**	H	*AR*	NC	5977	r	**V**	H	*VW*	OY
5937	r	**V**	H	*VW*	OY	5978	r	**V**	H	*VW*	OY
5939	r	**V**	H	*VW*	OY	5980	r	**V**	H	*VW*	OY
5940	u	**V**	H	*VW*	OY	5981	s		H	*VX*	MA
5941	r	**V**	H	*VW*	OY	5983	s	**V**	H	*VX*	MA
5943	rw	**V**	H	*VW*	OY	5984	r	**V**	H	*VW*	OY
5944		**AR**	H	*AR*	NC	5985		**AR**	H	*AR*	NC
5945	r	**V**	H	*VW*	OY	5986	r	**V**	H	*VW*	OY
5946	r	**V**	H	*VW*	OY	5987	r	**V**	H	*VW*	OY
5947	s pt	**V**	H	*VX*	MA	5988	r	**V**	H	*VW*	OY

5989	t	**V**	H	*VX*	MA
5991	s	**V**	H	*VX*	MA
5993	*	**AR**	H	*AR*	NC
5994	r	**V**	H	*VX*	MA
5995	s		H	*VX*	MA
5996	s pt	**V**	H	*VX*	MA
5997	r	**V**	H	*VW*	OY
5998		**AR**	H	*AR*	NC
5999	s	**V**	H	*VX*	MA
6000	t	**V**	H	*VX*	MA
6001	u	**V**	H	*VW*	OY
6002	†	**V**	H	*VW*	OY
6005	r	**V**	H	*VX*	MA
6006		**AR**	H	*AR*	NC
6008	s	**V**	H	*VX*	MA
6009	r	**V**	H	*VW*	OY
6010	s	**V**	H	*VX*	MA
6011	s	**V**	H	*VX*	MA
6012	r	**V**	H	*VW*	OY
6013	s		H	*VX*	MA
6014	s pt		H	*VX*	MA
6015	t	**V**	H	*VX*	MA
6016	r	**V**	H	*VW*	OY
6018	t	**V**	H	*VX*	MA
6021	r	**V**	H	*VW*	OY
6022	s	**V**	H	*VX*	MA
6024	s	**V**	H	*VX*	MA
6025	t	**V**	H	*VX*	MA
6026	s	**V**	H	*VX*	MA
6027	u	**V**	H	*VW*	OY
6028		**AR**	H	*AR*	NC
6029	r	**V**	H	*VW*	OY
6030	t	**V**	H	*VX*	MA
6031	r	**V**	H	*VW*	OY
6034		**AR**	H	*AR*	NC
6035	t		H	*VX*	MA
6036	*	**AR**	H	*AR*	NC
6037		**AR**	H	*AR*	NC
6038	s	**V**	H	*VX*	MA
6041	s	**V**	H	*VX*	MA
6042		**AR**	H	*AR*	NC
6043	†	**V**	H	*VW*	OY
6045	†w	**V**	H	*VW*	OY
6046	s	**V**	H	*VX*	MA
6047	†n*	**V**	H	*VW*	OY
6049	r	**V**	H	*VW*	OY
6050	s		H	*VX*	MA
6051	r	**V**	H	*VW*	OY
6052	tw		H	*VX*	MA
6053	*	**AR**	H	*AR*	NC
6054	r	**V**	H	*VW*	OY
6055	†	**V**	H	*VW*	OY
6056	†	**V**	H	*VW*	OY
6057	r	**V**	H	*VW*	OY
6059	s	**V**	H	*VX*	MA
6060	u	**V**	H	*VW*	OY
6061	s pt	**V**	H	*VX*	MA
6062	†	**V**	H	*VW*	OY
6063	†w	**V**	H	*VW*	OY
6064	s	**V**	H	*VX*	MA
6065	r	**V**	H	*VW*	OY
6066	s		H	*VX*	MA
6067	s pt	**V**	H	*VX*	MA
6073	s	**V**	H	*VX*	MA
6100	†*	**V**	H	*VW*	OY
6101	r	**V**	H	*VW*	OY
6102	r	**V**	H	*VW*	OY
6103		**AR**	H	*AR*	NC
6104	r	**V**	H	*VW*	OY
6105	tpt	**V**	H	*VX*	MA
6106	r	**V**	H	*VW*	OY
6107	r	**V**	H	*VW*	OY
6110			H	*AR*	NC
6111	†	**V**	H	*VW*	OY
6112	s pt	**V**	H	*VX*	MA
6113	†	**V**	H	*VW*	OY
6115	s		H	*VX*	MA
6116	†	**V**	H	*VW*	OY
6117	t	**V**	H	*VX*	MA
6119	s	**V**	H	*VX*	MA
6120	s	**V**	H	*VX*	MA
6121	†	**V**	H	*VW*	OY
6122	s	**V**	H	*VX*	MA
6123		**AR**	H	*AR*	NC
6124	s pt		H	*VX*	MA
6134	†	**V**	H	*VW*	OY
6135	s		H	*VX*	MA
6136	r	**V**	H	*VW*	OY
6137	s pt	**V**	H	*VW*	MA
6138	†	**V**	H	*VW*	OY
6139	n*		H	*AR*	NC
6141	u	**V**	H	*VW*	OY
6142	†*	**V**	H	*VW*	OY
6144	†*	**V**	H	*VW*	OY
6145	s pt	**V**	H	*VW*	OY
6146	*	**AR**	H	*AR*	NC
6147	r	**V**	H	*VW*	OY
6148	s		H	*VW*	MA
6149	u	**V**	H	*VW*	OY
6150	s		H	*VX*	MA
6151	†*	**V**	H	*VW*	OY
6152	*	**AR**	H	*AR*	NC

6153	†	**V**	H	*VW*	OY		6170	s	**V**	H	*VX*	MA
6154	r pt		H	*VX*	MA		6171	†	**V**	H	*VW*	OY
6155	*	**AR**	H	*AR*	NC		6172	s	**V**	H	*VX*	MA
6157	s	**V**	H	*VX*	MA		6173	s	**V**	H	*VX*	MA
6158	r	**V**	H	*VW*	OY		6174			H	*AR*	NC
6159	s pt	**V**	H	*VX*	MA		6175	r	**V**	H	*VW*	OY
6160	*	**AR**	H	*AR*	NC		6176	t	**V**	H	*VX*	MA
6161	†*	**V**	H	*VW*	OY		6177	s	**V**	H	*VX*	MA
6162	s pt	**V**	H	*VX*	MA		6178	s		H	*VX*	MA
6163	r	**V**	H	*VW*	OY		6179	r	**V**	H	*VW*	OY
6164	†	**V**	H	*VW*	OY		6180	†w	**V**	H	*VW*	OY
6165	r	**V**	H	*VW*	OY		6181	†wn	**V**	H	*VW*	OY
6166			H	*AR*	NC		6182	s	**V**	H	*VX*	MA
6167		**AR**	H	*AR*	NC		6183	s	**V**	H	*VX*	MA
6168	s		H	*VX*	MA		6184	s	**V**	H	*VX*	MA

AC2D (TSO)   OPEN STANDARD

Dia. AC217. Mark 2D. Air conditioned (Stones). Rebuilt from FO with new style 2+2 seats. –/58 2T. (–/58 1T*). B4 bogies. d. ETH 5X.

Lot No. 30821 Derby 1971–72. 33.5t.

* One toilet converted to store room for use of attendant on sleeping car services.

6200	(3198)		H		ZN		6212	(3176)		H		ZN
6202	(3191)	*	H		ZN		6213	(3208)		H		ZN
6203	(3180)		H		ZN		6219	(3213)		H		ZN
6206	(3183)		H		ZN		6221	(3173)		H		ZN
6207	(3204)		H		ZN		6226	(3203)		H		ZN

GX51   BRAKE GENERATOR VAN

Dia. GX501. Mark 1. Renumbered 1989 from BR departmental series. Converted from NDA in 1973 to three-phase supply brake generator van for use with HST trailers. Modified 1999 for use with loco-hauled stock. B5 bogies.

Lot No. 30400 Pressed Steel 1958.

6310   (81448, 975325)   **CH** RV *ON*   CP

AX51   GENERATOR VAN

Dia. AX501. Mark 1. Converted from NDA in 1992 to generator vans for use on Anglo-Scottish sleeping car services. Now normally used on trains hauled by steam locomotives. B4 bogies. ETH75.

6311. Lot No. 30162 Pressed Steel 1958. 37.25t.
6312. Lot No. 30224 Cravens 1956. 37.25t.
6313. Lot No. 30484 Pressed Steel 1958. 37.25t.

6313 is leased to the Venice Simplon Orient Express.

6311	(80903, 92911)	**B**	RS	*ON*	BN
6312	(81023, 92925)	**PC**	FS	*ON*	SZ
6313	(81553, 92167)	**PC**	P	*ON*	SL

GS5 (HSBV)   HST BARRIER VEHICLE

Various diagrams. Renumbered from BR departmental series or converted from various types. B4 bogies (Commonwealth bogies *).

6330. Mark 2A. Lot No. 30786 Derby 1968. 32t.
6334. Mark 1. Lot No. 30400 Pressed Steel 1957–8. 31.5t.
6336/8/44. Mark 1. Lot No. 30715 Gloucester 1962. 31t.
6340. Mark 1. Lot No. 30669 Swindon 1962. 36t.
6346. Mark 2A. Lot No. 30777 Derby 1967. 31.5t.
6348. Mark 1. Lot No. 30163 Pressed Steel 1957. 31.5t.

6330	(14084, 975629)		**G**	A	*A*	LA
6334	(81478, 92128)		**P**	P	*P*	NL
6336	(81591, 92185)		**G**	A	*A*	LA
6338	(81581, 92180)		**G**	A	*A*	LA
6340	(21251, 975678)	*	**G**	A	*A*	LA
6344	(81263, 92080)		**B**	A	*A*	EC
6346	(9422)		**B**	A	*A*	EC
6348	(81233, 92963)		**G**	A	*A*	LA

GF5 (MFBV)   MARK 4 BARRIER VEHICLE

Various diagrams. Converted from FK* or BSO. B4 bogies.

6352/3. Mark 2A. Lot No. 30774 Derby 1968. 33t.
6354/5. Mark 2C. Lot No. 30820 Derby 1970. 32t.
6358-9. Mark 2A. Lot No. 30788 Derby 1968. 31.5t.

6352	(13465, 19465)	*	**GN**	H	*GN*	BN
6353	(13478, 19478)	*	**GN**	H	*GN*	BN
6354	(9459)		**GN**	H	*GN*	BN
6355	(9477)		**GN**	H	*GN*	BN
6358	(9432)		**GN**	H	*GN*	BN
6359	(9429)		**GN**	H	*GN*	BN

GF5 (BV)   DMU/EMU* BARRIER VEHICLE

Various diagrams. Converted 1992 from BSO or BG*.

6360. Mark 2A. Lot No. 30777 Derby 1967. B4 bogies. 31.5t.
6361. Mark 2C. Lot No. 30820 Derby 1970. B4 bogies. 32t.
6364. Mark 1. Lot No. 30039 Derby 1954. BR Mark 1 bogies. 32t.
6365. Mark 1. Lot No. 30323 Pressed Steel 1957. BR Mark 1 bogies. 32t.

6360	(9420)		**RR**	P	*P*	NL
6361	(9460)		**RR**	P	*P*	NL
6364	(80565)	*	**RR**	P	*P*	TS
6365	(81296, 84296)	*	**RR**	P	*P*	TS

GS5 (HSBV)   HST BARRIER VEHICLE

Dia. GS507. Mark 1. Converted from BG in 1994–5. B4 bogies.

6392. Lot No. 30715 Gloucester 1962. 29.5t.
6393/6/7. Lot No. 30716 Gloucester 1962. 29.5t.
6394. Lot No. 30162 Pressed Steel 1956–57. 30.5t.
6395. Lot No. 30484 Pressed Steel 1958. 30.5t.
6398/9. Lot No. 30400 Pressed Steel 1957–58. 30.5t.

6392	(81588, 92183)	**P**	P	*P*	LA
6393	(81609, 92196)	**P**	P	*P*	LA
6394	(80878, 92906)	**P**	P	*P*	NL
6395	(81506, 92148)	**P**	P	*P*	NL
6396	(81606, 92195)	**P**	P	*P*	LA
6397	(81600, 92190)	**P**	P	*P*	NL
6398	(81471, 92126)	**P**	P	*P*	NL
6399	(81367, 92994)	**P**	P	*P*	NL

AG2C (TSOT)   OPEN STANDARD (TROLLEY)

Dia. AG201. Mark 2C. Converted from TSO by removal of one seating bay and replacing this by a counter with a space for a trolley. Adjacent toilet removed and converted to steward's washing area/store. Pressure ventilated. –/54 1T. B4 bogies. ETH 4.

Lot No. 30795 Derby 1969–70. 32.5t.

6528	(5592)	**M**	WC	*ON*	CS

AG2D (TSOT)   OPEN STANDARD (TROLLEY)

Dia. AG202. Mark 2D. Converted from TSO by removal of one seating bay and replacing this by a counter with a space for a trolley. Adjacent toilet removed and converted to steward's washing area/store. Air conditioned. Stones equipment. –/54 1T. B4 bogies. ETH 5.

Lot No. 30822 Derby 1971. 33t.

6609	(5698)	H	KN
6619	(5655)	H	KN

AN1F (RLO)   SLEEPER RECEPTION CAR

Dia. AN101 (AN102*). Mark 2F. Converted from FO, these vehicles consist of pantry, microwave cooking facilities, seating area for passengers, telephone booth and staff toilet. 6703–8 also have a bar. Converted at RTC, Derby (6700), Ilford (6701–5) and Derby (6706–8). Air conditioned. 6700/1/3/5/–8 have Stones equipment and 6702/4 have Temperature Ltd. equipment. 26/– 1T. B4 bogies. p. q. d. ETH 5X.

6700–2/4/8. Lot No. 30859 Derby 1973–74. 33.5t.
6703/5–7. Lot No. 30845 Derby 1973. 33.5t.

6700	(3347)		**SS**	H	*SR*	IS
6701	(3346)	*	**SS**	H	*SR*	IS
6702	(3421)	*	**SS**	H	*SR*	IS
6703	(3308)		**SS**	H	*SR*	IS
6704	(3310)		**SS**	H	*SR*	IS
6705	(3310, 6430)		**SS**	H	*SR*	IS
6706	(3283, 6421)		**SS**	H	*SR*	IS
6707	(3276, 6418)		**SS**	H	*SR*	IS
6708	(3370)		**SS**	H	*SR*	IS

AN1D (RMBF)   MINIATURE BUFFET CAR

Dia. AN103. Mark 2D. Converted from TSOT by the removal of another seating bay and fitting a proper buffet counter with boiler and microwave oven. Now converted to first class with new seating. Air conditioned. Stones equipment. 30/– 1T. B4 bogies. p. q. d. ETH 5.

Lot No. 30822 Derby 1971. 33 t.

6720	(5622, 6652)	**FG**	H	*GW*	OO
6721	(5627, 6660)	**FG**	H	*GW*	OO
6722	(5736, 6661)	**FG**	H	*GW*	OO
6723	(5641, 6662)	**FG**	H	*GW*	OO
6724	(5721, 6665)	**FG**	H	*GW*	OO

AC2F (TSO)   OPEN STANDARD

Dia. AC224. Mark 2F. Renumbered from FO and declassified in 1985–6. Converted 1990 to TSO with mainly unidirectional seating and power-operated sliding doors. Air conditioned. 6800–14 were converted by BREL Derby and have Temperature Ltd. air conditioning. 6815–29 were converted by RFS Industries Doncaster and have Stones air conditioning. –/74 2T. B4 bogies. d. ETH 5X.

6800–07. 6810–12. 6813–14. 6819/22/28. Lot No. 30859 Derby 1973–74. 33 t.
6808–6809. Lot No. 30873 Derby 1974–75. 33.5 t.
6815–18. 6820–21. 6823–27. 6829. Lot No. 30845 Derby 1973. 33 t.

6800	(3323, 6435)	**AR**	H	*AR*	NC
6801	(3349, 6442)	**AR**	H	*AR*	NC
6802	(3339, 6439)		H	*AR*	NC
6803	(3355, 6443)	**AR**	H	*AR*	NC
6804	(3396, 6449)		H	*AR*	NC
6805	(3324, 6436)	**AR**	H	*AR*	NC
6806	(3342, 6440)	**AR**	H	*AR*	NC
6807	(3423, 6452)		H	*AR*	NC
6808	(3430, 6454)	**AR**	H	*AR*	NC
6809	(3435, 6455)	**AR**	H	*AR*	NC
6810	(3404, 6451)	**AR**	H	*AR*	NC
6811	(3327, 6437)	**AR**	H	*AR*	NC
6812	(3394, 6448)	**AR**	H	*AR*	NC
6813	(3410, 6463)		H	*AR*	NC
6814	(3422, 6465)	**AR**	H	*AR*	NC
6815	(3282, 6420)	**AR**	H	*AR*	NC

6816	(3316, 6461)	**AR** H	*AR*	NC
6817	(3311, 6431)	**AR** H	*AR*	NC
6818	(3298, 6427)	**AR** H	*AR*	NC
6819	(3365, 6446)	**AR** H	*AR*	NC
6820	(3320, 6434)	**AR** H	*AR*	NC
6821	(3281, 6458)	**AR** H	*AR*	NC
6822	(3376, 6447)	**AR** H	*AR*	NC
6823	(3289, 6424)	**AR** H	*AR*	NC
6824	(3307, 6429)	**AR** H	*AR*	NC
6825	(3301, 6460)	**AR** H	*AR*	NC
6826	(3294, 6425)	**AR** H	*AR*	NC
6827	(3306, 6428)	**AR** H	*AR*	NC
6828	(3380, 6464)	**AR** H	*AR*	NC
6829	(3288, 6423)	**AR** H	*AR*	NC

NM51   MERSEYRAIL SANDITE COACH

Dia. NM504. Mark 1. Former Class 501 750 V d.c. third rail EMU driving trailers converted for use as Sandite/de-icing coaches. BR Mark 1 Bogies.

Lot No. 30328 Eastleigh 1958.   . t.

6910	(75178, 977346)	**MS** RK	*RK*	BD
6911	(75180, 977348)	**MS** RK	*RK*	BD

AH2Z (BSOT)
OPEN BRAKE STANDARD (MICRO-BUFFET)

Dia. AH203. Mark 2. Converted from BSO by removal of one seating bay and replacing this by a counter with a space for a trolley. Adjacent toilet removed and converted to a steward's washing area/store. –/23 0T. B4 bogies. ETH 4.

Lot No. 30757 Derby 1966. 31t.

9100	(9405)	v	**RR** H		LT
9101	(9398)	v	**RR** H		TM
9104	(9401)	v	**G** MH	*ON*	RL

AE21 (BSO)   OPEN BRAKE STANDARD

Dia. AE201. Mark 1. –/39 1T. BR Mark 1 bogies. ETH 3.

Lot No. 30170 Doncaster 1955–56. 34t.

9274 v   **CH** NY *ON*   NY

AE2Z (BSO)   OPEN BRAKE STANDARD

Dia. AE203. Mark 2. These vehicles use the same body shell as the Mark 2 BFK and have first class seat spacing and wider tables. Pressure ventilated. –/31 1T. B4 bogies. ETH 4.

Lot No. 30757 Derby 1966. 31.5t.

9385 v   **LN** H   LT | 9388 v   **LN** H   LT

AE2A (BSO)   OPEN BRAKE STANDARD

Dia. AE204. Mark 2A. These vehicles use the same body shell as the Mark 2A BFK and have first class seat spacing and wider tables. Pressure ventilated. – /31 1T. B4 bogies. ETH 4.

9417–21. Lot No. 30777 Derby 1970. 31.5t.
9428–35. Lot No. 30820 Derby 1970. 31.5t.

9417	**FT** RV *ON*	CP		9434	**RR** H		ZN
9421	**RR** H	PY		9435	**RR** H		KN
9428	**DR** DR *DR*	KD					

AE2C (BSO)   OPEN BRAKE STANDARD

Dia. AE205. Mark 2C. Pressure ventilated. –/31 1T. B4 bogies. ETH 4.

Lot No. 30798 Derby 1970. 32t.

Non-Standard Livery: 9440 is in Royal blue with white lining.

9440 d	**0** WC *ON*	CS		9448 d	**M** WC *ON*	CS

AE2D (BSO)   OPEN BRAKE STANDARD

Dia. AE206. Mark 2D. Air conditioned (Stones). –/31 1T. B4 bogies. pg. ETH 5.

r Refurbished with new interior panelling.
s Refurbished with new seating –/22 1TD.

Lot No. 30824 Derby 1971. 33t.

9479 dr		H	*VX*	MA	9488 ds	**FG** H	*GW*	OO
9480 d		H		ZN	9489 dr	**V** H	*VX*	MA
9481 ds	**FG**	H	*GW*	OO	9490 ds	**FG** H	*GW*	OO
9483		H		PY	9492 d	H		ZN
9484 d		H		CP	9493 ds	**FG** H	*GW*	OO
9485		CW		MM	9494 ds	**FG** H	*GW*	OO
9486		H		PY				

AE2E (BSO)   OPEN BRAKE STANDARD

Dia. AE207. Mark 2E. Air conditioned (Stones). –/32 1T. B4 bogies. d. pg. ETH 5.

Lot No. 30838 Derby 1972. 33t.

r Refurbished with new interior panelling.
s Refurbished with modified design of seat headrest and new interior panelling.

9496 r	H	*VX*	MA	9501	H		ZN
9497 r	H	*VX*	MA	9502 s	**V** H	*VX*	MA
9498 r	**V** H	*VX*	MA	9503 s	**V** H	*VX*	MA
9500 r	H	*VX*	MA	9504 s	**V** H	*VX*	MA

9505	s		H	VX	MA	9508	s	V H	VX	MA
9506	s	V	H	VX	MA	9509	s	V H	VX	MA
9507	s	V	H	VX	MA					

AE2F (BSO)   OPEN BRAKE STANDARD

Dia. AE208. Mark 2F. Air conditioned (Temperature Ltd.). All now refurbished with power-operated vestibule doors, new panels and seat trim. All now further refurbished with carpets and new m.a. sets. –/32 1T. B4 bogies. d. pg. ETH5X.

Lot No. 30861 Derby 1974. 34 t.

9513		V	H	VX	MA	9526	n	H	VX	MA
9516	n	V	H	VX	MA	9527	n	V H	VX	MA
9520	n	V	H	VX	MA	9529	n	V H	VX	MA
9521		V	H	VX	MA	9531		V H	VX	MA
9522		V	H	VX	MA	9537	n	V H	VX	MA
9523		V	H	VX	MA	9538		V H	VX	MA
9524	n	V	H	VX	MA	9539		V H	VX	MA
9525		V	H	VX	MA					

AF2F (DBSO)   DRIVING OPEN BRAKE STANDARD

Dia. AF201. Mark 2F. Air conditioned (Temperature Ltd.). Push & pull (t.d.m. system). Converted from BSO, these vehicles originally had half cabs at the brake end. They have since been refurbished and have had their cabs widened and the cab-end gangways removed. –/30 1W 1T. B4 bogies. d. pg. Cowcatchers. ETH 5X.

9701–9710. Lot No. 30861 Derby 1974. Converted Glasgow 1979. Disc brakes. 34 t.
9711–9713. Lot No. 30861 Derby 1974. Converted Glasgow 1985. 34 t.
9714. Lot No. 30861 Derby 1974. Converted Glasgow 1986. Disc brakes. 34 t.

9701	(9528)	AR	H AR	NC	9709	(9515)	AR	H AR	NC
9702	(9510)	AR	H AR	NC	9710	(9518)		H AR	NC
9703	(9517)	AR	H AR	NC	9711	(9532)	AR	H AR	NC
9704	(9512)	AR	H AR	NC	9712	(9534)	AR	H AR	NC
9705	(9519)		H AR	NC	9713	(9535)	AR	H AR	NC
9707	(9511)	AR	H AR	NC	9714	(9536)	AR	H AR	NC
9708	(9530)	AR	H AR	NC					

AE4E (BUO)   UNCLASSIFIED OPEN BRAKE

Dia. AE401. Mark 2E. Converted from TSO with new seating for use on Anglo-Scottish overnight services by Railcare, Wolverton. Air conditioned. Stones equipment. B4 bogies. d. –/31 1T. ETH 4X.

9801–9803. Lot No. 30837 Derby 1972. 33.5 t.
9804–9810. Lot No. 30844 Derby 1972–73. 33.5 t.

9800	(5751)	SS	H SR	IS	9803	(5799)	SS	H SR	IS
9801	(5760)	SS	H SR	IS	9804	(5826)	SS	H SR	IS
9802	(5772)	SS	H SR	IS	9805	(5833)	SS	H SR	IS

9806	(5840)	**SS**	H	*SR*	IS	9809	(5890)	**SS**	H	*SR*	IS
9807	(5851)	**SS**	H	*SR*	IS	9810	(5892)	**SS**	H	*SR*	IS
9808	(5871)	**SS**	H	*SR*	IS					

AJ1G (RFM) RESTAURANT BUFFET FIRST (MODULAR)

Dia. AJ103 (10200/1 are Dia. AJ101). Mark 3A. Air conditioned. Converted from HST TRFKs, RFBs and FOs. Refurbished with table lamps and burgundy seat trim (except *). 18/– plus two seats for staff use (*24/–). BT10 bogies. p. q. d. ETH 14X.

10200–10211. Lot No. 30884 Derby 1977.
10212–10229. Lot No. 30878 Derby 1975–76. 39.8t.
10230–10260. Lot No. 30890 Derby 1979. 39.8t.

10200	(40519)	*		P	*AR*	NC	10229	(11059)	**V**	P	*VW*	MA
10201	(40520)	**V**		P	*VW*	OY	10230	(10021)	**V**	P	*VW*	PC
10202	(40504)	**V**		P	*VW*	MA	10231	(10016)	**V**	P	*VW*	OY
10203	(40506)	* **AR**	P	*AR*	NC	10232	(10027)	**V**	P	*VW*	OY
10204	(40502)	**V**		P	*VW*	MA	10233	(10013)	**V**	P	*VW*	PC
10205	(40503)	**V**		P	*VW*	OY	10234	(10004)	**V**	P	*VW*	OY
10206	(40507)	**V**		P	*VW*	MA	10235	(10015)	**V**	P	*VW*	OY
10207	(40516)	**V**		P	*VW*	PC	10236	(10018)	**V**	P	*VW*	PC
10208	(40517)	**V**		P	*VW*	MA	10237	(10022)	**V**	P	*VW*	MA
10209	(40508)	**V**		P	*VW*	PC	10238	(10017)	**V**	P	*VW*	OY
10210	(40509)	**V**		P	*VW*	PC	10240	(10003)	**V**	P	*VW*	OY
10211	(40510)	**V**		P	*VW*	PC	10241	(10009)	* **AR**	P	*AR*	NC
10212	(11049)	**V**		P	*VW*	MA	10242	(10002)	**V**	P	*VW*	OY
10213	(11050)	**V**		P	*VW*	MA	10245	(10019)	**V**	P	*VW*	PC
10214	(11034)	* **AR**	P	*AR*	NC	10246	(10014)	**V**	P	*VW*	PC
10215	(11032)	**V**		P	*VW*	PC	10247	(10011)	* **AR**	P	*AR*	NC
10216	(11041)	* **AR**	P	*AR*	NC	10248	(10005)	**V**	P	*VW*	OY
10217	(11051)	**V**		P	*VW*	MA	10249	(10012)	**V**	P	*VW*	PC
10218	(11053)	**V**		P	*VW*	MA	10250	(10020)	**V**	P	*VW*	OY
10219	(11047)	**V**		P	*VW*	PC	10251	(10024)	**V**	P	*VW*	OY
10220	(11056)	**V**		P	*VW*	OY	10252	(10008)	**V**	P	*VW*	OY
10221	(11012)	**V**		P	*VW*	PC	10253	(10026)	**V**	P	*VW*	PC
10222	(11063)	**V**		P	*VW*	MA	10254	(10006)	**V**	P	*VW*	PC
10223	(11043)	* **AR**	P	*AR*	NC	10255	(10010)	**V**	P	*VW*	OY
10224	(11062)	**V**		P	*VW*	MA	10256	(10028)	**V**	P	*VW*	MA
10225	(11014)	**V**		P	*VW*	OY	10257	(10007)	**V**	P	*VW*	PC
10226	(11015)	**V**		P	*VW*	MA	10258	(10023)	**V**	P	*VW*	MA
10227	(11057)	**V**		P	*VW*	PC	10259	(10025)	**V**	P	*VW*	OY
10228	(11035)	* **AR**	P	*AR*	NC	10260	(10001)	**V**	P	*VW*	MA

AJ1J (RFM) RESTAURANT BUFFET FIRST (MODULAR)

Dia. AJ105. Mark 4. Air conditioned. 20/– 1T. BT41 bogies. ETH 6X.

Lot No. 31045 Metro-Cammell 1989 onwards. 45.5t.

10300	**GN**	H	*GN*	BN	10302	**GN**	H	*GN*	BN
10301	**GN**	H	*GN*	BN	10303	**GN**	H	*GN*	BN

10304	**GN**	H *GN*	BN		10319	**GN**	H *GN*	BN
10305	**GN**	H *GN*	BN		10320	**GN**	H *GN*	BN
10306	**GN**	H *GN*	BN		10321	**GN**	H *GN*	BN
10307	**GN**	H *GN*	BN		10322	**GN**	H *GN*	BN
10308	**GN**	H *GN*	BN		10323	**GN**	H *GN*	BN
10309	**GN**	H *GN*	BN		10324	**GN**	H *GN*	BN
10310	**GN**	H *GN*	BN		10325	**GN**	H *GN*	BN
10311	**GN**	H *GN*	BN		10326	**GN**	H *GN*	BN
10312	**GN**	H *GN*	BN		10327	**GN**	H	ZC
10313	**GN**	H *GN*	BN		10328	**GN**	H *GN*	BN
10314	**GN**	H *GN*	BN		10329	**GN**	H *GN*	BN
10315	**GN**	H *GN*	BN		10330	**GN**	H *GN*	BN
10316	**GN**	H *GN*	BN		10331	**GN**	H *GN*	BN
10317	**GN**	H *GN*	BN		10332	**GN**	H *GN*	BN
10318	**GN**	H *GN*	BN		10333	**GN**	H *GN*	BN

AU4G (SLEP)   SLEEPING CAR WITH PANTRY

Dia. AU401. Mark 3A. Air conditioned. Retention toilets. 12 compartments with a fixed lower berth and a hinged upper berth, plus an attendants compartment. 2T BT10 bogies. ETH 7X.

Lot No. 30960 Derby 1981–83. 41t.

10500		SA		ZC		10538 d		P	KN
10501 d	**SS**	P	*SR*	IS		10539 d		P	KN
10502 d	**SS**	P	*SR*	IS		10540 d		P	MM
10503		SA		ZC		10542 d	**SS**	P	*SR*	IS
10504 d	**SS**	P	*SR*	IS		10543 d	**SS**	P	*SR*	IS
10506 d	**SS**	P	*SR*	IS		10544 d	**SS**	P	*SR*	IS
10507 d	**SS**	P	*SR*	IS		10546		P	MM
10508 d	**SS**	P	*SR*	IS		10547 d		P	IS
10510 d		P		IS		10548 d	**SS**	P	*SR*	IS
10513 d	**SS**	P	*SR*	IS		10549 d		P	MM
10514		SA		ZC		10550 d		P	MM
10515 d		P		IS		10551 d	**SS**	P	*SR*	IS
10516 d	**SS**	P	*SR*	IS		10553 d	**SS**	P	*SR*	IS
10519 d	**SS**	P	*SR*	IS		10554 d		P	ZD
10520 d	**SS**	P	*SR*	IS		10555 d		P	KN
10522 d	**SS**	P	*SR*	IS		10557 d		P	ZD
10523 d	**SS**	P	*SR*	IS		10559 d		P	KN
10526 d	**SS**	P	*SR*	IS		10560 d		P	MM
10527 d	**SS**	P	*SR*	IS		10561 d	**SS**	P	*SR*	IS
10529 d	**SS**	P	*SR*	IS		10562 d	**SS**	P	*SR*	IS
10530 d		P		MM		10563 d	**FG**	P	*GW*	PZ
10531 d	**SS**	P	*SR*	IS		10565 d	**SS**	P	*SR*	IS
10532 d	**FG**	P	*GW*	PZ		10566 d		P	MM
10533		P		MM		10569 d	**PC**	VS *ON*	SL
10534 d	**FG**	P	*GW*	PZ		10570		P	KN
10535 d		P		MM		10571		SA	BN
10536 d		P		KN		10572 d		P	MM
10537 d		P		MM		10574		RS	FK

10575		SA		ZC		10596 d		P		KN
10577	**BG**	P		ZD		10597 d	**SS**	P	*SR*	IS
10578		P		MM		10598 d	**SS**	P	*SR*	IS
10579	**BG**	P		KN		10600 d	**SS**	P	*SR*	IS
10580 d	**SS**	P	*SR*	IS		10601		P		MM
10582 d		P		ZD		10602		P		MM
10583 d	**FG**	P	*GW*	PZ		10604		P		ZD
10584 d	**FG**	P	*GW*	PZ		10605 d	**SS**	P	*SR*	IS
10586 d		P		KN		10607 d	**SS**	P	*SR*	IS
10588 d	**FG**	P	*GW*	PZ		10610 d	**SS**	P	*SR*	IS
10589 d	**FG**	P	*GW*	PZ		10612 d	**FG**	P	*GW*	PZ
10590 d	**FG**	P	*GW*	PZ		10613 d	**SS**	P	*SR*	IS
10592		P		KN		10614 d	**SS**	P	*SR*	IS
10593 d		P		KN		10616 d	**FG**	P	*GW*	PZ
10594 d	**FG**	P	*GW*	PZ		10617 d	**SS**	P	*SR*	IS

AS4G (SLE/SLED*) SLEEPING CAR

Dia. AS403 (AS404*). Mark 3A. Air conditioned. Retention toilets. 13 compartments with a fixed lower berth and a hinged upper berth (* 11 compartments with a fixed lower berth and a hinged upper berth + one compartment for a disabled person). 2T. BT10 bogies. ETH 6X.

Notes:

10664/7/9/76/7/81/94/5/8/721 were sold to the Danish State Railways (DSB) when they were numbered in the UIC system. They have since returned to Britain.

10729 is leased to Venice Simplon-Orient Express.

Lot No. 30961 Derby 1980–84. 43.5t.

10646 d		RS		FK		10676	**DS**	CW		ZC
10647 d		P		KN		10677	**DS**	CW		ZN
10648 d*	**SS**	P	*SR*	IS		10678	**BG**	P		KN
10649 d		P		KN		10679	**BG**	P		KN
10650 d*	**SS**	P	*SR*	IS		10680 d*	**SS**	P	*SR*	IS
10651 d		P		ZD		10681	**DS**	A		KN
10653 d		P		MM		10682 d		P		ZD
10654 d		P		MM		10683 d	**SS**	P	*SR*	IS
10655		SA		ZC		10686 d		P		MM
10657		SA		ZC		10687 d		P		MM
10658 d		P		KN		10688 d	**SS**	P	*SR*	IS
10660 d		P		ZD		10689 d*	**SS**	P	*SR*	IS
10662 d		P		ZD		10690 d	**SS**	P	*SR*	IS
10663 d		P	*SR*	IS		10691 d		P		MM
10664	**DS**	A		KN		10692 d		P		MM
10666 d*	**SS**	P	*SR*	IS		10693 d	**SS**	P	*SR*	IS
10667	**DS**	CW		ZC		10694	**DS**	CW		ZC
10668 d		P		MM		10695	**DS**	CW		ZN
10669	**DS**	CW		ZN		10697 d		P		KN
10675 d	**SS**	P	*SR*	IS		10698	**DS**	CW		ZC

10699	d*SS	P	SR	IS	10717	d	P		MM
10701	d	P		KN	10718	d*SS	P	SR	IS
10702		SA		ZC	10719	d*SS	P	SR	IS
10703	d SS	P	SR	IS	10720		P		KN
10704	d	AE	AE	ZA	10721	DS	CW		ZN
10706	d*SS	P	SR	IS	10722	d*SS	P	SR	IS
10708	d	P		MM	10723	d*SS	P	SR	IS
10709	d	P		MM	10724		SA		FK
10710	d	P		KN	10726		SA		ZC
10711	d	P		MM	10727		SA		ZC
10712	d	P		MM	10729	M	SA	ON	CP
10713	d	P		MM	10730	d	P		MM
10714	d*SS	P	SR	IS	10731	d	P		KN
10715	d	P		MM	10732	d	P		KN
10716	d	P		ZD					

AD1G (FO)   OPEN FIRST

Dia. AD108. Mark 3A. Air conditioned. All now refurbished with table lamps and new seat cushions and trim. 48/– 2T (* 48/– 1T 1TD). BT10 bogies. d. ETH 6X.

11005–7 were open composites 11905–7 for a time.

Lot No. 30878 Derby 1975–76. 34.3t.

11005		V	P	VW	PC	11031	V	P	VW	MA
11006		V	P	VW	PC	11033	V	P	VW	PC
11007		V	P	VW	PC	11036	V	P	VW	MA
11011	*	V	P	VW	MA	11037	V	P	VW	PC
11013		V	P	VW	PC	11038	V	P	VW	PC
11016		V	P	VW	PC	11039	V	P	VW	PC
11017		V	P	VW	PC	11040	V	P	VW	MA
11018		V	P	VW	MA	11042	V	P	VW	MA
11019		V	P	VW	PC	11044	V	P	VW	MA
11020		V	P	VW	MA	11045	V	P	VW	PC
11021		V	P	VW	PC	11046	V	P	VW	PC
11023		V	P	VW	PC	11048	V	P	VW	MA
11024		V	P	VW	MA	11052	V	P	VW	MA
11026		V	P	VW	MA	11054	V	P	VW	PC
11027		V	P	VW	MA	11055	V	P	VW	PC
11028		V	P	VW	MA	11058	V	P	VW	MA
11029		V	P	VW	MA	11060	V	P	VW	PC
11030		V	P	VW	MA					

AD1H (FO)   OPEN FIRST

Dia. AD109. Mark 3B. Air conditioned. Inter-City 80 seats. All now refurbished with table lamps and new seat cushions and trim. 48/– 2T. BT10 bogies. d. ETH 6X.

Lot No. 30982 Derby 1985. 36.5t.

11064	**V**	P	*VW*	MA		11083 p	**V**	P	*VW*	MA
11065	**V**	P	*VW*	PC		11084 p	**V**	P	*VW*	MA
11066	**V**	P	*VW*	MA		11085 p	**V**	P	*VW*	MA
11067	**V**	P	*VW*	PC		11086 p	**V**	P	*VW*	PC
11068	**V**	P	*VW*	MA		11087 p	**V**	P	*VW*	MA
11069	**V**	P	*VW*	MA		11088 p	**V**	P	*VW*	PC
11070	**V**	P	*VW*	MA		11089 p	**V**	P	*VW*	PC
11071	**V**	P	*VW*	PC		11090 p	**V**	P	*VW*	MA
11072	**V**	P	*VW*	PC		11091 p	**V**	P	*VW*	MA
11073	**V**	P	*VW*	MA		11092 p	**V**	P	*VW*	MA
11074	**V**	P	*VW*	MA		11093 p	**V**	P	*VW*	PC
11075	**V**	P	*VW*	MA		11094 p	**V**	P	*VW*	MA
11076	**V**	P	*VW*	MA		11095 p	**V**	P	*VW*	MA
11077	**V**	P	*VW*	MA		11096 p	**V**	P	*VW*	PC
11078	**V**	P	*VW*	PC		11097 p	**V**	P	*VW*	MA
11079	**V**	P	*VW*	MA		11098 p	**V**	P	*VW*	PC
11080	**V**	P	*VW*	MA		11099 p	**V**	P	*VW*	PC
11081	**V**	P	*VW*	PC		11100 p	**V**	P	*VW*	PC
11082	**V**	P	*VW*	PC		11101 p	**V**	P	*VW*	MA

AD1J (FO)   OPEN FIRST

Dia. AD111. Mark 4. Air conditioned. 46/– 1T. BT41 bogies. ETH 6X.

11264–71 were cancelled.

Lot No. 31046 Metro-Cammell 1989–92. 39.7t.

11200		**GN**	H	*GN*	BN		11224		**GN**	H	*GN*	BN
11201	p	**GN**	H	*GN*	BN		11225	p	**GN**	H	*GN*	BN
11202		**GN**	H	*GN*	BN		11226		**GN**	H	*GN*	BN
11203	p	**GN**	H	*GN*	BN		11227	p	**GN**	H	*GN*	BN
11204	p	**GN**	H	*GN*	BN		11228	p	**GN**	H	*GN*	BN
11205		**GN**	H	*GN*	BN		11229	p	**GN**	H	*GN*	BN
11206		**GN**	H	*GN*	BN		11230		**GN**	H	*GN*	BN
11207	p	**GN**	H	*GN*	BN		11231	p	**GN**	H	*GN*	BN
11208		**GN**	H	*GN*	BN		11232		**GN**	H	*GN*	BN
11209		**GN**	H	*GN*	BN		11233	p	**GN**	H	*GN*	BN
11210		**GN**	H	*GN*	BN·		11234		**GN**	H	*GN*	BN
11211	p	**GN**	H	*GN*	BN		11235	p	**GN**	H	*GN*	BN
11212		**GN**	H	*GN*	BN		11236		**GN**	H	*GN*	BN
11213	p	**GN**	H	*GN*	BN		11237	p	**GN**	H	*GN*	BN
11214	p	**GN**	H	*GN*	BN		11238		**GN**	H	*GN*	BN
11215		**GN**	H	*GN*	BN		11239	p	**GN**	H	*GN*	BN
11216		**GN**	H	*GN*	BN		11240		**GN**	H	*GN*	BN
11217	p	**GN**	H	*GN*	BN		11241		**GN**	H	*GN*	BN
11218		**GN**	H	*GN*	BN		11242	p	**GN**	H	*GN*	BN
11219	p	**GN**	H	*GN*	BN		11243	p	**GN**	H	*GN*	BN
11220		**GN**	H	*GN*	BN		11244		**GN**	H	*GN*	BN
11221	p	**GN**	H	*GN*	BN		11245	p	**GN**	H	*GN*	BN
11222	p	**GN**	H	*GN*	BN		11246	p	**GN**	H	*GN*	BN
11223		**GN**	H	*GN*	BN		11247	p	**GN**	H	*GN*	BN

11248	**GN**	H *GN*	BN	11259 p	**GN**	H *GN*	BN	
11249 p	**GN**	H *GN*	BN	11260	**GN**	H *GN*	BN	
11250	**GN**	H *GN*	BN	11261 p	**GN**	H *GN*	BN	
11251 p	**GN**	H *GN*	BN	11262	**GN**	H *GN*	BN	
11252	**GN**	H *GN*	BN	11263 p	**GN**	H *GN*	BN	
11253 p	**GN**	H *GN*	BN	11272	**GN**	H *GN*	BN	
11254	**GN**	H *GN*	BN	11273	**GN**	H *GN*	BN	
11255 p	**GN**	H *GN*	BN	11274	**GN**	H *GN*	BN	
11256	**GN**	H *GN*	BN	11275	**GN**	H *GN*	BN	
11257 p	**GN**	H *GN*	BN	11276	**GN**	H *GN*	BN	
11258	**GN**	H *GN*	BN					

AC2G (TSO)   OPEN STANDARD

Dia. AC213 (AC220 z). Mark 3A. Air conditioned. All refurbished with modified seat backs and new layout and now further refurbished with new seat trim. – /76 2T (s –/70 2T 2W, z –/70 1TD 1T 2W). BT10 (* BREL T4) bogies. d. ETH 6X.

Note: 12169–72 were converted from open composites 11908–10/22, formerly FOs 11008–10/22.

Lot No. 30877 Derby 1975–77. 34.3t.

12004	**V**	P *VW*	MA	12035	**V**	P *VW*	PC	
12005	**V**	P *VW*	PC	12036 s	**V**	P *VW*	PC	
12007	**V**	P *VW*	MA	12037	**V**	P *VW*	PC	
12008	**V**	P *VW*	MA	12038	**V**	P *VW*	PC	
12009	**V**	P *VW*	MA	12040	**V**	P *VW*	PC	
12010	**V**	P *VW*	MA	12041	**V**	P *VW*	PC	
12011	**V**	P *VW*	PC	12042 s	**V**	P *VW*	PC	
12012	**V**	P *VW*	PC	12043	**V**	P *VW*	MA	
12013	**V**	P *VW*	MA	12044	**V**	P *VW*	MA	
12014	**V**	P *VW*	PC	12045	**V**	P *VW*	MA	
12015	**V**	P *VW*	PC	12046	**V**	P *VW*	PC	
12016	**V**	P *VW*	PC	12047 z	**V**	P *VW*	PC	
12017	**V**	P *VW*	MA	12048	**V**	P *VW*	PC	
12019	**V**	P *VW*	PC	12049	**V**	P *VW*	PC	
12020	**V**	P *VW*	PC	12050 s	**V**	P *VW*	PC	
12021	**V**	P *VW*	PC	12051	**V**	P *VW*	PC	
12022	**V**	P *VW*	MA	12052	**V**	P *VW*	MA	
12023	**V**	P *VW*	PC	12053	**V**	P *VW*	MA	
12024 s	**V**	P *VW*	PC	12054 s	**V**	P *VW*	MA	
12025	**V**	P *VW*	MA	12055	**V**	P *VW*	PC	
12026	**V**	P *VW*	PC	12056	**V**	P *VW*	PC	
12027	**V**	P *VW*	MA	12057	**V**	P *VW*	MA	
12028	**V**	P *VW*	MA	12058	**V**	P̦ *VW*	PC	
12029	**V**	P *VW*	MA	12059 s	**V**	P *VW*	MA	
12030	**V**	P *VW*	PC	12060	**V**	P *VW*	PC	
12031	**V**	P *VW*	PC	12061 s	**V**	P *VW*	PC	
12032	**V**	P *VW*	PC	12062	**V**	P *VW*	PC	
12033 z	**V**	P *VW*	MA	12063	**V**	P *VW*	MA	
12034	**V**	P *VW*	MA	12064	**V**	P *VW*	PC	

12065	**V**	P	*VW*	MA	12117	**V**	P	*VW*	MA
12066	**V**	P	*VW*	MA	12118	**V**	P	*VW*	MA
12067	**V**	P	*VW*	MA	12119	**V**	P	*VW*	MA
12068	**V**	P	*VW*	MA	12120	**V**	P	*VW*	MA
12069	**V**	P	*VW*	MA	12121	**V**	P	*VW*	PC
12070	**V**	P	*VW*	PC	12122 z	**V**	P	*VW*	MA
12071	**V**	P	*VW*	PC	12123	**V**	P	*VW*	PC
12072	**V**	P	*VW*	MA	12124	**V**	P	*VW*	MA
12073	**V**	P	*VW*	MA	12125	**V**	P	*VW*	MA
12075	**V**	P	*VW*	PC	12126	**V**	P	*VW*	MA
12076	**V**	P	*VW*	PC	12127	**V**	P	*VW*	PC
12077	**V**	P	*VW*	PC	12128 s	**V**	P	*VW*	MA
12078	**V**	P	*VW*	MA	12129	**V**	P	*VW*	MA
12079	**V**	P	*VW*	PC	12130	**V**	P	*VW*	MA
12080	**V**	P	*VW*	PC	12131	**V**	P	*VW*	PC
12081	**V**	P	*VW*	PC	12132	**V**	P	*VW*	MA
12082	**V**	P	*VW*	PC	12133	**V**	P	*VW*	MA
12083	**V**	P	*VW*	MA	12134	**V**	P	*VW*	PC
12084	**V**	P	*VW*	MA	12135	**V**	P	*VW*	PC
12085 s	**V**	P	*VW*	MA	12136	**V**	P	*VW*	PC
12086 s	**V**	P	*VW*	MA	12137	**V**	P	*VW*	PC
12087 s	**V**	P	*VW*	PC	12138	**V**	P	*VW*	PC
12088 z	**V**	P	*VW*	PC	12139	**V**	P	*VW*	MA
12089	**V**	P	*VW*	MA	12140 z*	**V**	P	*VW*	PC
12090	**V**	P	*VW*	MA	12141	**V**	P	*VW*	PC
12091	**V**	P	*VW*	PC	12142 z	**V**	P	*VW*	PC
12092	**V**	P	*VW*	MA	12143	**V**	P	*VW*	PC
12093	**V**	P	*VW*	PC	12144 s	**V**	P	*VW*	PC
12094	**V**	P	*VW*	PC	12145	**V**	P	*VW*	MA
12095	**V**	P	*VW*	MA	12146	**V**	P	*VW*	PC
12096	**V**	P	*VW*	PC	12147	**V**	P	*VW*	PC
12097	**V**	P	*VW*	PC	12148	**V**	P	*VW*	PC
12098	**V**	P	*VW*	MA	12149	**V**	P	*VW*	PC
12099	**V**	P	*VW*	PC	12150	**V**	P	*VW*	PC
12100 z	**V**	P	*VW*	PC	12151	**V**	P	*VW*	PC
12101 s	**V**	P	*VW*	PC	12152	**V**	P	*VW*	PC
12102	**V**	P	*VW*	PC	12153	**V**	P	*VW*	PC
12103 s	**V**	P	*VW*	MA	12154	**V**	P	*VW*	MA
12104	**V**	P	*VW*	MA	12155 s	**V**	P	*VW*	PC
12105	**V**	P	*VW*	PC	12156	**V**	P	*VW*	MA
12106	**V**	P	*VW*	MA	12157	**V**	P	*VW*	MA
12107	**V**	P	*VW*	PC	12158	**V**	P	*VW*	PC
12108 s	**V**	P	*VW*	MA	12159	**V**	P	*VW*	PC
12109 s	**V**	P	*VW*	MA	12160 s	**V**	P	*VW*	PC
12110	**V**	P	*VW*	MA	12161 z	**V**	P	*VW*	MA
12111	**V**	P	*VW*	MA	12163	**V**	P	*VW*	MA
12112 z	**V**	P	*VW*	MA	12164	**V**	P	*VW*	PC
12113	**V**	P	*VW*	MA	12165	**V**	P	*VW*	MA
12114	**V**	P	*VW*	PC	12166	**V**	P	*VW*	PC
12115	**V**	P	*VW*	MA	12167	**V**	P	*VW*	PC
12116	**V**	P	*VW*	PC	12168 s	**V**	P	*VW*	PC

| 12169 s | **V** | P | *VW* | MA | | 12171 s | **V** | P | *VW* | PC |
| 12170 s | **V** | P | *VW* | MA | | 12172 s | **V** | P | *VW* | PC |

Al2J (TSOE)   OPEN STANDARD (END)

Dia. Al201. Mark 4. Air conditioned. –/74 2T. BT41 bogies. ETH 6X.

Lot No. 31047 Metro-Cammell 1989–91. 39.5t.

12232 was converted from the original 12405.

12200	**GN**	H	*GN*	BN		12216	**GN**	H	*GN*	BN
12201	**GN**	H	*GN*	BN		12217	**GN**	H	*GN*	BN
12202	**GN**	H	*GN*	BN		12218	**GN**	H	*GN*	BN
12203	**GN**	H	*GN*	BN		12219	**GN**	H	*GN*	BN
12204	**GN**	H	*GN*	BN		12220	**GN**	H	*GN*	BN
12205	**GN**	H	*GN*	BN		12222	**GN**	H	*GN*	BN
12206	**GN**	H	*GN*	BN		12223	**GN**	H	*GN*	BN
12207	**GN**	H	*GN*	BN		12224	**GN**	H	*GN*	BN
12208	**GN**	H	*GN*	BN		12225	**GN**	H	*GN*	BN
12209	**GN**	H	*GN*	BN		12226	**GN**	H	*GN*	BN
12210	**GN**	H	*GN*	BN		12227	**GN**	H	*GN*	BN
12211	**GN**	H	*GN*	BN		12228	**GN**	H	*GN*	BN
12212	**GN**	H	*GN*	BN		12229	**GN**	H	*GN*	BN
12213	**GN**	H	*GN*	BN		12230	**GN**	H	*GN*	BN
12214	**GN**	H	*GN*	BN		12231	**GN**	H	*GN*	BN
12215	**GN**	H	*GN*	BN		12232	**GN**	H	*GN*	BN

AL2J (TSOD) OPEN STANDARD (DISABLED ACCESS)

Dia. AL201. Mark 4. Air conditioned. –/72 1TD 1W. BT41 bogies. p. ETH 6X.

Lot No. 31048 Metro-Cammell 1989–91. 39.4t.

12300	**GN**	H	*GN*	BN		12316	**GN**	H	*GN*	BN
12301	**GN**	H	*GN*	BN		12317	**GN**	H	*GN*	BN
12302	**GN**	H	*GN*	BN		12318	**GN**	H	*GN*	BN
12303	**GN**	H	*GN*	BN		12319	**GN**	H	*GN*	BN
12304	**GN**	H	*GN*	BN		12320	**GN**	H	*GN*	BN
12305	**GN**	H	*GN*	BN		12321	**GN**	H	*GN*	BN
12306	**GN**	H	*GN*	BN		12322	**GN**	H	*GN*	BN
12307	**GN**	H	*GN*	BN		12323	**GN**	H	*GN*	BN
12308	**GN**	H	*GN*	BN		12324	**GN**	H	*GN*	BN
12309	**GN**	H	*GN*	BN		12325	**GN**	H	*GN*	BN
12310	**GN**	H	*GN*	BN		12326	**GN**	H	*GN*	BN
12311	**GN**	H	*GN*	BN		12327	**GN**	H	*GN*	BN
12312	**GN**	H	*GN*	BN		12328	**GN**	H	*GN*	BN
12313	**GN**	H	*GN*	BN		12329	**GN**	H	*GN*	BN
12314	**GN**	H	*GN*	BN		12330	**GN**	H	*GN*	BN
12315	**GN**	H	*GN*	BN						

AC2J (TSO) OPEN STANDARD

Dia. AC214. Mark 4. Air conditioned. –/74 2T. BT41 bogies. ETH 6X.

Lot No. 31049 Metro-Cammell 1989 onwards. 39.9t.

12405 is the second coach to carry that number. It was built from the bodyshell originally intended for 12221. The original 12405 is now 12232. 12490–12512 were cancelled.

12400	**GN**	H *GN*	BN	12441	**GN**	H *GN*	BN
12401	**GN**	H *GN*	BN	12442	**GN**	H *GN*	BN
12402	**GN**	H *GN*	BN	12443	**GN**	H *GN*	BN
12403	**GN**	H *GN*	BN	12444	**GN**	H *GN*	BN
12404	**GN**	H *GN*	BN	12445	**GN**	H *GN*	BN
12405	**GN**	H *GN*	BN	12446	**GN**	H *GN*	BN
12406	**GN**	H *GN*	BN	12447	**GN**	H *GN*	BN
12407	**GN**	H *GN*	BN	12448	**GN**	H *GN*	BN
12408	**GN**	H *GN*	BN	12449	**GN**	H *GN*	BN
12409	**GN**	H *GN*	BN	12450	**GN**	H *GN*	BN
12410	**GN**	H *GN*	BN	12451	**GN**	H *GN*	BN
12411	**GN**	H *GN*	BN	12452	**GN**	H *GN*	BN
12412	**GN**	H *GN*	BN	12453	**GN**	H *GN*	BN
12413	**GN**	H *GN*	BN	12454	**GN**	H *GN*	BN
12414	**GN**	H *GN*	BN	12455	**GN**	H *GN*	BN
12415	**GN**	H *GN*	BN	12456	**GN**	H *GN*	BN
12416	**GN**	H *GN*	BN	12457	**GN**	H *GN*	BN
12417	**GN**	H *GN*	BN	12458	**GN**	H *GN*	BN
12418	**GN**	H *GN*	BN	12459	**GN**	H *GN*	BN
12419	**GN**	H *GN*	BN	12460	**GN**	H *GN*	BN
12420	**GN**	H *GN*	BN	12461	**GN**	H *GN*	BN
12421	**GN**	H *GN*	BN	12462	**GN**	H *GN*	BN
12422	**GN**	H *GN*	BN	12463	**GN**	H *GN*	BN
12423	**GN**	H *GN*	BN	12464	**GN**	H *GN*	BN
12424	**GN**	H *GN*	BN	12465	**GN**	H *GN*	BN
12425	**GN**	H *GN*	BN	12466	**GN**	H *GN*	BN
12426	**GN**	H *GN*	BN	12467	**GN**	H *GN*	BN
12427	**GN**	H *GN*	BN	12468	**GN**	H *GN*	BN
12428	**GN**	H *GN*	BN	12469	**GN**	H *GN*	BN
12429	**GN**	H *GN*	BN	12470	**GN**	H *GN*	BN
12430	**GN**	H *GN*	BN	12471	**GN**	H *GN*	BN
12431	**GN**	H *GN*	BN	12472	**GN**	H *GN*	3N
12432	**GN**	H *GN*	BN	12473	**GN**	H *GN*	BN
12433	**GN**	H *GN*	BN	12474	**GN**	H *GN*	BN
12434	**GN**	H *GN*	BN	12475	**GN**	H *GN*	BN
12435	**GN**	H *GN*	BN	12476	**GN**	H *GN*	BN
12436	**GN**	H *GN*	BN	12477	**GN**	H *GN*	BN
12437	**GN**	H *GN*	BN	12478	**GN**	H *GN*	BN
12438	**GN**	H *GN*	BN	12479	**GN**	H *GN*	BN
12439	**GN**	H *GN*	BN	12480	**GN**	H *GN*	BN
12440	**GN**	H *GN*	BN	12481	**GN**	H *GN*	BN

12482	**GN**	H *GN*	BN		12522	**GN**	H *GN*	BN
12483	**GN**	H *GN*	BN		12523	**GN**	H *GN*	BN
12484	**GN**	H *GN*	BN		12524	**GN**	H *GN*	BN
12485	**GN**	H *GN*	BN		12525	**GN**	H *GN*	BN
12486	**GN**	H *GN*	BN		12526	**GN**	H *GN*	BN
12487	**GN**	H *GN*	BN		12527	**GN**	H *GN*	BN
12488	**GN**	H *GN*	BN		12528	**GN**	H *GN*	BN
12489	**GN**	H *GN*	BN		12529	**GN**	H *GN*	BN
12513	**GN**	H *GN*	BN		12530	**GN**	H *GN*	BN
12514	**GN**	H *GN*	BN		12531	**GN**	H *GN*	BN
12515	**GN**	H *GN*	BN		12532	**GN**	H *GN*	BN
12516	**GN**	H *GN*	BN		12533	**GN**	H *GN*	BN
12517	**GN**	H *GN*	BN		12534	**GN**	H *GN*	BN
12518	**GN**	H *GN*	BN		12535	**GN**	H *GN*	BN
12519	**GN**	H *GN*	BN		12536	**GN**	H *GN*	BN
12520	**GN**	H *GN*	BN		12537	**GN**	H *GN*	BN
12521	**GN**	H *GN*	BN		12538	**GN**	H *GN*	BN

AA11 (FK)   CORRIDOR FIRST

Dia. AA101. Mark 1. 42/– 2T. ETH 3.

13225–13230. Lot No. 30381 Swindon 1959. B4 bogies. 33t.
13318–13341. Lot No. 30667 Swindon 1962. Commonwealth bogies. 36t.

f Fitted with fluorescent lighting.

13225	k	**RR**	H	EC		13318			RS *SO*	ZA
13227	xk	**CH**	RV *ON*	CP		13321	x	**M**	WC *ON*	CS
13228	xk	**M**	BK	BT		13331	vf	**N**	LW	CP
13229	xk	**M**	BK *ON*	BT		13341	f	**WR**RS *SO*	ZA
13230	xk	**M**	BK *ON*	BT						

AA1A (FK)   CORRIDOR FIRST

Dia. AA106. Mark 2A. Pressure ventilated. 42/– 2T. B4 bogies. ETH 4.

Lot No. 30774 Derby 1968. 33t.

13440	v	**G**	MH *ON*	RL

AA1D (FK)   CORRIDOR FIRST

Dia. AA109. Mark 2D. Air conditioned (Stones). 42/– 2T. B4 bogies. ETH 5.

Lot No. 30825 Derby 1971–72. 34.5t.

13582		E	KN		13604	RS	BN
13585		RV	CP		13607	RS	FK

AB11 (BFK)   CORRIDOR BRAKE FIRST

Dia. AB101. Mark 1. 24/– 1T. Commonwealth bogies. ETH 2.

17007. Lot No. 30382 Swindon 1959. 35t.

17013–17019. Lot No. 30668 Swindon 1961. 36t.
17023. Lot No. 30718 Swindon 1963. Metal window frames. 36t.

Originally numbered 14007/13/15/18/19/23.

17007	x	**PC**	MN	*OS*	SL	17018	v	**CH**	BM	*ON*	TM
17013		**M**	FS	*OS*	SZ	17019	x	**M**	NE	*OS*	BQ
17015	x	**BG**	RS	*ON*	BN	17023	x	**G**	RS	*ON*	BN

AB1A (BFK)   CORRIDOR BRAKE FIRST

Dia. AB103. Mark 2A. Pressure ventilated. 24/– 1T. B4 bogies. ETH 4.

17056–17077. Lot No. 30775 Derby 1967–8. 32t.
17086–17102. Lot No. 30786 Derby 1968. 32t.

Originally numbered 14056–102. 17090 was numbered 35503 for a time when declassified.

17056	**CH**	RV	*ON*	CP	17090	v	**RR**	H		TM
17058	**N**	H		KN	17091	v	**RR**	H		LT
17064	v	**RR**	H		LT	17096		**G**	MN	*OS*	SL
17077	**FT**	RV	*ON*	CP	17099	v	**RR**	H		LT
17086	**FT**	RV	*ON*	CP	17102		**M**	WC	*ON*	CS

AB1D (BFK)   CORRIDOR BRAKE FIRST

Dia. AB106. Mark 2D. Air conditioned (Stones equipment). 24/– 1T. B4 Bogies. ETH 5.

Lot No. 30823 Derby 1971–72. 33.5t.

Non-Standard Livery: 17141 & 17164 are as **WV** without lining.

Originally numbered 14141–72.

17141	**0**	RS		FK	17163			H		KN
17144		RK	*SO*	DY	17164	**0**	RV	*ON*	CP
17146		RK	*SO*	DY	17165		RS		FK
17148		CW		MM	17166		H		PY
17151		VS		CP	17167	**VN**	VS	*ON*	CP
17153	**WR**	RS		CS	17168	**M**	WC	*ON*	CS
17155		CW		MM	17169		RS		CS
17156		RS		DY	17170		RS		DY
17159	**CH**	RV	*ON*	CP	17171		E		CL
17161		E		OM	17172		RS		FK

AE1G (BFO)   OPEN BRAKE FIRST

Dia. AE101. Mark 3B. Air conditioned. Fitted with hydraulic handbrake. Refurbished with table lamps and burgundy seat trim. 36/– 1T (w 35/– 1T) BT10 bogies. pg. d. ETH 5X.

Lot No. 30990 Derby 1986. 35.81t.

17173	**V**	P	*VW*	PC	17175	w	**V**	P	*VW*	PC
17174	**V**	P	*VW*	PC						

AB31 (BCK)   CORRIDOR BRAKE COMPOSITE

Dia. AB301 (AB302*). Mark 1. There are two variants depending upon whether the standard class compartments have armrests. Each vehicle has two first class and three standard class compartments. 12/18 2T (12/24 2T *). ETH 2.

21224. Lot No. 30245. Metro-Cammell 1958. B4 bogies. 33t.
21236–21246. Lot No. 30669 Swindon 1961–62. Commonwealth bogies. 36t.
21252–21256. Lot No. 30731 Derby 1963. Commonwealth bogies. 37t.
21266–21272. Lot No. 30732 Derby 1964. Commonwealth bogies. 37t.

21224	**RB**	VS	*ON*	CP		21256	x **M**	WC *ON*	CS
21236	v **M**	ER	*OS*	ZG		21266	*	FS		CS
21241	x **M**	BK	*ON*	BT		21268	*	FS		CS
21245	x **CC**	RS	*ON*	BN		21269	* **WV**	RS	*ON*	BN
21246	**BG**	RS	*ON*	BN		21272	x* **CH**	RV	*ON*	CP
21252	v **G**	MH	*ON*	RL					

AA21 (SK)   CORRIDOR STANDARD

Dia. AA201 (AA202*). Mark 1. There are two variants depending upon whether the standard class compartments have armrests. Each vehicle has eight compartments. All remaining vehicles have metal window frames and melamine interior panelling. Commonwealth bogies. –/48 2T (–/64 2T *). ETH 4.

25729–25893. Lot No. 30685 Derby 1961–62. 36t.
25955. Lot No. 30686 Derby 1962. 36t.
26013. Lot No. 30719 Derby 1962. 37t.

Non-Standard Livery: 26013 is Pilkington's K (green with white/red chevron and light blue block).

f Facelifted with fluorescent lighting.
t Rebuilt internally as TSO using components from 4936. -/64 2T.

These coaches were renumbered 18729–19013 for a time.

25729	x*f **CH**	WC *ON*	TM		25862	x	**M**	WC *ON*	CS
25756	x **M**	WC *ON*	CS		25893	x	**CH**	WC *ON*	TM
25767	x **CH**	WC *ON*	TM		25955	x*f **M**	WC *ON*	CS
25806	xt **M**	WC *ON*	CS		26013	x	**O**	WC *ON*	CS
25808	x **M**	WC *ON*	CS					

AB21 (BSK)   CORRIDOR BRAKE STANDARD

Dia. AB201 (AB202*). Mark 1. There are two variants depending upon whether the standard class compartments have armrests. Each vehicle has four compartments. Lots 30699, 30721 and 30728 have metal window frames and melamine interior panelling. –/24 1T (–/32 1T*). ETH2.

g Fitted with an e.t.s. generator.

34525. Lot No. 30095 Wolverton 1955. Commonwealth bogies. 36 t.
34991. Lot No. 30229 Metro-Cammell 1956–57. Commonwealth bogies. 36 t.
35185–35207. Lot No. 30427 Wolverton 1959. B4 bogies. 33t.
35317–35333. Lot No. 30699 Wolverton 1962–63. Commonwealth bogies. 37t.
35407, 35452–35486. Lot No. 30721 Wolverton 1963. Commonwealth Bogies. 37t.
35449. Lot No. 30728 Wolverton 1963. Commonwealth bogies. 37t.

Non-Standard Livery: 35322 and 35407 are in London & North Western Railway livery.

34525	g	**M**	GS		CS	35457	v	**M**	IE *OS*	NY
34991	*	**PC**	VS	*ON*	SL	35459	x	**M**	WC *ON*	CS
35185	x	**M**	BK	*ON*	BT	35461	x	**CH**	RV *OS*	CP
35207	x*	**CC**	VS	*OS*	SL	35463	v	**M**	WC *OS*	CS
35317	x	**G**	WT	*ON*	CS	35465	x	**WV**	LW *OS*	CP
35322	x	**O**	SH	*ON*	CJ	35467	v	**M**	SV *OS*	KR
35329	v	**G**	MH	*ON*	RL	35468	v	**M**	NR *OS*	YM
35333	x	**CH**	24	*OS*	DI	35469	xg	**CC**	RS *ON*	BN
35407	xg	**O**	SH	*ON*	CJ	35470	v	**CH**	BM *OS*	TM
35449	x	**CH**	14	*OS*	BQ	35476	v	**CC**	62 *OS*	SK
35452		**RR**	H		CP	35479	v	**M**	SV *OS*	KR
35453	x	**CH**	RV	*ON*	CP	35486	v	**M**	SV *OS*	KR

AB2A/AB2C (BSK)   CORRIDOR BRAKE STANDARD

Dia. AB204. Mark 2A (c 2C). Pressure ventilated. Renumbered from BFK. –/24 1T. B4 (g B5) bogies. ETH 4.

35507/8/11. Lot No. 30796 Derby 1969–70. 32.5t.
35510/12–14. Lot No. 30775 Derby 1967–68. 32t.
35515–18. Lot No. 30786 Derby 1968. 32t.

* Cage removed from brake compartment.
g Fitted with an e.t.s. generator.

35507	(14123, 17123)	c	**RR**	CM		KN
35508	(14128, 17128)	c	**RR**	RV		CP
35510	(14075, 17075)		**RR**	H		KN
35511	(14130, 17130)	g	**G**	RA		CP
35512	(14057, 17057)	*	**RR**	H		CP
35513	(14063, 17063)	*	**RR**	H	*CA*	CF
35514	(14069, 17069)	*	**RR**	H		CP
35515	(14079, 17079)	*	**RR**	H	*CA*	CF
35516	(14080, 17080)	*	**RR**	H	*CA*	CF
35517	(14088, 17088)	*	**RR**	H		CP
35518	(14097, 17097)	*	**RR**	H	*CA*	CF

NAMED COACHES

The following miscellaneous coaches carry names:

1659	CAMELOT	5193	CLAN MACLEOD
1683	Carol	5212	CAPERKAILZIE
3066	CHATSWORTH	5275	Wendy
3068	BEAULIEU	5307	Beverley
3069	ALNWICK	5350	Dawn
3105	JULIA	5364	Andrea
3125	LOCH SHIEL	5365	Deborah
3130	PAMELA	5373	Felicity
3174	GLAMIS	5376	Michaela
3181	MONARCH	5378	Sarah
3182	WARWICK	9385	BALMACARA
3188	SOVEREIGN	9388	BAILECHAUL
3240	PENDENNIS	9417	Ellen
3247	CHATSWORTH	10569	LEVIATHAN
3267	BELVOIR	17007	MERCATOR
3273	ALNWICK	17077	Catherine
3275	HARLECH	17086	Georgina
5132	CLAN MUNRO	21224	DIRECTORS CAR
5154	CLAN FRASER	35449	ELIZABETH

Mark 1 Stock. Miniature Buffet Car (RMB) No. 1813 at Worcester Shrub Hill on 26th June 1999. This vehicle carries BR carmine & cream livery.

Stephen Widdowson

Corridor Brake Composite (BCK) No. 21272 is pictured at Hereford on 29th May 2000. BR chocolate & cream livery is carried, as used by the GWR and later adopted by the Western Region of British Railways for named trains.

Stephen Widdowson

▲ **Mark 2 Stock.** Pullman Brake First (PFB) No. 586 'DERWENTWATER' stands at Carnforth T&RSMD during November 2000. The coach had just received a repaint into Pullman Car Company umber & cream, a livery which it has never previously carried. **James Shuttleworth**

▼ **Mark 2B Stock.** Royal Household Couchette No. 2905, in Royal Train purple livery, stands at Old Oak Common on 5th August 2000. **Stephen Widdowson**

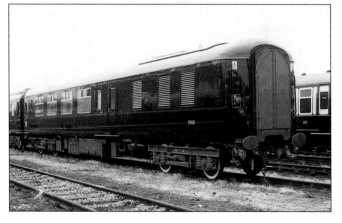

▲ **Mark 2E Stock.** BR maroon liveried Open Standard (TSO) No. 5756 is pictured stabled at Carnforth on 11th March 2000. **Martyn Hilbert**

▼ Open Brake Standard (BSO) No. 9500, in Intercity livery, is pictured at Birmingham International on 14th May 1998. **Stephen Widdowson**

Mark 2F Stock. Virgin Trains liveried Buffet Open First (RFB) No. 1215 leaves Carlisle in the formation of the 16.33 Glasgow Central–London Paddington on 25th June 2000.

K. Conkey

Anglia Railways liveried Driving Open Brake Standard (DBSO) No. 9714 at Ipswich on 5th May 2000.

D. Ford

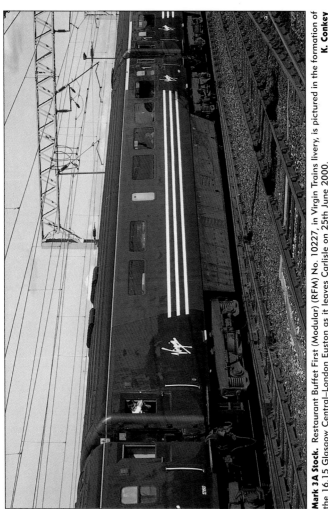

Mark 3A Stock. Restaurant Buffet First (Modular) (RFM) No. 10227, in Virgin Trains livery, is pictured in the formation of the 16.15 Glasgow Central–London Euston as it leaves Carlisle on 25th June 2000. **K. Conkey**

▲ Scotrail 'Caledonian Sleeper' liveried Sleeping Car with Pantry (SLEP) No. 10526 at Glasgow Central on 17th July 2000. **D. Ford**

▼ **Mark 3B Stock.** Virgin Trains liveried Open First (FO) No. 11097 leaves Carlisle as part of the 17.30 Glasgow Central–London Euston on 16th July 2000. **K. Conkey**

Mark 4 Stock. Great North Eastern Railway liveried Open First (FO) No. 11238 reaches the end of its journey as it enters London King's Cross with the 12.00 from Edinburgh on 13th June 2000.　**K. Conkey**

▲ **High Speed Train Trailer Cars.** Trailer Buffet First (TRFB) No. 40720, in Great North Eastern Railway livery, forms part of the 07.55 from Inverness as it enters London King's Cross on 13th June 2000. **K. Conkey**

▼ First Great Western liveried Trailer Standard (TS) No. 42008 pauses at Reading in the formation of a London Paddington bound servce. The date is 11th August 2000. **David Brown**

▲ **Non-Passenger Carrying Coaching Stock.** Post Office Sorting Van (POS) No. 80346 stabled at Carlisle on 26th June 2000. All Travelling Post Office vehicles carry Royal Mail livery. **K. Conkey**

▼ Driving Brake Van (DLV) No. 82215, in Great North Eastern Railway livery, arrives at York with a London King's Cross bound service on 4th September 1999. **Stephen Widdowson**

Virgin Trains liveried Driving Brake Van (DLV) No. 82148 'International Spring Fair' leads the 10.45 Liverpool Lime Street–London Euston service as it approaches Headstone Lane on 17th August 2000. These vehicles are, along with the Mark 4 variant, often referred to as Driving Van Trailers or DVTs.

David Brown

Rail express systems liveried Propelling Control Vehicle No. 94315 at Carlisle on 26th June 2000.

K. Conkey

Carrying Rail express systems livery but without the logo, High Security Brake Van No. 94504 passes Abbotswood Junction in the formation of a southbound Royal Mail service on 13th June 2000. **Stephen Widdowson**

▲ Plain red liveried High Security General Utility Van No. 95734 stabled at Carlisle on 30th June 2000. **K. Conkey**

▼ First Great Western liveried Motorail Van No. 96604 at Reading on 20th June 2000. The ivory and white stripes applied to First Great Western liveried passenger carrying stock, are not carried by these vehicles. **D. Ford**

▲ **Saloons.** Former London & North Western Railway (LNWR) Dining Saloon No. 159 operates as part of a special charter train set. The coach, which carries LNWR livery, is seen at Ascot on 17th June 1999. **D. Ford**

▼ **Pullman Car Company Series Stock.** Pullman Parlour First 'LUCILLE' at London Victoria on 12th May 2000. **David Brown**

2.2. HIGH SPEED TRAIN TRAILER CARS

HSTs normally run in formations of 7 or 8 trailer cars with a Class 43 power car at each end. All trailer cars are classified Mark 3 and have BT10 bogies with disc brakes and central door locking. Heating is by a 415V three-phase supply and vehicles have air conditioning. Max. Speed is 125 m.p.h.

All vehicles underwent a mid-life refurbishment in the 1980s, and a further refurbishment programme was completed in November 2000, each train operating company having a different scheme as follows:

First Great Western. Green seat covers and extra partitions between seat bays.
Great North Eastern Railway. New ceiling lighting panels and brown seat covers. First class vehicles have table lamps and imitation walnut plastic end panels.
Virgin Cross-Country. Green seat covers. Standard class vehicles have four seats in the centre of each carriage replaced with a luggage stack.
Virgin West Coast. Red seat covers in first class and light blue seat covers in standard class.
Midland Mainline. Grey seat covers, redesigned seat squabs, side carpeting and two seats in the centre of each carriage replaced with a luggage stack.

All vehicles except TRFK 40501/40513 and TRFM 40619 have been included in this programme.

Tops Type Codes

TOPS type codes for HST trailer cars are made up as follows:

(1) Two letters denoting the layout of the vehicle as follows:

GH	Open
GJ	Open with Guard's compartment.
GK	Buffet
GL	Kitchen
GN	Buffet

(2) A digit for the class of passenger accommodation

1	First
2	Standard (formerly second)
4	Unclassified

(3) A suffix relating to the build of coach.

G	Mark 3

Operator Codes

The normal operator codes are given in brackets after the TOPS codes. These are as follows:

TF	Trailer First	TRFK	Trailer Kitchen First
TGS	Trailer Guard's Standard	TRFM	Trailer Modular Buffet First
TRB	Trailer Buffet First	TRSB	Trailer Buffet Standard
TRFB	Trailer Buffet First	TS	Trailer Standard

GN4G (TRB)   TRAILER BUFFET FIRST

Dia. GN401. Converted from TRSB by fitting first class seats. Renumbered from 404xx series by subtracting 200. 23/–. p. q.

40204–40228. Lot No. 30883 Derby 1976–77. 36.12 t.
40231. Lot No. 30899 Derby 1978–79. 36.12 t.

40204	**FG**	A	*GW*	PM	40210	**FG**	A	*GW*	PM
40205	**FG**	A	*GW*	PM	40213	**FG**	A		ZC
40206	**FG**	A	*GW*	PM	40221	**FG**	A	*GW*	PM
40207	**FG**	A	*GW*	PM	40228	**FG**	A	*GW*	PM
40208	**FG**	A	*GW*	PM	40231	**FG**	A	*GW*	PM
40209	**FG**	A	*GW*	PM					

GK2G (TRSB)   TRAILER BUFFET STANDARD

Dia. GK202. Renumbered from 400xx series by adding 400. –/33 1W. p. q.

40401–40427. Lot No. 30883 Derby 1976–77. 36.12 t.
40429–40437. Lot No. 30899 Derby 1978–79. 36.12 t.

40411/2/32–4 were numbered 40211/2/32–4 for a time when fitted with first class seats.

40401	**V**	P	*VX*	LA	40423	**V**	P	*VX*	LA
40402	**V**	P	*VX*	LA	40424	**V**	P	*VX*	LA
40403	**V**	P	*VX*	LA	40425	**V**	P	*VX*	LA
40411	**V**	P	*VX*	LA	40426	**V**	P	*VX*	LA
40412	**V**	P	*VX*	LA	40427	**V**	P	*VX*	LA
40414	**V**	P	*VX*	LA	40429	**V**	P	*VX*	LA
40415	**V**	P	*VX*	LA	40430	**V**	P	*VX*	LA
40416	**V**	P	*VX*	LA	40432	**V**	P	*VX*	LA
40417	**V**	P	*VX*	LA	40433	**V**	P	*VX*	LA
40418	**V**	P	*VX*	LA	40434	**V**	P	*VX*	LA
40419	**V**	P	*VX*	LA	40435	**V**	P	*VX*	LA
40420	**V**	P	*VX*	LA	40436	**V**	P	*VX*	LA
40422	**V**	P	*VX*	LA	40437	**V**	P	*VX*	LA

GL1G (TRFK)   TRAILER KITCHEN FIRST

Dia. GL101. Reclassified from TRUK. p. q. 24/–.

Lot No. 30884 Derby 1976–77. 37 t.

40501		P		ZD	40513	P	ZD

GK1G (TRFM)   TRAILER MODULAR BUFFET FIRST

Dia. GK102. Converted to modular catering from TRFB 40719. 17/– 1T. p. q.

Lot No. 30921 Derby 1978–79. 38.16 t.

40619	P	*VX*	LA

GK1G (TRFB) TRAILER BUFFET FIRST

Dia. GK101. These vehicles have larger kitchens than the 402xx and 404xx series vehicles, and are used in trains where full meal service is required. They were renumbered from the 403xx series (in which the seats were unclassified) by adding 400 to previous number. 17/– (*12/– + one seat for staff use). p. q.

40700–40721. Lot No. 30921 Derby 1978–79. 38.16 t.
40722–40735. Lot No. 30940 Derby 1979–80. 38.16 t.
40736–40753. Lot No. 30948 Derby 1980–81. 38.16 t.
40754–40757. Lot No. 30966 Derby 1982. 38.16 t.

40700	**MM**	P	*MM*	NL		40730	**MM**	P	*MM*	NL
40701	**MM**	P	*MM*	NL		40731	**FG**	A	*GW*	LA
40702	**MM**	P	*MM*	NL		40732	**V**	A	*VW*	LA
40703	**FG**	A	*GW*	LA		40733	**FG**	A	*GW*	LA
40704	**GN**	A	*GN*	EC		40734	**FG**	A	*GW*	PM
40705	**GN**	A	*GN*	EC		40735	**GN**	A	*GN*	EC
40706	**GN**	A	*GN*	EC		40736	**FG**	A	*GW*	LA
40707	**FG**	A	*GW*	LA		40737	**GN**	A	*GN*	EC
40708	**MM**	P	*MM*	NL		40738	**FG**	A	*GW*	LA
40709	**FG**	A	*GW*	LA		40739	**FG**	A	*GW*	PM
40710	**FG**	A	*GW*	LA		40740	**GN**	A	*GN*	EC
40711	**GN**	A	*GN*	EC		40741	**MM**	P	*MM*	NL
40712	**FG**	A	*GW*	LA		40742	**V**	A	*VW*	LA
40713	**FG**	A	*GW*	LA		40743	**FG**	A	*GW*	LA
40714	**FG**	A	*GW*	PM		40744	**FG**	A	*GW*	PM
40715	**FG**	A	*GW*	PM		40745	**FG**	A	*GW*	LA
40716	**FG**	A	*GW*	PM		40746	**MM**	P	*MM*	NL
40717	**FG**	A	*GW*	PM		40747	**FG**	A	*GW*	PM
40718	**FG**	A	*GW*	LA		40748	**GN**	A	*GN*	EC
40720	**GN**	A	*GN*	EC		40749	**MM**	P	*MM*	NL
40721	**FG**	A	*GW*	LA		40750	**GN**	A	*GN*	EC
40722	**FG**	A	*GW*	LA		40751	**MM**	P	*MM*	NL
40723 *	**V**	A	*VW*	LA		40752	**FG**	A	*GW*	LA
40724	**FG**	A	*GW*	PM		40753	**MM**	P	*MM*	NL
40725	**FG**	A	*GW*	LA		40754	**MM**	P	*MM*	NL
40726	**FG**	A	*GW*	LA		40755	**FG**	A	*GW*	LA
40727	**FG**	A	*GW*	LA		40756	**MM**	P	*MM*	NL
40728	**MM**	P	*MM*	NL		40757	**FG**	A	*GW*	LA
40729	**MM**	P	*MM*	NL						

GH1G (TF) TRAILER FIRST

Dia. GH102. 48/– 2T (w 47/– 2T 1W).

41003–41056. Lot No. 30881 Derby 1976–77. 33.66 t.
41057–41120. Lot No. 30896 Derby 1977–78. 33.66 t.
41121–41148. Lot No. 30938 Derby 1979–80. 33.66 t.
41149–41166. Lot No. 30947 Derby 1980. 33.66 t.

41167–41169. Lot No. 30963 Derby 1982. 33.66 t.
41170. Lot No. 30967 Derby 1982. Former prototype vehicle. 33.66 t.
41179/80. Lot No. 30884 Derby 1976–77. 33.60 t.

s Fitted with centre luggage stack. 46/– 2T 1TD 1W.
41170 was converted from 41001. 41179/80 have been converted from 40505 and 40511 respectively.

No.						No.				
41003	p	**FG**	A	*GW*	LA	41051		**FG**	A	*GW*	LA
41004		**FG**	A	*GW*	PM	41052		**FG**	A	*GW*	LA
41005	p	**FG**	A	*GW*	PM	41055		**FG**	A	*GW*	LA
41006		**FG**	A	*GW*	PM	41056		**FG**	A	*GW*	LA
41007	p	**FG**	A	*GW*	PM	41057		**MM**	P	*MM*	NL
41008		**FG**	A	*GW*	PM	41058	s	**MM**	P	*MM*	NL
41009	p	**FG**	A	*GW*	PM	41059	w	**V**	P	*VX*	LA
41010		**FG**	A	*GW*	PM	41060		**FG**	A		ZC
41011	p	**FG**	A	*GW*	PM	41061		**MM**	P	*MM*	NL
41012		**FG**	A	*GW*	PM	41062	w	**MM**	P	*MM*	NL
41013	p	**FG**	A	*GW*	PM	41063		**MM**	P	*MM*	NL
41014		**FG**	A	*GW*	PM	41064	s	**MM**	P	*MM*	NL
41015	p	**FG**	A	*GW*	PM	41065		**FG**	A	*GW*	LA
41016		**FG**	A	*GW*	PM	41066	p	**V**	A	*VW*	LA
41017	p	**FG**	A	*GW*	PM	41067	s	**MM**	P	*MM*	NL
41018		**FG**	A	*GW*	PM	41068	s	**MM**	P	*MM*	NL
41019	p	**FG**	A	*GW*	PM	41069	s	**MM**	P	*MM*	NL
41020		**FG**	A	*GW*	PM	41070	s	**MM**	P	*MM*	NL
41021	p	**FG**	A	*GW*	PM	41071		**MM**	P	*MM*	NL
41022		**FG**	A	*GW*	PM	41072	s	**MM**	P	*MM*	NL
41023	p	**FG**	A	*GW*	LA	41075		**MM**	P	*MM*	NL
41024		**FG**	A	*GW*	LA	41076	s	**MM**	P	*MM*	NL
41025	p	**V**	A	*VW*	LA	41077		**MM**	P	*MM*	NL
41026		**V**	A	*VW*	LA	41078		**MM**	P	*MM*	NL
41027	p	**FG**	A	*GW*	LA	41079		**MM**	P	*MM*	NL
41028		**FG**	A	*GW*	LA	41080	s	**MM**	P	*MM*	NL
41029	p	**FG**	A	*GW*	LA	41081	w	**V**	P	*VX*	LA
41030		**FG**	A	*GW*	LA	41083		**MM**	P	*MM*	NL
41031	p	**FG**	A	*GW*	LA	41084	s	**MM**	P	*MM*	NL
41032		**FG**	A	*GW*	LA	41085	w	**V**	P	*VX*	LA
41033	p	**FG**	A	*GW*	LA	41086	w	**V**	P	*VX*	LA
41034		**FG**	A	*GW*	LA	41087		**GN**	A	*GN*	EC
41035	p	**V**	A	*VW*	LA	41088	w	**GN**	A	*GN*	EC
41036	w	**V**	A	*VW*	LA	41089		**FG**	A	*GW*	LA
41037	p	**FG**	A	*GW*	LA	41090	w	**GN**	A	*GN*	EC
41038		**FG**	A	*GW*	LA	41091		**GN**	A	*GN*	EC
41039		**GN**	A	*GN*	EC	41092	w	**GN**	A	*GN*	EC
41040		**GN**	A	*GN*	EC	41093		**FG**	A	*GW*	LA
41041	ps	**MM**	P	*MM*	NL	41094		**FG**	A	*GW*	LA
41042		**FG**	A		ZC	41095	w	**V**	P	*VX*	LA
41043	w	**GN**	A	*GN*	EC	41096		**V**	P	*VX*	LA
41044		**GN**	A	*GN*	EC	41097	w	**GN**	A	*GN*	EC
41045	w	**V**	P	*VX*	LA	41098	w	**GN**	A	*GN*	EC
41046	s	**MM**	P	*MM*	NL	41099		**GN**	A	*GN*	EC

41100 w	**GN**	A	*GN*	EC		41137 p	**FG**	A	*GW*	PM
41101	**FG**	A	*GW*	LA		41138	**FG**	A	*GW*	PM
41102	**FG**	A	*GW*	LA		41139 p	**FG**	A	*GW*	LA
41103	**FG**	A	*GW*	LA		41140	**FG**	A	*GW*	LA
41104	**FG**	A	*GW*	LA		41141 p	**FG**	A	*GW*	PM
41105	**FG**	A	*GW*	PM		41142	**FG**	A	*GW*	PM
41106	**FG**	A	*GW*	PM		41143 p	**FG**	A	*GW*	LA
41107 w	**V**	P	*VX*	LA		41144	**FG**	A	*GW*	LA
41108 w	**V**	P	*VX*	LA		41145 p	**FG**	A	*GW*	PM
41109 w	**V**	P	*VX*	LA		41146	**FG**	A	*GW*	PM
41110	**FG**	A	*GW*	PM		41147 w	**V**	P	*VX*	LA
41111	**MM**	P	*MM*	NL		41148 w	**V**	P	*VX*	LA
41112	**MM**	P	*MM*	NL		41149 w	**V**	P	*VX*	LA
41113 s	**MM**	P	*MM*	NL		41150 w	**GN**	A	*GN*	EC
41114 w	**V**	P	*VX*	LA		41151	**GN**	A	*GN*	EC
41115 w	**V**	P	*VX*	LA		41152	**GN**	A	*GN*	EC
41116	**FG**	A	*GW*	LA		41153	**MM**	P	*MM*	NL
41117	**MM**	P	*MM*	NL		41154 s	**MM**	P	*MM*	NL
41118 w	**GN**	A	*GN*	EC		41155	**MM**	P	*MM*	NL
41119 w	**V**	P	*VX*	LA		41156	**MM**	P	*MM*	NL
41120	**GN**	A	*GN*	EC		41157	**FG**	A	*GW*	LA
41121 p	**FG**	A	*GW*	LA		41158	**FG**	A	*GW*	LA
41122	**FG**	A	*GW*	LA		41159 w	**V**	P	*VX*	LA
41123 p	**FG**	A	*GW*	PM		41160 w	**V**	P	*VX*	LA
41124	**FG**	A	*GW*	PM		41161 w	**V**	P	*VX*	LA
41125	**FG**	A	*GW*	PM		41162 w	**V**	P	*VX*	LA
41126 p	**FG**	A	*GW*	PM		41163 w	**V**	P	*VX*	LA
41127 p	**FG**	A	*GW*	PM		41164 p	**V**	A	*VW*	•LA
41128	**FG**	A	*GW*	PM		41165 w	**V**	P	*VX*	LA
41129 p	**FG**	A	*GW*	PM		41166 w	**V**	P	*VX*	LA
41130	**FG**	A	*GW*	PM		41167 w	**V**	P	*VX*	LA
41131 p	**FG**	A	*GW*	LA		41168 w	**V**	P	*VX*	LA
41132	**FG**	A	*GW*	LA		41169 w	**V**	P	*VX*	LA
41133 p	**FG**	A	*GW*	LA		41170	**GN**	A	*GN*	EC
41134	**FG**	A	*GW*	LA		41179	**FG**	A	*GW*	PM
41135 p	**FG**	A	*GW*	LA		41180	**FG**	A	*GW*	PM
41136	**FG**	A	*GW*	LA						

GH2G (TS)   TRAILER STANDARD

Dia. GH203. –/76 2T. (§ –/70 2T 2W).

42003–42090/42362. Lot No. 30882 Derby 1976–77. 33.60t.
42091–42250. Lot No. 30897 Derby 1977–79. 33.60t.
42251–42305. Lot No. 30939 Derby 1979–80. 33.60t.
42306–42322. Lot No. 30969 Derby 1982. 33.60t.
42323–42341. Lot No. 30983 Derby 1984–85. 33.60t.
42342/60. Lot No. 30949 Derby 1982. 33.47t. Converted from TGS.
42343/5. Lot No. 30970 Derby 1982. 33.47t. Converted from TGS.
42344/61. Lot No. 30964 Derby 1982. 33.47t. Converted from TGS.
42346/7/50/1. Lot No. 30881 Derby 1976–77. 33.66t. Converted from TF.

42348/9/63. Lot No. 30896 Derby 1977–78. 33.66t. Converted from TF.
42353/5–7. Lot No. 30967 Derby 1982. Ex prototype vehicles. 33.66t.
42352/4. Lot No. 30897 Derby 1977. Were TF from 1983 to 1992. 33.66 t.

s Centre luggage stack –/72 2T.
t Centre luggage stack –/72 2T. Fitted with pt.
u Centre luggage stack –/74 2T (w –72 2T 1W).
* disabled persons toilet and 5 tip-up seats. –/65 1T 1TD.
42158 was also numbered 41177 for a time when fitted with first class seats.

42003	**FG**	A	*GW*	PM	42046	**FG**	A	*GW*	LA
42004 *	**FG**	A	*GW*	LA	42047	**FG**	A	*GW*	LA
42005	**FG**	A	*GW*	PM	42048	**FG**	A	*GW*	LA
42006	**FG**	A	*GW*	PM	42049	**FG**	A	*GW*	LA
42007 *	**FG**	A	*GW*	LA	42050	**FG**	A	*GW*	LA
42008 *	**FG**	A	*GW*	PM	42051 §	**V**	A	*VW*	LA
42009	**FG**	A	*GW*	PM	42052	**V**	A	*VW*	LA
42010	**FG**	A	*GW*	PM	42053	**V**	A	*VW*	LA
42012 *	**FG**	A	*GW*	PM	42054	**FG**	A	*GW*	PM
42013	**FG**	A	*GW*	PM	42055	**FG**	A	*GW*	LA
42014	**FG**	A	*GW*	PM	42056	**FG**	A	*GW*	LA
42015 *	**FG**	A	*GW*	PM	42057	**GN**	A	*GN*	EC
42016	**FG**	A	*GW*	PM	42058	**GN**	A	*GN*	EC
42017	**FG**	A	*GW*	PM	42059	**GN**	A	*GN*	EC
42018 *	**FG**	A	*GW*	PM	42060	**FG**	A	*GW*	PM
42019	**FG**	A	*GW*	PM	42061	**FG**	A	*GW*	PM
42020	**FG**	A	*GW*	PM	42062 *	**FG**	A	*GW*	LA
42021 *	**FG**	A	*GW*	PM	42063	**GN**	A	*GN*	EC
42022	**FG**	A	*GW*	PM	42064	**GN**	A	*GN*	EC
42023	**FG**	A	*GW*	PM	42065	**GN**	A	*GN*	EC
42024 *	**FG**	A	*GW*	PM	42066 *	**FG**	A	*GW*	LA
42025	**FG**	A	*GW*	PM	42067	**FG**	A	*GW*	LA
42026	**FG**	A	*GW*	PM	42068	**FG**	A	*GW*	LA
42027	**FG**	A	*GW*	PM	42069 *	**FG**	A	*GW*	PM
42028	**FG**	A	*GW*	PM	42070	**FG**	A	*GW*	PM
42029	**FG**	A	*GW*	PM	42071	**FG**	A	*GW*	PM
42030 *	**FG**	A	*GW*	PM	42072	**FG**	A	*GW*	PM
42031	**FG**	A	*GW*	PM	42073	**FG**	A	*GW*	PM
42032	**FG**	A	*GW*	PM	42074	**FG**	A	*GW*	PM
42033	**FG**	A	*GW*	LA	42075	**FG**	A	*GW*	PM
42034	**FG**	A	*GW*	LA	42076	**FG**	A	*GW*	LA
42035	**FG**	A	*GW*	LA	42077	**FG**	A	*GW*	LA
42036	**V**	A	*VW*	LA	42078	**FG**	A	*GW*	LA
42037	**V**	A	*VW*	LA	42079	**FG**	A	*GW*	PM
42038	**V**	A	*VW*	LA	42080	**FG**	A	*GW*	PM
42039	**FG**	A	*GW*	LA	42081 *	**FG**	A	*GW*	LA
42040	**FG**	A	*GW*	LA	42082 *	**FG**	A		ZC
42041	**FG**	A	*GW*	LA	42083	**FG**	A	*GW*	LA
42042	**FG**	A	*GW*	LA	42084 s	**V**	P	*VX*	LA
42043	**FG**	A	*GW*	LA	42085 t	**V**	P	*VX*	LA
42044	**FG**	A	*GW*	LA	42086 s	**V**	P	*VX*	LA
42045	**FG**	A	*GW*	LA	42087 s	**V**	P	*VX*	LA

42088 s	**V**	P	*VX*	LA	42140 u	**MM**	P	*MM*	NL
42089	**FG**	A	*GW*	PM	42141 u	**MM**	P	*MM*	NL
42090 s	**V**	P	*VX*	LA	42143	**FG**	A	*GW*	LA
42091 s	**V**	P	*VX*	LA	42144	**FG**	A	*GW*	LA
42092 s	**V**	P	*VX*	LA	42145	**FG**	A	*GW*	LA
42093 s	**V**	P	*VX*	LA	42146	**GN**	A	*GN*	EC
42094 s	**V**	P	*VX*	LA	42147 u	**MM**	P	*MM*	NL
42095 s	**V**	P	*VX*	LA	42148 u	**MM**	P	*MM*	NL
42096	**FG**	A	*GW*	LA	42149 u	**MM**	P	*MM*	NL
42097 §	**V**	A	*VW*	LA	42150	**GN**	A	*GN*	EC
42098	**FG**	A	*GW*	PM	42151 uw	**MM**	P	*MM*	NL
42099	**FG**	A	*GW*	LA	42152 u	**MM**	P	*MM*	NL
42100 u	**MM**	P	*MM*	NL	42153 u	**MM**	P	*MM*	NL
42101 uw	**MM**	P	*MM*	NL	42154		A	*GN*	EC
42102 u	**MM**	P	*MM*	NL	42155 uw	**MM**	P	*MM*	NL
42103 s	**V**	P	*VX*	LA	42156 u	**MM**	P	*MM*	NL
42104	**GN**	A	*GN*	EC	42157 u	**MM**	P	*MM*	NL
42105 s	**V**	P	*VX*	LA	42158	**GN**	A	*GN*	EC
42106	**GN**	A	*GN*	EC	42159 s	**V**	P	*VX*	LA
42107	**FG**	A	*GW*	LA	42160 s	**V**	P	*VX*	LA
42108 s	**V**	P	*VX*	LA	42161 s	**V**	P	*VX*	LA
42109 s	**V**	P	*VX*	LA	42162 s	**V**	P	*VX*	LA
42110 s	**V**	P	*VX*	LA	42163 uw	**MM**	P	*MM*	NL
42111 u	**MM**	P	*MM*	NL	42164 u	**MM**	P	*MM*	NL
42112 u	**MM**	P	*MM*	NL	42165 u	**MM**	P	*MM*	NL
42113 u	**MM**	P	*MM*	NL	42166 t	**V**	P	*VX*	LA
42115 t	**V**	P	*VX*	LA	42167 s	**V**	P	*VX*	LA
42116 s	**V**	P	*VX*	LA	42168 t	**V**	P	*VX*	LA
42117 s	**V**	P	*VX*	LA	42169 s	**V**	P	*VX*	LA
42118	**FG**	A	*GW*	PM	42170 s	**V**	P	*VX*	LA
42119 u	**MM**	P	*MM*	NL	42171	**GN**	A	*GN*	EC
42120 u	**MM**	P	*MM*	NL	42172	**GN**	A	*GN*	EC
42121 u	**MM**	P	*MM*	NL	42173 s	**V**	P	*VX*	LA
42122	**V**	A	*VW*	LA	42174 s	**V**	P	*VX*	LA
42123 u	**MM**	P	*MM*	NL	42175 s	**V**	P	*VX*	LA
42124 u	**MM**	P	*MM*	NL	42176 t	**V**	P	*VX*	LA
42125 u	**MM**	P	*MM*	NL	42177 s	**V**	P	*VX*	LA
42126	**FG**	A	*GW*	LA	42178 t	**V**	P	*VX*	LA
42127 s	**V**	P	*VX*	LA	42179	**GN**	A	*GN*	EC
42128 s	**V**	P	*VX*	LA	42180	**GN**	A	*GN*	EC
42129	**FG**	A	*GW*	LA	42181	**GN**	A	*GN*	EC
42130 t	**V**	P	*VX*	LA	42182	**GN**	A	*GN*	EC
42131 u	**MM**	P	*MM*	NL	42183 *	**FG**	A	*GW*	LA
42132 u	**MM**	P	*MM*	NL	42184	**FG**	A	*GW*	LA
42133 u	**MM**	P	*MM*	NL	42185	**FG**	A	*GW*	LA
42134	**V**	A	*VW*	LA	42186	**GN**	A	*GN*	EC
42135 u	**MM**	P	*MM*	NL	42187 t	**V**	P	*VX*	LA
42136 u	**MM**	P	*MM*	NL	42188 s	**V**	P	*VX*	LA
42137 u	**MM**	P	*MM*	NL	42189 s	**V**	P	*VX*	LA
42138 *	**FG**	A	*GW*	PM	42190	**GN**	A	*GN*	EC
42139 u	**MM**	P	*MM*	NL	42191	**GN**	A	*GN*	EC

42192		**GN**	A	*GN*	EC	42243		**GN**	A	*GN*	EC
42193		**GN**	A	*GN*	EC	42244		**GN**	A	*GN*	EC
42194 uw		**MM**	P	*MM*	NL	42245		**FG**	A	*GW*	LA
42195 s		**V**	P	*VX*	LA	42246 s		**V**	P	*VX*	LA
42196		**FG**	A	*GW*	LA	42247 t		**V**	P	*VX*	LA
42197		**FG**	A	*GW*	PM	42248 s		**V**	P	*VX*	LA
42198		**GN**	A	*GN*	EC	42249 s		**V**	P	*VX*	LA
42199		**GN**	A	*GN*	EC	42250		**FG**	A	*GW*	LA
42200 *		**FG**	A	*GW*	LA	42251 *		**FG**	A	*GW*	PM
42201 *		**FG**	A	*GW*	LA	42252		**FG**	A	*GW*	LA
42202 *		**FG**	A	*GW*	LA	42253		**FG**	A	*GW*	LA
42203		**FG**	A	*GW*	LA	42254 s		**V**	P	*VX*	LA
42204		**FG**	A	*GW*	LA	42255 *		**FG**	A	*GW*	PM
42205 u		**MM**	P	*MM*	NL	42256		**FG**	A	*GW*	PM
42206 *		**FG**	A	*GW*	LA	42257		**FG**	A	*GW*	PM
42207 *		**FG**	A	*GW*	LA	42258 t		**V**	P	*VX*	LA
42208		**FG**	A	*GW*	LA	42259 *		**FG**	A	*GW*	PM
42209		**FG**	A	*GW*	LA	42260		**FG**	A	*GW*	PM
42210 u		**MM**	P	*MM*	NL	42261		**FG**	A	*GW*	PM
42211 *		**FG**	A	*GW*	PM	42262 s		**V**	P	*VX*	LA
42212		**FG**	A	*GW*	PM	42263		**FG**	A	*GW*	PM
42213		**FG**	A	*GW*	PM	42264 *		**FG**	A	*GW*	PM
42214		**FG**	A	*GW*	PM	42265		**FG**	A	*GW*	LA
42215		**GN**	A	*GN*	EC	42266 s		**V**	P	*VX*	LA
42216		**FG**	A	*GW*	LA	42267 *		**FG**	A	*GW*	PM
42217 t		**V**	P	*VX*	LA	42268 *		**FG**	A	*GW*	LA
42218 t		**V**	P	*VX*	LA	42269		**FG**	A	*GW*	PM
42219		**GN**	A	*GN*	EC	42270 s		**V**	P	*VX*	LA
42220 uw		**MM**	P	*MM*	NL	42271 *		**FG**	A	*GW*	LA
42221		**FG**	A	*GW*	LA	42272		**FG**	A	*GW*	LA
42222 t		**V**	P	*VX*	LA	42273		**FG**	A	*GW*	LA
42223 s		**V**	P	*VX*	LA	42274 t		**V**	P	*VX*	LA
42224 s		**V**	P	*VX*	LA	42275 *		**FG**	A	*GW*	LA
42225 u		**MM**	P	*MM*	NL	42276		**FG**	A	*GW*	LA
42226		**GN**	A	*GN*	EC	42277		**FG**	A	*GW*	LA
42227 u		**MM**	P	*MM*	NL	42278 s		**V**	P	*VX*	LA
42228 u		**MM**	P	*MM*	NL	42279 *		**FG**	A	*GW*	LA
42229 u		**MM**	P	*MM*	NL	42280		**FG**	A	*GW*	LA
42230 u		**MM**	P	*MM*	NL	42281		**FG**	A	*GW*	LA
42231 s		**V**	P	*VX*	LA	42282 s		**V**	P	*VX*	LA
42232 t		**V**	P	*VX*	LA	42283		**FG**	A	*GW*	LA
42233 s		**V**	P	*VX*	LA	42284		**FG**	A	*GW*	PM
42234 s		**V**	P	*VX*	LA	42285		**FG**	A	*GW*	PM
42235		**GN**	A	*GN*	EC	42286 s		**V**	P	*VX*	LA
42236		**FG**	A	*GW*	PM	42287 *		**FG**	A	*GW*	LA
42237 s		**V**	P	*VX*	LA	42288		**FG**	A	*GW*	LA
42238 s		**V**	P	*VX*	LA	42289		**FG**	A	*GW*	LA
42239 s		**V**	P	*VX*	LA	42290 t		**V**	P	*VX*	LA
42240		**GN**	A	*GN*	EC	42291 *		**FG**	A	*GW*	PM
42241		**GN**	A	*GN*	EC	42292 *		**FG**	A	*GW*	LA
42242		**GN**	A	*GN*	EC	42293		**FG**	A	*GW*	PM

42294 s	**V**	P	*VX*	LA		42318 s	**V**	P	*VX*	LA
42295 *	**FG**	A	*GW*	LA		42319 t	**V**	P	*VX*	LA
42296	**FG**	A	*GW*	LA		42320 s	**V**	P	*VX*	LA
42297	**FG**	A	*GW*	LA		42321 s	**V**	P	*VX*	LA
42298 s	**V**	P	*VX*	LA		42322 s	**V**	P	*VX*	LA
42299 *	**FG**	A	*GW*	PM		42323	**GN**	A	*GN*	EC
42300	**FG**	A	*GW*	PM		42324 uw	**MM**	P	*MM*	NL
42301	**FG**	A	*GW*	PM		42325	**FG**	A	*GW*	PM
42302 s	**V**	P	*VX*	LA		42326 s	**V**	P	*VX*	LA
42303 t	**V**	P	*VX*	LA		42327 uw	**MM**	P	*MM*	NL
42304 s	**V**	P	*VX*	LA		42328 uw	**MM**	P	*MM*	NL
42305 s	**V**	P	*VX*	LA		42329 uw	**MM**	P	*MM*	NL
42306 s	**V**	P	*VX*	LA		42330 s	**V**	P	*VX*	LA
42307 s	**V**	P	*VX*	LA		42331 uw	**MM**	P	*MM*	NL
42308 s	**V**	P	*VX*	LA		42332	**FG**	A	*GW*	PM
42309 s	**V**	P	*VX*	LA		42333	**FG**	A	*GW*	LA
42310 s	**V**	P	*VX*	LA		42334 s	**V**	P	*VX*	LA
42311 t	**V**	P	*VX*	LA		42335 uw	**MM**	P	*MM*	NL
42312 s	**V**	P	*VX*	LA		42336 s	**V**	P	*VX*	LA
42313 s	**V**	P	*VX*	LA		42337 uw	**MM**	P	*MM*	NL
42314 s	**V**	P	*VX*	LA		42338 s	**V**	P	*VX*	LA
42315 t	**V**	P	*VX*	LA		42339 uw	**MM**	P	*MM*	NL
42316 s	**V**	P	*VX*	LA		42340	**GN**	A	*GN*	EC
42317 s	**V**	P	*VX*	LA		42341 uw	**MM**	P	*MM*	NL

42342	(44082)			**V**	A	*VW*	LA
42343	(44095)			**FG**	A	*GW*	LA
42344	(44092)		*	**FG**	A	*GW*	PM
42345	(44096)		*	**FG**	A	*GW*	LA
42346	(41053)			**FG**	A	*GW*	PM
42347	(41054)		*	**FG**	A	*GW*	PM
42348	(41073)		*	**FG**	A	*GW*	LA
42349	(41074)			**FG**	A	*GW*	PM
42350	(41047)			**FG**	A	*GW*	LA
42351	(41048)			**FG**	A	*GW*	PM
42352	(42142, 41176)		u	**MM**	P	*MM*	NL
42353	(42001, 41171)	s		**V**	P	*VX*	LA
42354	(42114, 41175)			**GN**	A	*GN*	EC
42355	(42000, 41172)	§		**V**	A	*VW*	LA
42356	(42002, 41173)			**FG**	A	*GW*	PM
42357	(41002, 41174)			**V**	A	*VW*	LA
42360	(44084, 45084)			**FG**	A	*VW*	PM
42361	(44099)			**FG**	A	*GW*	PM
42362	(42011, 41178)			**FG**	A	*GW*	PM
42363	(41082)	s		**V**	P	*VX*	LA

GJ2G (TGS) TRAILER GUARD'S STANDARD

Dia. GJ205. –/65 1T (w –/63 1T 1W). pg.
44000. Lot No. 30953 Derby 1980. 33.47 t.
44001–44090. Lot No. 30949 Derby 1980–82. 33.47 t.
44091–44094. Lot No. 30964 Derby 1982. 33.47 t.

44097–44101. Lot No. 30970 Derby 1982. 33.47 t.

s t Fitted with centre luggage stack s –/63 1T, t –/61 1T.

44000	t	**V**	P	*VX*	LA	44048	s	**MM**	P	*MM*	NL
44001	w	**FG**	A	*GW*	LA	44049	w	**FG**	A	*GW*	LA
44002	w	**FG**	A	*GW*	PM	44050	s	**MM**	P	*MM*	NL
44003	w	**FG**	A	*GW*	PM	44051	s	**MM**	P	*MM*	NL
44004	w	**FG**	A	*GW*	PM	44052	s	**MM**	P	*MM*	NL
44005	w	**FG**	A	*GW*	PM	44053	t	**V**	P	*VX*	LA
44006	w	**FG**	A	*GW*	PM	44054	s	**MM**	P	*MM*	NL
44007	w	**FG**	A	*GW*	PM	44055	t	**V**	P	*VX*	LA
44008	w	**FG**	A	*GW*	PM	44056	w	**GN**	A	*GN*	EC
44009	w	**FG**	A	*GW*	PM	44057	t	**V**	P	*VX*	LA
44010	w	**FG**	A	*GW*	PM	44058	w	**GN**	A	*GN*	EC
44011	w	**FG**	A	*GW*	LA	44059	w	**FG**	A	*GW*	LA
44012		**V**	A	*VW*	LA	44060	t	**V**	P	*VX*	LA
44013	w	**FG**	A	*GW*	LA	44061	w	**GN**	A	*GN*	EC
44014	w	**FG**	A	*GW*	LA	44062	t	**V**	P	*VX*	LA
44015	w	**FG**	A	*GW*	LA	44063	w	**GN**	A	*GN*	EC
44016	w	**FG**	A	*GW*	LA	44064	w	**FG**	A	*GW*	LA
44017		**V**	A	*VW*	LA	44065	t	**V**	P	*VX*	LA
44018	w	**FG**	A	*GW*	LA	44066	w	**FG**	A	*GW*	LA
44019	w	**GN**	A	*GN*	EC	44067	w	**FG**	A	*GW*	PM
44020	w	**FG**	A	*GW*	PM	44068	t	**V**	P	*VX*	LA
44021	t	**V**	P	*VX*	LA	44069	t	**V**	P	*VX*	LA
44022	w	**FG**	A	*GW*	LA	44070	s	**MM**	P	*MM*	NL
44023	w	**FG**	A	*GW*	PM	44071	s	**MM**	P	*MM*	NL
44024	w	**FG**	A	*GW*	PM	44072	t	**V**	P	*VX*	LA
44025	w	**FG**	A	*GW*	LA	44073	s	**MM**	P	*MM*	NL
44026	w	**FG**	A	*GW*	PM	44074	t	**V**	P	*VX*	LA
44027	s	**MM**	P	*MM*	NL	44075	t	**V**	P	*VX*	LA
44028	w	**FG**	A	*GW*	LA	44076	t	**V**	P	*VX*	LA
44029	w	**FG**	A	*GW*	PM	44077	w	**GN**	A	*GN*	EC
44030	w	**FG**	A	*GW*	PM	44078	t	**V**	P	*VX*	LA
44031		**V**	A	*VW*	LA	44079	t	**V**	P	*VX*	LA
44032	w	**FG**	A	*GW*	PM	44080	w	**GN**	A	*GN*	EC
44033	w	**FG**	A	*GW*	LA	44081	t	**V**	P	*VX*	LA
44034	w	**FG**	A	*GW*	LA	44083	s	**MM**	P	*MM*	NL
44035	w	**FG**	A	*GW*	LA	44085	s	**MM**	P	*MM*	NL
44036	w	**FG**	A	*GW*	PM	44086	w	**FG**	A	*GW*	LA
44037	w	**FG**	A	*GW*	LA	44087	t	**V**	P	*VX*	LA
44038	w	**FG**	A	*GW*	PM	44088	t	**V**	P	*VX*	LA
44039	w	**FG**	A	*GW*	LA	44089	t	**V**	P	*VX*	LA
44040	w	**FG**	A	*GW*	PM	44090	t	**V**	P	*VX*	LA
44041	s	**MM**	P	*MM*	NL	44091	t	**V**	P	*VX*	LA
44042	t	**V**	P	*VX*	LA	44093	w	**FG**	A	*GW*	LA
44043	w	**FG**	A	*GW*	LA	44094	w	**GN**	A	*GN*	EC
44044	s	**MM**	P	*MM*	NL	44097	t	**V**	P	*VX*	LA
44045	w	**GN**	A	*GN*	EC	44098	w	**GN**	A	*GN*	EC
44046	s	**MM**	P	*MM*	NL	44100	t	**V**	P	*VX*	LA
44047	s	**MM**	P	*MM*	NL	44101	t	**V**	P	*VX*	LA

2.3. SALOONS

Several specialist passenger carrying vehicles, normally referred to as saloons are permitted to run on the Railtrack system. Many of these are to pre-nationalisation designs.

LNER GENERAL MANAGERS SALOON

Dia. AO133. Built 1945 by LNER, York. Gangwayed at one end with a verandah at the other. The interior has a dining saloon seating twelve, kitchen, toilet, office and nine seat lounge. 21/– 1T. B4 bogies. 75 m.p.h. ETH3. 35.7 t.

1999   (902260)   **M**   GS   *ON*   ML

GNR FIRST CLASS SALOON

Dia. AO132. Built 1912 by GNR, Doncaster. Contains entrance vestibule, lavatory, two seperate saloons, library and luggage space. Gresley bogies. 19/– 1T. 75 m.p.h. 29.4 t.

Non-Standard Livery: Teak.

4807   (807)   x   **0**   SH   *ON*   CJ

LNWR DINING SALOON

Dia. AO131. Built 1890 by LNWR, Wolverton. Mounted on the underframe of LMS GUV 37908 in the 1980s. Contains kitchen and dining area seating 12 at tables for two. Gresley bogies. 10/–. 75 m.p.h. 25.4 t.

Non-Standard Livery: London & North Western Railway.

5159   (159)   x   **0**   SH   *ON*   CJ

GENERAL MANAGER'S SALOON

Dia. AZ501. Renumbered 1989 from London Midland Region departmental series. Formerly the LMR General Manager's saloon. Rebuilt from LMS period 1 BFK M 5033 M to dia. 1654 and mounted on the underframe of BR suburban BS M 43232. Screw couplings have been removed. B4 bogies. 100 m.p.h. ETH2X.

LMS Lot No. 326 Derby 1927. 27.5 t.

Non-Standard Livery: Aircraft blue with gold lining.

6320   (5033, DM 395707) x   **0**   RV   *ON*   CP

GWR FIRST CLASS SALOON

Dia. AO103. Built 1930 by GWR, Swindon. Contains saloons at either end with body end observation windows, staff compartment, central kitchen and pantry/bar. Numbered DE321011 when in departmental service with British Railways. 20/– 1T. GWR bogies. 75 m.p.h. 34 t.

GWR Lot No. 1431 1930.

9004　　**CH**　RA　*ON*　　BN

WCJS OBSERVATION SALOON

Dia. AO102. Built 1892 by LNWR, Wolverton. Originally dining saloon mounted on six-wheel bogies. Rebuilt with new underframe with four-wheel bogies in 1927. Rebuilt 1960 as observation saloon with DMU end. Gangwayed at other end. The interior has a saloon, kitchen, guards vestibule and observation lounge. Gresley bogies. 19/– 1T. 28.5 t. 75 m.p.h.

Non-Standard Livery: London & North Western Railway.

45018 (484, 15555)　x　**0**　　SH　*ON*　　CJ

LMS INSPECTION SALOONS

Dia. QX035 (*QX504). Built as engineers inspection saloons. Non-gangwayed. Observation windows at each end. The interior layout consists of two saloons interspersed by a central lavatory/kitchen/guards section. BR Mark 1 bogies. 80 m.p.h. 31.5 t.

45020–45026. Lot No. LMS 1356 Wolverton 1944.
45029. Lot No. LMS 1327 Wolverton 1942.
999503–999504. Lot No. BR Wagon Lot. 3093 Wolverton 1957.

45026 & 999503 are currently hired to Racal-BRT who have contracted maintenance to the Severn Valley Railway.

45020	**E**	E	*ON*	TO
45026	v　**M**	E	*ON*	KR
45029	v　**E**	E	*ON*	ML
999503	v*　**M**	E	*ON*	KR
999504	v*　**E**	E	*ON*	TO

RAILFILMS KITCHEN/SLEEPING SALOON

Dia. AO　　. Converted from BR Mark 1 SK. Contains three sleeping cabins with showers and toilets and a large kitchen/pantry. Commonwealth bogies. 100 m.p.h. ETH 4.

Non-standard Livery: London & North Western Railway.

99884 (26208, 19208)　**0**　　RA　　　CP　　　　Car No. 84

ROYAL SCOTSMAN SALOONS

Built 1960 by Metro-Cammell as Pullman Parlour First (§Pullman Kitchen First) for East Coast Main Line services. Rebuilt 1990 as sleeping cars with four twin sleeping rooms (*§ three twin sleeping rooms and two single sleeping rooms at each end). Commonwealth bogies. 38.5 t.

99961 (324 AMBER) *	M	GS	*ON*	ML	STATE CAR 1
99962 (329 PEARL)	M	GS	*ON*	ML	STATE CAR 2
99963 (324 TOPAZ)	M	GS	*ON*	ML	STATE CAR 3
99964 (313 FINCH) §	M	GS	*ON*	ML	STATE CAR 4

Built 1960 by Metro-Cammell as Pullman Kitchen First for East Coast Main Line services. Rebuilt 1990 as observation car with open verandah seating 32. Commonwealth bogies. 38.5 t.

| 99965 (319 SNIPE) | M | GS | *ON* | ML | OBSERVATION CAR |

Built 1960 by Metro-Cammell as Pullman Kitchen First for East Coast Main Line services. Rebuilt 1993 as dining car. Commonwealth bogies. 38.5 t.

| 99967 (317 RAVEN) | M | GS | *ON* | ML | DINING CAR |

Mark 3A. Converted from SLEP at Carnforth Railway Restoration and Engineering Services in 1997. BT10 bogies. Attendant's and adjacent two sleeping compartments converted to generator room containing a 160 kW Volvo unit. In 99968 four sleeping compartments remain for staff use with another converted for use as a staff shower and toilet. The remaining five sleeping compartments have been replaced by two passenger cabins. In 99969 seven sleeping compartments remain for staff use. A further sleeping compartment, along with one toilet, have been converted to store rooms. The other two sleeping compartments have been combined to form a crew mess. ETH7X. 41.5 t.

Lot. No. 30960 Derby 1981–3.

| 99968 (10541) | M | GS | *ON* | ML | STATE CAR 5 |
| 99969 (10556) | M | GS | *ON* | ML | SERVICE CAR |

RAILFILMS 'LMS CLUB CAR'

Dia. AO239. Converted from BR Mark 1 TSO at Carnforth Railway Restoration and Engineering Services in 1994. Contains kitchenette, pantry, coupé, lounge/reception area with two setees and two dining saloons. 24/– 1T. Commonwealth bogies. 100 m.p.h. ETH 4.

Lot. No. 30724 York 1963. 37 t.

| 99993 (5067) | M | RA | *ON* | BN | LMS CLUB CAR |

BR INSPECTION SALOON

Dia. QX505. Mark 1. Short frames. Non-gangwayed. Observation windows at each end. The interior layout consists of two saloons interspersed by a central lavatory/kitchen/guards/luggage section. BR Mark 1 bogies. 90 m.p.h.

Lot No. BR Wagon Lot. 3379 Swindon 1960. 30.5 t.

| 999509 | E | E | *ON* | ML | |

2.4. PULLMAN CAR COMPANY SERIES

Pullman cars have never generally been numbered as such, although many have carried numbers, instead they have carried titles. However, a scheme of schedule numbers exists which generally lists cars in chronological order. In this section those numbers are shown followed by the cars title. Cars described as 'kitchen' contain a kitchen in addition to passenger accomodation and have gas cooking unless otherwise stated. Cars described as 'parlour' consist entirely of passenger accomodation. Cars described as 'brake' contain a compartment for the use of the guard and a luggage compartment in addition to passenger accommodation.

PULLMAN PARLOUR FIRST

Built 1927 by Midland Carriage and Wagon Company. Gresley bogies. 26/–. ETH 2. 41 t.

213 MINERVA   **PC** VS *ON* SL

PULLMAN BRAKE THIRD

Built 1928 by Metropolitan Carriage and Wagon Company. Gresley bogies. –/30. 37.5 t.

232 CAR No. 79   v **PC** NY *ON* NY

PULLMAN PARLOUR FIRST

Built 1928 by Metropolitan Carriage and Wagon Company. Gresley bogies. 24/–. ETH 4. 40 t.

239 AGATHA   **PC** VS   SL
243 LUCILLE   **PC** VS *ON* SL

PULLMAN KITCHEN FIRST

Built 1925 by BRCW. Rebuilt by Midland Carriage & Wagon Company in 1928. Gresley bogies. 20/–. ETH 4. 41 t.

245 IBIS   **PC** VS *ON* SL

PULLMAN PARLOUR FIRST

Built 1928 by Metropolitan Carriage and Wagon Company. Gresley bogies. 24/–. ETH 4.

254 ZENA   **PC** VS *ON* SL

PULLMAN KITCHEN FIRST

Built 1928 by Metropolitan Carriage and Wagon Company. Gresley bogies.
20/–. ETH 4. 42 t.

| 255 | IONE | **PC** | VS | *ON* | SL |

PULLMAN PARLOUR THIRD

Built 1931 by Birmingham Railway Carriage and Wagon Company. Gresley
bogies. –/42.

| 261 | CAR No. 83 | **PC** | VS | | SL |

PULLMAN KITCHEN COMPOSITE

Built 1932 by Metropolitan Carriage and Wagon Company. Originally included
in 6-Pul EMU. Electric cooking. EMU bogies. 12/16.

| 264 | RUTH | **PC** | VS | | SL |

PULLMAN KITCHEN FIRST

Built 1932 by Metropolitan Carriage and Wagon Company. Originally included
in 'Brighton Belle' EMUs but now used as hauled stock. Electric cooking. B5
(SR) bogies (§ EMU bogies). 20/–. ETH 2. 44 t.

280	AUDREY		**PC**	VS	*ON*	SL
281	GWEN		**PC**	VS	*ON*	SL
283	MONA	§	**PC**	VS		SL
284	VERA		**PC**	VS	*ON*	SL

PULLMAN PARLOUR THIRD

Built 1932 by Metropolitan Carriage and Wagon Company. Originally included
in 'Brighton Belle' EMUs. EMU bogies. –/56.

| 285 | CAR No. 85 | **PC** | VS | SL |
| 286 | CAR No. 86 | **PC** | VS | SL |

PULLMAN BRAKE THIRD

Built 1932 by Metropolitan Carriage and Wagon Company. Originally driving
motor cars in 'Brighton Belle' EMUs. Traction and control equipment removed
for use as hauled stock. EMU bogies. –/48.

288	CAR No. 88	**PC**	VS	SL
292	CAR No. 92	**PC**	VS	SL
293	CAR No. 93	**PC**	VS	SL

PULLMAN PARLOUR FIRST

Built 1951 by Birmingham Railway Carriage and Wagon Company. Gresley bogies. 32/–. ETH 3. 39 t.

301 PERSEUS   **PC** VS *ON* SL

Dia. AO415. Built 1952 by Pullman Car Company, Preston Park using underframe and bogies from 176 RAINBOW, the body of which had been destroyed by fire. Gresley bogies. 26/–. ETH 4. 38 t.

302 PHOENIX   **PC** VS *ON* SL

PULLMAN KITCHEN FIRST

Built 1951 by Birmingham Railway Carriage & Wagon Company. Gresley bogies. 22/–.

307 CARINA   **PC** VS   SL

PULLMAN PARLOUR FIRST

Built 1951 by Birmingham Railway Carriage & Wagon Company. Gresley bogies. 32/–. ETH 3. 39 t.

308 CYGNUS   **PC** VS *ON* SL

PULLMAN FIRST BAR

Built 1951 by Birmingham Railway Carriage & Wagon Company. Rebuilt 1999 by Blake Fabrications, Edinburgh with original timber-framed body replaced by a new fabricated steel body. Contains kitchen, bar, dining saloon and coupé. Electric cooking. Gresley bogies. 14/– 1T. ETH 3.

310 PEGASUS   **PC** RA *ON* BN

Also carries "THE TRIANON BAR" branding.

PULLMAN KITCHEN FIRST

Built by Metro-Cammell 1960/1 for East Coast Main-line services. Commonwealth bogies. 20/– 2T. ETH4. 41.2 t.

315	HERON	x	**PC**	FS		On loan to Great Central Railway
316	MAGPIE	x	**PC**	FS		CS
318	ROBIN	x	**PC**	NY	*ON*	NY
321	SWIFT	x	**PC**	FS		CS

PULLMAN PARLOUR FIRST

Built by Metro-Cammell 1960/1 for East Coast Main-line services. Commonwealth bogies. 29/– 2T. 38.5 t.

325 AMETHYST x **PC** FS   SZ
328 OPAL   x **PC** NY *ON* NY

PULLMAN KITCHEN SECOND

Built by Metro-Cammell 1960/1 for East Coast Main-line services. Commonwealth bogies. –/30 1T. 40 t.

335 CAR No. 335 x **PC** FS   SZ
337 CAR No. 337 x **PC** FS   CS

PULLMAN PARLOUR SECOND

Built by Metro-Cammell 1960/1 for East Coast Main-line services. Commonwealth bogies. –/42 2T. 38.5 t.

347 CAR No. 347 x **PC** FS   SZ
348 CAR No. 348 x **PC** FS   SZ
349 CAR No. 349 x **PC** FS   On loan to Kent & East Sussex Railway
350 CAR No. 350 x **PC** FS   SZ
351 CAR No. 351 x **PC** FS   SZ
352 CAR No. 352 x **PC** FS   SZ
353 CAR No. 353 x **PC** FS   SZ

PULLMAN FIRST BAR

Built by Metro-Cammell 1961 for East Coast Main-line services. Commonwealth bogies. 24/– + bar seating 1T. 38.5 t.

354 THE HADRIAN BAR x **PC** FS   SZ

2.5. PASSENGER COACHING STOCK AWAITING DISPOSAL

This list contains the last known locations of coaching stock awaiting disposal. The definition of which vehicles are "awaiting disposal" is somewhat vague, but generally speaking these are vehicles of types not now in normal service or vehicles which have been damaged by fire, vandalism or collision.

1644	CS	6339	EC
1650	CS	6343	HT
1652	CS	6345	EC
1655	CS	6347	ZN
1663	CS	6351	ZB
1670	CS	6356	ZB
1684	CS	6357	ZB
1688	CS	6362	LL
4858	CS	6363	LL
4860	CS	6390	ZB
4932	CS	6523	CS
4997	CS	6900	Cambridge Station Yard
5438	CD	6901	Cambridge Station Yard
5476	Neville Hill Up Sidings	9458	ZB
5505	CS	9482	NL
5533	Neville Hill Up Sidings	13306	CS
5574	Neville Hill Up Sidings	13320	CS
5585	Neville Hill Up Sidings	13323	CS
5595	Neville Hill Up Sidings	17039	CD
5645	CS	21265	CS
5709	CS	25837	CS
5712	CS	34952	SL
6335	LA	35509	ZH

2.6. 99xxx RANGE NUMBER CONVERSION TABLE

The following table is presented to help readers identify vehicles which may carry numbers in the 99xxx range, the former private owner number series which is no longer in general use.

99xxx	BR No.	99xxx	BR No.	99xxx	BR No.	99xxx	BR No.
99035	35322	99324	5714	99546	281	99723	35459
99041	35476	99325	5727	99566	3066	99782	17007
99052	45018	99326	4954	99568	3068	99792	17019
99053	9004	99327	5044	99670	546	99823	4832
99121	3105	99328	5033	99671	548	99824	4831
99125	3113	99329	4931	99672	549	99826	13229
99127	3117	99371	3128	99673	550	99827	3096
99128	3130	99405	35486	99674	551	99828	13230
99131	1999	99530	301	99675	552	99829	4856
99241	35449	99531	302	99676	553	99830	5028
99304	21256	99532	308	99677	586	99880	5159
99311	1882	99534	245	99678	504	99881	4807
99312	35463	99535	213	99679	506	99886	35407
99314	25729	99536	254	99680	17102	99887	2127
99315	25955	99537	280	99710	25767	99953	35468
99316	13321	99538	34991	99712	25893	99966	34525
99317	3766	99539	255	99713	26013	99970	232
99318	4912	99540	3069	99716	25808	99972	318
99319	14168	99541	243	99718	25862	99973	324
99321	5299	99542	889202	99721	25756	99974	328
99322	5600	99543	284	99722	25806	99995	35457
99323	5704	99545	80207				

2.7. PRESERVED LOCOMOTIVE SUPPORT COACHES TABLE

The following table lists support coaches and the BR numbers of the locomotives which they normally support at present. These coaches can spend considerable periods of time off the Railtrack network when the locomotives they support are not being used on that network.

17007	35028	35207	VS locos	35463	WC locos	35476	80098
17013	60103*	35333	6024	35465	46035§	35479	SV locos
17019	45407	35449	34027	35467	SV locos	35486	SV locos
17096	35028	35457	60532	35468	NR locos	80217	75014
21236	30828	35461	5029	35470	BM locos		

* Carries former LNER number 4472.
§ Carries original number D 172.

3. DIESEL MULTIPLE UNITS

USING THIS SECTION – LAYOUT OF INFORMATION

DMUs are listed in numerical order of class, then in numerical order of set –
using current numbers as allocated by the RSL. Individual 'loose' vehicles are
listed in numerical order after vehicles formed into fixed formations. Where
numbers carried are differ from those officially allocated these are noted in
class headings where appropriate. Where sets or vehicles have been
renumbered since the previous edition of this book, former numbering detail
is shown in parentheses. Each entry is laid out as in the following example:

Set No.	Detail	Livery	Owner	Operation	Depot	Formation		Name
150 257	r*	**AR**	P	*AR*	NC	52257	57257	QUEEN BOADICEA

CLASS HEADINGS

Principal details and dimensions are quoted for each class in metric and/or imperial
units as considered appropriate bearing in mind common usage in the UK.

All dimensions and weights are quoted for vehicles in an 'as new' condition
with all necessary supplies (e.g. oil, water, sand) on board. Dimensions are
quoted in the order Length – Width. All lengths quoted are over buffers or
couplers as appropriate. All width dimensions quoted are maxima. Details of
abbreviations used are found on p. 384.

DETAIL DIFFERENCES

Only detail differences which currently affect the areas and types of train which
vehicles may work are shown. All other detail differences are specifically
excluded. Where such differences occur within a class, these are shown either
in the heading information or alongside the individual set or vehicle number.
The following standard abbreviation is used:

r   Radio Electronic Token Block (RETB) equipment.

In all cases use of the above abbreviations indicates the equipment indicated
is normally operable. Meaning of non-standard abbreviations is detailed in
individual class headings.

LIVERY CODES

Livery codes are used to denote the various liveries carried. Readers should
note it is impossible in a publication of this size to list every livery variation
which currently exists. In particular items ignored for the purposes of this
book include minor colour variations, all numbering, lettering and branding
and omission of logos.

The descriptions below are thus a general guide only and may be subject to
slight variation between individual vehicles. Logos as appropriate for each
livery are normally deemed to be carried. A complete list of livery codes used

appears on page 371

OWNER CODES

Owner codes are used in this to denote the owners of vehicles listed. Most vehicles are leased by the TOCs from specialist leasing companies. A complete list of owner codes used appears on page 375.

OPERATION CODES

Operation codes are used to denote the normal usage of the vehicles listed – i.e. A guide to the services of which train operating company any vehicle will normally be used upon. Where vehicles are used for non revenue earning purposes, an indication to the normal type of usage is given in the class heading. Where no operation code is shown, vehicles are currently not in use. A complete list of operation codes used appears on page 380.

DEPOT & LOCATION CODES

Depot codes are used to denote the normal maintenance base of each operational vehicle. However, maintenance may be carried out at other locations and may also be carried out by mobile maintenance teams.

Location codes are used to denote common storage locations whilst the full place name is used for other locations. A complete list of depot and location codes used appears on page 381.

SET FORMATIONS

Regular set formations are shown where these are normally maintained. Readers should note set formations might be temporarily varied from time to time to suit maintenance and/or operational requirements. Vehicles shown as 'Spare' are not formed in any regular set formation.

NAMES

Only names carried with official sanction are listed. As far as possible names are shown in UPPER/lower case characters as actually shown on the name carried on the vehicle(s). Unless otherwise shown, complete units are regarded as named rather than just the individual car(s) which carry the name.

GENERAL INFORMATION

CLASSIFICATION AND NUMBERING

First generation ('Heritage') DMUs are classified in the series 100–139.
Second generation DMUs are classified in the series 140–199.
Diesel-electric multiple units are classified in the series 200–249.
Service units are classified in the series 930–999.
First and second generation individual cars are numbered in the series 50000–59999 and 79000–79999.

DEMU individual cars are numbered in the series 60000–60999, except for a few former EMU vehicles which retain their EMU numbers.

Service stock individual cars are numbered in the series 975000–975999 and 977000–977999, although this series is not exclusively used for DMU vehicles.

OPERATING CODES

These codes are used by train operating company staff to describe the various different types of vehicles and normally appear on data panels on the inner (i.e. non driving) ends of vehicles.

DM	Driving Motor.	MF	Motor First
DMB	Driving Motor Brake.	MS	Motor Standard.
DMBS	Driving Motor Brake Standard	MSLRB	Motor Standard with buffet
DMC	Driving Motor Composite.	or MSRB	
DMF	Driving Motor First.	T	Trailer..
DMS	Driving Motor Standard.	TC	Trailer Composite.
DT	Driving Trailer.	TCso	Trailer Composite (semi-open).
DTC	Driving Trailer Composite.		
DTS	Driving Trailer Standard.	TS	Trailer Standard.
DTCso	Driving Trailer Composite	TSRB	Trailer Standard with buffet (semi-open).

All vehicles are of open configuration except where shown. A semi-open vehicle features both open and compartment accommodation, with first class accommodation usually in compartments in composite vehicles. Where two vehicles of the same type are formed within the same unit, the above codes may be suffixed by (A) and (B) to differentiate between the vehicles. The suffix 'L' denotes vehicles with a lavatory compartment.

A composite is a vehicle containing both first and standard class accommodation, whilst a brake vehicle is a vehicle containing separate specific accommodation for the conductor.

DESIGN CODES AND DIAGRAM CODES

For each type of vehicle the RSL issues a seven character 'Design Code' consisting of two letters plus four numbers and a suffix letter. (e.g. DP2010A).

The first five characters of the Design Code are known as the 'Diagram Code' and these are quoted in this publication in sub-headings. The meaning of the various characters of the Design Code is as follows:

First Character

D   Diesel Multiple Unit vehicle.

Second Character

B	DEMU Driving motor passenger vehicle with brake compartment.
C	DEMU Driving motor passenger vehicle.
D	DEMU Non-driving motor passenger vehicle.
E	DEMU Driving motor trailer passenger vehicle.
F	DEMU Driving motor passenger vehicle (tilting).
G	DEMU Non-driving motor passenger vehicle (tilting).
H	DEMU Trailer passenger vehicle.
P	DMU (excl. DEMU) Driving motor passenger vehicle.
Q	DMU (excl. DEMU) Driving motor passenger vehicle with brake compartment.
R	DMU (excl. DEMU) Non-driving motor passenger vehicle.
S	DMU (excl. DEMU) Driving trailer passenger vehicle.
T	DMU (excl. DEMU) Trailer passenger vehicle.
X	DMU (excl. DEMU) Single unit railcar.
Z	All types of service vehicle.

Third Character

2	Standard class accommodation.
3	Composite accommodation.
5	No passenger accommodation.

Fourth & Fifth Characters

These distinguish between different designs of vehicle, each design being allocated a unique two digit number.

Special Note

Where vehicles have been declassified, the correct design code for a declassified vehicle is quoted in this publication, even though this may be at variance with RSL records, which do not always show the reality of the current position.

BUILD DETAILS

Lot Numbers

Vehicles ordered under the auspices of BR were allocated a Lot (batch) number when ordered and these are quoted in class headings and sub-headings.

ACCOMMODATION

The information given in class headings and sub-headings is in the form F/S nT (or TD) nW. For example 12/54 1T 1W denotes 12 first class and 54 standard class seats, 1 toilet and 1 wheelchair space. In declassified vehicles the capacity is still shown in terms of first and standard class seats whilst different types of seat remain fitted. TD denotes a toilet suitable for a disabled person.

3.1. DIESEL MECHANICAL & DIESEL HYDRAULIC UNITS

3.1.1. FIRST GENERATION UNITS

CLASS 101   METRO-CAMMELL

DMBS–DTSL–DMBS, DMBS–DTSL or DMBS–DMSL. First generation units which are scheduled for early withdrawal.

Construction: Aluminium alloy body on steel underframe.
Engines: Two Leyland 680/1 of 112 kW (150 h.p.) at 1800 r.p.m. per power car.
Transmission: Mechanical. Cardan shaft and freewheel to a four-speed epicyclic gearbox with a further cardan shaft to the final drive, each engine driving the inner axle of one bogie.
Brakes: Twin-pipe vacuum.
Gangways: British Standard (Midland scissors type). Within unit only.
Bogies: DD15 (motor) and DT11 (trailer).
Couplers: Screw couplings.
Dimensions: 18.49 x 2.82 m.
Seating Layout: 3+2 unidirectional (2+2 facing in first class).
Doors: Manually-operated slam.
Multiple Working: 'Blue Square' coupling code. First generation vehicles may be coupled together to work in multiple up to a maximum of 6 motor cars or 12 cars in total in a formation. First generation vehicles may not be coupled in multiple with second generation vehicles.
Maximum Speed: 70 m.p.h.

51175–51253. DMBS. Dia. DQ202. Lot No. 30467 1958–59. –/52. 32.5 t.
51426–51442. DMBS. Dia. DQ202. Lot No. 30500 1959. –/52. 32.5 t.
53164. DMBS. Dia. DQ202. Lot No. 30254 1957. –/52. 32.5 t.
53204. DMBS. Dia. DQ202. Lot No. 30259 1957. –/52. 32.5 t.
53253–53256. DMBS. Dia. DQ202. Lot No. 30266 1957. –/52. 32.5 t.
51800. DMBS. Dia. DQ202. Lot No. 30587 1959. –/52. 32.5 t.
53311. DMBS. Dia. DQ202. Lot No. 30275 1958. –/49. 32.5 t.
51496–51533. DMCL or DMSL. Dia. DP317 or DP210. Lot No. 30501 1959. –/72 1T (12/49 1T*). 32.5t.
51803. DMSL. Dia. DP210. Lot No. 30588 1959. –/72 1T. 32.5 t.
53160–53163. DMSL. Dia. DP214. Lot No. 30253 1956. –/72 1T. 32.5 t.
53170–53171. DMSL. Dia. DP214. Lot No. 30255 1957. –/72 1T. 32.5 t.
53266–53269. DMSL. Dia. DP210. Lot No. 30267 1957. –/72 1T. 32.5 t.
53322. DMCL. Dia. DP317. Lot No. 30276 1958. 12/49 1T. 32.5t.
54056. DTSL. DS206. Lot No. 30260 1957. –/72 1T. 25.5 t.
54347–54408. DTSL. Dia. DS206. Lot No. 30468 1958. –/72 1T. 25.5 t.

2 or 3-car Sets. DMBS–DTSL plus DMBS locked out of use on 3-car sets.

101 653	**RR**	A	*NW*	LO	51426	54358	
101 654	**RR**	A	*NW*	LO	51800	54408	51175
101 656	**RR**	A	*NW*	LO	51230	54056	51428
101 657	**RR**	A		LO (S)	53211	54085	
101 663	**RR**	A	*NW*	LO	51201	54347	51442
101 665	**RR**	A	*NW*	LO (S)	51429	54393	
Spare	**RR**	A		LO (S)	51179	54062	
Spare	**RR**	A		LO (S)		54091	

Twin Power Car Sets. DMBS–DMSL.

Non-Standard livery: Caledonian style blue with yellow/orange stripes.

101 676	**RR**	A	*NW*	LO	51205	51803
101 677	**RR**	A		LO (S)	51179	51496
101 679	**RR**	A	*NW*	LO	51244	51533
101 680	**RR**	A	*NW*	LO	53204	53163
101 681	**RR**	A	*NW*	LO	51228	51506
101 682	**RR**	A	*NW*	LO	53256	51505
101 683	**RR**	A	*NW*	LO	51177	53269
101 685	**G**	A	*NW*	LO	53164	53160
101 687	**S**	A	*NW*	LO	51247	51512
101 689	**S**	A	*NW*	LO	51185	51511
101 691	**S**	A	*NW*	LO	51253	53171
101 692	**O**	A	*NW*	LO	53253	53170
101 693	**S**	A	*NW*	LO	51192	53266
101 694	**S**	A	*NW*	LO	51188	53268
101 695	**S**	A	*NW*	LO	51226	51499
L840	**N**	A		LO (S)	53311	53322

CLASS 122   GLOUCESTER

This unit has recently been registered for mainline use.
DMBS.
Construction: Steel.
Engines: Two Leyland 1595 of 112 kW (150 h.p.) at 188 r.p.m.
Transmission: Mechanical. Cardan shaft and freewheel to a four-speed epicyclic gearbox with a further cardan shaft to the final drive, each engine driving the inner axle of one bogie.
Brakes: Twin-pipe vacuum.
Gangways: Non-gangwayed.
Bogies: DD10.
Couplers: Screw couplings.
Dimensions: 20.45 x 2.82 m.
Seating Layout: 3+2 facing.
Doors: Manually-operated slam.
Multiple Working: 'Blue Square' coupling code (see Class 101)
Maximum Speed: 70 m.p.h.

DMBS. Dia. DX202. Lot No. 30419 Gloucester 1958. –/65. 36.5 t.

122 003	**G**	PO	RL	55003

3.1.2. SECOND GENERATION UNITS

All units in this section have air brakes and are equipped with public address, with transmission equipment on driving and certain other vehicles and flexible diaphragm gangways. Except where otherwise stated, transmission is Voith 211r hydraulic with a cardan shaft to a Gmeinder GM190 final drive.

CLASS 142   PACER   BREL/LEYLAND

DMS–DMSL.

Construction: Steel. Built from Leyland National bus bodywork on four-wheeled underframes.
Engines: One Cummins LTA10-R of 172 kW (230 h.p.) at 2100 r.p.m. (* One Perkins 2006-TWH of 172 kW (230 h.p.) at 2100 r.p.m.) per car.
Couplers: BSI at outer ends, bar within unit.
Seating Layout: 3+2 mainly unidirectional bus style.
Dimensions: 15.66 x 2.80 m.
Gangways: Within unit only.   **Wheel Arrangement:** 1-A A-1.
Doors: Twin-leaf inward pivoting.   **Maximum Speed:** 75 m.p.h.
Multiple Working: Classes 142, 143, 144, 150, 153, 155, 156, 158, 159, 170.

55542–55591. DMS. Dia. DP234 (s DP271). Lot No. 31003 BREL Derby 1985–86. –/62. (s –/56, t –/55, u –/52) 23.26 t.
55592–55641. DMSL. Dia. DP235 (s DP272). Lot No. 31004 BREL Derby 1985–86. –/59 1T. (s –/50 1T) 24.97 t.
55701–55746. DMS. Dia. DP234 (s DP271). Lot No. 31013 BREL Derby 1986–87. –/62. (s –/56, t –/55, u –/52) 23.26 t.
55747–55792. DMSL. Dia. DP235 (s DP272). Lot No. 31014 BREL Derby 1986–87. –/59 1T. (s –/50 1T) 24.97 t.

s Fitted with 2+2 individual high-backed seating.
t DMS fitted with luggage rack, seating –/55.
u Fitted with 3+2 individual low-back seating.

142 001	t	GM	A	NW	NH	55542	55592
142 002		GM	A	NW	NH	55543	55593
142 003		GM	A	NW	NH	55544	55594
142 004	t	GM	A	NW	NH	55545	55595
142 005	t	GM	A	NW	NH	55546	55596
142 006		GM	A	NW	NH	55547	55597
142 007	t	GM	A	NW	NH	55548	55598
142 008	t	GM	A		ZC (S)	55549	55599
142 009	t	GM	A	NW	NH	55550	55600
142 010		GM	A	NW	NH	55551	55601
142 011	t	GM	A	NW	NH	55552	55602
142 012	t	GM	A	NW	NH	55553	55603
142 013		GM	A	NW	NH	55554	55604
142 014	t	GM	A	NW	NH	55555	55605
142 015	s	RR	A	NS	HT	55556	55606
142 016	s	RR	A	NS	HT	55557	55607
142 017	s	TW	A	NS	HT	55558	55608

142 018	s	**TW**	A	*NS*	HT	55559 55609
142 019	s	**TW**	A	*NS*	HT	55560 55610
142 020	s	**TW**	A	*NS*	HT	55561 55611
142 021	s	**TW**	A	*NS*	HT	55562 55612
142 022	s	**TW**	A	*NS*	HT	55563 55613
142 023	t	**NW**	A	*NW*	NH	55564 55614
142 024	s	**RR**	A	*NS*	HT	55565 55615
142 025	s	**NS**	A	*NS*	HT	55566 55616
142 026	s	**NS**	A	*NS*	HT	55567 55617
142 027	t	**GM**	A	*NW*	NH	55568 55618
142 028	t	**GM**	A	*NW*	NH	55569 55619
142 029		**GM**	A	*NW*	NH	55570 55620
142 030		**GM**	A	*NW*	NH	55571 55621
142 031	t	**GM**	A	*NW*	NH	55572 55622
142 032	t	**GM**	A	*NW*	NH	55573 55623
142 033	t	**RR**	A	*NW*	NH	55574 55624
142 034	t	**GM**	A	*NW*	NH	55575 55625
142 035	t	**GM**	A	*NW*	NH	55576 55626
142 036	t	**RR**	A	*NW*	NH	55577 55627
142 037	t	**GM**	A	*NW*	NH	55578 55628
142 038	t	**GM**	A	*NW*	NH	55579 55629
142 039	t	**GM**	A	*NW*	NH	55580 55630
142 040	t	**GM**	A	*NW*	NH	55581 55631
142 041	u	**MY**	A	*NW*	NH	55582 55632
142 042	u	**MY**	A	*NW*	NH	55583 55633
142 043	u	**MY**	A	*NW*	NH	55584 55634
142 044	u	**MY**	A	*NW*	NH	55585 55635
142 045	u	**MY**	A	*NW*	NH	55586 55636
142 046	u	**MY**	A	*NW*	NH	55587 55637
142 047	u	**MY**	A	*NW*	NH	55588 55638
142 048		**RR**	A	*NW*	NH	55589 55639
142 049		**GM**	A	*NW*	NH	55590 55640
142 050	s	**NS**	A	*NS*	HT	55591 55641
142 051	u	**MT**	A	*NW*	NH	55701 55747
142 052	u	**MT**	A	*NW*	NH	55702 55748
142 053	u	**MT**	A	*NW*	NH	55703 55749
142 054	u	**MT**	A	*NW*	NH	55704 55750
142 055	u	**MT**	A	*NW*	NH	55705 55751
142 056	u	**MT**	A	*NW*	NH	55706 55752
142 057	u	**MT**	A	*NW*	NH	55707 55753
142 058	u	**MT**	A	*NW*	NH	55708 55754
142 060	t	**GM**	A	*NW*	NH	55710 55756
142 061		**GM**	A	*NW*	NH	55711 55757
142 062	t	**GM**	A	*NW*	NH	55712 55758
142 063	t	**GM**	A	*NW*	NH	55713 55759
142 064	t	**GM**	A	*NW*	NH	55714 55760
142 065	s	**NS**	A	*NS*	HT	55715 55761
142 066	s	**NS**	A	*NS*	HT	55716 55762
142 067		**GM**	A	*NW*	NH	55717 55763
142 068	t	**GM**	A	*NW*	NH	55718 55764
142 069		**GM**	A	*NW*	NH	55719 55765

142 070	t	**GM**	A	*NW*	NH	55720	55766
142 071	s	**RR**	A	*NS*	HT	55721	55767
142 072		**RR**	A	*NS*	HT	55722	55768
142 073		**RR**	A	*NS*	HT	55723	55769
142 074		**RR**	A	*NS*	HT	55724	55770
142 075		**RR**	A	*NS*	HT	55725	55771
142 076		**RR**	A	*NS*	HT	55726	55772
142 077		**RR**	A	*NS*	HT	55727	55773
142 078	s	**RR**	A	*NS*	HT	55728	55774
142 079		**RR**	A	*NS*	HT	55729	55775
142 080		**RR**	A	*NS*	HT	55730	55776
142 081		**RR**	A	*NS*	HT	55731	55777
142 082		**RR**	A	*NS*	HT	55732	55778
142 083		**RR**	A	*CA*	CF	55733	55779
142 084	s*	**RR**	A	*NS*	HT	55734	55780
142 085	s	**RR**	A	*CA*	CF	55735	55781
142 086	s	**RR**	A	*CA*	CF	55736	55782
142 087	s	**RR**	A	*CA*	CF	55737	55783
142 088	s	**RR**	A	*CA*	CF	55738	55784
142 089	s	**RR**	A	*CA*	CF	55739	55785
142 090	s	**RR**	A	*CA*	CF	55740	55786
142 091	s	**RR**	A	*CA*	CF	55741	55787
142 092	s	**RR**	A	*CA*	CF	55742	55788
142 093	s	**RR**	A	*CA*	CF	55743	55789
142 094	s	**RR**	A	*CA*	CF	55744	55790
142 095	s	**RR**	A	*NS*	HT	55745	55791
142 096	s	**RR**	A	*CA*	CF	55746	55792

CLASS 143   PACER   ALEXANDER/BARCLAY

DMS–DMSL. Similar design to Class 142, but bodies built by W. Alexander with Barclay underframes.

Construction: Steel. Alexander bus bodywork on four-wheeled underframes.
Engines: One Cummins LTA10-R of 172 kW (230 h.p.) at 2100 r.p.m. per car.
Couplers: BSI at outer ends, bar couplers within unit.
Seating Layout: 3+2 mainly unidirectional bus style.
Dimensions: 15.55 x 2.70 m.

Gangways: Within unit only.	**Wheel Arrangement:** 1-A A-1.
Doors: Twin-leaf inward pivoting.	**Maximum Speed:** 75 m.p.h.

Multiple Working: Classes 142, 143, 144, 150, 153, 155, 156, 158, 159, 170.

DMS. Dia. DP236 Lot No. 31005 Barclay 1985–86. –/62 (s –/55). 24.5 t.
DMSL. Dia. DP237 Lot No. 31006 Barclay 1985–86. –/60 1T (s –/51 1T). 25.0 t.

s Fitted with 2+2 individual high-backed seating.

143 601	**RR**	RD	*WW*	CF	55642	55667	
143 602	**RR**	P	*CA*	CF	55651	55668	
143 603	**RR**	P	*CA*	CF	55658	55669	
143 604	**RR**	P	*CA*	CF	55645	55670	
143 605	**RR**	P	*CA*	CF	55646	55671	Crimestoppers

143 606	s	**VL**	P	*CA*	CF	55647	55672	
143 607		**RR**	P	*CA*	CF	55648	55673	
143 608	s	**VL**	P	*CA*	CF	55649	55674	
143 609		**RR**	BB	*CA*	CF	55650	55675	TOM JONES
143 610		**RR**	RD	*WW*	CF	55643	55676	
143 611		**AL**	P	*CA*	CF	55652	55677	
143 612		**RR**	P	*WW*	CF	55653	55678	
143 613		**AL**	P	*CA*	CF	55654	55679	
143 614		**RR**	RD	*WW*	CF	55655	55680	
143 615		**RR**	P	*CA*	CF	55656	55681	
143 616		**RR**	P	*CA*	CF	55657	55682	
143 617		**RR**	RI	*WW*	CF	55644	55683	
143 618		**RR**	RI	*WW*	CF	55659	55684	
143 619		**RR**	RI	*WW*	CF	55660	55685	
143 620		**RR**	P	*WW*	CF	55661	55686	
143 621		**RR**	P	*WW*	CF	55662	55687	
143 622		**RR**	P	*WW*	CF	55663	55688	
143 623		**RR**	P	*WW*	CF	55664	55689	
143 624		**RR**	P	*CA*	CF	55665	55690	
143 625		**RR**	P	*CA*	CF	55666	55691	

CLASS 144　　　　　PACER　　　　ALEXANDER/BREL

DMS–DMSL or DMS–MS–DMSL. As Class 143, but underframes built by BREL.

Construction: Steel. Alexander bus bodywork on four-wheeled underframes.
Engines: One Cummins LTA10-R of 172 kW (230 h.p.) at 2100 r.p.m. per car.
Couplers: BSI at outer ends, bar couplers within unit.
Seating Layout: 3+2 mainly unidirectional bus style.
Dimensions: 15.55 x 2.73 m.
Gangways: Within unit only.　　　　**Wheel Arrangement:** 1-A A-1.
Doors: Twin-leaf inward pivoting.　　**Maximum Speed:** 75 m.p.h.
Multiple Working: Classes 142, 143, 144, 150, 153, 155, 156, 158, 159, 170.

DMS. Dia. DP240 Lot No. 31015 BREL Derby 1986–87. –/62 1W. 24.2 t.
MS. Dia. DR205 Lot No. BREL Derby 31037 1987. –/73. 22.6 t.
DMSL. Dia. DP241 Lot No. BREL Derby 31016 1986–87. –/60 1T. 25.0 t.

Note: The centre cars of the 3-car units are owned by West Yorkshire PTE, although managed by Porterbrook Leasing Company.

144 001	**WY**	P	*NS*	NL	55801		55824
144 002	**WY**	P	*NS*	NL	55802		55825
144 003	**WY**	P	*NS*	NL	55803		55826
144 004	**WY**	P	*NS*	NL	55804		55827
144 005	**WY**	P	*NS*	NL	55805		55828
144 006	**WY**	P	*NS*	NL	55806		55829
144 007	**WY**	P	*NS*	NL	55807		55830
144 008	**WY**	P	*NS*	NL	55808		55831
144 009	**WY**	P	*NS*	NL	55809		55832
144 010	**WY**	P	*NS*	NL	55810		55833
144 011	**RR**	P	*NS*	NL	55811		55834
144 012	**RR**	P	*NS*	NL	55812		55835

144 013	**RR**	P	*NS*	NL	55813		55836
144 014	**WY**	P	*NS*	NL	55814	55850	55837
144 015	**WY**	P	*NS*	NL	55815	55851	55838
144 016	**WY**	P	*NS*	NL	55816	55852	55839
144 017	**WY**	P	*NS*	NL	55817	55853	55840
144 018	**WY**	P	*NS*	NL	55818	55854	55841
144 019	**WY**	P	*NS*	NL	55819	55855	55842
144 020	**WY**	P	*NS*	NL	55820	55856	55843
144 021	**WY**	P	*NS*	NL	55821	55857	55844
144 022	**WY**	P	*NS*	NL	55822	55858	55845
144 023	**WY**	P	*NS*	NL	55823	55859	55846

CLASS 150/0   SPRINTER   BREL

DMSL–MS–DMS. Prototype Sprinter.

Construction: Steel.
Engines: One Cummins NT-855-R4 of 213 kW (285 h.p.) at 2100 r.p.m. per car.
Bogies: BX8P (powered), BX8T (non-powered).
Couplers: BSI at outer end of driving vehicles, bar non-driving ends.
Seating Layout: 3+2 (mainly unidirectional).
Dimensions: 20.06 x 2.82 m (outer cars), 20.18 x 2.82 m (inner car).
Gangways: Within unit only.   **Wheel Arrangement:** 2-B – 2-B – B-2.
Doors: Single-leaf sliding.   **Maximum Speed:** 75 m.p.h.
Multiple Working: Classes 142, 143, 144, 150, 153, 155, 156, 158, 159, 170.

DMSL. Dia. DP230. Lot No. 30984 BREL York 1984. –/72 1T. 35.8 t.
MS. Dia. DR202. Lot No. 30986 BREL York 1984. –/92. 34.4 t.
DMS. Dia. DP231. Lot No. 30985 BREL York 1984. –/76. 35.6 t.

| 150 001 | r | **CO** | A | *CT* | TS | 55200 | 55400 | 55300 |
| 150 002 | r | **CO** | A | *CT* | TS | 55201 | 55401 | 55301 |

CLASS 150/1   SPRINTER   BREL

DMSL–DMS or DMSL–DMSL–DMS or DMSL–DMS–DMS.

Construction: Steel.
Engines: One Cummins NT855R5 of 213 kW (285 h.p.) at 2100 r.p.m. per car.
Bogies: BP38 (powered), BT38 (non-powered).
Couplers: BSI.
Seating Layout: 3+2 facing as built but 150010–150 132 were reseated with mainly unidirectional seating.
Dimensions: 19.74 x 2.82 m.
Gangways: Within unit only.   **Wheel Arrangement:** 2-B (– 2–B) – B-2.
Doors: Twin-leaf sliding..   **Maximum Speed:** 75 m.p.h.
Multiple Working: Classes 142, 143, 144, 150, 153, 155, 156, 158, 159, 170.

DMSL. Dia. DP238. Lot No. 31011 BREL York 1985–86. –/72 1T (s –/58 1TD, t –/71 1W 1T, u –/71 1T). 36.5 t.
DMS. Dia. DP239. Lot No. 31012 BREL York 1985–86. –/76 (s –/64). 38.45 t.

Notes: The centre cars of three-car units are Class 150/2 vehicles. For details see Class 150/2.
Units in **NW** livery have been refurbished with new seating.

150 010	ru	**CO**	A	*CT*	TS	52110	57226	57110
150 011	ru	**CO**	A	*CT*	TS	52111	52204	57111
150 012	ru	**CO**	A	*CT*	TS	52112	57206	57112
150 013	ru	**CO**	A	*CT*	TS	52113	52226	57113
150 014	ru	**CO**	A	*CT*	TS	52114	57204	57114
150 015	ru	**CO**	A	*CT*	TS	52115	52206	57115
150 016	ru	**CO**	A	*CT*	TS	52116	57212	57116
150 018	r	**CO**	A	*CT*	TS	52118	52220	57118
150 019	ru	**CO**	A	*CT*	TS	52119	57220	57119
150 101	ru	**CO**	A	*CT*	TS	52101	57101	
150 102	ru	**CO**	A	*CT*	TS	52102	57102	
150 103	ru	**CO**	A	*CT*	TS	52103	57103	
150 104	ru	**CO**	A	*CT*	TS	52104	57104	
150 105	ru	**CO**	A	*CT*	TS	52105	57105	
150 106	r	**CO**	A	*CT*	TS	52106	57106	
150 107	r	**CO**	A	*CT*	TS	52107	57107	
150 108	ru	**CO**	A	*CT*	TS	52108	57108	
150 109	ru	**CO**	A	*CT*	TS	52109	57109	
150 117	ru	**CO**	A	*CT*	TS	52117	57117	
150 120	t	**SL**	A	*SL*	BY	52120	57120	
150 121	ru	**CO**	A	*CT*	TS	52121	57121	
150 122	ru	**CO**	A	*CT*	TS	52122	57122	
150 123	t	**SL**	A	*SL*	BY	52123	57123	
150 124	ru	**CO**	A	*CT*	TS	52124	57124	
150 125	ru	**CO**	A	*CT*	TS	52125	57125	
150 126	ru	**CO**	A	*CT*	TS	52126	57126	
150 127	t	**SL**	A	*SL*	BY	52127	57127	Bletchley TMD
150 128	t	**SL**	A	*SL*	BY	52128	57128	
150 129	t	**SL**	A	*SL*	BY	52129	57129	MARSTON VALE
150 130	t	**SL**	A	*SL*	BY	52130	57130	
150 131	t	**SL**	A	*SL*	BY	52131	57131	LESLIE CRABBE
150 132	r	**CO**	A	*CT*	TS	52132	57132	
150 133	s	**NW**	A	*NW*	NH	52133	57133	
150 134	s	**NW**	A	*NW*	NH	52134	57134	
150 135	s	**NW**	A	*NW*	NH	52135	57135	
150 136	s	**NW**	A	*NW*	NH	52136	57136	
150 137	s	**NW**	A	*NW*	NH	52137	57137	
150 138	s	**NW**	A	*NW*	NH	52138	57138	
150 139	s	**NW**	A	*NW*	NH	52139	57139	
150 140	s	**NW**	A	*NW*	NH	52140	57140	
150 141	s	**NW**	A	*NW*	NH	52141	57141	
150 142	s	**NW**	A	*NW*	NH	52142	57142	
150 143	s	**NW**	A	*NW*	NH	52143	57143	
150 144	s	**NW**	A	*NW*	NH	52144	57144	
150 145	s	**NW**	A	*NW*	NH	52145	57145	
150 146	s	**NW**	A	*NW*	NH	52146	57146	
150 147	s	**NW**	A	*NW*	NH	52147	57147	

150 148	s	**NW**	A	*NW*	NH	52148	57148
150 149	s	**NW**	A	*NW*	NH	52149	57149
150 150	s	**NW**	A	*NW*	NH	52150	57150

CLASS 150/2   SPRINTER   BREL

DMSL–DMS.

Construction: Steel.
Engines: One Cummins NT855R5 of 213 kW (285 h.p.) at 2100 r.p.m. per car.
Bogies: BP38 (powered), BT38 (non-powered).
Couplers: BSI.
Seating Layout: 3+2 mainly unidirectional seating.
Dimensions: 19.74 x 2.82 m.
Gangways: Throughout.   **Wheel Arrangement:** 2-B – B-2.
Doors: Twin-leaf sliding.   **Maximum Speed:** 75 m.p.h.
Multiple Working: Classes 142, 143, 144, 150, 153, 155, 156, 158, 159, 170.

DMSL. Dia. DP242. Lot No. 31017 BREL York 1986–87. –/73 1T (s –/70 1TD). 35.8 t.
DMS. Dia. DP243. Lot No. 31018 BREL York 1986–87. –/76 (* –/68, s –/62). 34.9 t.

Units in **NW** livery have been refurbished with new Chapman seating.

150 201	s	**NW**	A	*NW*	NH	52201	57201	
150 202		**CO**	A	*CT*	TS	52202	57202	
150 203	s	**NW**	A	*NW*	NH	52203	57203	
150 205	s	**NW**	A	*NW*	NH	52205	57205	
150 207	s	**NW**	A	*NW*	NH	52207	57207	
150 208		**RR**	P	*SR*	HA	52208	57208	
150 210		**CO**	A	*CT*	TS	52210	57210	
150 211	s	**NW**	A	*NW*	NH	52211	57211	
150 213	r*	**PS**	P	*AR*	NC	52213	57213	LORD NELSON
150 214		**CO**	A	*CT*	TS	52214	57214	
150 215	s	**NW**	A	*NW*	NH	52215	57215	
150 216		**CO**	A	*CT*	TS	52216	57216	
150 217	r*	**PS**	P	*AR*	NC	52217	57217	OLIVER CROMWELL
150 218	s	**NW**	A	*NW*	NH	52218	57218	
150 219	r	**RR**	P	*WW*	CF	52219	57219	
150 221	r	**RR**	P	*WW*	CF	52221	57221	
150 222	s	**NW**	A	*NW*	NH	52222	57222	
150 223	s	**NW**	A	*NW*	NH	52223	57223	
150 224	s	**NW**	A	*NW*	NH	52224	57224	
150 225	s	**NW**	A	*NW*	NH	52225	57225	
150 227	r*	**PS**	P	*AR*	NC	52227	57227	SIR ALF RAMSEY
150 228	tu	**RR**	P	*NS*	NL	52228	57228	
150 229	r*	**PS**	P	*AR*	NC	52229	57229	GEORGE BORROW
150 230	r	**RR**	P	*WW*	CF	52230	57230	
150 231	r*	**PS**	P	*AR*	NC	52231	57231	KING EDMUND
150 232	r	**RR**	P	*WW*	CF	52232	57232	
150 233	r	**RR**	P	*WW*	CF	52233	57233	
150 234	r	**RR**	P	*WW*	CF	52234	57234	
150 235	r*	**PS**	P	*AR*	NC	52235	57235	CARDINAL WOLSEY

150 236	r	**RR**	P	*WW*	CF	52236	57236	
150 237	r*	**PS**	P	*AR*	NC	52237	57237	HEREWARD THE WAKE
150 238		**RR**	P	*WW*	CF	52238	57238	
150 239	r	**RR**	P	*WW*	CF	52239	57239	
150 240	r	**RR**	P	*WW*	CF	52240	57240	
150 241	r	**RR**	P	*WW*	CF	52241	57241	
150 242	r	**RR**	P	*WW*	CF	52242	57242	
150 243	r	**RR**	P	*WW*	CF	52243	57243	
150 244	r	**RR**	P	*WW*	CF	52244	57244	
150 245	r	**RR**	P	*NS*	NL	52245	57245	
150 246	r	**RR**	P	*WW*	CF	52246	57246	
150 247	r	**RR**	P	*WW*	CF	52247	57247	
150 248	r	**RR**	P	*WW*	CF	52248	57248	
150 249	r	**RR**	P	*WW*	CF	52249	57249	
150 250		**RR**	P	*SR*	HA	52250	57250	
150 251	r	**RR**	P	*WW*	CF	52251	57251	
150 252		**RR**	P	*SR*	HA	52252	57252	
150 253	r	**RR**	P	*WW*	CF	52253	57253	
150 254	r	**RR**	P	*WW*	CF	52254	57254	
150 255	r*	**AR**	P	*AR*	NC	52255	57255	HENRY BLOGG
150 256		**SR**	P	*SR*	HA	52256	57256	
150 257	r*	**AR**	P	*AR*	NC	52257	57257	QUEEN BOADICEA
150 258		**RR**	P	*SR*	HA	52258	57258	
150 259		**RR**	P	*SR*	HA	52259	57259	
150 260		**RR**	P	*SR*	HA	52260	57260	
150 261	r	**RR**	P	*WW*	CF	52261	57261	
150 262		**RR**	P	*SR*	HA	52262	57262	
150 263	r	**RR**	P	*WW*	CF	52263	57263	
150 264		**RR**	P	*SR*	HA	52264	57264	
150 265	r	**RR**	P	*WW*	CF	52265	57265	
150 266	r	**RR**	P	*WW*	CF	52266	57266	
150 267	r	**RR**	P	*WW*	CF	52267	57267	
150 268		**RR**	P	*NS*	NL	52268	57268	
150 269		**RR**	P	*NS*	NL	52269	57269	
150 270		**RR**	P	*NS*	NL	52270	57270	
150 271		**RR**	P	*NS*	NL	52271	57271	
150 272		**RR**	P	*NS*	NL	52272	57272	
150 273		**RR**	P	*NS*	NL	52273	57273	
150 274		**RR**	P	*NS*	NL	52274	57274	
150 275		**RR**	P	*NS*	NL	52275	57275	
150 276		**RR**	P	*NS*	NL	52276	57276	
150 277		**RR**	P	*NS*	NL	52277	57277	
150 278	r	**RR**	P	*WW*	CF	52278	57278	
150 279		**RR**	P	*CA*	CF	52279	57279	
150 280		**RR**	P	*CA*	CF	52280	57280	
150 281		**RR**	P	*CA*	CF	52281	57281	
150 282		**RR**	P	*CA*	CF	52282	57282	
150 283		**RR**	P	*SR*	HA	52283	57283	
150 284		**RR**	P	*SR*	HA	52284	57284	
150 285		**SR**	P	*SR*	HA	52285	57285	
Spare		**CO**	A	*CT*	TS		57209	

CLASS 153   SUPER SPRINTER   LEYLAND BUS

DMSL. Converted by Hunslet-Barclay, Kilmarnock from Class 155 two-car units.

Construction: Steel. Built from Leyland National bus parts on bogied underframes.
Engine: One Cummins NT855R5 of 213 kW (285 h.p.) at 2100 r.p.m.
Bogies: One P3-10 (powered) and one BT38 (non-powered).
Couplers: BSI.
Seating Layout: 2+2 facing/unidirectional.
Dimensions: 23.21 x 2.70 m.
Gangways: Throughout.   **Wheel Arrangement:** 2-B.
Doors: Single-leaf sliding plug.   **Maximum Speed:** 75 m.p.h.
Multiple Working: Classes 142, 143, 144, 150, 153, 155, 156, 158, 159, 170.

52301–52335. DMSL. Dia. DX203. Lot No. 31026 1987–88. Converted under
    Lot No. 31115 1991–2. –/72 1TD 1W (* –/66 1TD 1W). 41.2 t.
57301–57335. DMSL. Dia. DX203. Lot No. 31027 1987–88. Converted under
    Lot No. 31115 1991–2. –/72 1TD (* –/66 1TD). 41.2 t.

Notes:

Cars numbered in the 573XX series were renumbered by adding 50 to their
original number so that the last two digits correspond with the set number.
Central Trains units have been fitted with new seating.
Wales & West units have been reseated with seats removed from that
company's Class 158 units.

153 301		**RR**	A	*NS*	NL	52301
153 302	r	**RR**	A	*WW*	CF	52302
153 303	r	**RR**	A	*WW*	CF	52303
153 304		**RR**	A	*NS*	NL	52304
153 305	r	**RR**	A	*WW*	CF	52305
153 306	r*	**PS**	P	*AR*	NC	52306	EDITH CAVELL
153 307		**RR**	A	*NS*	NL	52307
153 308	r	**RR**	A	*WW*	CF	52308
153 309	r*	**PS**	P	*AR*	NC	52309	GERARD FIENNES
153 310		**NW**	P	*NW*	NH	52310
153 311	r*	**PS**	P	*AR*	NC	52311	JOHN CONSTABLE
153 312	r	**RR**	A	*WW*	CF	52312
153 313		**NW**	P	*NW*	NH	52313
153 314	r*	**PS**	P	*AR*	NC	52314	DELIA SMITH
153 315		**RR**	A	*NS*	NL	52315
153 316		**NW**	P	*NW*	NH	52316
153 317		**RR**	A	*NS*	NL	52317
153 318	r	**RR**	A	*WW*	CF	52318
153 319		**RR**	A	*NS*	NL	52319
153 320	r	**RR**	P	*CT*	TS	52320
153 321	r	**PS**	P	*CT*	TS	52321
153 322	r*	**RR**	P	*AR*	NC	52322	BENJAMIN BRITTEN
153 323	r	**RR**	P	*CT*	TS	52323
153 324		**NW**	P	*NW*	NH	52324

153 325	r	**RR**	P	*CT*	TS	52325	
153 326	r*	**PS**	P	*AR*	NC	52326	TED ELLIS
153 327	r	**RR**	A	*WW*	CF	52327	
153 328		**RR**	A	*NS*	NL	52328	
153 329	r	**RR**	P	*CT*	TS	52329	
153 330		**NW**	P	*NW*	NH	52330	
153 331		**RR**	A	*NS*	NL	52331	
153 332		**NW**	P	*NW*	NH	52332	
153 333	r	**RR**	P	*CT*	TS	52333	
153 334	r	**RR**	P	*CT*	TS	52334	
153 335	r*	**PS**	P	*AR*	NC	52335	MICHAEL PALIN
153 351		**RR**	A	*NS*	NL	57351	
153 352		**RR**	A	*NS*	NL	57352	
153 353	r	**RR**	A	*WW*	CF	57353	
153 354	r	**RR**	P	*CT*	TS	57354	
153 355	r	**RR**	A	*WW*	CF	57355	
153 356	r	**RR**	P	*CT*	TS	57356	
153 357		**RR**	A	*NS*	NL	57357	
153 358		**NW**	P	*NW*	NH	57358	
153 359		**NW**	P	*NW*	NH	57359	
153 360		**RR**	P	*NW*	NH	57360	
153 361		**RR**	P	*NW*	NH	57361	
153 362	r	**RR**	A	*WW*	CF	57362	
153 363		**RR**	P	*NW*	NH	57363	
153 364	r	**RR**	P	*CT*	TS	57364	
153 365	r	**RR**	P	*CT*	TS	57365	
153 366	r	**RR**	P	*CT*	TS	57366	
153 367		**RR**	P	*NW*	NH	57367	
153 368	r	**RR**	A	*WW*	CF	57368	
153 369	r	**RR**	P	*CT*	TS	57369	
153 370	r	**RR**	A	*WW*	CF	57370	
153 371	r	**RR**	P	*CT*	TS	57371	
153 372	r	**RR**	A	*WW*	CF	57372	
153 373	r	**RR**	A	*WW*	CF	57373	
153 374	r	**RR**	A	*WW*	CF	57374	
153 375	r	**RR**	P	*CT*	TS	57375	
153 376	r	**RR**	P	*CT*	TS	57376	
153 377	r	**RR**	A	*WW*	CF	57377	
153 378		**RR**	A	*NS*	NL	57378	
153 379	r	**RR**	P	*CT*	TS	57379	
153 380	r	**RR**	A	*WW*	CF	57380	
153 381	r	**RR**	P	*CT*	TS	57381	
153 382	r	**RR**	A	*WW*	CF	57382	
153 383	r	**RR**	P	*CT*	TS	57383	
153 384	r	**RR**	P	*CT*	TS	57384	
153 385	r	**RR**	P	*CT*	TS	57385	

CLASS 155   SUPER SPRINTER   LEYLAND BUS

DMSL–DMS.

Construction: Steel. Built from Leyland National bus parts on bogied underframes.
Engines: One Cummins NT855R5 of 213 kW (285 h.p.) at 2100 r.p.m. per car
Bogies: One P3-10 (powered) and one BT38 (non-powered).
Couplers: BSI.
Seating Layout: 2+2 facing/unidirectional.
Dimensions: 23.21 x 2.70 m.
Gangways: Throughout.   **Wheel Arrangement:** 2-B – B-2.
Doors: Single-leaf sliding plug.   **Maximum Speed:** 75 m.p.h.
Multiple Working: Classes 142, 143, 144, 150, 153, 155, 156, 158, 159, 170.

DMSL. Dia. DP248. Lot No. 310571988. –/80 1TD 1W. 39.0 t.
DMS. Dia. DP249. Lot No. 31058 1988. –/80. 38.7 t.

Note: These units are owned by West Yorkshire PTE, although managed by Porterbrook Leasing Company.

155 341	**WY**	P	*NS*	NL	52341	57341
155 342	**WY**	P	*NS*	NL	52342	57342
155 343	**WY**	P	*NS*	NL	52343	57343
155 344	**WY**	P	*NS*	NL	52344	57344
155 345	**WY**	P	*NS*	NL	52345	57345
155 346	**WY**	P	*NS*	NL	52346	57346
155 347	**WY**	P	*NS*	NL	52347	57347

CLASS 156   SUPER SPRINTER   METRO-CAMMELL

DMSL–DMS.

Construction: Steel.
Engines: One Cummins NT855R5 of 213 kW (285 h.p.) at 2100 r.p.m. per car
Bogies: One P3-10 (powered) and one BT38 (non-powered).
Couplers: BSI.
Seating Layout: 2+2 facing/unidirectional.
Dimensions: 23.03 x 2.73 m.
Gangways: Throughout.   **Wheel Arrangement:** 2-B – B-2.
Doors: Single-leaf sliding plug.   **Maximum Speed:** 75 m.p.h.
Multiple Working: Classes 142, 143, 144, 150, 153, 155, 156, 158, 159, 170.

DMSL. Dia. DP244. Lot No. 31028 1988–89. –/74 (†* –/72, st$ –/70, u –/68) 1TD 1W. 36.1 t.
DMS. Dia. DP245. Lot No. 31029 1987–89. –/76 (q –/78,· † –/74, tu$§ –/72) 35.5 t.

Notes: 156 500–514 are owned by Strathclyde PTE, although managed by Angel Train Contracts.
Units in **RE**, **RN** or **NS** livery have been fitted with new seating.

156 401	r*	**RE**	P	*CT*	TS	52401	57401
156 402	r*	**RE**	P	*CT*	TS	52402	57402
156 403	r*	**RE**	P	*CT*	TS	52403	57403

156 404	r*	**RE**	P	*CT*	TS	52404	57404	
156 405	r*	**RE**	P	*CT*	TS	52405	57405	
156 406	r*	**RE**	P	*CT*	TS	52406	57406	
156 407	r*	**CT**	P	*CT*	TS	52407	57407	
156 408	r*	**RE**	P	*CT*	TS	52408	57408	
156 409	r*	**RE**	P	*CT*	TS	52409	57409	
156 410	r*	**RE**	P	*CT*	TS	52410	57410	
156 411	r*	**RE**	P	*CT*	TS	52411	57411	
156 412	r*	**RE**	P	*CT*	TS	52412	57412	
156 413	r*	**RE**	P	*CT*	TS	52413	57413	
156 414	r*	**RE**	P	*CT*	TS	52414	57414	
156 415	r*	**RE**	P	*CT*	TS	52415	57415	
156 416	r*	**RE**	P	*CT*	TS	52416	57416	
156 417	r*	**RE**	P	*CT*	TS	52417	57417	
156 418	r*	**RE**	P	*CT*	TS	52418	57418	
156 419	r*	**RE**	P	*CT*	TS	52419	57419	
156 420	s	**RN**	P	*NW*	NH	52420	57420	
156 421	s	**RN**	P	*NW*	NH	52421	57421	
156 422	r*	**RE**	P	*CT*	TS	52422	57422	
156 423	s	**RN**	P	*NW*	NH	52423	57423	
156 424	s	**RN**	P	*NW*	NH	52424	57424	
156 425	s	**RN**	P	*NW*	NH	52425	57425	
156 426	s	**RN**	P	*NW*	NH	52426	57426	
156 427	s	**RN**	P	*NW*	NH	52427	57427	
156 428	s	**RN**	P	*NW*	NH	52428	57428	
156 429	s	**RN**	P	*NW*	NH	52429	57429	
156 430	t	**SC**	A	*SR*	CK	52430	57430	
156 431	t	**SC**	A	*SR*	CK	52431	57431	
156 432	t	**SC**	A	*SR*	CK	52432	57432	
156 433	t	**SC**	A	*SR*	CK	52433	57433	The Kilmarnock Edition
156 434	t	**SC**	A	*SR*	CK	52434	57434	
156 435	t	**SC**	A	*SR*	CK	52435	57435	
156 436	†	**SC**	A	*SR*	CK	52436	57436	
156 437	rt	**SC**	A	*SR*	CK	52437	57437	
156 438		**PS**	A	*NS*	NL	52438	57438	
156 439	rt	**SC**	A	*SR*	CK	52439	57439	
156 440	s	**RN**	P	*NW*	NH	52440	57440	
156 441	s	**RN**	P	*NW*	NH	52441	57441	
156 442	rt	**SC**	A	*SR*	CK	52442	57442	
156 443	q	**NS**	A	*NS*	HT	52443	57443	
156 444	q	**NS**	A	*NS*	HT	52444	57444	
156 445	u	**SC**	A	*SR*	CK	52445	57445	
156 446	rt	**SR**	A	*SR*	CK	52446	57446	
156 447	ru	**SR**	A	*SR*	CK	52447	57447	
156 448	q	**NS**	A	*NS*	HT	52448	57448	
156 449	ru	**SR**	A	*SR*	CK	52449	57449	
156 450	t	**SR**	A	*SR*	CK	52450	57450	
156 451		**PS**	A	*NS*	HT	52451	57451	
156 452	s	**RN**	P	*NW*	NH	52452	57452	
156 453	ru	**SR**	A	*SR*	CK	52453	57453	
156 454	q	**NS**	A	*NS*	HT	52454	57454	

156 455	s	**RN**	P	*NW*	NH	52455 57455
156 456	rt	**SR**	A	*SR*	CK	52456 57456
156 457	rt	**SR**	A	*SR*	CK	52457 57457
156 458	t	**SR**	A	*SR*	CK	52458 57458
156 459	s	**RN**	P	*NW*	NH	52459 57459
156 460	s	**RN**	P	*NW*	NH	52460 57460
156 461	s	**RN**	P	*NW*	NH	52461 57461
156 462	r	**PS**	A	*SR*	CK	52462 57462
156 463	q	**NS**	A	*NS*	HT	52463 57463
156 464	s	**RN**	P	*NW*	NH	52464 57464
156 465	u	**PS**	A	*SR*	CK	52465 57465
156 466	s	**RN**	P	*NW*	NH	52466 57466
156 467	r	**SR**	A	*SR*	CK	52467 57467
156 468		**PS**	A	*NS*	NL	52468 57468
156 469	q	**NS**	A	*NS*	HT	52469 57469
156 470	q	**NS**	A	*NS*	NL	52470 57470
156 471	q	**NS**	A	*NS*	NL	52471 57471
156 472	q	**NS**	A	*NS*	NL	52472 57472
156 473	q	**PS**	A	*NS*	NL	52473 57473
156 474	rt	**SR**	A	*SR*	CK	52474 57474
156 475	q	**SR**	A	*NS*	NL	52475 57475
156 476	rt	**PS**	A	*SR*	CK	52476 57476
156 477	rt	**SR**	A	*SR*	CK	52477 57477
156 478	t	**SR**	A	*SR*	CK	52478 57478
156 479	q	**NS**	A	*NS*	NL	52479 57479
156 480	q	**NS**	A	*NS*	NL	52480 57480
156 481	q	**NS**	A	*NS*	NL	52481 57481
156 482	q	**NS**	A	*NS*	NL	52482 57482
156 483		**PS**	A	*NS*	NL	52483 57483
156 484	q	**NS**	A	*NS*	NL	52484 57484
156 485	ru	**SR**	A	*SR*	CK	52485 57485
156 486	q	**NS**	A	*NS*	NL	52486 57486
156 487	q	**NS**	A	*NS*	NL	52487 57487
156 488	q	**NS**	A	*NS*	NL	52488 57488
156 489	q	**NS**	A	*NS*	NL	52489 57489
156 490	q	**NS**	A	*NS*	NL	52490 57490
156 491	q	**NS**	A	*NS*	NL	52491 57491
156 492	r†	**SR**	A	*SR*	CK	52492 57492
156 493	rt	**SR**	A	*SR*	CK	52493 57493
156 494	§	**SC**	A	*SR*	CK	52494 57494
156 495	ru	**SC**	A	*SR*	CK	52495 57495
156 496	ru	**SR**	A	*SR*	CK	52496 57496
156 497	q	**NS**	A	*NS*	NL	52497 57497
156 498	q	**NS**	A	*NS*	NL	52498 57498
156 499	rt	**SR**	A	*SR*	CK	52499 57499
156 500	u	**SC**	A	*SR*	CK	52500 57500
156 501		**SC**	A	*SR*	CK	52501 57501
156 502		**SC**	A	*SR*	CK	52502 57502
156 503		**SC**	A	*SR*	CK	52503 57503
156 504		**SC**	A	*SR*	CK	52504 57504
156 505		**SC**	A	*SR*	CK	52505 57505

156 506	**SC**	A	*SR*	CK	52506	57506
156 507	**SC**	A	*SR*	CK	52507	57507
156 508	**SC**	A	*SR*	CK	52508	57508
156 509	**SC**	A	*SR*	CK	52509	57509
156 510	**SC**	A	*SR*	CK	52510	57510
156 511	**SC**	A	*SR*	CK	52511	57511
156 512	**SC**	A	*SR*	CK	52512	57512
156 513	**SC**	A	*SR*	CK	52513	57513
156 514	**SC**	A	*SR*	CK	52514	57514

CLASS 158/0   BREL

DMSL (B)–DMSL (A) or DMCL–DMSL or DMCL–MSL–DMSL.

Construction: Welded aluminium.
Engines: 158 701–158 814: One Cummins NTA855R of 260 kW (350 h.p.) at 1900 r.p.m. per car.
158 863–158 872: One Cummins NTA855R of 300 kW (400 h.p.) at 2100 r.p.m. per car.
158 815–158 862: One Perkins 2006-TWH of 260 kW (350 h.p.) at 1900 r.p.m. per car.
Bogies: One BREL P4 (powered) and one BREL T4 (non-powered) per car.
Couplers: BSI.
Seating Layout: 2+2 facing/unidirectional in standard class and in ScotRail first class. 2+2 facing in Northern Spirit first class, 2+1 facing/unidirectional in Virgin Cross-Country first class.
Dimensions: 22.57 x 2.70 m.
Gangways: Throughout.   **Wheel Arrangement:** 2-B – B-2.
Doors: Twin-leaf swing plug.   **Maximum Speed:** 90 m.p.h.
Multiple Working: Classes 142, 143, 144, 150, 153, 155, 156, 158, 159, 170.

DMSL (B). Dia. DP252. Lot No. 31051 BREL Derby 1989–92. –/68 1TD 1W. (†–/66 1TD 1W). Public telephone and trolley space. 38.5 t.
MSL. Dia. DR207. Lot No. 31050 BREL Derby 1991. 37.1 t. –/70 2T. 37.1 t.
DMSL (A). Dia. DP251 Lot No. 31052 BREL Derby 1989–92. –/70 († –/68; § 32/32) 1T. 37.8 t.

The above details refer to the "as built" condition. The following DMSL(B) have now been converted to DMCL as follows:

52701–52744 (Scotrail/Northern Spirit). Dia. DP318. 15/51 1TD 1W (*15/53 1TD 1W).
52747–52751. (Virgin Cross-Country). Dia. DP323. 9/51 1TD 1W.
52757–52759. (First North-Western). Dia. DP333. 16/51 1TD 1W.
52760–779/781. (Northern Spirit 2-car Units). Dia. DP331. 16/48 1TD 1W.
52798–814 (Northern Spirit 3-car Units). Dia. DP332. 32/32 1TD 1W.

s Refurbished with new shape seat cushions. Fitted with table lamps in first class. Units in **CT** livery have also been fitted with new shape seat cusions.
† Fitted with new seating.
Non-standard Livery: 158 867 is in prototype Wales & West Passenger Trains livery of grey, orange, light blue and dark blue with orange doors.

---

158 701	*	**SR**	P	*SR*	HA	52701	57701
158 702	*	**SR**	P	*SR*	HA	52702	57702	BBC Scotland – 75 Years
158 703	*	**SR**	P	*SR*	HA	52703	57703
158 704	*	**SR**	P	*SR*	HA	52704	57704
158 705	*	**SR**	P	*SR*	HA	52705	57705
158 706	*	**SR**	P	*SR*	HA	52706	57706
158 707		**SR**	P	*SR*	HA	52707	57707	Far North Line 125th ANNIVERSARY
158 708	*	**SR**	P	*SR*	HA	52708	57708
158 709	*	**SR**	P	*SR*	HA	52709	57709
158 710	*	**SR**	P	*SR*	HA	52710	57710
158 711	*	**SR**	P	*SR*	HA	52711	57711
158 712	*	**SR**	P	*SR*	HA	52712	57712
158 713	*	**SR**	P	*SR*	HA	52713	57713
158 714	*	**SR**	P	*SR*	HA	52714	57714
158 715	*	**SR**	P	*SR*	HA	52715	57715	Haymarket
158 716	*	**SR**	P	*SR*	HA	52716	57716
158 717	*	**SR**	P	*SR*	HA	52717	57717
158 718	*	**SR**	P	*SR*	HA	52718	57718
158 719	*	**SR**	P	*SR*	HA	52719	57719
158 720	*	**SR**	P	*SR*	HA	52720	57720
158 721	*	**SR**	P	*SR*	HA	52721	57721
158 722	*	**SR**	P	*SR*	HA	52722	57722
158 723	*	**SR**	P	*SR*	HA	52723	57723
158 724		**SR**	P	*SR*	HA	52724	57724
158 725	*	**SR**	P	*SR*	HA	52725	57725
158 726	*	**SR**	P	*SR*	HA	52726	57726
158 727	*	**SR**	P	*SR*	HA	52727	57727
158 728	*	**SR**	P	*SR*	HA	52728	57728
158 729	*	**SR**	P	*SR*	HA	52729	57729
158 730	*	**SR**	P	*SR*	HA	52730	57730
158 731	*	**SR**	P	*SR*	HA	52731	57731
158 732	*	**SR**	P	*SR*	HA	52732	57732
158 733	*	**SR**	P	*SR*	HA	52733	57733
158 734	*	**SR**	P	*SR*	HA	52734	57734
158 735	*	**SR**	P	*SR*	HA	52735	57735
158 736	*	**SR**	P	*SR*	HA	52736	57736
158 737		**TX**	P	*NS*	NL	52737	57737
158 738	*	**SR**	P	*SR*	HA	52738	57738
158 739		**SR**	P	*SR*	HA	52739	57739
158 740	*	**SR**	P	*SR*	HA	52740	57740
158 741	*	**SR**	P	*SR*	HA	52741	57741
158 742		**RE**	P	*NS*	NL	52742	57742
158 743		**RE**	P	*NS*	NL	52743	57743
158 744		**TX**	P	*NS*	NL	52744	57744
158 745	†	**WW**	P	*WW*	CF	52745	57745	Pont Britannia
158 746	†	**WW**	P	*WW*	CF	52746	57746
158 747		**RE**	P	*VX*	NH	52747	57747
158 748		**RE**	P	*VX*	NH	52748	57748
158 749		**RE**	P	*VX*	NH	52749	57749
158 750		**RE**	P	*VX*	NH	52750	57750

158 751		**RE**	P	*VX*	NH	52751	57751	
158 752		**NW**	P	*NW*	NH	52752	57752	
158 753		**NW**	P	*NW*	NH	52753	57753	
158 754		**NW**	P	*NW*	NH	52754	57754	
158 755		**NW**	P	*NW*	NH	52755	57755	
158 756		**NW**	P	*NW*	NH	52756	57756	
158 757		**NW**	P	*NW*	NH	52757	57757	
158 758		**NW**	P	*NW*	NH	52758	57758	
158 759		**NW**	P	*NW*	NH	52759	57759	
158 760	s	**TX**	P	*NS*	NL	52760	57760	
158 761	s	**TX**	P	*NS*	NL	52761	57761	
158 762	s	**TX**	P	*NS*	NL	52762	57762	
158 763	s	**TX**	P	*NS*	NL	52763	57763	
158 764	s	**TX**	P	*NS*	NL	52764	57764	
158 765	s	**TX**	P	*NS*	NL	52765	57765	
158 766	s	**TX**	P	*NS*	NL	52766	57766	
158 767	s	**TX**	P	*NS*	NL	52767	57767	
158 768	s	**TX**	P	*NS*	NL	52768	57768	
158 769	s	**TX**	P	*NS*	NL	52769	57769	
158 770	s	**TX**	P	*NS*	NL	52770	57770	
158 771	s	**TX**	P	*NS*	HT	52771	57771	
158 772	s	**TX**	P	*NS*	NL	52772	57772	
158 773	s	**TX**	P	*NS*	NL	52773	57773	
158 774	s	**TX**	P	*NS*	NL	52774	57774	
158 775	s	**TX**	P	*NS*	HT	52775	57775	
158 776	s	**TX**	P	*NS*	HT	52776	57776	
158 777	s	**TX**	P	*NS*	HT	52777	57777	
158 778	s	**TX**	P	*NS*	HT	52778	57778	
158 779	s	**TX**	P	*NS*	HT	52779	57779	
158 781	s	**TX**	P	*NS*	HT	52781	57781	
158 782	r	**RE**	A	*CT*	TS	52782	57782	
158 783	r	**CT**	A	*CT*	TS	52783	57783	
158 787	r	**CT**	A	*CT*	TS	52787	57787	
158 788	r	**RE**	A	*CT*	TS	52788	57788	
158 795	r	**CT**	A	*CT*	TS	52795	57795	
158 798	s	**TX**	P	*NS*	HT	52798	58715	57798
158 799	s	**TX**	P	*NS*	HT	52799	58716	57799
158 800	s	**TX**	P	*NS*	HT	52800	58717	57800
158 801	s	**TX**	P	*NS*	HT	52801	58701	57801
158 802	s	**TX**	P	*NS*	HT	52802	58702	57802
158 803	s	**TX**	P	*NS*	HT	52803	58703	57803
158 804	s	**TX**	P	*NS*	HT	52804	58704	57804
158 805	s	**TX**	P	*NS*	HT	52805	58705	57805
158 806	s	**TX**	P	*NS*	HT	52806	58706	57806
158 807	s	**TX**	P	*NS*	HT	52807	58707	57807
158 808	s	**TX**	P	*NS*	HT	52808	58708	57808
158 809	s	**TX**	P	*NS*	HT	52809	58709	57809
158 810	s	**TX**	P	*NS*	HT	52810	58710	57810
158 811	s	**TX**	P	*NS*	HT	52811	58711	57811
158 812	s	**TX**	P	*NS*	HT	52812	58712	57812
158 813	s	**TX**	P	*NS*	HT	52813	58713	57813

158 814	s	TX	P	NS	HT	52814	58714	57814
158 815	†	RE	A	WW	CF	52815	57815	
158 816	†	RE	A	WW	CF	52816	57816	
158 817	†	RE	A	WW	CF	52817	57817	
158 818	†	RE	A	WW	CF	52818	57818	
158 819	†	RE	A	WW	CF	52819	57819	
158 820	†	RE	A	WW	CF	52820	57820	
158 821	†	RE	A	WW	CF	52821	57821	
158 822	†	RE	A	WW	CF	52822	57822	
158 823	†	RE	A	WW	CF	52823	57823	
158 824	†	RE	A	WW	CF	52824	57824	
158 825	†	RE	A	WW	CF	52825	57825	
158 826	†	RE	A	WW	CF	52826	57826	
158 827	†	RE	A	WW	CF	52827	57827	
158 828	†	RE	A	WW	CF	52828	57828	
158 829	†	RE	A	WW	CF	52829	57829	
158 830	†	RE	A	WW	CF	52830	57830	
158 831	†	RE	A	WW	CF	52831	57831	
158 832	†	RE	A	WW	CF	52832	57832	
158 833	†	RE	A	WW	CF	52833	57833	
158 834	†	RE	A	WW	CF	52834	57834	
158 835	†	RE	A	WW	CF	52835	57835	
158 836	†	RE	A	WW	CF	52836	57836	
158 837	†	RE	A	WW	CF	52837	57837	
158 838	†	RE	A	WW	CF	52838	57838	
158 839	†	RE	A	WW	CF	52839	57839	
158 840	†	RE	A	WW	CF	52840	57840	
158 841	†	RE	A	WW	CF	52841	57841	
158 842	†	RE	A	WW	CF	52842	57842	
158 843	†	RE	A	WW	CF	52843	57843	
158 844	r	CT	A	CT	TS	52844	57844	
158 845	r	CT	A	CT	TS	52845	57845	
158 846	r	CT	A	CT	TS	52846	57846	
158 847	r	RE	A	CT	TS	52847	57847	
158 848	r	CT	A	CT	TS	52848	57848	
158 849	r	CT	A	CT	TS	52849	57849	
158 850	r	CT	A	CT	TS	52850	57850	
158 851	r	CT	A	CT	TS	52851	57851	
158 852	r	CT	A	CT	TS	52852	57852	
158 853	r	CT	A	CT	TS	52853	57853	
158 854	r	CT	A	CT	TS	52854	57854	
158 855	r	RE	A	CT	TS	52855	57855	
158 856	r	CT	A	CT	TS	52856	57856	
158 857	r	CT	A	CT	TS	52857	57857	
158 858	r	CT	A	CT	TS	52858	57858	
158 859	r	CT	A	CT	TS	52859	57859	
158 860	r	CT	A	CT	TS	52860	57860	
158 861	r	RE	A	CT	TS	52861	57861	
158 862	r	CT	A	CT	TS	52862	57862	
158 863	†	RE	A	WW	CF	52863	57863	
158 864	†	RE	A	WW	CF	52864	57864	

158 865	†	**RE**	A	*WW*	CF	52865 57865
158 866	†	**RE**	A	*WW*	CF	52866 57866
158 867	†	**0**	A	*WW*	CF	52867 57867
158 868	†	**RE**	A	*WW*	CF	52868 57868
158 869	†	**RE**	A	*WW*	CF	52869 57869
158 870	†	**RE**	A	*WW*	CF	52870 57870
158 871	†	**RE**	A	*WW*	CF	52871 57871
158 872	†	**RE**	A	*WW*	CF	52872 57872

CLASS 158/9   BREL

DMSL–DMS. Units leased by West Yorkshire PTE. Details as for Class 158/0 except for seating layout and toilets.

DMSL. Dia. DP252. Lot No. 31051 BREL Derby 1990–92. –/70 1TD 1W. Public telephone and trolley space. 38.1 t.

DMS. Dia. DP251. Lot No. 31052 BREL Derby 1990–92. –/72 and luggage area. 37.8 t.

Note: These units are leased by West Yorkshire PTE and are managed by Porterbrook Leasing Company.

158 901	**WY**	P	*NS*	NL	52901 57901
158 902	**WY**	P	*NS*	NL	52902 57902
158 903	**WY**	P	*NS*	NL	52903 57903
158 904	**WY**	P	*NS*	NL	52904 57904
158 905	**WY**	P	*NS*	NL	52905 57905
158 906	**WY**	P	*NS*	NL	52906 57906
158 907	**WY**	P	*NS*	NL	52907 57907
158 908	**WY**	P	*NS*	NL	52908 57908
158 909	**YN**	P	*NS*	NL	52909 57909
158 910	**WY**	P	*NS*	NL	52910 57910

CLASS 158/0   BREL

DMSL(B)–DMSL(A)–DMSL(A) or DMSL(B)–DMSL(A)–DMSL(B). Three car units formed by Central Trains from former 2-car units. For details see above.

158 951	r	**CT**	A	*CT*	TS	52780 57780 57784
158 952	r	**CT**	A	*CT*	TS	52785 57785 52786
158 953	r	**CT**	A	*CT*	TS	52790 57790 57796
158 954	r	**CT**	A	*CT*	TS	52791 57791 57786
158 955	r	**CT**	A	*CT*	TS	52792 57792 52796
158 956	r	**CT**	A	*CT*	TS	52793 57793 52784
158 957	r	**CT**	A	*CT*	TS	52794 57794 52789
158 958	r	**CT**	A	*CT*	TS	52797 57797 57789

CLASS 159   BREL

DMCL–MSL–DMSL. Built as Class 158. Converted before entering passenger service to Class 159 by Rosyth Dockyard.

Construction: Welded aluminium.
Engines: One Cummins NTA855R of 300 kW (400 h.p.) at 2100 r.p.m. per car.
Bogies: One BREL P4 (powered) and one BREL T4 (non-powered) per car.
Couplers: BSI.
Seating Layout: 2+2 facing/unidirectional (standard class), 2+1 facing (first class).
Dimensions: 23.21 x 2.82 m.
Gangways: Throughout.   **Wheel Arrangement:** 2-B – B-2 – B-2.
Doors: Twin-leaf swing plug.   **Maximum Speed:** 90 m.p.h.
Multiple Working: Classes 142, 143, 144, 150, 153, 155, 156, 158, 159, 170.

DMCL. Dia. DP322. Lot No. 31051 BREL Derby 1992–93. 24/28 1TD 1W. 38.5 t.
MSL. Dia. DR209. Lot No. 31050 BREL Derby 1992–93. 38 t. –/72 2T.
DMSL. Dia. DP260. Lot No. 31052 BREL Derby 1992–93. –/72 1T and luggage area. 37.8 t.

159 001	**NT** P	*SW*	SA	52873	58718	57873	CITY OF EXETER
159 002	**NT** P	*SW*	SA	52874	58719	57874	CITY OF SALISBURY
159 003	**SW** P	*SW*	SA	52875	58720	57875	TEMPLECOMBE
159 004	**NT** P	*SW*	SA	52876	58721	57876	BASINGSTOKE AND DEANE
159 005	**SW** P	*SW*	SA	52877	58722	57877	
159 006	**SW** P	*SW*	SA	52878	58723	57878	
159 007	**SW** P	*SW*	SA	52879	58724	57879	
159 008	**SW** P	*SW*	SA	52880	58725	57880	
159 009	**SW** P	*SW*	SA	52881	58726	57881	
159 010	**SW** P	*SW*	SA	52882	58727	57882	
159 011	**SW** P	*SW*	SA	52883	58728	57883	
159 012	**NT** P	*SW*	SA	52884	58729	57884	
159 013	**SW** P	*SW*	SA	52885	58730	57885	
159 014	**SW** P	*SW*	SA	52886	58731	57886	
159 015	**NT** P	*SW*	SA	52887	58732	57887	
159 016	**SW** P	*SW*	SA	52888	58733	57888	
159 017	**NT** P	*SW*	SA	52889	58734	57889	
159 018	**NT** P	*SW*	SA	52890	58735	57890	
159 019	**NT** P	*SW*	SA	52891	58736	57891	
159 020	**NT** P	*SW*	SA	52892	58737	57892	
159 021	**NT** P	*SW*	SA	52893	58738	57893	
159 022	**NT** P	*SW*	SA	52894	58739	57894	

CLASS 165/0   NETWORK TURBO   BREL

DMCL–DMS or DMCL–MS–DMS.

Construction: Welded aluminium.
Engines: One Perkins 2006-TWH of 260 kW (350 h.p.) at 1900 r.p.m. per car.
Bogies: BREL P3-17 (powered), BREL T3-17 (non-powered).
Couplers: BSI.

Seating Layout: 3+2 facing/unidirectional (standard class), 2+2 facing (first class).
Dimensions: 23.50 x 2.85 m.
Gangways: Within unit only.   **Wheel Arrangement:** 2-B (– B-2) – B-2.
Doors: Twin-leaf swing plug.   **Maximum Speed:** 75 m.p.h.
Multiple Working: Classes 165, 166, 168.

58801–58822. 58873–58878. DMCL. Dia. DP319. Lot No. 31087 BREL York 1990. 16/72 1T. 37.0 t.
58823–58833. DMCL. Dia. DP320. Lot No. 31089 BREL York 1991–92. 24/60 1T. 37.0 t.
MS. Dia. DR208. Lot No. 31090 BREL York 1991–92. –/106. 37.0 t.
DMS. Dia. DP253. Lot No. 31088 BREL York 1991–92. –/98. 37.0 t.

Note: 165 006–039 are fitted with tripcocks for working over London Underground tracks between Harrow-on-the-Hill and Amersham.

165 001	**NT**	A	*TT*	RG	58801		58834
165 002	**NT**	A	*TT*	RG	58802		58835
165 003	**NT**	A	*TT*	RG	58803		58836
165 004	**NT**	A	*TT*	RG	58804		58837
165 005	**NT**	A	*TT*	RG	58805		58838
165 006	**NT**	A	*CR*	AL	58806		58839
165 007	**NT**	A	*CR*	AL	58807		58840
165 008	**NT**	A	*CR*	AL	58808		58841
165 009	**NT**	A	*CR*	AL	58809		58842
165 010	**NT**	A	*CR*	AL	58810		58843
165 011	**NT**	A	*CR*	AL	58811		58844
165 012	**NT**	A	*CR*	AL	58812		58845
165 013	**NT**	A	*CR*	AL	58813		58846
165 014	**NT**	A	*CR*	AL	58814		58847
165 015	**NT**	A	*CR*	AL	58815		58848
165 016	**NT**	A	*CR*	AL	58816		58849
165 017	**NT**	A	*CR*	AL	58817		58850
165 018	**NT**	A	*CR*	AL	58818		58851
165 019	**NT**	A	*CR*	AL	58819		58852
165 020	**NT**	A	*CR*	AL	58820		58853
165 021	**NT**	A	*CR*	AL	58821		58854
165 022	**NT**	A	*CR*	AL	58822		58855
165 023	**NT**	A	*CR*	AL	58873		58867
165 024	**NT**	A	*CR*	AL	58874		58868
165 025	**NT**	A	*CR*	AL	58875		58869
165 026	**NT**	A	*CR*	AL	58876		58870
165 027	**NT**	A	*CR*	AL	58877		58871
165 028	**NT**	A	*CR*	AL	58878		58872
165 029	**NT**	A	*CR*	AL	58823	55404	58856
165 030	**NT**	A	*CR*	AL	58824	55405	58857
165 031	**NT**	A	*CR*	AL	58825	55406	58858
165 032	**NT**	A	*CR*	AL	58826	55407	58859
165 033	**NT**	A	*CR*	AL	58827	55408	58860
165 034	**NT**	A	*CR*	AL	58828	55409	58861
165 035	**NT**	A	*CR*	AL	58829	55410	58862

165 036	**NT**	A	*CR*	AL	58830	55411	58863
165 037	**NT**	A	*CR*	AL	58831	55412	58864
165 038	**NT**	A	*CR*	AL	58832	55413	58865
165 039	**NT**	A	*CR*	AL	58833	55414	58866

CLASS 165/1   NETWORK TURBO   BREL

DMCL–DMS or DMCL–MS–DMS.

Construction: Welded aluminium.
Engines: One Perkins 2006-TWH of 260 kW (350 h.p.) at 1900 r.p.m. per car.
Bogies: BREL P3-17 (powered), BREL T3-17 (non-powered).
Couplers: BSI.
Seating layout: 3+2 facing/unidirectional (standard class), 2+2 facing (first class).
Dimensions: 23.50 x 2.85 m.
Gangways: Within unit only.   **Wheel Arrangement:** 2-B (– B-2) – B-2.
Doors: Twin-leaf swing plug.   **Maximum Speed:** 90 m.p.h.
Multiple Working: Classes 165, 166, 168.

58953–58969. DMCL. Dia. DP320. Lot No. 31098 BREL York 1992. 16/66 1T. 37.0 t.
58879–58898. DMCL. Dia. DP319. Lot No. 31096 BREL York 1992. 16/72 1T. 37.0 t.
MS. Dia. DR208. Lot No. 31099 BREL 1992. –/106. 37.0 t.
DMS. Dia. DP253. Lot No. 31097 BREL 1992. –/98. 37.0 t.

165 101	**NT**	A	*TT*	RG	58953	55415	58916
165 102	**NT**	A	*TT*	RG	58954	55416	58917
165 103	**NT**	A	*TT*	RG	58955	55417	58918
165 104	**NT**	A	*TT*	RG	58956	55418	58919
165 105	**NT**	A	*TT*	RG	58957	55419	58920
165 106	**NT**	A	*TT*	RG	58958	55420	58921
165 107	**NT**	A	*TT*	RG	58959	55421	58922
165 108	**NT**	A	*TT*	RG	58960	55422	58923
165 109	**NT**	A	*TT*	RG	58961	55423	58924
165 110	**NT**	A	*TT*	RG	58962	55424	58925
165 111	**NT**	A	*TT*	RG	58963	55425	58926
165 112	**NT**	A	*TT*	RG	58964	55426	58927
165 113	**NT**	A	*TT*	RG	58965	55427	58928
165 114	**NT**	A	*TT*	RG	58966	55428	58929
165 116	**NT**	A	*TT*	RG	58968	55430	58931
165 117	**NT**	A	*TT*	RG	58969	55431	58932
165 118	**NT**	A	*TT*	RG	58879	58933	
165 119	**NT**	A	*TT*	RG	58880	58934	
165 120	**NT**	A	*TT*	RG	58881	58935	
165 121	**NT**	A	*TT*	RG	58882	58936	
165 122	**NT**	A	*TT*	RG	58883	58937	
165 123	**NT**	A	*TT*	RG	58884	58938	
165 124	**NT**	A	*TT*	RG	58885	58939	
165 125	**NT**	A	*TT*	RG	58886	58940	
165 126	**NT**	A	*TT*	RG	58887	58941	
165 127	**NT**	A	*TT*	RG	58888	58942	
165 128	**NT**	A	*TT*	RG	58889	58943	

165 129	**NT**	A	*TT*	RG	58890	58944	
165 130	**NT**	A	*TT*	RG	58891	58945	
165 131	**NT**	A	*TT*	RG	58892	58946	
165 132	**NT**	A	*TT*	RG	58893	58947	
165 133	**NT**	A	*TT*	RG	58894	58948	
165 134	**NT**	A	*TT*	RG	58895	58949	
165 135	**NT**	A	*TT*	RG	58896	58950	
165 136	**NT**	A	*TT*	RG	58897	58951	
165 137	**NT**	A	*TT*	RG	58898	58952	
Spare	**NT**	A	*TT*	ZC (S)		55429	58930

CLASS 166   NETWORK EXPRESS TURBO   ABB

DMCL (A)–MS–DMCL (B). Built for Paddington–Oxford/Newbury services. Air
conditioned.

Construction: Welded aluminium.
Engines: One Perkins 2006-TWH of 260 kW (350 h.p.) at 1900 r.p.m. per car.
Bogies: BREL P3-17 (powered), BREL T3-17 (non-powered).
Couplers: BSI.
Seating Layout: 3+2 facing/unidirectional (standard class) with 20 standard
class seats in 2+2 format in DMCL(B), 2+2 facing (first class).
Dimensions: 23.50 x 2.85 m.

Gangways: Within unit only.	**Wheel Arrangement:** 2-B – B-2 – B-2.
Doors: Twin-leaf swing plug.	**Maximum Speed:** 90 m.p.h.

Multiple Working: Classes 165, 166, 168.

DMCL (A). Dia. DP321. Lot No. 31116 ABB York 1992–3. 16/75 1T. 40.62 t.
MS. Dia. DR209. Lot No. 31117 ABB York 1992–93. –/96. 38.04 t.
DMCL (B). Dia. DP321. Lot No. 31116 ABB York 1992–93. 16/72 1T. 40.64 t.

166 201	**TT**	A	*TT*	RG	58101	58601	58122
166 202	**TT**	A	*TT*	RG	58102	58602	58123
166 203	**TT**	A	*TT*	RG	58103	58603	58124
166 204	**TT**	A	*TT*	RG	58104	58604	58125
166 205	**NT**	A	*TT*	RG	58105	58605	58126
166 206	**TT**	A	*TT*	RG	58106	58606	58127
166 207	**NT**	A	*TT*	RG	58107	58607	58128
166 208	**NT**	A	*TT*	RG	58108	58608	58129
166 209	**NT**	A	*TT*	RG	58109	58609	58130
166 210	**NT**	A	*TT*	RG	58110	58610	58131
166 211	**NT**	A	*TT*	RG	58111	58611	58132
166 212	**NT**	A	*TT*	RG	58112	58612	58133
166 213	**NT**	A	*TT*	RG	58113	58613	58134
166 214	**NT**	A	*TT*	RG	58114	58614	58135
166 215	**TT**	A	*TT*	RG	58115	58615	58136
166 216	**NT**	A	*TT*	RG	58116	58616	58137
166 217	**NT**	A	*TT*	RG	58117	58617	58138
166 218	**NT**	A	*TT*	RG	58118	58618	58139
166 219	**NT**	A	*TT*	RG	58119	58619	58140
166 220	**NT**	A	*TT*	RG	58120	58620	58141
166 221	**TT**	A	*TT*	RG	58121	58621	58142

CLASS 168   CLUBMAN   ADTRANZ

DMSL (A)–MSL–MS–DMSL (B). Air conditioned.

Construction: Welded aluminium bodies with bolt-on steel ends.
Engines: One MTU 6R183TD13H of 315 kW (422 h.p.) at 1900 r.p.m. per car.
Transmission: Hydraulic. Voith T211rzze to ZF final drive.
Bogies: One Adtranz P3–23 and one BREL T3–23 per car.
Couplers: BSI.
Seating Layout: 2+2 facing/unidirectional.
Dimensions: 23.62 x 2.69 m (driving cars), 23.61 x 2.69 m (centre cars).
Gangways: Within unit only.
Wheel Arrangement: 2-B (– B-2 – B-2) – B-2.
Doors: Twin-leaf swing plug.   **Maximum Speed:** 100 m.p.h.
Multiple Working: Classes 165, 166, 168.

58151–58155. DMSL(A). Dia. DP270. Adtranz Derby 1997–98. –/60 1TD 1W.
    43.7 t.
58156–58163. DMSL(A). Dia. DP280. Adtranz Derby 2000. –/59 1TD 2W. 43.7 t.
58651–58655. MSL. Dia. DR211. Adtranz Derby 1998. –/73 1T. 41.0 t.
58656–58660. MS. Dia. DR211. Adtranz Derby 1998. –/77. 40.5 t.
58661–58663. MS. Dia. DR211. Adtranz Derby 2000. –/76. 42.4 t.
58251–58255. DMSL(B). Dia. DP270. Adtranz Derby 1998. –/66 1T. 43.6 t.
58256–58263. DMSL(B). Dia. DP281. Adtranz Derby 2000. –/69 1T. 43.6 t.

Notes:

Fitted with tripcocks for working over London Underground tracks between
Harrow-on-the-Hill and Amersham.
58656–60 were formerly numbered 58451–6.

168 001	**CR**	P	*CR*	AL	58151	58651	58251
168 002	**CR**	P	*CR*	AL	58152	58652	58252
168 003	**CR**	P	*CR*	AL	58153	58653	58253
168 004	**CR**	P	*CR*	AL	58154	58654	58254
168 005	**CR**	P	*CR*	AL	58155	58655	58255
168 106	**CR**	P	*CR*	AL	58156	58656	58256
168 107	**CR**	P	*CR*	AL	58157	58657	58257
168 108	**CR**	P	*CR*	AL	58158	58658	58258
168 109	**CR**	P	*CR*	AL	58159	58659	58259
168 110	**CR**	P	*CR*	AL	58160	58660	58260
168 111	**CR**	H	*CR*	AL	58161	58661	58261
168 112	**CR**	H	*CR*	AL	58162	58662	58262
168 113	**CR**	H	*CR*	AL	58163	58663	58263

CLASS 170   TURBOSTAR   ADTRANZ

Various formations. Air conditioned.

Construction: Welded aluminium bodies with bolt-on steel ends.
Engines: One MTU 6R183TD13H of 315 kW (422 h.p.) at 1900 r.p.m. per car.
Transmission: Hydraulic. Voith T211rzze to ZF final drive.

Bogies: One Adtranz P3–23 and one BREL T3–23 per car.
Couplers: BSI.
Seating Layout: facing/unidirectional (2+2 in standard class and in first class on Class 170/1, 2+1 in first class on Class 170/2 and 170/4).
Dimensions: 23.62 x 2.69 m (driving cars), 23.61 x 2.69 m (centre cars).
Gangways: Within unit only.   **Wheel Arrangement:** 2-B (– B-2) – B-2.
Doors: Twin-leaf swing plug.   **Maximum Speed:** 100 m.p.h.
Multiple Working: Classes 142, 143, 144, 150, 153, 155, 156, 158, 159, 170.

Class 170/1. Midland Mainline Units. DMCL–DMCL.

DMCL (A). Dia. DP324. Adtranz Derby 1998–1999. 12/45 1TD 2W. 45.19 t.
DMCL (B). Dia. DP325. Adtranz Derby 1998–1999. 12/52 1T. Catering point.
   45.22 t

170 101	**MM**	P	*MM*	DY	50101	79101
170 102	**MM**	P	*MM*	DY	50102	79102
170 103	**MM**	P	*MM*	DY	50103	79103
170 104	**MM**	P	*MM*	DY	50104	79104
170 105	**MM**	P	*MM*	DY	50105	79105
170 106	**MM**	P	*MM*	DY	50106	79106
170 107	**MM**	P	*MM*	DY	50107	79107
170 108	**MM**	P	*MM*	DY	50108	79108
170 109	**MM**	P	*MM*	DY	50109	79109
170 110	**MM**	P	*MM*	DY	50110	79110
170 111	**MM**	P	*MM*	DY	50111	79111
170 112	**MM**	P	*MM*	DY	50112	79112
170 113	**MM**	P	*MM*	DY	50113	79113
170 114	**MM**	P	*MM*	DY	50114	79114
170 115	**MM**	P	*MM*	DY	50115	79115
170 116	**MM**	P	*MM*	DY	50116	79116
170 117	**MM**	P	*MM*	DY	50117	79117

MCLRMB. Dia. DR3 . Adtranz Derby 2001.   / : 1T + carvery bar.   .   t.
These cars will be formed into ten Midland mainline sets in 2001.

55101	55103	55105	55107	55109
55102	55104	55106	55108	55110

Class 170/2. Anglia Railways Units. DMCL–MSLRB–DMSL.

DMCL. Dia. DP326. Adtranz Derby 1999. 30/3 1TD 2W. 44.30 t.
MSLRB. Dia. DR212. Adtranz Derby 1999. –/58 1T. Buffet and conductor's office 42.76 t.
DMSL. Dia. DP274. Adtranz Derby 1999. –/66 1T. 44.70 t.

170 201	**AN**	P	*AR*	NC	50201	56201	79201
170 202	**AN**	P	*AR*	NC	50202	56202	79202
170 203	**AN**	P	*AR*	NC	50203	56203	79203
170 204	**AN**	P	*AR*	NC	50204	56204	79204
170 205	**AN**	P	*AR*	NC	50205	56205	79205
170 206	**AN**	P	*AR*	NC	50206	56206	79206
170 207	**AN**	P	*AR*	NC	50207	56207	79207
170 208	**AN**	P	*AR*	NC	50208	56208	79208

Class 170/3. South West Trains Units. DMCL–DMCL.

DMCL(A). Dia. DP329. Adtranz Derby 2000. 9/43 1TD 2W. 45.80 t.
DMCL(B). Dia. DP330. Adtranz Derby 2000. 9/53 1T. 45.80 t.

170 301	**SW**	P	*SW*	SA	50301	79301
170 302	**SW**	P	*SW*	SA	50302	79302
170 303	**SW**	P	*SW*	SA	50303	79303
170 304	**SW**	P	*SW*	SA	50304	79304
170 305	**SW**	P	*SW*	SA	50305	79305
170 306	**SW**	P	*SW*	SA	50306	79306
170 307	**SW**	P	*SW*	SA	50307	79307
170 308	**SW**	P	*SW*	SA	50308	79308

Class 170/4. ScotRail Units. DMCL–MS–DMCL.

DMCL(A). Dia. DP329. Adtranz Derby 1999–2000. 9/43 1TD 2W. 45.80 t.
MS. Dia. DR213. Adtranz Derby 1999–2000. –/76. 43.00 t.
DMCL(B). Dia. DP330. Adtranz Derby 1999–2000. 9/53 1T. 45.80 t.

Non-Standard Livery: Cars 56414 and 56415 are in advertising livery for "The Herald" and "The Sunday Herald" respectively. The outer cars are in **SR** livery.

170 401	**SR**	P	*SR*	HA	50401	56401	79401
170 402	**SR**	P	*SR*	HA	50402	56402	79402
170 403	**SR**	P	*SR*	HA	50403	56403	79403
170 404	**SR**	P	*SR*	HA	50404	56404	79404
170 405	**SR**	P	*SR*	HA	50405	56405	79405
170 406	**SR**	P	*SR*	HA	50406	56406	79406
170 407	**SR**	P	*SR*	HA	50407	56407	79407
170 408	**SR**	P	*SR*	HA	50408	56408	79408
170 409	**SR**	P	*SR*	HA	50409	56409	79409
170 410	**SR**	P	*SR*	HA	50410	56410	79410
170 411	**SR**	P	*SR*	HA	50411	56411	79411
170 412	**SR**	P	*SR*	HA	50412	56412	79412
170 413	**SR**	P	*SR*	HA	50413	56413	79413
170 414	**0**	P	*SR*	HA	50414	56414	79414
170 415	**0**	P	*SR*	HA	50415	56415	79415
170 416	**SR**	H	*SR*	HA	50416	56416	79416
170 417	**SR**	H	*SR*	HA	50417	56417	79417
170 418	**SR**	H	*SR*	HA	50418	56418	79418
170 419	**SR**	H	*SR*	HA	50419	56419	79419
170 420	**SR**	H	*SR*	HA	50420	56420	79420
170 421	**SR**	H	*SR*	HA	50421	56421	79421
170 422	**SR**	H	*SR*	HA	50422	56422	79422
170 423	**SR**	H	*SR*	HA	50423	56423	79423
170 424	**SR**	H	*SR*	HA	50424	56424	79424

Class 170/4. ScotRail Units. DMSL–MS–DMSL.

DMSL(A). Dia. DP284. Adtranz Derby 2001. –/55 1TD 2W. 45.80 t.
MS. Dia. DR213. Adtranz Derby 2001. –/76. 43.00 t.
DMSL(B). Dia. DP285. Adtranz Derby 2001. –/67 1T. 45.80 t.

170 470	**SP**	P			50470	56470	79470
170 471	**SP**	P			50471	56471	79471

Class 170/5. Central Trains 2-car Units. DMSL–DMSL.

DMSL(A). Dia. DP275. Adtranz Derby 1999–2000. –/55 1TD 2W. 45.80 t.
DMSL(B). Dia. DP276. Adtranz Derby 1999–2000. –/73 1T. 46.80 t.

170 501	r	**CT**	P	*CT*	TS	50501 79501
170 502	r	**CT**	P	*CT*	TS	50502 79502
170 503	r	**CT**	P	*CT*	TS	50503 79503
170 504	r	**CT**	P	*CT*	TS	50504 79504
170 505	r	**CT**	P	*CT*	TS	50505 79505
170 506	r	**CT**	P	*CT*	TS	50506 79506
170 507	r	**CT**	P	*CT*	TS	50507 79507
170 508	r	**CT**	P	*CT*	TS	50508 79508
170 509	r	**CT**	P	*CT*	TS	50509 79509
170 510	r	**CT**	P	*CT*	TS	50510 79510
170 511	r	**CT**	P	*CT*	TS	50511 79511
170 512	r	**CT**	P	*CT*	TS	50512 79512
170 513	r	**CT**	P	*CT*	TS	50513 79513
170 514	r	**CT**	P	*CT*	TS	50514 79514
170 515	r	**CT**	P	*CT*	TS	50515 79515
170 516	r	**CT**	P	*CT*	TS	50516 79516
170 517	r	**CT**	P	*CT*	TS	50517 79517
170 518	r	**CT**	P	*CT*	TS	50518 79518
170 519	r	**CT**	P	*CT*	TS	50519 79519
170 520	r	**CT**	P	*CT*	TS	50520 79520
170 521	r	**CT**	P	*CT*	TS	50521 79521
170 522	r	**CT**	P	*CT*	TS	50522 79522
170 523	r	**CT**	P	*CT*	TS	50523 79523

Class 170/6. Central Trains 3-car Units. DMSL–MS–DMSL.

DMSL(A). Dia. DP275. Adtranz Derby 2000. –/55 1TD 2W. 45.80 t.
MS. Dia. DR214. Adtranz Derby 2000. –/74. 43.00 t.
DMSL(B). Dia. DP276. Adtranz Derby 2000. –/73 1T. 46.80 t.

170 630	r	**CT**	P	*CT*	TS	50630	56630 79630
170 631	r	**CT**	P	*CT*	TS	50631	56631 79631
170 632	r	**CT**	P	*CT*	TS	50632	56632 79632
170 633	r	**CT**	P	*CT*	TS	50633	56633 79633
170 634	r	**CT**	P	*CT*	TS	50634	56634 79634
170 635	r	**CT**	P	*CT*	TS	50635	56635 79635
170 636	r	**CT**	P	*CT*	TS	50636	56636 79636
170 637	r	**CT**	P	*CT*	TS	50637	56637 79637
170 638	r	**CT**	P	*CT*	TS	50638	56638 79638
170 639	r	**CT**	P	*CT*	TS	50639	56639 79639

CLASS 175   CORADIA 1000   ALSTOM

Construction: Steel.
Engines: One Cummins N14 of 335 kW (450 h.p.).
Transmission: Hydraulic. Voith T211rzze to ZF final drive.
Bogies:
Couplers: Scharfenberg.
Seating Layout: 2+2 facing/unidirectional.
Dimensions: 23.71 x 2.73 m (driving cars), 23.03 x 2.73 m (centre cars).
Gangways: Within unit only.   **Wheel Arrangement:** 2-B (– B-2) – B-2.
Doors: Single-leaf swing plug.   **Maximum Speed:** 100 m.p.h.
Multiple Working: Classes 175, 180.

Class 175/0. DMSL–DMSL. 2-car units.

DMSL(A). Dia. DP278. Alstom Birmingham 1999–2000. –/54 1TD 2W. 51.00 t.
DMSL(B). Dia. DP279. Alstom Birmingham 1999–2000. –/64 1T. 51.00 t.

175 001	**FN**	A	NW	CH	50701	79701	
175 002	**FN**	A	NW	CH	50702	79702	
175 003	**FN**	A	NW	CH	50703	79703	
175 004	**FN**	A	NW	CH	50704	79704	
175 005	**FN**	A	NW	CH	50705	79705	
175 006	**FN**	A	NW	CH	50706	79706	
175 007	**FN**	A	NW	CH	50707	79707	
175 008	**FN**	A	NW	CH	50708	79708	Valhalla
175 009	**FN**	A	NW	CH	50709	79709	
175 010	**FN**	A	NW	CH	50710	79710	
175 011	**FN**	A	NW	CH	50711	79711	

Class 175/1. DMSL(A)–MSL–DMSL(B). 3-car units.

DMSL(A). Dia. DP278. Alstom Birmingham 1999–2001. –/54 1TD 2W. 51.00 t.
MSL. Dia. DR216. Alstom Birmingham 1999–2001. –/68 1T. 43 t 68 1T. 47.50 t.
DMSL(B). Dia. DP279. Alstom Birmingham 1999–2001. –/64 1T. 51.00 t.

175 101	**FN**	A	NW	CH	50751	56751	79751
175 102	**FN**	A	NW	CH	50752	56752	79752
175 103	**FN**	A	NW	CH	50753	56753	79753
175 104	**FN**	A	NW	CH	50754	56754	79754
175 105	**FN**	A	NW	CH	50755	56755	79755
175 106	**FN**	A	NW	CH	50756	56756	79756
175 107	**FN**	A	NW	CH	50757	56757	79757
175 108	**FN**	A			50758	56758	79758
175 109	**FN**	A			50759	56759	79759
175 110	**FN**	A	NW	CH	50760	56760	79760
175 111	**FN**	A	NW	CH	50761	56761	79761
175 112	**FN**	A			50762	56762	79762
175 113	**FN**	A			50763	56763	79763
175 114	**FN**	A			50764	56764	79764
175 115	**FN**	A			50765	56765	79765
175 116	**FN**	A			50766	56766	79766

CLASS 180   CORADIA 1000   ALSTOM

New units under construction for First Great Western.

Construction: Steel.
Engines: One Cummins QSK19 of 560 kW (750 h.p.) at 2100 r.p.m.
Transmission: Hydraulic. Voith T312br to Voith final drive.
Bogies: Alstom MB2.
Couplers: Scharfenberg.
Seating Layout: facing/unidirectional (2+2 in standard class and 2+1 in first class.
Dimensions: 23.71 x 2.73 m (driving cars), 23.03 x 2.73 m (centre cars).
Gangways: Within unit only.
Wheel Arrangement: 2-B – B-2 – B-2 – B-2 – B-2.
Doors: Single-leaf swing plug.   **Maximum Speed:** 125 m.p.h.
Multiple Working: Classes 175, 180.

DMSL(A). Dia. DP282. Alstom Birmingham 2000–01. –/46 2W 1TD. 53.00 t.
MFL. Dia. DR101. Alstom Birmingham 2000–01. 42/– 1T 1W + catering point. 51.50 t.
MSL. Dia. DR217. Alstom Birmingham 2000–01. –/68 1T. 51.50 t.
MSLRB. Dia. DR218 Alstom Birmingham 2000–01. –/56 1T. 51.50 t.
DMSL(B). Dia. DP283. Alstom Birmingham 2000–01. –/56 1T. 53.00 t.

180 101	**FW**	W	*TC*	OM	50901	54901	55901	56901 59901
180 102		W			50902	54902	55902	56902 59902
180 103		W			50903	54903	55903	56903 59903
180 104		W			50904	54904	55904	56904 59904
180 105		W			50905	54905	55905	56905 59905
180 106		W			50906	54906	55906	56906 59906
180 107		W			50907	54907	55907	56907 59907
180 108		W			50908	54908	55908	56908 59908
180 109		W			50909	54909	55909	56909 59909
180 110		W			50910	54910	55910	56910 59910
180 111		W			50911	54911	55911	56911 59911
180 112		W			50912	54912	55912	56912 59912
180 113		W			50913	54913	55913	56913 59913
180 114		W			50914	54914	55914	56914 59914

3.2. DIESEL ELECTRIC UNITS

The following features are standard to ex-BR Southern Region diesel-electric multiple unit power cars (Classes 201–207):

Construction: Steel.
Engine: One English Electric 4SRKT Mk. 2 of 450 kW (600 h.p.) at 850 r.p.m.
Main Generator: English Electric EE824.
Traction Motors: Two English Electric EE507 mounted on the inner bogie.
Bogies: SR Mk. 4. (Former EMU TSL vehicles have Commonwealth bogies).
Couplers: Drophead buckeye.
Doors: Manually operated slam.
Brakes: Electro-pneumatic and automatic air.
Maximum Speed: 75 m.p.h.
Multiple Working: Other ex BR Southern Region DEMU vehicles.

CLASS 201/202   'HASTINGS'   BR

DMBS–2TSL–TSRB–TSL–DMBS.

Unit made up from 2 Class 201 short-frame cars and 2 Class 202 long-frame cars. The 'Hastings' units were made with narrow body-profiles for use on the section between Tonbridge and Battle which had tunnels of restricted loading gauge. These tunnels were converted to single track operation in the 1980s thus allowing standard loading gauge stock to be used. The set also contains a Class 411 EMU trailer (not Hastings line gauge).

Gangways: Within unit only.
Seating Layout: 2+2 facing.
Dimensions: 18.36 x 2.50 m (60000/60501), 20.34 x 2.50 m. (60118/60529) 20.34 x 2.82 m (69337/70262).

60000. DMBS. Dia DB203. Lot No. 30329 Eastleigh 1957. –/22. 54 t.
60501. TSL. Dia DB204. Lot No. 30331 Eastleigh 1957. –/52 2T. 29 t.
70262. TSL (ex Class 411/5 EMU). Dia. DH208. Lot No. 30455 Eastleigh 1958–99. –/64 2T. 33.78 t.
69337. TSRB (ex Class 422 EMU). Dia. DH209. Lot No. 30805 York 1970. –/40. 35 t.
60529. TSL. Dia DH203. Lot No. 30397 Eastleigh 1957. –/60 2T. 30 t.
60118. DMBS. Dia DB203. Lot No. 30395 Eastleigh 1957. –/30. 55 t.

201 001   **G** HD *ON* SE   60000 60501 70262 69337 60529 60118

Names:

| 60000 | Hastings | | 60118 | Tunbridge Wells |

CLASS 205/0 (3H)   'HAMPSHIRE'   BR

DMBS–TSL–DTCsoL or DMBS–DTCsoL.

Gangways: Non-gangwayed.
Seating Layout: 3+2 facing or compartments.
Dimensions: 20.33 x 2.82 m (DMBS), 20.28 x 2.82 m (TS), 20.36 x 2.82 m (DTCsoL).

60111/117/154. DMBS. Dia DB203. Lot No. 30332 Eastleigh 1957. –/52. 56 t.
60122–124. DMBS. Dia DB203. Lot No. 30540 Eastleigh 1958–59. –/52. 56 t.
60146–151. DMBS. Dia DB204. Lot No. 30671 Eastleigh 1960–62. –/42. 56 t.
60650–670. TS. Dia DH203. Lot No. 30542 Eastleigh 1958–59. –/104. 30 t.
60673–678. TS. Dia DH203. Lot No. 30672 Eastleigh 1960–62. –/104. 30 t.
60800. DTCsoL. Dia DE301. Lot No. 30333 Eastleigh 1956–57. 13/50 2T. 32 t.
60811. DTCsoL. Dia DE302. Lot No. 30333 Eastleigh 1956–57. 19/50 2T. 32 t.
60820. DTCsoL. Dia DE301. Lot No. 30399 Eastleigh 1957–58. 13/50 2T. 32 t.
60823/824. DTCsoL. Dia DE301. Lot No. 30541 Eastleigh 1958–59. 13/50 2T. 32 t.
60827–832. DTCsoL. Dia DE303. Lot No. 30673 Eastleigh 1960–62. 13/62 2T. (13/60 2T 60827, 13/57 2T 60831) 32 t.

205 001	CX	P	SC	SU	60154		60800
205 009	CX	P	SC	SU	60108	60658	60808
205 012	CX	P	SC	SU	60111		60811
205 018	CX	P	SC	SU	60117	60674	60828
205 024	N	P	SC	SU (S)	60123		60823
205 025	CX	P	SC	SU	60124		60824
205 028	CX	P	SC	SU	60146	60673	60827
205 032	CX	P	SC	SU	60150		60831
205 033	CX	P	SC	SU	60151	60678	60832
Spare	CX	P	SC	ZG (S)	60650		
Spare	G	HD	ON	SE	60122	60668	
Spare	N	P	SC	SU (S)	60670		
Spare	N	P	SC	SU (S)	60677		

CLASS 205/2 (3H)   'HAMPSHIRE'   B

DMBS–TSL (ex Class 411/5 EMU)–DTSL. Refurbished 1980. Fluorescent lighting. PA.

Details as for Class 205/0 except:

Gangways: Within unit only.
Seating Layout: 3+2 facing.

DMBS. Dia. DB203. Lot No. 30332 Eastleigh 1957. –/39. 57 t.
TSL. Dia. DH207. Converted from loco-hauled TS 4059 Lot No. 30149 Swindon 1955–57. –/64 2T. 33.78 t.
DTSL. Dia. DE204. Lot No. 30333 Eastleigh 1957. –/76 2T. 32 t.
Note: This unit normally operates as a 2-car set in winter.

205 205	CX	P	SC	SU	60110	71634	60810

CLASS 207/0 (2D)   'OXTED'   BR

DMBS–DTS (formerly DMBS–TCsoL–DTS).

This class was built for the Oxted line and therefore referred to as 'Oxted' units. They were made with a narrower body-profile which also allowed them to be used through the restricted loading-gauge Somerhill Tunnel between Tonbridge and Grove Junction (Tunbridge Wells). This tunnel was converted to single track operation in the 1980s thus allowing standard loading gauge stock to be used.

Gangways: Non-gangwayed.
Seating Layout: 3+2 facing or compartments.
Dimensions: 20.33 x 2.74 m. (DMBS/TCsoL), 20.32 x 2.74 m. (DTS).

DMBS. Dia DB205. Lot No. 30625 Eastleigh 1962. –/42. 56 t.
60616. TCsoL. Dia DH301. Lot No. 30626 Eastleigh 1962. 24/42 1T. 31 t.
60916. DTS. Dia DE201. Lot No. 30627 Eastleigh 1962. –/76. 32 t.

207 017	**CX** P	*SC*	SU	60142		60916
Spare	**G** HD	*ON*	SE	60138	60616	

CLASS 207/1 (3D)   'OXTED'   BR

DMBS–TSL–DTS.
Gangwayed sets with a Class 411 EMU trailer in the centre.

Gangways: Within unit only.
Seating Layout: 2+2 facing.
Dimensions: 20.34 x 2.74 m. (DMBS), 20.32 x 2.74 m. (DTS).

DMBS. Dia DB205. Lot No. 30625 Eastleigh 1962. –/40. 56 t.
70286. TSL. Dia. DH206. Lot No. 30455 Eastleigh /64 2T. 33.78 t.
70547/9. TSL. Dia. DH206. Lot No. 30620 Eastleigh 1960–61 –/64 2T. 33.78 t.
DTS. Dia DE201. Lot No. 30627 Eastleigh 1962. –/75. 32 t.

Note: These units normally operate as 2-car sets in winter.

207 201	**CX** P	*SC*	SU	60129	70286	60901	Ashford Fayre
207 202	**CX** P	*SC*	SU	60130	70549	60904	Brighton Royal Pavilion
207 203	**CX** P	*SC*	SU	60127	70547	60903	

CLASS 220   VOYAGER   BOMBARDIER

DMS–MSRB–MS–DMF. New units under construction for Virgin Cross-Country.

Construction: Steel.
Engine: Cummins of 750 h.p. (560 kW) at 1800 r.p.m.
Transmission: Two Alstom ONIX 800 three-phase traction motors of 275 kW.
Braking: Rheostatic and electro-pneumatic.
Bogies: Bombardier B5005.
Couplers: Dellner.
Seating Layout: 2+2 mainly unidirectional (standard class, 2+1 facing/unidirectional (first class).
Dimensions: 23.85 x 2.73 m. (outer cars), 22.82 x 2.73 m. (inner cars).
Gangways: Within unit only.
Wheel Arrangement: 1A-A1 – 1A-A1 – 1A-A1 – 1A-A1.
Doors: Single-leaf swing plug.
Maximum Speed: 125 m.p.h.
Multiple Working: Classes 220, 221.

DMS. Dia DC201. Bombardier BN/Prorail 2000–01. –/42 1TD 1W.   .   t.
MSRB. Dia. DD201. Bombardier BN/Prorail 2000–01. –/58.   .   t.
MS. Dia. DD202. Bombardier BN/Prorail 2000–01. –/62 1TD 1W.   .   t.
DMF. Dia DC101. Bombardier BN/Prorail 2000–01. 26/– 1TD 1W.   .   t.

220 001	**VT**	HX	60301	60201	60701	60401
220 002	**VT**	HX	60302	60202	60702	60402
220 003	**VT**	HX	60303	60203	60703	60403
220 004	**VT**	HX	60304	60204	60704	60404
220 005	**VT**	HX	60305	60205	60705	60405
220 006		HX	60306	60206	60706	60406
220 007		HX	60307	60207	60707	60407
220 008		HX	60308	60208	60708	60408
220 009		HX	60309	60209	60709	60409
220 010		HX	60310	60210	60710	60410
220 011		HX	60311	60211	60711	60411
220 012		HX	60312	60212	60712	60412
220 013		HX	60313	60213	60713	60413
220 014		HX	60314	60214	60714	60414
220 015		HX	60315	60215	60715	60415
220 016		HX	60316	60216	60716	60416
220 017		HX	60317	60217	60717	60417
220 018		HX	60318	60218	60718	60418
220 019		HX	60319	60219	60719	60419
220 020		HX	60320	60220	60720	60420
220 021		HX	60321	60221	60721	60421
220 022		HX	60322	60222	60722	60422
220 023		HX	60323	60223	60723	60423
220 024		HX	60324	60224	60724	60424
220 025		HX	60325	60225	60725	60425
220 026		HX	60326	60226	60726	60426
220 027		HX	60327	60227	60727	60427

220 028	HX	60328	60228	60728	60428
220 029	HX	60329	60229	60729	60429
220 030	HX	60330	60230	60730	60430
220 031	HX	60331	60231	60731	60431
220 032	HX	60332	60232	60732	60432
220 033	HX	60333	60233	60733	60433
220 034	HX	60334	60234	60734	60434

Name:

60203 Maiden Voyager

CLASS 221   VOYAGER   BOMBARDIER

DMS–MSRB–MS(–MS)–DMF. New tilting units under construction for Virgin Cross-Country (5-car units) and Virgin West Coast (4-car units).

Construction: Steel.
Engine: Cummins of 750 h.p. (560 kW) at 1800 r.p.m.
Transmission: Two Alstom ONIX 800 three-phase traction motors of 275 kW.
Braking: Rheostatic and electro-pneumatic.
Bogies: Bombardier HVP.
Couplers: Dellner.
Seating Layout: 2+2 mainly unidirectional (standard class, 2+1 facing/unidirectional (first class).
Dimensions: 23.85 x 2.73 m. (outer cars), 22.82 x 2.73 m. (inner cars).
Gangways: Within unit only.
Wheel Arrangement: 1A-A1 – 1A-A1 – 1A-A1 (– 1A-A1) – 1A-A1.
Doors: Single-leaf swing plug.
Maximum Speed: 125 m.p.h.
Multiple Working: Classes 220, 221.

DMS. Dia DF201. Bombardier Prorail 2000–01. –/42 1TD 1W.   .   t.
MSRB. Dia. DG201. Bombardier Prorail 2000–01. –/58.   .   t.
MS. Dia. DDG02. Bombardier Prorail 2000–01. –/62 1TD 1W.   .   t.
DMF. Dia DF101. Bombardier Prorail 2000–01. 26/– 1TD 1W.   .   t.

221 001	HX	60351	60851	60951	60751	60451
221 002	HX	60352	60852	60952	60752	60452
221 003	HX	60353	60853	60953	60753	60453
221 004	HX	60354	60854	60954	60754	60454
221 005	HX	60355	60855	60955	60755	60455
221 006	HX	60356	60856	60956	60756	60456
221 007	HX	60357	60857	60957	60757	60457
221 008	HX	60358	60858	60958	60758	60458
221 009	HX	60359	60859	60959	60759	60459
221 010	HX	60360	60860	60960	60760	60460
221 011	HX	60361	60861	60961	60761	60461
221 012	HX	60362	60862	60962	60762	60462
221 013	HX	60363	60863	60963	60763	60463
221 014	HX	60364	60864	60964	60764	60464
221 015	HX	60365	60865	60965	60765	60465
221 016	HX	60366	60866	60966	60766	60466

221 017	HX	60367	60867	60967	60767	60467
221 018	HX	60368	60868	60968	60768	60468
221 019	HX	60369	60869	60969	60769	60469
221 020	HX	60370	60870	60970	60770	60470
221 021	HX	60371	60871	60971	60771	60471
221 022	HX	60372	60872	60972	60772	60472
221 023	HX	60373	60873	60973	60773	60473
221 024	HX	60374	60874	60974	60774	60474
221 025	HX	60375	60875	60975	60775	60475
221 026	HX	60376	60876	60976	60776	60476
221 027	HX	60377	60877	60977	60777	60477
221 028	HX	60378	60878	60978	60778	60478
221 029	HX	60379	60879	60979	60779	60479
221 030	HX	60380	60880	60980	60780	60480
221 031	HX	60381	60881	60981	60781	60481
221 032	HX	60382	60882	60982	60782	60482
221 033	HX	60383	60883	60983	60783	60483
221 034	HX	60384	60884	60984	60784	60484
221 035	HX	60385	60885	60985	60785	60485
221 036	HX	60386	60886	60986	60786	60486
221 037	HX	60387	60887	60987	60787	60487
221 038	HX	60388	60888	60988	60788	60488
221 039	HX	60389	60889	60989	60789	60489
221 040	HX	60390	60890	60990	60790	60490
221 041	HX	60391		60991	60791	60491
221 042	HX	60392		60992	60792	60492
221 043	HX	60393		60993	60793	60493
221 044	HX	60394		60994	60794	60494

3.3. SERVICE DMUS

This section lists vehicles not used for passenger-carrying purposes. Some vehicles are numbered in the special service stock number series or in the internal user series (An internal user vehicle is a vehicle specifically for use in one location/area which is not otherwise permitted over the Railtrack network without special authority).

CLASS 101   INTERNAL USER OFFICE VEHICLE

DT. Converted 1990 from Class 101 DTC. Gangwayed.

Construction: Steel underframe and aluminium alloy body.
Maximum Speed: 70 m.p.h.
Bogies: DT11.   **Couplings:** Screw.
Brakes: Twin pipe vacuum.   **Multiple Working:** Blue Square.
Doors: Manually operated slam.   **Dimensions:** 18.49 x 2.82 x 3.85 m.

Note: Allocated Internal User number 042222, but this is not carried.

54342. DT. Dia. DZ5??. Lot No. 30468 Metro-Cammell. 1958. 22.5 t.

Spare   **BG**   NS   NL(S)   54342

CLASS 114/1   ROUTE LEARNING UNIT

MB–DT. Converted 1992 from Class 114/1. Gangwayed within unit.

Construction: Steel.
Engines: Two Leyland TL11/40 of 153 kW (205 h.p.) at 1950 r.p.m. per car.
Transmission: Mechanical. Cardan shaft and freewheel to a four-speed epicyclic gearbox with a further cardan shaft to the final drive, each engine driving the inner axle of one bogie.
Maximum Speed: 70 m.p.h.   **Couplings:** Screw.
Bogies: DD9 + DT9.   **Multiple Working:** Blue Square.
Brakes: Twin pipe vacuum.   **Dimensions:** 20.45 x 2.82 x 3.87 m.
Doors: Manually operated slam/roller shutter.

Non-Standard Livery: Grey, red and green.

977775. DMB. Dia. DZ518. Lot No. 30209 Derby 1957. 39.0 t.
977776. DT. Dia. DZ516. Lot No. 30210 Derby 1957. 29.2 t.

-      **0**   E   TE(S)   977775 977776

CLASS 122   ROUTE LEARNING UNIT

DM. Converted 1995 from DMBS. Non gangwayed single car with cab at each end.

Construction: Steel.
Engines: Two Leyland 1595 of 112 kW (150 h.p.) at 1800 r.p.m.
Transmission: Mechanical. Cardan shaft and freewheel to a four-speed

epicyclic gearbox with a further cardan shaft to the final drive, each engine driving the inner axle of one bogie.

Maximum Speed: 75 m.p.h.
Bogies: DD10.
Brakes: Twin pipe vacuum.
Doors: Manually operated slam.
Couplings: Screw.
Multiple Working: Blue Square.
Dimensions: 20.45 x 2.82 x 3.87 m.

Note: Allocated number 977941, but this number is not carried.

55012. DM. Dia. DZ5??. Lot No. 30419 Gloucester 1958. Converted by ABB Doncaster 1995. 36.5 t.

| - | | **LH** | E | *E* | | TE | 55012 |

CLASS 930   SANDITE/DE-ICING UNIT

DMB–T–DMB. Converted 1993 from Class 205. Gangwayed within unit. Sandite trailer 977870 is replaced by de-icing trailer 977364 as required.

Construction: Steel.
Engine: One English Electric 4SRKT Mk. 2 of 450 kW (600 h.p.) at 850 r.p.m. per power car.
Transmission: Electric. Two English Electric EE507 traction motors mounted on the bogie at the non-driving end of each power car.
Maximum Speed: 75 m.p.h.   **Bogies:** SR Mk. 4.
Brakes: Electro-pneumatic and automatic air.
Doors: Manually operated slam.   **Couplings:** Drophead buckeye.
Multiple Working: Classes 201–207.
Dimensions: 20.33 x 2.82 x 3.87 m. (DMB); 20.28 x 2.82 x 3.87 m.

977939–977940. DMB. Dia. DZ537. Lot No. 30671 Eastleigh 1962. 56.0 t.
977870. T. Dia. DZ533. Lot No. 30542 Eastleigh 1960. 30.5 t.

| 930 301 | | **RO** | RK | *RK* | | SU | 977939 977870 977940 |

CLASS 960   ULTRASONIC TESTING/TRACTOR UNIT

DM–DM. Converted 1986 from Class 101. Gangwayed within unit. Often operates with either 975091 or 999602 as a centre car.

Construction: Steel underframe and aluminium alloy body.
Engines: Two Leyland 680/1 of 112 kW (150 h.p.) at 1800 r.p.m. per car.
Transmission: Mechanical. Cardan shaft and freewheel to a four-speed epicyclic gearbox with a further cardan shaft to the final drive, each engine driving the inner axle of one bogie.
Maximum Speed: 70 m.p.h.
Bogies: DD15.
Brakes: Air.
Doors: Manually operated slam.
Couplings: Screw.
Multiple Working: Blue Square.
Dimensions: 18.49 x 2.82 x 3.85 m.

977391. DM. Dia. DZ503. Lot No. 30500 Metro-Cammell. 1959. 32.5 t.
977392. DM. Dia. DZ503. Lot No. 30254 Metro-Cammell. 1956. 32.5 t.

| - | | **SO** | RK | *SO* | | RG | 977391 977392 |

▲ Regional Railways liveried Class 101 No. 101 653 passes the site of the former Heeley Carriage Sidings whilst working the 16.15 Sheffield–Manchester Piccadilly service on 27th May 2000. **Wolfram Stein**

▼ Merseytravel liveried Class 142 No. 142 052 is far from home as it passes through Carlisle with a southbound empty stock working. The date is 25th June 2000. **K. Conkey**

▲ Carrying the new Cardiff Valley Lines livery, Class 143 No. 143 606 is pictured at Cardiff Central on 9th November 2000 whilst working the 11.02 Coryton–Maesteg. **Bob Sweet**

▼ 3-car Class 144 No. 144 014, in West Yorkshire PTE livery, passes Gascoigne Wood with a Leeds–Hull train on 30th March 2000. **Ian A. Lyall**

▲ Class 117 and 121 DMUs have now been withdrawn from Bedford–Bletchley services in favour of Class 150/1s. Class 150/1 No. 150 131, in Silverlink livery, is seen here at Bletchley on 5th August 2000 shortly before working the 19.22 service to Bedford. **Martyn Hilbert**

▼ The North Western Trains livery, albeit with First North Western branding, is now being applied to Class 150/2s on refurbishment. 150 207 is pictured leaving Leyland with the 17.05 Blackpool North–Manchester Piccadilly on 19th August 2000. • **Martyn Hilbert**

▲ A pair of Class 153s, Nos. 153 332 and 153 330, enter Lancaster on 30th September 2000 whilst forming the 15.00 Barrow-in-Furness–Manchester Airport.
Dave McAlone

▼ West Yorkshire PTE liveried Class 155 No. 155 344 approaches Manston Crossing with the 09.23 Manchester Victoria–Selby on 5th October 1999.
John G. Teasdale

Northern Spirit liveried Class 156 No. 156 448 is pictured south of Armathwaite on 27th July 2000 with the 16.48 Carlisle–Leeds.
K. Conkey

▲ Class 156 No. 156 449, in Scotrail livery, passes Enterkinfoot, north of Dumfries, on 26th July 2000 with the 13.07 Carlisle–Glasgow Central. **K. Conkey**

▼ Northern Spirit units which are used on Transpennine Express services have a distinctive colour scheme applied. One of the units which carries the livery, 3-car Class 158 No. 158 799, is seen passing through Horbury Cutting on 16th October 2000. **G.W. Morrison**

Wales & West 'Alphaline' liveried Class 158 No. 158 746 is about to enter Parsons Tunnel, near Teignmouth, whilst forming the 11.45 Penzance–Cardiff Central service on 29th April 2000.

John Chalcraft

A pair of Class 159 units Nos. 159 007, in South West Trains livery, and 159 017, in the old Network SouthEast livery, are pictured forming the 12.35 London Waterloo–Exeter St Davids service as they pull away from Clapham Junction. The date is 20th April 2000.

K. Conkey

▲ Class 165 'Turbo' No. 165 127 approaches Bath Spa with the 13.40 Oxford–Bristol Temple Meads service on 5th May 1999. The Network SouthEast livery, still carried by this unit, is now obsolescent. **John Chalcraft**

▼ The recently introduced Thames Trains livery is seen here on Class 166 No. 166 201 as it pauses at Reading whilst forming the 15.15 Oxford–London Paddington service on 29th September 2000. **D. Ford**

▲ Chiltern Railways liveried Class 168/1 No. 168 109 passes West Ruislip with the 11.30 Birmingham Snow Hill–London Marylebone 'Clubman' service. The outer cars of these units are, in reality, Class 170s with Class 168 interiors.

David Brown

▼ Class 170 No. 170 102 passes through Cricklewood with the 11.56 Nottingham–London St Pancras on 7th April 2000. This unit carries Midland Mainline livery. **K. Conkey**

▲ Anglia Railways liveried Class 170 No. 170 208 forms the 12.32 Basingstoke–Chelmsford at Winchfield on 19th July 2000. This is one of a number Basingstoke to East Anglia services recently introduced by Anglia Railways.　　**David Brown**

▼ Central Trains liveried Class 170 No. 170 636 nears the end of its journey as it passes Alexandra Dock Junction, west of Newport, with the 10.28 Nottingham–Cardiff Central on 30th June 2000.　　**Rodney Lissenden**

▲ After much delay, units of Class 175 are now entering service with First North Western. Carrying First Group livery, No. 175 006 is seen here near Stableford, Staffordshire whilst working a Birmingham to Holyhead service. The date is 19th July 2000. **Hugh Ballantyne**

▼ Connex South Central liveried Class 205 No. 205 009 stables between duties at Selhurst T&RSMD on 16th November 1999. **Brian Denton**

▲ Testing of the first Class 220 Virgin 'Voyager' DEMU has recently commenced in Belgium, where the class are under construction. The first unit is pictured here between trials on the Belgian network.　　　　**Daniel Moens**

▼ Loadhaul liveried Class 122 'bubble' car, No. 55012, is used on route learning duties. In this capacity, it was pictured at Brocklesby on 7th July 1999.

Ian A. Lyall

Croydon Tramlink. Carrying 'Necafé' advertising livery, car No. 2533 passes through East Croydon whilst working a Route 2 service from Croydon–Beckenham Junction. **Peter Fox**

Manchester Metrolink. One of the recently built Ansaldo cars, No. 2002 is pictured on Eccles New Road on 22nd July 2000, the first day of normal service on the Eccles extension.
Peter Fox

▲ **Strathclyde PTE Underground.** Cars Nos. 105, 206 and 128 are pictured in a 3-car formation outside the depot at Broomloan on 15th May 1999.   **Ross Aitken**

▼ **Tyne and Wear Metro.** Two units pass at West Jesmond on 8th April 2000. On the left, unit No. 4012 carries red and yellow livery and is working a Newcastle Airport bound service, whilst the unit on the right, No. 4002, is in advertising livery and working a service destined for South Shields.   **Rodney Lissenden**

CLASS 960   TEST UNIT

DM–DM. Converted 1991 from Class 101. Gangwayed within unit.

Construction: Steel underframe and aluminium alloy body.
Engines: Two Leyland 680/1 of 112 kW (150 h.p.) at 1800 r.p.m. per car.
Transmission: Mechanical. Cardan shaft and freewheel to a four-speed epicyclic gearbox with a further cardan shaft to the final drive, each engine driving the inner axle of one bogie.
Maximum Speed: 70 m.p.h.

Bogies: DD15.	**Couplings:** Screw.
Brakes: Twin pipe vacuum.	**Multiple Working:** Blue Square.
Doors: Manually operated slam.	**Dimensions:** 18.49 x 2.82 x 3.85 m.

977693. DM. Dia. DZ503. Lot No. 30261 Metro-Cammell. 1957. 32.5 t.
977694. DM. Dia. DZ503. Lot No. 30276 Metro-Cammell. 1958. 32.5 t.

-		**S0**	RK	*SO*	BY	977693	977694		Iris 2

CLASS 960   SANDITE UNIT

DMB. Converted 1991/93 from Class 121. Non gangwayed.

Construction: Steel.
Engines: Two Leyland 1595 of 112 kW (150 h.p.) at 1800 r.p.m.
Transmission: Mechanical. Cardan shaft and freewheel to a four-speed epicyclic gearbox with a further cardan shaft to the final drive, each engine driving the inner axle of one bogie.
Maximum Speed: 70 m.p.h.

Bogies: DD10.	**Couplings:** Screw.
Brakes: Twin pipe vacuum.	**Multiple Working:** Blue Square.
Doors: Manually operated slam.	**Dimensions:** 20.45 x 2.82 x 3.87 m.

977722-977723. DMB. Dia. DZ515. Lot No. 30518 Pressed Steel 1960. 38.0 t.
977858–60/66/73. DMB. Dia. DZ526. Lot No. 30518 Pressed Steel 1960. 38.0 t.

960 002	**N**	RK		AL(S)	977722
55024	**M**	RK	*RK*	AL	977858
960 011	**RK**	RK		AF	977859
960 012	**N**	RK	*RK*	AF	977860
960 013	**R0**	RK		RG(S)	977866
960 014	**N**	RK		RG(S)	977873
960 021	**R0**	RK	*RK*	AL	977723

CLASS 960   SANDITE UNIT

DMB. Converted 1991 from Class 122 vehicle. Non gangwayed.

Construction: Steel.
Engines: Two Leyland 1595 of 112 kW (150 h.p.) at 1800 r.p.m.
Transmission: Mechanical. Cardan shaft and freewheel to a four-speed epicyclic gearbox with a further cardan shaft to the final drive, each engine driving the inner axle of one bogie.

Maximum Speed: 70 m.p.h.
Bogies: DD10.
Brakes: Twin pipe vacuum.
Doors: Manually operated slam.
Couplings: Screw.
Multiple Working: Blue Square.
Dimensions: 20.45 x 2.82 x 3.87 m.

975042. DMB. Dia. DX516. Lot No. 30419 Gloucester 1958. 36.5 t.

960 015	**RO**	RK *RK*	AL	975042

CLASS 960/9   SANDITE/ROUTE LEARNING UNIT

DM. Converted 1993 from Class 101 vehicles. Gangwayed within unit.

Construction: Steel underframe and aluminium alloy body.
Engines: Two Leyland 680/1 of 112 kW (150 h.p.) at 1800 r.p.m. per car.
Transmission: Mechanical. Cardan shaft and freewheel to a four-speed epicyclic gearbox with a further cardan shaft to the final drive, each engine driving the inner axle of one bogie.   **Maximum Speed:** 70 m.p.h.
Bogies: DD15.
Brakes: Twin pipe vacuum.
Doors: Manually operated slam.
Couplings: Screw.
Multiple Working: Blue Square.
Dimensions: 18.49 x 2.82 x 3.85 m.

977895. DM. Dia. DZ503. Lot No. 30275 Metro-Cammell. 1958. 32.5 t.
977896/900. DM. Dia. DZ504. Lot No. 30276 Metro-Cammell. 1958. 32.5 t.
977897/901/903. DM. Dia. DZ503. Lot No. 30259 Metro-Cammell. 1957. 32.5 t.
977898. DM. Dia. DZ515. Lot No. 30256 Metro-Cammell. 1957. 32.5 t.
977899. DM. Dia. DZ503. Lot No. 30500 Metro-Cammell. 1959. 32.5 t.
977902. DM. Dia. DZ503. Lot No. 30261 Metro-Cammell. 1957. 32.5 t.
977904. DM. Dia. DZ503. Lot No. 30270 Metro-Cammell. 1957. 32.5 t.

960 991	**N**	RK	LO(S)	977895	977896
960 992	**BG**	RK	LO(S)	977897	977898
960 993	**BG**	RK	LO(S)	977899	977900
960 994	**BG**	RK	LO(S)	977901	977902
960 995	**BG**	RK	LO(S)	977903	977904

UNCLASSIFIED   DE-ICING UNIT

T. Converted 1960 from 4-Sub EMU vehicle. Non gangwayed. Operates with 977939/40.

Construction: Steel.
Maximum Speed: 70 m.p.h.
Bogies: Central 43 inch.
Brakes: Electro-pneumatic and automatic air.
Doors: Manually operated slam.
Couplings: Drophead buckeye.
Multiple Working: SR system.
Dimensions:

977364. T. Dia. EZ520. Southern Railway Eastleigh 1946. 29.0 t.

-	**RO**	RK *RK*	SU	977364

UNCLASSIFIED — DE-ICING UNIT

T. Converted 1960 from 4-Sub EMU vehicle. Non gangwayed. Operates with 977939/40.

Construction: Steel.
Maximum Speed: 70 m.p.h.   **Couplings:** Drophead buckeye.
Bogies: Central 43 inch.   **Multiple Working:** SR system.
Brakes: Electro-pneumatic and automatic air.
Doors: Manually operated slam.   **Dimensions:**

977364. T. Dia. EZ520. Southern Railway Eastleigh 1946. 29.0 t.

| - | **RO** | RK | *RK* | SU | 977364 |

UNCLASSIFIED — TRACK ASSESSMENT UNIT

DM–DM. Purpose built service unit. Gangwayed within unit.

Construction: Steel.
Engine: One Cummins NT-855-RT5 of 213 kW (285 h.p.) at 2100 r.p.m. per power car.
Transmission: Hydraulic. Voith T211r with cardan shafts to Gmeinder GM190 final drive.
Maximum Speed: 75 m.p.h.   **Couplers:** BSI automatic.
Bogies: BP38 (powered), BT38 (non-powered).
Brakes: Electro-pneumatic.   **Dimensions:** 20.06 x 2.82 x 3.77 m.
Doors: Manually operated slam & power operated sliding.
Multiple Working: Classes 142, 143, 144, 150, 153, 155, 156, 158, 159, 170.

Non-Standard Livery: Grey, red and blue.

999600. DM. Dia. DZ536. Lot No. 4060 BREL York 1987. 36.5 t.
999601. DM. Dia. DZ536. Lot No. 4061 BREL York 1987. 36.5 t.

| - | **O** | RK | *SO* | NC | 999600 999601 |

UNCLASSIFIED — ULTRASONIC TEST UNIT

T. Converted 1986 from Class 432 EMU. Gangwayed. Operates with 977391/2.

Construction: Steel.   **Maximum Speed:** 70 m.p.h.
Bogies: SR Mk. 6.   **Couplings:** Screw.
Brakes: Twin pipe vacuum.   **Multiple Working:** Blue Square.
Doors: Manually operated slam.   **Dimensions:** 19.66 x 2.82 x 3.90 m.

999602. T. Dia. DZ531. Lot No. 30862 York 1974. 55.5 t.

| - | **SO** | SO | *SO* | ZA | 999602 |

3.4. DMUS AWAITING DISPOSAL

The list below comprises vehicles awaiting disposal which are stored on the Railtrack network, together with vehicles stored at other locations (e.g. repair facilites) which, although awaiting disposal, remain Railtrack registered. This includes vehicles for which sales have been agreed, but collection by the new owner had not been made at the time of going to press.

Class 100

977191	**B**	?	ZC	

Class 101

101 660	**RR**	A	PY	51213 54343
101 678	**RR**	A	PY	51210 53746
101 684	**S**	A	PY	51188 53268
101 686	**S**	A	PY	51231 51500
101 690	**S**	A	PY	51435 53177
L835	**RR**	A	PY	51432 51498
L842	**N**	A	ZA	53314 53327
Spare:	**RR**	A	PY	51189 51463 53228 54055
Spare:	**RR**	A	PY	54061 54352 54365
Spare:	**BG**	A	PY	54350
Spare	**RR**	A	BP	59303
Spare	**G**	A	BP	59539

Class 117

117 301	**RR**	A	PY	51353		51395	L704	**N**	A	PY	51341	51383
117 306	**RR**	A	AL	51369		51411	L706	**N**	A	PY	51366	51408
117 308	**RR**	A	PY	51371		51413	L707	**N**	A	PY	51335	51377
117 310	**RR**	A	PY	51373	59486	51381	L720	**N**	A	PY	51354	51396
117 311	**RR**	A	PY	51352		51376	L721	**N**	A	PY	51363	51405
117 313	**RR**	A	PY	51339		51382	Spare	**RR**	A	PY	59492 59500	59505
117 701	**N**	A	PY	51350		51392	Spare	**RR**	A	PY	59509 59521	
L702	**N**	A	PY	51356		51398	Spare	**N**	A	PY	51358	51400

Class 121

121 027	**SL**	A	PY	55027		121 031	**N**	A	PY	55031
121 029	**SL**	A	PY	55029						

Class 141

141 105	**WY**	CW	ZF	55505 55525		141 113	**WY**	CW	ZF	55513 55533	
141 112	**WY**	CW	ZF	55512 55532			**SO**	CW	ZA	55518 55538	

Class 951

977696	**N**	RK	ZG

4. ELECTRIC MULTIPLE UNITS

USING THIS SECTION – LAYOUT OF INFORMATION

25 kV a.c. 50 Hz overhead Electric Multiple Units and 'Versatile' EMUs (units capable of utilising more than one type of electrical supply system) are listed in numerical order of class number, then in numerical order of set number – using official numbers as allocated by the Rolling Stock Library. Individual 'loose' vehicles are listed in numerical order after vehicles formed into fixed formations. Where numbers carried are different to those officially allocated, these are noted in class headings where appropriate.

750 V dc third rail EMUs are normally listed in numerical order of set numbers actually carried. Where such numbers consist of a four digit number only, these have been derived from the official six digit RSL number by omitting the first two digits of the class number (e.g. 423 401 carries 3401).

Where sets or vehicles have been renumbered since the previous edition of this book, former numbering detail is shown alongside current detail.

Each entry is laid out as in the following example:

Set No.	Detail	Livery	Owner	Operation	Allocation	Formation			
1706	†	**CX**	A	*SC*	Bl	76094	63035	70713	76040

Eurostar EMUs are listed in numerical order of set numbers actually carried. Each entry is laid out as shown in the example above, except that formation details for individual units are not shown as formations of these articulated units are fixed.

Service EMUs (i.e those not normally used in revenue-earning service) are listed in numerical order of class number, then in numerical order of set number – using official numbers as allocated by the Rolling Stock Library.

CLASS HEADINGS

Principal details and dimensions are quoted for each class in metric and/or imperial units as considered appropriate bearing in mind common UK usage. Abbreviations used are shown in Section 6.9.

All dimensions and weights are quoted for vehicles in an 'as new' condition with all necessary supplies on board. Dimensions are quoted in the order Length – Width – Height. All lengths quoted are over buffers or couplings as appropriate. All width and height dimensions quoted are maxima. Height of vehicles is quoted over body, ignoring pantographs (where fitted).

Bogie Types are quoted in the format motored/non-motored (e.g BP20/BT13 denotes BP20 motored bogies and BT non-motored bogies).

Unless noted to the contrary, all vehicles listed have bar couplings at non-driving ends and tread brakes.

DETAIL DIFFERENCES

Only detail differences which currently affect the areas and types of train which vehicles may work are shown. All other detail differences are specifically excluded. Where such differences occur within a class or part class, these are shown alongside the individual set or vehicle number. Meaning of abbreviations is detailed in individual class headings.

LIVERY CODES

Livery codes are used in this publication to denote the various liveries carried by vehicles. Readers should note it is impossible in a publication of this size to list every livery variation which currently exists. In particular items ignored for the purposes of this book include:

- Minor colour variations;
- Omission of logos:
- All numbering, lettering and branding.

The descriptions quoted are thus a general guide only and may be subject to slight variation between individual vehicles. Logos as appropriate for each livery are normally deemed to be carried.

A complete list of livery codes used in this publication appears in Section 6.1.

OWNER CODES

Owner codes are used in this publication to denote the owners of vehicles listed. Most vehicles are leased by the TOCs from specialist leasing companies.

A complete list of owner codes used in this publication appears in Section 6.2.

OPERATION CODES

Operation codes are used in this publication to denote the normal usage of the vehicles listed – i.e. A guide to the services of which train operating company any vehicle will normally be used upon. Where vehicles are used for non revenue earning purposes, an indication to the normal type of usage is given in the class heading.

Where no operation code is shown, a unit/vehicle is not currently in use. In this instance, the symbol (S) – denoting stored – will appear immediately after the location code.

Where an operation code is shown, but a unit/vehicle is also shown as stored – then the unit/vehicle remains available for use (i.e. on lease, but is currently out of use).

Readers should appreciate some units/vehicles are only operational for certain periods of the year (e.g. Sandite and De-Icing units). As such units/vehicles are normally stored at other times of the year, locations during such store periods are not shown in this publication.

A complete list of operation codes used in this publication appears in Section 6.4.

ALLOCATION & LOCATION CODES

Allocation codes are used to denote the normal maintenance base of each operational vehicle. However, maintenance may be carried out at other locations and may also be carried out by mobile maintenance teams.

Location codes are used to denote the current actual location of stored vehicles. A location code will always be followed by (S) to denote stored.

A complete list of allocation and location codes used in this publication appears in Section 6.5.

SET FORMATIONS

Set formations shown are those normally maintained. Readers should note some set formations might be temporarily varied from time to time to suit maintenance and/or operational requirements. Vehicles shown as 'Spare' are not formed in any regular set formation.

NAMES

Only names carried with official sanction are listed in this publication. As far as possible names are shown in UPPER/lower case characters as actually shown on the name carried on the vehicle(s). Inscriptions carried on crests and/or plates additional to the main name are not shown. Complete units are regarded as named rather than just the individual car(s) which carry the name.

GENERAL INFORMATION

CLASSIFICATION AND NUMBERING

25 kV a.c. 50 Hz and 'Versatile' EMUs are classified in the series 300–399.

750 V d.c. third rail EMUs are classified in the series 400–599.

Service EMUs are classified in the series 900–949.

EMU individual cars are numbered in the series 61000–78999, except for vehicles used on the Isle of Wight – which are numbered in a separate series.

Prior to privatisation, Service Stock individual cars were numbered in the series 975000–975999 and 977000–977999, although this series was not used exclusively for EMU vehicles. Since privatisation, use of these series has been sporadic, vehicles often now retaining their former numbers.

Where a vehicle carries an incorrect number which duplicates another correct number, the actual number carried is shown followed by ‖ to indicate a duplicate number. Correct number details are noted in the class heading.

Any vehicle constructed or converted to replace another vehicle following accident damage and carrying the same number as the original vehicle is denoted by the suffix [2] in this publication.

OPERATING CODES

These codes are used by TOC staff to describe the various different types of vehicles and normally appear on data panels on the non-driving ends of vehicles.

ATC	Auxiliary Equipment Trailer Composite
ATS	Auxiliary Equipment Trailer Standard
BDBS	Battery Driving Trailer Brake Standard
BDMS	Battery Driving Motor Standard
BDTC	Battery Driving Trailer Composite
BDTS	Battery Driving Trailer Standard
DM	Driving Motor
DMBS	Driving Motor Brake Standard
DMC	Driving Motor Composite
DMF	Driving Motor First
DMFRK	Driving Motor First with Kitchen
DMLF	Driving Motor Lounge First
DMLV	Driving Motor Luggage Van
DMS	Driving Motor Standard
DT	Driving Trailer
DTB	Driving Trailer Brake
DTBS	Driving Trailer Brake Standard
DTC	Driving Trailer Composite
DTF	Driving Trailer First
DTV	Driving Trailer Van
DTS	Driving Trailer Standard
M	Motor
MB	Motor Brake
MBLS	Motor Brake Restaurant Buffet Lounge Standard
MBS	Motor Brake Standard
MF	Motor First
MFD	Motor First with Disabled accommodation
MS	Motor Standard
MSD	Motor Standard with Disabled accommodation
PMB	Pantograph Motor Buffet Standard
PMS	Pantograph Motor Standard
PMV	Pantograph Motor Van
PTF	Pantograph Trailer First
PTS	Pantograph Trailer Standard
PTSRMB	Pantograph Trailer Standard with Buffet/Shop
TAV	Trailer Auxiliary Equipment Van
TBC	Trailer Brake Composite
TBF	Trailer Brake First
TBS	Trailer Brake Standard
TC	Trailer Composite
TF	Trailer First

TFH	Trailer First with Handbrake
TRBS	Trailer Restaurant Buffet Standard
TS	Trailer Standard
TSD	Trailer Standard with Disabled Persons' toilet.
TSH	Trailer Standard with Handbrake
TSW	Trailer Standard with Wheelchair Accommodation

The letters 'O' (denoting Open), 'K' (denoting Corridor) or 'L' (denoting Lavatory) may be added to the above codes on some vehicle data panels. Where two vehicles of the same type are formed within the same unit, the above codes may be suffixed by (A) and (B) to differentiate between the vehicles.

A composite is a vehicle containing both first and standard class accommodation, although first class accommodation on some EMU vehicles has now all been permanently declassified. A brake vehicle is a vehicle containing separate specific accommodation for the conductor (as opposed to the use of rear or intermediate cabs on some units).

Single motor coach 25 kV a.c. 50 Hz overhead EMUs (except Class 306) all have the pantograph mounted on the motor coach. Units with more than one motor coach have the pantograph mounted on a trailer car denoted as shown above.

DESIGN CODES AND DIAGRAM CODES

For each type of vehicle the Rolling Stock Library issues a seven character 'Design Code' consisting of two letters plus four numbers and a suffix letter. (e.g. EF2110A). The first five characters of the Design Code are known as the 'Diagram Code' and these are quoted in this publication in sub-headings. The meaning of the various characters of the Design Code is as follows: .

First Character
| E | Electric Multiple Unit |
| L | Eurostar Unit |

Second Character (EMU vehicles)
A	Driving Motor
B	Driving Motor Brake
C	Non-driving Motor
D	Non-driving Motor Brake
E	Driving Trailer
F	Battery Driving Trailer
G	Driving Trailer Brake
H	Trailer
I	Battery Driving Motor
J	Trailer Brake
N	Trailer Buffet
O	Battery Driving Trailer Brake
P	Trailer with Handbrake
X	Driving Motor Van
Z	All types of service vehicle

Second Character (Eurostar vehicles)
| A | Driving Motor |

B	Non-driving Motor
C	Trailer (with train manager's compartment) – position 3
D	Trailer – position 4
E	Trailer (with public telephone) – position 5
F	Trailer – position 6
G	Kitchen/Bar
H	Trailer – position 8
J	Trailer (with public telephone) – position 9
K	Trailer (with staff compartment) – position 10

Third Character

1	First class accommodation
2	Standard class accommodation
3	Composite accommodation
4	Unclassified accommodation
5	No passenger accommodation

Fourth & Fifth Characters

These distinguish between different designs of vehicle, each design being allocated a unique two digit number.

Special Note

Where vehicles have been declassified, the correct design code for a declassified vehicle is quoted in this publication, even though this may be at variance with RSL records, which do not always show the reality of the current position.

ACCOMMODATION

The information given in class headings and sub-headings is in the form F/S nT (or TD) nW. For example 12/54 1T 1W denotes 12 first class and 54 standard class seats, 1 toilet and 1 wheelchair space.

Except where otherwise noted, seating is 3+2 (i.e. three seats on one side of the gangway plus two on the other side) in standard class open vehicles, 2+2 in first class open vehicles, 8 per compartment in standard class and 6 per compartment in first class. Stock noted as being of 'Express' configuration has 2+2 seating in standard class vehicles and 2+1 seating in first class vehicles.

BUILD DETAILS

Lot Numbers

Vehicles ordered under the auspices of BR were allocated a Lot (batch) number when ordered and these are quoted in class headings and sub-headings.

Builders/Heavy Maintenance Providers

Abbreviations used to denote builders and heavy maintenance providers are shown in Section 6.8.

4.1. 25 kV a.c. 50 Hz OVERHEAD & 'VERSATILE' UNITS

Supply System: Except where otherwise stated, all units in this section operate on 25 kV a.c. 50 Hz overhead only.

CLASS 303   PRESSED STEEL

DTS–MBS–BDTS. Gangwayed within unit. 2+2 (*3+2) seating.

Construction: Steel.
Traction Motors: Four Metropolitan Vickers MV155 of 155 kW each.
Dimensions: 20.18 x 2.82 x 3.86 m.
Maximum Speed: 75 m.p.h.   **Doors:** Power operated sliding.
Couplings: Buckeye.   **Bogies:** Gresley ED3/ET3.
Multiple Working: Classes 303–312 only.

61481–61515. MBS. Dia. ED220. Lot No. 30580 Pressed Steel 1959–60. –/48. 56.4 t.
61812–61867. MBS. Dia. ED220. Lot No. 30630 Pressed Steel 1960–61. –/48. 56.4 t.
75566–75600. DTS. Dia. EE241. Lot No. 30579 Pressed Steel 1959–60. –/56. 34.4 t.
75601–75635. BDTS. Dia. EF217. Lot No. 30581 Pressed Steel 1959–60. –/56. 38.4 t.
75746–75801. DTS. Dia. EE241 (* EE206). Lot No. 30629 Pressed Steel 1960–61. –/56 (* –/83). 34.4 (* 34.5) t.
75802–75857. BDTS. Dia. EF217. Lot No. 30631 Pressed Steel 1960–61. –/56. 38.4 t.

303 001	S	A	SR	GW	75566	61481	75601
303 003	S	A	SR	GW	75568	61483	75603
303 004	S	A	SR	GW	75569	61484	75604
303 006	S	A	SR	GW	75571	61486	75606
303 008	S	A	SR	GW	75573	61488	75608
303 009	S	A	SR	GW	75574	61504	75609
303 010	S	A	SR	GW	75575	61490	75610
303 011	S	A	SR	GW	75576	61491	75611
303 012	S	A	SR	GW	75577	61492	75612
303 013	S	A	SR	GW	75578	61493	75613
303 014	S	A	SR	GW	75579	61494	75614
303 016	S	A	SR	GW	75750	61496	75616
303 019	SC	A	SR	GW	75584	61499	75619
303 020	S	A	SR	GW	75585	61500	75620
303 021	SC	A	SR	GW	75586	61501	75621
303 023	SC	A	SR	GW	75588	61503	75623
303 024	S	A		GW(S)	75589	61489	75624
303 025	S	A	SR	GW	75572	61505	75625
303 027	S	A	SR	GW	75592	61507	75627

303 028	S	A		GW(S)	75600	61813	75845
303 032	S	A	SR	GW	75597	61512	75632
303 033	S	A	SR	GW	75595	61860	75817
303 034	S	A	SR	GW	75599	61514	75634
303 037	S	A	SR	GW	75781	61508	75803
303 040	S	A	SR	GW	75581	61816	75806
303 043	S	A	SR	GW	75766	61819	75809
303 045	S	A	SR	GW	75755	61821	75811
303 047	S	A	SR	GW	75757	61823	75813
303 054	S	A	SR	GW	75764	61830	75820
303 055	S	A	SR	GW	75765	61831	75821
303 058	S	A		CK(S)	75768	61834	75824
303 061	S	A		GW(S)	75771	61837	75827
303 065	S	A	SR	GW	75775	61841	75831
303 070	S	A	SR	GW	75780	61846	75836
303 077	S	A	SR	GW	75787	61853	75843
303 079	S	A	SR	GW	75789	61855	75635
303 080	S	A	SR	GW	75790	61856	75846
303 083	S	A	SR	GW	75793	61859	75849
303 085	S	A	SR	GW	75795	61861	75851
303 087	SC	A	SR	GW	75797	61863	75853
303 088	S	A	SR	GW	75798	61864	75854
303 089	S	A	SR	GW	75799	61865	75855
303 090	S	A	SR	GW	75800	61866	75856
303 091	S	A	SR	GW	75801	61867	75857
Spare	S	A	SR	GW(S)		61832	75822
Spare	S	A	SR	YO(S)	75590		
Spare	* BG	A		PY(S)	75773		

Name (carried on MBS):

303 089   COWAL HIGHLAND GATHERING 1894–1994

CLASS 305   BR

BDTC (declassified)–MBS–DTS or BDTS–MBS–TS–DTS. Gangwayed within unit.

Construction: Steel.
Traction Motors: Four GEC WT380 of 153 kW each.
Dimensions: 20.35 (BDTC, BDTS & DTS) or 20.29 (MBS & TS) x 2.82 x 3.84 m.
Maximum Speed: 75 m.p.h.   **Doors:** Manually operated slam.
Couplings: Buckeye.   **Bogies:** Gresley ED5/ET5.
Multiple Working: Classes 303–312 only.

61410–61428. MBS. Dia. ED216. Lot No. 30567 Doncaster 1960. –/76 (*–/58; †–/72). 56.5 t.
70356–70374. TS. Dia. EH223. Lot No. 30568 Doncaster 1960. –/86 1T. 31.5 t.
75424–75442. BDTS. Dia. EF2??. Lot No. 30566 Doncaster 1960. –/80) 1T. 36.5 t.
75443–75461. DTS. Dia. EE220. Lot No. 30569 Doncaster 1960. –/88 . 32.7 t.

| 305 501 | † RR | A | SR | GW | 75424 | 61410 | 70356 | 75443 |
| 305 502 | † RR | A | SR | GW | 75425 | 61421 | 70357 | 75444 |

305 508	†	**RR**	A	*SR*	GW	75431	61417	70363	75450
305 517	†	**RR**	A	*SR*	GW	75440	61426	70372	75459
305 519	†	**RR**	A	*SR*	GW	75442	61428	70374	75461

CLASS 306 METRO-CAMMELL/BRCW

DMS–TBS–DTS. Non gangwayed. 2+2 seating. Original supply system 1500V d.c. overhead, converted 1960–61. Retained for special workings only, not used in normal service.

Construction: Steel.
Traction Motors: Four Crompton Parkinson of 155 kW each.
Dimensions: 19.24 (DMS & DTS) or 17.40 (TBS) x 2.89 x 3.84 m.
Maximum Speed: 70 m.p.h.   **Doors:** Power operated sliding.
Couplings: Screw.   **Bogies:** LNER ED6/ET6.
Multiple Working: Classes 303–312 only.

65201–65292. DMS. Dia. EA203. Lot No. 363 Metro-Cammell 1949. –/62. 51.7t.
65401–65492. TBS. Dia. EJ201. Lot No. 365 BRCW 1949. –/46. 26.4 t.
65601–65692. DTS. Dia. EE211. Lot No. 364 Metro-Cammell 1949. –/60. 27.9 t.

306 017	**G**	H	*GE*	IL(S)	65217	65417	65617

CLASS 308 BR

BDTC (declassified)–MBS–DTS. Gangwayed within unit. Originally 4-car units, but surviving TS cars are all now awaiting disposal.

Construction: Steel.
Traction Motors: Four English Electric 536A of 143.5 kW each.
Dimensions: 19.88 (BDTC & DTS) or 19.35 (MBS & TS) x 2.82 x 3.86 m.
Maximum Speed: 75 m.p.h.   **Doors:** Manually operated slam.
Couplings: Buckeye.   **Bogies:** Gresley ED5/ET5.
Multiple Working: Classes 303–312 only.

61883–61891. MBS. Dia. ED216. Lot No. 30653 York 1961–62. –/76. 55.0 t.
61893–61915. MBS. Dia. ED216. Lot No. 30653 York 1961–62. –/76. 55.0 t.
75878–75886. BDTC. Dia. EF304. Lot No. 30652 York 1961–62. 24/50 1T. 36.3 t.
75887–75895. DTS. Dia. EE220. Lot No. 30655 York 1961–62. –/88. 33.0 t.
75896–75928. BDTC. Dia. EF304. Lot No. 30656 York 1961–62. 24/50 1T. 36.3 t.
75929–75961. DTS. Dia. EE220. Lot No. 30659 York 1961–62. –/88. 33.0 t.

308 136	**WY**	A	*NS*	NL	75881	61886	75890
308 137	**WY**	A	*NS*	NL	75882	61887	75891
308 138	**WY**	A	*NS*	NL	75883	61888	75892
308 141	**WY**	A	*NS*	NL	75886	61891	75895
308 143	**WY**	A	*NS*	NL	75897	61893	75930
308 144	**WY**	A		ZF(S)	75890	61894	75931
308 145	**WY**	A	*NS*	NL	75899	61895	75932
308 147	**WY**	A	*NS*	NL	75901	61897	75934
308 152	**WY**	A	*NS*	NL	75913	61902	75939
308 153	**WY**	A	*NS*	NL	75907	61903	75940
308 154	**WY**	A	*NS*	NL(S)	75908	61904	75941

308 155	**WY**	A	*NS*	NL(S)	75909	61905	75942
308 157	**WY**	A	*NS*	NL	75915	61907	75944
308 158	**WY**	A	*NS*	NL	75912	61908	75945
308 159	**WY**	A	*NS*	NL	75906	61909	75946
308 161	**WY**	A	*NS*	NL	75911	61911	75948
308 162	**WY**	A	*NS*	NL	75916	61884	75949
308 163	**WY**	A	*NS*	NL	75917	61913	75950
308 164	**WY**	A	*NS*	NL	75918	61914	75951
308 165	**WY**	A	*NS*	NL	75919	61915	75952
Spare	**WY**	A		PY(S)	75879		
Spare	**WY**	A		ZH(S)		61912	75888

CLASS 310   BR

Various formations, see below. Gangwayed within unit. Disc brakes.

Construction: Steel.
Traction Motors: Four English Electric 546 of 201.5 kW each.
Dimensions: 20.18 x 2.82 x 3.86 m.
Maximum Speed: 75 m.p.h.   **Doors:** Manually operated slam.
Couplings: Buckeye.   **Bogies:** B4.
Multiple Working: Classes 303–312 only.

Note: 310 081 carries car numbers 76991, 62526, 71210, 78042 in error on
one side only.

62071–62120. MBS. Dia. ED219. Lot No. 30746 Derby 1965–67. –/68. 57.2 t.
70731–70780. TS. Dia. EH232. Lot No. 30747 Derby 1965–67. –/98. 31.7 t.
76130–76179. BDTS. Dia. EF211. Lot No. 30745 Derby 1965–67. –/80 2T. 37.3 t.
76180/181/183–186/190–195/198–205/208/209/211/213–223/225/227/229.
   DTC. Dia. EE306. Lot No. 30748 Derby 1965–67. 25/43 2T. 34.4 t.
76182/187–189/196/197/206/207/210/212/224. DTS. Dia. EE237. Lot No.
   30748 Derby 1965–67. Converted from DTC. –/75 2T. 34.4 t.
76228. BDTS. Dia. EF210. Lot No. 30748 Derby 1967. Converted from DTC.
   –/68 2T. 34.5 t.
76998. BDTS. Dia. EF214. Lot No. 30747 Derby 1965–67. Converted from TS.
   –/75 2T. 35.0 t.

Class 310/0. 4-car units. BDTS–MBS–TS–DTC (declassified).

310 046	**N**	H	*C2*	EM	76130	62071	70731	76180
310 047	**N**	H	*C2*	EM	76131	62072	70732	76181
310 049	**N**	H	*C2*	EM	76133	62074	70734	76183
310 050	**N**	H	*C2*	EM	76134	62075	70735	76184
310 051	**N**	H	*C2*	EM	76135	62076	70736	76185
310 052	**N**	H	*C2*	EM	76136	62077	70737	76186
310 057	**N**	H		EM(S)	76141	62082	70742	76191
310 058	**N**	H	*C2*	EM	76142	62083	70743	76192
310 059	**N**	H	*C2*	EM	76143	62084	70744	76205
310 060	**N**	H	*C2*	EM	76144	62085	70745	76194
310 064	**N**	H	*C2*	EM	76148	62089	70749	76198
310 066	**N**	H	*C2*	EM	76228	62091	70751	76200
310 067	**N**	H	*C2*	EM	76151	62092	70752	76201

310 068	**N**	H	*C2*	EM	76152	62093	70753	76202
310 069	**N**	H	*C2*	EM	76153	62094	70754	76203
310 070	**N**	H	*C2*	EM	76154	62095	70755	76204
310 074	**N**	H	*C2*	EM	76145	62099	70759	76208
310 075	**N**	H	*C2*	EM	76159	62100	70760	76209
310 077	**N**	H	*C2*	EM	76161	62102	70762	76211
310 079	**N**	H	*C2*	EM	76163	62104	70764	76222
310 080	**N**	H	*C2*	EM	76164	62105	70765	76214
310 081	**N**	H	*C2*	EM	76165	62106	70766	76215
310 082	**N**	H	*C2*	EM	76166	62107	70767	76216
310 083	**N**	H	*C2*	EM	76167	62108	70768	76217
310 084	**N**	H	*C2*	EM	76168	62109	70769	76206
310 085	**N**	H	*C2*	EM	76169	62110	70770	76219
310 086	**N**	H	*C2*	EM	76170	62111	70771	76220
310 087	**N**	H	*C2*	EM	76171	62112	70772	76221
310 088	**N**	H	*C2*	EM	76172	62113	70773	76213
310 089	**N**	H		EM(S)	76173	62114	70774	76223
310 091	**N**	H	*C2*	EM	76175	62116	70776	76225
310 092	**N**	H	*C2*	EM	76176	62117	70777	76226
310 093	**N**	H	*C2*	EM	76177	62118	70778	76190
310 094	**N**	H	*C2*	EM	76998	62119	70780	76193
310 095	**N**	H	*C2*	EM	76179	62120	70779	76229
Spare	**N**	H		EM(S)				76218

Name (carried on MBS):

310 058   Chafford Hundred.

Class 310/1. 3-car units. BDTS–MBS–DTS (*DTC (declassified)).

310 101		**RR**	H	*C2*	EM	76157	62098	76207
310 102		**RR**	H	*C2*	EM	76139	62080	76189
310 104		**RR**	H	*C2*	EM	76162	62103	76212
310 105		**RR**	H	*C2*	EM	76174	62115	76224
310 106		**RR**	H		EM(S)	76156	62097	
310 107		**RR**	H	*C2*	EM	76146	62087	76196
310 108		**RR**	H	*C2*	EM	76132	62073	76182
310 109		**RR**	H	*C2*	EM	76137	62078	76187
310 110		**RR**	H	*C2*	EM	76138	62079	76188
310 111		**RR**	H	*C2*	EM	76147	62088	76197
310 112	*	**RR**	H	*C2*	EM	76140	62086	76227
310 113	*	**RR**	H	*C2*	EM	76158	62090	76195
Spare		**RR**	H		EM(S)		62101	
Spare		**RR**	H		SN(S)	76160		76210

CLASS 312   BREL

BDTS–MBS–TS–DTC. Gangwayed within unit. Disc brakes. All DTC vehicles operated by c2c are declassified.

Construction: Steel.
Traction Motors: Four English Electric 546 of 201.5 kW each.
Dimensions: 20.18 x 2.82 x 3.86 m.
Maximum Speed: 90 m.p.h.   **Doors:** Manually operated slam.
Couplings: Buckeye.   **Bogies:** B4.
Multiple Working: Classes 303–312 only.

Note: 76949 carries number 76946 in error on one side only.

Class 312/0. Built to operate on 25 kV 50 Hz a.c. overhead only.

62484–62509. MBS. Dia. ED212. Lot No. 30864 BREL York 1977–78. –/68. 56.0 t.
62657–62560. MBS. Dia. ED214. Lot No. 30892 BREL York 1976. –/68. 56.0 t.
71168–71193. TS. Dia. EH209. Lot No. 30865 BREL York 1977–78. –/98. 30.5 t.
71277–71280. TS. Dia. EH209. Lot No. 30893 BREL York 1976. –/98. 30.5 t.
76949–76974. BDTS. Dia. EF213. Lot No. 30863 BREL York 1977–78. –/84 1T. 34.9 t.
76994–76997. BDTS. Dia. EF213. Lot No. 30891 BREL York 1976. –/84 1T. 34.9 t.
78000–78025. DTC. Dia. EE305. Lot No. 30866 BREL York 1977–78. 25/47 2T. 33.0 t.
78045–78048. DTC. Dia. EE305. Lot No. 30894 BREL York 1976. 25/47 2T. 33.0 t.

312 701	GE	A	GE	IL	76949	62484	71168	78000
312 702	GE	A	GE	IL	76950	62485	71169	78001
312 703	GE	A	GE	IL	76951	62486	71170	78002
312 704	GE	A	GE	IL	76952	62487	71171	78003
312 705	GE	A	GE	IL	76953	62488	71172	78004
312 706	GE	A	GE	IL	76954	62489	71173	78005
312 707	GE	A	GE	IL	76955	62490	71174	78006
312 708	GE	A	C2	EM	76956	62491	71175	78007
312 709	GE	A	GE	IL	76957	62492	71176	78008
312 710	GE	A	GE	IL	76958	62493	71177	78009
312 711	GE	A	GE	IL	76959	62494	71178	78010
312 712	GE	A	GE	IL	76960	62495	71179	78011
312 713	GE	A	GE	IL	76961	62496	71180	78012
312 714	GE	A	GE	IL	76962	62497	71181	78013
312 715	GE	A	GE	IL	76963	62498	71182	78014
312 716	GE	A	GE	IL	76964	62499	71183	78015
312 717	GE	A	GE	IL	76965	62500	71184	78016
312 718	GE	A	GE	IL	76966	62501	71185	78017
312 719	GE	A	GE	IL	76967	62502	71186	78018
312 720	GE	A	GE	IL	76968	62503	71187	78019
312 721	GE	A	GE	IL	76969	62504	71188	78020
312 722	GE	A	GE	IL	76970	62505	71189	78021
312 723	GE	A	GE	IL	76971	62506	71190	78022
312 724	GE	A	GE	IL	76972	62507	71191	78023
312 725	N	A	C2	EM	76973	62509	71193	78025
312 726	N	A	C2	EM	76974	62508	71192	78024
312 727	N	A	C2	EM	76994	62657	71277	78045
312 728	N	A	C2	EM	76995	62658	71278	78046
312 729	N	A	C2	EM	76996	62659	71279	78047
312 730	N	A	C2	EM	76997	62660	71280	78048

Class 312/1. Built to operate on 25 kV 50 Hz a.c. or 6.25 kV 50 Hz a.c. overhead.

62510–62528. MBS. Dia. ED213. Lot No. 30868 BREL York 1975–76. –/68. 56.0 t.
71194–71212. TS. Dia. EH209. Lot No. 30869 BREL York 1975–76. –/98. 30.5 t.
76975–76993. BDTS. Dia. EF213. Lot No. 30867 BREL York 1975–76. –/84 2T. 34.9 t.
78026–78044. DTC. Dia. EE305. Lot No. 30870 BREL York 1975–76. 25/47 2T. 33.0 t.

312 781	N	A	C2	EM	76975	62510	71194	78026
312 782	N	A	C2	EM	76976	62511	71195	78027
312 783	N	A	C2	EM	76977	62512	71196	78028
312 784	N	A	C2	EM	76978	62513	71197	78029
312 785	N	A	C2	EM	76979	62514	71198	78030
312 786	N	A	C2	EM	76980	62515	71199	78031
312 787	N	A	C2	EM	76981	62516	71200	78032
312 788	N	A	C2	EM	76982	62517	71201	78033
312 789	N	A	C2	EM	76983	62518	71202	78034
312 790	N	A	C2	EM	76984	62519	71203	78035
312 791	N	A	C2	EM	76985	62520	71204	78036
312 792	N	A	C2	EM	76986	62521	71205	78037
312 793	N	A	C2	EM	76987	62522	71206	78038
312 794	N	A	C2	EM	76988	62523	71207	78039
312 795	N	A	C2	EM	76989	62524	71208	78040
312 796	N	A	C2	EM	76990	62525	71209	78041
312 797	N	A	C2	EM	76991	62526	71210	78042
312 798	N	A	C2	EM	76992	62527	71211	78043
312 799	N	A	C2	EM	76993	62528	71212	7804

CLASS 313   BREL

DMS–PTS–BDMS. Gangwayed within unit. End doors. Disc and rheostatic braking.

Construction: Steel underframe, aluminium alloy body and roof.
Supply System: 25 kV 50 Hz a.c. overhead or 750 V d.c. third rail.
Traction Motors: Four GEC G310AZ of 82.125 kW each per motor car.
Dimensions: 19.80 (DMS & BDMS) or 19.92 (PTS) x 2.82 x 3.58 m.
Maximum Speed: 75 m.p.h.   **Doors:** Power operated sliding.
Couplers: Tightlock.   **Bogies:** BREL BX1.
Multiple Working: Classes 313–323.
Notes: 71217 carries number 71277 in error on one side only.

62529–62592. DMS. Dia. EA204. Lot No. 30879 BREL York 1976–77. –/74. 36.4 t.
62593–62656. BDMS. Dia. EI201. Lot No. 30885 BREL York 1976–77. –/74. 37.6 t.
71213–71276. PTS. Dia. EH210. Lot No. 30880 BREL York 1976–77. –/84 (*–/80). 30.5 t.

Class 313/0. Operated by West Anglia Great Northern Railway.

Note: † Refurbished 1998 onwards by Adtranz Ilford with high back seats.

Advertising Liveries:
- 313 024/027/043/057/064 'WAGN Family Travelcard'
- 313 050 'WAGN Daytripper Ticket'
- 313 060 'Intalink'

313 018	†	U	H	*WN*	HE	62546	71230	62610
313 024	†	AL	H	*WN*	HE	62552	71236	62616
313 025	†	N	H	*WN*	HE	62553	71237	62617
313 026	†	N	H	*WN*	HE	62554	71238	62618
313 027	†	AL	H	*WN*	HE	62555	71239	62619
313 028	†	U	H	*WN*	HE	62556	71240	62620
313 029	†	U	H	*WN*	HE	62557	71241	62621
313 030	†	U	H	*WN*	HE	62558	71242	62622
313 031		N	H	*WN*	HE	62559	71243	62623
313 032	†	U	H	*WN*	HE	62560	71244	62643
313 033	†	U	H	*WN*	HE	62561	71245	62625
313 035	†	U	H	*WN*	HE	62563	71247	62627
313 036	†	U	H	*WN*	HE	62564	71248	62628
313 037	†	U	H	*WN*	HE	62565	71249	62629
313 038	†	U	H	*WN*	HE	62566	71250	62630
313 039	†	U	H	*WN*	HE	62567	71251	62631
313 040		N	H	*WN*	HE	62568	71252	62632
313 041		N	H	*WN*	HE	62569	71253	62633
313 042	†	N	H	*WN*	HE	62570	71254	62634
313 043	†	AL	H	*WN*	HE	62571	71255	62635
313 044	†	U	H	*WN*	HE	62572	71256	62636
313 045	†	N	H	*WN*	HE	62573	71257	62637
313 046		N	H	*WN*	HE	62574	71258	62638
313 047	†	U	H	*WN*	HE	62575	71259	62639
313 048	†	N	H	*WN*	HE	62576	71260	62640
313 049		N	H	*WN*	HE	62577	71261	62641
313 050	†	AL	H	*WN*	HE	62578	71262	62649
313 051	†	U	H	*WN*	HE	62579	71263	62624
313 052	†	N	H	*WN*	HE	62580	71264	62644
313 053	†	N	H	*WN*	HE	62581	71265	62645
313 054	†	N	H	*WN*	HE	62582	71266	62646
313 055	†	N	H	*WN*	HE	62583	71267	62647
313 056		U	H	*WN*	HE	62584	71268	62648
313 057	†	AL	H	*WN*	HE	62585	71269	62642
313 058	†	N	H	*WN*	HE	62586	71270	62650
313 059	†	U	H	*WN*	HE	62587	71271	62651
313 060	†	AL	H	*WN*	HE	62588	71272	62652
313 061	†	N	H	*WN*	HE	62589	71273	62653
313 062	†	N	H	*WN*	HE	62590	71274	62654
313 063	†	N	H	*WN*	HE	62591	71275	62655
313 064	†	AL	H	*WN*	HE	62592	71276	62656

Class 313/1. Operated by Silverlink Train Services. No power cable between the two motor coaches, hence equipped with additional shoegear. Units are renumbered and reclassified from Class 313/0 upon completion of facelift by Railcare Wolverton, retaining last two digits of previous number.

Number Former No.

313 101	313 001	*	**SL**	H	*SL*	BY	62529	71213	62593
313 102	313 002	*	**SL**	H	*SL*	BY	62530	71214	62594
313 103	313 003	*	**SL**	H	*SL*	BY	62531	71215	62595
313 104	313 004	*	**SL**	H	*SL*	BY	62532	71216	62596
313 105	313 005	*	**SL**	H	*SL*	BY	62533	71217	62597
313 106	313 006	*	**SL**	H	*SL*	BY	62534	71218	62598
	313 007	*	**N**	H	*SL*	BY	62535	71219	62599
313 108	313 008	*	**SL**	H	*SL*	BY	62536	71220	62600
313 109	313 009	*	**SL**	H	*SL*	BY	62537	71221	62601
313 110	313 010	*	**SL**	H	*SL*	BY	62538	71222	62602
313 111	313 011	*	**SL**	H	*SL*	BY	62539	71223	62603
313 112	313 012	*	**SL**	H	*SL*	BY	62540	71224	62604
	313 013		**N**	H	*SL*	BY	62541	71225	62605
313 114	313 014	*	**SL**	H	*SL*	BY	62542	71226	62606
313 115	313 015	*	**SL**	H	*SL*	BY	62543	71227	62607
	313 016		**N**	H	*SL*	BY	62544	71228	62608
313 117	313 017	*	**SL**	H	*SL*	BY	62545	71229	62609
	313 019		**N**	H	*SL*	BY	62547	71231	62611
313 120	313 020	*	**SL**	H	*SL*	BY	62548	71232	62612
313 121	313 021	*	**SL**	H	*SL*	BY	62549	71233	62613
313 122	313 022	*	**SL**	H	*SL*	BY	62550	71234	62614
313 123	313 023	*	**SL**	H	*SL*	BY	62551	71235	62615
313 134	313 034	*	**SL**	H	*SL*	BY	62562	71246	62626

Name (carried on PTS):

313 109   Arnold Leah   313 120   PARLIAMENT HILL

CLASS 314   BREL

DMS–PTS–DMS. Gangwayed within unit. End doors. Disc brakes.

Construction: Steel underframe, aluminium alloy body and roof.
Traction Motors: Four Brush TM61-53 or GEC G310AZ of 82.125 kW each per motor car.
Dimensions: 19.80 (DMS or 19.92 (PTS) x 2.82 x 3.58 m.
Maximum Speed: 75 m.p.h.   **Doors:** Power operated sliding.
Couplers: Tightlock.   **Bogies:** BREL BX1.
Multiple Working: Classes 313–323.

64583–64613 (Odd numbers). DMS(A). Dia. EA206. Lot No. 30912 BREL York 1979. –/68. 34.5 t.
64584–64614 (Even numbers). DMS(B). Dia. EA206. Lot No. 30912 BREL York 1979. –/68. 34.5 t.
64588[*]. DMS(B). Dia. EA206. Lot No. 30908 BREL York 1978–80. Rebuilt Railcare Glasgow 1996 from Class 507 DMS. –/72. 35.6 t.
71450–71465. PTS. Dia. EH211. Lot No. 30913 BREL York 1979. –/76. 33.0 t.

Units 314 201–314 206. Brush traction motors.

314 201	S	A	SR	GW	64583 71450 64584
314 202	S	A	SR	GW	64585 71451 64586
314 203	SC	A	SR	GW	64587 71452 64588²
314 204	SC	A	SR	GW	64589 71453 64590
314 205	SC	A	SR	GW	64591 71454 64592
314 206	SC	A	SR	GW	64593 71455 64594

Units 314 207–314 216. GEC traction motors.

314 207	S	A	SR	GW	64595 71456 64596
314 208	S	A	SR	GW	64597 71457 64598
314 209	S	A	SR	GW	64599 71458 64600
314 210	SC	A	SR	GW	64601 71459 64602
314 211	SC	A	SR	GW	64603 71460 64604
314 212	SC	A	SR	GW	64605 71461 64606
314 213	S	A	SR	GW	64607 71462 64608
314 214	S	A	SR	GW	64609 71463 64610
314 215	SC	A	SR	GW	64611 71464 64612
314 216	SC	A	SR	GW	64613 71465 64614

Name (carried on PTS):

314 203   European Union

CLASS 315   BREL

DMS–TS–PTS–DMS. Gangwayed within unit. End doors. Disc brakes.

Construction: Steel underframe, aluminium alloy body and roof.
Traction Motors: Four GEC G310AZ or Brush TM61-53) of 82.125 kW each per motor car.
Dimensions: 19.80 (DMS) or 19.92 (TS & PTS) x 2.82 x 3.58 m.
Maximum Speed: 75 m.p.h.   **Doors:** Power operated sliding.
Couplers: Tightlock.   **Bogies:** BREL BX1.
Multiple Working: Classes 313–323.

Advertising Livery:
• 315 844/845 'WAGN Family Travelcard'.

64461–64581 (Odd numbers). DMS(A). Dia. EA207. Lot No. 30902 BREL York 1980–81. –/74. 35.0 t.
64462–64582 (Even numbers). DMS(B). Dia. EA207. Lot No. 30902 BREL York 1980–81. –/74. 35.0 t.
71281–71341. TS. Dia. EH216. Lot No. 30904 BREL York 1980–81. –/86. 25.5 t.
71389–71449. PTS. Dia. EH217. Lot No. 30903 BREL York 1980–81. –/84. 32.0 t.

Units 315 801–315 841. Brush electrical equipment.

315 801	GE	H	GE	IL	64461 71281 71389 64462
315 802	GE	H	GE	IL	64463 71282 71390 64464
315 803	GE	H	GE	IL	64465 71283 71391 64466
315 804	GE	H	GE	IL	64467 71284 71392 64468
315 805	GE	H	GE	IL	64469 71285 71393 64470

315 806	**GE**	H	*GE*	IL	64471	71286	71394	64472
315 807	**GE**	H	*GE*	IL	64473	71287	71395	64474
315 808	**GE**	H	*GE*	IL	64475	71288	71396	64476
315 809	**GE**	H	*GE*	IL	64477	71289	71397	64478
315 810	**GE**	H	*GE*	IL	64479	71290	71398	64480
315 811	**GE**	H	*GE*	IL	64481	71291	71399	64482
315 812	**GE**	H	*GE*	IL	64483	71292	71400	64484
315 813	**GE**	H	*GE*	IL	64485	71293	71401	64486
315 814	**GE**	H	*GE*	IL	64487	71294	71402	64488
315 815	**GE**	H	*GE*	IL	64489	71295	71403	64490
315 816	**GE**	H	*GE*	IL	64491	71296	71404	64492
315 817	**GE**	H	*GE*	IL	64493	71297	71405	64494
315 818	**GE**	H	*GE*	IL	64495	71298	71406	64496
315 819	**GE**	H	*GE*	IL	64497	71299	71407	64498
315 820	**GE**	H	*GE*	IL	64499	71300	71408	64500
315 821	**GE**	H	*GE*	IL	64501	71301	71409	64502
315 822	**GE**	H	*GE*	IL	64503	71302	71410	64504
315 823	**GE**	H	*GE*	IL	64505	71303	71411	64506
315 824	**GE**	H	*GE*	IL	64507	71304	71412	64508
315 825	**GE**	H	*GE*	IL	64509	71305	71413	64510
315 826	**GE**	H	*GE*	IL	64511	71306	71414	64512
315 827	**GE**	H	*GE*	IL	64513	71307	71415	64514
315 828	**GE**	H	*GE*	IL	64515	71308	71416	64516
315 829	**GE**	H	*GE*	IL	64517	71309	71417	64518
315 830	**GE**	H	*GE*	IL	64519	71310	71418	64520
315 831	**GE**	H	*GE*	IL	64521	71311	71419	64522
315 832	**GE**	H	*GE*	IL	64523	71312	71420	64524
315 833	**GE**	H	*GE*	IL	64525	71313	71421	64526
315 834	**GE**	H	*GE*	IL	64527	71314	71422	64528
315 835	**GE**	H	*GE*	IL	64529	71315	71423	64530
315 836	**GE**	H	*GE*	IL	64531	71316	71424	64532
315 837	**GE**	H	*GE*	IL	64533	71317	71425	64534
315 838	**GE**	H	*GE*	IL	64535	71318	71426	64536
315 839	**GE**	H	*GE*	IL	64537	71319	71427	64538
315 840	**GE**	H	*GE*	IL	64539	71320	71428	64540
315 841	**GE**	H	*GE*	IL	64541	71321	71429	64542

Units 315 842–315 861. GEC electrical equipment.

315 842	**GE**	H	*GE*	IL	64543	71322	71430	64544
315 843	**GE**	H	*GE*	IL	64545	71323	71431	64546
315 844	**AL**	H	*WN*	HE	64547	71324	71432	64548
315 845	**AL**	H	*WN*	HE	64549	71325	71433	64550
315 846	**U**	H	*WN*	HE	64551	71326	71434	64552
315 847	**U**	H	*WN*	HE	64553	71327	71435	64554
315 848	**U**	H	*WN*	HE	64555	71328	71436	64556
315 849	**U**	H	*WN*	HE	64557	71329	71437	64558
315 850	**U**	H	*WN*	HE	64559	71330	71438	64560
315 851	**U**	H	*WN*	HE	64561	71331	71439	64562
315 852	**U**	H	*WN*	HE	64563	71332	71440	64564
315 853	**U**	H	*WN*	HE	64565	71333	71441	64566
315 854	**U**	H	*WN*	HE	64567	71334	71442	64568

315 855	U	H	*WN*	HE	64569	71335	71443	64570
315 856	U	H	*WN*	HE	64571	71336	71444	64572
315 857	U	H	*WN*	HE	64573	71337	71445	64574
315 858	U	H	*WN*	HE	64579	71338	71446	64580
315 859	N	H	*WN*	HE	64577	71339	71447	64578
315 860	N	H	*WN*	HE	64575	71340	71448	64576
315 861	N	H	*WN*	HE	64581	71341	71449	64582

CLASS 317   BREL

Various formations, see below. Gangwayed throughout. Disc brakes.

Construction: Steel.
Traction Motors: Four GEC G315BZ of 247.5 kW each.
Dimensions: 20.13 (DTS & DTC) or 20.18 (ATC, ATS & PMS) x 2.82 x 3.58 m.
Maximum Speed: 100 m.p.h.   **Doors:** Power operated sliding.
Couplers: Tightlock.   **Bogies:** BREL BP20/BT13.
Multiple Working: Classes 313–323.

Notes: Four (unspecified) Class 317/1 units are hired from West Anglia Great Northern to Thameslink Rail on a fortnightly basis.
Four (unspecified) Class 317/1 units are hired from West Anglia Great Northern to c2c Rail pending further commissioning of Class 357 units.

Class 317/1. Pressure heating & ventilation. DTS(A)–PMS–ATC († ATS)–DTS(B).

62661–62708. PMS. Dia. EC208. Lot No. 30958 BREL York 1981–82. –/79. 49.8 t.
71577–71624. ATC. Dia. EH307. Lot No. 30957 BREL Derby 1981–82. 22/46 2T. 28.8 t.
77000–77047. DTS(A). Dia. EE216. Lot No. 30955 BREL York 1981–82. –/74. 29.4 t.
77048–77095. DTS(B). Dia. EE235 (*EE232). Lot No. 30956 York 1981–82. –/70. (* –/71). 29.3 t.

317 301	LS	A	*WN*	HE	77024	62661	71577	77048
317 302	LS	A	*WN*	HE	77001	62662	71578	77049
317 303	LS	A	*WN*	HE	77002	62663	71579	77050
317 304	LS	A	*WN*	HE	77003	62664	71580	77051
317 305	LS	A	*WN*	HE	77004	62665	71581	77052
317 306	LS	A	*WN*	HE	77005	62666	71582	77053
317 307	LS	A	*WN*	HE	77006	62667	71583	77054
317 311	LS	A	*WN*	HE	77010	62697	71587	77058
317 312	LS	A	*WN*	HE	77011	62672	71588	77059
317 313	LS	A	*WN*	HE	77012	62673	71589	77060
317 315	N	A	*WN*	HE	77014	62675	71591	77062
317 316	N	A	*WN*	HE	77015	62676	71592	77063
317 317	N	A	*WN*	HE	77016	62677	71593	77064
317 318	N	A	*WN*	HE	77017	62678	71594	77065
317 320	N	A	*WN*	HE	77019	62680	71596	77067
317 321	N	A	*WN*	HE	77020	62681	71597	77068
317 324	N	A	*WN*	HE	77023	62684	71600	77071
317 325	N	A	*WN*	HE	77000	62685	71601	77072
317 326	N	A	*WN*	HE	77025	62686	71602	77073

317 327		**N**	A	*WN*	HE	77026	62687	71603	77074
317 328		**N**	A	*WN*	HE	77027	62688	71604	77075
317 330		**N**	A	*WN*	HE	77043	62704	71606	77077
317 331		**N**	A	*WN*	HE	77030	62691	71607	77078
317 333		**N**	A	*WN*	HE	77032	62693	71609	77080
317 334		**N**	A	*WN*	HE	77033	62694	71610	77081
317 335		**N**	A	*WN*	HE	77034	62695	71611	77082
317 336		**N**	A	*WN*	HE	77035	62696	71612	77083
317 337	*	**N**	A	*WN*	HE	77036	62671	71613	77084
317 338	*	**N**	A	*WN*	HE	77037	62698	71614	77085
317 339	*	**N**	A	*WN*	HE	77038	62699	71615	77086
317 340	*	**N**	A	*WN*	HE	77039	62700	71616	77087
317 341	*	**N**	A	*WN*	HE	77040	62701	71617	77088
317 342	*	**N**	A	*WN*	HE	77041	62702	71618	77089
317 343	*	**N**	A	*WN*	HE	77042	62703	71619	77090
317 344	*	**N**	A	*WN*	HE	77029	62690	71620	77091
317 345	*	**N**	A	*WN*	HE	77044	62705	71621	77092
317 346	*	**N**	A	*WN*	HE	77045	62706	71622	77093
317 347	*	**N**	A	*WN*	HE	77046	62707	71623	77094
317 348	*	**N**	A	*WN*	HE	77047	62708	71624	77095

Class 317/6. Convection heating. DTS–PMS–ATS–DTC.

62846–62865. PMS. Dia. EC222. Lot No. 30996 BREL York 1985–86. Refurbished Railcare Wolverton 1998–99. –/70. 50.1 t.

62886–62889. PMS. Dia. EC222. Lot No. 31009 BREL York 1987. Refurbished Railcare Wolverton 1998–99. –/70. 50.1 t.

71734–71753. ATS. Dia. EH247. Lot No. 30997 BREL York 1985–86. Refurbished Railcare Wolverton 1998–99. –/62 2T. 28.8 t.

71762–71765. ATS. Dia. EH247. Lot No. 31010 BREL York 1987. Refurbished Railcare Wolverton 1998–99. –/62 2T. 28.8 t.

77200–77219. DTS. Dia. EE247. Lot No. 30994 BREL York 1985–86. Refurbished Railcare Wolverton 1998–99. –/64. 29.3 t.

77280–77283. DTS. Dia. EE247. Lot No. 31007 BREL York 1987. Refurbished Railcare Wolverton 1998–99. –/64. 29.3 t.

77220–77239. DTC. Dia. EE375. Lot No. 30995 BREL York 1985–86. Refurbished Railcare Wolverton 1998–99. 24/48. 29.3 t.

77284–77287. DTC. Dia. EE375. Lot No. 31008 BREL York 1987. Refurbished Railcare Wolverton 1998–99. 24/48. 29.3 t.

317 649	**WN**	A	*WN*	HE	77200	62846	71734	77220
317 650	**WN**	A	*WN*	HE	77201	62847	71735	77221
317 651	**WN**	A	*WN*	HE	77202	62848	71736	77222
317 652	**WN**	A	*WN*	HE	77203	62849	71739	77223
317 653	**WN**	A	*WN*	HE	77204	62850	71738	77224
317 654	**WN**	A	*WN*	HE	77205	62851	71737	77225
317 655	**WN**	A	*WN*	HE	77206	62852	71740	77226
317 656	**WN**	A	*WN*	HE	77207	62853	71742	77227
317 657	**WN**	A	*WN*	HE	77208	62854	71741	77228
317 658	**WN**	A	*WN*	HE	77209	62855	71743	77229
317 659	**WN**	A	*WN*	HE	77210	62856	71744	77230
317 660	**WN**	A	*WN*	HE	77211	62857	71745	77231

317 661	**WN**	A	*WN*	HE	77212	62858	71746	77232
317 662	**WN**	A	*WN*	HE	77213	62859	71747	77233
317 663	**WN**	A	*WN*	HE	77214	62860	71748	77234
317 664	**WN**	A	*WN*	HE	77215	62861	71749	77235
317 665	**WN**	A	*WN*	HE	77216	62862	71750	77236
317 666	**WN**	A	*WN*	HE	77217	62863	71752	77237
317 667	**WN**	A	*WN*	HE	77218	62864	71751	77238
317 668	**WN**	A	*WN*	HE	77219	62865	71753	77239
317 669	**WN**	A	*WN*	HE	77280	62886	71762	77284
317 670	**WN**	A	*WN*	HE	77281	62887	71763	77285
317 671	**WN**	A	*WN*	HE	77282	62888	71764	77286
317 672	**WN**	A	*WN*	HE	77283	62889	71765	77287

Class 317/7. Refurbished units equipped with vertical luggage stacks for use on 'Stansted Express' services between London Liverpool Street and Stansted Airport. 'Express' Stock. Air conditioning. DTS–PMS–ATS–DTC.

62661–62708. PMS. Dia. EC232. Lot No. 30958 BREL York 1981-82. Refurbished Railcare Wolverton 2000. –/62. 49.8 t.
71577–71624. ATS. Dia. EH256. Lot No. 30957 BREL Derby 1981-82. Refurbished Railcare Wolverton 2000. –/42 + 4. 1W 1T 1TD. 28.8 t.
77000–77047. DTS. Dia. EE285. Lot No. 30955 BREL York 1981-82. Refurbished Railcare Wolverton 2000. –/52 plus catering point. 29.4 t.
77048–77095. DTC. Dia. EE301. Lot No. 30956 York 1981–82. Refurbished Railcare Wolverton 2000. 22/16 plus catering point. 29.3 t.

Number Former No.

317 708	317 308	**SX**	A	*WN*	HE	77007	62668	71584	77055
317 709	317 309	**SX**	A	*WN*	HE	77008	62669	71585	77056
317 710	317 310	**SX**	A	*WN*	HE	77009	62670	71586	77057
317 714	317 314	**SX**	A	*WN*	HE	77013	62674	71590	77061
317 719	317 319	**SX**	A	*WN*	HE	77018	62679	71595	77066
317 722	317 392	**SX**	A	*WN*	HE	77021	62682	71598	77069
317 723	317 393	**SX**	A	*WN*	HE	77022	62683	71599	77070
317 729	317 329	**SX**	A	*WN*	HE	77028	62689	71605	77076
317 732	317 332	**SX**	A	*WN*	HE	77031	62692	71608	77079

CLASS 318   BREL

DTS(B)–PMS–DTS(A). Gangwayed throughout. Disc brakes.

Construction: Steel.
Traction Motors: Four Brush TM 2141 of 268 kW each.
Dimensions: 20.13 (DTS) or 20.18 (PMS) x 2.82 x 3.77 m.
Maximum Speed: 90 m.p.h.   **Doors:** Power operated sliding.
Couplers: Tightlock.   **Bogies:** BREL BP20/BT13.
Multiple Working: Classes 313–323.

Notes: All equipped with controlled emission toilet to permit use on the Argyle Line.
*‡ – Conductor-operated door controls (to permit use on Edinburgh–North Berwick services).

62866–62885. PMS. Dia. EC207. Lot No. 30998 BREL York 1985–86. –/79. 50.9 t.
62890. PMS. Dia. EC207. Lot No. 31019 BREL York 1987. –/79. 50.9 t.
77240–77259. DTS(A). Dia. EE227. Lot No. 30999 BREL York 1985–86. –/66 1T
   1W. 30.0 t.
77260–77279. DTS(B). Dia. EE228. Lot No. 31000 BREL York 1985–86. –/71
   (†‡ –/74). 26.6 t.
77288. DTS(A). Dia. EE227. Lot No. 31020 BREL York 1987. –/66 1T 1W. 30.0 t.
77289. DTS(B). Dia. EE228. Lot No. 31021 BREL York 1987. –/71. 26.6 t.

318 250		**SC**	H	*SR*	GW	77260	62866	77240
318 251	†	**SC**	H	*SR*	GW	77261	62867	77241
318 252	‡	**SC**	H	*SR*	GW	77262	62868	77242
318 253		**SC**	H	*SR*	GW	77263	62869	77243
318 254		**SC**	H	*SR*	GW	77264	62870	77244
318 255		**SC**	H	*SR*	GW	77265	62871	77245
318 256	*	**SC**	H	*SR*	GW	77266	62872	77246
318 257		**SC**	H	*SR*	GW	77267	62873	77247
318 258		**SC**	H	*SR*	GW	77268	62874	77248
318 259		**SC**	H	*SR*	GW	77269	62875	77249
318 260		**SC**	H	*SR*	GW	77270	62876	77250
318 261		**SC**	H	*SR*	GW	77271	62877	77251
318 262		**SC**	H	*SR*	GW	77272	62878	77252
318 263		**SC**	H	*SR*	GW	77273	62879	77253
318 264		**SC**	H	*SR*	GW	77274	62880	77254
318 265		**SC**	H	*SR*	GW	77275	62881	77255
318 266		**SC**	H	*SR*	GW	77276	62882	77256
318 267		**SC**	H	*SR*	GW	77277	62883	77257
318 268		**SC**	H	*SR*	GW	77278	62884	77258
318 269		**SC**	H	*SR*	GW	77279	62885	77259
318 270		**SC**	H	*SR*	GW	77289	62890	77288

Names (carried on PMS):

318 256   North Berwick Flyer 1850 – 2000
318 259   Citizens' Network |318 266   STRATHCLYDER

CLASS 319   BREL

Various formations, see below. Gangwayed within unit. End doors. Disc brakes.

Construction: Steel.
Supply System: 25 kV 50 Hz a.c. overhead and/or 750 V d.c. third rail.
Traction Motors: Four GEC G315BZ of 247.5 kW each.
Dimensions: 20.13 (DTC & DTS) or 20.18 (ATS & PMS) x 2.82 x 3.77 m.
Maximum Speed: 100 m.p.h.   **Doors:** Power operated sliding.
Couplers: Tightlock.   **Bogies:** BREL P7-4/T3-7.
Multiple Working: Classes 313–323.

Advertising Liveries:
• 319 214/215/218/220 'Family Zone'.
• 319 422 'Luton Airport Parkway'.

Class 319/0. DTS(A)–PMS–ATS–DTS(B). 25 kV 50 Hz a.c. overhead or 750 V d.c. third rail supply.

Note: Two (non specified) units are hired from Connex South Central to Thameslink Rail on a daily basis.

62891–62903. PMS. Dia. EC209. Lot No. 31023 BREL York 1987–8. –/77 2T. 51.0 t.

71772–71784. ATS. Dia. EH234. Lot No. 31024 BREL York 1987–8. –/77 2T. 31.0 t.

77290–77314 (Even numbers). DTS(B). Dia. EE234. Lot No. 31025 BREL York 1987–8. –/78. 30.0 t.

77291–77315 (Odd numbers). DTS(A). Dia. EE233. Lot No. 31022 BREL York 1987–8. –/82. 30.0 t.

319 001	**CX**	P	*SC*	SU	77291	62891	71772	77290
319 002	**CX**	P	*SC*	SU	77293	62892	71773	77292
319 003	**CX**	P	*SC*	SU	77295	62893	71774	77294
319 004	**CX**	P	*SC*	SU	77297	62894	71775	77296
319 005	**CX**	P	*SC*	SU	77299	62895	71776	77298
319 006	**CX**	P	*SC*	SU	77301	62896	71777	77300
319 007	**CX**	P	*SC*	SU	77303	62897	71778	77302
319 008	**CX**	P	*SC*	SU	77305	62898	71779	77304
319 009	**CX**	P	*SC*	SU	77307	62899	71780	77306
319 010	**CX**	P	*SC*	SU	77309	62900	71781	77308
319 011	**CX**	P	*SC*	SU	77311	62901	71782	77310
319 012	**CX**	P	*SC*	SU	77313	62902	71783	77312
319 013	**CX**	P	*SC*	SU	77315	62903	71784	77314

Names (carried on ATS):

319 005	Partnership For Progress	319 011	John Ruskin College
319 008	Cheriton	319 013	The Surrey Hills
319 009	Coquelles		

Class 319/2. DTS–PMB–ATS–DTC. 750 V d.c. third rail with provision for 25 kV a.c. 50 Hz overhead supply. 'Express' stock operated by Connex South Central on the London Victoria–Brighton route.

62904–62910. PMB. Dia. EN262. Lot No. 31023 BREL York 1987–8. Refurbished Railcare Wolverton 1996. –/60 2T. 51.0 t.

71785–71791. ATS. Dia. EH212. Lot No. 31024 BREL York 1987–8. Refurbished Railcare Wolverton 1996. –/52 1T 1TD. 31.0 t.

77316–77328 (Even numbers). DTC. Dia. EE374. Lot No. 31025 BREL York 1987–8. Refurbished Railcare Wolverton 1996. 18/36. 29.0 t.

77317–77329 (Odd numbers). DTS. Dia. EE244. Lot No. 31022 BREL York 1987–8. Refurbished Railcare Wolverton 1996. –/64. 29.7 t.

319 214	**AL**	P	*SC*	SU	77317	62904	71785	77316
319 215	**AL**	P	*SC*	SU	77319	62905	71786	77318
319 216	**CX**	P	*SC*	SU	77321	62906	71787	77320
319 217	**CX**	P	*SC*	SU	77323	62907	71788	77322
319 218	**AL**	P	*SC*	SU	77325	62908	71789	77324
319 219	**CX**	P	*SC*	SU	77327	62909	71790	77326
319 220	**AL**	P	*SC*	SU	77329	62910	71791	77328

Names (carried on ATS):

319 215   London |319 218 Croydon
319 217   Brighton

Class 319/3. DTS(A)–PMS–ATS–DTS(B). 25 kV 50 Hz a.c. overhead or 750 V d.c. third rail supply. Operated by Thameslink Rail on the 'City Metro' Luton–Sutton route.

63043–63062, 63098–63098. PMS. Dia. EC214. Lot No. 31064 BREL York 1990. –/79. 50.3 t.

71929–71948, 71979–71984. ATS. Dia. EH238. Lot No. 31065 BREL York 1990. –/74 2T. 33.1 t.

77458–77496, 77974–77984 (Even numbers). DTS(B). Dia. EE240. Lot No. 31066 BREL York 1990. –/78. 29.7 t.

77459–77497, 77973–77983 (Odd numbers). DTS(A). Dia. EE240. Lot No. 31063 BREL York 1990. –/70. 29.0 t.

319 361	**TR**	P	*TR*	SU	77459	63043	71929	77458
319 362	**TR**	P	*TR*	SU	77461	63044	71930	77460
319 363	**TR**	P	*TR*	SU	77463	63045	71931	77462
319 364	**TR**	P	*TR*	SU	77465	63046	71932	77464
319 365	**TR**	P	*TR*	SU	77467	63047	71933	77466
319 366	**TR**	P	*TR*	SU	77469	63048	71934	77468
319 367	**TR**	P	*TR*	SU	77471	63049	71935	77470
319 368	**TR**	P	*TR*	SU	77473	63050	71936	77472
319 369	**TR**	P	*TR*	SU	77475	63051	71937	77474
319 370	**TR**	P	*TR*	SU	77477	63052	71938	77476
319 371	**TR**	P	*TR*	SU	77479	63053	71939	77478
319 372	**TR**	P	*TR*	SU	77481	63054	71940	77480
319 373	**TR**	P	*TR*	SU	77483	63055	71941	77482
319 374	**TR**	P	*TR*	SU	77485	63056	71942	77484
319 375	**TR**	P	*TR*	SU	77487	63057	71943	77486
319 376	**TR**	P	*TR*	SU	77489	63058	71944	77488
319 377	**TR**	P	*TR*	SU	77491	63059	71945	77490
319 378	**TR**	P	*TR*	SU	77493	63060	71946	77492
319 379	**TR**	P	*TR*	SU	77495	63061	71947	77494
319 380	**TR**	P	*TR*	SU	77497	63062	71948	77496
319 381	**TR**	P	*TR*	SU	77973	63093	71979	77974
319 382	**TR**	P	*TR*	SU	77975	63094	71980	77976
319 383	**TR**	P	*TR*	SU	77977	63095	71981	77978
319 384	**TR**	P	*TR*	SU	77979	63096	71982	77980
319 385	**TR**	P	*TR*	SU	77981	63097	71983	77982
319 386	**TR**	P	*TR*	SU	77983	63098	71984	77984

Class 319/4. DTC–PMS–ATS–DTS. 25 kV 50 Hz a.c. overhead or 750 V d.c. third rail supply. Operated by Thameslink Rail on the 'Cityflier' Bedford–Gatwick Airport–Brighton route.

62911–62936. PMS. Dia. EC209. Lot No. 31023 BREL York 1987–88. –/77 2T. 51.0 t.

62961–62974. PMS. Dia. EC209. Lot No. 31039 BREL York 1988. –/77 2T. 51.0 t.

71792–71817. ATS. Dia. EH234. Lot No. 31024 BREL York 1987–88. –/77 2T. 34.0 t.

71866–71879. ATS. Dia. EH234. Lot No. 31040 BREL York 1988. –/77 2T. 34.0 t.
77330–77380 (Even numbers). DTS. Dia. EE234. Lot No. 31025 BREL York 1987–88. –/78. 30.0 t.
77331–77381 (Odd numbers). DTC. Dia. EE314. Lot No. 31022 BREL York 1987–88. 12/54. 30.0 t.
77430–77456 (Even numbers). DTS. Dia. EE234. Lot No. 31041 BREL York 1988. –/74. 30.0 t.
77431–77457 (Odd numbers). DTC. Dia. EE314. Lot No. 31038 BREL York 1988. 12/54. 30.0 t.

319 421	**TR**	P	*TR*	SU	77331	62911	71792	77330
319 422	**AL**	P	*TR*	SU	77333	62912	71793	77332
319 423	**TR**	P	*TR*	SU	77335	62913	71794	77334
319 424	**TR**	P	*TR*	SU	77337	62914	71795	77336
319 425	**TR**	P	*TR*	SU	77339	62915	71796	77338
319 426	**TR**	P	*TR*	SU	77341	62916	71797	77340
319 427	**TR**	P	*TR*	SU	77343	62917	71798	77342
319 428	**TR**	P	*TR*	SU	77345	62918	71799	77344
319 429	**TR**	P	*TR*	SU	77347	62919	71800	77346
319 430	**TR**	P	*TR*	SU	77349	62920	71801	77348
319 431	**TR**	P	*TR*	SU	77351	62921	71802	77350
319 432	**TR**	P	*TR*	SU	77353	62922	71803	77352
319 433	**TR**	P	*TR*	SU	77355	62923	71804	77354
319 434	**TR**	P	*TR*	SU	77357	62924	71805	77356
319 435	**TR**	P	*TR*	SU	77359	62925	71806	77358
319 436	**TR**	P	*TR*	SU	77361	62926	71807	77360
319 437	**TR**	P	*TR*	SU	77363	62927	71808	77362
319 438	**TR**	P	*TR*	SU	77365	62928	71809	77364
319 439	**TR**	P	*TR*	SU	77367	62929	71810	77366
319 440	**TR**	P	*TR*	SU	77369	62930	71811	77368
319 441	**TR**	P	*TR*	SU	77371	62931	71812	77370
319 442	**TR**	P	*TR*	SU	77373	62932	71813	77372
319 443	**TR**	P	*TR*	SU	77375	62933	71814	77374
319 444	**TR**	P	*TR*	SU	77377	62934	71815	77376
319 445	**TR**	P	*TR*	SU	77379	62935	71816	77378
319 446	**TR**	P	*TR*	SU	77381	62936	71817	77380
319 447	**TR**	P	*TR*	SU	77431	62961	71866	77430
319 448	**TR**	P	*TR*	SU	77433	62962	71867	77432
319 449	**TR**	P	*TR*	SU	77435	62963	71868	77434
319 450	**TR**	P	*TR*	SU	77437	62964	71869	77436
319 451	**TR**	P	*TR*	SU	77439	62965	71870	77438
319 452	**TR**	P	*TR*	SU	77441	62966	71871	77440
319 453	**TR**	P	*TR*	SU	77443	62967	71872	77442
319 454	**TR**	P	*TR*	SU	77445	62968	71873	77444
319 455	**TR**	P	*TR*	SU	77447	62969	71874	77446
319 456	**TR**	P	*TR*	SU	77449	62970	71875	77448
319 457	**TR**	P	*TR*	SU	77451	62971	71876	77450
319 458	**TR**	P	*TR*	SU	77453	62972	71877	77452
319 459	**TR**	P	*TR*	SU	77455	62973	71878	77454
319 460	**TR**	P	*TR*	SU	77457	62974	71879	77456

CLASS 320   BREL

DTS(A)–PMS–DTS(B). Gangwayed within unit. Disc brakes.

Construction: Steel.
Traction Motors: Four Brush TM2141 of 268 kW each.
Dimensions: 19.95 (DTS) or 19.92 (PMS) x 2.82 x 3.78 m.
Maximum Speed: 75 m.p.h.   **Doors:** Power operated sliding.
Couplers: Tightlock.   **Bogies:** BREL P7-4/T3-7.
Multiple Working: Classes 313–323.

63021–63042. PMS. Dia. EC212. Lot No. 31062 BREL York 1990. –/77. 52.1 t.
77899–77920. DTS(A). Dia. EE238. Lot No. 31060 BREL York 1990. –/77. 30.7 t.
77921–77942. DTS(B). Dia. EE239. Lot No. 31061 BREL York 1990. –/76 31.7 t.

320 301	S	H	*SR*	GW	77899	63021	77921
320 302	S	H	*SR*	GW	77900	63022	77922
320 303	S	H	*SR*	GW	77901	63023	77923
320 304	S	H	*SR*	GW	77902	63024	77924
320 305	S	H	*SR*	GW	77903	63025	77925
320 306	SC	H	*SR*	GW	77904	63026	77926
320 307	SC	H	*SR*	GW	77905	63027	77927
320 308	SC	H	*SR*	GW	77906	63028	77928
320 309	SC	H	*SR*	GW	77907	63029	77929
320 310	SC	H	*SR*	GW	77908	63030	77930
320 311	SC	H	*SR*	GW	77909	63031	77931
320 312	SC	H	*SR*	GW	77910	63032	77932
320 313	SC	H	*SR*	GW	77911	63033	77933
320 314	SC	H	*SR*	GW	77912	63034	77934
320 315	SC	H	*SR*	GW	77913	63035	77935
320 316	SC	H	*SR*	GW	77914	63036	77936
320 317	SC	H	*SR*	GW	77915	63037	77937
320 318	SC	H	*SR*	GW	77916	63038	77938
320 319	SC	H	*SR*	GW	77917	63039	77939
320 320	SC	H	*SR*	GW	77918	63040	77940
320 321	SC	H	*SR*	GW	77919	63041	77941
320 322	SC	H	*SR*	GW	77920	63042	77942

Names (carried on PMS):

320 305	GLASGOW SCHOOL OF ART 1844–150–1994
320 306	Model Rail Scotland
320 308	High Road 20th Anniversary 2000
320 309	Radio Clyde 25th Anniversary
320 311	The Royal College of Physicians and Surgeons of Glasgow
320 321	The Rt. Hon. John Smith, QC, MP
320 322	Festive Glasgow Orchid

CLASS 321   BREL

Various formations, see below. Gangwayed within unit. Disc brakes.

Construction: Steel.
Traction Motors: Four Brush TM2141 of 268 kW each.
Dimensions: 19.95 (DTC & DTS) or 19.92 (ATS & PMS) x 2.82 x 3.78 m.
Maximum Speed: 100 m.p.h.   **Doors:** Power operated sliding.
Couplers: Tightlock.   **Bogies:** BREL P7-4/T3-7.
Multiple Working: Classes 313–323.

Advertising Liveries:
• 321 319/327/328/329/330 'Braintree Freeport'.

Class 321/3. DTC–PMS–ATS–DTS. Small first class area.

62975–63020, 63105–63124. PMS. Dia. EC210. Lot No. 31054 BREL York 1988–90. –/79 (* –/82). 51.5 t.
71880–71925, 71991–72010. ATS. Dia. EH235. Lot No. 31055 BREL York 1988–90. –/74 (* –/75). 2T. 28.0 t.
77853–77898, 78280–78299. DTS. Dia. EE236. Lot No. 31056 BREL York 1988–90. –/78. 29.1 t.
78049–78094, 78131–78150. DTC. Dia. EE308. Lot No. 31053 BREL York 1988–90. 12/56 (* 16/57). 29.3 t.

321 301	*	GE	H	GE	IL	78049	62975	71880	77853
321 302	*	GE	H	GE	IL	78050	62976	71881	77854
321 303	*	GE	H	GE	IL	78051	62977	71882	77855
321 304	*	GE	H	GE	IL	78052	62978	71883	77856
321 305	*	GE	H	GE	IL	78053	62979	71884	77857
321 306	*	GE	H	GE	IL	78054	62980	71885	77858
321 307	*	GE	H	GE	IL	78055	62981	71886	77859
321 308	*	GE	H	GE	IL	78056	62982	71887	77860
321 309	*	GE	H	GE	IL	78057	62983	71888	77861
321 310	*	GE	H	GE	IL	78058	62984	71889	77862
321 311	*	GE	H	GE	IL	78059	62985	71890	77863
321 312	*	GE	H	GE	IL	78060	62986	71891	77864
321 313		GE	H	GE	IL	78061	62987	71892	77865
321 314		GE	H	GE	IL	78062	62988	71893	77866
321 315		GE	H	GE	IL	78063	62989	71894	77867
321 316		GE	H	GE	IL	78064	62990	71895	77868
321 317		GE	H	GE	IL	78065	62991	71896	77869
321 318		GE	H	GE	IL	78066	62992	71897	77870
321 319		AL	H	GE	IL	78067	62993	71898	77871
321 320		GE	H	GE	IL	78068	62994	71899	77872
321 321	*	GE	H	GE	IL	78069	62995	71900	77873
321 322		GE	H	GE	IL	78070	62996	71901	77874
321 323		GE	H	GE	IL	78071	62997	71902	77875
321 324		GE	H	GE	IL	78072	62998	71903	77876
321 325		GE	H	GE	IL	78073	62999	71904	77877
321 326		GE	H	GE	IL	78074	63000	71905	77878
321 327		AL	H	GE	IL	78075	63001	71906	77879
321 328		AL	H	GE	IL	78076	63002	71907	77880

321 329	**AL**	H	*GE*	IL	78077	63003	71908	77881
321 330	**AL**	H	*GE*	IL	78078	63004	71909	77882
321 331	**GE**	H	*GE*	IL	78079	63005	71910	77883
321 332	**GE**	H	*GE*	IL	78080	63006	71911	77884
321 333	**GE**	H	*GE*	IL	78081	63007	71912	77885
321 334	**GE**	H	*GE*	IL	78082	63008	71913	77886
321 335	**GE**	H	*GE*	IL	78083	63009	71914	77887
321 336	**GE**	H	*GE*	IL	78084	63010	71915	77888
321 337	**GE**	H	*GE*	IL	78085	63011	71916	77889
321 338	**GE**	H	*GE*	IL	78086	63012	71917	77890
321 339	**GE**	H	*GE*	IL	78087	63013	71918	77891
321 340	**GE**	H	*GE*	IL	78088	63014	71919	77892
321 341	**GE**	H	*GE*	IL	78089	63015	71920	77893
321 342	**GE**	H	*GE*	IL	78090	63016	71921	77894
321 343	**GE**	H	*GE*	IL	78091	63017	71922	77895
321 344	**GE**	H	*GE*	IL	78092	63018	71923	77896
321 345	**GE**	H	*GE*	IL	78093	63019	71924	77897
321 346	**GE**	H	*GE*	IL	78094	63020	71925	77898
321 347	**GE**	H	*GE*	IL	78131	63105	71991	78280
321 348	**GE**	H	*GE*	IL	78132	63106	71992	78281
321 349	**GE**	H	*GE*	IL	78133	63107	71993	78282
321 350	**GE**	H	*GE*	IL	78134	63108	71994	78283
321 351	**GE**	H	*GE*	IL	78135	63109	71995	78284
321 352	**GE**	H	*GE*	IL	78136	63110	71996	78285
321 353	**GE**	H	*GE*	IL	78137	63111	71997	78286
321 354	**GE**	H	*GE*	IL	78138	63112	71998	78287
321 355	**GE**	H	*GE*	IL	78139	63113	71999	78288
321 356	**GE**	H	*GE*	IL	78140	63114	72000	78289
321 357	**GE**	H	*GE*	IL	78141	63115	72001	78290
321 358	**GE**	H	*GE*	IL	78142	63116	72002	78291
321 359	**GE**	H	*GE*	IL	78143	63117	72003	78292
321 360	**GE**	H	*GE*	IL	78144	63118	72004	78293
321 361	**GE**	H	*GE*	IL	78145	63119	72005	78294
321 362	**GE**	H	*GE*	IL	78146	63120	72006	78295
321 363	**GE**	H	*GE*	IL	78147	63121	72007	78296
321 364	**GE**	H	*GE*	IL	78148	63122	72008	78297
321 365	**GE**	H	*GE*	IL	78149	63123	72009	78298
321 366	**GE**	H	*GE*	IL	78150	63124	72010	78299

Names (carried on ATS):

321 312   Southend-on-Sea
321 321   NSPCC ESSEX FULL STOP
321 334   Amsterdam
321 336   GEOFFREY FREEMAN ALLEN
321 351   GURKHA

Class 321/4. DTC–PMS–ATS–DTS. Large first class area. All First Great Eastern operated DTC have 12 first class seats declassfied.

Advertising Livery:
• 321 428 'Birmingham Daytripper Ticket'.

63063–63092, 63099–63104, 63125–63136. PMS. Dia. EC210. Lot No. 31068 BREL York 1989–90. –/79. 51.5 t.
63082². PMS. Dia. EC210. Adtranz Crewe 1998. –/79. 51.5 t.
71949–71978, 71985–71990, 72011–72022. ATS. Dia. EH235. Lot No. 31069 BREL York 1989–90. –/74 2T. 28.0 t.
71966². ATS. Dia. EH235. Adtranz Crewe 1998. –/74 2T. 28.0 t.
77943–77972, 78274–78279, 78300–78311. DTS. Dia. EE236. Lot No. 31070 BREL York 1989–90. –/78. 29.1 t.
77960². DTS. Dia. EE236. Adtranz Crewe 1998. –/78. 29.1 t.
78095–78130/151–78162. DTC. Dia. EE309. Lot No. 31067 BREL York 1989–90. 28/40. 29.3 t.
78114². DTC. Dia. EE309. Adtranz Crewe 1998. 28/40. 29.3 t.

321 401	**SL**	H	*SL*	BY	78095	63063	71949	77943
321 402	**SL**	H	*SL*	BY	78096	63064	71950	77944
321 403	**SL**	H	*SL*	BY	78097	63065	71951	77945
321 404	**SL**	H	*SL*	BY	78098	63066	71952	77946
321 405	**N**	H	*SL*	BY	78099	63067	71953	77947
321 406	**SL**	H	*SL*	BY	78100	63068	71954	77948
321 407	**N**	H	*SL*	BY	78101	63069	71955	77949
321 408	**N**	H	*SL*	BY	78102	63070	71956	77950
321 409	**N**	H	*SL*	BY	78103	63071	71957	77951
321 410	**N**	H	*SL*	BY	78104	63072	71958	77952
321 411	**SL**	H	*SL*	BY	78105	63073	71959	77953
321 412	**N**	H	*SL*	BY	78106	63074	71960	77954
321 413	**SL**	H	*SL*	BY	78107	63075	71961	77955
321 414	**N**	H	*SL*	BY	78108	63076	71962	77956
321 415	**N**	H	*SL*	BY	78109	63077	71963	77957
321 416	**N**	H	*SL*	BY	78110	63078	71964	77958
321 417	**N**	H	*SL*	BY	78111	63079	71965	77959
321 418	**N**	H	*SL*	BY	78112	63080	71968	77962
321 419	**N**	H	*SL*	BY	78113	63081	71967	77961
321 420	**SL**	H	*SL*	BY	78114²	63082²	71966²	77960²
321 421	**SL**	H	*SL*	BY	78115	63083	71969	77963
321 422	**N**	H	*SL*	BY	78116	63084	71970	77964
321 423	**N**	H	*SL*	BY	78117	63085	71971	77965
321 424	**N**	H	*SL*	BY	78118	63086	71972	77966
321 425	**N**	H	*SL*	BY	78119	63087	71973	77967
321 426	**N**	H	*SL*	BY	78120	63088	71974	77968
321 427	**N**	H	*SL*	BY	78121	63089	71975	77969
321 428	**AL**	H	*SL*	BY	78122	63090	71976	77970
321 429	**SL**	H	*SL*	BY	78123	63091	71977	77971
321 430	**SL**	H	*SL*	BY	78124	63092	71978	77972
321 431	**SL**	H	*SL*	BY	78151	63125	72011	78300
321 432	**SL**	H	*SL*	BY	78152	63126	72012	78301
321 433	**SL**	H	*SL*	BY	78153	63127	72013	78302

321 434	**SL**	H	*SL*	BY	78154	63128	72014	78303
321 435	**SL**	H	*SL*	BY	78155	63129	72015	78304
321 436	**SL**	H	*SL*	BY	78156	63130	72016	78305
321 437	**SL**	H	*SL*	BY	78157	63131	72017	78306
321 438	**GE**	H	*GE*	IL	78158	63132	72018	78307
321 439	**GE**	H	*GE*	IL	78159	63133	72019	78308
321 440	**GE**	H	*GE*	IL	78160	63134	72020	78309
321 441	**GE**	H	*GE*	IL	78161	63135	72021	78310
321 442	**GE**	H	*GE*	IL	78162	63136	72022	78311
321 443	**GE**	H	*GE*	IL	78125	63099	71985	78274
321 444	**GE**	H	*GE*	IL	78126	63100	71986	78275
321 445	**GE**	H	*GE*	IL	78127	63101	71987	78276
321 446	**GE**	H	*GE*	IL	78128	63102	71988	78277
321 447	**GE**	H	*GE*	IL	78129	63103	71989	78278
321 448	**GE**	H	*GE*	IL	78130	63104	71990	78279

Names (carried on ATS):

321 407	HERTFORDSHIRE WRVS
321 439	Chelmsford Cathedral Festival
321 444	Essex Lifeboats

Class 321/9. DTS(A)–PMS–ATS–DTS(B). Leased by West Yorkshire PTE from International Bank of Scotland. Managed by Porterbrook Leasing Company.

63153–63155. PMS. Dia. EC216. Lot No. 31109 BREL York 1991. –/79. 51.5 t.
72128–72130. ATS. Dia. EH240. Lot No. 31110 BREL York 1991. –/74 2T. 28.0 t.
77990–77992. DTS(A). Dia. EE277. Lot No. 31108 BREL York 1991. –/78. 29.3 t.
77993–77995. DTS(B). Dia. EE277. Lot No. 31111 BREL York 1991. –/78. 29.1 t.

321 901	**WY**	P	*NS*	NL	77990	63153	72128	77993
321 902	**WY**	P	*NS*	NL	77991	63154	72129	77994
321 903	**WY**	P	*NS*	NL	77992	63155	72130	77995

CLASS 322   BREL

DTC–PMS–ATS–DTS. Gangwayed within unit. Disc brakes.

Construction: Steel.
Traction Motors: Four Brush TM2141 of 268 kW each.
Dimensions: 19.83 (DTC & DTS) or 19.92 (ATS & PMS) x 2.82 x 3.78 m.
Maximum Speed: 100 m.p.h.   **Doors:** Power operated sliding.
Couplers: Tightlock.   **Bogies:** BREL P7-4/T3-7.
Multiple Working: Classes 313–323.

Non-Standard Livery:
•   322 481–483 carry 'Stansted Skytrain' livery (grey with a yellow stripe).

Advertising Livery:
•   322 485 'Stansted Express'.

78163–78167. DTC. Dia. EE313. Lot No. 31094 BREL York 1990. 35/22. 30.4 t.
63137–63141. PMS. Dia. EC215. Lot No. 31092 BREL York 1990. –/70. 52.3 t.
72023–72027. ATS. Dia. EH239. Lot No. 31093 BREL York 1990. –/60 2T. 29.5 t.
77985–77989. DTS. Dia. EE242. Lot No. 31091 BREL York 1990. –/65. 29.8 t.

322 481	0	H	WN	HE	78163	72023	63137	77985
322 482	0	H	WN	HE	78164	72024	63138	77986
322 483	0	H	WN	HE	78165	72025	63139	77987
322 484	NW	H	WN	HE	78166	72026	63140	77988
322 485	AL	H	WN	HE	78167	72027	63141	77989

CLASS 323   HUNSLET-TPL

DMS(A)–PTS–DMS(B). Gangwayed within unit. Disc brakes.

Construction: Welded aluminium alloy.
Traction Motors: Four Holec DMKT 52/24 of 146 kW per motor car.
Dimensions: 23.37 (DMS) or 23.44 (PTS) x 2.80 x . m.
Maximum Speed: 90 m.p.h.   **Doors:** Power operated sliding plug.
Couplers: Tightlock.   **Bogies:** SRP BP62/BT52
Multiple Working: Classes 313–323.

64001–64043. DMS(A). Dia. EA272. Lot No. 31112 Hunslet TPL 1992–93. –/98
(* –/82). 41.0 t.
72201–72243. PTS. Dia. EH296. Lot No. 31113 Hunslet TPL 1992–93. –/88
(* –/80) 1T. 39.4 t.
65001–65043. DMS(B). Dia. EA272. Lot No. 31114 Hunslet TPL 1992–93. –/98
(* –/82). 41.0 t.

323 201		CO	P	CT	SI	64001	72201	65001
323 202		CO	P	CT	SI	64002	72202	65002
323 203		CO	P	CT	SI	64003	72203	65005
323 204		CO	P	CT	SI	64004	72204	65004
323 205		CO	P	CT	SI	64005	72205	65003
323 206		CO	P	CT	SI	64006	72206	65006
323 207		CO	P	CT	SI	64007	72207	65007
323 208		CO	P	CT	SI	64008	72208	65008
323 209		CO	P	CT	SI	64009	72209	65009
323 210		CO	P	CT	SI	64010	72210	65010
323 211		CO	P	CT	SI	64011	72211	65011
323 212		CO	P	CT	SI	64012	72212	65012
323 213		CO	P	CT	SI	64013	72213	65013
323 214		CO	P	CT	SI	64014	72214	65014
323 215		CO	P	CT	SI	64015	72215	65015
323 216		CO	P	CT	SI	64016	72216	65016
323 217		CO	P	CT	SI	64017	72217	65017
323 218		CO	P	CT	SI	64018	72218	65018
323 219		CO	P	CT	SI	64019	72219	65019
323 220		CO	P	CT	SI	64020	72220	65020
323 221		CO	P	CT	SI	64021	72221	65021
323 222		CO	P	CT	SI	64022	72222	65022
323 223	*	GM	P	NW	LG	64023	72223	65023
323 224	*	NW	P	NW	LG	64024	72224	65024
323 225	*	GM	P	NW	LG	64025	72225	65025
323 226		GM	P	NW	LG	64026	72226	65026
323 227		GM	P	NW	LG	64027	72227	65027
323 228		GM	P	NW	LG	64028	72228	65028

323 229	GM	P	NW	LG	64029	72229	65029
323 230	GM	P	NW	LG	64030	72230	65030
323 231	GM	P	NW	LG	64031	72231	65031
323 232	GM	P	NW	LG	64032	72232	65032
323 233	NW	P	NW	LG	64033	72233	65033
323 234	GM	P	NW	LG	64034	72234	65034
323 235	GM	P	NW	LG	64035	72235	65035
323 236	GM	P	NW	LG	64036	72236	65036
323 237	GM	P	NW	LG	64037	72237	65037
323 238	GM	P	NW	LG	64038	72238	65038
323 239	GM	P	NW	LG	64039	72239	65039
323 240	CO	P	CT	SI	64040	72340	65040
323 241	CO	P	CT	SI	64041	72341	65041
323 242	CO	P	CT	SI	64042	72342	65042
323 243	CO	P	CT	SI	64043	72343	65043

CLASS 325 ABB

DTV(A)–PMV–TAV–DTV(B). Royal Mail units. Non gangwayed. Disc brakes.

Construction: Steel.
Supply System: 25 kV 50 Hz a.c. overhead or 750 V d.c. third rail.
Traction Motors: Four GEC G315BZ of 247.5 kW each.
Dimensions: 20.35 x 2.82 x . m.   **Doors:** Roller shutter.
Maximum Speed: 100 m.p.h.   **Bogies:** ABB P7-4/T3-7.
Couplers: Buckeye.   **Multiple Working:** Within class only.

68300–68330 (Even numbers). DTV(A). Dia. EE503. Lot No. 31144 ABB Derby 1995. Load capacity 12.0 t. 29.2 t.
68340–68355. PMV. Dia. EC501. Lot No. 31145 ABB Derby 1995. Load capacity 12.0 t. 49.5 t.
68360–68375. TAV. Dia. EH501. Lot No. 31146 ABB Derby 1995. Load capacity 12.0 t. 30.7 t.
68301–68331 (Odd numbers). DTV(B). Dia. EE503. Lot No. 31144 ABB Derby 1995. Load capacity 12.0 t. 29.1 t.

325 001	RM	RM	E	CE	68300	68340	68360	68301
325 002	RM	RM	E	CE	68302	68341	68361	68303
325 003	RM	RM	E	CE	68304	68342	68362	68305
325 004	RM	RM	E	CE	68306	68343	68363	68307
325 005	RM	RM	E	CE	68308	68344	68364	68309
325 006	RM	RM	E	CE	68310	68345	68365	68311
325 007	RM	RM	E	CE	68312	68346	68366	68313
325 008	RM	RM	E	CE	68314	68347	68367	68315
325 009	RM	RM	E	CE	68316	68348	68368	68317
325 010	RM	RM	E	CE	68318	68349	68369	68319
325 011	RM	RM	E	CE	68320	68350	68370	68321
325 012	RM	RM	E	CE	68322	68351	68371	68323
325 013	RM	RM	E	CE	68324	68352	68372	68325
325 014	RM	RM	E	CE	68326	68353	68373	68327
325 015	RM	RM	E	CE	68328	68354	68374	68329
325 016	RM	RM	E	CE	68330	68355	68375	68331

Names (carried on one DTV per side):

325 002   Royal Mail North Wales and North West
325 006   John Grierson
325 008   Peter Howarth C.B.E.

CLASS 332   SIEMENS

Various formations, see below. 'Express' stock. Gangwayed within unit. Disc brakes. Air conditioned.

Construction: Steel.
Traction Motors: Two Siemens monomotors of 350 kW each per motor car.
Dimensions: 23.74 (DMF/DMS) or 23.15 (TS/PTS) x 2.75 x . m.
Maximum Speed: 160 km/h.   **Doors:** Power operated sliding plug.
Couplers: Scharfenberg.   **Bogies:** CAF.
Multiple Working: Within class only.

Advertising Liveries:
- 78402, 78405, 78406, 78408, 78410, 78412, 78414, 78416, 78419, 78421, 78423, 78425, 78427 all carry 'Vodafone' advertising livery. Other cars are livery **HE**.

Units 332 001–332 007. DMF–TS–PTS–DMS.

63400–63406. PTS. Dia. EH243. CAF 1997–98. –/44 1T 1W. 45.6 t.
72400–72413. TS. Dia. EH245. CAF 1997–98. –/56. 35.8 t.
78400–78412 (Even numbers). DMF. Dia. EA1??. CAF 1997–98. Converted 1998 from DMS. 26/–. 48.8 t.
78401–78413 (Odd numbers). DMS. Dia. EA243. CAF 1997–98. –/48. 48.8 t.

332 001	**HE**	HE	*HE*	OH	78400	72412	63400	78416
332 002	0	HE	*HE*	OH	78402	72409	63401	78403
332 003	0	HE	*HE*	OH	78404	72407	63402	78405
332 004	0	HE	*HE*	OH	78406	72405	63403	78407
332 005	0	HE	*HE*	OH	78408	72411	63404	78409
332 006	0	HE	*HE*	OH	78410	72410	63405	78411
332 007	0	HE	*HE*	OH	78412	72401	63406	78413

Units 332 008–332 014. DMS–TS–PTS–DMF.

63407–63413. PTS. Dia. EH243. CAF 1997–98. –/44 1T 1W. 45.6 t.
72400–72413. TS. Dia. EH245. CAF 1997–98. –/56. 35.8 t.
78414–78426 (Even numbers). DMS. Dia. EA244. CAF 1997–98. –/48. 48.8 t.
78415–78427 (Odd numbers). DMF. Dia. EA1??. CAF 1997–98. Converted 1998 from DMS. 14/– 1W. 48.8 t.

332 008	0	HE	*HE*	OH	78414	72413	63407	78415
332 009	**HE**	HE	*HE*	OH	78401	72400	63408	78417
332 010	0	HE	*HE*	OH	78418	72402	63409	78419
332 011	0	HE	*HE*	OH	78420	72403	63410	78421
332 012	0	HE	*HE*	OH	78422	72404	63411	78423
332 013	0	HE	*HE*	OH	78424	72408	63412	78425
332 014	0	HE	*HE*	OH	78426	72406	63413	78427

CLASS 333   SIEMENS

DMS(A)–PTS–DMS(B). Gangwayed within unit. Disc brakes. Air conditioned. Currently undergoing acceptance trials prior to entry into service with Northern Spirit. Eight TS cars are on order to augment eight 3-car units to 4-cars.

Construction: Steel.
Traction Motors: Two Siemens monomotors of 350 kW each per motor car.
Dimensions: 23.74 (DMS) or 23.15 (PTS) x 2.75 x 3.78 m.
Maximum Speed: 160 km/h.   **Doors:** Power operated sliding plug.
Couplers: Scharfenberg.   **Bogies:** CAF design.
Multiple Working: Within class only.

63461–63468. TS. Dia. EH2??. CAF 2001. –/102.
74461–74476. PTS. Dia. EH264. CAF 2000. –/73 (7). 1TD 2W. 46.7 t.
78451–78481 (Odd numbers). DMS(A). Dia. EA278. CAF 2000. –/90. 50.6 t.
78452–78482 (Even numbers). DMS(B). Dia. EA278. CAF 2000. –/90. 50.6 t.

333 001	**YN**	A		NL(S)	78451	74461	63461	78452
333 002	**YN**	A	*TC*	NL	78453	74462	63462	78454
333 003	**YN**	A	*TC*	NL	78455	74463	63463	78456
333 004	**YN**	A	*TC*	NL	78457	74464	63464	78458
333 005	**YN**	A	*TC*	NL	78459	74465	63465	78460
333 006	**YN**	A		WU(S)	78461	74466	63466	78462
333 007	**YN**	A		NL(S)	78463	74467	63467	78464
333 008	**YN**	A		WU(S)	78465	74468	63468	78466
333 009	**YN**	A		WU(S)	78467	74469		78468
333 010	**YN**	A	*TC*	NL	78469	74470		78470
333 011	**YN**	A		WU(S)	78471	74471		78472
333 012	**YN**	A		WU(S)	78473	74472		78474
333 013	**YN**	A		WU(S)	78475	74473		78476
333 014	**YN**	A		WU(S)	78477	74474		78478
333 015	**YN**	A		WU(S)	78479	74475		78480
333 016	**YN**	A		WU(S)	78481	74476		78482

CLASS 334   JUNIPER   ALSTOM

DMS(A)–PTS–DMS(B). Gangwayed within unit. Disc brakes. Air conditioned. 2+2 seating in the DMS vehicles, 3+2 seating in the PTS vehicle. Currently undergoing acceptance trials prior to entry into service with ScotRail.

Construction: Steel.
Traction Motors: Two Alstom ONIX 800 of 270 kW each per motor car.
Dimensions: 21.16 (DMS) or 19.94 (PTS) x 2.80 x 3.77. m.
Doors: Power operated sliding plug.
Maximum Speed: 100 m.p.h.   **Bogies:** Alstom LTB3/TBP3.
Couplers: Tightlock.   **Multiple Working:** Within class only.

64101–64140. DMS(A). Dia. EA215. Alstom Birmingham 1999–2000. –/64. 42.6 t.
65101–65140. DMS(B). Dia. EA215. Alstom Birmingham 1999–2000. –/64. 42.6 t.
74301–74340. PTS. Dia.EH255. Alstom Birmingham 1999–2000. –/55. 1TD. 2W. 39.4 t.

334 001	**SC**	H	*TC*	GW	64101	74301	65101
334 002	**SC**	H	*TC*	GW	64102	74302	65102
334 003	**SC**	H		PC(S)	64103	74303	65103
334 004	**SP**	H		PC(S)	64104	74304	65104
334 005	**SP**	H	*TC*	GW	64105	74305	65105
334 006	**SP**	H	*TC*	GW	64106	74306	65106
334 007	**SP**	H		KN(S)	64107	74307	65107
334 008	**SP**	H		PC(S)	64108	74308	65108
334 009	**SP**	H		PC(S)	64109	74309	65109
334 010	**SP**	H	*TC*	GW	64110	74310	65110
334 011	**SP**	H		PC(S)	64111	74311	65111
334 012	**SP**	H	*TC*	GW	64112	74312	65112
334 013	**SP**	H		PC(S)	64113	74313	65113
334 014	**SP**	H		KN(S)	64114	74314	65114
334 015	**SP**	H	*TC*	GW	64115	74315	65115
334 016	**SP**	H		PC(S)	64116	74316	65116
334 017	**SP**	H		PC(S)	64117	74317	65117
334 018		H			64118	74318	65118
334 019	**SP**	H		PC(S)	64119	74319	65119
334 020	**SP**	H		GW(S)	64120	74320	65120
334 021		H			64121	74321	65121
334 022		H			64122	74322	65122
334 023	**SP**	H		PC(S)	64123	74323	65123
334 024		H			64124	74324	65124
334 025		H			64125	74325	65125
334 026		H			64126	74326	65126
334 027		H			64127	74327	65127
334 028		H			64128	74328	65128
334 029		H			64129	74329	65129
334 030		H			64130	74330	65130
334 031		H			64131	74331	65131
334 032		H			64132	74332	65132
334 033		H			64133	74333	65133
334 034		H			64134	74334	65134
334 035		H			64135	74335	65135
334 036		H			64136	74336	65136
334 037		H			64137	74337	65137
334 038		H			64138	74338	65138
334 039		H			64139	74339	65139
334 040		H			64140	74340	65140

CLASS 357   ELECTROSTAR   ADTRANZ

DMS(A)–PTS–MS–DMS(B). Gangwayed within unit. Disc and regenerative braking. Air conditioning. Currently in the process of entering service with c2c Rail.

Construction: Welded aluminium alloy underframe, side and roof. Steel ends. All sections bolted together.
Supply System: 25 kV a.c. 50Hz overhead (with provision for 750 V d.c. third rail).   **Bogies:** Adtranz P3-25/ T3-25.

Traction Motors: Two Adtranz of 250 kW each per motor car.
Dimensions: 20.40 (DMS) or 19.99 (MS & PTS) x 2.80 x 3.78 m.
Maximum Speed: 100 m.p.h.   **Doors:** Power operated sliding plug.
Multiple Working: Within class.   **Couplers:** Tightlock.

Class 357/0. Owned by Porterbrook Leasing.

67651–67696. DMS(A). Dia. EA273. Adtranz Derby 1999–2000. –/71. 40.7 t.
67751–67796. DMS(B). Dia. EA214. Adtranz Derby 1999–2000. –/71. 40.7 t.
74051–74096. PTS. Dia. EH215. Adtranz Derby 1999–2000. –/62 1TD 2W. 36.7 t.
74151–74196. MS. Dia. EC225. Adtranz Derby 1999–2000. –/78 . 39.5 t.

357 001	LS	P	TC	EM	67651	74051	74151	67751
357 002	LS	P	TC	EM	67652	74052	74152	67752
357 003	LS	P	TC	PY(S)	67653	74053	74153	67753
357 004	LS	P		PY(S)	67654	74054	74154	67754
357 005	LS	P		ZD(S)	67655	74055	74155	67755
357 006	LS	P		PY(S)	67656	74056	74156	67756
357 007	LS	P		ZD(S)	67657	74057	74157	67757
357 008	LS	P		ZD(S)	67658	74058	74158	67758
357 009	LS	P		ZD(S)	67659	74059	74159	67759
357 010	LS	P		EM(S)	67660	74060	74160	67760
357 011	LS	P	C2	EM	67661	74061	74161	67761
357 012	LS	P	C2	EM	67662	74062	74162	67762
357 013	LS	P	C2	EM	67663	74063	74163	67763
357 014	LS	P	C2	EM	67664	74064	74164	67764
357 015	LS	P	C2	EM	67665	74065	74165	67765
357 016	LS	P		PY(S)	67666	74066	74166	67766
357 017	LS	P	TC	EM	67667	74067	74167	67767
357 018	LS	P		EM(S)	67668	74068	74168	67768
357 019	LS	P	C2	EM	67669	74069	74169	67769
357 020	LS	P	TC	EM	67670	74070	74170	67770
357 021	LS	P	TC	EM	67671	74071	74171	67771
357 022	LS	P	TC	EM	67672	74072	74172	67772
357 023	LS	P	C2	EM	67673	74073	74173	67773
357 024	LS	P	TC	EM	67674	74074	74174	67774
357 025	C2	P		EM(S)	67675	74075	74175	67775
357 026	LS	P	C2	EM	67676	74076	74176	67776
357 027	C2	P		EM(S)	67677	74077	74177	67777
357 028	LS	P	C2	EM	67678	74078	74178	67778
357 029	LS	P		PY(S)	67679	74079	74179	67779
357 030	LS	P	TC	EM	67680	74080	74180	67780
357 031	LS	P	TC	EM(S)	67681	74081	74181	67781
357 032	LS	P	TC	EM(S)	67682	74082	74182	67782
357 033	LS	P	C2	EM	67683	74083	74183	67783
357 034	LS	P	TC	EM	67684	74084	74184	67784
357 035	LS	P	C2	EM	67685	74085	74185	67785
357 036	LS	P	C2	EM	67686	74086	74186	67786
357 037	LS	P	TC	EM	67687	74087	74187	67787
357 038	LS	P	C2	EM	67688	74088	74188	67788
357 039	LS	P	C2	EM	67689	74089	74189	67789
357 040	LS	P		EM	67690	74090	74190	67790

357 041	LS	P		PY(S)	67691	74091	74191	67791
357 042	LS	P	TC	EM	67692	74092	74192	67792
357 043	LS	P		EM(S)	67693	74093	74193	67793
357 044	LS	P	TC	EM	67694	74094	74194	67794
357 045	LS	P		EM(S)	67695	74095	74195	67795
357 046	LS	P		EM(S)	67696	74096	74196	67796

Class 357/2. Owned by Angel Trains.

68601–68628. DMS(A). Dia. EA273. Adtranz Derby 2001. –/71. 40.7 t.
68701–68728. DMS(B). Dia. EA214. Adtranz Derby 2001. –/71. 40.7 t.
74601–74628. PTS. Dia. EH215. Adtranz Derby 2001. –/62 1TD 2W. 36.7 t.
74701–74728. MS. Dia. EC225. Adtranz Derby 2001. –/78 . 39.5 t.

357 201	A	68601	74601	74701	68701
357 202	A	68602	74602	74702	68702
357 203	A	68603	74603	74703	68703
357 204	A	68604	74604	74704	68704
357 205	A	68605	74605	74705	68705
357 206	A	68606	74606	74706	68706
357 207	A	68607	74607	74707	68707
357 208	A	68608	74608	74708	68708
357 209	A	68609	74609	74709	68709
357 210	A	68610	74610	74710	68710
357 211	A	68611	74611	74711	68711
357 212	A	68612	74612	74712	68712
357 213	A	68613	74613	74713	68713
357 214	A	68614	74614	74714	68714
357 215	A	68615	74615	74715	68715
357 216	A	68616	74616	74716	68716
357 217	A	68617	74617	74717	68717
357 218	A	68618	74618	74718	68718
357 219	A	68619	74619	74719	68719
357 220	A	68620	74620	74720	68720
357 221	A	68621	74621	74721	68721
357 222	A	68622	74622	74722	68722
357 223	A	68623	74623	74723	68723
357 224	A	68624	74624	74724	68724
357 225	A	68625	74625	74725	68725
357 226	A	68626	74626	74726	68726
357 227	A	68627	74627	74727	68727
357 228	A	68628	74628	74728	68728

CLASS 365   NETWORKER   ABB

DMC(A)–TSD–TS–DMC(B) or DMC(A)–TSD–PTS–DMC(B). 'Express' stock. Gangwayed within unit. Disc, rheostatic and regenerative braking.

Construction: Welded aluminium alloy.
Supply System: 25 kV a.c. 50 Hz overhead with provision for 750 V d.c. third rail or 750 V d.c. third rail with provision for 25 kV a.c. 50 Hz overhead.
Traction Motors: Four GEC-Alsthom G354CX of 157 kW each per motor car.
Dimensions: 20.89 (DMC) or 20.06 (TS & TSD) x 2.81 x 3.77 m.

Maximum Speed: 100 m.p.h.   **Doors:** Power operated sliding plug.
Couplers: Tightlock.   **Bogies:** ABB P3–16/T3-16.
Multiple Working: Classes 365, 465 and 466.

65894–65934. DMC(A). Dia. EA301. Lot No. 31133 ABB York 1994–95. 12/56. 46.7 t.
65935–65975. DMC(B). Dia. EA301. Lot No. 31136 ABB York 1994–95. 12/56. 46.7 t.
72240–72320 (Even numbers). PTS. Dia. EH298. Lot No. 31135 ABB York 1994–95. –/68 1T. 34.6 t.
72241–72321 (Odd numbers). TSD. Dia. EH298. Lot No. 31134 ABB York 1994–95. –/59 1TD 1W. 32.9 t.

Units 365 001–365 516. DMC(A)–TSD–TS–DMC(B). 750 V d.c. third rail with provision for 25 kV a.c. 50 Hz overhead supply.

365 501	**CS**	H	*SE*	RE	65894	72241	72240	65935
365 502	**CS**	H	*SE*	RE	65895	72243	72242	65936
365 503	**CS**	H	*SE*	RE	65896	72245	72244	65937
365 504	**CS**	H	*SE*	RE	65897	72247	72246	65938
365 505	**CS**	H	*SE*	RE	65898	72249	72248	65939
365 506	**CS**	H	*SE*	RE	65899	72251	72250	65940
365 507	**CS**	H	*SE*	RE	65900	72253	72252	65941
365 508	**CS**	H	*SE*	RE	65901	72255	72254	65942
365 509	**CS**	H	*SE*	RE	65902	72257	72256	65943
365 510	**CS**	H	*SE*	RE	65903	72259	72258	65944
365 511	**CS**	H	*SE*	RE	65904	72261	72260	65945
365 512	**CS**	H	*SE*	RE	65905	72263	72262	65946
365 513	**CS**	H	*SE*	RE	65906	72265	72264	65947
365 514	**CS**	H	*SE*	RE	65907	72267	72266	65948
365 515	**CS**	H	*SE*	RE	65908	72269	72268	65949
365 516	**CS**	H	*SE*	RE	65909	72271	72270	65950

Names (carried on one side of each DMC):

365 505   Spirit of Ramsgate
365 515   Spirit of Dover

Units 365 517–365 541. DMC(A)–TSD–PTS–DMC(B). 25 kV a.c. 50 Hz overhead with provision for 750 V d.c. third rail supply.

365 517	**NT**	H	*WN*	HE	65910	72273	72272	65951
365 518	**NT**	H	*WN*	HE	65911	72275	72274	65952
365 519	**NT**	H	*WN*	HE	65912	72277	72276	65953
365 520	**NT**	H	*WN*	HE	65913	72279	72278	65954
365 521	**NT**	H	*WN*	HE	65914	72281	72280	65955
365 522	**NT**	H	*WN*	HE	65915	72283	72282	65956
365 523	**NT**	H	*WN*	HE	65916	72285	72284	65957
365 524	**NT**	H	*WN*	HE	65917	72287	72286	65958
365 525	**NT**	H	*WN*	HE	65918	72289	72288	65959
365 526	**NT**	H	*WN*	HE	65919	72291	72290	65960
365 527	**NT**	H	*WN*	HE	65920	72293	72292	65961
365 528	**NT**	H	*WN*	HE	65921	72295	72294	65962
365 529	**NT**	H	*WN*	HE	65922	72297	72296	65963
365 530	**NT**	H	*WN*	HE	65923	72299	72298	65964

365 531	**NT**	H	*WN*	HE	65924	72301	72300	65965
365 532	**NT**	H	*WN*	HE	65925	72303	72302	65966
365 533	**NT**	H	*WN*	HE	65926	72305	72304	65967
365 534	**NT**	H	*WN*	HE	65927	72307	72306	65968
365 535	**NT**	H	*WN*	HE	65928	72309	72308	65969
365 536	**NT**	H	*WN*	HE	65929	72311	72310	65970
365 537	**NT**	H	*WN*	HE	65930	72313	72312	65971
365 538	**NT**	H	*WN*	HE	65931	72315	72314	65972
365 539	**NT**	H	*WN*	HE	65932	72317	72316	65973
365 540	**NT**	H	*WN*	HE	65933	72319	72318	65974
365 541	**NT**	H	*WN*	HE	65934	72321	72320	65975

CLASS 375   ELECTROSTAR   ADTRANZ

Various formations, see below. Gangwayed throughout. Disc and regenerative braking. Air conditioned. Currently undergoing acceptance trials prior to entry into service.

Construction: Welded aluminium alloy underframe, side and roof. Steel ends. All sections bolted together.
Supply System: 25 kV a.c. 50 Hz overhead and/or 750 V d.c. third rail. 750 V d.c only units also have provision for 25 kV a.c. 50 Hz overhead supply.
Traction Motors: Two Adtranz of 250 kW each per motor car.
Dimensions: 20.40 (DMS) or 19.99 (MS & PTS) x 2.80 x 3.78 m.
Maximum Speed: 100 m.p.h.   **Doors:** Power operated sliding plug.
Couplers: Tightlock.   **Multiple Working:** Within class.
Bogies: Adtranz P3-25/T3-25.

Class 375/3. 750 V d.c. only 3-car 'Express' units for Connex South Eastern. DMS(A)–PTS–DMS(B).

67921–67930. DMS(A). Dia. EA277. Adtranz Derby 2000–01. –/64. . t.
67931–67940. DMS(B). Dia. EA277. Adtranz Derby 2000–01. –/64. . t.
74351–74360. PTS. Dia. EH254. Adtranz Derby 2000–01. –/56 1TD 2W. . t.

375 301	H	67921	74351	67931
375 302	H	67922	74352	67932
375 303	H	67923	74353	67933
375 304	H	67924	74354	67934
375 305	H	67925	74355	67935
375 306	H	67926	74356	67936
375 307	H	67927	74357	67937
375 308	H	67928	74358	67938
375 309	H	67929	74359	67939
375 310	H	67930	74360	67940

Class 375/3. 750 V d.c. only 3-car 'Express' units for Connex South Central. DMS(A)–PTS–DMS(B).

?. DMS(A). Dia. EA277. Adtranz Derby 2000–01. –/64. . t.
?. DMS(B). Dia. EA277. Adtranz Derby 2000–01. –/64. . t.
?. PTS. Dia. EH254. Adtranz Derby 2000–01. –/56 1TD 2W. . t.

375 311	H

375 312	H						
375 313	H						
375 314	H						
375 315	H						
375 316	H						
375 317	H						
375 318	H						
375 319	H						
375 320	H						
375 321	H						
375 322	H						
375 323	H						
375 324	H						
375 325	H						
375 326	H						
375 327	H						
375 328	H						
375 329	H						
375 330	H						
375 331	H						
375 332	H						
375 333	H						
375 334	H						
375 335	H						
375 336	H						
375 337	H						
375 338	H						

Class 375/6. Dual Voltage 4-car 'Express' units for Connex South Eastern. DMS(A)–PTS–MS–DMS(B).

67801–67830. DMS(A). Dia. EA275. Adtranz Derby 1999–2000. –/60. 46.2 t.
67851–67880. DMS(B). Dia. EA275. Adtranz Derby 1999–2000. –/60. 46.2 t.
74201–74230. PTS. Dia. EH252. Adtranz Derby 1999–2000. –/56 1TD 2W. 40.7 t.
74251–74280. MS. Dia. EC230. Adtranz Derby 1999–2000. –/66 1T. 40.5 t.

375 601	U	H	TC	AF	67801	74201	74251	67851
375 602	U	H		ZD(S)	67802	74202	74252	67852
375 603	U	H		ZD(S)	67803	74203	74253	67853
375 604	U	H	TC	AF	67804	74204	74254	67854
375 605	U	H	TC	AF	67805	74205	74255	67855
375 606	U	H	TC	AF	67806	74206	74256	67856
375 607	U	H		ZD(S)	67807	74207	74257	67857
375 608	U	H		ZD(S)	67808	74208	74258	67858
375 609	U	H		ZD(S)	67809	74209	74259	67859
375 610	U	H		ZD(S)	67810	74210	74260	67860
375 611	U	H		ZD(S)	67811	74211	74261	67861
375 612	U	H		ZD(S)	67812	74212	74262	67862
375 613	U	H		ZD(S)	67813	74213	74263	67863
375 614	U	H	TC	VM	67814	74214	74264	67864
375 615	U	H		ZD(S)	67815	74215	74265	67865
375 616	U	H		ZD(S)	67816	74216	74266	67866

375 617	U	H	ZD(S)	67817	74217	74267	67867
375 618	U	H	ZD(S)	67818	74218	74268	67868
375 619	U	H	ZD(S)	67819	74219	74269	67869
375 620	U	H	ZD(S)	67820	74220	74270	67870
375 621	U	H	ZD(S)	67821	74221	74271	67871
375 622	U	H	ZD(S)	67822	74222	74272	67872
375 623	U	H	ZD(S)	67823	74223	74273	67873
375 624	U	H	ZD(S)	67824	74224	74274	67874
375 625	U	H	ZD(S)	67825	74225	74275	67875
375 626	U	H	ZD(S)	67826	74226	74276	67876
375 627	U	H	ZD(S)	67827	74227	74277	67877
375 628	U	H	ZD(S)	67828	74228	74278	67878
375 629	U	H	ZD(S)	67829	74229	74279	67879
375 630	U	H	ZD(S)	67830	74230	74280	67880

Class 375/7. 750 V d.c. only 4-car 'Express' units for Connex South Eastern. DMS(A)–PTS–MS–DMS(B).

67831–67845. DMS(A). Dia. EA276. Adtranz Derby 2000–01. –/60. . t.
67881–67895. DMS(B). Dia. EA276. Adtranz Derby 2000–01. –/60. t.
74231–74245. PTS. Dia. EH253. Adtranz Derby 2000–01. –/56 1TD 2W. . t.
74281–74295. MS. Dia. EC231. Adtranz Derby 2000–01. –/66 1T. . t.

375 701	H		67831	74281	74231	67881
375 702	H		67832	74282	74232	67882
375 703	H		67833	74283	74233	67883
375 704	H		67834	74284	74234	67884
375 705	H		67835	74285	74235	67885
375 706	H		67836	74281	74236	67886
375 707	H		67837	74287	74237	67887
375 708	H		67838	74288	74238	67888
375 709	H		67839	74289	74239	67889
375 710	H		67840	74290	74240	67890
375 711	H		67841	74291	74241	67891
375 712	H		67842	74292	74242	67892
375 713	H		67843	74293	74243	67893
375 714	H		67844	74294	74244	67894
375 715	H		67845	74295	74245	67895

Class 375/7. 750 V d.c. only 4-car 'Express' units for Connex South Central. DMS(A)–PTS–MS–DMS(B).

?. DMS(A). Dia. EA276. Adtranz Derby 2000–01. –/60. . t.
?. DMS(B). Dia. EA276. Adtranz Derby 2000–01. –/60. t.
?. PTS. Dia. EH253. Adtranz Derby 2000–01. –/56 1TD 2W. . t.
?. MS. Dia. EC231. Adtranz Derby 2000–01. –/66 1T. . t.

375 716	H
375 717	H
375 718	H
375 719	H
375 720	H
375 721	H
375 722	H

375 723	H
375 724	H
375 725	H
375 726	H
375 727	H
375 728	H
375 729	H
375 730	H
375 731	H
375 732	H
375 733	H
375 734	H

CLASS 390 PENDOLINO-BRITANNICO ALSTOM

DMFRK–MFD–PTF–MF–TS–MSD–PTSRMB–MSD–DMS. 'Express' stock. Tilting units under construction for Virgin West Coast. Gangwayed within unit. Disc, rheostatic and regenerative braking. Air conditioned.

Construction: Welded aluminium alloy.
Supply System: 25 kV a.c. 50 Hz overhead.
Traction Motors: Two Alstom ONIX 800 of 425 kW each per motor car.
Dimensions: 23.05 (DMS & DMRFK) or 23.90 (other cars) x 2.73 x 3.56 m.
Maximum Speed: 140 m.p.h.   **Doors:** Power operated sliding plug.
Couplers: Dellner.   **Multiple Working:** Within class.
Bogies: FIAT-SIG.

69101–69153. DMRFK. Dia. EA102. Alstom Birmingham 2001–02. 18/–. 55.6 t
69201–69253. DMS. Dia. EA281. Alstom Birmingham 2001–02. –/46 1T. 51.0 t.
69401–69453. MFD. Dia. EC101. Alstom Birmingham 2001–02. 37/– 1TD 1W. 52.0 t.
69501–69553. PTF. Dia EH162. Alstom Birmingham 2001–02. 44/– 1T. 50.1 t.
68801–68853. TS. Dia EH258. Alstom Birmingham 2001–02. –/76 1T. 45.5 t.
69601–69653. MF. Dia. EC103. Alstom Birmingham 2001–02.44/– 1T. 51.8 t.
69701–69753. MSD(A). Dia. EC234. Alstom Birmingham 2001–02. –/62 1TD1W. 50.0 t.
69801–69853. PTSRMB. Dia. EH259. Alstom Birmingham 2001–02. –/50. 52.0t.
69901–69944. MSD(B). Dia. EC235. Alstom Birmingham 2001–02. –/62 1TD 1W. 51.7 t.

390 001	**VT**	A	69101	69401	69501	69601	68801
				69701	69801	69901	69201
390 002	**VT**	A	69102	69402	69502	69602	68802
				69702	69802	69902	69202
390 003		A	69103	69403	69503	69603	68803
				69703	69803	69903	69203
390 004		A	69104	69404	69504	69604	68804
				69704	69804	69904	69204
390 005		A	69105	69405	69505	69605	68805
				69705	69805	69905	69205
390 006		A	69106	69406	69506	69606	68806
				69706	69806	69906	69206

390 007	A	69107	69407	69507	69607	68807
			69707	69807	69907	69207
390 008	A	69108	69408	69508	69608	68808
			69708	69808	69908	69208
390 009	A	69109	69409	69509	69609	68809
			69709	69809	69909	69209
390 010	A	69110	69410	69510	69610	68810
			69710	69810	69910	69210
390 011	A	69111	69411	69511	69611	68811
			69711	69811	69911	69211
390 012	A	69112	69412	69512	69612	68812
			69712	69812	69912	69212
390 013	A	69113	69413	69513	69613	68813
			69713	69813	69913	69213
390 014	A	69114	69414	69514	69614	68814
			69714	69814	69914	69214
390 015	A	69115	69415	69515	69615	68815
			69715	69815	69915	69215
390 016	A	69116	69416	69516	69616	68816
			69716	69816	69916	69216
390 017	A	69117	69417	69517	69617	68817
			69717	69817	69917	69217
390 018	A	69118	69418	69518	69618	68818
			69718	69818	69918	69218
390 019	A	69119	69419	69519	69619	68819
			69719	69819	69919	69219
390 020	A	69120	69420	69520	69620	68820
			69720	69820	69920	69220
390 021	A	69121	69421	69521	69621	68821
			69721	69821	69921	69221
390 022	A	69122	69422	69522	69622	68822
			69722	69822	69922	69222
390 023	A	69123	69423	69523	69623	68823
			69723	69823	69923	69223
390 024	A	69124	69424	69524	69624	68824
			69724	69824	69924	69224
390 025	A	69125	69425	69525	69625	68825
			69725	69825	69925	69225
390 026	A	69126	69426	69526	69626	68826
			69726	69826	69926	69226
390 027	A	69127	69427	69527	69627	68827
			69727	69827	69927	69227
390 028	A	69128	69428	69528	69628	68828
			69728	69828	69928	69228
390 029	A	69129	69429	69529	69629	68829
			69729	69829	69929	69229
390 030	A	69130	69430	69530	69630	68830
			69730	69830	69930	69230
390 031	A	69131	69431	69531	69631	68831
			69731	69831	69931	69231

390 032	A	69132	69432	69532	69632	68832
			69732	69832	69932	69232
390 033	A	69133	69433	69533	69633	68833
			69733	69833	69933	69233
390 034	A	69134	69434	69534	69634	68834
			69734	69834	69934	69234
390 035	A	69135	69435	69535	69635	68835
			69735	69835	69935	69235
390 036	A	69136	69436	69536	69636	68836
			69736	69836	69936	69236
390 037	A	69137	69437	69537	69637	68837
			69737	69837	69937	69237
390 038	A	69138	69438	69538	69638	68838
			69738	69838	69938	69238
390 039	A	69139	69439	69539	69639	68839
			69739	69839	69939	69239
390 040	A	69140	69440	69540	69640	68840
			69740	69840	69940	69240
390 041	A	69141	69441	69541	69641	68841
			69741	69841	69941	69241
390 042	A	69142	69442	69542	69642	68842
			69742	69842	69942	69242
390 043	A	69143	69443	69543	69643	68843
			69743	69843	69943	69243
390 044	A	69144	69444	69544	69644	68844
			69744	69844	69944	69244
390 045	A	69145	69445	69545	69645	68845
			69745	69845	69945	69245
390 046	A	69146	69446	69546	69646	68846
			69746	69846	69946	69246
390 047	A	69147	69447	69547	69647	68847
			69747	69847	69947	69247
390 048	A	69148	69448	69548	69648	68848
			69748	69848	69948	69248
390 049	A	69149	69449	69549	69649	68849
			69749	69849	69949	69249
390 050	A	69150	69450	69550	69650	68850
			69750	69850	69950	69250
390 051	A	69151	69451	69551	69651	68851
			69751	69851	69951	69251
390 052	A	69152	69452	69552	69652	68852
			69752	69852	69952	69252
390 053	A	69153	69453	69553	69653	68853
			69753	69853	69953	69253

4.2. 750 V d.c. THIRD RAIL UNITS

Supply System: 660–850 V d.c. third rail unless otherwise stated.

CLASSES 411 & 412 (3-or 4-Cep/Bep)   BR

Various formations, see below. 'Express' stock. Gangwayed throughout.

Construction: Steel.
Traction Motors: Two English Electric 507 of 185 kW each per motor car.
Dimensions: 20.34 x 2.82 x 3.83 m.
Maximum Speed: 90 m.p.h.   **Doors:** Manually operated slam.
Couplings: Buckeye.   **Multiple Working:** SR type.
Bogies: Mk. 4 (* Mk. 3B; † Mk. 6)/Commonwealth († B5 (SR)).

61229–61239 (Odd numbers). DMS(A). Dia. EA264. Lot No. 30449 Eastleigh 1958. –/64. 44.2 t.
61230–61240 (Even numbers). DMS(B). Dia. EA264. Lot No. 30449 Eastleigh 1958. –/64. 43.5 t.
61305–61409 (Odd numbers). DMS(A). Dia. EA264. Lot No. 30454 Eastleigh 1958–59. –/64. 44.2 t.
61304–61408 (Even numbers). DMS(B). Dia. EA264. Lot No. 30454 Eastleigh 1958–59. –/64. 43.5 t.
61694–61810 (Even numbers). DMS(A). Dia. EA264. Lot No. 30619 Eastleigh 1960–61. –/64. 44.2 t.
61695–61811 (Odd numbers). DMS(B). Dia. EA264. Lot No. 30619 Eastleigh 1960–61. –/64. 43.5 t.
61948–61960 (Even numbers). DMS(A). Dia. EA264. Lot No. 30708 Eastleigh 1963. –/64. 44.2 t.
61949–61961 (Odd numbers). DMS(B). Dia. EA264. Lot No. 30708 Eastleigh 1963. –/64. 43.5 t.
69341–69347. TRBS. Dia. EN261. Built as TRB to Lot No. 30622 Eastleigh 1961. Converted BREL Swindon 1982–84. –/24 plus 9 chairs 1T. 35.5 t.
70033–70036. TBC. Dia. EJ361. Lot No. 30109 Eastleigh 1956. 24/6 2T. 36.2 t.
70044. TBC. Dia. EJ361. Lot No. 30639 Eastleigh 1961. 24/6 2T. 36.2 t.
70229–70234. TBC. Dia. EJ361. Lot No. 30450 Eastleigh 1958. 24/6 2T. 36.2 t.
70235–70240. TBC. Dia. EJ361. Lot No. 30451 Eastleigh 1958. 24/6 2T. 36.2 t.
70241–70242. TBC. Dia. EJ361. Lot No. 30640 Eastleigh 1961. 24/6 2T. 36.2 t.
70260–70302. TS. Dia. EH282. Lot No. 30455 Eastleigh 1958–59. –/64 2T. 31.5 t.
70303–70355. TS. Dia. EH282. Lot No. 30456 Eastleigh 1958–59. –/64 2T. 31.5 t.
70503–70551. TS. Dia. EH282. Lot No. 30620 Eastleigh 1960–61. –/64 2T. 31.5 t.
70552–70610. TS. Dia. EH282. Lot No. 30621 Eastleigh 1960–61. –/64 2T. 31.5 t.
70653–70659. TS. Dia. EH282. Lot No. 30709 Eastleigh 1963. –/64 2T. 31.5 t.
70660–70666. TS. Dia. EH282. Lot No. 30710 Eastleigh 1963. –/64 2T. 31.5 t.
71625–71636. TS. Dia. EH284. Converted BREL Swindon 1981–82 from loco-hauled TSO of various lots. –/64 2T. 33.6 t.
71711–71712. TS. Dia. EH284. Converted BREL Swindon 1983–84 from loco-hauled TSO of various lots. –/64 2T. 33.6 t.

Class 411/9 (3-Cep). DMS(A)–TBC–DMS(B).

1101		N	P	*SE*	RM	61331	70316	61330
1102		N	P	*SE*	RM	61231	70604	61232
1103	*	N	P	*SE*	RM	61750	70580	61751
1104	*	N	P	*SE*	RM	61760	70585	61761
1105	*	N	P	*SE*	RM	61952	70655	61953
1106		N	P	*SE*	RM	61365	70333	61364
1107		N	P	*SE*	RM	61343	70327	61380
1108		N	P	*SE*	RM	61399	70350	61398
1109		N	P	*SE*	RM	61409	70355	61408
1110		N	P	*SE*	RM	61323	70312	61322
1111		N	P	*SE*	RM	61339	70320	61338
1112		N	P	*SE*	RM	61369	70335	61368
1113		N	P	*SE*	RM	61371	70336	61370
1114		N	P	*SE*	RM	61377	70339	61376
1115	*	N	P	*SE*	RM	61718	70564	61719
1116	*	N	P	*SE*	RM	61756	70589	61757
1117	*	N	P	*SE*	RM	61704	70557	61705
1118	*	N	P	*SE*	RM	61708	70559	61709

(Class continued with 1507)

CLASS 421 (4-Cig/3-Cop)   BR

Various formations, see below. 'Express' stock. Gangwayed throughout.

Construction: Steel.
Traction Motors: Four English Electric 507 of 185 kW each.
Dimensions: 20.19 x 2.82 x 3.86 m.
Maximum Speed: 90 m.p.h.
Doors: Manually operated slam.   **Multiple Working:** SR type.
Couplings: Buckeye.   **Bogies:** Mk. 4 or Mk. 6/B5 (SR).

Note: d – Experimentally equipped with central door locking.

62017–62070. MBS. Dia. ED264. Lot No. 30742 York 1964–65. –/56. 49.0 t.
62277–62286. MBS. Dia. ED264. Lot No. 30804 York 1970. –/56. (§ 1W) 49.0 t.
62287–62316. MBS. Dia. ED 264. Lot No. 30808 York 1970. –/56. (§ 1W) 49.0 t.
62355–62425. MBS. Dia. ED264. Lot No. 30816 York 1970. –/56. (§ 1W) 49.0 t.
62430. MBS. Dia. ED264. Lot No. 30829 York 1972. –/56. 49.0 t.
70260–70302. TS. Dia. EH282. Lot No. 30455 Eastleigh 1958–59. –/64 2T. 31.5 t.
  Class 411/5 cars.
70503–70551. TS. Dia. EH282. Lot No. 30620 Eastleigh 1960–61. –/64 2T. 31.5 t.
  Class 411/5 cars.
70695–70730. TS. Dia. EH287. Lot No. 30730 York 1964–65. –/72. 31.5 t.
70967–70996 TS. Dia. EH287 (• EH275). Lot No. 30809 York 1970–71. –/72. 31.5t.
71035–71105. TS. Dia. EH287. Lot No. 30817 York 1970. –/72. 31.5t.
71106. TS. Dia. EH287. Lot No. 30830 York 1972. –/72. 31.5t.
71766–71770. TS. Dia. EH287. Built as EMU TSRB to Lot No. 30744 York 1963–
  66. Converted BRML Eastleigh 1985–87. –/72. 31.5 t.
71926. TS. Dia. EH287. Built as EMU TSRB to Lot No. 30744 York 1963–66.
  Converted BRML Eastleigh 1988. –/72. 31.5t.

71927–71928. TS. Dia. EH287. Built as EMU TSRB to Lot No. 30805 York 1970. Converted BRML Eastleigh 1988. –/72. 31.5t.

76022–76075. DTC(B). Dia. EE369. Lot No. 30740 York 1964–65. 18/36 2T.

76076–76129. DTC(A) (†‡ DTS). Dia. EE369 (†‡ EE282). Lot No. 30741 York 1964–65. 18/36 († –/54; ‡ –/60) 2T. 35.5 t.

76561–76570. DTC(A) (†‡ DTS; § DTS(A)). Dia. EE369 (†‡ EE283; § EE245). Lot No. 30802 York 1970 (§ Rebuilt Wessex Traincare/Alstom Eastleigh 1997– 98). 18/36 (*12/42; †–/54; ‡§ –/60) 2(§ 1)T. 35.5 t.

76571–76580. DTC(B) (§ DTS(B)). Dia. EE369 (§ EE246). Lot No. 30802 York 1970 (§ Rebuilt Wessex Traincare/Alstom Eastleigh 1997–98). 18/36 2(§ 1)T. 35.5 t.

76581–76610. DTC(A) (†‡ DTS; § DTS(A)). Dia. EE369 (§ EE245). Lot No. 30806 York 1970 (§ Rebuilt Wessex Traincare/Alstom Eastleigh 1997–98). 18/36 (*12/42; † –/54; ‡§–/60) 2(§ 1)T. 35.5 t.

76611–76640. DTC(B) (§ DTS(B)). Dia. EE369 (§ EE246). Lot No. 30807 York 1970 (§ Rebuilt Wessex Traincare/Alstom Eastleigh 1997–98). 18/36 2(§1)T. 35.5 t.

76788–76858. DTC(B) (§ DTS(B)). Dia. EE369 (§ EE246). Lot No. 30815 York 1970–72. (§ Rebuilt Wessex Traincare/Alstom Eastleigh 1997–98). 18/36 2T. 35.5 t.

76859. DTC(A). Dia. EE369. Lot No. 30827 York 1972. 12/42 2T. 35.5 t.

76860. DTC(B). Dia. EE369. Lot No. 30828 York 1972. 12/42 2T. 35.5 t.

Class 421/5 (4-Cig). DTC(A)–MBS-TS–DTC(B). 'Greyhound' units with additional stage of field weakening to improve the maximum attainable speed. Mk. 6 motor bogies.

1301	**ST**	H	*SW*	FR	76595	62301	70981	76625
1302	**ST**	H	*SW*	FR	76584	62290	70970	76614
1303	**ST**	H	*SW*	FR	76581	62287	70967	76611
1304	**ST**	H	*SW*	FR	76583	62289	70969	76613
1305	**ST**	H	*SW*	FR	76717	62355	71035	76788
1306	**ST**	H	*SW*	FR	76723	62361	71041	76794
1307	**ST**	H	*SW*	FR	76586	62292	70972	76616
1308	**ST**	H	*SW*	FR	76627	62298	70978	76622
1309	**ST**	H	*SW*	FR	76594	62300	70980	76624
1310	**ST**	H	*SW*	FR	76567	62283	71926	76577
1311	**ST**	H	*SW*	FR	76561	62277	71927	76571
1312	**ST**	H	*SW*	FR	76562	62278	71928	76572
1313	**ST**	H	*SW*	FR	76596	62302	70982	76626
1314	**ST**	H	*SW*	FR	76588	62294	70974	76618
1315	**ST**	H	*SW*	FR	76608	62314	70994	76638
1316	**ST**	H	*SW*	FR	76585	62291	70971	76615
1317	**ST**	H	*SW*	FR	76597	62303	70983	76592
1318	**ST**	H	*SW*	FR	76590	62296	70976	76620
1319	**ST**	H	*SW*	FR	76591	62297	70977	76621
1320	**ST**	H	*SW*	FR	76593	62299	70979	76623
1321	**ST**	H	*SW*	FR	76589	62295	70975	76619
1322	**ST**	H	*SW*	FR	76587	62293	70973	76617

Class 421/8 (4-Cig). DTC(A)–MBS–TS–DTC(B). 'Greyhound' units with additional stage of field weakening to improve the maximum attainable speed. Mk. 6 motor bogies. Former Class 422 units with TRBS replaced by Class 411/5 TS.

1392	**ST**	P	*SW*	FR	76811	62378	70273	76740
1393	**ST**	P	*SW*	FR	76746	62384	70527	76817
1394	**ST**	P	*SW*	FR	76726	62364	70663	76797
1395	**ST**	P	*SW*	FR	76850	62417	70662	76779
1396	**ST**	P	*SW*	FR	76803	62370	70531	76732
1397	**ST**	P	*SW*	FR	76749	62387	70515	76820
1398	**ST**	P	*SW*	FR	76819	62386	70292	76748
1399	**ST**	P	*SW*	FR	76747	62385	70508	76818

Class 421/7 (3-Cop). DTS(A)–MBS–DTS(B). 3-car units for Connex South Central Brighton–Portsmouth 'Coastway' route. Mk. 6 motor bogies.

1401	§	**CX**	P	*SC*	BI	76568	62284	76578
1402	§	**CX**	P	*SC*	BI	76564	62280	76574
1403	§	**CX**	P	*SC*	BI	76563	62279	76573
1404	§	**CX**	P	*SC*	BI	76602	62308	76632
1405	§	**CX**	P	*SC*	BI	76565	62281	76575
1406	§	**CX**	P	*SC*	BI	76728	62366	76799
1407	§	**CX**	P	*SC*	BI	76729	62367	76800
1408	§	**CX**	P	*SC*	BI	76750	62388	76821
1409	§	**CX**	P	*SC*	BI	76569	62285	76579
1410	§	**CX**	P	*SC*	BI	76734	62372	76805
1411	§	**CX**	P	*SC*	BI	76570	62286	76580

Name (Carried on MBS):

1408	Littlehampton Progress 2000
1409	Operation Perseus

(Class continued with 1701)

CLASS 411 (4-Cep)   BR

For details see pages 288.

Class 411/5 (4-Cep). 4-car units. DMS(A)–TBC–TS–DMS(B).

1507	**ST**	P	*SW*	FR	61363	70332	70289	61362
1509	**N**	P	*SE*	RM	61335	70318	70275	61334
1511	**N**	P	*SE*	RM	61367	70334	70291	61366
1512	**ST**	P	*SW*	FR	61321	70311	70268	61320
1517	**N**	P	*SW*	FR	61317	70309	70266	61316
1518	**N**	P		ZG(S)	61333	70317	70274	61332
1519	**ST**	P	*SW*	FR	61403	70352	70536	61402
1527	**N**	P		BM(S)	61237	70239	70233	61238
1531	**ST**	P	*SW*	FR	61233	70237	70231	61234
1533	**ST**	P	*SW*	FR	61393	70347	71627	61385
1534	**ST**	P	*SW*	FR	61405	70353	71626	61404
1535	**ST**	P	*SW*	FR	61397	70349	71629	61396
1537	**ST**	P	*SW*	FR	61229	70235	70229	61230
1538	**ST**	P	*SW*	FR	61307	70304	70261	61306

1539		**ST**	P	*SW*	FR	61401	70351	71632	61400
1544		**ST**	P	*SW*	FR	61315	70308	70265	61349
1547		**ST**	P	*SW*	FR	61329	70578	70272	61328
1548		**ST**	P	*SW*	FR	61375	70338	70295	61374
1550		**ST**	P	*SW*	FR	61313	70307	70264	61312
1551		**N**	P	*SE*	RM	61325	70313	70270	61324
1553		**N**	P	*SW*	FR	61728	70306	70263	61350
1555		**ST**	P	*SW*	FR	61311	70326	70283	61310
1557		**N**	P		CJ(S)	61337	70331	70288	61360
1560		**N**	P	*SE*	RM	61387	70344	70301	61386
1562		**N**	P	*SE*	RM	61407	70236	70241	61406
1563	*	**ST**	P	*SW*	FR	61740	70575	70526	61741
1564	*	**N**	P	*SE*	RM	61788	70599	70550	61789
1565	*	**ST**	P	*SW*	FR	61762	70586	71711	61763
1566	*	**ST**	P	*SW*	FR	61722	70566	70517	61723
1568	*	**ST**	P	*SW*	FR	61766	70588	70539	61767
1570	*	**N**	P	*SE*	RM	61738	70574	70525	61739
1571	*	**N**	P	*SW*	FR	61806	70608	71636	61807
1573	*	**ST**	P	*SW*	FR	61726	70568	70519	61727
1574	*	**N**	P	*SE*	RM	61792	70601	71635	61793
1575	*	**N**	P	*SE*	RM	61768	70583	70540	61769
1576	*	**N**	P	*SE*	RM	61770	70590	70541	61771
1578	*	**ST**	P	*SW*	FR	61700	70555	70506	61701
1581	*	**ST**	P	*SW*	FR	61784	70597	70548	61785
1582	*	**N**	P	*SE*	RM	61748	70603	71630	61797
1584	*	**N**	P	*SE*	RM	61752	70581	70532	61753
1585	*	**N**	P	*SE*	RM	61710	70560	70511	61711
1586	*	**N**	P	*SE*	RM	61714	70562	70513	61715
1587	*	**N**	P	*SE*	RM	61764	70587	71625	61765
1588	*	**N**	P	*SE*	RM	61720	70044	70520	61721
1590	*	**N**	P	*SE*	RM	61696	70553	70504	61697
1591	*	**N**	P	*SE*	RM	61790	70600	70551	61791
1592	*	**N**	P	*SE*	RM	61778	70594	70545	61779
1593	*	**N**	P	*SE*	RM	61730	70570	70521	61731
1594	*	**N**	P	*SE*	RM	61754	70582	70533	61755
1599	*	**N**	P	*SE*	RM	61706	70558	70509	61707
1602	*	**CX**	P	*SE*	RM	61958	70565	70279	61959
1606	*	**N**	P		AF(S)	61694	70552		61695
1607	*	**N**	P	*SE*	RM	61698	70554	70505	61699
1609	*	**N**	P	*SE*	RM	61744	70577	70528	61745
1611	*	**N**	P	*SE*	RM	61758	70584	70537	61759
1612	*	**ST**	P	*SW*	FR	61794	70602	70535	61795
1614	*	**N**	P	*SE*	RM	61702	70556	70507	61703
1615	*	**N**	P	*SE*	RM	61956	70657	70664	61957
1616	*	**N**	P	*SE*	RM	61950	70654	70543	61951
1617	*	**N**	P		CJ(S)	61800	70605	70661	61801
1697	†	**ST**	P	*SW*	FR	61373	70337	70294	61372
1698	†	**N**	P	*SW*	FR	61355	70343	70300	61384
1699	†	**N**	P	*SW*	FR	61712	70561	70512	61713
Spare	*	**N**	P		BM(S)	61734			61735
Spare		**N**	P		ZG(S)			70503	

CLASS 421 (4-Cig)   BR

For details see pages 289–290.

Class 421/3 (4-Cig). DTC(A)/(†‡DTS)–MBS–TS–DTC(B). Mk. 4 motor bogies.

1701		U	A	SE	RM	76087	62028	70706	76033
1702	†	CX	A	SC	BI	76101	62042	70720	76047
1703	†	CX	A	SC	BI	76097	62038	70716	76043
1704	†	CX	A	SC	BI	76092	62033	70711	76038
1705	†	CX	A	SC	BI	76076	62017	70695	76022
1706	†	CX	A	SC	BI	76094	62035	70713	76040
1707	†	CX	A	SC	BI	76084	62025	70703	76030
1708	†	CX	A	SC	BI	76110	62051	70729	76056
1709	†	CX	A	SC	BI	76103	62044	70722	76049
1710	†	CX	A	SC	BI	76078	62019	70697	76024
1711	‡	CX	A	SC	BI	76114	62055	71766	76060
1712	†	CX	A	SC	BI	76079	62020	70698	76025
1713	†	CX	A	SC	BI	76128	62069	71767	76074
1714	†	CX	A	SC	BI	76077	62018	70696	76023
1717	†	CX	A	SC	BI	76083	62024	70702	76029
1719	†	CX	A	SC	BI	76116	62057	70719	76062
1720	†	CX	A	SC	BI	76098	62039	71769	76044
1721	†	CX	A	SC	BI	76090	62031	70709	76036
1722	‡	CX	A	SC	BI	76106	62047	70725	76052
1724	†	CX	A	SC	BI	76120	62061	71770	76066
1725	†	CX	A	SC	BI	76088	62029	70707	76034
1726	†	CX	A	SC	BI	76109	62050	70728	76055
1727	†	CX	A	SC	BI	76111	62052	70730	76057
1731	†	CX	A	SC	BI	76095	62036	70714	76041
1733	†	CX	A	SC	BI	76122	62063	71047	76068
1734	†	CX	A	SC	BI	76063	62054	71044	76059
1735	†	CX	A	SC	BI	76117	62058	71050	76051
1736	†	U	A	SC	BI	76124	62065	71052	76070
1737	†	U	A	SC	BI	76121	62062	71058	76067
1738	†	CX	A	SC	BI	76129	62064	71046	76069
1739	†	CX	A	SC	BI	76123	62070	71066	76075
1740	†	CX	A	SC	BI	76126	62067	71097	76072
1741	†	CX	A	SC	BI	76089	62030	70708	76035
1742		U	A	SE	RM	76086	62027	70705	76032
1743	†	CX	A	SC	BI	76118	62059	71065	76064
1744	†	CX	A	SC	BI	76127	62068	71064	76073
1745	†	CX	A	SC	BI	76085	62026	70704	76031
1746	‡	CX	A	SC	BI	76091	62032	70710	76037
1747	†	CX	A	SC	BI	76093	62034	70712	76026
1748		U	A	SE	RM	76115	62056	71067	76061
1750	†	CX	A	SC	BI	76080	62021	70699	76039
1751	†	CX	A	SC	BI	76125	62066	71051	76071
1752	†	CX	A	SC	BI	76119	62060	70717	76065
1753	†	CX	A	SC	BI	76102	62043	70721	76048
Spare		N	A		AF(S)				76058

Spare   **N**   A   PY(S)   62053 71068

Class 421/4 (4-Cig). DTC(A)/(†‡DTS)–MBS–TS–DTC(B). Mk. 6 motor bogies.

1801	†	**CX**	P	*SC*	BI	76848	71095	62415	76777
1802	†	**CX**	P	*SC*	BI	76754	62392	71072	76825
1803	†	**CX**	A	*SC*	BI	76780	62418	71098	76851
1804	†	**CX**	A	*SC*	BI	76778	62416	71096	76849
1805	†	**CX**	A	*SC*	BI	76782	62420	71100	76853
1806	*	**N**	H	*SE*	RM	76783	62421	71101	76854
1807	*	**N**	H	*SE*	RM	76784	62422	71102	76855
1808	*	**N**	H	*SE*	RM	76785	62423	71103	76856
1809	*	**N**	H	*SE*	RM	76786	62424	71104	76857
1810	*	**N**	H	*SE*	RM	76787	62425	71105	76858
1811	*	**N**	H	*SE*	RM	76781	62419	71099	76852
1812	*d	**N**	H	*SE*	RM	76757	62395	71075	76828
1813	*	**N**	H	*SE*	RM	76859	62430	71106	76860
1831	†	**CX**	A	*SC*	BI	76598	62304	70984	76628
1832	†	**CX**	A	*SC*	BI	76719	62357	71037	76790
1833	†	**CX**	A	*SC*	BI	76582	62288	70968	76612
1834	†	**CX**	A	*SC*	BI	76566	62282	70988	76576
1835	†	**CX**	A	*SC*	BI	76601	62307	70987	76631
1837	†	**CX**	A	*SC*	BI	76722	62360	71040	76793
1839	*	**N**	H	*SE*	RM	76607	62313	70993	76637
1840	*	**N**	H	*SE*	RM	76724	62362	71042	76795
1841	*	**N**	H	*SE*	RM	76603	62309	70989	76633
1842	*	**N**	H	*SE*	RM	76725	62363	71043	76796
1843	*	**N**	H	*SE*	RM	76731	62369	71049	76802
1845	†	**CX**	A	*SC*	BI	76599	62305	70985	76718
1846	†	**CX**	A	*SC*	BI	76737	62375	71055	76808
1847	†	**CX**	A	*SC*	BI	76600	62306	70986	76630
1848	†	**CX**	A	*SC*	BI	76605	62311	70991	76635
1850	†	**CX**	A	*SC*	BI	76629	62356	71036	76789
1851	†	**CX**	A	*SC*	BI	76721	62359	71039	76792
1853	†	**CX**	A	*SC*	BI	76606	62312	70992	76636
1854	†	**CX**	A	*SC*	BI	76738	62376	71056	76809
1855	†	**CX**	A	*SC*	BI	76720	62358	71038	76791
1856	†	**CX**	A	*SC*	BI	76739	62377	71057	76810
1857	†	**CX**	A	*SC*	BI	76610	62316	70996	76640
1858	‡	**CX**	A	*SC*	BI	76604	62310	70990	76634
1859	‡	**CX**	A	*SC*	BI	76727	62365	71045	76798
1860	‡	**CX**	A	*SC*	BI	76752	62390	71070	76823
1861	‡	**CX**	A	*SC*	BI	76735	62373	71053	76806
1862	†	**CX**	A	*SC*	BI	76736	62374	71054	76807
1863	†	**CX**	A	*SC*	BI	76742	62380	71060	76813
1864	†	**CX**	A	*SC*	BI	76741	62379	71059	76812
1865	†	**CX**	A	*SC*	BI	76745	62383	71063	76639
1866	†	**CX**	A	*SC*	BI	76743	62381	71061	76814
1867	†	**CX**	A	*SC*	BI	76744	62382	71062	76815
1868	†	**CX**	A	*SC*	BI	76751	62389	71069	76822
1869	†	**CX**	A	*SC*	BI	76753	62391	71071	76804
1870	*	**CX**	H	*SE*	RM	76108	62409	71089	76842

1871	*	**N**	H	*SE*	RM	76756	62394	71074	76827
1872	*	**N**	H	*SE*	RM	76771	62396	71076	76829
1873	*	**N**	H	*SE*	RM	76759	62397	71077	76830
1874	†	**CX**	A	*SC*	BI	76755	62393	71073	76826
1876	*	**N**	H	*SE*	RM	76761	62399	71079	76832
1877	*	**N**	H	*SE*	RM	76763	62401	71081	76834
1878	*	**N**	H	*SE*	RM	76768	62406	71086	76839
1879	*	**N**	H	*SE*	RM	76760	62398	71078	76831
1880		**ST**	H	*SW*	FR	76770	62408	71088	76841
1881		**ST**	H	*SW*	FR	76762	62400	71080	76833
1882		**ST**	H	*SW*	FR	76765	62403	71083	76836
1883		**ST**	H	*SW*	FR	76764	62402	71082	76835
1884		**ST**	H	*SW*	FR	76767	62405	71085	76838
1885		**ST**	H	*SW*	FR	76769	62407	71087	76840
1886		**ST**	H	*SW*	FR	76772	62410	71090	76843
1887		**ST**	H	*SW*	FR	76766	62404	71084	76837
1888		**N**	H	*SW*	FR	76773	62411	71091	76844
1889		**ST**	H	*SW*	FR	76774	62412	71092	76845
1890		**ST**	H	*SW*	FR	76775	62413	71093	76846
1891		**ST**	H	*SW*	FR	76776	62414	71094	76847
Spare	•	**BG**	A		ZG(S)			70995	

Class 421/6 (4-Cig). DTS–MBS–TS–DTC(B). Mk. 6 motor bogies.

1901	†	**CX**	P	*SC*	BI	76082	62023	70701	76028
1902	†	**CX**	P	*SC*	BI	76100	62041	71768	76046
1903	†	**CX**	A	*SC*	BI	76081	62022	70700	76027
1904	†	**CX**	A	*SC*	BI	76107	62048	70726	76053
1905	‡	**CX**	A	*SC*	BI	76099	62040	70718	76045
1906	†	**CX**	A	*SC*	BI	76105	62046	70724	76113
1907	†	**CX**	A	*SC*	BI	76104	62045	70723	76050
1908	†	**CX**	A	*SC*	BI	76096	62037	70715	76042

CLASS 412 (4-Bep) BR

For details see pages 288.

Class 412 (4-Bep). DMS(A)–TBC–TRBS–DMS(B).

2301	†	**ST**	P	*SW*	FR	61804	70607	69341	61805
2302	†	**ST**	P	*SW*	FR	61774	70592	69342	61809
2303	†	**ST**	P	*SW*	FR	61954	70656	69343	61955
2304	†	**ST**	P	*SW*	FR	61736	70573	69344	61737
2305	†	**ST**	P	*SW*	FR	61798	70354	69345	61799
2306	†	**ST**	P	*SW*	FR	61808	70609	69346	61775
2307	†	**ST**	P	*SW*	FR	61802	70606	69347	61803

CLASS 442 (5-Wes)   WESSEX   BREL

DTF–TS–MBLS–TSW–DTS. 'Express' stock. Gangwayed throughout. Air conditioned.

Construction: Steel.
Traction Motors: Four English Electric 546 of 300 kW each.
Dimensions: 23.15 (DTF & DTS) or 23.00 (MBLS, TS & TSW) x 2.74 x 3.81m.
Doors: Power operated sliding plug.
Maximum Speed: 100 m.p.h.   **Bogies:** Mk. 6/T4.
Couplings: Buckeye.   **Multiple Working:** SR type.

62937–62960. MBLS. Dia. ED268. Lot No. 31034 BREL Derby 1988–89. Modified Adtranz Crewe 1998. –/30 (*–/35) 1W. 55.2 t.
71818–71841. TS. Dia. EH288. Lot No. 31032 BREL Derby 1988–89. –/80 2T. 35.3 t.
71842–71865. TSW. Dia. EH289. Lot No. 31033 BREL Derby 1988–89. –/76 1W 2T. 35.4 t.
77382–77405. DTF. Dia. EE160. Lot No. 31030 BREL Derby 1988–89. 50/– 1T. 39.1 t.
77406–77429. DTS. Dia. EE273. Lot No. 31031 BREL Derby 1988–89. –/78 1T. 39.1 t.

2401	*	**SW**	A	*SW*	BM	77382	71818	62937	71842	77406
2402	*	**SW**	A	*SW*	BM	77383	71819	62938	71843	77407
2403	*	**SW**	A	*SW*	BM	77384	71820	62941	71844	77408
2404	*	**SW**	A	*SW*	BM	77385	71821	62939	71845	77409
2405	*	**SW**	A	*SW*	BM	77386	71822	62944	71846	77410
2406	*	**SW**	A	*SW*	BM	77389	71823	62942	71847	77411
2407	*	**SW**	A	*SW*	BM	77388	71824	62943	71848	77412
2408	*	**SW**	A	*SW*	BM	77387	71825	62945	71849	77413
2409	*	**SW**	A	*SW*	BM	77390	71826	62946	71850	77414
2410	*	**SW**	A	*SW*	BM	77391	71827	62948	71851	77415
2411	*	**SW**	A	*SW*	BM	77392	71828	62940	71858	77422
2412		**SW**	A	*SW*	BM	77393	71829	62947	71853	77417
2413		**SW**	A	*SW*	BM	77394	71830	62949	71854	77418
2414		**SW**	A	*SW*	BM	77395	71831	62950	71855	77419
2415	*	**SW**	A	*SW*	BM	77396	71832	62951	71856	77420
2416	*	**SW**	A	*SW*	BM	77397	71833	62952	71857	77421
2417	*	**SW**	A	*SW*	BM	77398	71834	62953	71852	77416
2418		**SW**	A	*SW*	BM	77399	71835	62954	71859	77423
2419	*	**SW**	A	*SW*	BM	77400	71836	62955	71860	77424
2420	*	**SW**	A	*SW*	BM	77401	71837	62956	71861	77425
2421	*	**SW**	A	*SW*	BM	77402	71838	62957	71862	77426
2422	*	**SW**	A	*SW*	BM	77403	71839	62958	71863	77427
2423	*	**SW**	A	*SW*	BM	77404	71840	62959	71864	77428
2424	*	**SW**	A	*SW*	BM	77405	71841	62960	71865	77429

Names (carried on MBLS):

2401	BEAULIEU		2404	BOROUGH OF WOKING
2402	COUNTY OF HAMPSHIRE		2405	CITY OF PORTSMOUTH
2403	THE NEW FOREST		2406	VICTORY

2407	THOMAS HARDY	2418	WESSEX CANCER TRUST
2408	COUNTY OF DORSET	2419	BBC SOUTH TODAY
2409	BOURNEMOUTH ORCHESTRAS	2420	CITY SOUTHAMPTON
2410	MERIDIAN TONIGHT	2422	OPERATION OVERLORD
2412	SPECIAL OLYMPICS	2423	COUNTY OF SURREY
2415	MARY ROSE	2424	GERRY NEWSOM
2416	MUM IN A MILLION 1997 – DOREEN SCANLON		

CLASS 423 (4-Vep/4-Vop)   BR

Various formations, see below. Gangwayed throughout.

Construction: Steel.
Traction Motors: Four English Electric 507 of 185 kW each.
Dimensions: 20.18 x 2.82 x 3.84 m.   **Doors:** Manually operated slam.
Maximum Speed: 90 m.p.h.   **Multiple Working:** SR type.
Couplings: Buckeye.   **Bogies:** Mk. 4/B5 (SR).

62121–62140. MBS. Dia. ED266. Lot No. 30760 Derby 1967. –/76. 49.0 t.
62182–62216. MBS. Dia. ED266. Lot No. 30773 York 1967–68. –/76. 49.0 t.
62217–62266. MBS. Dia. ED266. Lot No. 30794 York 1968–69. –/76. 49.0 t.
62267–62276. MBS. Dia. ED266. Lot No. 30800 York 1970. –/76. 49.0 t.
62317–62354. MBS. Dia. ED266. Lot No. 30813 York 1970–73. –/76. 49.0 t.
62435–62475. MBS. Dia. ED266. Lot No. 30851 York 1973–74. –/76. 49.0 t.
70781–70800. TS. Dia. EH291. Lot No. 30759 Derby 1967. –/98. 31.5 t.
70872–70906. TS. Dia. EH291. Lot No. 30772 York 1967–68. –/98. 31.5 t.
70907–70956. TS. Dia. EH291. Lot No. 30793 York 1968–69. –/98. 31.5 t.
70957–70966. TS. Dia. EH291. Lot No. 30801 York 1970. –/98. 31.5 t.
70997–71034. TS. Dia. EH291. Lot No. 30812 York 1970–73. –/98. 31.5 t.
71115–71155. TS. Dia. EH291. Lot No. 30852 York 1973–74. –/98. 31.5 t.
76230–76269. DTC. Dia. EE373. Lot No. 30758 York 1967. 18/46 (†§ 12/52)1T. 35.0 t.
76275. DTS. Dia. EE266. Built as loco-hauled vehicle to Lot No. 30086 Eastleigh 1953–55. Converted to Lot No. 30764 York 1966. –/64. 32.0 t.
76333–76402. DTC (*‡ DTS). Dia. EE373 (* EE281; ‡ EE278). Lot No. 30771 York 1967–68. (*Converted Adtranz, Chart Leacon 1999–2000). 18/46 († 12/52)1T ; (* –/70; ‡ –/88 0T). 32.5 t.
76441–76540. DTC. Dia. EE373. Lot No. 30792 York 1968–69. 18/46 (†‡ 12/52) 1T. 32.5 t.
76541–76560. DTC. Dia. EE373. Lot No. 30799 York 1970. 18/46 († 12/52) 1T. 32.5 t.
76641–76716. DTC. Dia. EE373. Lot No. 30811 York 1970–73. 18/46 († 12/52) 1T. 32.5 t.
76861–76942. DTC. Dia. EE368. Lot No. 30853 York 1973–74. 18/46 († 12/52) 1T. 32.5 t.

Class 423/1 (4-Vep). DTC–MBS–TS–DTC.

3401	**ST**	H	*SW*	WD	76230	62276	70781	76231
3402	**ST**	H	*SW*	WD	76233	62123	70782	76232
3403	**CX**	H	*SC*	BI	76234	62254	70783	76235
3404	**ST**	H	*SW*	WD	76378	62261	70894	76236

3405		ST	H	SW	WD	76239	62271	70785	76238
3406		ST	H	SW	WD	76241	62130	70786	76240
3407		ST	H	SW	WD	76243	62348	70787	76242
3408		ST	H	SW	WD	76244	62435	70788	76245
3409		ST	H	SW	WD	76246	62239	70789	76247
3410		ST	H	SW	WD	76369	62442	70790	76249
3411		ST	H	SW	WD	76250	62342	70791	76251
3412	†	CX	A	SE	RM	76252	62340	70792	76253
3413		ST	H	SW	WD	76255	62441	70793	76254
3414		ST	H	SW	WD	76257	62446	70794	76248
3415		N	H	SW	WD	76258	62462	70795	76259
3416	†	CX	A	SE	RM	76261	62451	70796	76260
3417		ST	H	SW	WD	76262	62236	70797	76263
3418		ST	H	SW	WD	76265	62133	70875	76264
3419		ST	H	SW	WD	76267	62354	70799	76266
3420		ST	H	SW	WD	76269	62349	70800	76268
3421	†	CX	A	SE	RM	76889	62449	71129	76890
3422	†	CX	A	SE	RM	76372	62201	70891	76371
3423	†	CX	A	SE	RM	76452	62222	70912	76451
3424	†	CX	A	SE	RM	76354	62185	70882	76353
3425		ST	H	SW	WD	76338	62192	70874	76358
3426		ST	H	SW	WD	76386	62208	70898	76385
3427		ST	H	SW	WD	76374	62184	70892	76373
3428		ST	H	SW	WD	76454	62223	70913	76453
3429		ST	H	SW	WD	76334	62202	70872	76333
3430		ST	H	SW	WD	76348	62189	70879	76347
3431		ST	H	SW	WD	76458	62182	70915	76457
3432		ST	H	SW	WD	76400	62225	70905	76399
3433		ST	H	SW	WD	76444	62215	70908	76443
3434		ST	H	SW	WD	76462	62218	70917	76461
3435		CX	P	SC	BI	76342	62228	70876	76341
3436		CX	P	SC	BI	76350	62190	70880	76349
3437		CX	P	SC	BI	76346	62186	70878	76345
3445	†	CX	A	SE	RM	76450	62242	70911	76449
3446	†	CX	A	SE	RM	76532	62243	70952	76531
3447	†	CX	A	SE	RM	76380	62199	70895	76379
3448	†	CX	A	SE	RM	76376	62221	70886	76375
3449	†	CX	A	SE	RM	76336	62205	70873	76335
3450	†	CX	A	SE	RM	76460	62203	70916	76459
3451	†	N	A	SE	RM	76488	62240	70930	76487
3452	†	CX	A	SE	RM	76340	62183	71021	76690
3453	†	CX	A	SE	RM	76382	62226	70896	76381
3454	†	CX	A	SE	RM	76390	62200	70798	76389
3455		ST	H	SW	WD	76388	62206	70899	76387
3456		ST	H	SW	WD	76456	62210	70914	76455
3457		ST	H	SW	WD	76392	62197	70901	76391
3458		ST	H	SW	WD	76394	62209	70902	76393
3459		ST	H	SW	WD	76396	62224	70903	76395
3466		ST	H	SW	WD	76464	62214	70918	76463
3467		ST	H	SW	WD	76446	62217	70909	76445
3468		ST	H	SW	WD	76448	62267	70910	76447

3469		**ST**	H	*SW*	WD	76546	62219	70959	76545
3470		**ST**	H	*SW*	WD	76496	62220	70934	76495
3471	†	**CX**	A	*SE*	RM	76498	62269	70935	76497
3472	†	**CX**	A	*SE*	RM	76500	62244	70936	76499
3473	‡	**CX**	A	*SE*	RM	76502	62245	70937	76339
3474	†	**CX**	A	*SE*	RM	76504	62246	70938	76503
3475	†	**CX**	A	*SE*	RM	76552	62270	70962	76551
3479		**CX**	H	*SC*	BI	76655	62272	71004	76656
3480		**ST**	H	*SW*	WD	76474	62323	70923	76473
3481		**ST**	H	*SW*	WD	76647	62324	70900	76648
3482		**CX**	H	*SC*	BI	76657	62320	71005	76658
3483		**CX**	H	*SC*	BI	76661	62233	71007	76662
3484		**CX**	H	*SC*	BI	76476	62325	70924	76475
3485		**CX**	H	*SC*	BI	76508	62327	70940	76507
3486		**CX**	H	*SC*	BI	76478	62234	70925	76477
3487	†	**CX**	A	*SC*	BI	76645	62250	70941	76509
3488		**CX**	H	*SC*	BI	76663	62235	71008	76664
3489		**CX**	H	*SC*	BI	76665	62251	71009	76666
3490		**CX**	H	*SC*	BI	76695	62328	71024	76696
3491	†	**CX**	A	*SE*	RM	76337	62436	70927	76481
3492	†	**CX**	A	*SE*	RM	76667	62344	71010	76668
3493	†	**CX**	A	*SE*	RM	76669	62237	71011	76670
3494	†	**CX**	A	*SE*	RM	76675	62330	71014	76676
3495	†	**CX**	A	*SE*	RM	76699	62331	71026	76700
3496	†	**CX**	A	*SE*	RM	76673	62334	71013	76674
3497	†	**CX**	A	*SE*	RM	76671	62346	71012	76672
3498	†	**CX**	A	*SE*	RM	76701	62333	71027	76702
3499	†	**CX**	A	*SE*	RM	76901	62347	71135	76902
3500	†	**CX**	A	*SE*	RM	76470	62455	70921	76469
3501		**CX**	P	*SC*	BI	76512	62332	70942	76511
3503		**CX**	P	*SC*	BI	76681	62231	71017	76682
3504		**CX**	P	*SC*	BI	76711	62351	71032	76712
3505		**CX**	P	*SC*	BI	76472	62352	70922	76471
3508		**ST**	H	*SW*	WD	76643	62273	70998	76644
3509		**ST**	H	*SW*	WD	76560	62275	70966	76559
3510		**ST**	H	*SW*	WD	76641	62318	70997	76642
3511	†	**CX**	A	*SE*	RM	76893	62135	70999	76646
3512		**CX**	P	*SC*	BI	76679	62337	71016	76680
3514		**CX**	P	*SC*	BI	76683	62136	71018	76684
3515		**CX**	P	*SC*	BI	76544	62319	70958	76543
3516		**ST**	H	*SW*	WD	76693	62268	71023	76694
3517		**CX**	P	*SC*	BI	76685	62338	71019	76686
3518		**CX**	P	*SC*	BI	76689	62343	70887	76363
3519		**ST**	H	*SW*	WD	76556	62274	70964	76555
3520		**ST**	H	*SW*	WD	76697	62131	71025	76698
3521	†	**N**	A	*SE*	RM	76484	62345	70928	76483
3523		**CX**	H	*SC*	BI	76651	62139	71002	76652
3524		**CX**	H	*SC*	BI	76466	62322	70919	76370
3529		**CX**	H	*SC*	BI	76659	62257	71006	76660
3530		**CX**	H	*SC*	BI	76468	62256	70920	76467
3531		**CX**	H	*SC*	BI	76649	62230	71001	76650

3535		**CX**	P	*SC*	BI	76677	62335	71015	76678
3536		**ST**	H	*SW*	WD	76384	62207	70897	76383
3539		**ST**	H	*SW*	WD	76861	62122	71115	76862
3540		**ST**	H	*SW*	WD	76863	62128	71116	76864
3542		**ST**	H	*SW*	WD	76480	62127	70926	76479
3543	†	**N**	A	*SC*	BI	76899	62137	71134	76900
3544	†	**CX**	A	*SE*	RM	76892	62454	71131	76894
3545	†	**CX**	A	*SE*	RM	76875	62121	71122	76876
3546		**CX**	P	*SC*	BI	76687	62339	71020	76688
3547	†	**N**	A	*SE*	RM	76895	62126	71132	76896
3548	†	**N**	A	*SE*	RM	76903	62452	71136	76904
3549		**CX**	P	*SC*	BI	76707	62132	71030	76708
3551		**CX**	P	*SC*	BI	76465	62456	71033	76714
3552		**ST**	H	*SW*	WD	76715	62353	71034	76716
3553	†	**N**	A	*SE*	RM	76913	62241	71141	76914
3554	†	**CX**	A	*SE*	RM	76905	62461	71137	76906
3555		**ST**	H	*SW*	WD	76865	62140	71117	76866
3556	†	**CX**	A	*SE*	RM	76885	62457	71127	76886
3557		**ST**	H	*SW*	WD	76869	62437	71119	76870
3558		**ST**	H	*SW*	WD	76352	62447	70881	76351
3559		**ST**	H	*SW*	WD	76486	62439	70929	76485
3560	†	**CX**	A	*SE*	RM	76897	62191	71133	76898
3561		**ST**	H	*SW*	WD	76867	62453	71118	76868
3562	†	**CX**	A	*SE*	RM	76907	62129	71138	76908
3563		**ST**	H	*SW*	WD	76873	62438	71121	76874
3564	†	**CX**	A	*SE*	RM	76883	62458	71126	76884
3565	†	**CX**	A	*SE*	RM	76877	62134	71123	76878
3566	†	**CX**	A	*SE*	RM	76916	62443	71142	76916
3567		**ST**	H	*SW*	WD	76871	62138	71120	76872
3568	†	**CX**	A	*SE*	RM	76887	62440	71128	76888
3569		**ST**	H	*SW*	WD	76344	62448	70877	76343
3570	†	**CX**	A	*SE*	RM	76909	62187	71139	76910
3571	†	**CX**	A	*SE*	RM	76927	62463	71148	76928
3572	†	**CX**	A	*SE*	RM	76879	62468	71124	76880
3573	†	**CX**	A	*SE*	RM	76919	62444	71144	76920
3574	†	**CX**	A	*SE*	RM	76929	62464	71149	76930
3575	†	**CX**	A	*SE*	RM	76931	62469	71150	76932
3576		**ST**	H	*SW*	WD	76362	62196	70890	76361
3577	†	**CX**	A	*SE*	RM	76933	62459	71151	76934
3578		**ST**	H	*SW*	WD	76356	62193	70883	76355
3579	†	**CX**	A	*SE*	RM	76935	62471	71152	76936
3580		**ST**	H	*SW*	WD	76360	62195	70885	76359
3581		**ST**	H	*SW*	WD	76366	62198	70888	76365
3582	†	**CX**	A	*SE*	RM	76891	62472	71130	76275
3583	†	**CX**	A	*SE*	RM	76937	62450	71153	76938
3584	†	**CX**	A	*SE*	RM	76881	62473	71125	76882
3585	†	**CX**	A	*SE*	RM	76939	62445	71154	76940
3586	†	**CX**	A	*SE*	RM	76921	62474	71145	76922
3587	†	**CX**	A	*SE*	RM	76925	62465	71147	76926
3588	†	**CX**	A	*SE*	RM	76923	62467	71146	76924
3589	†	**CX**	A	*SE*	RM	76911	62466	71140	76912

3590	†	**CX**	A	*SE*	RM	76941	62460	71155	76942
3591	†	**CX**	A	*SE*	RM	76917	62475	71143	76918
3801	†	**CX**	P	*SE*	RM	76522	62229	70947	76521
3802	†	**CX**	P	*SE*	RM	76534	62188	70953	76533
3803	†	**CX**	P	*SE*	RM	76494	62263	70933	76493
3804	†	**CX**	P	*SE*	RM	76368	62204	70889	76367
3805	†	**CX**	P	*SE*	RM	76540	62211	70956	76539
3806	†	**CX**	P	*SE*	RM	76538	62212	70955	76537
3807	†	**CX**	P	*SE*	RM	76542	62264	70957	76541
3808	†	**CX**	P	*SE*	RM	76550	62248	70961	76549
3809		**N**	P	*SW*	WD	76516	62253	70944	76515
3810		**N**	P	*SW*	WD	76709	62252	71031	76710
3811		**N**	P	*SW*	WD	76514	62249	70943	76513
3812		**ST**	P	*SW*	WD	76703	62238	71028	76704
Spare		**N**	H		WD(S)		62470		

Class 423/2 (4-Vop). DTS–MBS–TS–DTS. Declassified units for Connex South Central 'South London Metro' services.

Notes: 70904^ǁ in unit 3903 is actually 70954.

No.	Former No.								
3901	3439	*	**CX**	P	*SC*	BI	76402	62227	70906	76401
3902	3533	*	**CX**	P	*SC*	BI	76364	62260	70949	76525
3903	3462	*	**CX**	P	*SC*	BI	76536	62213	70904^ǁ	76535
3904	3513	*	**CX**	P	*SC*	BI	76691	62336	71022	76692
3905	3463	*	**CX**	P	*SC*	BI	76398	62266	70904	76397
3906	3550	*	**CX**	P	*SC*	BI	76490	62350	70931	76489
3907	3534	*	**CX**	P	*SC*	BI	76506	62259	70939	76505
3908	3464	*	**CX**	P	*SC*	BI	76442	62265	70907	76441
3909	3522	*	**CX**	P	*SC*	BI	76705	62341	71029	76706
3910	3438	*	**CX**	P	*SC*	BI	76530	62262	70951	76529
3911	3476	*	**CX**	P	*SC*	BI	76548	62247	70960	76547
3912	3442	*	**CX**	P	*SC*	BI	76492	62216	70932	76491
3913	3478	*	**CX**	P	*SC*	BI	76653	62125	71003	76654
3914	3527	*	**CX**	P	*SC*	BI	76520	62326	70946	76519
3915	3526	*	**CX**	P	*SC*	BI	76524	62255	70948	76523
3916	3528	*	**CX**	P	*SC*	BI	76518	62258	70945	76517
3917	3507	*	**CX**	P	*SC*	BI	76558	62232	70965	76557
3918	3532	*	**CX**	P	*SC*	BI	76528	62321	70950	76527
3919	3506	*	**CX**	P	*SC*	BI	76554	62317	70963	76553

CLASS 455   BREL

DTS–MS–TS–DTS. Gangwayed throughout. Disc brakes .

Construction: Steel (MS & DTS); Steel underframe, aluminium alloy body and roof (TS).
Traction Motors: Four GEC507-20J of 185 kW each.
Dimensions: 19.92 x 2.82 x 3.77 (3.58 Class 455/7 TSO) m.
Maximum Speed: 75 m.p.h.   **Couplers:** Tightlock.
Doors: Power operated sliding.
Bogies: BP27/BT13 (Classes 455/8 and 455/9) or BX1 (Class 455/7).

Multiple Working: Classes 455–456.

Class 455/7. Built as 3-car units, augmented with ex-Class 508 TSO. Pressure heating & ventilation.

62783–62825. MS. Dia. EC203. Lot No. 30975 BREL York 1984–85. –/84. 45.0 t.
71526–71568. TS. Dia. EH219. Lot No. 30944 BREL York 1977–80. –/86. 25.5 t.
77727–77812. DTS. Dia. EE218. Lot No. 30976 BREL York 1984–85. –/74. 29.5 t.

5701	**N**	P	*SW*	WD	77727	62783	71545	77728
5702	**N**	P	*SW*	WD	77729	62784	71547	77730
5703	**N**	P	*SW*	WD	77731	62785	71540	77732
5704	**N**	P	*SW*	WD	77733	62786	71548	77734
5705	**ST**	P	*SW*	WD	77735	62787	71565	77736
5706	**N**	P	*SW*	WD	77737	62788	71534	77738
5707	**N**	P	*SW*	WD	77739	62789	71536	77740
5708	**N**	P	*SW*	WD	77741	62790	71560	77742
5709	**N**	P	*SW*	WD	77743	62791	71532	77744
5710	**N**	P	*SW*	WD	77745	62792	71566	77746
5711	**N**	P	*SW*	WD	77747	62793	71542	77748
5712	**N**	P	*SW*	WD	77749	62794	71546	77750
5713	**N**	P	*SW*	WD	77751	62795	71567	77752
5714	**ST**	P	*SW*	WD	77753	62796	71539	77754
5715	**ST**	P	*SW*	WD	77755	62797	71535	77756
5716	**ST**	P	*SW*	WD	77757	62798	71564	77758
5717	**N**	P	*SW*	WD	77759	62799	71528	77760
5718	**N**	P	*SW*	WD	77761	62800	71557	77762
5719	**ST**	P	*SW*	WD	77763	62801	71558	77764
5720	**ST**	P	*SW*	WD	77765	62802	71568	77766
5721	**ST**	P	*SW*	WD	77767	62803	71553	77768
5722	**ST**	P	*SW*	WD	77769	62804	71533	77770
5723	**ST**	P	*SW*	WD	77771	62805	71526	77772
5724	**ST**	P	*SW*	WD	77773	62806	71561	77774
5725	**ST**	P	*SW*	WD	77775	62807	71541	77776
5726	**ST**	P	*SW*	WD	77777	62808	71556	77778
5727	**ST**	P	*SW*	WD	77779	62809	71562	77780
5728	**ST**	P	*SW*	WD	77781	62810	71527	77782
5729	**ST**	P	*SW*	WD	77783	62811	71550	77784
5730	**ST**	P	*SW*	WD	77785	62812	71551	77786
5731	**ST**	P	*SW*	WD	77787	62813	71555	77788
5732	**ST**	P	*SW*	WD	77789	62814	71552	77790
5733	**ST**	P	*SW*	WD	77791	62815	71549	77792
5734	**ST**	P	*SW*	WD	77793	62816	71531	77794
5735	**ST**	P	*SW*	WD	77795	62817	71563	77796
5736	**ST**	P	*SW*	WD	77797	62818	71554	77798
5737	**ST**	P	*SW*	WD	77799	62819	71544	77800
5738	**ST**	P	*SW*	WD	77801	62820	71529	77802
5739	**ST**	P	*SW*	WD	77803	62821	71537	77804
5740	**ST**	P	*SW*	WD	77805	62822	71530	77806
5741	**ST**	P	*SW*	WD	77807	62823	71559	77808
5742	**ST**	P	*SW*	WD	77809	62824	71543	77810
5750	**ST**	P	*SW*	WD	77811	62825	71538	77812

Names:

5711	SPIRIT OF RUGBY
5731	VARIETY CLUB
5735	The Royal Borough of Kingston
5750	Wimbledon Train Care

Class 455/8. Pressure heating & ventilation.

Non Standard/Advertising Liveries:
• 5860/70 'South West Trains'.
• 5864 'Royal British Legion Poppy Appeal'.

62709–62782. MS. Dia. EC203. Lot No. 30973 BREL York 1982–84. –/84. 45.6 t.
71637–71710. TS. Dia. EH221. Lot No. 30974 BREL York 1982–84. –/84. 27.1 t.
77579–77726. DTS. Dia. EE218. Lot No. 30972 BREL York 1982–84. –/74. 29.5 t.

5801	N	H	*SC*	SU	77579	62709	71637	77580
5802	CX	H	*SC*	SU	77581	62710	71664	77582
5803	CX	H	*SC*	SU	77583	62711	71639	77584
5804	CX	H	*SC*	SU	77585	62712	71640	77586
5805	CX	H	*SC*	SU	77587	62713	71641	77588
5806	CX	H	*SC*	SU	77589	62714	71642	77590
5807	N	H	*SC*	SU	77591	62715	71643	77592
5808	N	H	*SC*	SU	77593	62716	71644	77594
5809	N	H	*SC*	SU	77595	62717	71645	77596
5810	CX	H	*SC*	SU	77597	62718	71646	77598
5811	CX	H	*SC*	SU	77599	62719	71647	77600
5812	CX	H	*SC*	SU	77601	62720	71648	77602
5813	N	H	*SC*	SU	77603	62721	71649	77604
5814	CX	H	*SC*	SU	77605	62722	71650	77606
5815	CX	H	*SC*	SU	77607	62723	71651	77608
5816	N	H	*SC*	SU	77609	62724	71652	77633
5817	N	H	*SC*	SU	77611	62725	71653	77612
5818	N	H	*SC*	SU	77613	62726	71654	77614
5819	N	H	*SC*	SU	77615	62727	71655	77616
5820	CX	H	*SC*	SU	77617	62728	71656	77618
5821	CX	H	*SC*	SU	77619	62729	71657	77620
5822	N	H	*SC*	SU	77621	62730	71658	77622
5823	N	H	*SC*	SU	77623	62731	71659	77624
5824	N	H	*SC*	SU	77637	62732	71660	77626
5825	N	H	*SC*	SU	77627	62733	71661	77628
5826	N	H	*SC*	SU	77629	62734	71662	77630
5827	N	H	*SC*	SU	77610	62735	71663	77632
5828	N	H	*SC*	SU	77631	62736	71638	77634
5829	N	H	*SC*	SU	77635	62737	71665	77636
5830	N	H	*SC*	SU	77625	62743	71666	77638
5831	N	H	*SC*	SU	77639	62739	71667	77640
5832	N	H	*SC*	SU	77641	62740	71668	77642
5833	N	H	*SC*	SU	77643	62741	71669	77644
5834	N	H	*SC*	SU	77645	62742	71670	77646
5835	N	H	*SC*	SU	77647	62738	71671	77648
5836	N	H	*SC*	SU	77649	62744	71672	77650
5837	N	H	*SC*	SU	77651	62745	71673	77652

5838	N	H	*SC*	SU	77653	62746	71674	77654
5839	N	H	*SC*	SU	77655	62747	71675	77656
5840	N	H	*SC*	SU	77657	62748	71676	77658
5841	N	H	*SC*	SU	77659	62749	71677	77660
5842	N	H	*SC*	SU	77661	62750	71678	77662
5843	N	H	*SC*	SU	77663	62751	71679	77664
5844	N	H	*SC*	SU	77665	62752	71680	77666
5845	N	H	*SC*	SU	77667	62753	71681	77668
5846	N	H	*SC*	SU	77669	62754	71682	77670
5847	ST	P	*SW*	WD	77671	62755	71683	77672
5848	ST	P	*SW*	WD	77673	62756	71684	77674
5849	ST	P	*SW*	WD	77675	62757	71685	77676
5850	N	P	*SW*	WD	77677	62758	71686	77678
5851	N	P	*SW*	WD	77679	62759	71687	77680
5852	N	P	*SW*	WD	77681	62760	71688	77682
5853	N	P	*SW*	WD	77683	62761	71689	77684
5854	N	P	*SW*	WD	77685	62762	71690	77686
5855	N	P	*SW*	WD	77687	62763	71691	77688
5856	N	P	*SW*	WD	77689	62764	71692	77690
5857	N	P	*SW*	WD	77691	62765	71693	77692
5858	N	P	*SW*	WD	77693	62766	71694	77694
5859	N	P	*SW*	WD	77695	62767	71695	77696
5860	AL	P	*SW*	WD	77697	62768	71696	77698
5861	N	P	*SW*	WD	77699	62769	71697	77700
5862	N	P	*SW*	WD	77701	62770	71698	77702
5863	N	P	*SW*	WD	77703	62771	71699	77704
5864	AL	P	*SW*	WD	77705	62772	71700	77706
5865	N	P	*SW*	WD	77707	62773	71701	77708
5866	N	P	*SW*	WD	77709	62774	71702	77710
5867	N	P	*SW*	WD	77711	62775	71703	77712
5868	N	P	*SW*	WD	77713	62776	71704	77714
5869	N	P	*SW*	WD	77715	62777	71705	77716
5870	AL	P	*SW*	WD	77717	62778	71706	77718
5871	N	P	*SW*	WD	77719	62779	71707	77720
5872	N	P	*SW*	WD	77721	62780	71708	77722
5873	N	P	*SW*	WD	77723	62781	71709	77724
5874	N	P	*SW*	WD	77725	62782	71710	77726

Class 455/9. Convection heating.

Non Standard/Advertising Liveries:
• 5904 'South West Trains'.

62826–62845. MS. Dia. EC206. Lot No. 30992 BREL York 1985. –/84. 45.6 (†48.0) t.
71714–71733. TS. Dia. EH224. Lot No. 30993 BREL York 1985. –/84. 27.1 t.
77813–77852. DTS. Dia. EE226. Lot No. 30991 BREL York 1985. –/74. 29.5 t.

5901	ST	P	*SW*	WD	77813	62826	71714	77814
5902	ST	P	*SW*	WD	77815	62827	71715	77816
5903	ST	P	*SW*	WD	77817	62828	71716	77818
5904	AL	P	*SW*	WD	77819	62829	71717	77820
5905	ST	P	*SW*	WD	77821	62830	71725	77822

▲ Old Strathclyde PTE liveried Class 303 No. 303 008 departs from Glasgow Central on 17th July 2000 with a Wemyss Bay service. **D. Ford**

▼ Only a few units of Class 305 now remain in service. One of them, Regional Railways liveried No. 305 519, waits to enter Slateford station whilst forming the 17.50 North Berwick–Kirknewton service on 9th May 2000. **Ross Aitken**

▲ A Skipton–Leeds service, formed of West Yorkshire PTE liveried Class 308 No. 308 163, pauses at Bingley on 20th April 2000. **Les Nixon**

▼ LTS Rail operated slam-door stock still carries Network SouthEast livery. Here, Class 312 No. 312 798 passes Shadwell with the 09.50 London Fenchurch Street–Southend Central on 28th August 2000. **Hugh Ballantyne**

▲ Whilst the livery design is similar, Silverlink liveried units are branded 'metro' or 'county' dependant upon the services on which they are used. Silverlink metro branded Class 313 No. 313 103 is pictured forming a Willesden–Clapham Junction service at Kensington Olympia on 26th June 2000. **D. Ford**

▼ Stathclyde PTE liveried Class 314 No. 314 212 leaves Glasgow Central with a Newton service. The date is 17th July 2000. **D. Ford**

▲ A pair of First Great Eastern liveried Class 315 units, Nos. 315 818 and 315 825, pass Pudding Mill Lane Docklands Light Railway station on 10th April 2000 whilst forming an empty caoching stock train from London Liverpool Street.

Alex Dasi-Sutton

▼ Class 317s operated by LTS Rail carry modified form of Network SouthEast livery, the main alteration to which is the red stripe having been replaced with a green stripe. A example of this livery is seen here on No. 317 311 as is enters Bethnal Green with the 10.19 London Liverpool Street–Cambridge on 17th June 2000. **K. Conkey**

▲ West Anglia Great Northern (WAGN) Railway liveried Class 317 No. 317 664 passes through Stratford on 31st March 2000 with an empty coaching stock train.
Ross Aitken

▼ Strathclyde PTE liveried Class 318 No. 318 252 waits to form its next train at Glasgow Central on 16th September 2000. **Stephen Widdowson**

▲ The 13.31 Luton–Sutton pauses at Cricklewood on 23rd September 2000 formed of Class 319 No. 319 429 in Thameslink livery. **K. Conkey**

▼ Class 320 No. 320 319 stands at Springburn on 13th August 1999. The unit had just arrived with an empty coaching stock train from Yoker EMUD and was later to form a service to Milngavie. **Hugh Ballantyne**

▲ First Great Eastern liveried Class 321 No. 321 302 passes Witham with the 10.25 Clacton–London Liverpool Street service on 25th August 2000. **Alan Sargeant**

▼ North Western Trains liveried Class 323 No. 323 233 is pictured departing from Manchester Piccadilly on 11th May 2000. **G.W. Morrison**

▲ Royal Mail liveried Class 325 No. 325 014 passes Durham with a Shieldmuir–London Royal Mail service on 26th July 1999.   **Ian A. Lyall**

▼ Heathrow Express Class 332 units, Nos. 332 010 and 332 005, leave London Paddington with the 13.25 to Heathrow Airport on 30th August 2000. The leading car of this formation has had Heathrow Express all-over vinyls applied.

Hugh Ballantyne

▲ Class 333 No. 333 001 at Neville Hill on 22nd March 2000. These units carry the livery used on Northern Spirit units which operate on services funded by West Yorkshire PTE consisting of red with a silver 'N' in place of the usual colours of turquoise and lime green. **G.W. Morrison**

▼ LTS Rail liveried Class 357s Nos. 357 023 and 357 019 pass Shadwell on a test run from London Fenchurch Street on 28th August 2000. It is expected that units of this class will be put into c2c livery by the application of vinyls.
Hugh Ballantyne

▲ Network SouthEast liveried Class 365 No. 365 540 is pictured passing through Welwyn Garden City with the 07.51 London Kings Cross–Cambridge semi-fast service on 24th July 1999. **David Brown**

▼ Class 375 'Electrostar' No. 375 603 is pictured in a plain white livery which is carried by these units prior to the application of vinyls. The location was Brighton, where the unit was put on public display for three days from April 18th 2000 when this picture was taken. **Chris Wilson**

▲ Stagecoach liveried Class 411/5 (4-Cep) No. 1538 and Class 423/1 (4-Vep) No. 3567 pass East Wimbledon with the 16.40 London Waterloo–Portsmouth Harbour via Eastleigh on 5th May 2000. **David Brown**

▼ Two Class 421 (4-Cig) units, Nos. 1801 and 1724, near Redhill with the 15.02 London Victoria–Bognor Regis & Portsmouth Harbour on 29th July 2000. Both units carry Connex livery. **Alex Dasi-Sutton**

▲ South West Trains liveried Class 442 No. 2406 crosses Holes Bay Causeway as it leaves Poole whilst forming a London Waterloo–Weymouth service on 26th August 1999. **John Chalcraft**

▼ Connex liveried Class 423 No. 3492 at Swanley on 5th May 2000 with the 10.41 London Victoria–Faversham service. **Rodney Lissenden**

▲ Advertising liveries are becoming a common sight, being carried by units of various classes of EMUs. Here, South West Trains operated Class 455/9 No. 5904 displays its own example as it pulls away from New Malden with the 09.32 London Waterloo–Richmond–Kingston–London Waterloo circular service. **David Brown**

▼ South West Trains liveried Class 458 'Juniper' No. 8005 near New Malden with 14.20 London Waterloo–Alton on 28th June 2000.　　　　**Alex Dasi-Sutton**

▲ Class 456 No. 456 006, in Network SouthEast livery, approaches Wandsworth Road on 9th November 1999 with the 12.10 London Victoria–London Bridge.

K. Conkey

▼ Gatwick Express liveried Class 460 No. 460 004 is pictured near Horley on 23rd September 2000 whilst forming the 14.00 London Victoria–Gatwick Airport. These units only carry the last two digits of the set number. **Chris Wilson**

▲ Connex liveried Class 465 No. 465 017 at Swanley with the 10.43 London Blackfriars–Sevenoaks service on 5th May 2000. The blue visable on the upper bodyside of this unit is due to the original Network SouthEast livery being covered by the application of Connex vinyls on the lower bodyside only. **Rodney Lissenden**

▼ Class 483 No. 483 004 arriving at Ryde St Johns Road with 09.13 Shanklin–Ryde Pier Head on 18th July 2000. The unit carries Island Line 'Dinosaur' livery.
Martyn Hilbert

▲ Merseytravel liveried Class 507 No. 507 004 pulls into Capenhurst with a Liverpool–Chester service on 19th July 2000. **George Allsop**

▼ Class 373 'Eurostar' set Nos. 3003/4 form the 11.23 London Waterloo–Paris Nord near Marden on 27th May 2000. **Brian Denton**

5906	**ST**	P	*SW*	WD	77823	62831	71719	77824
5907	**ST**	P	*SW*	WD	77825	62832	71720	77826
5908	**ST**	P	*SW*	WD	77827	62833	71721	77828
5909	**ST**	P	*SW*	WD	77829	62834	71722	77830
5910	**ST**	P	*SW*	WD	77831	62835	71723	77832
5911	**ST**	P	*SW*	WD	77833	62836	71724	77834
5912	† **ST**	P	*SW*	WD	77835	62837		77836
5913	**ST**	P	*SW*	WD	77837	62838	71726	77838
5914	**ST**	P	*SW*	WD	77839	62839	71727	77840
5915	**ST**	P	*SW*	WD	77841	62840	71728	77842
5916	**ST**	P	*SW*	WD	77843	62841	71729	77844
5917	**ST**	P	*SW*	WD	77845	62842	71730	77846
5918	**ST**	P	*SW*	WD	77847	62843		77848
5919	**ST**	P	*SW*	WD	77849	62844	71718	77850
5920	**ST**	P	*SW*	WD	77851	62845	71733	77852
Spare	**ST**	P		ZG(S)	71731	71732		

CLASS 458 (4-Jop)   JUNIPER   ALSTOM

DMC(A)–PTS–MS–DMC(B). Gangwayed throughout. Disc and regenerative brakes. Air conditioned. Currently in the process of entering service with South West Trains.

Construction: Steel.
Supply System: 750 V d.c. third rail with provision for 25 kV a.c. 50 Hz overhead.
Traction Motors: Two Alstom ONIX 800 of 270 kW each per motor car.
Dimensions: 21.16 (DMC) or 19.94 (MS & PTS) x 2.80 x 3.77. m.
Maximum Speed: 100 m.p.h.   **Doors:** Power operated sliding plug.
Couplers: Tightlock.   **Bogies:** ACR.
Multiple Working: Within class.
67601–67630. DMC(A). Dia. EA302. Alstom Birmingham 1998–2000. 12/63. 45.2 t.
67701–67730. DMC(B). Dia. EA303. Alstom Birmingham 1998–2000. 12/63. 45.2 t.
74001–74030. PTS. Dia. EH250. Alstom Birmingham 1998–2000. –/49 1TD 2W. 33.3 t.
74101–74130. MS. Dia. EC226. Alstom Birmingham 1998–2000. –/75 1T. 40.6 t.

8001	**U**	P		WD	67601	74001	74101	67701
8002	**SW**	P		WB(S)	67602	74002	74102	67702
8003	**SW**	P		WB(S)	67603	74003	74103	67703
8004	**SW**	P		WB(S)	67604	74004	74104	67704
8005	**SW**	P	*SW*	WD	67605	74005	74105	67705
8006	**SW**	P	*SW*	WD	67606	74006	74106	67706
8007	**SW**	P		WD(S)	67607	74007	74107	67707
8008	**SW**	P		WD(S)	67608	74008	74108	67708
8009	**SW**	P		WD(S)	67609	74009	74109	67709
8010	**SW**	P		WD	67610	74010	74110	67710
8011	**SW**	P		WD	67611	74011	74111	67711
8012	**SW**	P		WD	67612	74012	74112	67712
8013	**SW**	P	*TC*	WD	67613	74013	74113	67713

8014	**SW**	P	*TC*	WD	67614	74014	74114	67714
8015	**SW**	P		ZG(S)	67615	74015	74115	67715
8016	**SW**	P		ZG(S)	67616	74016	74116	67716
8017	**SW**	P		KN(S)	67617	74017	74117	67717
8018	**SW**	P		KN(S)	67618	74018	74118	67718
8019	**SW**	P		KN(S)	67619	74019	74119	67719
8020	**SW**	P		KN(S)	67620	74020	74120	67720
8021	**SW**	P			67621	74021	74121	67721
8022	**SW**	P			67622	74022	74122	67722
8023	**SW**	P			67623	74023	74123	67723
8024	**SW**	P			67624	74024	74124	67724
8025	**SW**	P			67625	74025	74125	67724
8026	**SW**	P			67626	74026	74126	67726
8027	**SW**	P			67627	74027	74127	67727
8028	**SW**	P			67628	74028	74128	67728
8029	**SW**	P			67629	74029	74129	67729
8030	**SW**	P			67630	74030	74130	67730

CLASS 488   **BR**

Various formations, see below. 'Express' stock. Gangwayed throughout. Air conditioned.

Construction: Steel.
Dimensions: 20.38 x 2.84 x 3.79 m.   **Doors:** Manually operated slam.
Maximum Speed: 90 m.p.h.   **Bogies:** B4.
Couplings: Buckeye.   **Multiple Working:** SR type.

Advertising Livery:
* 8203/04/07/08/10, 8304/05/10/14/19 'Continental Airlines'.

72500–72509. TFH. Dia. EP101. Built as loco-hauled vehicles to Lot No. 30859 Derby 1973–74. Converted BREL Eastleigh 1983–84. 41/– 1T. 35.0 t.
72602–14/16–18/20–44/46/47. TSH. Dia. EP201. Built as loco-hauled vehicles to Lot No. 30860 Derby 1973–74. Converted BREL Eastleigh 1983–84. –/48 1T (* 1W). 35.0 t.
72615/19/45. TSH. Dia. EP201. Built as loco-hauled vehicles to Lot No. 30846 Derby 1973. Converted BREL Eastleigh 1983–84. –/48 1T. 35.0 t.
72701–72718. TS. Dia. EH290. Built as loco-hauled vehicles to Lot No. 30860 Derby 1973–74. Converted BREL Eastleigh 1983–84. –/48 1T. 35.0 t.

CLASS 488/2. 2-car units. TFH–TSH.

8201	*	**GX**	P	*GX*	SL	72500	72638
8202	*	**GX**	P	*GX*	SL	72501	72617
8203	*	**AL**	P	*GX*	SL	72502	72640
8204	*	**AL**	P		PY(S)	72503	72641
8205	*	**GX**	P	*GX*	SL	72504	72628
8206	*	**GX**	P	*GX*	SL	72505	72629
8207	*	**AL**	P	*GX*	SL	72506	72642
8208	*	**AL**	P	*GB*	PY(S)	72507	72643
8209	*	**GX**	P		ZG(S)	72508	72644
8210	*	**AL**	P	*GX*	SL	72509	72635

CLASS 488/3. 3-car units. TFH–TS–TSH.

8302	**GX**	P	*GX*	SL	72602	72701	72604
8303	**GX**	P		PY(S)	72603	72702	72608
8304	**AL**	P	*GX*	SL	72606	72703	72611
8305	**AL**	P		PY(S)	72605	72704	72609
8306	**GX**	P	*GX*	SL	72607	72705	72610
8307	**GX**	P	*GX*	SL	72612	72706	72613
8308	**GX**	P		PY(S)	72614	72707	72615
8309	**GX**	P	*GX*	SL	72616	72708	72639
8310	**AL**	P	*GX*	SL	72618	72709	72619
8311	**GX**	P		ZG(S)	72620	72710	72621
8312	**GX**	P	*GB*	PY(S)	72622	72711	72623
8313	**GX**	P		ZG(S)	72624	72712	72625
8314	**AL**	P		PY(S)	72626	72713	72627
8315	**GX**	P	*GB*	PY(S)	72636	72714	72645
8316	**GX**	P	*GX*	SL	72630	72715	72631
8317	**GX**	P	*GX*	SL	72632	72716	72633
8318	**GX**	P		PY(S)	72634	72717	72637
8319	**AL**	P		PY(S)	72646	72718	72647

CLASS 489   BR

DMLV. Gangwayed at non-driving end only. Luggage vans which operate in conjunction with Class 488.

Construction: Steel.
Traction Motors: Two English Electric 507 of 185 kW each.
Dimensions: 20.45 x 2.82 x 3.86 m.   **Doors:** Manually operated slam.
Maximum Speed: 90 m.p.h.   **Bogies:** B4.
Couplings: Buckeye.   **Multiple Working:** SR type.

68500–68509. DMLV. Dia. EB501. Built as DMBS to Lot No. 30452 Eastleigh 1959. Converted BREL Eastleigh 1983–84. 40.5 t.

9101	**GX**	P	*GX*	SL	68500
9102	**GX**	P		PY(S)	68501
9103	**GX**	P	*GX*	SL	68502
9104	**GX**	P		ZG(S)	68503
9105	**GX**	P	*GX*	SL	68504
9106	**GX**	P	*GX*	SL	68505
9107	**GX**	P	*GX*	SL	68506
9108	**GX**	P		PY(S)	68507
9109	**GX**	P	*GX*	SL	68508
9110	**GX**	P	*GX*	SL	68509

CLASS 424   CLASSIC   ADTRANZ

DTS. Gangwayed within unit. Prototype of a scheme to rebuild Mark 1 design units.

Construction: Steel.
Dimensions: **Doors:** Power operated sliding.

Maximum Speed: 90 m.p.h.   **Bogies:** B5 (SR).
Couplers: Tightlock.   **Multiple Working:**

Non Standard Livery:
• Silver with black window surrounds.

76112. DTS. Dia. EE280. Built as DTCso to Lot No. 30741 York 1963–66. Rebuilt
Adtranz Derby 1997. –/77. 34.0 t.

424 001	**0**	A	ZD(S)	76112	

CLASS 438 (4-TC)   BR

DTS–TBS–TCK–DTS. 'Express' stock. Gangwayed throughout.

Dimensions: 20.18 x 2.82 x 3.81 m.   **Doors:** Manually operated slam.
Maximum Speed: 90 m.p.h.   **Bogies:** B5 (SR).
Couplings: Buckeye.   **Multiple Working:** SR type.

Non Standard Numbering:
• 438 417 carries abbreviated unit number 417.

70812/826. TBS. Dia. EJ260. Built as loco-hauled BSK to Lot No. 30229 Metro-
Cammell 1955–57 Rebuilt to Lot No. 30765 York 1966–67. –/32. 1T. 33.5 t.
70860. TCK. Dia. EH363. Built as loco-hauled FK to Lot No. 30019 Swindon
1952. Rebuilt to Lot No. 30766 York 1966–67. 30/16. 2T. 33.5 t.
76301–76327. DTS. Dia. EE266. Built as loco-hauled TSO to Lot No. 30219
Swindon 1955–57.Rebuilt to Lot No. 30764 York 1966–67. –/64. 32.0 t.

438 417	**B**	CM	*ON*	KN(S)	76301	70826	70860	76302
Spare	**N**	VS	*ON*	SL(S)	76327		
Spare	**B**	CM	*ON*	KN(S)		70812		

CLASS 456   BREL

DMS–DTS. Gangwayed within unit. Disc brakes.

Construction: Steel.
Traction Motors: Two GEC507-20J of 185 kW each.
Dimensions: 19.95 x 2.82 x . m.
Maximum Speed: 75 m.p.h.   **Doors:** Power operated sliding.
Couplers: Tightlock.   **Bogies:** BREL P7/T3.
Multiple Working: Classes 455–456.

64735–64758. DMS. Dia. EA267. Lot No. 31073 BREL York 1990–91. –/79. 41.1 t.
78250–78273. DTS. Dia. EE276. Lot No. 31074 BREL York 1990–91. –/73. 31.4 t.

456 001	**N**	P	*SC*	SU	64735	78250
456 002	**N**	P	*SC*	SU	64736	78251
456 003	**N**	P	*SC*	SU	64737	78252
456 004	**N**	P	*SC*	SU	64738	78253
456 005	**N**	P	*SC*	SU	64739	78254
456 006	**N**	P	*SC*	SU	64740	78255
456 007	**N**	P	*SC*	SU	64741	78256
456 008	**N**	P	*SC*	SU	64742	78257

456 009	N	P	*SC*	SU	64743	78258
456 010	N	P	*SC*	SU	64744	78259
456 011	N	P	*SC*	SU	64745	78260
456 012	N	P	*SC*	SU	64746	78261
456 013	N	P	*SC*	SU	64747	78262
456 014	N	P	*SC*	SU	64748	78263
456 015	N	P	*SC*	SU	64749	78264
456 016	N	P	*SC*	SU	64750	78265
456 017	N	P	*SC*	SU	64751	78266
456 018	N	P	*SC*	SU	64752	78267
456 019	N	P	*SC*	SU	64753	78268
456 020	N	P	*SC*	SU	64754	78269
456 021	N	P	*SC*	SU	64755	78270
456 022	N	P	*SC*	SU	64756	78271
456 023	N	P	*SC*	SU	64757	78272
456 024	CX	P	*SC*	SU	64758	78273

Name (carried on DTS):

456 024   Sir Cosmo Bonsor

CLASS 460 (8-Gat)   JUNIPER   ALSTOM

DMF–TF–TC–MS(A)–MS(B)–TS–MS(C)–DMS. 'Express' stock. Gangwayed within unit. Disc and regenerative brakes. Currently in the process of entering service with Gatwick Express.

Construction: Steel.
Traction Motors: Two Alstom ONIX 800 of 270 kW each per motor car.
Dimensions: 21.01 (DMF & DMS) or 19.94 (other cars) x 2.80 x 3.77. m.
Maximum Speed: 100 m.p.h.   **Doors:** Power operated sliding plug.
Couplers: Scharfenberg.   **Bogies:** ACR.
Multiple Working:

Non Standard Numbering:
• Abbreviated unit numbers comprising the last two digits only are carried on vehicle ends. The full six-digit numbers are carried on driving vehicles adjacent to the cab door.

67901–67908. DMF. Dia. EA101. Alstom Birmingham. 1999–2000. 10/– . 42.6 t.
67911–67918. DMS. Dia. EA274. Alstom Birmingham 1999–2000. –/56. 45.3 t.
74401–74408. TF. Dia. EH161. Alstom Birmingham 1999–2000. 28/– 1TD 1W. 33.5 t.
74411–74418. TC. Dia. EH364. Alstom Birmingham 1999–2000. 9/42 1T. 34.9 t.
74421–74428. MS(A). Dia. EC227. Alstom Birmingham 1999–2000. –/60. 42.5 t.
74431–74438. MS(B). Dia. EC228 . Alstom Birmingham 1999–2000. –/60. 42.5 t.
74441–74448. TS. Dia. EH251. Alstom Birmingham 1999–2000. –/38 1TD 1W. 35.2 t.
74451–74458. MS(C). Dia. EC229 . Alstom Birmingham 1999–2000. –/60. 40.5 t.

| 460 001 | U | P | | SL | 67901 | 74401 | 74411 | 74421 | 74431 | 74441 |
| | | | | | | 74451 | 67911 | | | |

460 002 **GV**	P		SL	67902	74402	74412	74422	74432	74442
					74452	67912			
460 003 **GV**	P	*GX*	SL	67903	74403	74413	74423	74433	74443
					74453	67913			
460 004 **GV**	P	*GX*	SL	67904	74404	74414	74424	74434	74444
					74454	67914			
460 005 **GV**	P	*GX*	SL	67905	74405	74415	74425	74435	74445
					74455	67915			
460 006 **GV**	P	*GX*	SL	67906	74406	74416	74426	74436	74446
					74456	67916			
460 007 **GV**	P	*TC*	SL	67907	74407	74417	74427	74437	74447
					74457	67917			
460 008 **GV**	P	*TC*	SL	67908	74408	74418	74428	74438	74448
					74458	67918			

CLASS 465 NETWORKER BREL/ABB/GEC-ALSTHOM

DMS–TS(A)–TS(B)–DMS. Gangwayed within unit. Disc, rheostatic and regenerative braking.

Construction: Welded aluminium alloy.
Traction Motors: Four Brush TIM 970 or GEC-Alsthom G352BY of 280 kW each per motor car.
Dimensions: 20.89 (DMS) or 20.06 (other cars) x 2.81 x 3.77 m.
Maximum Speed: 75 m.p.h.   **Doors:** Power operated sliding plug.
Couplers: Tightlock.
Bogies: BREL P3/T3 (Class 465/1), SRP BP62/BT52 (Class 465/2).
Multiple Working: Classes 365, 465 & 466. Couplers within units on Class 465/2 cars are not compatible with Classes 465/0 and 465/1.

64759–64858. DMS. Dia. EA268. Lot No. 31100 BREL York 1992–93. –/86 (* –/74). 39.2 t.
65700–65799. DMS. Dia. EA269. Lot No. 31103 GEC-Alsthom Birmingham 1992–93. –/86. 38.9 t.
65800–65893. DMS. Dia. EA268. Lot No. 31130 ABB York 1993–94. –/86. 39.0 t.
72028–72126 (Even numbers). TS(A). Dia. EH293. Lot No. 31102 BREL York 1992–93. –/90 (* –/80). 30.4 t.
72029–72127 (Odd numbers). TS(B). Dia. EH292. Lot No. 31101 BREL York 1992–93. –/86 (* –/76). 30.5 t.
72719–72817 (Odd numbers). TS(A). Dia. EH294. Lot No. 31104 GEC-Alsthom Birmingham 1992–93. –/86. 30.2 t.
72720–72818 (Even numbers). TS(B). Dia. EH295. Lot No. 31105 GEC-Alsthom Birmingham 1992–93. –/90. 29.1 t.
72900–72992 (Even numbers). TS(A). Dia. EH293. Lot No. 31132 ABB York 1993–94. –/90. 29.5 t.
72901–72993 (Odd numbers). TS(B). Dia. EH294. Lot No. 31131 ABB York 1993–94. –/86. 30.2 t.

Class 465/0. Brush traction motors.

465 001	**CS**	H	*SE*	SG	64759	72028	72029	64809
465 002	**CS**	H	*SE*	SG	64760	72030	72031	64810
465 003	**CS**	H	*SE*	SG	64761	72032	72033	64811

465 004		**NT**	H	*SE*	SG	64762	72034	72035	64812
465 005		**NT**	H	*SE*	SG	64763	72036	72037	64813
465 006		**CS**	H	*SE*	SG	64764	72038	72039	64814
465 007		**CS**	H	*SE*	SG	64765	72040	72041	64815
465 008		**CS**	H	*SE*	SG	64766	72042	72043	64816
465 009		**CS**	H	*SE*	SG	64767	72044	72045	64817
465 010		**CS**	H	*SE*	SG	64768	72046	72047	64818
465 011		**CS**	H	*SE*	SG	64769	72048	72049	64819
465 012		**CS**	H	*SE*	SG	64770	72050	72051	64820
465 013		**CS**	H	*SE*	SG	64771	72052	72053	64821
465 014	*	**CS**	H	*SE*	SG	64772	72054	72055	64822
465 015		**CS**	H	*SE*	SG	64773	72056	72057	64823
465 016		**CS**	H	*SE*	SG	64774	72058	72059	64824
465 017		**CS**	H	*SE*	SG	64775	72060	72061	64825
465 018		**CS**	H	*SE*	SG	64776	72062	72063	64826
465 019		**CS**	H	*SE*	SG	64777	72064	72065	64827
465 020		**CS**	H	*SE*	SG	64778	72066	72067	64828
465 021		**NT**	H	*SE*	SG	64779	72068	72069	64829
465 022		**NT**	H	*SE*	SG	64780	72070	72071	64830
465 023		**NT**	H	*SE*	SG	64781	72072	72073	64831
465 024		**NT**	H	*SE*	SG	64782	72074	72075	64832
465 025		**NT**	H	*SE*	SG	64783	72076	72077	64833
465 026		**NT**	H	*SE*	SG	64784	72078	72079	64834
465 027		**NT**	H	*SE*	SG	64785	72080	72081	64835
465 028		**NT**	H	*SE*	SG	64786	72082	72083	64836
465 029		**NT**	H	*SE*	SG	64787	72084	72085	64837
465 030		**NT**	H	*SE*	SG	64788	72086	72087	64838
465 031		**NT**	H	*SE*	SG	64789	72088	72089	64839
465 032		**NT**	H	*SE*	SG	64790	72090	72091	64840
465 033		**NT**	H	*SE*	SG	64791	72092	72093	64841
465 034		**NT**	H	*SE*	SG	64792	72094	72095	64842
465 035		**NT**	H	*SE*	SG	64793	72096	72097	64843
465 036		**NT**	H	*SE*	SG	64794	72098	72099	64844
465 037		**NT**	H	*SE*	SG	64795	72100	72101	64845
465 038		**NT**	H	*SE*	SG	64796	72102	72103	64846
465 039		**NT**	H	*SE*	SG	64797	72104	72105	64847
465 040		**NT**	H	*SE*	SG	64798	72106	72107	64848
465 041		**NT**	H	*SE*	SG	64799	72108	72109	64849
465 042		**NT**	H	*SE*	SG	64800	72110	72111	64850
465 043		**NT**	H	*SE*	SG	64801	72112	72113	64851
465 044		**NT**	H	*SE*	SG	64802	72114	72115	64852
465 045		**NT**	H	*SE*	SG	64803	72116	72117	64853
465 046		**NT**	H	*SE*	SG	64804	72118	72119	64854
465 047		**NT**	H	*SE*	SG	64805	72120	72121	64855
465 048		**NT**	H	*SE*	SG	64806	72122	72123	64856
465 049		**NT**	H	*SE*	SG	64807	72124	72125	64857
465 050		**NT**	H	*SE*	SG	64808	72126	72127	64858

Class 465/1. Brush traction motors.

465 151		**NT**	H	*SE*	SG	65800	72900	72901	65847
465 152		**NT**	H	*SE*	SG	65801	72902	72903	65848

465 153	**NT**	H	*SE*	SG	65802	72904	72905	65849
465 154	**NT**	H	*SE*	SG	65803	72906	72907	65850
465 155	**NT**	H	*SE*	SG	65804	72908	72909	65851
465 156	**NT**	H	*SE*	SG	65805	72910	72911	65852
465 157	**NT**	H	*SE*	SG	65806	72912	72913	65853
465 158	**NT**	H	*SE*	SG	65807	72914	72915	65854
465 159	**NT**	H	*SE*	SG	65808	72916	72917	65855
465 160	**NT**	H	*SE*	SG	65809	72918	72919	65856
465 161	**NT**	H	*SE*	SG	65810	72920	72921	65857
465 162	**NT**	H	*SE*	SG	65811	72922	72923	65858
465 163	**NT**	H	*SE*	SG	65812	72924	72925	65859
465 164	**NT**	H	*SE*	SG	65813	72926	72927	65860
465 165	**NT**	H	*SE*	SG	65814	72928	72929	65861
465 166	**NT**	H	*SE*	SG	65815	72930	72931	65862
465 167	**NT**	H	*SE*	SG	65816	72932	72933	65863
465 168	**NT**	H	*SE*	SG	65817	72934	72935	65864
465 169	**NT**	H	*SE*	SG	65818	72936	72937	65865
465 170	**NT**	H	*SE*	SG	65819	72938	72939	65866
465 171	**NT**	H	*SE*	SG	65820	72940	72941	65867
465 172	**NT**	H	*SE*	SG	65821	72942	72943	65868
465 173	**NT**	H	*SE*	SG	65822	72944	72945	65869
465 174	**NT**	H	*SE*	SG	65823	72946	72947	65870
465 175	**NT**	H	*SE*	SG	65824	72948	72949	65871
465 176	**NT**	H	*SE*	SG	65825	72950	72951	65872
465 177	**NT**	H	*SE*	SG	65826	72952	72953	65873
465 178	**NT**	H	*SE*	SG	65827	72954	72955	65874
465 179	**NT**	H	*SE*	SG	65828	72956	72957	65875
465 180	**NT**	H	*SE*	SG	65829	72958	72959	65876
465 181	**NT**	H	*SE*	SG	65830	72960	72961	65877
465 182	**NT**	H	*SE*	SG	65831	72962	72963	65878
465 183	**NT**	H	*SE*	SG	65832	72964	72965	65879
465 184	**NT**	H	*SE*	SG	65833	72966	72967	65880
465 185	**NT**	H	*SE*	SG	65834	72968	72969	65881
465 186	**NT**	H	*SE*	SG	65835	72970	72971	65882
465 187	**NT**	H	*SE*	SG	65836	72972	72973	65883
465 188	**NT**	H	*SE*	SG	65837	72974	72975	65884
465 189	**NT**	H	*SE*	SG	65838	72976	72977	65885
465 190	**NT**	H	*SE*	SG	65839	72978	72979	65886
465 191	**NT**	H	*SE*	SG	65840	72980	72981	65887
465 192	**NT**	H	*SE*	SG	65841	72982	72983	65888
465 193	**NT**	H	*SE*	SG	65842	72984	72985	65889
465 194	**NT**	H	*SE*	SG	65843	72986	72987	65890
465 195	**NT**	H	*SE*	SG	65844	72988	72989	65891
465 196	**NT**	H	*SE*	SG	65845	72990	72991	65892
465 197	**NT**	H	*SE*	SG	65846	72992	72993	65893

Class 465/2. GEC-Alsthom traction motors.

465 201	**NT**	A	*SE*	SG	65700	72719	72720	65750
465 202	**NT**	A	*SE*	SG	65701	72721	72722	65751
465 203	**NT**	A	*SE*	SG	65702	72723	72724	65752
465 204	**NT**	A	*SE*	SG	65703	72725	72726	65753

465 205	**NT**	A	*SE*	SG	65704	72727	72728	65754
465 206	**NT**	A	*SE*	SG	65705	72729	72730	65755
465 207	**NT**	A	*SE*	SG	65706	72731	72732	65756
465 208	**NT**	A	*SE*	SG	65707	72733	72734	65757
465 209	**NT**	A	*SE*	SG	65708	72735	72736	65758
465 210	**NT**	A	*SE*	SG	65709	72737	72738	65759
465 211	**NT**	A	*SE*	SG	65710	72739	72740	65760
465 212	**NT**	A	*SE*	SG	65711	72741	72742	65761
465 213	**NT**	A	*SE*	SG	65712	72743	72744	65762
465 214	**NT**	A	*SE*	SG	65713	72745	72746	65763
465 215	**NT**	A	*SE*	SG	65714	72747	72748	65764
465 216	**NT**	A	*SE*	SG	65715	72749	72750	65765
465 217	**NT**	A	*SE*	SG	65716	72751	72752	65766
465 218	**NT**	A	*SE*	SG	65717	72753	72754	65767
465 219	**NT**	A	*SE*	SG	65718	72755	72756	65768
465 220	**NT**	A	*SE*	SG	65719	72757	72758	65769
465 221	**NT**	A	*SE*	SG	65720	72759	72760	65770
465 222	**NT**	A	*SE*	SG	65721	72761	72762	65771
465 223	**NT**	A	*SE*	SG	65722	72763	72764	65772
465 224	**NT**	A	*SE*	SG	65723	72765	72766	65773
465 225	**NT**	A	*SE*	SG	65724	72767	72768	65774
465 226	**NT**	A	*SE*	SG	65725	72769	72770	65775
465 227	**NT**	A	*SE*	SG	65726	72771	72772	65776
465 228	**NT**	A	*SE*	SG	65727	72773	72774	65777
465 229	**NT**	A	*SE*	SG	65728	72775	72776	65778
465 230	**NT**	A	*SE*	SG	65729	72777	72778	65779
465 231	**NT**	A	*SE*	SG	65730	72779	72780	65780
465 232	**NT**	A	*SE*	SG	65731	72781	72782	65781
465 233	**NT**	A	*SE*	SG	65732	72783	72784	65782
465 234	**NT**	A	*SE*	SG	65733	72785	72786	65783
465 235	**NT**	A	*SE*	SG	65734	72787	72788	65784
465 236	**NT**	A	*SE*	SG	65735	72789	72790	65785
465 237	**NT**	A	*SE*	SG	65736	72791	72792	65786
465 238	**NT**	A	*SE*	SG	65737	72793	72794	65787
465 239	**NT**	A	*SE*	SG	65738	72795	72796	65788
465 240	**NT**	A	*SE*	SG	65739	72797	72798	65789
465 241	**NT**	A	*SE*	SG	65740	72799	72800	65790
465 242	**NT**	A	*SE*	SG	65741	72801	72802	65791
465 243	**NT**	A	*SE*	SG	65742	72803	72804	65792
465 244	**NT**	A	*SE*	SG	65743	72805	72806	65793
465 245	**NT**	A	*SE*	SG	65744	72807	72808	65794
465 246	**NT**	A	*SE*	SG	65745	72809	72810	65795
465 247	**NT**	A	*SE*	SG	65746	72811	72812	65796
465 248	**NT**	A	*SE*	SG	65747	72813	72814	65797
465 249	**NT**	A	*SE*	SG	65748	72815	72816	65798
465 250	**NT**	A	*SE*	SG	65749	72817	72818	65799

CLASS 466   NETWORKER   GEC-ALSTHOM

DMS–DTS. Gangwayed within unit. Disc, rheostatic and regenerative braking.
466 017 has experimental 2+2 seating.

Construction: Welded aluminium alloy.
Traction Motors: Four GEC-Alsthom G352BY of 280 kW each.
Dimensions: 20.89 (DMS) or 20.06 (DTS) x 2.81 x 3.77 m.
Maximum Speed: 75 m.p.h.   **Doors:** Power operated sliding plug.
Couplers: Tightlock.   **Bogies:** SRP BP62/BT52.
Multiple Working: Classes 365, 465 & 466.

64860–64902. DMS. Dia. EA271. Lot No. 31128 GEC-Alsthom Birmingham
1993–94. –/86 (* –/72). 38.8 t.
78312–78354. DTS. Dia. EE279. Lot No. 31129 GEC-Alsthom Birmingham 1993–
94. –/82 (* –/68). 33.2 t.

466 001		**NT**	A	*SE*	SG	64860	78312
466 002		**NT**	A	*SE*	SG	64861	78313
466 003		**NT**	A	*SE*	SG	64862	78314
466 004		**NT**	A	*SE*	SG	64863	78315
466 005		**NT**	A	*SE*	SG	64864	78316
466 006		**NT**	A	*SE*	SG	64865	78317
466 007		**NT**	A	*SE*	SG	64866	78318
466 008		**NT**	A	*SE*	SG	64867	78319
466 009		**NT**	A	*SE*	SG	64868	78320
466 010		**NT**	A	*SE*	SG	64869	78321
466 011		**NT**	A	*SE*	SG	64870	78322
466 012		**NT**	A	*SF*	SG	64871	78323
466 013		**NT**	A	*SE*	SG	64872	78324
466 014		**NT**	A	*SE*	SG	64873	78325
466 015		**NT**	A	*SE*	SG	64874	78326
466 016		**NT**	A	*SE*	SG	64875	78327
466 017	*	**NT**	A	*SE*	SG	64876	78328
466 018		**NT**	A	*SE*	SG	64877	78329
466 019		**NT**	A	*SE*	SG	64878	78330
466 020		**NT**	A	*SE*	SG	64879	78331
466 021		**NT**	A	*SE*	SG	64880	78332
466 022		**NT**	A	*SE*	SG	64881	78333
466 023		**NT**	A	*SE*	SG	64882	78334
466 024		**NT**	A	*SE*	SG	64883	78335
466 025		**NT**	A	*SE*	SG	64884	78336
466 026		**NT**	A	*SE*	SG	64885	78337
466 027		**NT**	A	*SE*	SG	64886	78338
466 028		**NT**	A	*SE*	SG	64887	78339
466 029		**NT**	A	*SE*	SG	64888	78340
466 030		**NT**	A	*SE*	SG	64889	78341
466 031		**NT**	A	*SE*	SG	64890	78342
466 032		**NT**	A	*SE*	SG	64891	78343
466 033		**NT**	A	*SE*	SG	64892	78344
466 034		**NT**	A	*SE*	SG	64893	78345
466 035		**NT**	A	*SE*	SG	64894	78346

466 036	**NT**	A	*SE*	SG	64895	78347
466 037	**NT**	A	*SE*	SG	64896	78348
466 038	**NT**	A	*SE*	SG	64897	78349
466 039	**NT**	A	*SE*	SG	64898	78350
466 040	**NT**	A	*SE*	SG	64899	78351
466 041	**NT**	A	*SE*	SG	64900	78352
466 042	**NT**	A	*SE*	SG	64901	78353
466 043	**NT**	A	*SE*	SG	64902	78354

CLASS 483   METRO-CAMMELL

DMS(A)–DMS(B). Non gangwayed. End doors. Converted from vehicles purchased from London Transport in 1988.

Construction: Steel.
Traction Motors: Two Crompton Parkinson/GEC/BTH LT100 of 125 kW each per motor car.
Dimensions: 15.94 x 2.65 x 2.88 m.   **Doors:** Power operated sliding.
Maximum Speed: 45 m.p.h.   **Bogies:** LT design.
Couplings: Wedglock.   **Multiple Working:** Within class.

Non Standard Liveries/Numbering:
• This entire class carries abbreviated unit numbers comprising the last three digits of the official RSL number only.
• 007 is in London Transport style red livery.

121–129. DMS(A). Dia. EA265. Metro-Cammell 1938. Rebuilt to Lot No. 31071 BRML Eastleigh 1989–92. –/42. 27.5 t.
221–229. DMS(B). Dia. EA266. Metro-Cammell 1938. Rebuilt to Lot No. 31072 BRML Eastleigh 1989–92. –/42. 27.5 t.

483 002	**IL**	H	*IL*	RY	122	225	RAPTOR
483 003	**N**	H	*IL*	RY(S)	123	221	
483 004	**IL**	H	*IL*	RY	124	224	T. REX
483 006	**IL**	H	*IL*	RY	126	226	TERRY
483 007	**O**	H	*IL*	RY	127	227	
483 008	**IL**	H	*IL*	RY	128	228	
483 009	**IL**	H	*IL*	RY	129	229	

CLASS 507   BR

BDMS–TS–DMS. Gangwayed within unit. End doors. Disc & rheostatic braking.

Construction: Steel underframe, aluminium alloy body and roof.
Traction Motors: Four GEC G310AZ of 82.125 kW per motor car.
Dimensions: 20.02 (BDMS & DMS) or 19.92 (TS) x 2.82 x 3.58 m.
Maximum Speed: 75 m.p.h.   **Doors:** Power operated sliding.
Couplers: Tightlock.   **Bogies:** BREL BX1.
Multiple Working: Classes 507 & 508.

Note: Fitted with de-icing equipment.

64367–64399. BDMS. Dia. EI202. Lot No. 30906 York 1978–80. –/74. 37.1 t.
64405–64437. DMS. Dia. EA201. Lot No. 30908 York 1978–80. –/74. 35.6 t.

71342–71374. TS. Dia. EH205. Lot No. 30907 York 1978–80. –/82. 25.6 t.

507 001	**MT**	A	*ME*	BD	64367	71342	64405
507 002	**MT**	A	*ME*	BD	64368	71343	64406
507 003	**MY**	A	*ME*	BD	64369	71344	64407
507 004	**MT**	A	*ME*	BD	64388	71345	64408
507 005	**MY**	A	*ME*	BD	64371	71346	64409
507 006	**MY**	A	*ME*	BD	64372	71347	64410
507 007	**MT**	A	*ME*	BD	64373	71348	64411
507 008	**MT**	A	*ME*	BD	64374	71349	64412
507 009	**MT**	A	*ME*	BD	64375	71350	64413
507 010	**MT**	A	*ME*	BD	64376	71351	64414
507 011	**MT**	A	*ME*	BD	64377	71352	64415
507 012	**MT**	A	*ME*	BD	64378	71353	64416
507 013	**MT**	A	*ME*	BD	64379	71354	64417
507 014	**MT**	A	*ME*	BD	64380	71355	64418
507 015	**MT**	A	*ME*	BD	64381	71356	64419
507 016	**MT**	A	*ME*	BD	64382	71357	64420
507 017	**MT**	A	*ME*	BD	64383	71358	64421
507 018	**MT**	A	*ME*	BD	64384	71359	64422
507 019	**MT**	A	*ME*	BD	64385	71360	64423
507 020	**MT**	A	*ME*	BD	64386	71361	64424
507 021	**MT**	A	*ME*	BD	64387	71362	64425
507 023	**MT**	A	*ME*	BD	64389	71364	64427
507 024	**MT**	A	*ME*	BD	64390	71365	64428
507 025	**MT**	A	*ME*	BD	64391	71366	64429
507 026	**MT**	A	*ME*	BD	64392	71367	64430
507 027	**MT**	A	*ME*	BD	64393	71368	64431
507 028	**MT**	A	*ME*	BD	64394	71369	64432
507 029	**MT**	A	*ME*	BD	64395	71370	64433
507 030	**MT**	A	*ME*	BD	64396	71371	64434
507 031	**MT**	A	*ME*	BD	64397	71372	64435
507 032	**MT**	A	*ME*	BD	64398	71373	64436
507 033	**MT**	A	*ME*	BD	64399	71374	64437

CLASS 508 BREL

DMS–TS–BDMS. Gangwayed within unit. End doors. Disc & rheostatic braking.

Construction: Steel underframe, aluminium alloy body and roof.
Traction Motors: Four GEC G310AZ of 82.125 kW per motor car.
Dimensions: 20.02 (DMS & BDMS) or 19.92 (TS) x 2.82 x 3.58 m.
Maximum Speed: 75 m.p.h.　　**Doors:** Power operated sliding.
Couplers: Tightlock.　　**Bogies:** BREL BX1.
Multiple Working: Classes 507 & 508.

64649–64691. DMS. Dia. EA208 (*EA211). Lot No. 30979 BREL York 1979–80 (* Facelifted 1998–99 by Wessex Traincare/Alstom Eastleigh). –/68 (*–/66). 36.2 t.
64692–64734. BDMS. Dia. EI203 (*EI204). Lot No. 30981 BREL York 1979–80 (Facelifted 1998–99 by Wessex Traincare/Alstom Eastleigh). –/68 (*–/74). 36.6 t.

71483–71525. TS. Dia. EH218 (*EH246). Lot No. 30980 BREL York 1979–80 (Facelifted 1998–99 by Wessex Traincare/Alstom Eastleigh). –/86 (*–/79). 26.7 t.

Class 508/1. Standard design.

508 102	**MT**	A	*ME*	WK(S)	64650	71484	64693
508 103	**MT**	A	*ME*	BD	64651	71485	64694
508 104	**MT**	A	*ME*	BD	64652	71486	64695
508 108	**MT**	A	*ME*	NB(S)	64656	71490	64699
508 110	**MT**	A	*ME*	BD(S)	64658	71492	64701
508 111	**MT**	A	*ME*	BD	64659	71493	64702
508 112	**MT**	A	*ME*	BD	64660	71494	64703
508 114	**MT**	A	*ME*	BD	64662	71496	64705
508 115	**MT**	A	*ME*	BD	64663	71497	64706
508 117	**MT**	A	*ME*	BD	64665	71499	64708
508 118	**MT**	A	*ME*	BD(S)	64666	71500	64709
508 120	**MT**	A	*ME*	KK(S)	64668	71502	64711
508 122	**MT**	A	*ME*	KK(S)	64670	71504	64713
508 123	**MT**	A	*RK*	ZA(S)	64671	71505	64714
508 124	**MT**	A	*ME*	BD	64672	71506	64715
508 125	**MT**	A	*ME*	BD	64673	71507	64716
508 126	**MT**	A	*ME*	BD	64674	71508	64717
508 127	**MY**	A	*ME*	BD	64675	71509	64718
508 128	**MT**	A	*ME*	BD	64676	71510	64719
508 130	**MT**	A	*ME*	BD	64678	71512	64721
508 131	**MT**	A	*ME*	KK(S)	64679	71513	64722
508 134	**MT**	A	*ME*	BD	64682	71516	64725
508 135	**MT**	A	*ME*	NB(S)	64683	71517	64726
508 136	**MT**	A	*ME*	BD	64684	71518	64727
508 137	**MT**	A	*ME*	BD	64685	71519	64728
508 138	**MT**	A	*ME*	BD	64686	71520	64729
508 139	**MT**	A	*ME*	BD	64687	71521	64730
508 140	**MT**	A	*ME*	BD	64688	71522	64731
508 141	**MT**	A	*ME*	BD	64689	71523	64732
508 142	**MT**	A	*ME*	WK(S)	64690	71524	64733
508 143	**MT**	A	*ME*	BD	64691	71525	64734

Class 508/2. Facelifted units for Connex South Eastern.

508 201	*	**CX**	A	*SE*	GI	64649	71483	64692
508 202	*	**CX**	A	*SE*	GI	64653	71487	64696
508 203	*	**CX**	A	*SE*	GI	64654	71488	64697
508 204	*	**CX**	A	*SE*	GI	64655	71489	64698
508 205	*	**CX**	A	*SE*	GI	64657	71491	64700
508 206	*	**CX**	A	*SE*	GI	64661	71495	64714
508 207	*	**CX**	A	*SE*	GI	64664	71498	64707
508 208	*	**CX**	A	*SE*	GI	64667	71501	64710
508 209	*	**CX**	A	*SE*	GI	64669	71503	64712
508 210	*	**CX**	A	*SE*	GI	64677	71511	64720
508 211	*	**CX**	A	*SE*	GI	64680	71514	64723
508 212	*	**CX**	A	*SE*	GI	64681	71515	64724

4.3. EUROSTAR UNITS (CLASS 373)

Eurostar units were built for and are normally used on services between Britain and Continental Europe via the Channel Tunnel. Apart from such workings units may be used as follows::

- Four SNCF-owned units (3203/04/27/28) have been removed from the Eurostar pool as surplus, and are now largely used on services within Continental Europe only. However, these sets continue to make occasional appearances on their former duties.

- Four 8-car sets are hired on a daily basis to the gner for its 'White Rose' services between London King's Cross and York. Although these trains are scheduled to be formed of units 3301–04, other units may appear from time to time as dictated by maintenance requirements.

Each train consists of two Eurostar units coupled, with a motor car at each driving end. Services starting from/terminating at London Waterloo International are formed of two 10-car units coupled, whilst those to/from other British destinations (yet to commence) will be formed of two 8-car units coupled. All units are articulated with an extra motor bogie on the coach adjacent to the motor car.

DM–MS–4TS–RB–2TF–TBF. or DM–MS–3TS–RB–TF–TBF. Gangwayed within pair of units. Air conditioned.
Construction: Steel.
Supply Systems: 25 kV a.c. 50 Hz overhead or 3000 V d.c. overhead or 750 V d.c. third rail (* also equipped for 1500 V d.c. overhead operation).
Wheel Arrangement: Bo–Bo + Bo–2–2–2–2–2–2–2–2–2.
Length: 22.15 m (DM), 21.85 m (MSOL & TBFOL), 18.70 m (other cars).
Maximum Speed: 300 km/h.
Built: 1992-93 by GEC-Alsthom/Brush/ANF/De Dietrich/BN Construction/ACEC.
Note: DM vehicles carry the set numbers indicated below.

10-Car Sets. Built for services starting from/terminating at London Waterloo. Individual vehicles in each set are allocated numbers 7xxxx0 + 7xxxx1 + 7xxxx2 + 7xxxx3 + 7xxxx4 + 7xxxx5 + 7xxxx6 + 7xxxx8 + 7xxxx9, where xxxx denotes the set number.

Advertising Liveries:
- 3005/06 '102 Dalmations'.
- 3011/12 'Notre Dame de Paris'.

73xxx0 series. DM. Dia. LA501. Lot No. 31118 1992–95. 68.5 t.
73xxx1 series. MS. Dia. LB202. Lot No. 31119 1992–95. –/48 2T. 44.6 t.
73xxx2 series. TS. Dia. LC202. Lot No. 31120 1992–95. –/58 1T. 28.1 t.
73xxx3 series. TS. Dia. LD202. Lot No. 31121 1992–95. –/58 2T. 29.7 t.
73xxx4 series. TS. Dia. LE202. Lot No. 31122 1992–95. –/58 1T. 28.3 t.
73xxx5 series. TS. Dia. LF202. Lot No. 31123 1992–95. –/58 2T. 29.2 t.
73xxx6 series. RB. Dia. LG502. Lot No.31124 1992–95. 31.1 t.
73xxx7 series. TF. Dia. LH102. Lot No. 31125 1992–95. 39/– 1T. 29.6 t.
73xxx8 series. TF. Dia. LJ102. Lot No. 31126 1992–95. 39/– 1T. 32.2 t.
73xxx9 series.TBF. Dia. LK102. Lot No. 31127 1992–95. 25/– 1TD. 39.4 t.

3001	**EU**	EU	*EU*	NP	3202*	**EU**	SF	*EU*	LY
3002	**EU**	EU	*EU*	NP	3203	**EU**	SF	*EU*	LY
3003	**EU**	EU	*EU*	NP	3204	**EU**	SF	*EU*	LY
3004	**EU**	EU	*EU*	NP	3205	**EU**	SF	*EU*	LY
3005	**AL**	EU	*EU*	NP	3206	**EU**	SF	*EU*	LY
3006	**AL**	EU	*EU*	NP	3207*	**EU**	SF	*EU*	LY
3007	**EU**	EU	*EU*	NP	3208*	**EU**	SF	*EU*	LY
3008	**EU**	EU	*EU*	NP	3209*	**EU**	SF	*EU*	LY
3009	**EU**	EU	*EU*	NP	3210*	**EU**	SF	*EU*	LY
3010	**EU**	EU	*EU*	NP	3211	**EU**	SF	*EU*	LY
3011	**AL**	EU	*EU*	NP	3212	**EU**	SF	*EU*	LY
3012	**AL**	EU	*EU*	NP	3213	**EU**	SF	*EU*	LY
3013	**EU**	EU	*EU*	NP	3214	**EU**	SF	*EU*	LY
3014	**EU**	EU	*EU*	NP	3215*	**EU**	SF	*EU*	LY
3015	**EU**	EU	*EU*	NP	3216*	**EU**	SF	*EU*	LY
3016	**EU**	EU	*EU*	NP	3217	**EU**	SF	*EU*	LY
3017	**EU**	EU	*EU*	NP	3218	**EU**	SF	*EU*	LY
3018	**EU**	EU	*EU*	NP	3219	**EU**	SF	*EU*	LY
3019	**EU**	EU	*EU*	NP	3220	**EU**	SF	*EU*	LY
3020	**EU**	EU	*EU*	NP	3221	**EU**	SF	*EU*	LY
3021	**EU**	EU	*EU*	NP	3222	**EU**	SF	*EU*	LY
3022	**EU**	EU	*EU*	NP	3223*	**EU**	SF	*EU*	LY
3101	**EU**	SB	*EU*	FF	3224*	**EU**	SF	*EU*	LY
3102	**EU**	SB	*EU*	FF	3225*	**EU**	SF	*EU*	LY
3103	**EU**	SB	*EU*	FF	3226*	**EU**	SF	*EU*	LY
3104	**EU**	SB	*EU*	FF	3227	**EU**	SF	*EU*	LY
3105	**EU**	SB	*EU*	FF	3228	**EU**	SF	*EU*	LY
3106	**EU**	SB	*EU*	FF	3229*	**EU**	SF	*EU*	LY
3107	**EU**	SB	*EU*	FF	3230*	**EU**	SF	*EU*	LY
3108	**EU**	SB	*EU*	FF	3231	**EU**	SF	*EU*	LY
3201	* **EU**	SF	*EU*	LY	3232	**EU**	SF	*EU*	LY

8-Car Sets. Built for Regional Eurostar services. Individual vehicles in each set are allocated numbers 7xxxx0 + 7xxxx1 + 7xxxx3 + 7xxxx2 + 7xxxx5 + 7xxxx6 + 7xxxx7 + 7xxxx9, where xxxx denotes the set number.

733xx0 series. DM. Dia. LA502. 68.5 t.
733xx1 series. MS. Dia. LB203. –/48 1T. 44.6 t.
733xx3 series. TS. Dia. LD203. –/58 2T. 29.7 t.
733xx2 series. TS. Dia. LC203. –/58 1T. 28.1 t.
733xx5 series. TS. Dia. LF203. –/58 1T. 29.2 t.
733xx6 series. RB. Dia. LG503. 31.1 t.
733xx7 series. TF. Dia. LH103. 39/– 1T. 29.6 t.
733xx9 series. TBF. Dia. LK103. 18/– 1TD. 39.4 t.

3301	**GN**	EU	*GN*	NP	3308	**EU**	EU	*EU*	NP(S)
3302	**GN**	EU	*GN*	NP	3309	**EU**	EU	*GN*	NP
3303	**GN**	EU	*GN*	NP	3310	**EU**	EU	*GN*	NP
3304	**GN**	EU	*GN*	NP	3311	**EU**	EU	*GN*	NP
3305	**EU**	EU	*GN*	NP	3312	**EU**	EU	*GN*	NP
3306	**EU**	EU	*GN*	NP	3313	**EU**	EU	*EU*	NP(S)
3307	**EU**	EU	*EU*	NP(S)	3314	**EU**	EU	*EU*	NP(S)

Spare DM:

3999   **EU**   EU   *EU*   NP

Names:

3303 The White Rose
3304 The White Rose

4.4. SERVICE UNITS

CLASS 316   TEST UNIT

BDB–M–DT. Gangwayed within unit. Converted from Class 307. Test bed for Class 323 electrical equipment.

Construction: Steel.
Supply System: 25 kV a.c. 50 Hz overhead or 750 V d.c. third rail.
Traction Motors: Four Holec DMKT52/24 of 146 kW each.
Dimensions: 20.31 (BDB & DT) or 20.18 (M) x 2.82 x 3.86 m.
Maximum Speed: 75 m.p.h.   **Doors:** Manually operated slam.
Couplings: Buckeye.   **Bogies:** Gresley ED7/B4.

61018. M. Dia. EZ5?? . Lot No. 30203 Eastleigh 1954–56. Converted BR, Derby 1992. ??.?? t.
75018. DT. Dia. EZ5?? . Lot No. 30206 Eastleigh 1954–56. Converted BR, Derby 1992. ??.?? t.
75118. BDB. Dia. EZ5?? . Lot No. 30205 Eastleigh 1954–56. Converted BR, Derby 1992. ??.?? t.

316 997	**BG**	SO		EH(S)	75118	61018	75018

CLASS 930/0   SANDITE/DE-ICING UNIT

DMB–DMB. Gangwayed within unit. Converted from Class 405.

Construction: Steel.   **Supply System:** 750 V d.c. third rail.
Traction Motors: Two English Electric 507 of 185 kW each per car.
Dimensions: 19.05 x 2.74 x 3.99 m.   **Doors:** Manually operated slam.
Maximum Speed: 75 m.p.h.   **Bogies:** Central 43 inch.
Couplings: Buckeye.   **Multiple Working:** SR type.

977586/587/604/605. DMB. Dia. EZ512. Lot No. 3231 Southern Railway Eastleigh 1947. 39.0 t.
975588/589/592/595/597–600/602/603. DMB. Dia. EZ512 Lot No. 1060. Southern Railway Eastleigh 1941. 39.0 t.
975590/591/596/601. DMB. Dia. EZ512. Lot No. 3384 Eastleigh 1948. 39.0 t.
975593/594. DMB. Dia. EZ512. Lot No. 3618 Eastleigh 1950. 39.0 t.
975896/897. DMB. Dia. EZ512. Lot No. 3506 Eastleigh 1950. 39.0 t.

930 002	**RK**	RK	*RK*	RM	975896	975897
930 003	**RO**	RK	*RK*	SU	975594	975595
930 004	**RO**	RK	*RK*	WD	975586	975587
930 005	**RK**	RK	*RK*	WD	975588	975589
930 006	**RO**	RK	*RK*	WD	975590	975591
930 007	**RO**	RK	*RK*	GI	975592	975593
930 008	**RK**	RK	*RK*	GI	975596	975597
930 009	**RK**	RK	*RK*	BI	975604	975599
930 010	**RK**	RK	*RK*	BI	975600	975601
930 011	**RO**	RK	*RK*	SU	975602	975603
Spare	**RO**	RK		AF(S)	975598	975605

CLASS 930/0   SANDITE/DE-ICING TRAILER

DT. Non gangwayed. Converted from Class 416/2.

Construction: Steel.
Dimensions: 20.44 x 2.82 x 3.86 m.   **Bogies:** Mark 3D.
Maximum Speed: 75 m.p.h.   **Doors:** Manually operated slam.
Couplings: Buckeye with additional Tightlock at non driving ends only.
Multiple Working: With Classes 317 and 319.

975578/579. DT. Dia. EZ526. Lot No. 30117 Eastleigh 1954. 32.5 t.

| 930 078 | **RO** | RK | *RK* | HE | 977578 |
| 930 079 | **N** | RK | | ZA(S) | 977579 |

CLASS 930/0   ROUTE LEARNING UNIT

DM–TB–DM. Gangwayed within unit. Converted from Class 411/4.

Construction: Steel.
Supply System: 750 V d.c. third rail.
Traction Motors: Two English Electric 507 of 185 kW each per motor car.
Dimensions: 20.34 x 2.82 x 3.83 m.
Maximum Speed: 90 m.p.h.   **Doors:** Manually operated slam.
Couplings: Buckeye.   **Bogies:** Mk. 4/Commonwealth.
Multiple Working: SR type.

977861. DM. Dia. EZ536. Lot No. 30111 Eastleigh 1956. 44.2 t.
977862. TB. Dia. EZ542. Lot No. 30110 Eastleigh 1956. 36.2 t.
977863. DM. Dia. EZ536. Lot No. 30108 Eastleigh 1956. 43.5 t.

| 930 082 | **CX** | SC | *OT* | SU | 977861 | 977862 | 977863 |

CLASS 930/1   TRACTOR UNIT

DMB–DMB. Gangwayed within unit.

Construction: Steel.
Supply System: 750 V d.c. third rail.
Traction Motors: Two English Electric 507 of 185 kW each per car.
Dimensions: 20.42 x 2.82 x 3.86 m.
Maximum Speed: 90 m.p.h.   **Doors:** Manually operated slam.
Couplings: Buckeye.   **Multiple Working:** SR type.
Bogies: Mk. 4 or Mk. 3B/Commonwealth.

977207. DMB. Dia. EZ522. Lot No. 30388 Eastleigh 1958. 40.5 t.
977609. DMB. Dia. EZ522. Lot No. 30617 Eastleigh 1961. 40.5 t.

| 930 101 | **N** | RK | | AF(S) | 977207 | 977609 |

CLASS 930/1   SANDITE UNIT

DMB–DMB. Gangwayed within unit. Converted from Class 416.

Construction: Steel.
Supply System: 750 V d.c. third rail.
Traction Motors: Two English Electric 507 of 185 kW each per car.
Dimensions: 19.23 x 2.74 x 3.99 m.   **Doors:** Manually operated slam.
Maximum Speed: 75 m.p.h.   **Bogies:** Central 40 inch.
Couplings: Buckeye.   **Multiple Working:** SR type.

977533. DMB. Dia. EZ512. Lot No. 4016 Eastleigh 1954–55. 40.5 t.
977534. DMB. Dia. EZ512. Lot No. 4099 Eastleigh 1955–56. 40.5 t.

930 102	**RK**	RK	*RK*	FR	977533	977534

CLASS 930/2   SANDITE/DE-ICING UNIT

DMB–DMB. Gangwayed within unit. Converted from Class 416/2.

Construction: Steel.
Supply System: 750 V d.c. third rail.
Traction Motors: Two English Electric 507 of 185 kW each per car.
Dimensions: 20.44 x 2.82 x 3.86 m.   **Doors:** Manually operated slam.
Maximum Speed: 75 m.p.h.   **Bogies:** Mk. 3B.
Couplings: Buckeye.   **Multiple Working:** SR type.

977566/567. DMB. Dia. EZ525. Lot No. 30116 Eastleigh 1954–55. 40.5 t.
977804/864. DMB. Dia. EZ522. Lot No. 30119 Eastleigh 1954. 40.5 t.
977805/865/871. DMB. Dia. EZ522. Lot No. 30167 Eastleigh 1955. 40.5 t.
977872/924/925. DMB. Dia. EZ522. Lot. No. 30314. Eastleigh 1956–58. 40.5 t.
977874/875. DMB. Dia. EZ522. Lot No. 30114 Eastleigh 1954. 40.5 t.

930 201	**RO**	RK	*RK*	FR	977566	977567
930 202	**RK**	RK	*RK*	FR	977804	977805
930 203	**RO**	RK	*RK*	RM	977864	977865
930 204	**RK**	RK	*RK*	RM	977874	977875
930 205	**RO**	RK	*RK*	RM	977871	977872
930 206	**RO**	RK	*RK*	WD	977924	977925

CLASS 931   ROUTE LEARNING UNIT

DT–DMB or DMB–DT. Gangwayed within unit. Converted from Class 416/2.

Construction: Steel.
Supply System: 750 V d.c. third rail.
Traction Motors: Two English Electric 507 of 185 kW each.
Dimensions: 20.44 x 2.82 x 3.86 m.   **Doors:** Manually operated slam.
Maximum Speed: 75 m.p.h.   **Bogies:** Mk. 3B.
Couplings: Buckeye.   **Multiple Working:** SR type.

977856. DT. Dia. EZ541. Lot No. 30168 Eastleigh 1955. 30.5 t.
977857. DMB. Dia. EZ522. Lot No. 30167 Eastleigh 1955. 40.5 t.
977917. DMB. Dia. EZ541. Lot No. 30119 Eastleigh 1954. 40.5 t.
977918. DT. Dia. EZ541. Lot No. 30120 Eastleigh 1954. 30.5 t.

| 931 001 | **N** | SE | *OT* | RM | 977856 | 977857 |
| 931 002 | **N** | SE | *OT* | RM | 977917 | 977918 |

CLASS 931   TRACTOR UNIT

DMB–DMB. Gangwayed within unit. Converted from Class 416/2.

Construction: Steel.
Supply System: 750 V d.c. third rail.
Traction Motors: Two English Electric 507 of 185 kW each per car.
Dimensions: 20.44 x 2.82 x 3.86 m.   **Doors:** Manually operated slam.
Maximum Speed: 75 m.p.h.   **Bogies:** Mk. 3B.
Couplings: Buckeye.   **Multiple Working:** SR type.

977559/560. DMB. Dia. EZ525. Lot No. 30116 Eastleigh 1954-55. 40.5 t.

| 931 062 | **N** | SE | *OT* | RM | 977559 977560 | The Sprinkler |

CLASS 931   TRACTOR UNIT

DM. Non gangwayed. Previously Class 419.

Construction: Steel.
Supply System: 750 V d.c. third rail or battery power.
Traction Motors: Four English Electric 507 of 185 kW each.
Dimensions: 19.64 x 2.82 x 3.86 m.   **Doors:** Manually operated slam.
Maximum Speed: 90 m.p.h.   **Bogies:** Mk. 3B.
Couplings: Buckeye.   **Multiple Working:** SR type.

68002. DM. Dia. EX560. Lot No. 30458 Eastleigh 1959. 45.5 t.

| 931 092 | **N** | P | *SW* | BM | 68002 |

CLASS 932   TEST UNIT

DM–TB–T–DM. Gangwayed throughout. Converted from Class 411. Test units for manufacturers' traction packages.

Construction: Steel.
Supply System: 750 V d.c. third rail (* or 15 kV a.c. 16.67 Hz overhead; † or 25 kV a.c. 50 Hz overhead).
Traction Motors: Adtranz. († Two English Electric 507 of 185 kW each (61948); Alstom (61949).
Dimensions: 20.34 x 2.82 x 3.83 m.

Maximum Speed: **Doors:** Manually operated slam.
Couplings: Buckeye.   **Multiple Working:** SR type.
Bogies: Mk. 4 /Commonwealth.

Non Standard Liveries:
- 932 545 is Adtranz blue with a white stripe.
- 932 620 has one side of each car painted in GEC-Alsthom white and orange livery and the other side of each car painted in livery **P**.)

Note: 932 545 is currently based at the Adtranz works at Västerås, Sweden.

61358/359. DM. Dia. EZ???. Lot No. 30454 Eastleigh 1958–59. ??.?? t.
61948/949. DM. Dia. EZ???. Lot No. 30708 Eastleigh 1963. ??.?? t.
70330. TB. Dia. EZ???. Lot No. 30456 Eastleigh 1958–59. ??.?? t.
70653. TB. Dia. EZ???. Lot No. 30709 Eastleigh 1963. ??.?? t.

932 545	*	**0**	P	*AD*	Sweden	61359	70330	61358
932 620	†	**0**	P	*AM*	IL	61948	70653	70660	61949

CLASS 936/0   SANDITE UNIT

DM–DTB. Gangwayed throughout. Converted from Class 501.

Construction: Steel.
Supply System: 750 V d.c. third rail.
Traction Motors: Four GEC of 137 kW each.
Dimensions: 18.47 x 2.90 x 3.86 m.   **Doors:** Manually operated slam.
Maximum Speed: 70 m.p.h.   **Bogies:** BR2.
Couplings: Buckeye.   **Multiple Working:** Within class only.

977349. DM. Dia. EZ504. Lot No. 30326 Eastleigh 1957–58. 48.0 t.
977350. DTB. Dia. EZ506. Lot No. 30328 Eastleigh 1957–58. 30.5 t.

936 003	**MS**	RK	*RK*	BD	977349	977350

CLASS 936/1   SANDITE UNIT

DT–MB–DT. Non gangwayed. Converted from Class 311.

Construction: Steel.
Supply System: 25 kV a.c. 50 Hz overhead.
Traction Motors: Four AEI of 165 kW each.
Dimensions: 20.18 x 2.82 x 3.86 m.
Maximum Speed: 75 m.p.h.   **Doors:** Power operated sliding.
Couplings: Buckeye.   **Bogies:** Gresley ED3/ET3.
Multiple Working: Classes 303–312.

977844/847. DT. Dia. EZ543. Lot No. 30767 Cravens 1967. 34.4 t.
977845/848. MB. Dia. EZ544. Lot No. 30768 Cravens 1967. 56.4 t.
977846/849. DT. Dia. EZ543. Lot No. 30769 Cravens 1967. 38.4 t.

936 103	**R0**	RK	CK(S)	977844	977845	977846
936 104	**R0**	RK	CK(S)	977847	977848	977849

CLASS 937   SANDITE UNIT

BDT–MB–DT. Gangwayed within unit. Converted from Class 308.

Supply System: 25 kV a.c. 50 Hz overhead.

For details see Class 308.

977876/926. BDT. Dia. EZ545. Lot No. 30656 York 1961. 36.3 t.
977877/927. MB. Dia. EZ546. Lot No. 30657 York 1961. 55.0 t.
977878/928. DT. Dia. EZ547. Lot No. 30659 York 1961. 33.0 t.

| 937 990 | N | RK | RK | EM | 977876 | 977877 | 977878 |
| 937 991 | N | RK | RK | IL | 977926 | 977927 | 977928 |

UNCLASSIFIED   GENERATOR CAR

QXA. Gangwayed throughout. Converted from Class 438.

Construction: Steel.
Dimensions: 20.18 x 2.82 x 3.81 m.
Maximum Speed: 90 m.p.h.   **Doors:** Manually operated slam.
Couplings: Buckeye.   **Bogies:** B5 (SR).

977335. QXA. Dia. QX174. Lot No. 30764 York 1966–67. 32.0 t.

| – | SO | SO | SO | ZA | 977335 |

UNCLASSIFIED   TRACK RECORDING CAR

T. London Underground Ltd. Track Recording Car. Converted from 1973 tube stock.

Dimensions:
Maximum Speed: 70 m.p.h.   **Doors:** Power operated sliding.
Couplings: Buckeye.   **Bogies:** LT design.
Non Standard Livery: White with blue lower body stripe and red doors.
Note: Also carries LUL number TRC666.

999666. T. Dia. EZ548. Metro-Cammell 1974. Converted BREL Derby 1987. 23.8 t.

| – | 0 | LU | OT | WR | 999666 |

4.5. EMUS AWAITING DISPOSAL

The list below comprises vehicles awaiting disposal which are stored on the Railtrack network, together with vehicles stored at other locations (e.g. repair facilites) which, although awaiting disposal, remain Railtrack registered. This includes vehicles for which sales have been agreed, but collection by the new owner had not been made at the time of going to press.

25 kV a.c. 50 Hz OVERHEAD UNITS

Complete Units:

302 201	N	H	PY(S)	75085	61060	70060	75033	
302 204	N	H	PY(S)	75088	61063	70063	75036	
302 213	N	H	PY(S)	75097	61072	70072	75060	
302 216	N	H	PY(S)	75100	61075	70075	75063	
302 218	N	H	PY(S)	75191	61077	70077	75065	
302 221	N	H	PY(S)	75194	61080	70080	75068	
302 225	N	H	PY(S)	75198	61084	70084	75072	
302 226	N	H	PY(S)	75199	61085	70085	75073	
302 227	N	H	PY(S)	75325	61193	70193	75250	
302 228	N	H	PY(S)	75201	61087	70087	75075	
302 230	N	H	PY(S)	75205	61091	70091	75079	
305 506	GM	A	PY(S)	75429	61415	75448		
305 511	GM	A	PY(S)	75434	61420	75453		
305 516	GM	A	PY(S)	75439	61425	75458		
309 613	RN	A	PY(S)	75639	61934	71756	75978	
309 616	RN	A	PY(S)	75642	61937	71759	75981	
309 617	RN	A	PY(S)	75643	61938	71760	75982	
309 623	RN	A	PY(S)	75641	61927	71758	7598J	
309 624	AL	A	PY(S)	75965	61928	70256	75972	
309 627	RN	A	PY(S)	75644	61931	70259	75975	

Spare Cars:

Cl. 302	N	H	PY(S)	75197	75071			
Cl. 307	BG	E	KN(S)	75023				
Cl. 308	N	A	PY(S)	70612	70621	70622	70631	70640
Cl. 310/1	PM	H	KN(S)	70733	70747	70748	70757	70763

750 V d.c. THIRD RAIL UNITS

Complete Units:

4308	N	H	PY(S)	61275	75395		
5001	G	H	KN(S)	14001	15207	15101	14002

5. LOCO-HAULED NON-PASSENGER-CARRYING COACHING STOCK

The notes shown for locomotive-hauled passenger stock generally apply also to non-passenger-carrying coaching stock (often abbreviated to NPCCS).

TOPS TYPE CODES

TOPS type codes for NPCCS are made up as follows:

(1) Two letters denoting the type of the vehicle:

AX	Nightstar generator van
AY	Eurostar barrier Vehicle
NA	Propelling control vehicle.
NB	High security brake van (100 m.p.h.).
NC	Gangwayed brake van modified for newspaper conveyance (100 m.p.h.).
ND	Gangwayed brake van (90 m.p.h.).
NE	Gangwayed brake van (100 m.p.h.).
NF	Gangwayed brake van with guard's safety equipment removed.
NG	Motorail loading wagon.
NH	Gangwayed brake van (110 m.p.h.).
NI	High security brake van (110 m.p.h.).
NJ	General utility van (90 m.p.h.).
NK	High security general utility van (100 m.p.h.).
NL	Newspaper van.
NN	Courier vehicle.
NO	General utility van (100 m.p.h. e.t.h. wired).
NP	General utility van for post office use or Motorail van (110 m.p.h.).
NR	BAA container van (100 m.p.h.).
NS	Post office sorting van.
NT	Post office stowage van.
NU	Brake post office stowage van.
NV	Motorail van (side loading).
NW	Barrier vehicle for DMU/EMU.
NX	Motorail van (100 m.p.h.).
NY	Exhibition van.
NZ	Driving brake van (also known as driving van trailer).
QS	EMU translator vehicle.
YR	Ferry van (special Southern Region version of NJ with two pairs of side doors instead of three).

(2) A third letter denoting the brake type:

A	Air braked
V	Vacuum braked
X	Dual braked

OPERATING CODES

The normal operating codes are given in parentheses after the TOPS type codes. These are as follows:

BG   Gangwayed brake van.
BPOT   Brake post office stowage van.
DLV   Driving brake van (also known as driving van trailer – DVT).
GUV   General utility van.
PCV   Propelling control van.
POS   Post office sorting van.
POT   Post office stowage van.

AK51 (RK)   KITCHEN CAR

Dia. AK503. Mark 1. Converted 1989 from RBR. Fluorescent lighting. Commonwealth bogies. ETH 2X.

Lot No. 30628 Pressed Steel 1960–61. 39 t.

Note: Kitchen cars have traditionally been numbered in the NPCCS series, but have passenger coach diagram numbers!

80041	(1690)	x	**CC**	RS	*ON*	BN

NN   COURIER VEHICLE

Dia. NN504. Mark 1. Converted 1986–7 from BSKs. One compartment retained for courier use. Roller shutter doors. ETH 2.

80207. Lot No. 30721 Wolverton 1963. Commonwealth bogies. 37 t.
80204/11–17/23. Lot No. 30699 Wolverton 1962. Commonwealth bogies. 37 t.
80220. Lot No. 30573 Gloucester 1960. B4 bogies. 33 t.

Non-Standard Livery: 80211 is purple.

80204	(35297)	x	**M**	62		SK
80207	(35466)	x	**PC**	VS	*ON*	SL
80211	(35296)		**O**	RS		FK
80213	(35316)	x	**CH**	RV	*ON*	CP
80217	(35299)	x	**M**	14	*OS*	NY
80220	(35276)	x	**G**	WT		BQ
80223	(35331)	x	**RY**	RS		DY

Name: 80207 is branded 'BAGGAGE CAR No.11'.

NP/NW   POST OFFICE GUV/BARRIER VEHICLE

Dia. NP502. Mark 1. Converted 1991–93 from newspaper vans. Short frames (57'). Originally converted from GUV. Fluorescent lighting, toilet and gangways fitted. Load 14 t. B5 bogies. ETH 3X.

NWA – Converted to barrier vehicle for DMU/EMU in 2000.

Lot No. 30922 Wolverton or Doncaster 1977–78. 31 t.

80251	(86467, 94017)	NWA	**E**	E	*E*	CF
80252	(86718, 94022)	NWA	**E**	E	*E*	CF
80253	(86170, 94018)		**RM**	E		OM
80254	(86082, 94012)	x	**RM**	E		OM

80255	(86098, 94019)	x	**RM** E		OM
80256	(86408, 94013)	x	**RM** E		OM
80258	(86651, 94002)		**RM** E		OM
80259	(86845, 94005)	x	**RM** E		OM

NS (POS) POST OFFICE SORTING VAN

Used in travelling post office (TPO) trains. Mark 1. Various diagrams. Pressure ventilated. Fluorescent lighting. B5 bogies. ETH 4X.

80319–80327. Dia. NS504. Lot No. 30778 York 1968–69. 35 t.
80331–80337. Dia. NS505. Lot No. 30779 York 1968–69. 35 t.
80339–80355. Dia. NS506. Lot No. 30780 York 1968–69. 35 t.
80356–80380. Dia. NS501. Lot No. 30839 York 1972–73. 37 t.

80319	**RM** E	*E*	EN	80353	**RM** E	*E*	EN
80320	**RM** E	*E*	EN	80354	**RM** E	*E*	BK
80321	**RM** E	*E*	BK	80355	**RM** E	*E*	EN
80322	**RM** E	*E*	EN	80356	**RM** E	*E*	BK
80323	**RM** E	*E*	EN	80357	**RM** E	*E*	BK
80324	**RM** E	*E*	EN	80358	**RM** E	*E*	EN
80325	**RM** E	*E*	EN	80359	**RM** E	*E*	BK
80326	**RM** E	*E*	EN	80360	**RM** E	*E*	EN
80327	**RM** E	*E*	BK	80361	**RM** E	*E*	EN
80331	**RM** E	*E*	EN	80362	**RM** E	*E*	EN
80332	**RM** E	*E*	EN	80363	**RM** E	*E*	BK
80333	**RM** E	*E*	EN	80364	**RM** E	*E*	BK
80334	**RM** E	*E*	BK	80365	**RM** E	*E*	EN
80337	**RM** E	*E*	EN	80366	**RM** E	*E*	EN
80339	**RM** E	*E*	BK	80367	**RM** E	*E*	EN
80340	**RM** E	*E*	BK	80368	**RM** E	*E*	BK
80341	**RM** E	*E*	EN	80369	**RM** E	*E*	EN
80342	**RM** E	*E*	EN	80370	**RM** E	*E*	BK
80343	**RM** E	*E*	BK	80371	**RM** E	*E*	BK
80344	**RM** E	*E*	BK	80372	**RM** E	*E*	EN
80345	**RM** E	*E*	EN	80373	**RM** E	*E*	EN
80346	**RM** E	*E*	EN	80374	**RM** E	*E*	EN
80347	**RM** E	*E*	EN	80375	**RM** E	*E*	BK
80348	**RM** E	*E*	BK	80376	**RM** E	*E*	BK
80349	**RM** E	*E*	EN	80377	**RM** E	*E*	EN
80350	**RM** E	*E*	BK	80378	**RM** E	*E*	EN
80351	**RM** E	*E*	EN	80379	**RM** E	*E*	EN
80352	**RM** E	*E*	BK	80380	**RM** E	*E*	BK

Names:

80320	The Borders Mail	80360	Derek Carter
80327	George James	80367	M.G. Berry
80337	Brian Quinn	80368	George Economou

80381–80395. Lot No. 30900 Wolverton 1977. Dia NS531. Converted from SK. 38 t.

| 80381 | (25112) | **RM** E | *E* | EN | 80382 | (25109) | **RM** E | *E* | EN |

80383	(25033)	**RM** E	*E*	EN	80390	(25047)	**RM** E	*E*	EN
80384	(25078)	**RM** E	*E*	EN	80392	(25082)	**RM** E	*E*	EN
80385	(25083)	**RM** E	*E*	EN	80393	(25118)	**RM** E	*E*	EN
80386	(25099)	**RM** E	*E*	EN	80394	(25156)	**RM** E	*E*	EN
80387	(25045)	**RM** E	*E*	EN	80395	(25056)	**RM** E	*E*	EN
80389	(25103)	**RM** E		ZG					

Name:
80390 Ernie Gosling

NT (POT)   POST OFFICE STOWAGE VAN

Mark 1. Open vans used for stowage of mail bags in conjunction with POS.

Lot No. 30488 Wolverton 1959. Dia. NT502. Originally built with nets for
   collecting mail bags in motion. Equipment now removed. B5 bogies. ETH
   3. 35 t.

| 80400 | **RM** E | *E* | BK | 80402 | **RM** E | *E* | BK |
| 80401 | **RM** E | *E* | BK | | | | |

The following eight vehicles were converted at York from BSK to lot 30143
(80403) and 30229 (80404–80414). No new lot number was issued. Dia. NT503.
B5 bogies. 35 t. (* Dia. NT501 BR2 bogies 38 t.). ETH 3 (3X*).

80403	(34361)		**RM** E	*E*	BK	80411	(35003)	*	**RM** E	*E*	EN
80404	(35014)		**RM** E	*E*	BK	80412	(35002)	*	**RM** E	*E*	EN
80405	(35009)		**RM** E	*E*	BK	80413	(35004)	*	**RM** E	*E*	EN
80406	(35022)		**RM** E	*E*	EN	80414	(35005)	*	**RM** E	*E*	EN

Lot No. 30781 York 1968. Dia. NT505. Pressure ventilated. B5 bogies. ETH 4.
   34 t.

80415	**RM** E	*E*	EN	80421	**RM** E	*E*	EN
80416	**RM** E	*E*	EN	80422	**RM** E	*E*	EN
80417	**RM** E	*E*	EN	80423	**RM** E	*E*	EN
80419	**RM** E	*E*	EN	80424	**RM** E	*E*	EN
80420	**RM** E	*E*	BK				

Lot No. 30840 York 1973. Dia. NT504. Pressure ventilated. fluorescent
   lighting. B5 bogies. ETH 4X. 35 t.

80425	**RM** E	*E*	BK	80428	**RM** E	*E*	EN
80426	**RM** E	*E*	EN	80429	**RM** E	*E*	BK
80427	**RM** E	*E*	EN	80430	**RM** E	*E*	EN

Lot No. 30901 Wolverton 1977. converted from SK. Dia. NT521. Pressure ven
   tilated. Fluorescent lighting. B5 bogies. ETH 4X. 35 t.

80431	(25104)	**RM** E	*E*	EN	80436	(25077)	**RM** E	*E*	EN
80432	(25071)	**RM** E	*E*	EN	80437	(25068)	**RM** E	*E*	EN
80433	(25150)	**RM** E	*E*	BK	80438	(25139)	**RM** E	*E*	BK
80434	(25119)	**RM** E	*E*	EN	80439	(25127)	**RM** E	*E*	BK
80435	(25117)	**RM** E	*E*	EN					

NU (BPOT)   BRAKE POST OFFICE STOWAGE VAN

Dia. NU502. Mark 1. As NT but with brake compartment. Pressure ventilated. B5 bogies. ETH4.

Lot No. 30782 York 1968. 36 t.

80456	**RM** E	*E*	EN		80458	**RM** E	*E*	EN
80457	**RM** E	*E*	EN					

ND (BG)   GANGWAYED BRAKE VAN (90 m.p.h.)

Dia. ND501. Mark 1. Short frames (57'). Load 10t. All vehicles were built with BR Mark 1 bogies. ETH 1. Vehicles numbered 81xxx had 3000 added to the original numbers to avoid confusion with Class 81 locomotives. The full lot number list is listed here for reference purposes with renumbered vehicles. No unmodified vehicles remain in service.

80525. Lot No. 30009 Derby 1952–53. 31 t.
80621. Lot No. 30046 York 1954. 31.5 t.
80700. Lot No. 30136 Metro-Cammell 1955. 31.5 t.
80731–80791. Lot No. 30140 BRCW 1955–56. 31.5 t.
80826–80848. Lot No. 30144 Cravens 1955. 31.5 t.
80855–80960. Lot No. 30162 Pressed Steel 1956–57. 32 t.
80971–81014. Lot No. 30173 York 1956. 31.5 t.
81025–81051. Lot No. 30224 Cravens 1956. 31.5 t.
81055–81175. Lot No. 30228 Metro-Cammell 1957–58. 31.5 t.
81182–81188. Lot No. 30234 Cravens 1956–57. 31.5 t.
81205–81265. Lot No. 30163 Pressed Steel 1957. 31.5 t.
81266–81309. Lot No. 30323 Pressed Steel 1957. 32 t.
81316–81497. Lot No. 30400 Pressed Steel 1957–58. 32 t.
81498–81568. Lot No. 30484 Pressed Steel 1958. 32 t.
81590. Lot No. 30715 Gloucester 1962. 31 t.
81604–81606. Lot No. 30716 Gloucester 1962. 31 t.

The following vehicle is an ND rebogied with Commonwealth bogies and adapted for use as exhibition van 1998 at Lancastrian Carriage & Wagon Co. Ltd. 33 t.

81025	(81025, 84025)	**G**	RA	*ON*	BN

Name: 81025 VALIANT

NZ (DLV)   DRIVING BRAKE VAN (110 m.p.h.)

Dia. NZ501. Mark 3B. Air conditioned. T4 bogies. dg. ETH 5X.

Lot No. 31042 Derby 1988. 45.18 t.

82101	**V**	P	*VW*	OY		82106	**V**	P	*VW*	OY
82102	**V**	P	*VW*	OY		82107	**V**	P	*VW*	PC
82103	**V**	P	*VW*	OY		82108	**V**	P	*VW*	PC
82104	**V**	P	*VW*	PC		82109	**V**	P	*VW*	PC
82105	**V**	P	*VW*	PC		82110	**V**	P	*VW*	PC

82111	**V**	P	*VW*	PC	82132	**V**	P	*VW*	OY
82112	**V**	P	*VW*	PC	82133	**V**	P	*VW*	OY
82113	**V**	P	*VW*	OY	82134	**V**	P	*VW*	OY
82114	**V**	P	*VW*	MA	82135	**V**	P	*VW*	MA
82115	**V**	P	*VW*	MA	82136	**V**	P	*VW*	MA
82116	**V**	P	*VW*	PC	82137	**V**	P	*VW*	MA
82117	**V**	P	*VW*	PC	82138	**V**	P	*VW*	PC
82118	**V**	P	*VW*	OY	82139	**V**	P	*VW*	PC
82119	**V**	P	*VW*	MA	82140	**V**	P	*VW*	MA
82120	**V**	P	*VW*	MA	82141	**V**	P	*VW*	MA
82121	**V**	P	*VW*	PC	82142	**V**	P	*VW*	MA
82122	**V**	P	*VW*	MA	82143	**V**	P	*VW*	OY
82123	**V**	P	*VW*	PC	82144	**V**	P	*VW*	OY
82124	**V**	P	*VW*	PC	82145	**V**	P	*VW*	MA
82125	**V**	P	*VW*	PC	82146	**V**	P	*VW*	MA
82126	**V**	P	*VW*	OY	82147	**V**	P	*VW*	MA
82127	**V**	P	*VW*	OY	82148	**V**	P	*VW*	PC
82128	**V**	P	*VW*	OY	82149	**V**	P	*VW*	PC
82129	**V**	P	*VW*	OY	82150	**V**	P	*VW*	PC
82130	**V**	P	*VW*	MA	82151	**V**	P	*VW*	OY
82131	**V**	P	*VW*	OY	82152	**V**	P	*VW*	MA

Names:

82101	101 Squadron
82115	Liverpool John Moores University
82120	Liverpool Chamber of Commerce
82121	Carlisle Cathedral
82124	The Girls' Brigade
82126	G8 Summit Birmingham 1998
82127	Abraham Darby
82132	INDUSTRY 96 West Midlands
82134	Sir Henry Doulton 1820–1897
82135	Spirit of Cumbria
82147	The Red Devils
82148	International Spring Fair

NZ (DLV)   DRIVING BRAKE VAN (140 m.p.h.)

Dia. NZ502. Mark 4. Air conditioned. Swiss-built (SIG) bogies. dg. ETH 6X.

Lot No. 31043 Metro-Cammell 1988. 45.18 t.

82200	**GN**	H	*GN*	BN	82210	**GN**	H	*GN*	BN
82201	**GN**	H	*GN*	BN	82211	**GN**	H	*GN*	BN
82202	**GN**	H	*GN*	BN	82212	**GN**	H	*GN*	BN
82203	**GN**	H	*GN*	BN	82213	**GN**	H	*GN*	BN
82204	**GN**	H	*GN*	BN	82214	**GN**	H	*GN*	BN
82205	**GN**	H	*GN*	BN	82215	**GN**	H	*GN*	BN
82206	**GN**	H	*GN*	BN	82216	**GN**	H	*GN*	BN
82207	**GN**	H	*GN*	BN	82217	**GN**	H	*GN*	BN
82208	**GN**	H	*GN*	BN	82218	**GN**	H	*GN*	BN
82209	**GN**	H	*GN*	BN	82219	**GN**	H	*GN*	BN

82220	**GN**	H	*GN*	BN		82226	**GN**	H	*GN*	BN
82221	**GN**	H	*GN*	BN		82227	**GN**	H	*GN*	BN
82222	**GN**	H	*GN*	BN		82228	**GN**	H	*GN*	BN
82223	**GN**	H	*GN*	BN		82229	**GN**	H	*GN*	BN
82224	**GN**	H	*GN*	BN		82230	**GN**	H	*GN*	BN
82225	**GN**	H	*GN*	BN		82231	**GN**	H	*GN*	BN

NB   HIGH SECURITY BRAKE VAN

Dia. NB501. Mark 1. Converted at WB from ND in 1985. Gangways removed. B4 bogies.

Lot No. 30400 Pressed Steel 1957–58. 32 t.

| 84387 | (81387, 80461) | x | **B** | E | | CW |
| 84477 | (81477, 80463) | x | **B** | E | | CW |

NJ (GUV)   GENERAL UTILITY VAN

Dia. NJ501. Mark 1. Short frames. Load 14 t. Screw couplings. These vehicles had 7000 added to the original numbers to avoid confusion with Class 86 locomotives. The full lot number list is listed here for reference purposes with renumbered vehicles. No unmodified vehicles remain in service. All vehicles were built with BR Mark 2 bogies. ETH 0 or 0X*.

86081–86499. Lot No. 30417 Pressed Steel 1958–59. 30 t.
86508–86518. Lot No. 30343 York 1957. 30 t.
86521–86651. Lot No. 30403 York/Glasgow 1958–60. 30 t.
86656–86834. Lot No. 30565 Pressed Steel 1959. 30 t.
86836–86978. Lot No. 30616 Pressed Steel 1959–60. 30 t.

NE/NH (BG)   GANGWAYED BRAKE VAN (100/110 m.p.h.)

NE are ND but rebogied with B4 bogies suitable for 100 m.p.h. NH are identical but are allowed to run at 110 m.p.h. with special maintenance of the bogies. For lot numbers refer to original number series. Deduct 1.5t from weights. All NHA are *pg. ETH 1 (1X*).

Non-standard Livery: 92116 is purple.

92100	(81391)		to		RV	CP
92111	(81432)		NHA		H	CP
92114	(81443)		NHA		H	LT
92116	(81450)		to	**0**	RS	FK
92125	(81470)		to		DR	SD
92146	(81498)		NHA		H	LT
92159	(81534)		NHA		H	PY
92174	(81567)		NHA		H	PY
92175	(81568)		pg		H	CP
92193	(81604)		pg		E	Preston station
92194	(81606)		to		H	PY
92234	(81336, 84336)	*		**RX**	E	DY
92238	(81563, 84563)			**RY**	E	DY
92261	(80988)	x*		**RY**	E	BK

NE (BG)   GANGWAYED BRAKE VAN (100 m.p.h.)

As ND but rebogied with Commonwealth bogies suitable for 100 m.p.h. ETH 1 (1X*). For lot numbers refer to original number series. Add 1.5 t to weights to allow for the increased weight of the Commonwealth bogies.

92302	(81501, 84501)		**RX**	E	HY
92303	(81427, 84427)		**RX**	E	DY
92306	(81217, 84217)	*	**RY**	E	HY
92309	(81043, 84043)	x*	**RX**	E	Arpley Yard
92311	(81453, 84453)	x	**RY**	E	CW
92312	(81548, 84548)		**RX**	E	CL
92314	(80777)	x*	**RY**	E	CW
92316	(80980)	x*	**RY**	E	CL
92319	(81055, 84055)	*	**RY**	E	CL
92321	(81566, 84566)		**RY**	E	FK
92323	(80832)	*	**R**	E	CL
92324	(81087, 84087)		**RY**	E	CL
92325	(80791)		**RY**	E	HY
92328	(80999)	x*	**RY**	E	CL
92329	(81001, 84001)	*	**RY**	E	CL
92330	(80995)	x*	**RY**	E	CL
92332	(80845)	*	**RX**	E	CL
92333	(80982)	*	**RY**	E	HY
92337	(81140, 84140)	*	**RX**	E	CL
92340	(81059, 84059)	*	**RY**	E	CL
92341	(81316, 84316)	x	**RY**	E	HY
92343	(81505, 84505)	x	**R**	E	CL
92344	(81154, 84154)	*	**RY**	E	CL
92345	(81083, 84083)	x*	**RY**	E	CL
92346	(81091, 84091)		**RY**	E	HY
92347	(81326, 84326)		**RX**	E	DY
92348	(81075, 84075)	x*	**R**	E	CL
92350	(81049, 84049)	*	**RY**	E	DY
92353	(81323, 84323)		**R**	E	HY
92355	(81517, 84517)	x	**RX**	E	DY
92356	(81535, 84535)	x		E	HY
92357	(81136, 84136)		**RX**	E	HY
92362	(81188, 84188)	x	**RY**	E	CL
92363	(81294, 84294)	x	**RY**	E	CW
92364	(81030, 84030)	x*	**R**	E	CL
92365	(81122, 84122)		**RX**	E	CL
92366	(81551, 84551)		**RX**	E	CL
92369	(80960)	x*		E	Doncaster West Yard
92370	(81324, 84324)		**RX**	E	HY
92377	(80928)	*	**RX**	E	DY
92379	(80914)	*	**RX**	E	CL
92380	(81247, 84247)	*	**R**	E	CL
92381	(81476, 84476)		**RX**	E	HY
92382	(81561, 84561)		**RX**	E	DY

92384	(80893)		**RY**	E	CW
92385	(81261, 84261)	x*	**RY**	E	CL
92389	(81026, 84026)	*	**RY**	E	CL
92390	(80834)	*		E	CL
92392	(80861)	*	**RY**	E	CL
92395	(81274, 84274)			E	CL
92398	(80859)	x*	**RY**	E	CL
92400	(81211, 84211)	*		E	CW
92401	(81280, 84280)	x	**RX**	E	HY
92402	(81099, 84099)	*	**RY**	E	HY
92404	(81051, 84051)	x		E	CL
92410	(81469, 84469)	x		E	CW
92412	(81354, 84354)	*	**RY**	E	CW
92413	(81472, 84472)	x	**RY**	E	CW
92415	(81388, 84388)		**RX**	E	CL
92416	(81250, 84250)	*	**RY**	E	HY
92417	(80885)	*	**RX**	E	CL

NF (BG)   GANGWAYED BRAKE VAN (100 m.p.h.)

As NE but with emergency equipment removed. For details and lot numbers refer to original number series. 92530/42 have B4 bogies whilst the rest have Commonwealth bogies.

b (Dia. NB501). High security brake van. Converted at Wembley Heavy Repair Depot from ND 1985. Gangways removed. Now used for movement of materials between EWS maintenance depots.

92530	(81461, 84461)	xb	**RX**	E	*E*	EN
92542	(81207, 92942)		**RX**	E		CL
92804	(81339, 92304)	x	**RX**	E		CL
92805	(81590, 92305)	x	**RX**	E		CL
92810	(81105, 92310)		**RX**	E		CL
92815	(80848, 92315)	*	**RX**	E		CU
92817	(80836, 92317)	x	**RX**	E		CL
92822	(80771, 92322)	x	**RX**	E		Arpley Yard
92827	(80842, 92327)	x	**RX**	E		CL
92831	(81365, 92331)	x	**RX**	E		HY
92842	(81397, 92342)	x	**RY**	E		HY
92852	(81182, 92352)	*	**RX**	E		DY
92854	(81353, 92354)	x	**RX**	E		Arpley Yard
92859	(81275, 92359)	*	**RX**	E		DY
92861	(81463, 92361)		**R**	E		CL
92867	(81293, 92367)	x	**RX**	E		CU
92872	(81362, 92372)	x	**RY**	E		CW
92873	(81528, 92373)		**RX**	E		HY
92876	(81374, 92376)	*	**RX**	E		CL
92886	(80843, 92386)	x	**RX**	E		CL
92897	(80700, 92397)	x*	**RY**	E		HY

NE/NH (BG) GANGWAYED BRAKE VAN (100/110 m.p.h.)

Renumbered from 920xx series by adding 900 to number to avoid conflict with Class 92 locos. Class continued from 92261.

92901	(80855, 92001)	NHA		H		PY
92904	(80867, 92004)	*pg	G	VS		SL
92908	(80895, 92008)	NHA		H		PY
92912	(80910, 92012)	*pg		H		KN
92923	(80971, 92023)	*pg		H		LT
92927	(81061, 92027)	NHA		H		LT
92928	(81064, 92028)	NHA		H		LT
92929	(81077, 92029)	NHA		LW		CP
92931	(81102, 92031)	NHA		H		PY
92933	(81123, 92033)	NHA		H		NC
92934	(81142, 92034)	NHA		H		LT
92935	(81150, 92035)	*pg		H		PY
92936	(81158, 92036)	NHA		H		CP
92937	(81165, 92037)	NHA		H		LT
92938	(81173, 92038)	NHA		H		PY
92939	(81175, 92039)	NHA		H		LT
92940	(81186, 92040)	pg		H		IS
92946	(81214, 92046)	NHA		H		PY
92948	(81218, 92048)	NHA		H		PY
92961	(81231, 92061)			H		LT
92986	(81282, 92086)	to		H		CP
92988	(81284, 92088)	to		H		LT
92991	(81308, 92091)	to		II		LT
92998	(81381, 92098)	NHA		H		LT

NL/NW   NEWSPAPER VAN/BARRIER VEHICLE

Dia. NL501. Mark 1. Short frames (57'). Converted from NJ (GUV). Fluorescent lighting, toilets and gangways fitted. Load 14 t. All except 94003/6/25/8 out of use. B5 Bogies. ETH 3X.

NWA – Converted to barrier vehicle for DMU/EMU in 2000.

Lot No. 30922 Wolverton or Doncaster 1977–78. 31 t.

94003	(86281, 93999)	x	**RX**	GW	*GW*	OO
94004	(86156, 85504)		**RY**	E		OM
94006	(86202, 85506)		**RX**	GW	*GW*	OO
94007	(86572, 85507)		**B**	E		OM
94009	(86144, 85509)		**RY**	E		OM
94010	(86151, 85510)	x	**RX**	E		OM
94011	(86437, 85511)		**RX**	E		OM
94016	(86317, 85516)	x	**B**	E		OM
94020	(86220, 85520)	x	**RY**	E		OM
94021	(86204, 85521)	x	**B**	E		OM
94024	(86106, 85524)		**B**	E		OM
94025	(86377, 85525)	NWA	**E**	E	*E*	CF

94026	(86703, 85526)	x	**RY**	E		OM
94027	(86732, 85527)		**R**	E		FK
94028	(86733, 85528)	NWA	**E**	E	*E*	CF
94029	(86740, 85529)	x	**RY**	E		OM
94030	(86746, 85530)	x	**B**	E		OM
94032	(86730, 85532)		**RX**	E		OM

NKA   HIGH SECURITY GENERAL UTILITY VAN

Dia. NK501. Mark 1. These vehicles are GUVs further modified with new floors, three roller shutter doors per side and the end doors removed. For lot Nos. see original number series. Commonwealth bogies. Add 2 t to weight. ETH0X.

94100	(86668, 95100)	**RX**	E	*E*	BK
94101	(86142, 95101)	**RX**	E	*E*	BK
94102	(86762, 95102)	**RX**	E	*E*	BK
94103	(86956, 95103)	**RX**	E	*E*	BK
94104	(86942, 95104)	**RX**	E	*E*	EN
94106	(86353, 95106)	**RX**	E	*E*	BK
94107	(86576, 95107)	**RX**	E	*E*	EN
94108	(86600, 95108)	**RX**	E	*E*	BK
94110	(86393, 95110)	**RX**	E	*E*	BK
94111	(86578, 95111)	**RX**	E	*E*	EN
94112	(86673, 95112)	**RX**	E	*E*	EN
94113	(86235, 95113)	**RX**	E	*E*	BK
94114	(86081, 95114)	**RX**	E	*E*	BK
94116	(86426, 95116)	**RX**	E	*E*	BK
94117	(86534, 95117)	**RX**	E	*E*	BK
94118	(86675, 95118)	**RX**	E	*E*	EN
94119	(86167, 95119)	**RX**	E	*E*	EN
94121	(86518, 95121)	**RX**	E	*E*	BK
94123	(86376, 95123)	**RX**	E	*E*	BK
94126	(86692, 95126)	**RX**	E	*E*	BK
94132	(86607, 95132)	**RX**	E	*E*	EN
94133	(86604, 95133)	**RX**	E	*E*	BK
94137	(86610, 95137)	**RX**	E	*E*	EN
94138	(86212, 95138)	**RX**	E	*E*	EN
94140	(86571, 95140)	**RX**	E	*E*	BK
94146	(86648, 95146)	**RX**	E	*E*	BK
94147	(86091, 95147)	**RX**	E	*E*	BK
94148	(86416, 95148)	**RX**	E	*E*	EN
94150	(86560, 95150)	**RX**	E	*E*	BK
94153	(86798, 95153)	**RX**	E	*E*	EN
94155	(86820, 95155)	**RX**	E	*E*	EN
94157	(86523, 95157)	**RX**	E	*E*	EN
94160	(86581, 95160)	**RX**	E	*E*	BK
94164	(86104, 95164)	**RX**	E	*E*	EN
94166	(86112, 95166)	**RX**	E	*E*	BK
94168	(86914, 95168)	**RX**	E	*E*	BK
94170	(86395, 95170)	**RX**	E	*E*	BK
94172	(86429, 95172)	**RX**	E	*E*	EN

94174	(86852, 95174)	**RX**	E	*E*	EN
94175	(86521, 95175)	**RX**	E	*E*	BK
94176	(86210, 95176)	**RX**	E	*E*	EN
94177	(86411, 95177)	**RX**	E	*E*	BK
94180	(86362, 95141)	**RX**	E	*E*	EN
94182	(86710, 95182)	**RX**	E	*E*	BK
94190	(86624, 95350)	**RX**	E	*E*	EN
94191	(86596, 95351)	**RX**	E	*E*	BK
94192	(86727, 95352)	**RX**	E	*E*	EN
94193	(86514, 95353)	**RX**	E	*E*	EN
94195	(86375, 95355)	**RX**	E	*E*	BK
94196	(86478, 95356)	**RX**	E	*E*	BK
94197	(86508, 95357)	**RX**	E	*E*	BK
94198	(86195, 95358)	**RX**	E	*E*	BK
94199	(86854, 95359)	**RX**	E	*E*	BK
94200	(86207, 95360)	**RX**	E	*E*	EN
94202	(86563, 95362)	**RX**	E	*E*	BK
94203	(86345, 95363)	**RX**	E	*E*	BK
94204	(86715, 95364)	**RX**	E	*E*	BK
94205	(86857, 95365)	**RX**	E	*E*	BK
94207	(86529, 95367)	**RX**	E	*E*	BK
94208	(86656, 95368)	**RX**	E	*E*	EN
94209	(86390, 95369)	**RX**	E	*E*	BK
94211	(86713, 95371)	**RX**	E	*E*	EN
94212	(86728, 95372)	**RX**	E	*E*	EN
94213	(86258, 95373)	**RX**	E	*E*	EN
94214	(86367, 95374)	**RX**	E	*E*	BK
94215	(86862, 94077)	**RX**	E	*E*	BK
94216	(86711, 93711)	**RX**	E	*E*	EN
94217	(86131, 93131)	**RX**	E	*E*	BK
94218	(86541, 93541)	**RX**	E	*E*	BK
94221	(86905, 93905)	**RX**	E	*E*	BK
94222	(86474, 93474)	**RX**	E	*E*	EN
94223	(86660, 93660)	**RX**	E	*E*	BK
94224	(86273, 93273)	**RX**	E	*E*	BK
94225	(86849, 93849)	**RX**	E	*E*	BK
94226	(86525, 93525)	**RX**	E	*E*	BK
94227	(86585, 93585)	**RX**	E	*E*	BK
94228	(86511, 93511)	**RX**	E	*E*	BK
94229	(86720, 93720)	**RX**	E	*E*	BK

NAA   PROPELLING CONTROL VEHICLE

Dia. NA508. Mark 1. Class 307 driving trailers converted for use in propelling mail trains out of termini. Fitted with roller shutter doors. Equipment fitted for communication between cab of PCV and locomotive. B5 bogies. ETH 2X.

Lot No. 30206 Eastleigh 1954–556. Converted at Hunslet-Barclay, Kilmarnock 1994–6.

94302	(75124)	**RX**	E	*E*	BK	94304	(75107)	**RX**	E	*E*	EN
94303	(75131)	**RX**	E	*E*	EN	94305	(75104)	**RX**	E	*E*	EN

94306	(75112)	**RX** E	*E*	BK	94325	(75113)	**RX** E	*E*	EN
94307	(75127)	**RX** E	*E*	EN	94326	(75123)	**RX** E	*E*	BK
94308	(75125)	**RX** E	*E*	EN	94327	(75116)	**RX** E	*E*	EN
94309	(75130)	**RX** E	*E*	EN	94331	(75022)	**RX** E	*E*	BK
94310	(75119)	**RX** E	*E*	EN	94332	(75011)	**RX** E	*E*	EN
94311	(75105)	**RX** E	*E*	EN	94333	(75016)	**RX** E	*E*	EN
94312	(75126)	**RX** E	*E*	BK	94334	(75017)	**RX** E	*E*	EN
94313	(75129)	**RX** E	*E*	BK	94335	(75032)	**RX** E	*E*	BK
94314	(75109)	**RX** E	*E*	BK	94336	(75031)	**RX** E	*E*	EN
94315	(75132)	**RX** E	*E*	EN	94337	(75029)	**RX** E	*E*	EN
94316	(75108)	**RX** E	*E*	EN	94338	(75008)	**RX** E	*E*	EN
94317	(75117)	**RX** E	*E*	EN	94339	(75024)	**RX** E	*E*	BK
94318	(75115)	**RX** E	*E*	EN	94340	(75012)	**RX** E	*E*	BK
94319	(75128)	**RX** E	*E*	EN	94341	(75007)	**RX** E	*E*	BK
94320	(75120)	**RX** E	*E*	EN	94342	(75005)	**RX** E	*E*	BK
94321	(75122)	**RX** E	*E*	EN	94343	(75027)	**RX** E	*E*	EN
94322	(75111)	**RX** E	*E*	BK	94344	(75014)	**RX** E	*E*	BK
94323	(75110)	**RX** E	*E*	EN	94345	(75004)	**RX** E	*E*	EN
94324	(75103)	**RX** E	*E*	EN					

NBA   HIGH SECURITY BRAKE VAN (100 m.p.h.)

Dia. NB501. Mark 1. These vehicles are NEs further modified with sealed gangways, new floors, built-in tail lights and roller shutter doors. For lot Nos. see original number series. B4 bogies. 31.4 t. ETH 1X.

94400	(81224, 92954)	**RX**	E	*E*	BK
94401	(81277, 92224)	**RX**	E	*E*	EN
94403	(81479, 92629)	**RX**	E	*E*	BK
94404	(81486, 92135)	**RX**	E	*E*	BK
94405	(80890, 92233)	**RX**	E	*E*	EN
94406	(81226, 92956)	**RX**	E	*E*	BK
94407	(81223, 92553)	**RX**	E	*E*	BK
94408	(81264, 92981)	**RX**	E	*E*	BK
94410	(81205, 92941)	**RX**	E	*E*	EN
94411	(81378, 92997)	**RX**	E	*E*	EN
94412	(81210, 92945)	**RX**	E	*E*	EN
94413	(80909, 92236)	**RX**	E	*E*	EN
94414	(81377, 92996)	**RX**	E	*E*	BK
94415	(81309, 92992)	**RX**	E	*E*	EN
94416	(80929, 92746)	**RX**	E	*E*	BK
94418	(81248, 92244)	**RX**	E	*E*	BK
94420	(81325, 92263)	**RX**	E	*E*	BK
94422	(81516, 92651)	**RX**	E	*E*	BK
94423	(80923, 92914)	**RX**	E	*E*	BK
94424	(81400, 92103)	**RX**	E	*E*	EN
94427	(80894, 92754)	**RX**	E	*E*	BK
94428	(81550, 92166)	**RX**	E	*E*	BK
94429	(80870, 92232)	**RX**	E	*E*	EN
94431	(81401, 92604)	**RX**	E	*E*	BK
94432	(81383, 92999)	**RX**	E	*E*	EN

94433	(81495, 92643)	**RX**	E	*E*	EN
94434	(81268, 92584)	**RX**	E	*E*	EN
94435	(81485, 92134)	**RX**	E	*E*	EN
94436	(81237, 92565)	**RX**	E	*E*	BK
94437	(81403, 92208)	**RX**	E	*E*	EN
94438	(81425, 92251)	**RX**	E	*E*	BK
94439	(81480, 92130)	**RX**	E	*E*	BK
94440	(81497, 92645)	**RX**	E	*E*	BK
94441	(81492, 92140)	**RX**	E	*E*	BK
94442	(80932, 92723)	**RX**	E	*E*	BK
94443	(81473, 92127)	**RX**	E	*E*	BK
94444	(81484, 92133)	**RX**	E	*E*	BK
94445	(81444, 92615)	**RX**	E	*E*	EN
94446	(80857, 92242)	**RX**	E	*E*	EN
94447	(81515, 92266)	**RX**	E	*E*	EN
94448	(81541, 92664)	**RX**	E	*E*	BK
94449	(81536, 92747)	**RX**	E	*E*	BK
94450	(80927, 92915)	**RX**	E	*E*	BK
94451	(80955, 92257)	**RX**	E	*E*	EN
94452	(81394, 92602)	**RX**	E	*E*	BK
94453	(81170, 92239)	**RX**	E	*E*	EN
94454	(81465, 92124)	**RX**	E	*E*	EN
94455	(81239, 92264)	**RX**	E	*E*	BK
94458	(81255, 92974)	**RX**	E	*E*	BK
94459	(81490, 92138)	**RX**	E	*E*	BK
94460	(81266, 92983)	**RX**	E	*E*	EN
94461	(81487, 92136)	**RX**	E	*E*	EN
94462	(81289, 92270)	**RX**	E	*E*	EN
94463	(81375, 92995)	**RX**	E	*E*	EN
94464	(81240, 92262)	**RX**	E	*E*	EN
94465	(81481, 92131)	**RX**	E	*E*	BK
94466	(81236, 92964)	**RX**	E	*E*	EN
94467	(81245, 92969)	**RX**	E	*E*	BK
94468	(81259, 92978)	**RX**	E	*E*	BK
94469	(81260, 92979)	**RX**	E	*E*	BK
94470	(81442, 92113)	**RX**	E	*E*	EN
94471	(81518, 92152)	**RX**	E	*E*	BK
94472	(81256, 92975)	**RX**	E	*E*	BK
94473	(81262, 92272)	**RX**	E	*E*	EN
94474	(81452, 92618)	**RX**	E	*E*	EN
94475	(81208, 92943)	**RX**	E	*E*	EN
94476	(81209, 92944)	**RX**	E	*E*	BK
94477	(81494, 92642)	**RX**	E	*E*	BK
94478	(81488, 92637)	**RX**	E	*E*	EN
94479	(81482, 92132)	**RX**	E	*E*	BK
94480	(81411, 92608)	**RX**	E	*E*	EN
94481	(81493, 92641)	**RX**	E	*E*	BK
94482	(81491, 92639)	**RX**	E	*E*	EN
94483	(81500, 92647)	**RX**	E	*E*	EN
94484	(81426, 92110)	**RX**	E	*E*	BK
94485	(81496, 92644)	**RX**	E	*E*	EN

94486	(81254, 92973)	**RX**	E	*E*	BK
94487	(81413, 92609)	**RX**	E	*E*	BK
94488	(81405, 92105)	**RX**	E	*E*	BK
94490	(81409, 92606)	**RX**	E	*E*	EN
94492	(80888, 92721)	**RX**	E	*E*	BK
94493	(80944, 92919)	**RX**	E	*E*	BK
94494	(81451, 92617)	**RX**	E	*E*	BK
94495	(80871, 92755)	**RX**	E	*E*	BK
94496	(81514, 92650)	**RX**	E	*E*	BK
94497	(80877, 92717)	**RX**	E	*E*	BK
94498	(81225, 92555)	**RX**	E	*E*	BK
94499	(81258, 92577)	**RX**	E	*E*	BK

NBA/NIA HIGH SECURITY BRAKE VAN (100/110 m.p.h.)

Dia. NB501 or NI501. Mark 1. These vehicles are NEs further modified with sealed gangways, new floors, built-in tail lights and roller shutter doors. For lot Nos. see original number series. B4 bogies. 31.4 t. ETH 1X.

These vehicles are identical to the 94400–94499 series. Certain vehicles are being given a special maintenance regime whereby tyres are reprofiled more frequently than normal and are then allowed to run at 110 m.p.h. Vehicles from the 94400 series upgraded to 110 m.p.h. are being renumbered in this series. Vehicles are NBA (100 m.p.h.) unless marked NIA (110 m.p.h.)

94500	(81457, 92121)	NIA	**RX**	E	*E*	ML
94501	(80891, 92725)		**RX**	E	*E*	BK
94502	(80924, 92720)	NIA	**RX**	E	*E*	ML
94503	(80873, 92709)	NIA	**RX**	E	*E*	ML
94504	(80935, 92748)	NIA	**RX**	E	*E*	BK
94505	(81235, 92750)	NIA	**RX**	E	*E*	ML
94506	(80958, 92922)	NIA	**RX**	E	*E*	ML
94507	(80876, 92505)	NIA	**RX**	E	*E*	ML
94508	(80887, 92722)	NIA	**RX**	E	*E*	BK
94509	(80897, 92509)	NIA	**RX**	E	*E*	ML
94510	(80945, 92265)		**RX**	E	*E*	BK
94511	(81504, 92714)	NIA	**RX**	E	*E*	ML
94512	(81265, 92582)		**RX**	E	*E*	BK
94513	(81257, 92576)		**RX**	E	*E*	BK
94514	(81459, 92122)	NIA	**RX**	E	*E*	ML
94515	(80916, 92513)	NIA	**RX**	E	*E*	ML
94516	(81267, 92211)	NIA	**RX**	E	*E*	ML
94517	(81489, 92243)	NIA	**RX**	E	*E*	BK
94518	(81346, 92258)		**RX**	E	*E*	BK
94519	(80930, 92916)	NIA	**RX**	E	*E*	ML
94520	(80940, 92917)	NIA	**RX**	E	*E*	ML
94521	(80900, 92510)	NIA	**RX**	E	*E*	ML
94522	(80880, 92907)	NIA	**RX**	E	*E*	ML
94523	(81509, 92649)	NIA	**RX**	E	*E*	BK
94524	(81454, 94457)	NIA	**RX**	E	*E*	BK
94525	(80902, 92229)	NIA	**RX**	E	*E*	ML

94526	(80941, 92518)	NIA	**RX**	E	*E*	ML
94527	(80924, 92728)	NIA	**RX**	E	*E*	BK
94528	(81404, 92267)		**RX**	E	*E*	BK
94529	(80959, 92252)	NIA	**RX**	E	*E*	BK
94530	(81511, 94409)	NIA	**RX**	E	*E*	ML
94531	(80879, 94456)	NIA	**RX**	E	*E*	ML
94532	(81423, 94489)	NIA	**RX**	E	*E*	BK
94533	(80937, 94425)	NIA	**RX**	E	*E*	BK
94534	(80908, 94430)	NIA	**RX**	E	*E*	BK
94535	(80858, 94419)	NIA	**RX**	E	*E*	BK
94536	(80936, 94491)	NIA	**RX**	E	*E*	BK
94537	(81230, 94421)	NIA	**RX**	E	*E*	BK
94538	(81283, 94426)	NIA	**RX**	E	*E*	BK

NO (GUV)   GENERAL UTILITY VAN (100 m.p.h.)

Dia. NO513. Mark 1. For lot Nos. see original number series. Commonwealth bogies except where shown otherwise. Add 2 t to weight. ETH 0X.

95105	(86126, 93126)		**RX**	E	CU
95109	(86269, 93269)	x	**B**	E	CU
95120	(86468, 93468)	x	**RY**	E	CU
95124	(86836, 93836)	x	**R**	E	CU
95125	(86143, 93143)	x	**B**	E	CU
95128	(86764, 93764)	x	**RY**	E	CW
95129	(86347, 93347)	x	**RY**	E	CW
95135	(86249, 93249)	x	**RY**	E	CU
95145	(86293, 93293)	x	**RX**	E	CU
95152	(86969, 93969)	x	**RY**	E	CU
95165	(86262, 93262)	x	**RX**	E	CU

NCX   NEWSPAPER VAN (100 m.p.h.)

Dia. NC501. Mark 1. BGs modified to carry newspapers. As EWS does not now carry newspaper traffic these are now all out of use. For lot Nos. refer to original number series. Commonwealth bogies. Add 2 t to weight. ETH3 (3X*).

95201	(80875)	x	**RX**	E	HY
95211	(80949)	x	**RY**	E	CL
95227	(81292, 95310)	x	**RX**	E	HY
95228	(81014, 95332)	x	**RX**	E	NC
95230	(80525, 95321)	x	**RX**	E	DY

NAA   PROPELLING CONTROL VEHICLE

Dia. NA508. Mark 1. Class 307 driving trailers converted for use in propelling mail trains out of termini. Fitted with roller shutter doors. Equipment was fitted for communication between cab of PCV and locomotive but this is now isolated and the vehicles are in use as for movement of materials between EWS maintenance depots. B5 bogies. ETH 2X.

Lot No. 30206 Eastleigh 1954–556. Converted at RTC, Derby 1993.

95300	(75114, 94300)	**RX**	E	*E*	EN	
95301	(75102, 94301)	**RX**	E	*E*	EN	

NRX   BAA CONTAINER VAN (100 m.p.h.)

Dia. NR503. Mark 1. Modified for carriage of British Airports Authority containers with roller shutter doors and roller floors and gangways removed. For lot Nos. see original number series. Now used for movement of materials between EWS maintenance depots. Commonwealth bogies. Add 2 t to weight. ETH3.

95400	(80621, 95203)	x	**RX**	E	*E*	CD
95410	(80826, 95213)	x	**E**	E	*E*	EN

NKA   HIGH SECURITY GENERAL UTILITY VAN

Dia. NK502. Mark 1. These vehicles are GUVs further modified with new floors, two roller shutter doors per side, middle doors sealed and end doors removed. For lot Nos. see original number series. Commonwealth bogies. Add 2 t to weight. ETH 0X.

95715	(86174, 95115)	**R**	E	*E*	EN
95727	(86323, 95127)	**R**	E	*E*	EN
95734	(86462, 95134)	**RX**	E	*E*	EN
95739	(86172, 95139)	**R**	E	*E*	EN
95743	(86485, 95143)	**RX**	E	*E*	EN
95749	(86265, 95149)	**R**	E	*E*	EN
95754	(86897, 95154)	**R**	E	*E*	EN
95758	(86499, 95158)	**RX**	E	*E*	EN
95759	(86084, 95159)	**RX**	E	*E*	EN
95761	(86205, 95161)	**RX**	E	*E*	EN
95762	(86122, 95162)	**RX**	E	*E*	EN
95763	(86407, 95163)	**R**	E	*E*	EN

NX/NV (GUV)   MOTORAIL VAN (100 m.p.h.)

Dia. NX501. Mark 1. For details and lot numbers see original number series. ETH 0 (0X*).

Note: 96101 has a new prototype body built 1998 by Marcroft Engineering with side loading and one end sealed (Dia. NV501).

96100	(86734, 93734)	*B5		H		KN
96101	(86741, 93741)	*B5	FT	H		PY
96110	(86738, 93738)	*C		H	E	CF
96112	(86750, 93750)	*C		H		LT
96130	(86736, 93736)	*C		H		KN
96131	(86737, 93737)	*C		H		KN
96132	(86754, 93754)	*C		H		LT
96133	(86685, 93685)	C		H		LT
96134	(86691, 93691)	C		H		LT
96135	(86755, 93755)	C		H		CP
96136	(86735, 93735)	C		H		LT
96137	(86748, 93748)	C	B	H		ZN
96139	(86751, 93751)	C		H	VW	MA
96162	(86647, 93647)	*C		H		LT
96163	(86646, 93646)	*C		H		KN
96164	(86880, 93880)	*C		H		LT
96165	(86784, 93784)	*C		H		KN
96166	(86834, 93834)	*C		H		KN
96167	(86756, 93756)	*C		H		KN
96168	(86978, 93978)	*C		H		LT
96170	(86159, 93159)	x*C		H		KN
96171	(86326, 93326)	x*C		H		LT
96172	(86363, 93363)	x*C		H		KN
96173	(86440, 93440)	x*C		H		KN
96174	(86453, 93453)	x*C		H		LT
96175	(86628, 93628)	x*C		H		KN
96176	(86641, 93641)	x*C		H		KN
96178	(86782, 93782)	*C		H		KN
96179	(86910, 93910)	*C		H		LT
96181	(86875, 93875)	*C		H		LT
96182	(86944, 93944)	*C		H		CP
96185	(86083, 93083)	x*C		H		LT
96186	(86087, 93087)	x*C		H		LT
96187	(86168, 93168)	x*C		H		LT
96188	(86320, 93320)	x*C		H		KN
96189	(86447, 93447)	x*C		H		LT
96190	(86448, 93448)	x*C		H		LT
96191	(86665, 93665)	x*C		H		KN
96192	(86669, 93669)	x*C		H		KN
96193	(86874, 93874)	x*C		H		LT
96194	(86949, 93949)	x*C		H		LT
96195	(86958, 93958)	x*C		H		LT

NP (GUV)   MOTORAIL VAN (110 m.p.h.)

Dia. NP503. Mark 1. Vehicles modified with concertina end doors. For details
and lot numbers see original number series. B5 Bogies. ETH 0X.

96210	(86355, 96159)	H	LT
96212	(86443, 96161)	H	LT
96218	(86286, 96151)	H	LT

AX5G — NIGHTSTAR GENERATOR VAN

Dia. AX502. Mark 3A. Generator vans converted from sleeping cars for use on 'Nightstar' services. Designed to operate between two Class 37/6 locomotives. Gangways removed. Two Cummins diesel generator groups providing a 1500 V train supply. Hydraulic parking brake. 61-way ENS interface jumpers. BT10 bogies.

Lot No. 30960 Derby 1981–83. 46.01 t.

96371	(10545, 6371)	**EP**	EU	*EU*	NP
96372	(10564, 6372)	**EP**	EU	*EU*	NP
96373	(10568, 6373)	**EP**	EU	*EU*	NP
96374	(10585, 6374)	**EP**	EU	*EU*	NP
96375	(10587, 6375)	**EP**	EU	*EU*	NP

AY5 (BV) — EUROSTAR BARRIER VEHICLE

Dia. AY501. Mark 1. Converted from GUVs. Bodies removed. B4 bogies.

96380–96382/9. Lot No. 30417 Pressed Steel 1958–59. 40t.
96383. Lot No. 30565 Pressed Steel 1959. 40t.
96384/6/7. Lot No. 30616 Pressed Steel 1959–60. 40t.
96385. Lot No. 30343 York 1957. 40t.
96388. Lot No. 30403 Glasgow 1958–60. 40t.

96380	(86386, 6380)	**B**	EU	*EU*	NP
96381	(86187, 6381)	**B**	EU	*EU*	NP
96382	(86295, 6382)	**B**	EU	*EU*	NP
96383	(86664, 6383)	**B**	EU	*EU*	NP
96384	(86955, 6384)	**B**	EU	*EU*	NP
96385	(86515, 6385)	**B**	EU	*EU*	NP
96386	(86859, 6386)	**B**	EU	*EU*	NP
96387	(86973, 6387)	**B**	EU	*EU*	NP
96388	(86562, 6388)	**B**	EU	*EU*	NP
96389	(86135, 6389)	**B**	EU	*EU*	NP

NG — MOTORAIL LOADING WAGON

Dia. NG 503. These vehicles have been converted and renumbered from weltrol wagons and were used for loading purposes.

Built Swindon 1960. Wagon Lot No. 3102 (3192*).

96452	(B900917)		H	LT
96453	(B900926)	*	H	LT

NVA — MOTORAIL VAN (100 m.p.h.)

Dia. NV502. Mark 1. Built 1998–9 by Marcroft Engineering using underframe and running gear from Motorail GUVs. Side loading with one end sealed. The vehicles run in pairs and access is available to the adjacent vehicle. For details and lot numbers see original number series. B5 bogies. ETH 0X.

96602	(86097, 96150)	**FG**	H	*GW*	PZ
96603	(86334, 96155)	**FG**	H	*GW*	PZ
96604	(86337, 96156)	**FG**	H	*GW*	PZ
96605	(86344, 96157)	**FG**	H	*GW*	PZ
96606	(86324, 96213)	**FG**	H	*GW*	PZ
96607	(86351, 96215)	**FG**	H	*GW*	PZ
96608	(86385, 96216)	**FG**	H	*GW*	PZ
96609	(86327, 96217)	**FG**	H	*GW*	PZ

NY EXHIBITION VAN

Various interiors. Converted from various vehicle types. Electric heating from shore supply. Livery varies according to job being undertaken.

Converted Salisbury 1981 from RBs of Lot No. 30636 Pressed Steel 1962. Club cars. Dia NY523/4 respectively. Commonwealth bogies.

99645	(1765)	v	**0**	E	FK
99646	(1766)	v	**0**	E	FK

Converted Railway Age, Crewe 1996 from TSO to Lot No. 30822 Derby 1971. B4 bogies.

99662	(5689)	**0**	RS	FK

Converted Railway Age, Crewe 1996 from SO to Lot No. 30821 Derby 1971. Originally FO. B4 bogies.

99663	(3194, 6223)	**0**	RS	FK
99664	(3189, 6231)	**0**	RS	FK

Converted Railway Age, Crewe 1996 from TSO to Lot No. 30837 Derby 1972. B4 bogies.

99665	(5755)	**0**	RS	FK

Converted Railway Age, Crewe 1996 from FO to Lot No. 30843 Derby 1972–73. B4 bogies.

99666	(3250)	**0**	RS	FK

YR FERRY VAN

Dia. YR025. This vehicle was built to a wagon lot although the design closely resembles that of NJ except it only has two sets of doors per side. Short Frames (57'). Load 14 t. Commonwealth bogies.

Built Eastleigh 1958. Wagon Lot. No. 2849. 30 t.

889202	**PC**	VS	*ON*	SL

Name: 889202 is branded 'BAGGAGE CAR No.8'.

QSA   EMU TRANSLATOR VEHICLES

These vehicles are numbered in the former BR departmental number series but are included here as they are owned by leasing companies and used by them for moving their vehicles around the national system in the same way as other vehicles included in this book. Various diagrams. Converted from Mark 1 TSO, RSOs, RUOs and BSKs.

975864. Lot No. 30054 Eastleigh 1951–54. BR Mark 1 bogies.
975867. Lot No. 30014 York 1950–51. BR Mark 1 bogies.
975875. Lot No. 30143 Charles Roberts 1954–55. BR Mark 1 bogies.
975871–975978. Lot No. 30647 Wolverton 1959–61. Commonwealth bogies.
977087. Lot No. 30229 Metro–Cammell 1955–57. Commonwealth bogies.

975864	(3849)		H	*H*	IL
975867	(1006)		H	*H*	IL
975875	(34643)		H	*H*	IL
975971	(1054)	**P**	P	*P*	CJ
975972	(1039)	**P**	P	*P*	CJ
975973	(1021)	**P**	P	*P*	CJ
975974	(1030)	**N**	A	*A*	IL
975975	(1042)	**P**	P	*P*	CJ
975976	(1033)		A		KN
975977	(1023)		A		KN
975978	(1025)	**N**	A	*A*	IL
977087	(34971)		H	*H*	IL

5.2. TEST TRAIN COACHES

LABORATORY & TESTING COACHES

These coaches are used for research, development, testing and inspection on the Railtrack network. Many are fitted with sophisticated technical equipment. They are numbered in the former BR departmental number series.

Non-Standard Livery: 975000/46/76/428/54 are in BR research white and red with a grey stripe.

Laboratory Coach. Converted from BR Mark 1 RSO. Lot No. 30014 York 1950–51. B4 bogies.

975000	(1003)	**0**	AE	ZA

Laboratory Coach. Converted from BR Mark 1 BSK. Lot No. 30021 Eastleigh 1950–52. B4 bogies.

975046	(34249)	**0**	AE	ZA

Tribometer Driving Trailer Coach. Converted from BR Mark 1 BSK. Lot No. 30060 GRCW 1954–55. B4 bogies.

975076	(34500)	**0**	AE	ZA

Structure Gauging Driving Trailer Coach. Converted from BR Mark 1 BSK. Lot No. 30699 Wolverton 1961–63. B4 bogies.

975081	(35313)	**SO**	RK	*SO*	ZA

Overhead Line Equipment Test Coach. Can either be locomotive hauled or included between DMU vehicles 977391/2. Converted from BR Mark 1 BSK Lot No. 30142 Gloucester 1954–5. B4 bogies.

975091	(34615)	**SO**	RK	*SO*	ZA

Structure Gauging Train Dormitory and Generator Coach. Converted from BR Mark 1 BCK Lot No. 30732 Derby 1962–4. B4 bogies.

975280	(21263)	**SO**	RK	*SO*	ZA

Test Coach. Converted from BR Mark 2 FK Lot No. 30734 Derby 1962–64. B4 bogies.

975290	(13396)	**SO**	SO	*SO*	ZA

Test Coach. Converted from BR Mark 1 BSK Lot No. 30699 Wolverton 1961–63. Commonwealth bogies.

975397	(35386)	**SO**	SO	*SO*	ZA

Test Coach. Converted from BR Mark 1 BSK Lot No. 30223 Charles Roberts 1955–56. B5 bogies.

975422	(34875)	**SO**	SO	*SO*	ZA

Laboratory/Generator Coach. Converted from BR Mark 1 BSO Lot No. 30170

Doncaster 1954–56. B4 bogies.

975428 (9236)	**0**	SO		ZA

Laboratory/Generator Coach. Converted from BR Mark 1 BG Lot No. 30725 GRCW 1962–63. B4 bogies.

975547 (81617)	**0**	SO		ZA

Test Coach. Converted from Mark 3 TRUB Lot No. 30849 Derby 1972–3. BT10 bogies.

975984 (10000, 40000)	**SO**	SO	*SO*	ZA

High Speed Track Recording Train Generator Coach. Converted from Class 438 750 V d.c. third rail EMU driving trailer. Lot No. 30764. York 1965–67. B5 (SR) bogies.

977335 (76277)	**SO**	SO	*SO*	ZA

High Speed Track Recording Train Dormitory Coach. Converted from BR Mark 2 BSO. Lot No 30757 Derby 1965–66. B4 bogies.

977337 (9395)	**SO**	SO	*SO*	ZA

High Speed Track Recording Train Brake & Stores Coach. Converted from Mark 2 BSO. Lot No. 30757 Derby 1965–66. B4 bogies.

977338 (9387)	**SO**	RK	*SO*	ZA

Laboratory Coach. Converted from BR Mark 2 TSO. Lot No. 30751 Derby 1965–67. B4 bogies.

977469 (5190)	**AE**	AE	*AE*	ZA

Test Train Staff and Dormitory Coach. Converted from BR Mark 3 SLEP. Lot No. 30960 Derby 1979–83. BT10 bogies.

977855 (10576)	**SO**	RK	*SO*	ZA

Test Coach. Converted from BR Inspection Saloon. BR Wagon Lot No. 3095. Swindon 1957. B4 bogies.

999506		RK		ZA

Track Recording Coach. Converted from BR Inspection Saloon. BR Wagon Lot No. 3379. Swindon 1960. B4 bogies.

999508	**SO**	RK	*SO*	ZA

High Speed Track Recording Coach. Can either be locomotive hauled (accompanied by 977335/7/8) or included between DMU vehicles 977391/2. Purpose built Mark 2. B4 bogies.

999550	**RK**	RK	*SO*	ZA

TEST TRAIN BRAKE FORCE RUNNERS

These vehicles are included in test trains to provide brake force. Those listed are numbered in the former BR departmental number series and are not used for any other purposes. Other vehicles included in this book may also be similarly used on a temporary basis if required. Converted from BR Mark 1

BSK, RKB, RB, RU, FOs and BR Mark 2 TSO, SO, FK, BFKs.

975051. Lot No. 30025 Wolverton 1950–52. B4 bogies.
977084. Lot No. 30514 Cravens 1958–61. B5 bogies.
977085. Lot No. 30633 Swindon 1959–62. Commonwealth bogies.
977193. Lot No. 30632 Swindon 1959–61. Commonwealth bogies.
977331. Lot No. 30721 Swindon 1961–63. Commonwealth bogies.
977387/468/70/773/801/2. Lot No. 30751 Derby 1964–7. B4 bogies.
977388. Lot No. 30242 Doncaster 1955–56. B4 bogies.
977389. Lot No. 30091 Doncaster 1953–54. B4 bogies.
977390/546. Lot No. 30810 Derby 1969–70. B4 bogies.
977449/50/594. Lot No. 30472 BRCW 1957–59. B4 bogies.
977595. Lot No. 30825 Derby 1969–72. B4 bogies.
977788/94/5. Lot No. 30823 Derby 1969–72. B4 bogies.
977789. Lot No. 30837 Derby 1971–72. B4 bogies.
977790/1/2/6. Lot No. 30844 Derby 1972–73. B4 bogies.
977793. Lot No. 30795 Derby 1969–70. B4 bogies.
977905. Lot No. 30573 GRCW 1959–60. B4 bogies.

Non-Standard Livery: 977387 is BR blue and grey lined out in white with a red stripe. 977773 is blue and grey with a cream stripe. 977788–94 are Adtranz White with yellow stripe.

975051	(34133)	**B**	E	*E*	CE
977084	(1505)	**B**	E	*E*	CE
977085	(336, 1637)	**B**	E	*E*	CE
977193	(1989)	**B**	E	*E*	CE
977331	(35444)	**BG**	RC		ZH
977387	(5195)	**O**	SO		ZA
977388	(3071)	**BG**	RC		ZH
977389	(3049)	**BG**	RC		ZH
977390	(3164, 6410)	**B**	E	*E*	CE
977449	(3086)	**B**	E	*E*	CE
977450	(3087)	**B**	E	*E*	CE
977468	(5169)	**SO**	SO	*SO*	ZA
977470	(5134)	**SO**	SO	*SO*	ZA
977546	(3165, 6416)	**BG**	RC		ZH
977594	(3093)	**BG**	RC		ZH
977595	(13573)	**BG**	E	*E*	CE
977773	(5182)	**O**	RK		ZA
977788	(17157)	**O**	AD	*AD*	ZF
977789	(5765)	**O**	AD	*AD*	ZF
977790	(5830)	**O**	AD	*AD*	ZF
977791	(5855)	**O**	AD	*AD*	ZF
977792	(5856)	**O**	AD	*AD*	ZF
977793	(5596)	**O**	AD	*AD*	ZF
977794	(17139)	**O**	AD	*AD*	ZF
977795	(17162)	**BG**	RC		ZH
977796	(5898)	**BG**	RC		ZH
977801	(5153)	**SO**	RK	*SO*	ZA
977802	(5176)	**SO**	RK	*SO*	ZA
977905	(35292, 80215)	**SO**	SO	*SO*	ZA

5.3. NPCCS AWAITING DISPOSAL

This list contains the last known locations of NPCCS vehicles awaiting disposal. The definition of which vehicles are "awaiting disposal" is somewhat vague, but generally speaking these are vehicles of types not now in normal service or vehicles which have been damaged by fire, vandalism or collision.

80330	Bristol Pylle Hill
80336	Bristol East Yard
80338	Bristol East Yard
80735	Perth Holding Sidings
80865	Hornsey Sand Terminal
84197	Worksop
84361	Cambridge Coalfields Sidings
84364	Doncaster West Yard
84382	Cambridge Coalfields Sidings
84519	Crewe Coal Sidings
93180	Derby South Dock Siding
93234	Hayes & Harlington
93358	Mossend Yard
93446	Crewe South Yard
93457	Cricklewood Rubbish Terminal
93482	Bedford Civil Engineers Sidings
93542	Hayes & Harlington
93579	DY
93723	Bletchley T&RSMD
93930	Crewe South Yard
95366	Bristol East Yard
96177	CP
99648	Eastleigh East Yard
975991	Crewe Coal Sidings
977144	PY
977182	Eastleigh Down CS
977183	Eastleigh Down CS
977359	ZN
977399	NL
977510	FK
977781	DY
977782	DY
977783	DY
977784	DY
977914	DY
977916	DY

6. CODES

6.1. LIVERY CODES

Note: Loco-hauled coaching stock vehicles are in Intercity (light grey/red stripe/white stripe/dark grey) livery unless otherwise indicated. For traditional two-colour carrige liveries the colour of the lower half of the bodyside is stated first.

* denotes an obsolescent livery style no longer normally used for repaints.

Code	Description
Code	*Description*
AE	AEA Technology (Dark blue with white stripe).
AL	Advertising livery (See class heading for details).
AN	Anglia Railways (White/turquoise with blue vignette).
AR	Anglia Railways (Turquoise blue with white stripe).
B*	BR (Blue).
BG*	BR (Blue and grey lined out in white).
BL*	BR (Blue with yellow cabs, grey roof, large numbers).
BR*	BR (Blue with red solebar stripe).
C2	c2c (Blue, with grey doors).
CC	BR (Carmine & cream lined out in black & gold) ('blood & custard').
CE*	BR Engineers (Yellow & grey with black cab doors and window surrounds).
CH	BR Western Region/GWR (Chocolate & cream).
CO	Centro (Grey/green with light blue, white & yellow stripes).
CR	Chiltern Railways (Blue and white with a thin red stripe).
CS	Connex (Blue with yellow lower body and blue solebar).
CT	Central Trains (Two-tone green with yellow doors. Blue flash at vehicle ends. Thin red stripe at vehicle ends and at cantrail level).
CX	Connex (White with yellow lower body and blue solebar).
DG*	BR Departmental (Plain dark grey with black cab doors and window surrounds).
DR	Direct Rail Services (Dark blue with light blue roof).
DS	Danske Statsbaner (Blue and red with moon and star motifs).
E	English Welsh & Scottish Railway (Maroon bodyside & roof with gold stripe, gold reflective stripe at solebar level).
EG	Eurotunnel (Two-tone grey and white).
EN	Enron Teesside Operations (Trafalgar blue with red solebar stripe).
EP	European Passenger Services (Two-tone grey with dark blue roof).
ET	Eurotunnel (Two-tone grey and white with green and blue bands).
EU	Eurostar (White with dark blue & yellow stripes).
F*	BR Trainload Freight (Two-tone grey with black cab doors and window surrounds. No logos).
FA*	BR Trainload Construction (Two-tone grey with black cab doors and window surrounds. Yellow & blue chequered logo).
FC*	BR Trainload Coal (Two-tone grey with black cab doors and window surrounds. Black & yellow logo).
FD*	BR Railfreight Distribution (Two-tone grey with black cab doors and

FE* Railfreight Distribution International (Two tone-grey with black cab doors and dark blue roof. Red & yellow logo).

FF* Freightliner (Two-tone grey with black cab doors and window surrounds. Freightliner logo).

FG First Great Western (Green and ivory with thin green and broad gold stripes).

FL Freightliner (Dark green with yellow cabs).

FM* BR Trainload Metals (Two-tone grey with black cab doors and window surrounds. Yellow & blue chevrons logo).

FN First North Western (Indigo blue with pink and white stripes).

FO* BR Railfreight (Grey bodyside, yellow cabs, red buffer beam, large double-arrow logo).

FP* BR Trainload Petroleum (Two-tone grey with black cab doors and window surrounds. Yellow & blue waves logo).

FQ* BR Railfreight (Grey bodyside, yellow cabs, red buffer beam/stripe at solebar level, large double-arrow logo).

FR Fragonset Railways (Black with silver roof and a red bodyside band lined out in white).

FT Forward Trust Rail (Blue and white lined out in straw).

FW First Great Western (Indigo blue with white roof and gold, pink and white stripes)

FX Felixstowe Dock & Railway Company (Blue, with a green stripe picked out in white).

FY Foster Yeoman (Blue/silver. Cast numberplates).

G* BR (Plain green, with white stripe on main line locomotives).

G BR Southern Region/SR (Green with straw stripe on coaching stock).

GB GB Railfreight (Blue with orange cantrail & solebar stripes, orange cabs).

GE First Great Eastern (Grey, green, blue and white).

GG* BR (Two-tone green).

GL First Great Western (Green with gold stripe).

GM Greater Manchester PTE (Light grey/dark grey with red and white stripes).

GN Great North Eastern Railway (Dark blue with a red stripe).

GS Great Scottish & Western Railway (Maroon).

GV Gatwick Express (Red, white & Indigo blue with mauve & blue doors).

GW* Great Western Railway (Green, lined out in black & orange. Cast numberplates).

GX Gatwick Express (Dark grey/white/burgundy/white).

GY Eurotunnel (Grey and yellow).

HA Hanson Quarry Products (Dark blue and silver).

HB* Hunslet-Barclay (Two-tone grey with red solebar).

HE Heathrow Express (Silver grey and indigo blue with black window surrounds).

HN Harry Needle Railroad Company (Grey/orange, lined out in black).

I* BR InterCity (Dark grey/white/red/light grey and yellow lower cabsides).

IL Island Line (Light blue, with desert illustrations featuring dinosaurs, camels etc).

IM*	BR Mainline (Dark grey/white/red/light grey).
IS*	BR InterCity Swallow (Dark grey/white/red/white).
LH*	BR Loadhaul (Black with orange cabsides).
LN	LNER Tourist (green & cream).
LS*	LTS Rail (Grey/white/green/white/blue/white).
M	BR Maroon lined out in straw and black).
MA	Maintrain (Light blue).
MD	Ministry of Defence (Black).
MG*	BR Mainline Freight (Two-tone grey with black cab doors and window surrounds).
ML*	BR Mainline Freight (Aircraft blue with silver stripe).
MM	Midland Main Line (Teal green with cream lower body sides and three orange stripes).
MR	Mendip Rail (Green, red & silver).
MS*	Mersey Travel departmental (Yellow/black).
MT*	Mersey Travel (Yellow/white with grey and black stripes).
MY	Mersey Travel (Yellow/white with grey stripe).
N*	BR Network South East (Grey/white/red/white/blue/white).
NB	Provincial services (As **NW** but with the red stripe repainted blue).
NS	Northern Spirit (Turquoise blue with lime green 'N').
NT*	BR Network South East (Grey/red/white/blue/white).
NW	North West Trains (Blue with gold cant rail stripe and star).
O	Non standard liveries (See class heading for details).
P	Porterbrook Leasing Company (Purple & grey).
PC*	Pullman Car Company (Umber & cream with gold lettering).
PM*	Provincial Midline (Dark blue/grey with dark blue & grey stripes).
PS	Provincial (Dark blue/grey with light blue & white stripes).
R*	Plain red.
RB	Riviera Trains (Oxford blue & cream, lined out in gold).
RE*	Provincial Express (Light grey/buff/dark grey with white, dark blue & light blue stripes).
RF*	RFS (E) (Light grey with yellow and blue stripes).
RG*	BR Parcels (Dark grey and red).
RK	Railtrack (Green and blue).
RL	RMS Locotech (Blue & red).
RM	Royal Mail. (Red with Yellow stripes above solebar)
RN*	North West Regional Railways (Dark blue/grey with green & white stripes).
RO*	Railtrack (Orange with white and grey stripes).
RP	Royal Train (Claret, lined out in red and black).
RR*	Regional Railways (Dark Blue/Grey with light blue & white stripes, three narrow dark blue stripes at cab ends).
RT	RT Rail (Black, lined out in red).
RX	Rail express systems (Dark grey and red with or without blue markings).
RY	BR parcels sector. Red with yellow stripes above solebar.
S*	Strathclyde PTE (Orange/black lined out in white).
SB*	Belgian National Railways (SNCB/NMBS-style blue with yellow stripes).
SC	Strathclyde PTE (Carmine & cream lined out in black and gold – not lined out on Class 334).

SL   Silverlink (Indigo blue with white stripe, green lower body & yellow doors).
SO   Serco Railtest (Red/grey).
SP   Strathclyde Passenger Transport (Carmine and cream, with a turqouise stripe).
SR   ScotRail (White, terracotta, purple and aquamarine).
SS   ScotRail Caledonian Sleepers (Two-tone purple with silver stripe).
ST   Stagecoach South West Trains (White/orange/white/red/white/blue/white).
SW   South West Trains (White/black/orange/red/blue, with red doors).
SX   Stansted Express (Two-tone metallic blue with grey doors)
T*   Transrail (Two-tone grey with Transrail logos).
TC*   BR Engineers/Transrail. (Yellow & grey with black cab doors and window surrounds. Transrail logo).
TR   Thameslink Rail (Dark blue with a broad orange stripe and two narrower white bodyside stripes plus white cantrail stripe).
TW   Tyne & Wear PTE (White/yellow with blue stripe).
TX   Northern Spirit Trans-Pennine Express (Plum with yellow 'N').
U   Undercoat (White or grey undercoat).
V   Virgin Trains (red with black doors extending into bodysides, three white lower bodysides stripes).
VL   Valley Lines. (Dark green & red with white & light green stripes. Light green doors).
VN   Venice Simplon Orient Express 'Northern Belle' (Crimson lake and cream).
VP   Virgin Trains (Black with a large black & white chequered flag on the bodyside).
VT   Virgin Trains (Silver, with black window surrounds, white cant-rail stripe and red roof. Red is swept down at unnit ends. Black and white striped doors).
WA   Wabtec Rail (Black).
WN   West Anglia Great Northern Railway (White with blue, grey and orange stripes).
WR   Waterman Railways (Maroon with cream stripes).
WV   Waterman Railways VIP (West Coast Joint Stock-style lined purple lake).
WW   Wales & West Passenger Trains (Grey, orange, light blue and dark blue with orange doors)
WY*   West Yorkshire PTE (Red/cream with thin yellow stripe).
Y   Plain yellow.
YN   West Yorkshire PTE (Red with light grey N).
YO*   Foster Yeoman (Blue/silver/blue. Cast numberplates).

6.2. OWNER CODES

Code	Owner
14	75014 Locomotive Operators Group.
24	6024 Preservation Society Ltd.
50	The Fifty Fund.
62	The Princess Royal Class Locomotive Trust Ltd.
90	Deltic 9000 Locomotives Ltd.
A	Angel Trains Ltd.
AD	Adtranz (DaimlerChrysler Rail Systems UK).
AE	AEA Technology plc.
AM	Alstom Ltd.
AR	Anglia Railways Train Services Ltd.
BB	Bridgend County Borough Council
BK	The Scottish Railway Preservation Society
BM	Birmingham Railway Museum Trust.
CA	Cardiff Railway Company Ltd.
CM	Cambrian Trains Ltd.
CN	The Carriage and Traction Company Ltd.
CW	Cotswold Rail Engineering Ltd.
DP	The Deltic Preservation Society Ltd.
DR	Direct Rail Services Ltd.
E	English Welsh & Scottish Railway Ltd.
EF	EWS Finance Ltd.
EN	East Lancashire Railway Trust Ltd.
EN	Enron Teesside Operations Ltd.
ER	Eastleigh Railway Preservation Society Ltd.
ET	Eurotunnel plc.
EU	Eurostar (UK) Ltd.
FL	Freightliner Ltd.
FR	Fragonset Railways Ltd.
FS	Flying Scotsman Railways Ltd.
FW	Great Western Trains Company Ltd.
FX	The Felixstowe Dock & Railway Company Ltd.
FY	Foster Yeoman Ltd.
GS	The Great Scottish & Western Railway Company Ltd.
H	HSBC Rail (UKI) Ltd.
HA	The Hanson Group Ltd.
HD	Hastings Diesels Ltd.
HE	British Airports Authority PLC.
HJ	Howard Johnston Engineering.
HL	Heritage Traction Leasing Ltd.
HN	Harry Needle Railroad Company Ltd.
HS	Harry Schneider.
HX	Halifax Asset Finance Ltd.
IE	Ian Storey Engineering
IR	Ian Riley Engineering.
JK	Dr. John Kennedy.
LU	London Underground Ltd.
LW	London & North Western Railway Company Ltd.

MA	Maintrain Ltd.
MD	Ministry of Defence.
ME	Merseyrail Electrics Ltd.
MH	Mid-Hants Railway plc.
MN	Merchant Navy Locomotive Preservation Society Ltd.
NE	North Eastern Locomotive Preservation Group Ltd.
NR	National Railway Museum
NS	Northern Spirit Ltd.
NY	North Yorkshire Moors Railway
P	Porterbrook Leasing Company Ltd.
PD	Project Defiance Limited.
PO	Privately owned (owner undisclosed).
RA	Railfilms plc.
RC	Railcare Ltd.
RD	Rhondda Cynon Taff District Council
RI	Rail Assets Investments Ltd.
RK	Railtrack
RL	RMS Locotech Ltd.
RM	Royal Mail.
RT	RT Rail Tours Ltd.
RS	Rail Charter Services
RV	Riviera Trains Ltd.
SB	SNCB/NMBS (Société Nationale des Chemins de fer Belges/ Nationale Maatschappij der belgische Spoorwegen).
SC	Connex South Central.
SE	Connex South Eastern
SF	SNCF (Société Nationale des Chemins de fer Français).
SH	Scottish Highland Railway Company Ltd.
SI	Sea Containers Railway Services Ltd.
SO	Serco Railtest Ltd.
SV	Severn Valley Railway Co. Ltd.
SW	South West Trains Ltd.
VS	Venice Simplon Orient Express Ltd.
VW	West Coast Trains Ltd.
W	Wiltshire Leasing Co. Ltd.
WA	Wabtec Rail Ltd.
WC	West Coast Railway Company Ltd.
WF	Western Falcon Rail.
WN	West Anglia Great Northern Railway Ltd.
WT	Wessex Trains Ltd.
X	Sold for scrap, awaiting collection or disposal.

6.3. LOCOMOTIVE OPERATING POOL CODES

Code	Pool
CDJD	Serco Railtest. Class 08.
CTLO	Cambrian Trains. Operational Fleet.
DFFT	Freightliner. Class 47 with 'Dock Mode'.
DFGC	Freightliner. Class 86/5.
DFGM	Freightliner. Class 66/5, general traffic.
DFHH	Freightliner. Class 66/5, Heavy Haul Division.
DFHZ	Freightliner. Class 57 (standard fuel capacity).
DFLC	Freightliner. Class 90/1.
DFLM	Freightliner. Class 47 (with multiple working equipment).
DFLS	Freightliner. Class 08.
DFLT	Freightliner. Class 47.
DFNC	Freightliner. Class 86/6.
DFRT	Freightliner. Class 66/5, Railtrack contract.
DFTZ	Freightliner. Class 57 (additional fuel capacity).
DHLT	Freightliner. Locomotives awaiting maintenance/repair.
GPSN	Eurostar (UK). Class 73.
GPSS	Eurostar (UK). Class 08.
GPSV	Eurostar (UK). Class 37.
HASS	ScotRail. Class 08.
HDXX	First North Western. Class 08.
HEBD	Merseyrail Electrics. Class 73.
HEXX	Merseyrail Electrics. Stored.
HFSL	Virgin Cross Country. Class 08.
HFSN	Virgin West Coast. Class 08.
HGSS	Maintrain. Class 08 (Tyseley)
HISE	Maintrain. Class 08 (Derby).
HISL	Maintrain. Class 08 (Neville Hill).
HJSE	First Great Western. Class 08 (Landore).
HJSL	First Great Western. Class 08 (Laira).
HJXX	First Great Western. Class 08 (Old Oak HST & St. Phillips Marsh).
HLSV	Cardiff Railway Company. Class 08. Hire locomotive.
HNRL	Harry Needle Railtrack Leasing. Hire locomotives.
HNRS	Harry Needle Railroad Company. Stored.
HPXX	Silverlink Train Services. Unspecified.
HQXX	West Anglia Great Northern Railway. Class 03.
HSSN	Anglia Railways. Class 08.
HWSU	Connex South Central. Class 09.
HWXX	Connex South Central. Stored.
HYSB	South West Trains. Standby locomotives.
IANA	Anglia Railways. Class 86.
ICCA	Virgin Cross Country. Class 86.
ICCP	Virgin Cross Country. Class 43.
IECA	Great North Eastern Railway. Class 91.
IECB	Great North Eastern Railway. Class 89.
IECP	Great North Eastern Railway. Class 43.
ILRA	Virgin Cross Country. Class 47.
IMLP	Midland Mainline. Class 43.

IVGA	Gatwick Express. Class 73/2.
IWCA	Virgin West Coast. Classes 87 & 90.
IWCP	Virgin West Coast. Class 43.
IWLA	First Great Western. Class 47.
IWPA	Virgin West Coast. Class 86.
IWRP	First Great Western. Class 43.
KCSI	Adtranz. Class 08 (Ilford).
KDSD	Adtranz. Class 08 (Doncaster).
KESE	Alstom. Class 08 (Eastleigh).
KGSS	Railcare. Class 08 (Glasgow).
KWSW	Railcare. Class 08 (Wolverton).
MBDL	Non TOC owned diesel locomotives.
MBEL	Non TOC owned electric locomotives.
MOLO	RT Rail Tours (Michael Owen).
QXXX	Railtrack.
RFSH	Wabtec. Hire fleet.
RTLO	Riviera Trains. Operational Fleet.
SAXL	HSBC Rail (UK). Off lease.
SBXL	Porterbrook Leasing. Off lease.
SCXL	Angel Trains. Off lease.
SDFR	Fragonset Railways. Operational locomotives.
WAAK	EWS. Class 67.
WBAH	EWS. Class 66 Anglia & Southern.
WBAI	EWS. Class 66 North Eastern (South).
WBAK	EWS. Class 66 Great Western.
WBAM	EWS. Class 66 Scotland, non-RETB equipped.
WBAN	EWS. Class 66 Midland.
WBAT	EWS. Class 66 North Eastern (North).
WBBM	EWS. Class 66 RETB equipped.
WCAI	EWS. Class 60 North Eastern (South).
WCAK	EWS. Class 60 Great Western.
WCAN	EWS. Class 60 Midland.
WCAT	EWS. Class 60 North Eastern (North).
WDAG	EWS. Class 59/2.
WEFE	EWS. Class 90 Freight.
WEOE	EWS. Class 86.
WEPE	EWS. Class 90 Royal Mail & Passenger.
WFAN	EWS. Class 58.
WGAI	EWS. Class 56 North Eastern (South).
WGAT	EWS. Class 56 North Eastern (North).
WHCD	EWS. Class 47.
WHCM	EWS. Class 47 Hired to ScotRail.
WHPT	EWS. New locomotives (pre-acceptance).
WHRD	EWS. Class 47 Special Trains.
WHTD	EWS. Class 47 Hired to Serco Railtest.
WHZX	EWS. Locomotives awaiting disposal.
WKAC	EWS. Class 37 Anglia & Southern.
WKAD	EWS. Class 37 Midlands & North West.
WKBM	EWS. Class 37 RETB equipped.
WKCD	EWS. Class 37/4 Hired to First North Western & Cardiff Railway.
WKGS	EWS. Class 37 Identified for possible hire to Spain.

WKSN	EWS. Class 37 Railtrack Sandite contract.	
WMAC	EWS. Class 31.	
WNWX	EWS. Main line locomotives – for major repairs.	
WNXX	EWS. Main line locomotives – stored.	
WNYX	EWS. Main line locomotives – authorised for component recovery.	
WNZX	EWS. Main line locomotives – awaiting disposal.	
WPAG	EWS. Class 73.	
WSAC	EWS. Class 33. Aberdeen area shunting/trip locomotives.	
WSAW	EWS. Shunting locomotives (on hire to Allied Steel & Wire).	
WSEM	EWS. Shunting locomotives (East Midlands).	
WSNE	EWS. Shunting locomotives (North East England).	
WSNW	EWS. Shunting locomotives (North West England).	
WSSC	EWS. Shunting locomotives (Scotland).	
WSSE	EWS. Shunting locomotives (London & South East England).	
WSSW	EWS. Shunting locomotives (South Wales).	
WSWM	EWS. Shunting locomotives (West Midlands).	
WSWS	EWS. Shunting locomotives (Wessex).	
WSWX	EWS. Shunting locomotives – Strategic Reserve.	
WSXX	EWS. Shunting locomotives – Stored.	
WSYH	EWS. Shunting locomotives (Yorkshire & Humberside).	
WSYX	EWS. Shunting locomotives – component recovery only.	
WTAE	EWS. Class 92 Dollands Moor–Wembley–Mossend–Doncaster & Crewe–Trafford Park Routes.	
WTWE	EWS. Class 92 Eurotunnel only.	
XHSD	Direct Rail Services. Operational locomotives.	
XHSS	Direct Rail Services. Stored locomotives.	
XYPA	Mendip Rail. Class 59/0.	
XYPO	Mendip Rail. Class 59/1.	
XYPS	Mendip Rail. Shunting locomotives.	

6.4. OPERATION CODES

Code	Operator
A	Angel Train Contracts
AD	Adtranz.
AE	AEA Technology.
AR	Anglia Railways
AM	Alstom.
AR	Anglia Railways.
CA	Cardiff Railway Company.
CR	Chiltern Railways.
CT	Central Trains.
C2	c2c Rail
DR	Direct Rail services.
E	English Welsh & Scottish Railway.
EU	Eurostar (UK).
GB	GB Railways.
GE	First Great Eastern.
GN	Great North Eastern Railway.
GX	Gatwick Express.
GW	First Great Western.
HE	Heathrow Express.
H	HSBC Rail
IL	Island Line.
ME	Merseyrail Electrics.
MM	Midland Mainline.
NS	Northern Spirit.
NW	First North Western.
ON	Normally used on special or charter services.
OT	Non revenue earning (e.g. Test Trains, Research, Route Learning).
OS	Locomotive support coach..
HE	Heathrow Express.
P	Porterbrook Leasing.
RK	Railtrack
RP	Royal train
SC	Connex South Central.
SE	Connex South Eastern.
SL	Silverlink.
SO	Serco Railtest.
SR	ScotRail.
SW	South West Trains.
TC	Undergoing tests prior to commissioning.
TR	Thameslink Rail.
VW	Virgin West Coast
VX	Virgin Cross Country
WN	West Anglia Great Northern.

6.5. ALLOCATION & LOCATION CODES

* denotes unofficial code.

Code	Location	Depot Operator
AF	Chart Leacon (Ashford, Kent) T&RSMD	Adtranz
AL	Aylesbury TMD	Chiltern Railways
AN	Allerton (Liverpool) T&RSMD	EWS
AY	Ayr SD	EWS
BC*	Bescot Yard	*Storage location only.*
BD	Birkenhead North T&RSMD	Merseyrail Electrics
BH	Barrow Hill T&RSMD	Harry Needle Railroad Company
BG*	Billingham T&RSMD	Enron Teesside Operations
BI	Brighton T&RSMD	Connex South Central
BK	Barton Hill (Bristol) T&RSMD	EWS
BM	Bournemouth T&RSMD	South West Trains
BN	Bounds Green (London) T&RSMD	Great North Eastern Railway
BP	Blackpool North Carrige Sidings	*Storage location only*
BQ	Bury T&RSMD	East Lancashire Railway
BS	Bescot (Walsall) TMD	EWS
BT	Bo'ness (West Lothian)	Bo'ness & Kinneil Railway
BW*	Barry WRD (closed)	*Storage location only*
BY	Bletchley T&RSMD	Silverlink Train Services
BZ	St. Blazey (Par) T&RSMD	EWS
CB*	Crewe Basford Hall Yard	*Storage location only*
CD	Crewe Diesel TMD	EWS
CE	Crewe International Electric T&RSMD	EWS
CF	Cardiff Canton (Loco) TMD	EWS
CF	Cardiff Canton (DMU) TMD	Wales & West
CG*	Crewe Gresty Lane Sidings	*Storage location only*
CH	Chester TMD	First North Western
CJ	Clapham Yard (London) CSD	South West Trains
CK	Corkerhill (Glasgow) TMD	ScotRail
CL	Carlisle Upperby (closed)	*Storage location only*
CO	Coquelles (France) T&RSMD	Eurotunnel
CP	Crewe Carriage T&RSMD	London & North Western Railway
CQ	Crewe (The Railway Age) T&RSMD	Carriage & Traction Company
CS	Carnforth T&RSMD	West Coast Railway Company
CT*	Chester WRD (closed)	*Storage location only*
CU*	Carlisle Currock WRD	*Storage location only*
CW*	Crewe South Yard	*Storage location only*
DD*	Doncaster Wood Yard	*Storage location only*
DE*	Dewsbury T&RSMD	RMS Locotech
DI	Didcot Railway Centre	Great Western Society
DR	Doncaster TMD	EWS
DY	Derby Etches Park T&RSMD	Maintrain
EC	Edinburgh Craigentinny T&RSMD	Great North Eastern Railway
EH	Eastleigh T&RSMD	EWS
EM	East Ham T&RSMD	c2c Rail
EN	Euston Downside CARMD (London)	EWS
FB	Ferrybridge T&RSMD	EWS

FD	Unallocated	Freightliner
FE	Unallocated	Freightliner
FF	Forest (Brussels) T&RSMD	SNCB/NMBS
FK	Ferme Park CSD	GNER
FR	Fratton T&RSMD	South West Trains
FW	Fort William SD	EWS
FX*	Felixstowe TMD	Felixstowe Dock & Railway Company
GD	Gateshead TMD (closed)	*Storage location only*
GI	Gillingham (Kent) T&RSMD	Connex South Eastern
GW	Shields Road (Glasgow) T&RSMD	ScotRail/Alstom
HA	Haymarket (Edinburgh) TMD	Scotrail
HE	Hornsey T&RSMD	West Anglia Great Northern
HG	Hither Green TMD	EWS
HH	Haworth TMD	Keighley & Worth Valley Railway
HM	Healey Mills (Wakefield) SD	EWS
HT	Heaton T&RSMD (Newcastle)	Northern Spirit
HY*	Hinksey Yard (Oxford)	*Storage location only*
IL	Ilford T&RSMD	First Great Eastern
IM	Immingham T&RSMD	EWS
IS	Inverness T&RSMD	ScotRail
IW*	Ipswich WRD	*Storage location only*
KD	Carlisle Kingmoor T&RSMD	Direct Rail Services
KK	Kirkdale SD	Merseyrail Electrics
KN	MoD, Defence Munitions, Kineton	Ministry of Defence
KR	Kidderminster T&RSMD	Severn Valley Railway
KY	Knottingley T&RSMD	EWS
LA	Laira (Plymouth) T&RSMD	First Great Western
LB*	Loughborough	Brush Traction
LE	Landore (Swansea) T&RSMD	First Great Western
LG	Longsight Electric (Manchester) T&RSMD	Cross Fleet
LO	Longsight Diesel (Manchester) TMD	First North Western
LL	Liverpool Downhill CSD	West Coast Traincare
LR	Leicester SD	EWS
LT*	MoD Longtown	Ministry of Defence
LY	Le Landy (Paris) T&RSMD	SNCF
MA	Manchester Longsight CARMD	West Coast Traincare
MD	Merehead T&RSMD	Mendip Rail
MG	Margam (Port Talbot) SD	EWS
MH	Millerhill (Edinburgh) SD	EWS
ML	Motherwell T&RSMD	EWS
MM*	Fire Service College, Moreton-in-Marsh	*Storage location only*
NB*	New Brighton EMU Sidings	*Storage location only*
NC	Norwich Crown Point T&RSMD	Anglia Railways
NL	Neville Hill InterCity (Leeds) T&RSMD	Maintrain
NL	Neville Hill DMU/EMU (Leeds) T&RSMD	Northern Spirit
NP	North Pole International (London) T&RSMD	Eurostar (UK)
NY	Grosmont T&RSMD	North Yorkshire Moors Railway
OC	Old Oak Common (London) TMD	EWS
OH	Old Oak Common Electric (London) T&RSMD	Siemens
OM	Old Oak Common (London) CARMD	First Great Western

OO	Old Oak Common HST T&RSMD (London)	First Great Western
OY	Oxley T&RSMD (Wolverhampton)	West Coast Traincare
PC	Polmadie T&RSMD (Glasgow)	West Coast Traincare
PM	St. Phillips Marsh (Bristol) T&RSMD	First Great Western
PY*	MoD, DERA, Pig's Bay (Shoeburyness)	*Storage location only*
PZ	Penzance CARMD	First Great Western
RG	Reading TMD	Thames Trains
RL	Ropley T&RSMD	Mid Hants Railway
RM	Ramsgate T&RSMD	Connex South Eastern
RY	Ryde (Isle of Wight) T&RSMD	Island Line
SA	Salisbury TMD	South West Trains
SD	Sellafield T&RSMD	Direct Rail Services
SE	St. Leonards T&RSMD	St. Leonards Railway Engineering.
SF	Stratford (London) SD	EWS
SG	Slade Green T&RSMD	Connex South Eastern
SI	Soho (Birmingham) T&RSMD	Maintrain
SK	Swanwick Junction (Derbyshire)	Midland Railway Centre
SL	Stewarts Lane (London) T&RSMD	Gatwick Express
SN*	Shoeburyness EMU Sidings	*Storage location only*
ST*	Southampton Maritime T&RSMD	Freightliner
SP	Springs Branch (Wigan) CRDC	EWS
SU	Selhurst (Croydon) T&RSMD	Connex South Central
SZ	Southall (Greater London)	Flying Scotsman Railways
TE	Thornaby T&RSMD	EWS
TM	Tyseley Museum T&RSMD	Birmingham Railway Museum/ Fragonset Railways
TO	Toton (Nottinghamshire) TMD	EWS
TS	Tyseley (Birmingham) T&RSMD	Maintrain
TT*	Toton Training School (Notts)	*Storage location only*
TY	Tyne Yard SD	EWS
VM*	Velim Test Track (Czech Republic)	
WA	Warrington Arpley SD	EWS
WB	Wembley CSD	*Storage location only*
WD	Wimbledon T&RSMD	South West Trains
WK*	West Kirkby	*Storage location only*
WN	Willesden (London) TMD	West Coast Train Care
WR*	West Ruislip T&RSMD	London Underground
WU*	Wakefield Euroterminal	*Storage location only*
YM	National Railway Museum (York)	Science Museum
ZA	Railway Technical Centre, Derby	Serco Railtest/AEA Technology/ Fragonset Railways
ZB	Doncaster Works	Wabtec
ZC	Crewe Works	Adtranz
ZD	Derby Litchurch Lane Works	Adtranz
ZF	Doncaster Works	Adtranz
ZG	Eastleigh Works	Alstom
ZH	Springburn Works, Glasgow	Railcare
ZI	Ilford	Adtranz
ZN	Wolverton Works	Railcare

6.6. DEPOT TYPE CODES

CARMD	Carriage Maintenance Depot.
CRDC	Component Recovery & Disposal Centre.
CSD	Carriage Servicing Depot.
SD	Servicing Depot.
TMD	Traction Maintenance Depot.
T&RSMD	Traction & Rolling Stock Depot.
WRD	Wagon Repair Depot.

6.7. GENERAL ABBREVIATIONS

a.c.	alternating current.
BR	British Railways.
BSI	Bergische Stahl Industrie.
d.c.	direct current.
DEMU	Diesel-electric multiple unit.
Dia.	Diagram number.
DMU	Diesel multiple unit (general term).
EMU	Electric multiple unit.
GNER	Great North Eastern Railway
GWR	Great Western Railway
H-B	Hunslet-Barclay.
h.p.	horse power.
HNRC	Harry Needle Railroad Co.
Hz	Hertz.
kN	kilonewtons.
km/h	kilometres per hour.
kW	kilowatts.
lbf	pounds force.
LT	London Transport.
LUL	London Underground Limited.
m.	metres.
mm.	millimetres.
m.p.h.	miles per hour.
RCH	Railway Clearing House.
r.p.m.	revolutions per minute.
RR	Rolls Royce.
RSL	Rolling Stock Library.
SR	BR Southern Region.
t.	tonnes.
T	Toilets.
TD	Toilets suitable for disabled passengers.
TDM	Time Division Multiplex.
V	volts.
w	wheelchair spaces.

6.8 BUILDER DETAILS

These are shown in class headings, the following abbreviations being used:

ABB Derby	ABB, Derby Carriage Works (now Adtranz Derby).
ABB Doncaster	ABB, Doncaster Works (now Adtranz Doncaster).
ABB York	ABB, York.
Adtranz Derby	Adtranz, Derby Carriage Works.
Alexander	Walter Alexander, Falkirk.
Alstom Birmingham	Alstom, Saltley, Birmingham.
Alstom Eastleigh	Alstom, Eastleigh Works.
Ashford	BR, Ashford Works.
Barclay	Andrew Barclay, Caledonia Works, Kilmarnock (now Hunslet-Barclay).
Bombardier BN	Bombardier BN, Brugge, Belgium.
Bombardier Prorail	Bombardier Prorail, Horbury Junction, Wakefield.
BRCW	Birmingham Railway Carriage & Wagon, Smethwick.
BREL Derby	BREL, Derby Carriage Works (later ABB, now Adtranz).
BREL Eastleigh	BREL, Eastleigh Works (later Wessex Traincare, now Alstom Eastleigh).
BREL Swindon	BREL, Swindon Works.
BREL Wolverton	BREL, Wolverton Works (now Railcare, Wolverton).
BREL York	BREL, York Works (later ABB York).
CAF	Construcciones y Auxiliar de Ferrocarriles, Zaragosa, Spain.
Cowlairs	BR, Cowlairs Works.
Cravens	Cravens, Sheffield.
Derby	BR, Derby Carriage Works (later BREL Derby, then ABB Derby, now Adtranz Derby).
Doncaster	BR, Doncaster Works (later BREL Doncaster, then BRML Doncaster, then ABB Doncaster, now Adtranz Doncaster).
Eastleigh	BR, Eastleigh Works (later BREL Eastleigh, then Wessex Traincare, now Alstom Eastleigh).
GEC-A Birmingham	GEC-Alsthom, Saltley, Birmingham (now Alstom Birmingham).
Gloucester	Gloucester Railway Carriage & Wagon, Gloucester.
Hunslet-Barclay	Hunslet-Barclay, Caledonia Works, Kilmarnock.
Hunslet TPL	Hunslet Transportation Projects, Leeds.
Lancing	SR, Lancing Works.
Leyland Bus	Leyland Bus, Workington.
Metro-Cammell	Metropolitan-Cammell, Saltley, Birmingham (later GEC-A Birmingham, now Alstom Birmingham).
Pressed Steel	Pressed Steel, Linwood.
Railcare Glasgow	Railcare, Springburn Works, Glasgow.
Railcare Wolverton	Railcare, Wolverton.
Charles Roberts	Charles Roberts, Horbury Junction, Wakefield (later Procor, now Bombardier Prorail).
SRP	Specialist Rail Products Ltd (A subsidiary of RFS Industries, Doncaster.
Swindon	BR, Swindon Works.
Wessex Traincare	Wessex Traincare, Eastleigh (now Alstom Eastleigh).
York	BR, York Carriage Works (later BREL York, then ABB York).

5. UK LIGHT RAIL SYSTEMS & METROS

5.1. BLACKPOOL & FLEETWOOD TRAMWAY

Until the opening of Manchester Metrolink, the Blackpool & Fleetwood Tramway was the only urban/inter-urban tramway system left in Britain. The infrastructure is owned by the local authorities and the tramway operated by Blackpool Transport Services Ltd.

System: 660 V d.c. overhead.
Depot & Workshops: Rigby Road, Blackpool.
Livery: Cream and green except where stated otherwise.

Notes: Numbers in brackets are pre-1968 numbers. All cars are single-deck unless stated otherwise.

OPEN BOAT CARS A1-1A

Built: 1934–5 by English Electric. 12 built (225–236).
Traction Motors: Two EE327 of 30 kW.
Seats: 56.

600	(225)	604	(230)	607	(236)
602	(227)	605	(233)		

REPLICA VANGUARD A1-1A

Built: 1987 by Blackpool & Fleetwood Tramway, Blackpool on underframe of one man car No. 7 which was itself converted from English Electric Railcoach 619 (282).
Traction Motors: Two EE327 of 30 kW.
Seats:

619

BRUSH RAILCOACHES A1-1A

Built: 1937 by Brush. 20 built (284–303).
Traction Motors: Two EE305 of 40 kW (*EE327 of 30 kW).
Seats: 48.

Note: 635 carries its original number 298.

621	(284)		**AL**	627	(290)	**Purple**	633	(296)		
622	(285)	*	**White**	630	(293)	**AL**	634	(297)		**AL**
623	(286)		**AL**	631	(294)		636	(299)		
625	(288)			632	(295)	**AL**	637	(300)		**AL**
626	(289)		**AL**							

CENTENARY CLASS — A1-1A

Built: 1984–7. Body by East Lancs. Coachbuilders, Blackburn. One man operated.
Traction Motors: Two EE305 of 40 kW.
Seats: 52.

* Rebuilt from GEC car 651.

641	AL	643	AL	645	AL	647	AL
642	AL	644	AL	646	AL	648 *	

CORONATION CLASS — Bo-Bo

Built: 1953 by Charles Roberts & Co., Wakefield. Resilient wheels. 25 built (304–328).
Traction motors: Four Crompton-Parkinson 92 of 34 kW.
Seats: 56.

660 (324)

PROGRESS TWIN CARS — A1-1A + 2-2

Built: Motor cars (671–677) rebuilt 1958–60 from English Electric railcoaches by Blackpool Corporation Transport. Driving trailers (681–687) built 1960 by Metro-Cammell.
Traction Motors: Two EE305 of 40 kW.
Seats: 53 + 53.

671+681 (271+T1)	674+684 (274+T4)	676+686 (276+T6)
672+682 (272+T2)	675+685 (275+T5)	677+687 (277+T7)
673+683 (273+T1)		

ENGLISH ELECTRIC RAILCOACHES — A1-1A

Built: Rebuilt 1958–60 from English Electric railcoaches. Originally ran with trailers.
Traction Motors: Two EE305 of 40 kW.
Seats: 48.

678 (278)	AL	679 (279)		680 (280)	AL

"BALLOON" DOUBLE DECKERS — A1-1A

Built: 1934–5 by English Electric. 700–712 were originally built with open tops, and 706 has now reverted to that condition and is named 'PRINCESS ALICE'.
Traction Motors: Two EE305 of 40 kW.
Seats: 94 (*† 92, ‡ 90, ¶ 88).

* Rebuilt with new front end design and air-conditioned cabs. Known as "Super Balloons" or "Millennium Class"

§ Converted to ice cream tram seating 78 with an ice cream sales area in one of the lower saloons.

o Rebuilt as open-topped double-decker setaing 82. Named "PRINCESS ALICE'

700	(237)		709	(246)	*	718	(255)	
701	(238)	‡	710	(247)		719	(256)	§ AL
702	(239)	¶	711	(248)	†	720	(257)	AL
703	(240)		712	(249)		721	(258)	AL
704	(241)	**AL**	713	(250)		722	(259)	‡ AL
706	(243)	o	715	(252)		723	(260)	† AL
707	(244)	*	716	(253)		724	(261)	
708	(245)	‡	717	(254)		726	(263)	AL

ILLUMINATED CARS

732	(168)	Rocket	Built: 1961	Seats: 47
733	(209)	Western Train loco. & tender	Built: 1962	Seats: 35
734	(174)	Western Train coach	Built: 1962	Seats: 60
735	(222)	Hovertram	Built: 1963	Seats: 99
736	(170)	HMS Blackpool	Built: 1965	Seats: 71

JUBILEE CLASS DOUBLE DECKERS

Built: Rebuilt 1979/82 from Balloon cars. Standard bus ends, thyristor control and stairs at each end. 761 has one door per side whereas 762 has two.
Traction Motors: Two EE305 of 40 kW.
Seats: 100.

761   (725, 262) **AL** | 762   (714, 251)

WORKS CARS

259	(748, 624)	Permanent way car	Converted: 1971
260	(751, 628, 291)	Crane car and rail carrier	Converted: 1973
752	(2, 1)	Rail grinder and snowplough	Converted: 19
754		New works car (unnumbered)	Built: 1993

VINTAGE CARS

Stockport 5	Double-decker	Built: 1901
Bolton 66	Bogie double-decker	Built: 1901
Blackpool & Fleetwood 40	Box car	Built: 1914
Blackpool & Fleetwood 147	Standard double-decker	Built: 1924
Glasgow 1245	Double-decker	Built: 1939

5.2 CROYDON TRAMLINK

This new system runs through central Croydon with lines to Wimbledon, Addington and Beckenham Junction/Elmers End. Operated by Tramlink Croydon Ltd.

System: 750 V d.c. overhead.
Depot & Workshops: Therapia Lane, Croydon.
Livery: Red and white.

SIX AXLE ARTICULATED CARS   Bo–2–Bo

Built: 1998-99 by Bombardier-Wien Schienenfahrzeuge, Austria.
Traction Motors: Four of 120 kW each.
Seats: 70.
Dimensions: 30.10 x 2.65 m.
Couplers: Scharfenberg.
Doors: Sliding plug.
Weight: 36.3 t.
Braking: Disc, regenerative and magnetic track.
Max. Speed: 80 km/h.

The following trams carry advertising livery:
• 2531 Addington Palace Country Club (purple)
• 2533 Nescafé (dark brown)
• 2542 Amey Construction (yellow)
• 2546 Whitgift Shopping Centre (blue)
• 2550 First Group (similar to **FN** – indigo blue with pink and white stripes).

2530	2534	2538	2542 **AL**	2546 **AL**	2550 **AL**
2531 **AL**	2535	2539	2543	2547	2551
2532	2536	2540	2544	2548	2552
2533 **AL**	2537	2541	2545	2549	2553

5.3. DOCKLANDS LIGHT RAILWAY

This is a light rail line running in London's East End between Bank, Tower Gateway and Stratford to Lewisham and Beckton. Originally owned by London Transport, it is now owned by DLR Ltd. and operated by DLR Management Ltd. Cars normally operate automatically using the Alcatel "Seltrack" moving block signalling system.

System: 750 V d.c. third rail (bottom contact).
Depots: Poplar, Beckton.
Workshops: Poplar
Livery: Red and blue.

CLASS B90   B–2–B

Built: 1991–2 by BN Construction, Brugge, Belgium. Chopper control.
Traction Motors: Two Brush of 140 kW.
Seats: 66.   **Weight:** 36 t.
Dimensions: 28.80 x 2.65 m.   **Braking:** Rheostatic.
Couplers: Scharfenberg.   **Max. Speed:** 80 km/h.
Doors: Sliding. End doors for staff use.

22	26	30	34	38	42
23	27	31	35	39	43
24	28	32	36	40	44
25	29	33	37	41	

CLASS B92   B–2–B

Built: 1992–5 by BN Construction, Brugge, Belgium. Chopper control.
Traction Motors: Two Brush of 140 kW.
Seats: 66.   **Weight:** 36 t.
Dimensions: 28.80 x 2.65 m.   **Braking:** Rheostatic.
Couplers: Scharfenberg.   **Max. Speed:** 80 km/h.
Doors: Sliding. End doors for staff use.

45 **AL**	53	61	69	77	85
46 **AL**	54	62	70	78	86
47 **AL**	55	63	71	79	87
48 **AL**	56	64	72 **AL**	80	88
49 **AL**	57	65	73	81	89
50 **AL**	58	66	74	82	90
51 **AL**	59	67 **AL**	75	83	91
52 **AL**	60	68 **AL**	76	84	

CLASS ?   B–2–B

To be built: by Bombardier Transportation, Brugge, Belgium.
Traction Motors: Two Brush of 140 kW.
Seats: 66.   **Weight:** 36 t.
Dimensions: 28.80 x 2.65 m.   **Braking:** Rheostatic.

Couplers: Scharfenberg.   **Max. Speed:** 80 km/h.
Doors: Sliding. End doors for staff use.

92	96	100	104	108	112
93	97	101	105	109	113
94	98	102	106	110	114
95	99	103	107	111	115

BATTERY/ELECTRIC WORKS LOCO   B

Built: 1991 by RFS Engineering, Kilnhurst.
Electrical Equipment:

Unnumbered

DIESEL SHUNTER   B

Built: 1962 by Ruston & Hornsby, Lincoln.
Engine:
Transmission: Mechanical.

Unnumbered

5.4. MANCHESTER METROLINK

This light rail system runs from Bury to Altrincham through the streets of Manchester, with a spur to Piccadilly. A new line has now opened to Salford Quays and Eccles. The system is franchised to the Altram consortium and the operation is subcontracted to Serco Metrolink.

System: 750 V d.c. overhead.
Depot & Workshops: Queens Road, Manchester.
Livery: White, dark grey and blue.

SIX-AXLE ARTICULATED CARS   Bo–2–Bo

Built: 1991–2 by Firema, Italy. Chopper control.
Traction Motors: Four GEC of 130 kW.
Seats: 84.
Dimensions: 29.00 x 2.65 m.
Couplers: Scharfenberg.
Doors: Sliding.
Weight: 45 t.
Braking: Rheostatic, regenerative, disc and emergency track.
Max. Speed: 80 km/h.

* Fitted with front valances, retractible couplers and controllable magnetic track brakes for running to Eccles.

1001		1015	* SPARKY
1002		1016	
1003		1017	
1004	THE ROBERT OWEN	1018	SIR MATT BUSBY
1005	*	1019	
1006		1020	THE DAVID GRAHAM C.B.E.
1007		1021	THE GREATER MANCHESTER
1008	MANCHESTER AIRPORT		RADIO
1009		1022	THE GRAHAM ASHWORTH
1010	* MANCHESTER CHAMPION	1023	
1011		1024	THE JOHN GREENWOOD
1012		1025	
1013	THE FUSILIER	1026	THE POWER
1014	THE CITY OF DRAMA		

SIX-AXLE ARTICULATED CARS   Bo–2–Bo

Built: 1999 by Ansaldo, Italy. Chopper control. Fitted with front valances, retractible couplers and controllable magnetic track brakes for running to Eccles.
Traction Motors: Four GEC of 130 kW.
Seats: 82.
Dimensions: 29.00 x 2.65 m.
Couplers: Scharfenberg.
Doors: Power operated sliding.
Weight: 45 t.

Braking: Rheostatic, regenerative, disc and magnetic track.
Max. Speed: 80 km/h.

2001	THE JOE CLARKE OBE
2002	
2003	TRAVELLER 2000
2004	
2005	
2006	CITY OF SALFORD 2000

SPECIAL PURPOSE VEHICLE

Built: 1991 by RFS Industries, Kilnhurst.
Engine: Caterpillar 3306 PCT of 170 kW.
Transmission: Mechanical. Rockwell T280.
Couplers: Scharfenberg.
Max. Speed: 40 km/h.

Unnumbered

5.5 MIDLAND METRO

This new operation runs from Birmingham Snow Hill to Wolverhampton along the former GWR line to Wolverhampton Low Level. On the approach to Wolverhampton it deviates from the former railway alignment to run on-street to the St. George's terminus. Operated by Travel West Midlands Ltd.

System: 750 V d.c. overhead.
Depot & Workshops: Wednesbury.
Livery: Dark blue and light grey with green stripe, yellow doors and red front end and roof.

SIX AXLE ARTICULATED CARS   Bo–2–Bo

Built: 1998–99 by Ansaldo Transporti, Italy.
Traction Motors: Four.
Seats: 58.
Dimensions: 24.00 x 2.65 m.
Couplers: Not equipped.
Doors: Power operated sliding plug.
Weight: 35.6 t.
Braking: Rheostatic, regenerative, disc and magnetic track.
Max. Speed: 75 km/h.

01	04	07	10	13	15
02	05	08	11	14	16
03	06	09	12		

5.6. STAGECOACH SUPERTRAM

This light rail system has three lines, to Halfway in the south east of Sheffield with a spur from Gleadless Townend to Herdings, to Middlewood in the north west with a spur from Hillsborough to Malin Bridge and to Meadowhall Interchange in the north east adjacent to the large shopping complex. Because of the severe gradients in Sheffield (up to 1 in 10), all axles are powered on the vehicles which are owned by South Yorkshire Light Rail Ltd., a subsidiary of South Yorkshire Passenger Transport Executive, but are mortgaged to Lloyd's Bank, whilst the operating company, South Yorkshire Supertram Ltd. has been leased to Stagecoach Holdings Ltd. for 27 years and is now known as Stagecoach Supertram.

System: 750 V d.c. overhead.
Depot & Workshops: Nunnery.
Livery: White with orange, red and blue stripes.

AL Advertising livery (JON)

EIGHT-AXLE ARTICULATED UNITS   B–B–B–B

Built: 1993–4 by Duewag, Düsseldorf, Germany.
Traction Motors: Four monomotors.
Seats: 88.
Dimensions: 34.75 x 2.65 m.
Couplers: Not equipped.
Doors: Sliding plug.
Weight: 52 t.
Braking: Rheostatic, regenerative, disc and emergency track.
Max. Speed: 50 m.p.h.

101	106	110	114	118	122
102	107	111	115	119	123
103	108	112	116	120 **AL**	124
104	109	113	117	121	125
105					

5.7. STRATHCLYDE PTE UNDERGROUND

This circular 4 foot gauge underground line in Glasgow is generally referred to as the "Subway" or the "Clockwork Orange". It is operated by Strathclyde PTE.

System: 600 V d.c. third rail.
Depot & Workshops: Broomloan.
Livery: Orange and black.

SINGLE POWER CARS　　　　　　　　Bo–Bo

Built: 1977–79 by Metropolitan Cammell, Birmingham. Refurbished 1993–95 by ABB Derby.
Traction Motors: Four GEC G312AZ of 35.6 kW each.
Seats: 36.
Dimensions: 12.81 x 2.34 m.
Couplers: Wedglock.
Doors: Sliding.
Weight: 19.62 t.
Maximum Speed: 54 km/h.

101	107	113	119	124	129
102	108	114	120	125	130
103	109	115	121	126	131
104	110	116	122	127	132
105	111	117	123	128	133
106	112	118			

INTERMEDIATE TRAILERS　　　　　　　　2–2

Built: 1992 by Hunslet-Barclay, Kilmarnock.
Seats: 40.
Dimensions: 12.70 x 2.34 m.
Couplers: Wedglock.
Doors: Sliding.
Weight: 17.25 t.
Maximum Speed: 54 km/h.

201	203	205	206	207	208
202	204				

BATTERY ELECTRIC WORKS LOCOS · Bo

Built: 1977 by Clayton Equipment, Hatton.
Battery: 96 cell Chloride lead acid.
Traction Motors: Two GEC G312AZ of 35.6 kW each.
Dimensions: 4.65 x ?.?? m.
Couplers: Wedglock.
Weight: 14.8 tonnes.
Braking:
Max. Speed:

L2   LOBEY DOSSER
L3   RANK BAJIN

BATTERY ELECTRIC WORKS LOCO · Bo

Built: 1974 by Clayton Equipment, Hatton. One of a pair of 3 ft. gauge locomotives for use on the Channel Tunnel construction project. Both were converted to 4 ft. gauge in 1976 or 1977 and used by contractors Taylor Woodrow
on the Strathclyde Underground modernisation between 1977 and 1980 before being stored at Taylor Woodrow, Southall. Both were purchased in a der-
elict condition by Strathclyde PTE in 1987, and one loco, L4, was rebuilt by
Clayton in 1988 from the parts recovered from these two locomotives. L4 was
further rebuilt by Hunslet-Barclay, Kilmarnock, in 1990 to make it compatible
with L2 and L3.
Battery: 96 cell Chloride lead acid.
Traction Motors: Two GEC G312AZ of 35.6 kW each.
Dimensions:
Couplers: Wedglock.
Weight:
Max. Speed:

L4   EL FIDELDO

5.8. TYNE AND WEAR METRO

System: 1500 V d.c. overhead.
Depot & Workshops: South Gosforth.

SIX-AXLE ARTICULATED UNITS   B–2–B

Built: 1978–81 by Metropolitan Cammell, Birmingham (4001/2 were built by Metropolitan Cammell in 1976 and rebuilt 1984–87 by Hunslet TPL, Leeds).
Traction Motors: Two Siemens of 187 kW each.
Seats: 68.   **Dimensions:** 27.80 x 2.65 m.
Couplers: BSI.   **Doors:** Sliding plug.
Weight: 39.0 t.   **Maximum Speed:** 80 km/h.
Livery: Red &Yellow unless otherwise indicated.

AL Advertising livery; **B** Blue and yellow; **G** Green and yellow.
0 Original 1975 livery with red stripe as used on test track.

4001	**0**	4019		4037		4055	**AL**	4073	
4002	**AL**	4020		4038		4056	**G**	4074	
4003		4021		4039	**AL**	4057		4075	**B**
4004	**G**	4022		4040		4058	**B**	4076	**B**
4005		4023	**G**	4041		4059		4077	
4006		4024		4042	**AL**	4060		4078	
4007		4025	**G**	4043		4061	**G**	4079	
4008	**B**	4026		4044		4062	**G**	4080	
4009		4027		4045	**AL**	4063	**AL**	4081	**B**
4010		4028		4046		4064		4082	**G**
4011		4029		4047	**B**	4065		4083	**B**
4012		4030		4048	**B**	4066	**B**	4084	
4013		4031	**B**	4049	**AL**	4067		4085	**B**
4014		4032		4050		4068		4086	**AL**
4015		4033		4051		4069		4087	**AL**
4016	**B**	4034		4052		4070		4088	
4017		4035	**B**	4053	**B**	4071		4089	
4018	**G**	4036	**G**	4054	**B**	4072	**G**	4090	

Names:

4026	George Stephenson	4065	Dame Catherine Cookson
4041	HARRY COWANS	4077	Robert Stephenson
4060	Thomas Bewick	4078	ELLEN WILKINSON

BATTERY/ELECTRIC WORKS LOCOS

Built: 1989–90 by Hunslet TPL, Leeds.
Traction Motors: Two Hunslet-Greenbat T9-4P of 67 kW each.
Dimensions: 9.00 x ?.?? m.   **Couplers:** BSI.
Weight: 26.25 t.   **Maximum Speed:** 50 km/h.
Livery: Green, with red solebar and black & yellow striped ends.

BL1	BL2	BL3

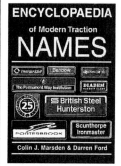